COUNTRY

100

ana

• Wagga Wagga

NEW SOUTH WALES

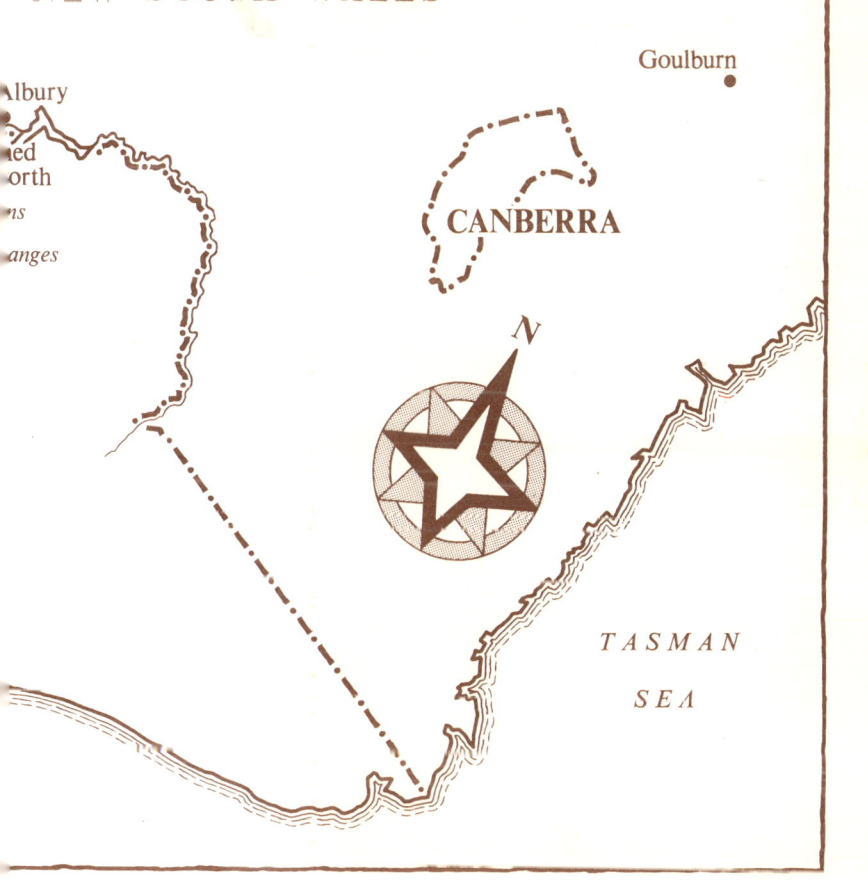

Goulburn

Albury

CANBERRA

N

TASMAN
SEA

Ned Kelly

Other books by Charles Osborne

KAFKA : A CRITICAL STUDY

THE COMPLETE OPERAS OF VERDI : A CRITICAL GUIDE

SWANSONG (poems : illustrated by Sidney Nolan)

FIFTY WORKS OF ENGLISH LITERATURE WE COULD DO WITHOUT (with Brigid Brophy and Michael Levey)

AUSTRALIAN STORIES OF TODAY (Ed.)

OPERA 66 (Ed.)

AUSTRALIA AND NEW ZEALAND : A HANDBOOK (Ed.)

NED KELLY

by

Charles Osborne

ANTHONY BLOND

Acknowledgment
Some of the photographs are reproduced by courtesy of The Hamlyn Publishing Group Ltd., Feltham, Middlesex.

*First published in Great Britain by
Anthony Blond Limited
56 Doughty Street, London, W.C.1*

© *Copyright* 1970 *Charles Osborne*

218 51124 8

*Printed in Great Britain by
Tonbridge Printers Ltd
Peach Hall Works, Tonbridge, Kent*

INTRODUCTION

There have been several books on Ned Kelly. Most of these have concerned themselves as much with the myth as with the man, and some of them have been written from a partisan viewpoint, depicting the Australian bushranger either as simply a vicious and cold-blooded thug or, more usually, as a potential political leader of genius. What I have attempted is to present the known facts about Kelly's life as objectively as possible. This has meant jettisoning many a good story to be found in earlier accounts of the Kelly Gang. It has also prevented me from inventing dialogue. The reader can safely assume that all dialogue in these pages is taken from contemporary statements. I have relied heavily on newspaper reports of the pursuit and capture of Kelly, as well as documents relating to his trial and to evidence given to the Royal Commission on the Victorian Police Force which was set up to inquire into the police's handling of the case.

Ned Kelly is still, of course, remembered in Australia. But it is not the man who is remembered, it is a myth-figure who is referred to with ironic affection and, at least in what is still called the Kelly Country of Victoria, jealously cherished and guarded from the prying foreign eyes of Melbourne and the outside world. It is easy to say that the Kelly-figure appeals to the Australian's anti-authoritarian feeling, to the egalitarianism that springs from the national inferiority complex, which in turn springs from the country's ashamed awareness of its convict beginnings. It is easy, and it is true. But it is not the whole truth. The other side of that particular truth is that even the most determinedly egalitarian society needs an object of worship, a hero who must first be sacrificed for his people, and then deified by them. Compared to, say, Jesus Christ, Ned Kelly may appear to exhibit certain defects, but there is no doubt that the Australian psyche makes essentially the same kind of use of him as another colonial people made of Jesus two thousand years earlier.

Kelly is an Australian hero, known to every Australian household. In Ireland, most people will hear of him for the first time when they see him played on the screen by Mick Jagger. But Kelly was as much an Irishman as he was an Australian, and a great deal of the sympathy accorded to him in north-east Victoria in the 1870s came from the Irish small settlers, some of them transported convicts who had served their sentence, some of them free immigrants who had left Ireland to escape the harsh British rule which had been dreaded in their country since Cromwell, only to find themselves still subjected to it in what they had hoped would be a brave new world. Ned Kelly was their unofficial spokesman.

What Australians choose to celebrate in Kelly are the daring and the gaiety of the bank raids at Euroa and Jerilderie, in which money was taken from institutions and distributed to individuals, and in which no person was injured. What they are also unable to forget, however, are the killings at Stringybark Creek, the murder of Aaron Sherritt (which criminal mentality would justify on the ground that Sherritt was an informer), and the intended wholesale massacre of police at Glenrowan, although at this encounter the only police to suffer wounds were Superintendent Hare and a black tracker. (It was police bullets which killed two innocent civilians.) Kelly was no real bushranger: it was not his profession to hold up and rob individuals. Nor was he the psychopathic killer he is sometimes made out to be. But that he was a killer is a fact that cannot be disputed, and the arguments he himself put forward in justification displayed an extremely stunted moral sense.

There are, however, Kelly supporters and enthusiasts in Australia today who claim that, far from possessing a criminal mentality, Kelly was, in fact, potentially a political leader. During a symposium held at the Adult Education Centre at Wangaratta, in Kelly Country, in 1967, the extreme opinion was voiced, unsupported by any evidence, that at Glenrowan in 1880 Kelly had intended to lead a rebellion and proclaim a new Republic of North-Eastern Victoria. Kelly, it was suggested, 'was forming a selector army. The plan was simple. The gang, with their armour, would act as the shock-troops – the tanks – of the army. They would give their best guns to the sympathizers. The Kellys, with their armour to protect them, would retain the obsolete guns they had acquired during their outlawry.'

The plan, apparently, was that, at a given signal, the sympathizers would ride into Glenrowan from all over the Kelly country, 'clutching the guns which had been given to them by the gang, to follow them in raids on the banks at Benalla, Wangaratta, possibly Beechworth. And then what? The Republic of Victoria? Holding the Governor to ransom? We don't know.' It is suggested that, when Kelly left the Glenrowan Inn, in the middle of the battle, it was to meet the sympathizers. 'The eye-witness accounts of this extraordinary meeting are confused and contradictory,' a contributor to the Wangaratta symposium stated. The fact is that there are no identified eye-witness accounts. Hearsay offers an army of either thirty or one hundred and fifty, and contributes, too, two fragments of speech from Kelly at this meeting: 'This is our fight,' and 'I am prepared to die.'

Since there were, at that moment, no more than sixteen armed police attacking the Glenrowan Inn, an organized Kelly army, even of as few as thirty, would have stood more than an even chance of defeating the police. There is no reason to believe that such an army ever existed, or that the secession of North-East Victoria from the Colony was ever proposed or even consciously envisaged by Ned Kelly.

Kelly was undoubtedly more than just a criminal. He lived in a time and place where the law, or its administration, tended to turn poor and desperate men into criminals. But that he was, to quote his modern Wangaratta advocate, 'a man of greater nobility and moral courage than anything [Australia has] hinted at in the past', is simply not worth serious consideration. He lived, he took risks, he died game. The man has ceased to exist, consumed in the flames of the legend. The legend will survive while Australia continues to have need of it.

* * *

The story of Ned Kelly begins somewhat earlier than 1855, the year of his birth: it emerges from eighteenth-century political unrest in Ireland, from the series of historical accidents which culminated in the creation of the colony of Victoria, and from social and economic conditions in the early years of the colony. When Kelly was born in Beveridge, about twenty-five miles from Melbourne, in June 1855, the colony of Victoria was itself no more than four years old. Until 1851, the settled southeastern area of Australia formed part of the colony of New South Wales, and was simply known as the Port Philip district. Port Philip Bay, on which Melbourne now stands, had been discovered and explored as early as 1802, and a settlement established there in 1803 was abandoned four months later. But Port Philip remained uninhabited by white settlers, except temporarily, until 1834, when a group of 'squatters' – farmers, graziers and adventurers – made a deal with the local aborigines by which they 'purchased' 600,000 acres of land. The British Home Office refused to recognize the transaction, declared the settlers to be trespassers on Crown property, and dispatched an official to take charge. In 1837 the settlement was given the name of Melbourne: the explorations which opened up the hinterland country ensured rapid development of the area, and by 1851, when Victoria became a separate colony with Melbourne as its chief town, there were an estimated 77,000 settlers and 5,000,000 sheep in the colony. Small farming towns had sprung up in the area to the north and north-east of Melbourne in rich, hilly, fertile country.

In the same year that Victoria, named after its sovereign, became a separate entity, gold was discovered in the colony, and the rush was on. The first finds in July 1851 were at Warrandyte, Clunes, Castlemaine, Ballarat and Bendigo, and before long the infant state was filled with gold diggers: men seeking easy wealth, dreamers, desperadoes, the greedy and the gullible. They deserted from ships, they flocked down from China, or across from California. In Melbourne, all but two members of the police force resigned and joined the rush to the gold fields. Within five years the colony's population had trebled. From Britain, a quarter of a million people arrived to seek a quick fortune. But the quick pickings, the areas where one could almost pick the gold off the ground, were soon exhausted. The majority of the miners found the search to be by no means an easy one. Many of them failed to discover gold, and had difficulty in paying their mining licence fee. At one of the gold diggings, Eureka, near Ballarat, 10,000 of the miners met in protest not only against the fee of thirty shillings, which they considered excessive, but also against the brutal methods employed by the Australian police, an organization largely composed of Irish bullies, in dealing with those miners who were unwilling or unable to pay it. The miners burned their licences, built a stockade, and ran up their own republican flag, a Southern Cross on a blue background. On Sunday, December 3rd, they were attacked by a joint force of police and army sent up from Melbourne, and the first and only battle of Australia's first and only civil war was fought. Thirty miners and five soldiers were killed before the miners were forced to surrender. One hundred and twenty-eight were arrested and tried. Though the leaders were acquitted, the bitterness engendered by the affair ran deep; the anti-police, anti-authority attitude of the Australian worker springs as much from the Eureka Stockade as from the country's convict beginnings. From the same source, incidentally, springs the illiberal White Australia policy: the presence of Chinese miners on the goldfields was jealously objected to, and in 1855 a special tax of £10 was levied on every Chinese entering Australia. Many of the discontented and disaffected miners left Australia, and a few of them took to the bush. The age of the great bushrangers in Victoria began.

The first Australian bushrangers were convicts who escaped from the settlements in New South Wales and Tasmania, but the Victorian breed of the 1850s and 60s were predominantly free settlers, or the shiftless sons of farmers, who found it more exciting to live by holding up coaches carrying gold, and by robbing banks and isolated farms, than by less arduous and more honest work. Between 1860 and 1875, approximately 300 men took to the road in emulation of the English highwayman. Ned Kelly is frequently referred to as 'the last of the bushrangers', but the Kelly Gang were not really bushrangers at all. Before considering what they were, it might be as well to acquaint oneself with the exploits of the more notorious of the Victorian bushrangers who preceded the Kellys and who, in a sense, set the scene for them. Almost without exception these men were not redressers of injustice as the Kellys liked to consider themselves, but ordinary criminals operating in the extraordinary conditions of a new, convict-based society, in an untamed country far from the laws and customs of Europe.

The first Victorian bushrangers were the Williams Gang, led by Jack Williams. They operated mainly in the Dandenong district, outside Melbourne, where they robbed farmers' homesteads as well as travellers on the road. They were finally cornered in a farmer's house they had raided on the Yarra

River, only a few miles from Melbourne, and forced to surrender after their leader was killed. The three surviving members of the gang were hanged in public. Most of Melbourne turned out to watch them die.

The gold rush of 1851 brought with it a great increase in lawlessness. One of the most violent criminals was Richard Burgess, who had been transported to Australia for housebreaking. Gaining his parole, or ticket-of-leave, he arrived on the goldfields at Ballarat where, after a desultory attempt at legitimate gold digging, he formed a gang to hold up the miners and tradesmen. Burgess never hesitated to kill when he thought it necessary. With the money from his robberies he lived a very gay social life in Melbourne, disappearing into the bush every so often to rob and murder. He was captured and spent some years in gaol, but when he was released he went to New Zealand where he teamed up with three other bushrangers. For some time they operated successfully, but in 1866, after they had murdered four travellers for the £300 in gold they carried, the gang was arrested. One turned Queen's evidence, and the other three, including Burgess, were hanged.

One of the most enterprising of the Victorian bushrangers was Joseph Grey, who planned the hold-up of an armed gold escort, conveying £10,000 in gold from the diggings to Melbourne. A month later, one of the gang betrayed the others to the police, but Grey himself was never caught.

Of all the Victorian bushrangers before Kelly, the most famous was Francis McCallum, known as Captain Melville. Convicted of theft in Scotland when he was twelve, he was transported to Tasmania where he spent eleven years. On his release, he made his way to the Victorian goldfields, where for over a year he robbed homesteads and solitary travellers. Occasionally he worked alone, but he also commanded a large gang. Captain Melville was gentlemanly in his manner, well-spoken and polite. He was eventually arrested while celebrating Christmas Eve in a brothel in Geelong, and died in his prison cell, strangled by his own scarf. The coroner's verdict of suicide was doubted by many.

Henry Garrett, an English convict, joined three others and robbed the Ballarat branch of the Bank of Victoria of £14,300. The gang divided the loot and split up. Garrett took a job as a station hand, waited until the hue-and-cry had died down, then retrieved his share of the spoils and sailed back to England with it. He lived in Oxford Street in an elegant apartment with a valet. The valet discovered a quantity of gold dust and some incriminating Australian papers in Garrett's desk, and informed the police. A police inspector from Victoria had already arrived in London to search for Garrett, and was now able to follow him. In the middle of the West End, the Inspector suddenly startled Garrett with a loud 'Coo-ee!', the Australian bush-call. Garrett lost his head and ran, but was caught. He was taken back to Melbourne to serve ten years in the prison hulks.

The last of the Victorian bushrangers, and a real link with Ned Kelly, was Harry Power. Power was an Irishman who came to Victoria during the gold rush days. Before long, he was sentenced to fourteen years' imprisonment for horse stealing and wounding a police officer. After serving the greater part of it, he escaped, took to the bush and supported himself by holding up coaches. His hideout was a cave in the hills behind the farmhouse of the Quinn family. One of the Quinns was Ned Kelly's mother, and the teenaged Ned is said to have accompanied Power on at least one of his exploits. In 1870, betrayed by one of the Quinns, Harry Power was captured and sent to gaol for fourteen years. His apprentice, Ned Kelly, was then about fifteen years old, and already on the brink of his own sad, violent and doomed career.

ONE

John Kelly, Ned's father, was born in Ireland, in County Tipperary, in 1820. As a young man, he worked as gamekeeper to an English landlord. In 1841, when he was twenty-one, he was convicted of stealing two pigs, and transported to Van Diemen's Land, as Tasmania was then called, for a term of seven years. He served most of his sentence working as a farmhand for free settlers, though he spent two months in chains in the dungeons for being discovered in a free settler's potato patch. After four years he was granted his ticket-of-leave, and soon made his way across to the mainland of Victoria. After spending some time in Melbourne, John, known as 'Red', moved twenty-four miles north to Beveridge, found employment as a labourer, and built himself a bark hut. It was in Beveridge that he met Ellen Quinn.

The Quinns were an Irish family who had emigrated to Australia as free settlers. James Quinn, from County Antrim, had brought with him his wife and ten children, and had rented a small farm at Wallan not far from Beveridge. His eldest daughter, Ellen, was eighteen when she met and fell in love with Red Kelly. The Quinns were not very keen on the idea of their daughter marrying an ex-convict, but the youngsters eloped on horseback to Melbourne where they were married on November 18th, 1850, by Father Gerald Ward at St Francis' Church in Lonsdale Street. Faced with the marriage, the Quinn parents accepted the situation and the young couple moved into Red's hut in Beveridge. The following year Red, like most people, joined the gold rush but soon became discouraged and returned to farming. After all, Beveridge was on the main road between Melbourne and the goldfields, and it was easy to sell horses and cattle. The Kellys' first child was born in 1851, but died in infancy. They had a daughter, Annie, in 1853, and in June, 1855 their first son, Edward (Ned) was born. There were to be five more children: Maggie (1857), Jim (1859), Dan (1861), Kate (1862), and Grace (1865). Red Kelly paid his brother Jim's passage to Australia from Tipperary, and the

(above) The Kelly home at Eleven Mile Creek, near Greta: a rough hut with a bark roof and earth floor.

(left) Dan Kelly, Ned's youngest brother: outlawed at 17, died at Glenrowan, aged 19.

Jim Kelly, whose five-year prison sentence for cattle stealing prevented him from being with the Kelly Gang. After the death of his brothers he supported his mother and lived quietly at Greta until his own death in 1946, aged 87.

Joe Byrne

Steve Hart

(a) (b)

(c)

(a) Ned Kelly in 1874, aged 19.
(b) Ned Kelly, pictured in the *Australasian Sketcher* after his capture at Glenrowan. Fantasy rather than reality, an elegant tameness quite uncharacteristic of him, intended perhaps to deflate Kelly's popular image.
(c) Supposedly taken after the fracas at Benalla in 1877, and circulated by police in the hunt for Kelly, this is in fact the photograph of 1874, with beard and moustache drawn on.

family was further enlarged by the marriage of two of Ellen's sisters, Kate and Jane, to two brothers, Jack and Tom Lloyd.

The first of this large clan to get into trouble with the police was sixteen-year-old Jimmy Quinn, uncle of Ned, who was then a baby. In December 1856 Jimmy Quinn was charged with being in illegal possession of a bullock. Owing to lack of evidence the charge was dismissed, but the damage had been done. The Quinns and Kellys, anti-police by Irish instinct, convinced themselves that as poor farmers they could never hope for justice from the rich man's police force. Whether Jimmy Quinn really stole the bullock hardly matters. A great amount of cattle and horse rustling was going on in the district, and the rich squatters used their influence to have additional police and detectives sent up from Melbourne to stamp it out. Inevitably, members of the Quinn, Lloyd and Kelly families were among those viewed with suspicion. A reward of £50 was offered for the capture of the gang believed to be stealing cattle, and it was not long before various Kellys and their inlaws found themselves in court. Jack Quinn was acquitted on two charges of stealing, but young Jimmy went to gaol for six weeks for assaulting a neighbour, and a further four months for illegal use of a horse. His brother-in-law Jack Lloyd was acquitted on a charge of brawling.

This was the world in which young Ned grew up: honesty was a mug's game, and survival depended on being smarter than the local police. Red Kelly, realizing that his convict past rendered him vulnerable, did his best to avert danger by moving with his family from Beveridge to Avenel, over fifty miles to the north. There he rented forty acres of grassland, and contrived to make some kind of a living selling butter and milk to the local shopkeepers. Ned and his sister Annie attended Richardson's Church of England School, which cost their father two shillings a week.

Meanwhile, the Kelly relatives continued to pop in and out of the local courts. Red's brother Jim was convicted of cattle stealing at Kilmore, between Wallan and Avenel, and sentenced to three years' imprisonment. At Beechworth, much further to the north-east, two of the young Quinns were in trouble: Jimmy went to gaol for a year for horse stealing, and Jack was accused of robbery under arms, a charge which carried the death sentence. He was acquitted.

The Kellys' first brush with the law came when Ned was ten years old, in 1865. It appears to have grown out of a feud between the Kellys and their Welsh neighbours, the Morgans. The Morgans owned seven hundred acres of rich pastureland, adjoining Red Kelly's forty rented acres, and there was no love lost between the two families. The Morgans looked down on the Kellys as little better than convicts, while the Kellys saw the Morgans as the type of rich squatter who could always command the police, and who were to a great extent responsible for the persecution of the lower classes by the law. Morgan suspected Red Kelly of stealing his cattle, and one day in May 1865 he arrived at the Kelly homestead accompanied by a police constable. They searched the house, and found the hide of a calf with the brand cut out. Red was arrested, convicted of being in illegal possession of the hide, and fined £25. Until the fine was paid he was to be confined in gaol. His wife Ellen sent young Ned off on horseback to Glenmore to appeal to her family, the Quinns, for help. But it was some weeks before the £25 could be scraped together, and by the time Red was released from gaol, he was a sick and broken man. From this time on, it was young Ned who was of most help to his mother on the farm. He had to give up going to school. At ten, he was forced to become a man, with adult responsibilities.

The following year, 1866, his father died at the age of 47, and the family had him buried in a home-made coffin in the cemetery at Avenel. In the opinion of the Kellys and the Quinns, his life had been shortened by the brutal treatment he had received at the hands of the police. To young Ned, the police were his natural enemies, and the tragic course of his short life was charted on this one fact of existence. He does not appear to have been an unruly child: he worked hard to help his mother at the farm, and he was once given a green silk sash with a gold fringe in recognition of his bravery when he plunged into a creek to rescue a farmer from drowning. But he must have been a serious child, for he was deprived of the opportunity not to be serious.

Only a few months after Red's death, Ellen Kelly was arrested for having used abusive and threatening language to her neighbours, the Morgans, and was fined £2 and ordered to keep the peace. The alternative was two days in gaol, so Ned found the money and even persuaded two farmers to act as guarantors for his mother's future good behaviour. With the help of those of their relatives who were not at that time in prison, the Kellys moved from Avenel to a hut on the banks of Eleven Mile Creek, between Benalla and Greta. The roughly constructed hut had a bark roof and an earthen floor, and was divided into rooms not by walls but by hessian bags. Ellen Kelly earned a meagre living by letting space to travellers, and providing meals. Ned continued to act as the man of the house. He had no choice: His father's brother, Jim Kelly, was serving a long gaol sentence for having set fire to his sister-in-law Kate Lloyd's house. Jim Kelly had, in fact, been sentenced to death by the harsh Judge Redmond Barry who was later to sentence Ned, but the Executive Council had commuted the sentence to fifteen years' imprisonment.

So far, Ned himself had kept out of the courts. But it is probable that he helped to supplement the family income by a little discreet horse stealing. He is believed, too, to have served as apprentice to the bushranger Harry Power. Police Superintendent Hare, who wrote a book about the part he played in the eventual capture of the Kelly gang, claimed that Ned had spoken to him of his association with Power:

> Ned Kelly ... was regarded as a horse and cattle stealer from his earliest boyhood. He was known to steal carriers' horses at night, 'plant' them in the bush until a reward was offered for their recovery, and then in the most innocent manner claim the reward. Afterwards he took to stealing and selling any horses he found straying about. When he was sixteen years of age he joined Power, although he never assisted in any of his sticking-up cases; still, he was with him on two or three occasions when Power committed some of his depredations. He merely took charge of Power's horses at a distance, but he could not be recognized by any of the victims, and consequently he was never tried for any offence in connection with him; but he served two or three sentences for horse and cattle stealing. When with Power, Ned Kelly was a flash, ill-looking young blackguard. He told me the reason he left him was because Power had such an ungovernable temper that he thought Power would shoot him. He told me that when they were riding in the mountains, Power swore at him to such an extent, without his giving

him any provocation, that he put spurs to his horse and galloped away home. It was generally supposed by the public that Ned Kelly gave the police some information which led to Power's arrest; but this is entirely untrue. Power would not at that time have trusted Kelly with the knowledge of his whereabouts. Power had a very poor opinion of Kelly's courage, and told me that once or twice Ned Kelly had suggested that they should surrender, more especially when Kelly and he were trying to steal some of Dr. Rowe's horses at Mount Battery Station, Mansfield, and Dr. Rowe fired on them with a long distance rifle. Power said Kelly turned deadly white and wished to surrender. He had the greatest difficulty in getting him off the ground, he was in such a fright.

Ned's first encounter with the law, however, was almost comical, and quite untypical of his later career. It arose from a quarrel with a Chinese named Ah Fook.

TWO

In October, 1869, a Chinese merchant, Ah Fook, encountered Mrs Kelly's eldest daughter, Annie, by the creek near the Kelly home, and asked her for a drink of water. Instead of going to the water tank, Annie took a ladle to the creek and offered Ah Fook the creek water to drink. Ah Fook threw the ladle to the ground, lost his temper and swore violently. The fourteen-year-old Ned, who was working in a nearby field, chased Ah Fook off their land, and the man rode into Benalla with a story that he had been the victim of robbery with violence. He told Sergeant Whelan that Ned had bailed him up, threatened to beat him, and stolen ten shillings. Whelan went out to Eleven Mile Creek, arrested Ned, and brought him, in handcuffs, to the Benalla gaol. After eleven days in gaol, Ned appeared in court on a charge of robbery with violence. Ah Fook gave evidence, claiming that Ned had hit him with a stick and said, 'I'm a bushranger. Hand over your money or I'll beat you to death.' But when it was established that Ah Fook had been carrying £25 on his person, his story that Ned had relieved him of only ten shillings seemed not to make sense. The case was dismissed.

Ned's next appearance in court was a more serious one. On May 4th, 1870, police arrested the fifteen-year-old youngster on two charges of robbery under arms. He had been recognized by witnesses as Harry Power's accomplice. A local newspaper reporting the court procedure said, 'Kelly seemed quite indifferent to the danger of his position. While casting eyes among the crowd, he smiled complacently and assumed a jaunty air. Previous to his appearance in court, and while confined in the lock-up, he "sang like a bird" and seemed quite proud. The misguided youth evidently considers himself a character to be admired.'

Evidently Ned was very badly frightened: the punishment for robbery under arms was death. But Sergeant Whelan of the Benalla police was unable to produce real evidence, so Ned was acquitted. He was then remanded in custody to Kyneton to face a similar charge. In Kyneton he was questioned by Superintendent C. H. Nicolson who had come up from Melbourne to attempt to suppress lawlessness in the north-east of Victoria. Again, due to lack of evidence, Ned was acquitted. Meanwhile, Superintendents Hare and Nicolson, acting on information received not from Ned but from his uncle Jack Lloyd in gaol, surprised Harry Power in his eyrie in the hills behind the Quinn homestead, and arrested him. In court, the vain old clown Power, when asked by the judge if he had anything to say, remarked, 'It is too bad, altogether too bad. Not content with trying to make me out a pitiful pilferer instead of the bold highwayman I actually was, some of these rags they call newspapers are actually endeavouring to decry my personal appearance. I am willing to bet the £15 the police took out of my pockets, and leave the decision to the ladies of Beechworth, that I am a better looking man than the whole lot of the reporters present in this court today.'

And then he went off to gaol for fifteen years.

Four months after he was acquitted on the charges of having aided Harry Power, Ned was arrested again. And this time, although the charge was a relatively trivial one, the police had evidence enough to convict him. A hawker named Jeremiah McCormack accused Ned of knocking him down and also of handing Mrs McCormack a parcel containing an indecent note and a pair of calf's testicles. (Several years later Ned gave his own account of the episode in his famous 'Jerilderie letter' [See p. 75]). The magistrate at Wangaratta sentenced him to three months at hard labour in Beechworth Gaol for assault, and a further three months, or £10 fine, for indecent behaviour. None of his relatives was able to produce a ready £10, so Ned went to gaol for six months. At Beechworth Gaol, a record was kept of the boy's appearance. It revealed him, at the age of fifteen years and three months, to be 5 ft. 10 in. in height, 11 stone 4 lb. in weight, sallow of complexion, with hazel eyes, dark-brown hair and broad features. His eyebrows met across the top of his nose, and there were nine scars on his head and hands.

There can be no doubt that his six months' sentence had a distinctly hardening effect on the already unruly youth. His continual claim in later years that he had been victimized by the police does in fact have some substance to it. A man called Ben Gould, who was involved in Ned's argument with McCormack, admitted that he had written the indecent note to

McCormack's wife, and McCormack himself, having laid the charge against Ned, then tried to withdraw it. But the police refused to allow the charge to be withdrawn: this was their first real chance to put young Kelly behind bars, and they were not willing to pass it up. After all, they had the support of Superintendent Nicolson:

> I expressed my opinion to the officer in charge of the district that, without oppressing the people or worrying them in any way, he should endeavour, when they had committed any crime, to bring them to justice and send them to Pentridge even on a paltry sentence, the object being to take their prestige away from them, which was as good an effect as being sent to prison with a very heavy sentence, because the prestige these men get up there from what is termed their 'flashness' helps to keep them together, and that is a very good way of taking the 'flashness' out of them.

Flashness Ned certainly possessed. He was already reputed to be one of the best horsemen in the district, he had an intimate knowledge of the country, the bush and the hills for miles around, he was a good shot and a plucky fighter. One could almost say he became a criminal through being treated as a potential criminal from childhood. The six months' gaol sentence served by the adolescent was decisive.

A few weeks after his release, Ned was arrested again on a charge of horse stealing. Again, his version of the facts is given in the Jerilderie letter. It appears that Ned's brother-in-law, Alec Gunn, was being visited by a friend, 'Wild' Wright, from Mansfield, when Ned arrived back at the homestead after his enforced six months' absence. Wright's mare strayed away just as he was about to return to Mansfield, so he borrowed a horse from Ned, on the understanding that Ned could use Wright's mare if and when it turned up. Ned found the mare, which had apparently been stolen from the postmaster at Mansfield, and rode it into and around the town of Wangaratta. The horse still bore its original brand, but no one challenged him, and Ned claimed he had no reason to suspect it had been stolen. But as he was riding back through Greta, he was stopped by Constable Hale. Claiming that he merely wanted the lad to sign documents relating to his release from gaol, Hale called Ned into the police station, and grabbed him as he dismounted, trying to fling him to the ground. In the ensuing struggle Hale drew his revolver, but Ned continued to fight. A number of men came to the Constable's aid, and eventually Ned was overpowered and tied hand and foot. It was then, he claimed, that Hale struck him across the face with his revolver.

The horse had been stolen at Mansfield while Ned was in gaol at Beechworth but this did not prevent the judge presiding at the Beechworth Assizes from sentencing Ned to three years' hard labour. 'Wild' Wright and Alec Gunn received lighter sentences of eighteen months each. In his Jerilderie letter, Ned claimed that the only witness produced by the police ('James Murdock who was recently hung in Wagga Wagga') had been bribed by Constable Hale, and that Hale had been 'tried several times for perjury'. His bitter conclusion was that 'it is a credit to a Policeman to convict an innocent man, but any mutt can pot a guilty one'.

The police interest in the Kelly family did not subside once Ned was got behind bars for three years. Some months later his young brothers Jim, aged twelve, and Dan, aged ten, were arrested on a charge of illegally using a horse. The charge was dismissed, but eighteen months later Jim, barely fourteen, was sent to prison for five years on a charge of cattle stealing.

Ned served the first part of his sentence in Beechworth Gaol, working every day with the chain gangs in the May Day Hills. In February 1873, he was transferred to Pentridge Prison, on the outskirts of Melbourne. From here he was transferred first to the prison hulk *Sacramento* and later to another hulk, the *Battery*. Every day, the convicts in these hulks were taken ashore to work in the quarries or to construct roads. Ned did not serve his full three years: one week was added when he was caught offering tobacco to a fellow-prisoner, but his generally good behaviour got him a remission. After two and a half years, he was free again. He returned home to find a few changes made in his familiar landscape. The railway was encroaching upon his territory, a number of his relatives were in gaol for stealing cattle or horses, and his mother had married again. Her new husband was George King, an immigrant from California, who seemed no more honest than any other member of the family. For the time being, honesty presented itself to Ned as a sensible way of life. 'I'd rather face the gallows than to go to gaol again,' he declared, and made his way to Mansfield where he took a job at the local sawmill.

He stayed in regular employment for nearly three years, rising to the position of overseer at the mill, and then went prospecting for gold on the King River, in company with his stepfather George King. He claimed they found some gold, but it seems more likely that they prospered by stealing horses and cattle from farmers in the King Valley. In fact, Ned admitted as much in his Jerilderie letter. In little more than a year, Kelly and his helpers stole two hundred horses, altered their brands, and sold them through agents in various towns, some of them across the border in New South Wales.

Twenty-seven of the wealthiest graziers in the district held a meeting at Moyhu, at the junction of the King River and Boggy Creek, and formed themselves into the North Eastern Stock Protection Society, offering rewards for information leading to the arrest of the thieves. But the poorer settlers were hardly likely to betray their own kind, and no one came forward to claim the reward.

It was at this time that Superintendent Nicolson visited the north-east of Victoria on a tour of inspection. 'I visited the notorious Mrs Kelly's on the road ... to Benalla,' he reported:

> She lived on a piece of cleared and partly cultivated land on the road-side, in an old wooden hut, with a large bark roof. The dwelling was divided into five apartments by partitions of blanketing, rags, etc. There were no men in the house, only children and two girls of about fourteen years of age, said to be her daughters. They all appeared to be existing in poverty and squalor.... She said her sons were out at work, but did not indicate where, and that their relatives seldom came near them. However, their communications with each other are known to the police. Until the gang referred to is rooted out of this neighbourhood, one of the most experienced and successful mounted-constables in the district will be required in charge at Greta.

On a visit to his mother in September 1877, Ned celebrated too riotously in Benalla, was arrested for drunkenness, and put in the cells overnight. The next morning, four policemen were detailed to escort him across the street to the courthouse. They were Sergeant Whelan, and Constables Lonigan, Fitzpatrick and O'Dea. A fight broke out when Fitzpatrick tried to handcuff Ned who knocked him aside and ran into a nearby bootmaker's shop. According to Ned, Fitzpatrick rushed into the shop and tried to choke him, while Lonigan grabbed him by the testicles. Peace was restored by a Mr McInness, owner of the local flour mill, who persuaded Ned to allow himself to be handcuffed and taken into court. Ned glared at Lonigan and promised: 'Well, Lonigan, I never shot a man yet. But if I ever do, so help me God, you'll be the first.'

In court, Ned accused the police of having doped his liquor. The flour-miller, McInness, who was a J.P., spoke up for him, and, as a result, the magistrate ignored police requests for a gaol sentence. Instead, he fined Kelly one shilling for being drunk and disorderly, £2 for assaulting the police, and £2 for resisting arrest. There was a further charge of 5s. compensation for the damage done to Constable Fitzpatrick's uniform.

THREE

The row between the local police and the Kelly clan continued. Ned's young brother Dan, now aged sixteen, was accused of stealing a saddle, but was able to produce a receipt and establish ownership. Old John Lloyd spent eight days in gaol on a charge of horse stealing before being released on lack of evidence. Shortly after he came out, the unfortunate man was accidentally killed by his nephew Tom in some high-spirited larking about in a pub. Dan Kelly, Tom Lloyd and young John Lloyd went to gaol for several months on charges of unlawfully entering, stealing and wilfully damaging. Life might have gone on like this for the Kellys for ever, still sentences and petty crimes endlessly succeeding one another, were it not for the absurd, cowardly and vain Constable Fitzpatrick who, in April 1878, decided to arrest Ned and Dan Kelly. In March, a warrant had been issued for Ned on charges of horse stealing and in April a second warrant was issued for Dan on similar charges. On April 15th, with a few drinks inside him to increase his courage, Constable Fitzpatrick rode out alone from Benalla to the Kelly homestead.

Giving evidence before the Royal Commission set up to investigate the Police Force of Victoria after the capture of the Kelly Gang, the Chief Commissioner of Police stated that the 'Kelly outrages' could be traced back to April 15, 1878, and Fitzpatrick's visit to the Kelly hut:

> For several years before the Kelly outbreak there is no doubt that the north-eastern district was a receptacle for horse stealers and cattle stealers and that they gave the police force a great deal of trouble. No outrages were committed in those days, but a wholesale system of cattle duffing was carried on extensively. This appears to have culminated in the disturbance at Greta, when Constable Fitzpatrick went out to serve a warrant on Dan Kelly for horse stealing. He arrived there, found Dan Kelly, and, in my opinion, foolishly allowed him to stay and have his dinner. In the meantime Ned Kelly,

Williamson, commonly called 'Bricky', and his brother-in-law Skillion arrived with two or three others of their confederates and friends. A disturbance immediately took place between these men and Constable Fitzpatrick, which resulted in Ned Kelly firing at him, and shooting him through the wrist.

Fitzpatrick fainted, and lay there in a semi-comatose state for some time while they cut the ball out of his wrist; it had been under the skin, and they allowed him to go. He rode off, and laboured under the idea that he was pursued by two of the outlaws, which I have ascertained was not the case.

By the time of the Royal Commission, Fitzpatrick had been dismissed from the police force because, according to the official report: 'He could not be trusted out of sight, and he never did his duty. He associated with the lowest people in town and was not a fit person to be in the police force.' Fitzpatrick gave his account of the evening of April 15th, 1878, under examination by the Royal Commission three years later:

When I first went to the place Dan was not there, only Mrs Kelly and some of the younger children of the place, and I entered into conversation for a while to see if there was any chance of Dan putting in an appearance. I drew Mrs Kelly's attention to the sound of someone cutting wood behind the hut on the creek where they lived; and I said 'I will go up and see who they are.' I went up there and found Williamson, a man that used to live with them, splitting rails, and asked him had he a licence, and he said no, he did not require one, splitting on selected land; so, after I had spent a few moments with him, I was heading for Greta. I was going straight there – the station I was *en route* for. I was on horseback. I had occasion to pass by Kelly's new hut at the time, the one they were living in at the time. As I was passing that, I noticed two horsemen entering the slip panels in front of the old hut. I rode round to where they were, and by the time I got round one of the men disappeared, and Skillion was holding one horse by the mane, and had the other horse, the one he had been riding, with the saddle and bridle on – he was holding that, and a third horse he had caught in the panel just after coming in. The horse that had been ridden had the bridle taken off. I asked Skillion who was riding the horse. He told me he did not know. I examined the mare, and saw it was the one Dan Kelly was riding two or three days previous to that when I had seen him. I said, 'That is Dan Kelly's mare,' and he said, 'Yes.' I said, 'Where is he?' and he said, 'Up at the house, I suppose,' that is the new hut. So I rode up to the place again, and called out 'Dan', and he came out, and as soon as I saw him I walked up to him. He had his hat and coat off, and a knife and fork in his hand. I said, 'I am going to arrest you on a charge of horse stealing, Dan.' He said, 'Very well, you will let me have something to eat before you take me?' I said, 'All right.' He said, 'I have been out riding all day.' He went back into the hut, and I followed him in. As soon as I went inside Mrs Kelly accosted me, calling me 'a deceitful little bugger'. She said she always thought I was. She said, 'You will not take him out of this tonight.' I said it was no use talking that way, that I had to do my duty; and Dan says, 'Shut up, mother, that is all right.' I was scarcely in the place three minutes, when Ned Kelly rushed in and fired a shot at me, and said 'Out of this, you bastard.'

Dan was sitting down to have something to eat. I was standing up alongside him, with my right side to him. Ned was about a yard and a half from me; he had just come from the side of the hut door. As soon as he had fired the first shot Mrs Kelly seized an old shovel that was at the fireplace, and rushed at me with it, and smashed my helmet completely in over my eyes; and as I raised my hand to keep off the shovel Ned fired a second shot, and it lodged in my wrist. With that I turned to draw my revolver, and just as I slewed to the right Dan Kelly had my revolver pointed at me. He had snatched it while my attention was drawn to his mother and Ned. Williamson had come to the door of the bedroom, and Skillion. They both had revolvers in there hands; they were not in the hut when I came in. Ned Kelly said, 'That will do, boys.' If he had known it was Fitzpatrick he would not have fired a bloody shot. I fell down on the floor insensible.

After I got up, Ned Kelly examined my hand and found a bullet in my wrist, and said, 'You must have it out of that;' and I asked him to let me go into Benalla to let the doctor take it out, and he refused; and I saw he was determined to take out the bullet. He wanted to take it out with a razor. and I took out my penknife and he held my hand and I took it out. It was not very deep in; it was a small-sized ball. I could not leave for some time. They kept me till eleven o'clock after I came round, and would not let me go.

Ned Kelly's own story, however, was that he was nowhere near the Kelly hut on Eleven Mile Creek at the time of the Fitzpatrick incident. When a party of police rode from Benalla some hours later to arrest the Kellys, they found no sign of Ned or Dan; Mrs Kelly claimed that she had not seen Ned for weeks and that Constable Fitzpatrick's injury had been accidental. Dr John Nicholson of Benalla, who examined Fitzpatrick's wrist at the time, reported that he had found two slight wounds 'which *might* have been produced by a bullet'. He also pointed out that there was a smell of brandy on the Constable.

The police arrested those who were present at the Kelly home: Mrs Kelly, Maggie Kelly's husband Bill Skillion, and the neighbour 'Bricky' Williamson. They were sent to gaol to await trial, and warrants were issued for the arrest of Ned and Dan: the charge was no longer horse stealing, it was attempted murder.

Since the formation of the Kelly Gang was a direct consequence of the Fitzpatrick incident, it is of some importance to try to discover exactly what happened in the Kelly hut on the evening of April 15th, 1878. Was Ned present, and did he shoot at Fitzpatrick? He had never pulled a gun on a man before, but a few months later he was to have no compunction about shooting to kill. In his Jerilderie letter he claims to have been 'over 400 miles from Greta', presumably horse stealing in New South Wales, and boasts 'It is not likely that I would fire three shots at Fitzpatrick and miss him at a yard-and-a-half.' As he admitted to other killings, it is at least possible that here he was telling the truth.

The Kellys claimed that Fitzpatrick was drunk, and that he drew his gun when Mrs Kelly angrily waved her fire shovel in his face. To frighten him, Dan announced that Ned had arrived and, when Fitzpatrick turned, grabbed his gun. The farm helpers, Williamson and Skillion, came in and helped to pacify Fitzpatrick who stayed to have a few drinks with them and eventually left at about 11 p.m.

It is certainly possible that this is what happened, and that, to explain why he had stayed so long a time, Fitzpatrick invented the story of his being held prisoner. He may also have preferred to think he had been attacked by Ned rather than disarmed by a mere sixteen-year-old. There is no way of telling; but, if a man is innocent until proven guilty, Ned remains innocent: Fitzpatrick's evidence ought never to have convicted anyone.

While Mrs Kelly, Skillion and Williamson were in gaol awaiting trial, the police made several raids on the Kelly farm in an attempt to discover evidence to support Fitzpatrick's story. A reward of £100 was offered for information regarding the whereabouts of Ned and Dan, but no such information was forthcoming. What has to be understood from the very outset about the Ned Kelly story is that, whether one chooses to regard him now as brutish criminal or political leader *manqué*, to almost the entire population of small farmers in Victoria, working-class and largely uneducated, he was at the time a hero, and anyone who informed on him would have been considered a traitor. Captain Standish, the Chief Commissioner of Police, admitted as much, with a slightly different emphasis, when he said to the Royal Commission:

> The Kellys, as is well known, had an enormous number of sympathizers in the district, and after their outrages there is not the slightest doubt that a great many respectable men were in dread of their lives, and were intimidated by a fear of the consequences from giving any information whatsoever to the police. Not only their lives and those of their families were in danger, but their cattle, and sheep, and horses, and property were liable to be stolen or destroyed; in addition to which there is not the slightest doubt that there was an enormous number of tradesmen in the district who were so benefited by the large increase of the police, and by the consequent expenditure, that they were only too glad that this unpleasant business was protracted for so many months. I may also state that a great many of the local papers never lost an opportunity of attacking the police in the most unjustifiable manner and on every possible occasion.

Mrs Kelly, Williamson and Skillion were held in custody for six months before being brought to trial in October, 1878. They were then found guilty of aiding and abetting the attempted murder of Constable Fitzpatrick. Judge Barry sentenced the two men to six years' imprisonment each, and Mrs Kelly to three years. Ned and Dan let it be known that they would be willing to surrender themselves if their mother were released, and the Beechworth magistrate to whom the offer was communicated was inclined to accept it. But the authorities and the police were determined not to bargain. In sentencing Mrs Kelly, Judge Barry had added: 'If your son Ned was here, I would make an example of him. I would give him a sentence of fifteen years.' So Ned and Dan continued to hide out in the hills of the Wombat Ranges where they were more than a match for any city-trained policeman. There they were joined by two friends, Joe Byrne and Steve Hart. The Kelly Gang had sidled into existence.

A newspaper reporter later described the Kellys' mountain hideout:

> The hut was situated on a rise in the middle of a basin bounded east by Ryan's Creek, west by high, steep mountains of the Wombat Ranges, north by a small creek flowing down between ranges, and south by a ridge. Reining in my horse on the crest of this ridge, I could not but be struck with wonderment that such a perfect settlement should have existed so long within half a dozen miles of selections, without being discovered. Farmer Jebb within four miles, and Harrison within six, assert they were not even aware the Kellys were in the vicinity, although the basin was so improved, they must have lived there many months. The basin contains 70 acres fenced in by sapling, dogleg and brush fences, the west side needing no fencing because of the steepness of the hill.
>
> Twenty acres immediately around the hut are cleared, the trees are ringed, and the timber – mainly swamp gum and peppermint – is placed in heaps ready for burning. The ground had even been raked so as to give every chance for the grass to grow. Bark had been removed from peppermints for the roof. In the creek to the north, there had been gold-digging mainly by sluicing. From appearances there had been gold in payable quantities; the workings were of the extent that four men must have worked for several months.

The hut was erected of bullet-proof logs, fully two feet in diameter, one on top of the other, crossed at ends. The door was six feet high by two feet six inches wide, and made of stiff slabs, and plated with iron nearly a quarter of an inch in thickness, which was loop-holed to fire through. The door is on the north side, opposite the gold workings in the creek, and a well built log chimney occupies the greater part of the west end of the hut. Such was the home of the Kelly gang for some months before the police murders. Its interior was fitted up just as substantially as its exterior, and in a manner calculated to stand a long siege, there having been every provision made for the storage of flour, beef, tea, sugar and other necessaries of life. To show that in fresh meat, at least, they were not wanting, we discovered portions of several carcasses, together with seven or eight heads of cattle, with bullet holes in the centre of the forehead, lying outside. These may have belonged to either 'scrubbers' out of the ranges, or the fat bullocks of some not far distant squatter or farmer, but most probably the latter. Empty jam and sardine tins, old powder flasks, cap boxes, broken shovels, old billy cans, glass bottles, door hinges and a great variety of other articles were to be seen all round the hut.

But the crowning wonder of all was the evident pains taken by the Kellys to improve themselves as marksmen. In every direction – taking the hut as a standing-point – we saw trees which were marked with bullets, from five to fifty having been fired into each, at ranges varying from twenty to four hundred yards. The bullets, being afterwards chopped out, were melted down and converted again into their former state. On one small tree, a circle of charcoal six inches in diameter had been traced, and into this two or three revolver bullets had been fired, one striking the black dot meant to represent the bullseye in the centre, and the other two being close to it. Some of the bullets had gone to a depth of four inches in the trees, and consequently a great deal of chopping had to be done to get them out. There was abundant evidence, too, to prove that, the more practice the outlaws had, the more they improved in the use of the rifle and revolver, the shooting at some marks on the trees being very wide, and on others remarkably straight, and dead into the bullseye.

At the time they took to the hills, Ned was twenty-three, and Dan seventeen. Ned was tall, well-built, and had already grown his full beard. Dan, by comparison, was a weedy youth, straight-haired, clean shaven and sallow of complexion. To him, understandably, brother Ned was something of a hero, and he accepted Ned's leadership without question. Superintendent Hare's view of Dan was that he 'was always known to be a cunning low little sneak, he would be prowling about half the night seeing what he could pick up; of course he knew every road, lane and mountain gully in the district, and could ride about the darkest night and find his way as if in his own garden.'

Steve Hart, one of the two other lads who joined the Kelly brothers in what they considered to be their fight against police injustice, was Dan Kelly's best friend. At the time of the formation of the gang, Steve was just under eighteen. He, too, was a local lad, born on his father's 200-acre farm near Wangaratta. Like so many of the settlers, his family was Irish in origin. Steve himself was a slight youth of average height, somewhat dandified in dress. His eyebrows were thick, his forehead low, his hair dark, straight and plentiful. After joining the gang he grew a beard. His one outstanding quality appears to have been his horsemanship. A number of people later described how he always jumped his horse over the gates at the railway crossing when riding in and out of Wangaratta. From being fond of horses, Steve naturally developed a propensity for horse stealing, and it was this which first led him into trouble with the police. In January 1877 he had been sentenced to twelve months in Beechworth gaol for illegally using other people's horses, so he was already an old lag when he joined the Kellys in the Warby Ranges in 1878.

The fourth member of the gang, Joe Byrne, was twenty-one years old, and also a native of the district. A slim, handsome youth, with light, wavy hair, he was known to be quiet, well behaved, but notoriously work-shy. His father, a carter and miner, had died while Joe was still a child, and his mother had struggled to bring up her six children in a slab hut in the Woodshed valley. A fourteen-year-old girl, whom he used to flirt with, spoke of him when she was an old woman seventy years later:

There was no harm in Joe. He was a nice boy. He brought me two young curlews, but the mother bird followed them down, and when it came night they commenced to squeal, so we let them go. Then he brought me a lamb. You never knew where he got it, and it followed us around for years, even after he himself was dead. He was a nice, quiet boy – not flash – and a fine horseman. He would come in at any old hour to stay for the night, and my father would say 'Whose horse have you got tonight? and Joe would tell him. He probably did a bit of cattle-duffing, just kill a cow where it stood, for the meat, but that was no great crime unless you were caught. A lot of people did it, and had good reason. He got in with Sherritt, and that was when the trouble began.

Joe was slightly better educated than Steve Hart or the Kelly brothers. As Superintendent Hare remarked of him, 'He was very fond of writing, and was a bit of a poet. A great deal of his writing fell into our hands. They were chiefly directed against the police.'

As the most literate of the four, it was Joe's job, when they were planning a robbery or a hold-up, to write out the plan of action in advance, so that they could decide what part each of them would play.

Joe Byrne's mate, Aaron Sherritt, a fascinatingly complex character, was a kind of unofficial fifth member of the Kelly Gang. Probably the most intelligent of them, Aaron elected not to follow his friends into a way of life beyond the law, but to play the double and doubly dangerous game of pretending to be a police informer. His method was to tell the police where the gang were to be found, then ride out and warn the gang so that they could move out in time. The police paid him well for his information which always seemed to be authentic even when they were not able successfully to act upon it. And the gang, knowing what Aaron had told the police, made their plans accordingly. There must have been, indeed there were times when both police and outlaws wondered uneasily just where Aaron's sympathies really lay. He was a close friend of Joe Byrne, yet for his money which he spent on drink and women, he was dependent upon the police. The temptation to throw in his lot completely on the side of law and order, and reward, must have been a strong one. Whether Aaron Sherritt eventually completely succumbed to it or not is still far from certain. What is certain is that Aaron had a healthy respect for Ned Kelly himself. 'I'm tougher than Joe', he told a police officer, 'and I can lick the two youngsters. But Ned's tougher than I am. I regard him as superhuman.' Kelly's mythic quality, so much written about after his death, had revealed itself already to his close associates.

Superintendent Hare tells that on one occasion, while talking to Aaron Sherritt, he inadvertently broke a twig off a tree, and began pulling off the leaves. Sherritt immediately stopped him, saying: 'You'd never do for a bushranger. If Ned Kelly saw any of his men break a twig off a tree when he was camped, he'd have an awful row with them.' Hare, and others, were astonished by Sherritt's physical toughness. Apparently, even on the coldest nights, he could sleep out of doors in the lightest of clothes. When people remarked on this to him, he would reply that Ned Kelly was ten times as hardy.

These were the men who camped out in the hills, not knowing what else they could do. The heavy sentences passed on Mrs Kelly, Skillion and Williamson conveyed plainly to the Kelly brothers that, if they were to allow themselves to fall into the hands of the police, they would go to gaol for a very long time. With two friends to share their exile from society, and a third to keep them informed of what the police were up to, the Kellys awaited the next move.

FOUR

The police continued their search for Ned and Dan Kelly, unaware, at the time, that it was a gang of four they were hunting. When hunter and hunted met at Stringybark Creek the point of no return was passed. Until then, if the Kelly boys had been captured they would have gone to gaol for a long stretch each; but, when they came out, however bitter they might have felt, they would hardly have been able to take to the bush and wage their own war against society. Society, in the 1870s, was already moving quickly in the direction of mechanization, improved communications, and even towards fairer conditions for all. The age of the bushranger was disappearing into distant memory as the train replaced the coach as a means of travel. The go-getters in Parliament were occasionally being joined by men with a social conscience. Had the Kellys been captured in 1878, we would probably not be able to remember the name of Ned Kelly today. But they were not captured, and the encounter between pursuers and pursued, the encounter in which farcically and tragically the pursuers momentarily became the pursued, ended in murder. From then on, the drama could have only one conclusion, and the wonder is only that it took nearly two years to be played out to the end.

After some months of unsuccessful searching for the Kelly boys, the police decided to concentrate on the hilly country between Greta and Mansfield, and two search parties were formed of four officers each: one party to operate from Greta, and one from Mansfield. The officer placed in charge of the Mansfield party was Sergeant Kennedy. Kennedy had the reputation of being a good bushman, with a detailed knowledge of the country around Mansfield. His three companions were Constable Michael Scanlan, Constable Lonigan and Constable McIntyre. Scanlan was said to know the country well, Lonigan had already been involved with Ned Kelly, having been one of the police who arrested him on his drunk and disorderly charge, and he also knew Dan well by sight. McIntyre, the youngest member of the party, was cook and general assistant. Early on the morning of Friday, October 25th, 1878, the four men set off on horseback from Mansfield improbably disguised as gold prospectors, and armed not only with their service revolvers but also with a Spencer revolving rifle, and a double-barrelled fowling piece. They took with them an additional pack-horse, and food supplies to last a week.

The fragmentary tales and wisps of reported conversations about the Kellys are numerous, and are still re-told and added to in the Kelly country of Victoria. Fact and rumour are by now indissolubly linked; but it may be true that, as they say, Constable Lonigan before he left remembered Ned's threat to him. 'If ever I shoot a man, it'll be you, Lonigan,' and twice rode back to say goodbye to his wife. And it may also be true that, as he rode off, Constable Scanlan called out to an acquaintance, 'If I don't come back, you can have my dog.'

The four policemen travelled all day, through bush and open country, past gullies, creeks, and even hilly ridges. By nightfall they had covered about twenty miles and decided to make camp in a clearing on the banks of Stringybark Creek. A tumble-down old wooden hut already stood there, evidence that at some time in the past gold-diggers had sought their fortune in the vicinity. The police party put up their tent and settled down for the night.

Next morning, the search began in earnest. Kennedy took Scanlan with him and rode out into the surrounding country, while McIntyre occupied himself with baking bread, and Lonigan simply looked after the horses. The morning was uneventful. At lunchtime, McIntyre and Lonigan heard the sharp report of a rifle, and went down to the creek to investigate. They found nothing, and apparently concluded they had been mistaken: perhaps it had been the cry of a bird, ringing out sharply in the bush silence. During the afternoon, McIntyre went off with his shotgun, shooting parrots. Towards sunset the two men collected deadwood to start a fire to stave off the cool of the evening as well as to help to guide Kennedy and Scanlan back to camp. They were sitting on a tree-trunk, lazily hypnotized by the flames when the Kelly Gang, at full strength of four, found them.

Had the Gang stumbled upon the police by accident, or had

Kelly been warned of the search-party? Superintendent Hare, in his memoirs, wrote:

> 'Sergeant Kennedy was a shrewd, intelligent man, and there is every reason to believe he had received information of a most positive nature as to where the Kellys were to be found, the information being supplied by a man whom I must call P——, a well-educated fellow who had held various responsible positions in the district, on the promise from Kennedy that if he arrested the offenders, the reward offered by the Government for their apprehension should be paid to him. It is also stated, that no sooner had P—— given this information to Kennedy and seen the police started in search of the bushrangers, than he went straight to the Kellys and told them that Kennedy was to camp in a certain spot in the Wombat Ranges.'

Whether Kelly had prior knowledge of the search party's whereabouts or not, the previous evening he had found their tracks in the bush, and traced them to the clearing by Stringybark Creek. Returning to his hide-out further up in the hills, he told his three colleagues of his find, and it was decided between them that they, the hunted, should bail up the hunters, and rob them of their weapons, which were superior to the old rifle and the revolvers which were all the Kellys carried at this time. According to Ned, there was no intention to kill the police: 'We saw they carried long firearms, and we knew our doom was sealed if we could not beat those before the others would come, as I knew the other party of police would soon join them and if they came on us at our camp they would shoot us down like dogs at our work. As we had only two guns we thought it best to try and bail those up, take their firearms and ammunition and horses, and we could stand a chance with the rest.'

For a detailed account of what happened at Stringybark Creek, one is dependent on the testimony of Constable Thomas McIntyre, the only one of the four police who survived the day. It was five in the afternoon, and he had just boiled a billy of tea, when he and Constable Lonigan were startled to hear a voice shouting 'Bail up! Hold up your hands!'

McIntyre quickly turned around and saw four men about forty yards away, all armed, with their guns pointing at Lonigan and himself. He immediately held out his arms horizontally, but Lonigan began to run, and one of the armed men, who later revealed himself as Ned Kelly, shot at him. Lonigan staggered a further four or five yards and then fell, 'breathing heavily and stertorously'. As Lonigan fell, Kelly transferred his gun to his left hand, and drew a revolver from his clothes with his right hand. He called out to McIntyre, 'Keep your hands up! Keep your hands up!' at which McIntyre raised his hands above his head.

Kelly and his companions advanced to within three yards of McIntyre, keeping him covered, three of them with shotguns and Kelly with his revolver. 'Have you got any firearms on you?' Kelly asked, and McIntyre replied that he had not. At this moment Lonigan, who had been writhing on the ground in pain, ceased to move, murmured 'Oh Christ, I'm shot,' and died. 'You must have a revolver,' Kelly continued to McIntyre. 'Where is it?' 'In the tent,' said McIntyre, and Dan Kelly, Steve Hart and Joe Byrne continued to keep him covered while Kelly searched him thoroughly.

Satisfied that McIntyre was unarmed, Ned Kelly leaped across a log, walked over to Lonigan's body and came back carrying Lonigan's revolver. 'Dear, oh dear,' he said, 'what a pity that bloke tried to get away.'

'It was plucky, all right,' said Dan. 'Did you see how he went for his revolver?'

Kelly entered the tent and collected McIntyre's revolver, calling to the others to leave McIntyre and follow him. The outlaws went into the tent, while a badly frightened McIntyre stayed where he was. To have made a break for it then would have been useless. He would certainly have been shot down before he could get across the clearing and into the bush.

Dan Kelly returned with a pair of handcuffs he had found in the tent, saying 'We'll put these on the beggar,' but McIntyre succeeded in convincing Ned that the handcuffs were unnecessary. 'Don't put them on him,' said Ned to his brother. 'This,' as he tapped his rifle, 'is a darn sight better than handcuffs.' He turned to McIntyre: 'Mind you don't try to get away, because if you do I'll shoot you – even if I had to track you to the police station to shoot you there.' 'The buggers'd soon put them on us, if they had us,' muttered Dan, as he and Ned walked back to the tent. Ned, now in reflective mood, sat down with his rifle across his knees, and called McIntyre across. 'This is a curious old gun for a man to carry about the country with him,' he said.

'It is,' replied McIntyre, 'but I dare say it's better than it looks.'

'It is that. I'll back it against any gun in the country. I can shoot a kangaroo at a hundred yards with it, and not miss a shot.' It was an old barrelled gun, with stock and barrel tied together with waxed string for three or four inches in front of the lock.

Looking across to Lonigan's body, Kelly asked, 'Who's that over there?'

'That's Lonigan.'

'No, it can't be Lonigan, can it? I know Lonigan.'

'It's Lonigan all right,' said McIntyre.

'Is it, indeed? Well, I'm glad of that. The bastard gave me a hiding in Benalla one day.'

Dan Kelly smirked at this. 'He won't lock any other poor bastards up now,' he said.

By this time, Joe Byrne was pouring the tea that McIntyre had made into shallow pannikins. He handed one to the policeman. 'Here, mate, have some tea.' The outlaws drank only after seeing McIntyre do so, Ned first asking, 'There's no poison in it, is there?' He then took the police party's fowling piece, drew the cartridges out, pricked the end of them, extracted the shot and threw it away, tore up the cartridges and replaced the charges with two bullets he took from the pocket of his trousers, one bullet for each cartridge. He handed the reloaded gun to Byrne. 'Here, Joe, you take that, and give me yours.' He turned to McIntyre, 'One of those bullets is for you if you don't do what I tell you.'

'Do you smoke, mate?' asked Byrne. 'Fill your pipe and have a smoke if you want to.' McIntyre did so, and gave some tobacco to Ned Kelly and Byrne when they asked for it. They sat about, smoking in silence for some minutes. Then Kelly said, 'Take your places, lads,' walked over to the fire, and concealed himself behind a tree-stump about three feet in height. Steve Hart took up a position in the tent, while Dan Kelly and Joe Byrne went to the edge of the clearing and hid in the long grass. From behind his log Ned called to McIntyre, 'You stand there,' indicating a spot near the fire. McIntyre did as he was told, and, while he was waiting for the other two policemen to return to camp, Ned engaged McIntyre in conversation. 'Who showed you this place?' he asked.

'No one showed it to us. It's well known to everybody around Mansfield.'

'How did you come here then?'

'We crossed Holland's Creek, and followed the blazed line.'

'Who are you, and what brought you here?'

'You know very well who we are.'

'What brought you here? I suppose you came after me?'

Since Kelly had not at this stage identified himself McIntyre decided to play dumb. He said, 'No, I don't know that we did come after you.'

'Well, you came after Ned Kelly, then?'

'Yes, we did.'

Tacitly admitting his identity, Ned burst out: 'You buggers came here to shoot me, I suppose.'

'No,' said McIntyre, reverting to officialese, 'We came to apprehend you.'

'Why did you bring so much firearms and ammunition?'

'We only brought the fowling piece to shoot kangaroos.'

'Who was that shooting down the creek today?'

'I was shooting at parrots.'

'That's very strange. Didn't you know we were here?'

'No, I didn't think you were within ten miles of this place. We thought you were over there.' And McIntyre pointed in the direction of Greta.

'When do you expect your mates back?'

'I don't think they'll get back tonight. They must have got bushed.'

'What are their names?'

'Sergeant Kennedy from Mansfield and Constable Scanlan from Benalla.'

'I've never heard of Kennedy, but I believe Scanlan is one of those flash bastards.'

'You're not going to shoot them down in cold blood, are you?'

'I'm not going to shoot them, but you'll have to get them to surrender. I won't fire at any man that holds his hands up and surrenders.'

'What about me?'

'What would I shoot you for? I could have killed you half

an hour ago when you were sitting on that log, if I'd wanted to. We were watching you both for quite a while. At first I thought you were a bugger called Flood, and it's a good job for you that you're not, because if you had been, I wouldn't have shot you, I'd have roasted you on that fire. There are four men in the police force that I'll roast alive if I ever lay hands on them. Fitzpatrick, Flood, Steele and Strachan. Strachan has been skiting that he'll take me single-handed. Huh!'

Kelly brooded on his four enemies awhile, and then said to McIntyre: 'How are your mates armed?'

'In the usual way.'

'What do you mean by that? Have they got revolvers?'

'Yes, they've got their revolvers with them.'

'Haven't they got a rifle with them?'

McIntyre hesitated, and Kelly continued: 'Come on, tell me the truth because if I find you're lying I'll put a hole in you.'

McIntyre was no hero. 'Yes,' he said, 'they've got a rifle.'

'What sort is it? Is it a breechloader?'

'Yes, it is.'

'Well, now, it looks as though you did come out to shoot me.'

'You can't blame the police. You know we've got our duty to do, and we have to come out after you if we're ordered to.'

'You're not ordered to go about the country shooting people. I know one of you buggers will shoot me one of these days. But before you do, I'll make some of you suffer. I'm no coward.' Kelly was silent for a moment, and then continued, 'That bloody Fitzpatrick is the cause of all this.'

'You can't blame us for what Fitzpatrick has done to you,' said McIntyre.

'No, but I almost swore after letting him go, that I'd never let another bloody police bastard go. If I let you go, you'll have to promise to leave the police force.'

'I will,' replied McIntyre hastily. 'My health has been bad, and I've been thinking of leaving the force and going home for some time. But if I get the other two to surrender what are you going to do?'

'You'd better get them to surrender,' said Kelly, 'because, if you don't, we'll shoot the bloody lot of you. But all we're after is their horses and firearms.' He was looking over at the creek as he spoke. His two guns were lying against the tree stump. Thinking that he might be able to get one of the guns, McIntyre took a short step towards Kelly, but Steve Hart, who had been watching from the tent, called out excitedly: 'Ned, look out, or that bugger will be on top of you.'

Ned turned around and addressed McIntyre coolly, 'You'd better not, mate, because if you do, you'll have had it.' He continued: 'Are there any other search parties out looking for me?'

'There's another party going to leave from Greta.'

'Who are they?'

'I don't know, but Sergeant Steele is in charge of them, and—'

'Shut up! Here they come,' muttered Kelly who had suddenly caught a glimpse of Kennedy and Scanlan about a hundred yards away down the creek. 'Here they are, lads,' he called to the other three. To McIntyre he said: 'Go and sit down on that log, and mind you don't give no alarm, or I'll put a hole in you.'

McIntyre obliged, but as his two colleagues advanced slowly on horseback, Kennedy leading and Scanlan ten or twelve yards behind, he stepped forward and called to them, 'Sergeant, you had better dismount and surrender. We're surrounded.' Immediately Kelly cried out, 'Bail up! Hold up your hands!'

Perhaps Kennedy thought a joke was being played on him. At first he smiled, and moved his hand casually to the gun which was buckled up in its case at his hip. As he did so, Kelly fired at him, but missed. The other outlaws then emerged from their hiding places, calling on Kennedy and Scanlan to put up their hands. Kennedy, and Scanlan who was still several yards behind him, quickly dismounted and attempted to take cover. The outlaws opened fire, and one of their first shots struck Scanlan. Seeing that the attention of the Kellys was momentarily diverted by his two armed colleagues, McIntyre seized the opportunity to make a getaway. Kennedy's horse, frightened by the shooting, had moved towards him. He quickly mounted and galloped off to the north, the direction in which the horse happened to be facing. Shots were fired after him, but he was not hit. After riding north until he had put the camp well behind him, he turned to the west, towards Benalla and Mansfield. He soon had to abandon his horse, or perhaps was thrown off it by the low branches of trees. In a state of fear bordering on panic, he scribbled in his note-book: 'Ned Kelly, Dan and two others stuck us up today when we were disarmed. Lonigan and Scanlan shot. I am hiding in wombat hole till dark. The lord have mercy upon me. Scanlan tried to get his gun out.'

McIntyre spent the night in the bush, and eventually reached Mansfield at three the following afternoon, where he reported what had occurred to the Inspector in charge. A search party was hastily organized, made up of police and civilians, and McIntyre accompanied them. They set out in the early evening, and at one or two o'clock the following morning they reached the camp and found the dead bodies of Constables Lonigan and Scanlan. They searched for Kennedy but did not succeed in finding him. The tent had been burnt down and any property and provisions not destroyed had been taken, with the exception of one tin plate.

It was another four days before the body of Sergeant Kennedy was found a mile away in the bush, one ear chewed off, probably by a wombat. According to Kelly, he had chased Kennedy through the bush, exchanging shots until finally Kennedy was brought down.

Witnesses at Kelly's trial in October 1880 were able to quote conversations with Ned in which he boasted of the killings at Stringybark Creek, though he did not like them to be referred to as murders. To George Stephens, a groom employed on a cattle station at Faithfull's Creek, four miles from Euroa, Kelly confided some of the details of the shooting of Sergeant Kennedy, only a few weeks after the event, on his way to rob the bank at Euroa.

'The reason Kennedy got so far was that I had taken up Scanlan's rifle, but had to throw it away again, as I did not know how to use it. I still followed Kennedy up. When he stepped out from behind a tree, I thought I was done for, as he fired and the ball grazed my ribs. I immediately fired and hit him in the shoulder as he was getting back behind the tree. Kennedy then ran, and I followed him. He wheeled round and rose his hands, and I fired and shot him through the chest. When I hit him in the shoulder, he must have dropped his revolver, and the blood running down his arm formed into a clot in his hand, which I took for his revolver. Knowing he had one shot left, when he wheeled round I thought he was going to fire, but I knew afterwards he was turning up his hands.'

To an itinerant hawker of drapery goods called James Gloster, who had also formed part of his captive audience at Faithfull's Creek, Kelly said he had had a long talk with Kennedy after he had wounded him, and that, as he 'did not like to leave him in a dying state,' he had shot Kennedy to end his misery, and had covered his body with a cloak, as a sign of respect.

The clearing at Stringybark Creek is as remote, desolate and inaccessible a spot today as it was in 1878. A few yards from the clearing the bush is thick and menacing, the tree-trunks close together and rising to heights of over thirty feet, the ferny undergrowth damp and tangled. It is by no means surprising that it took days to find Kennedy's body.

After the Stringybark Creek killings, there could be no turning back for the Kelly Gang. From then on, although Ned continued to assert his moral innocence as opposed to his legal guilt, it was clear that, when caught, as they inevitably would be, he and his gang would be convicted of murder. That it took nearly two years for this to happen speaks for the disorganization and demoralization of the Victoria police force as well as for the loyalty of many of the small freeholders in the north-east of the state to the four young men whom many still considered had been hounded into a life of crime.

There is no doubt that the Kellys lost some of their supporters after the killings at Stringybark Creek. To kill policemen was one thing, and the poor Irish settlers were no friends of police authority. But these policemen were human beings as well, because they happened all to be Irish. When they were buried in the cemetery at Mansfield, the Victoria Government and a great many private citizens subscribed the cost of expensive headstones, and a monument to the three troopers was erected in the town of Mansfield itself. Two of the Irish priests who officiated at the joint funeral, Fathers Kennedy and Scanlan, were cousins of Sergeant Kennedy and Constable Scanlan. Ned Kelly, son of Irish parents and protester against the injustice his forefathers had suffered, had not improved his image by slaughtering three Irishmen, despite the extenuating circumstances of their being policemen.

The authorities acted swiftly. Within a few days, the Victoria Government had obtained viceregal assent to a new

Act, the Felons' Apprehension Act, Victoria, 1878, which gave civilians the right to shoot outlaws on sight, and police the power to arrest anyone suspected of harbouring or assisting outlaws. The Kellys, Ned and Dan, and their two colleagues, Joe Byrne and Steve Hart, who at this time had not been properly identified and who were described under the names of Charles Brown and William King, were given a week to surrender at Mansfield and stand trial for murder. If they failed to appear, they were to be outlawed and could be apprehended and shot by anyone under the new act.

The Kelly Gang did not appear. They may not even have heard of the announcement in time to do so. Within a few days, notices offering £500 for their capture, dead or alive, appeared on notice boards and tree-trunks throughout the colony. Ned Kelly became Victoria's chief topic of conversation. The rich upper class voiced its disgusted condemnation of the criminals, while the middle and lower classes of both town and country were more ambivalent in attitude, or at any rate less united. The Church, too, was divided. Strongly in favour of the speedy apprehension of the murderers, church leaders were less certain that they approved of their parishioners being encouraged to become murderers themselves for the sake of a reward which rose from £500 first to £1,000 and then to £2,000.

A number of petty crimes were committed which were wrongly attributed to the Kellys, and of course there was a considerable increase in horse and cattle-stealing in and around the Kelly country. Spurious Kelly stories, and even documents, began to circulate. One such document was the letter sent to Monk, the sawmill owner who had been a member of the search party which found the bodies of Lonigan and Scanlan. It read:

To E. Monk.
  You think you have done a grate thing by searching for the traps, but you made a grate mistake for your friend Kennedy is gone although we made him confess many things you told him in confidence and we heard you say you could track us and our horses, but we will track you to hell but what we will have you. We will make your place a Government Camp when we come, and give them some more bodeys to

pack. What a fine thing it is to cut their ears off, but we will poke your eyes out.
>   Yours until we meet.
>   E. and D. Kelly

The style is not Kelly's, nor is the spelling. And he was fonder of the first person singular than plural. In any case, a man named Walter Lynch was sent to prison for two years for having written this particular threatening letter.

V. R.

£1,000 REWARD!!!
FOR THE KELLY GANG.

GO AND SEE
THE GREAT PICTURE
OF THE
NOTORIOUS BUSHRANGERS,
Painted by Fry from a photograph taken on the ground where the Murder of Sergeant Kennedy was committed.

Every Visitor will be presented with a photograph of the Notorious Ned Kelly.

Now on View opposite Theatre Royal.

Sergeant Michael Kennedy

Constable Thomas Lonigan

Constable Michael Scanlan

Constable Thomas McIntyre

The body of Sergeant Kennedy was found on the morning of 31st October 1878, four days after his death.

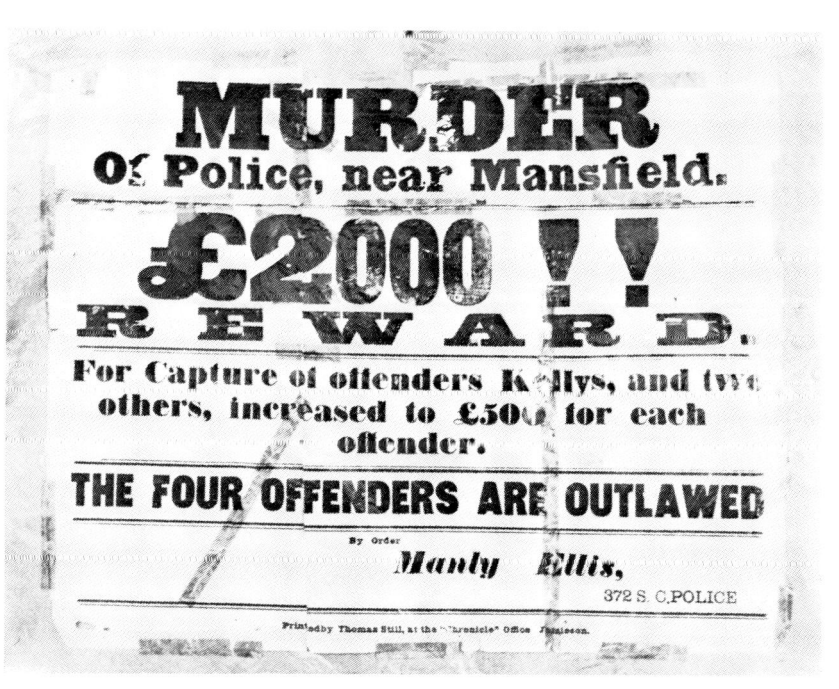

MURDER
Of Police, near Mansfield.
£2000!!
REWARD.

For Capture of offenders Kellys, and two others, increased to £500 for each offender.

THE FOUR OFFENDERS ARE OUTLAWED

By Order
Manly Ellis,
372 S. C. POLICE

Printed by Thomas Still, at the "Chronicle" Office Jamieson.

The reward was increased to £2,000 after the shootings at Stringybark Creek.

(left) The monument erected in Mansfield 'To the memory of three brave men'.

(below) The National Bank at Euroa.

FIVE

After the Stringybark encounter, the Kellys, Joe Byrne and Steve Hart rode off to their hut with the police horses and supplies they had commandeered. For the next couple of weeks they kept on the move, riding the police horses and accompanied by pack-horses. They had thought of crossing the Murray River into New South Wales and robbing a bank there, but at the point where they intended to cross, the Murray was at its highest for several years, and when they set off upstream to cross by punt, they found the punt had sunk. Temporarily abandoning the New South Wales project, the gang returned south. They were heard, and seen, to gallop through Wangaratta at four o'clock one morning, with two pack-horses and four spare horses. Resting in the familiar Warby Ranges, they then continued towards their hut, past Glenrowan. Here, in their own home country, there were still plenty of friends and sympathizers to keep them appraised of the movements of the police search parties, and to take them into their homes and given them food and shelter. The police in the area were under the charge of Superintendent Nicolson who had helped to capture the bushranger Harry Power some years earlier. Nicolson himself, with the aid of an aborigine tracker, had been attempting to trace the movements of the Kellys near the Murray River, but, meeting with no success, had returned to his headquarters at Benalla. On November 6th, the Chief Commissioner of Police, Captain Standish, came up from Melbourne to confer with Nicolson. The two men were dining together when they received a telegram from the Beechworth police, stating that the Kellys had been seen at Sebastopol. Standish and Nicolson attempted to send telegrams to Beechworth and to Melbourne, but found the lines from Benalla out of order. The Kelly sympathizers had been at work.

The entire Benalla police force was ordered to report by midnight, and set out for Beechworth in a special train at 1.30 a.m., arriving an hour and a half later to find a large party of armed civilians which had been organized to augment the police contingent. A posse of more than fifty men rode out of Beechworth into the hills of the Sebastopol district several miles away. Their objective was the hut of Aaron Sherritt, and their belief was that they would find the Kelly Gang sleeping there.

It was still quite dark, just before dawn, when they reached the brow of a hill and saw the hut in the valley below. A detachment was sent forward to place a cordon around the hut; Captain Standish remained on the hill with twelve men, ready to give chase if necessary, and Superintendent Nicolson with six men charged down the hill in a surprise attack. Leaping from his horse outside the hut, Nicolson rushed in through the door. As he did so, he stumbled against one of his constables whose gun went off. At the sound, the men surrounding the hut came racing towards it to join in the fight. Inside the hut, which had no windows, it was still completely dark. Men fought each other, bumped into tables and chairs, and finally one of them struck a match. After a while, it became evident to the police that they had been fighting themselves and that the hut was deserted.

Once this discovery had been made, the police lost no more time. Just over the next hill was the Byrne house, and it was by now suspected that young Joe Byrne was one of the Kelly brothers' two accomplices. Racing off to the Byrne house, a detachment of the police party awakened Mrs Byrne, Joe's mother. She was alone. Other police had gone off to search the homes of neighbours known or suspected to be sympathetic to the Kellys. By now it was morning. There were no outlaws to be caught, so the hungry police settled down in a paddock close to Mrs Byrne's house to eat their breakfast. They had got nothing out of Joe's mother: when told they would save her son from the gallows if he would inform on his three mates, she replied simply, 'He's made his bed, let him lie on it.'

The Sherritt hut, nearby, had been searched, and old John Sherritt now came to complain indignantly. Finally, his son, the tall, elegant Aaron Sherritt appeared, looking amused. A constable who recognized him introduced Aaron to the Superintendent of the Beechworth police as a man who knew the Kellys well, and who could be useful. Superintendent Sadleir questioned Aaron, and offered him a large share of the reward if he would help them to capture the Kellys. Aaron professed himself willing to co-operate, but in his turn questioned the policeman's authority to make such a bargain. Sadleir introduced him to Superintendent Nicolson who referred Aaron to Captain Standish. Standish rather off-handedly confirmed the police offer, and advised Aaron to remain on close terms with his friend Joe Byrne and to pass on any information he could obtain from Joe. Aaron had, in fact, for some time been keeping in with both police and Kellys, but it was from this moment, when he was, in the hearing of a large number of police constables, engaged as an informer, that his relationship with the police became somewhat more official, and that it became possible for the Gang to doubt whether his sympathies were entirely with them.

The Sebastopol raid had been a comic disaster, and the Kellys were still at large. Days passed, and it became clear that the police had completely lost track of them. Meanwhile, in their hideout in the hills, Ned and his companions planned the next move. This was to be a raid on the National Bank at Euroa.

The raid was planned with great care and precision down to the slightest detail. On Saturday, December 7th, Steve Hart made an exploratory visit to Euroa, a small, virtually one-street town of three hundred inhabitants, the centre of the surrounding agricultural district, and about thirty miles to the south-west of Benalla on the main railway-line from Melbourne to the New South Wales border. Steve strolled about the town noting the positions of the key buildings, bank, pub, police station, and then rode back into the hills to join Joe Byrne and the Kellys. On the following Monday, the Gang made their way to Euroa.

They called first, about midday, at Younghusband's Station, a large property and sheep station at Faithfull's Creek, four miles outside Euroa. One of the station-hands, Fitzgerald, was having lunch with his wife in the kitchen when a stranger appeared at the door and asked for Mr Macaulay, the manager. Fitzgerald replied that the manager was away, and asked if he could help, but the stranger walked away. He reappeared a few minutes later in the yard outside, with three companions, all leading horses. Still unconcerned, Fitzgerald went off to the stables, while two of the men entered the kitchen to the surprise of Mrs Fitzgerald who asked them who they were and what they wanted. One, Dan, did not reply but helped himself to some bread and jam. The other, the man who had first appeared on his own announced himself as Ned Kelly, and said he required food for himself and his friends, and for their horses. He assured Mrs Fitzgerald she had no cause to be alarmed. Mrs Fitzgerald called out to her husband who returned to the kitchen to find Kelly chatting amiably enough, but with a revolver in his hand. When they were joined a few moments later by a groom, Stephens, who greeted the strangers believing them to be there on business, Kelly said to him, 'I don't suppose you know who I am.'

'Perhaps you're Ned Kelly,' said Stephens. It had become the jocular remark to make to any stranger.

'That's a damn good guess,' replied Kelly flourishing the revolver he had been holding behind his back.

'I beg your pardon,' stammered Stephens. 'I thought you were joking.'

Everyone was highly amused at this exchange. Stephens then took the Kellys outside to feed their horses, and they were joined by Steve who announced that the station-hands were knocking off for lunch. Joe Byrne placed himself at the door of a large storeroom near the house, while Ned and Steve intercepted the station hands and marched them and Fitzgerald into the storeroom. The entire episode was carried off in an atmosphere of extreme affability, the station-hands being assured they would not be harmed as long as they did not try to escape. The storeroom door was locked, and Steve and Dan stood guard over it, while Ned and Joe were having lunch with Mrs Fitzgerald.

It was only a few minutes later that Mr Macaulay, the manager, returned to the station. As he approached the house he was astonished to find the place apparently deserted, and called out, 'Where is everybody?' From the storeroom, the voice of Fitzgerald replied, 'The Kellys are here,' and at that moment Ned himself appeared from the house and held up the manager, assuring him that they had no intention of stealing anything other than food for themselves and their horses, and a couple of hours' rest. Macaulay saw no point in objecting to this, and joined Ned, Joe and Mrs Fitzgerald for lunch in the kitchen where Ned, again suspicious, insisted on his food being tasted before he ate.

'There's far too much strychnine and arsenic about for a man to feel safe,' he said. 'D'you remember Morgan? He wouldn't eat anything except boiled eggs, and he wouldn't even touch those if the shells were cracked.'

After they had eaten, Ned and Joe took their turn to guard the prisoners in the storeroom while Dan and Steve had their lunch. During the afternoon, one or two of the station hands were allowed out at a time, and the four outlaws rested and slept at different times. Towards dusk, a travelling haberdasher named Gloster arrived at the station in his covered wagon. Unharnessing his horses and making camp in one of the fields, he walked up to the house to get some water to make tea, but encountered Ned and Dan who accompanied him back to the wagon, relieved him of a revolver and some fresh clothes from his stock, as well as perfume which they sprinkled over themselves, and invited the draper to join the party in the storeroom. During the evening, Ned showed himself perfectly willing to discuss his exploits with the assembled company, freely admitting to the shootings at Stringybark Creek, and reminiscing also about his earlier life and his family. Early next morning the twenty or so prisoners were allowed to have breakfast at the house after which they were locked up again. In the middle of the day, a party of visitors arrived in a horse and cart driven by a farmer named Casement, and they too were herded in with the station hands. While Joe Byrne stood guard, the Kelly brothers and Steve Hart grabbed axes and went off to cut down the telegraph wires that ran alongside the railway line not far from Faithfull's Creek. Four railway workers who were inquisitive or public-spirited enough to come up and demand to know what they were doing were taken prisoner and escorted to the storeroom.

Before they finally left Younghusband's property, Ned asked the manager, Macaulay, if he had an account at the bank in Euroa. Macaulay replied that he had, and Ned said, 'Write me a cheque then.' When Macaulay refused, Ned simply went to his desk, found a cheque book and tore a cheque from it. 'This'll do,' he said, putting it in his pocket. He was now ready for Euroa. Steve had already ridden off towards the town, Ned commandeered Casement's horse and cart, and set off after him, while Dan followed in the draper's wagon. Joe Byrne stayed behind to guard Younghusband's station and its staff and guests.

Steve Hart was first to arrive in Euroa. After having a look around the town, he went into a café a few doors from the National Bank, ate a meal, and waited for Ned and Dan to turn up. When they arrived, Steve led Dan and his wagon into the courtyard of the bank, while Ned left his horse and cart outside the front entrance. Ned's plan had been to walk up to the cashier with a cheque in his hand, pretending that he wanted it cashed. He entered the bank intending to do this, strode up to the cashier and was in the act of presenting his cheque when he saw Steve coming in from the back door. Retrieving his cheque, Ned presented a revolver instead at the startled cashier. Steve went behind the counter, held up the manager and two clerks and relieved them of the revolvers they carried. Ned crossed to the front door of the bank and closed it. The operation had been carefully timed: it was now just past closing time. Dan loitered about on guard outside the bank.

Mr Scott, the bank manager, had been just on his way out to attend a funeral, when the outlaws introduced themselves and Kelly demanded money from the cashier. Scott said to the cashier, 'I don't see how we can stop them taking the money, but we certainly won't give them anything.' He was, presumably, protecting his own position. Steve Hart ushered the staff into an office, while Ned asked Scott where his own apartment and his family were. Scott told him, and added, 'You be careful how you deal with my wife.'

'You be careful how you address Mr Kelly,' Steve Hart advised, as he returned from the office in which he had locked the cashier and the clerks.

'What's the matter with your wife?' asked Kelly. 'Is she nervous?'

'No,' admitted the manager, 'she's quite all right.'

'In that case,' said Kelly, 'you can take me out and introduce me.'

Scott preceded Ned down a corridor to his living quarters behind the bank office, where they found Mrs Scott dressing her several children for a walk. 'My dear,' said Scott, 'this is Mr Ned Kelly who has just held up the bank.' Ned assured Mrs Scott, who seemed not at all nervous but excited at the prospect of adventure, that there was no cause for her to worry. 'I want all of you to get ready for a drive out to Younghusband's Station,' he added. 'You won't come to any harm, and you'll only be away a few hours.'

Leaving Mrs Scott and her children to prepare for their unexpected outing, Kelly returned to the bank offices with the manager, and took possession of just under £2,000 in cash, thirty ounces of gold, a number of mortgages and other property documents, as well as two revolvers and a box of cartridges. Then everyone was herded into the bank yard for the trip to Faithfull's Creek. The party consisted of the bank staff, the manager's wife and seven children, Mrs Scott's mother, and two servant girls, one of whom had gone to school with Steve Hart and was intrigued and excited to discover he was now a member of the Kelly Gang. In order to accommodate so many people, Kelly appropriated the bank manager's horse and buggy. When they were ready to set off, Scott unexpectedly produced a bottle of whisky and invited the gang to join him in a swig, which they did.

The procession of three vehicles moved off. Dan Kelly drove the drapery hawker's cart, with the bank clerks and one of the servant girls as his passengers. The bank manager's family and children followed in their buggy with Mrs Scott at the reins. Ned had advised her not to try to raise an alarm, for her husband would be travelling behind in the third cart with Ned himself and the second servant girl. Steve Hart brought up the rear on horseback. They drove slowly through the town, occasionally exchanging greetings with passing citizens, who must have thought the bank manager was treating his family, his staff, and some visitors to a picnic in the country. On the way out of town they passed, without incident, the funeral which the bank manager had been going to attend.

The party arrived at Younghusband's Station at about six in the evening, and the women were asked to set about preparing a meal for thirty people. The prisoners already at the station were both astonished and amused that the Kellys had not only successfully robbed the bank but had also managed to kidnap everyone on the premises, and an atmosphere of gaiety and cameraderie developed. After supper, Ned talked at length to the company in answer to questions about his life, and his reasons for robbing and killing. He claimed never to have molested a working man or a farmer. His battle was against a corrupt police force, and an unjust social system. 'I'll rob the banks,' he said, 'and if I get my hands on any more mortgages, I'll burn them, the same as those I got this afternoon.' Later, when a bonfire was made of the outlaws' old clothing which they had exchanged for new at the station, Ned flung the bank documents into the flames.

Next day, when a half-burnt woman's hat was found among the ashes, the rumour began that one of the Gang, Steve Hart, occasionally rode dressed as a woman. There is no firm evidence that he did, nor does it seem at all likely. (A month later, a man named George Cherry reported to the police that the Gang had been seen at Patrick Quinn's, near Moyhu, and that Ned Kelly had then been dressed as a woman!)

In addition to Ned's talk, the Kelly's guests were entertained by exhibitions of trick riding by Dan, Joe and Steve. At last, around eight o'clock, the outlaws were ready to leave. Ned addressed the company, warning them to stay where they were for three hours. 'If anyone leaves within three hours, I'll shoot him dead. I can track you anywhere in this country, and I'm a man of my word.' He gave Mrs Fitzgerald a bulky envelope addressed to Mr Cameron, member of the Legislative Assembly, and asked her to post it for him. Then he and his three companions mounted, wheeled about and galloped off into the darkening night. They left behind them a company of people whose feelings towards them ranged from irritation through fear to uneasy admiration. Not one of them attempted to leave the Station before eleven o'clock, when the bank manager Mr Scott and his family returned to break the news in Euroa.

A few days later, on December 14th, Mrs Fitzgerald posted from Glenrowan the letter Kelly had given her. Its recipient, Donald Cameron, was a Member of Parliament who had spoken against the Felon's Apprehension Act which outlawed the Kellys. Here is the full text of the letter: the spelling, punctuation and underlinings (here italicized) are as in the original manuscript:

Dear Sir,

Take no offence if I take the opportunity of writing a few lines to you wherein I wish to state a few remarks concerning the case of Trooper Fitzpatrick against Mrs Kelly W. Skillion and W. Williamson and to state the facts of the case to you.

It seems impossible for me to get any justice without I make a statement to some one that will take notice of it as it is no use in me complaining about anything that the Police may choose to say or swear against me and the public in their ignorance and blindness will undoubtedly back them up to their utmost.

No doubt I am now placed in very peculiar circumstances and you might blame me for it but if you knew how I have been wronged and persecuted you would say I cannot be blamed.

In April last an information was (which must have come under your notice) sworn against me for shooting trooper Fitzpatrick which was false and my mother with an infant baby and brother-in-law and another neighbour was taken for aiding and abetting and attempting to murder him a charge of they are as purely innocent as the child unborn.

During my stay on the King River I run in a wild bull which I gave to Lydicher who afterwards sold him to Carr and he killed him for beef.

Sometime afterwards I was told I was blamed for stealing this bull from Whitty I asked Whitty on Moyhu racecourse why he blamed me for stealing his bull he said he had found his bull and *he* never blamed me for stealing him.

He said it was Farrell who told him that I stole the bull. Sometimes afterwards I heard again I was blamed for stealing a mob of calves from Whitty and Farrell which I never had anything to do with and along with this and other talk I began to think they wanted something to talk about.

Whitty and Burns not being satisfied with all the picked land on King River and Boggy Creek and the run of their stock on the certificate ground free and no one interfering with them. Paid heavy rent for all the open ground so as a poor man could not keep any stock and impounded every beast they could catch even off government roads if a poor man happened to leave his horse or bit of a poddy calf outside his paddock it would be impounded.

I have known over 60 head of horses to be in one day impounded by Whitty and Burns all belonging to poor men of the district they would have to leave their harvest or ploughing and go to Oxley and then perhaps not have money enough to release them and have to give a bill of sale or borrow the money which is no easy matter and along with all this sort of work Farrell the Policeman stole a horse from George King and has him in Whitty and Jeffrey's paddock until he left the force and this was the cause of me and my stepfather George King stealing Whitty's horses and selling them to Baumgarten and those other men the pick of them was sold to Howlong and the rest was sold to Baumgarten who was a perfect stranger to me and I believe an honest man.

No man had anything to do with the horses but me and George King William Cooke who was convicted for Whitty's horses had nothing to do with them nor was he ever in my company at Peterson the German's at Howlong.

The brands was altered by me and George King and the horses were sold as straight.

Anyman requiring horses would have bought them the same as those men and would have been potted the same and I consider Whitty ought to do something towards the release of those innocent men otherwise there will be a collision between me and him as I can to his satisfaction prove I took J. Welshe's black mare and the rest of the horses which I will prove to him in next issue and after those horses had been found and the row being over them I wrote a letter to Mr Swannell of Lake Rowan to advertise my horses for sale as I was intend to sell out.

I sold them afterwards at Benalla and the rest in New South Wales and left Victoria as I wished see to certain parts of the country and very shortly afterward there was a warrant for me and as I since hear the Police Sergeant Steel, Straughan and Fitzpatrick and others searched the Seven Mile and every other place in the district for me and a man named Newman who had escaped from the Wangaratta Police for months before the 15th of April. Therefore it was impossible for me to be in Victoria as every schoolboy knows me and on the 15th of April Fitzpatrick came to the Seven Mile and had some conversation with Williamson who was splitting on the hill seeing my brother and another man he rode down and had some conversation with this man whom he swore was William Skillion this man was not called in Beechworth as he could have proved Fitzpatrick's falsehood as Skillion and another man was away after horses at this time which can be proved by eight or nine witnesses the man who the trooper swore was Skillion can prove Williamson's innocence besides other important evidence which can be brought on the prisoners behalf.

The trooper after speaking to this man rode to the house and Dan came out he asked Dan to go to Greta with him Dan asked him what for and he said he had a warrant for him for stealing Whitty's horses.

They both went inside Dan was having something to eat trooper was impatient and Mrs. Kelly asked him what he wanted Dan for and he said he had a warrant for him.

Dan said produce your warrant and he said he had none it was only a telegram from Chiltern.

Mrs. Kelly said he need not go unless he liked without a warrant. She told him the trooper had no business on her premises without some authority besides his own word.

He pulled out his revolver and said he would blow her brains out if she interfered in the arrest Mrs. Kelly said if Ned was here he would ram the revolver down his throat.

To frighten the trooper Dan said Ned is coming now. The trooper looked around to see if it was true Dan dropped his knife and fork which shewed he had no murderous intention clapped Heenan's hug on him took his revolver and threw him and part of the door outside and kept him there until Skillion and Ryan came with horses which Dan sold that night the trooper left and invented some scheme to say he got shot which any man can see it is impossible for him to have been shot. He told Dan to clear out that Sergeant Steel or Detective Brown would be there before morning as Straughan was over the Murray trying to get up a case against Dan and the Lloyds as the Germans over the Murray would swear to any one and they will lag you guilty or not.

Next day Skillion, Williamson and Mrs. Kelly with an infant were taken and thrown into prison and were six months awaiting trial and no bail allowed and was convicted on the evidence of the meanest man that ever the sun shone on I have been told by Police that he is hardly ever sober also between him and his father they sold his sister to a Chinaman but he seems a strapping and rather genteel looking young man more fit to be a starcher to a laundry than a trooper, but to a keen observer he has the wrong appearance to have anything like a clear conscience or a manly heart the deceit is too plain to be seen in the white cabbage hearted looking face.

I heard nothing of this transaction until very close on the trial I being then over 400 miles from Greta.

I heard I was outlawed and £100 reward for me in Victoria and also hundreds of charges of horsestealing was against me besides shooting a trooper.

I came to Victoria and enquired after my brother and found him working with another man on Bullock Creek.

Heard how the Police used to be blowing that they would shoot me first and then cry surrender.

How they used to come to the house when there was no one there but women and Superintendent Smith used to say see all the men I have out today I will have as many more tomorrow and blow him into pieces as small as paper that is in our guns and they used to repeatedly rush into the house revolver in hand upset milk dishes empty the flour out on the ground break tins of eggs and even throw the meat out of the cask on to the floor and dirty and destroy all the provisions which can be proved and shove the girls in front of them into the rooms like dogs and abuse and insult them. Detective Ward and Constable Hayes took out their revolvers and threatened to shoot the girls and children whilst Mrs Skillion was absent, the oldest being with her.

The greatest murders and ruffians would not be guilty of such an action.

His sort of cruelty and disgraceful conduct to my brothers and sisters who had no protection coupled with the conviction of my mother and those innocent men certainly made my blood boil and don't think there is any man born could have the patience to suffer what I did.

They were not satisfied with frightening and insulting my sisters night and day and destroying their provisions and lagging my mother with an infant baby and those innocent men but should follow me and my brother who was innocent of having anything to do with any stolen horses into the wilds where he had been quietly digging and doing well neither molesting or interfering with any one.

And I was not there long and on the 25th of October I came on the tracks of Police horses between tabletop and the boys I crossed them and went to Emu Swamp and returning home I came on more Police tracks making for our camp.

I told my mates and me and my brother went out next morning and found Police camped at the shingle hut with long fire arms and we came to the conclusion our doom was sealed unless we could take their firearms, as we had nothing but a gun and a rifle, if they came on us at our work or camp we had no chance only to die like dogs as we thought the country was woven with Police and we might have a chance of fighting them if we had firearms as it generally takes 40 to one.

We approached the spring as close as we could get to the camp. The intervening space being clear we saw two men at the top they got up and one took a double barrel fowling piece and one drove the horses down and hobled them against the tent and we thought there was more men in the tent those being on sentry. We could have shot those two men without speaking but not wishing to take life we waited McIntyre laid the gun against the stump Lonigan sat on the log I advanced my brother Dan keeping McIntyre covered I called on them to throw up their hands McIntyre obeyed and never attempted to reach for his gun or revolver.

Lonigan ran to a battery of logs and put his head up to take aim at me when I shot him or he would have shot me as I knew well I asked who was in the tent McIntyre replied no one.

I approached the camp and took possession of their revolvers and fowling piece which I loaded with bullets instead of shot I told McIntyre I did not want to shoot him or any man that would surrender I explained Fitzpatrick's falsehood which no policeman can be ignorant of.

He said he knew Fitzpatrick had wronged us but he could not help it. He said he intended to leave the force on account of his bad health his life was insured the other two men who had no firearms came up when they heard the shot fired, and went back to our camp for fear the Police might call there in our absence and surprise us on our arrival.

My brother went back to the spring and I stopped at the top with McIntyre, Kennedy and Scanlan came up, McIntyre said he would get them to surrender if I spared their lives as well as his, I said I did not know either him Scanlan or Kennedy and had nothing against them and would not shoot any of them if they gave up their firearms and promise to leave the force as it was the meanest billet in the world they are worse than cold blooded murderers or hangmen.

He said he was sure they would never follow me any more. I gave him my word I would give them a chance McIntyre went up to Kennedy Scanlan being behind with a rifle and revolver I called on them to throw up their hands Scanlan slewed his horse around to gallop away but turned again, and as quick as thought fired at me with the rifle and was in the act of firing again when I shot him.

Kennedy alighted on the off side of his horse and got behind a tree and opened hot fire McIntyre got on Kennedy's horse and galloped away.

I could have shot him if I choose as he was right against me but rather than break my word I let him go.

My brother advanced from the spring Kennedy fired at him and ran as he found neither of us was dead.

I followed him he got behind another tree and fired at me again. I shot him in the arm-pit as he was behind the tree he dropped his revolver and ran again and slewed round and I fired with the gun again and shot him through the right chest as I did not know he had dropped his revolver and was turning to surrender he could not live or I would have let him go.

Had they been my own brothers I could not help shooting them, or else lie down and let them shoot me which they would have done had their bullets been directed as they intended them.

But as for handcuffing Kennedy to a tree or cutting his ear off, or brutally treating any one them, is a cruel falsehood.

If Kennedy's ear was cut off it has been done since. I put his cloak over him and left him as honourable as I could and if they were my own brothers I could not be more sorry for them with the exception of Lonigan I did not begrudge him what bit of lead he got as he was the flashest and meanest man that I had any account against him Fitzpatrick Sergeant Whelan Constable O'Day and King the bootmaker once tried to handcuff me at Benalla and when they could not Fitzpatrick tried to choke me. Lonigan caught me by the privates and would have killed me but was not able Mr

McInnis came up and I allowed him to put the handcuffs on when the Police were bested.

This cannot be called wilful murder for I was compelled to shoot them in my own defence or lie down like a cur and die.

Certainly their wives and children are to be pitied but those men came into the bush with the intention of shooting me down like a dog and yet they know and acknowledge I have been wronged.

And is my mother and her infant baby and my poor little brothers and sisters not to be pitied moreso who has got no alternative only to put up with brutal and unmanly conduct of the Police who have never had any relation or a mother or must have forgot them I was never convicted of horsestealing I was once arrested by Constable Hall and 14 more men in Greta and there was a subscription raised for Hall by persons who had too much money about Greta in honour of Hall arresting Wild Wright and Gunn.

Wright and Gunn were potted and Hall could not pot me for horsestealing but with the subscription money he gave £20 to James Murdock who has recently been hung in Wagga Wagga and on Murdock's evidence I was found guilty of receiving knowing to be stolen which I. Wright W. Ambrose J. Ambrose and W. Hatcher and W. Williamson and others can prove I was innocent of Knowing the mare to be stolen and I was once accused of taking a hawker of the name of McCormacks horse to pull another hawker named Ben Gould out of a bog.

Mr. Gould got up in the morning to feed his horses seen McCormack's horse and knew he had strayed sent his man in with him about two miles to where McCormack was camped in Greta.

Mr and Mrs McCormack came out and seen the waggons bogged and accused him of using the horse.

I told Gould that was for his good nature Mrs McCormack turned on me and accused me for catching the horse for Gould as Gould knew he was wicked and could not catch him himself. Me and my uncle was cutting and branding calves and Ben Gould wrapped up a pair of testicles wrote a note and gave it to me to give to Mrs McCormack McCormack said he would fight me I was then 14 years of age, I was getting off my horse and Mrs McCormack hit the horse he jumped forwards and my fist came in collision with McCormack's nose who swore he was standing 10 yards away from another man and the one hit knocked two men down, however ridiculous the evidence may seem I received 3 months or 10£ fine for hitting him and 3 months for delivering the parcel and bound to the peace for 12 months.

At the time I was taken by Hall and his 14 assistants, therefore I dare not strike any of them as Hall was a great cur, and as for Dan he never was tried for assaulting a woman Mr Butler PM sentenced him to 3 months without the option of a fine and one month or two pounds fine for wilfully destroying property a sentence which there is no law to uphold and yet they had to do their sentences and their prosecutor Mr D Goodman since got 4 years for perjury concerning the same property.

The Minister of Justice should enquire into this respecting their sentence and he will find a wrong jurisdiction given by Butler P.M. on the 19th of October 1877 at Benalla.

And these are the only charges was ever proved against either of us therefore we are falsely represented.

The report of bullets having being fired into the bodies of the troopers after their death is false and the coroner should be consulted *I have no intention of asking mercy for myself of any mortal man, or apologising, but I wish to give timely warning that if my people do not get justice and those innocents released from prison and the Police wear their uniforms I shall be forced to seek revenge of everything of the human race for the future.*

I will not take innocent life if justice is given but as it is the Police are afraid or ashamed to wear their uniform therefore every mans life is in danger as I was outlawed without any cause and cannot be no worse and have but once to die and if the public do not see justice done I will seek revenge for the name and character which has been given to me and my relations while God gives me strength to pull a trigger.

The witnesses which can prove Fitzpatrick's falsehood can be found by advertising and if this is not done immediately horrible disasters will follow. Fitzpatrick shall be the cause of greater slaughter to the rising generation than St. Patrick was to the snakes and frogs in Ireland.

For had I robbed, plundered, ravished and murdered everything I met my character could not be painted blacker than it is at present but thank God my conscience is as clear as the snow in Peru and as I hear a picked jury amongst which was a discharged Sergeant of Police was impanelled on the trial and David Lindsay who gave evidence for the Crown is a shantykeeper having no license and is liable to a heavy fine and keeps a book of information for the Police and *his* character needs no comment for he is capable of rendering Fitzpatrick any assistance he required for a conviction as he could be broke any time Fitzpatrick chose to inform on him.

I am really astonished to see members of the Legislative Assembly led astray by such articles as the Police for while an outlaw reigns their pocket swells, Tis double pay and country girls.

By concluding as I have no more paper unless I rob for it, if I get justice I will cry a go.

For I need no lead or powder to revenge my cause, and if words be louder I will oppose your laws.

With no offence (remember your railroads) and a sweet good bye

     from

          Edward Kelly
          a forced outlaw

SIX

The success of the Kelly's raid on the National Bank at Euroa was a great embarrassment to the Police. Acting on information received from one of their informers, Superintendent Nicolson sent all the men at his command to the banks of the Murray River, having been assured that the Gang was attempting to escape into New South Wales. In fact, the Gang was closer to home, rejoicing in the knowledge that there were, temporarily, no police in the vicinity. They shared out the spoils of the bank raid amongst their relatives and friends, promising them that there was plenty more where that came from. 'We've got an account at every bank in Australia,' Ned is reported to have said.

When the police returned some days later from their exhausting and unproductive search along the banks of the Murray, they found that the majority of local debts and fines had been settled up in crisp, new banknotes. Ned's sister, Mrs Skillion, boasted to a police sergeant at Wangaratta of her collection of 'nice new sovereigns'. A number of unlikely people were in possession of gold dust which they claimed to have found in abandoned mine workings. Disillusioned with his informers, Superintendent Nicolson claimed that the only reliable information he ever received about the outlaws came from Ned Kelly himself. He rounded up twenty known Kelly sympathizers, and gaoled them, but not one of them was willing or able to betray the Gang. It was becoming clear that the police were fighting a hopeless battle, and that their quarry was invariably more than just one leap ahead of them. Not only in the Kelly Country, but even in the City of Melbourne, the public came to consider the police as laughing-stocks. Newspapers and magazines not only ridiculed their inability to catch four young men but also published highly romanticized accounts of the exploits of the four outlaws. 'That four young fellows,' wrote one editor, 'should set at defiance every effort of that mighty Engine of Civilization, the Police Force, is one of the most extraordinary things of the age, as ridiculous as it is reproachful.'

Ned's letter to Cameron, the M.P., proved less helpful to his cause than he had hoped. Cameron referred it to the Chief Secretary who merely released an abridged version to the press, with all unflattering references to the police eliminated.

The Chief Commissioner of the Victorian Police Force, Captain Standish, travelled up to Euroa to discover for himself what progress Superintendent Nicolson was making. Finding Nicolson exhausted and dispirited, Standish sent him back to Melbourne and called on Superintendent Hare to take over the pursuit of the Kelly Gang. The Government, at the request of the banks, sent police to guard every branch in the colony.

At Benalla, meanwhile, Superintendent Hare acquainted himself with the situation locally, while his men continued to chase about the country to no purpose. Three weeks after the Euroa bank robbery, as the year 1879 began, all trails seemed cold, and Hare decided to concentrate on attempting to destroy the extensive though loosely organized network which he was convinced was keeping the Gang supplied with food and information about Police movements. But, although he was able to arrest a few more sympathizers, he could produce no evidence. After constant remands, and reappearances in court over several months, all of his prisoners were eventually given their freedom. During this time, the Chief Secretary received a letter from Ned Kelly:

Sir,
I take the liberty of addressing you with respect to the matter of myself, my brother and my two friends Hart and Byrne. And I take this opportunity to declare most positively that we did not kill the policemen in cold blood, as has been stated by that rascal McIntyre. We only fired on them to save ourselves, and we are not the cold-blooded murderers which people presume us to be. Circumstances have forced us to become what we are – outcasts and outlaws, and, bad as we are, we are not so bad as we are supposed to be.

But my chief reason for writing this is to tell you that you are committing a manifest injustice in imprisoning so many innocent people just because they are supposed to be friendly to us. There is not the least foundation for the charge of aiding and abetting us against any of them, and you may know this is correct, or we would not be obtaining our food as usual since they have been arrested.

Your policemen are cowards – every one of them. I have been with one party two hours while riding in the ranges and they did not know me.

I will show you that we are determined men, and I warn you that within a week we will leave your colony, but we will not leave it until we have made the country ring with the name of Kelly and taken terrible revenge for the injustice and oppression we have been subjected to. Beware, for we are now desperate men.

Edward Kelly.

For a few weeks, the Gang remained quiet, though occasionally one or another of them would be seen riding through a small country town or cantering along a bush road. One evening Joe Byrne, perhaps for a bet, appeared in the back bar of the Commercial Hotel at Beechworth, drank a glass of brandy and chatted to several acquaintances, before disappearing as quickly as he had come. For the most part, however, the Gang kept in hiding in the hills, and Ned himself worked at the composition of another lengthy apologia which he decided to have printed. One of Ned's cousins, Mary Miller, frequently rode out to their hideout at night, with food and supplies. She was an attractive young woman, and legend has it that she and Ned were lovers.

On the afternoon of February 4th, Dan Kelly and Joe Byrne visited Aaron Sherritt where he was working on a new selection in the middle of the Woolshed Ranges, and Joe explained that they were going to cross the Murray and make for Goulburn, a town in New South Wales, where a cousin of the Kelly boys lived. They would also stick up a bank in New South Wales. Perhaps Aaron would like to go along with them as a scout? Aaron considered the proposition, but finally decided against it. Joe said he understood, and he and Dan rode off. They did not, however, head north-east for Goulburn. Instead, they rode to the west, met Ned and Steve at a prearranged spot, then made their way north to the Murray which they crossed on a raft, a few miles from Yarrawonga. It took them four days, riding through desolate bush country by day and resting at night, to reach their objective. On the fourth evening they camped about two miles outside the small and straggling New South Wales town of Jerilderie, a community of no more than two hundred and fifty inhabitants. It was here, and not at Goulburn, as they had told Aaron (whom they no longer completely trusted), that they had designs upon the bank.

In spite of Jerilderie's small population, there was a pub for every fifty people, and in one of the five, Davidson's Hotel, about a mile or more outside the town, Dan and Joe had a meal and a few drinks that evening. After they had left and ridden off, Ned and Steve entered and ate a meal. A few hundred yards down the road in the direction of Jerilderie, the four joined company again and set off together for the police station. It was now quite late, and the two constables who resided at the station, together with the wife and children of one of them, were asleep. Having discovered in conversation at the pub the names of the two policemen, Senior Constable Devine and Constable Richards, Ned galloped up to the police station, shouting, 'Mr Devine, there's a row on at Davidson's Hotel. Come quick, or there'll be murder.'

The two policemen inside leapt out of bed and dressed quickly. Devine opened the front door, while Richards rushed round from his room at the back of the station. The four outlaws pushed their way in, held up the two constables and handcuffed them. Kelly demanded to know who else was in the building.

'Only my wife and children,' replied Devine, as he and Richards were forced into a cell already occupied by a drunk. The noise had aroused Mrs Devine who now appeared in her nightdress. Devine, who was certainly not devoid of courage, was inclined to be unco-operative, and Kelly told him it was his wife's presence alone which saved his life. He advised Devine to resign from the police force within a month, or he would come back and shoot him.

'How can I leave the force after all my years of service?' argued Devine. 'I've got my family to think of.'

Ned did not pursue the subject, but instead told Devine the two purposes of his visit to Jerilderie: to arrange for the printing of a statement he had written, and, of course, to rob the Bank of New South Wales.

Dan, Steve and Joe, guided by Mrs Devine, had searched the police station, commandeered some arms and ammunition, and stabled their horses. After Mrs Devine had been allowed to rejoin her children, the men in the front part of the station settled down for the night, the Gang standing guard by turns.

Next morning, which was Sunday, Kelly was determined that everything should appear to be as usual in Jerilderie and its police station. When Mrs Devine informed him that she was expected to prepare the courthouse opposite the station for the visiting priest who celebrated mass there every Sunday morning, Ned allowed her to go, but sent Dan with her. Dan, wearing Constable Richards' spare uniform, helped Mrs Devine arrange the pews and place flowers on the improvised altar, while, in the yard of the police station, Joe and Steve, who were grooming their horses, politely nodded their greetings to the priest and the members of his congregation as they arrived.

After lunch at the station, Joe Byrne donned a police uniform, and he and Dan patrolled the town in the company of Constable Richards whom they had released for the purpose and provided with an empty revolver. Richards, as instructed, introduced them to people they met as members of a special squad on their way to Victoria to help hunt the Kellys. The two special squad members showed particular interest in the Bank of New South Wales, a single-storied building adjoining the eastern end of the Royal Mail Hotel. They got back to the station to find everything in order, and Constable Richards was returned to his cell. In the evening three of the gang had a meal with Mrs Devine and the children, and then retired for the night. Joe Byrne, however, had changed into a tweed suit and disappeared at six o'clock. He rode off to Davidson's Hotel where he stayed for most of the evening, talking to the barmaid and discovering that, on this side of the border, the Kellys were highly popular. When he finally left Davidson's, Joe was far from sober, and had to be helped on to his horse. His reception by Ned back at the police station was far from cordial: 'Where the hell have you been? You'll ruin all our plans.'

The four outlaws were up and about very early on Monday morning. Joe, still in his tweed suit, took his and Ned's horses to the blacksmith to be shod. The blacksmith, impressed by the two splendid thoroughbreds, was inquisitive, but Joe cut his conversation short with, 'Do you mind getting on with your work? I'm in a hurry.' When the horses were shod, he told the blacksmith to charge his fee to the police account, and bought him a drink at the Royal Mail Hotel. He then went to the butcher's, and to the general store where he purchased sardines, before returning to the station where he found Chief Constable Devine still in his cell, Mrs Devine and the children locked in the dining-room, and Ned and Dan in uniform, ready and waiting, accompanied by Constable Richards with his empty revolver.

Shortly before noon, the group set out from the police station. Ned, Dan and Constable Richards, in uniform, walked, while Joe and Steve, in plain clothes, both rode and led the other two horses. As they walked, Constable Richards asked Ned who his most reliable man was. His brother? 'No,' said Ned. He pointed at Byrne. 'That bloke. He's as straight and as true as steel.'

At noon, they walked into the Royal Mail Hotel. The three men in uniform, the Kelly brothers and Richards, went in through the front entrance, while Joe and Steve rode into the back yard, dismounted, entered through the back door with their revolvers drawn, and shepherded everyone they could find towards the front of the hotel. The Chinese cook who protested was knocked on the head with a gun by Steve Hart, and hastily withdrew his protests.

In the parlour, Ned had called for the publican, Mr Cox. When Cox appeared, Constable Richards introduced the outlaws: 'This is Ned Kelly, this is Dan Kelly and the men with police guns are Joe Byrne and Steve Hart.'

Kelly said, 'I won't do you any harm, but what I want I must have. I need a room to put my prisoners in, as I'm going to stick up the bank next door.'

Cox assured Ned he could have any room in the house, and the dining-room near the front of the hotel was chosen. While Steve kept everyone in order, Dan stood at the front door capturing newcomers as they came in from the street. The dining-room was soon crowded, and Ned ordered the publican to serve drinks to all his guests, 'on the Kellys'. Addressing the assembled company, he announced, 'We don't want to hurt anyone, but if we have to shoot, we'll shoot to kill.' Dan flourished his revolver and added, 'The policeman we got this from is dead.' After a couple of drinks, Ned and Joe Byrne left to visit the bank next door.

At the bank, the manager, Mr Tarleton, was in his living quarters at the rear. The senior clerk, Mr Lyving, was at his desk, while the junior clerk, Mackie, stood outside in the street.

Joe Byrne entered through the back door as Ned came in by the front entrance. Joe stumbled in, pretending to be drunk, and, taking him for someone who had been chucked out of the pub, Lyving cried out 'What the devil do you mean coming in the back door like that? If you've got any business here, go round and come in at the front.' The customer who had made a legitimate entrance through the front door at this moment thrust a revolver at the clerk. 'Put up your hands,' he said, 'I'm Kelly.'

'I'll be blowed. You're kidding me.'

'Come on, quickly, what firearms have you got?'

'I haven't got any.'

The junior clerk, Mackie, came in from the street and was quickly covered by Joe Byrne who asked, 'Who are you?'

'My name's Mackie. I work here.'

'Are you Tarleton?' Kelly asked the senior clerk.

'No.'

'Where is he?'

'I suppose he's in his rooms at the back.'

'Let's go and see if you can find him,' said Kelly. Joe Byrne escorted Mackie to the pub, handed him over to Dan and Steve, and rejoined Ned at the bank where Lyving was rushing nervously from room to room looking for the manager whom he eventually found in his bath.

'Excuse me, sir,' Lyving said as he pushed open the bathroom door, 'but we're being held up. The Kellys are here.'

'Don't talk rubbish, man.'

'They've stuck up the police, too.'

Tarleton caught sight of Ned behind his chief clerk. 'You'd better come out of there,' said Ned. Steve Hart arrived from the pub, stood guard over Tarleton while he dressed and then took him back to the pub. Ned and Joe returned to the business section of the bank with Lyving, and ordered him to hand over all the cash on the premises.

'We haven't got very much,' said the clerk. 'It's all been sent away. We've only got about six or seven hundred pounds.'

'Oh no,' said Kelly. 'More like nine or ten thousand.'

'There's nothing like that amount. All we've got is the teller's cash.'

Ned went behind the counter to look at the teller's cash which consisted mainly of gold, silver, and coppers. He disappeared into the rear of the building, and came back a moment later with a sugar bag which he filled with the cash, amounting to just under £700. 'Now, where's the rest?' he asked, as he proceeded to look into a safe that was open.

'There's nothing there except a lot of papers and documents,' said Lyving. 'They're no use to you.'

Finding a drawer inside the safe locked, Ned commanded Lyving to open it.

'I can't,' said the clerk. 'Anyway, there's nothing of any use to you in there.'

Kelly insisted, and the clerk explained he could only half-open it, as it was a check-lock which required two keys of which he held one. He handed over his key, and Ned turned it in the lock. The drawer remained closed.

'I'll get a sledge-hammer from across the road,' said Joe Byrne.

'Wait a moment,' ordered Ned. 'Who's got the other key? Tarleton?'

'Yes,' replied Lyving, and Ned went next door to fetch the bank manager. As soon as he had gone, a customer walked into the bank, and was ordered by Joe to put his hands up, 'You'd better do as he says, old chap,' advised Lyving, as the newcomer hesitated. 'This is the Kelly gang.'

Ned returned with Tarleton whom he ordered to open the locked drawer. 'Who are you?' he demanded of the new arrival.

'My name's Elliott. I'm the schoolmaster. I've come to withdraw some money.'

Kelly was amused. 'You're too late,' he shouted. 'Ned Kelly has just withdrawn it all. Well, now,' he continued, as he saw what was in the drawer which Tarleton had just opened. 'So this is your six or seven hundred pounds is it?' It was clear that the drawer contained at least twice as much. 'Jump over here,' he commanded the schoolmaster.

'I can't jump over the counter.'

'You'll bloody well have to. Come on.'

Elliott scrambled across the counter and Ned ordered him to hold the sugar bag open as the contents of the drawer were emptied into it. 'Thank you,' said Ned. 'I think you ought to give your kids a holiday in honour of my visit. Is that all there is?' he continued, to Tarleton. 'No more bloody lies or I'll shoot you.'

Tarleton swore there was no more cash on the premises, but Ned asked, 'What about the bills and securities?' He took a steel box from a shelf. 'What's in this?'

'Mortgages, deeds of property and documents of that kind.'

'Good, I'll burn them.'

'Careful, my life insurance policy's in there,' cried Lyving. And Tarleton tried to assure Kelly that it would be pointless to destroy the documents, as copies were held at the head office of the bank in Sydney. Ned, however, seized a handful of documents to the dismay of Lyving who cried, 'For God's sake, don't burn my life policy.'

Ned allowed the clerk to retrieve his insurance policy. He was becoming confused and annoyed by all these papers. He wanted to destroy any evidence of monies owed to the bank by poor farmers, but was anxious not to destroy their assets by mistake.

'Look, Kelly,' said the bank manager. 'There's no sense in destroying those. You'll only get me into trouble. I give you my word of honour you have all the money there is here.'

Uncertain what to believe, Kelly flung the documents down, and said, 'I haven't got time now, but I'll be back to look at these. And, what's more, I'll burn every ledger in the place.' He and Joe then conducted Tarleton, Lyving and Elliott next door to the pub.

Leaving Joe to usher the three new prisoners into the hotel dining-room, Ned returned to the bank to examine the documents more carefully. As he left the pub, he saw two men just entering the bank. Following them, he rushed into the bank calling on them to bail up, but the two startled citizens ran through the bank. Ned chased them, and saw the second man run into the hotel where he was caught and made to join the others. 'What the bloody hell do you mean by running away when I tell you to bail up?' he shouted in a fury, 'Now, where's the other bugger?' When he realized that the other man had not run into the hotel, Ned raced outside, but returned a minute or two later, still furious. 'The bastard's got away,' he shouted. 'This isn't going to do our plans any good. What's his name?'

No one answered. 'By God, the shooting's going to begin now,' said Ned. 'Where's that big bugger I chased in here?'

Steve Hart pushed the man forward. A shopkeeper named Rankin, he was also the local J.P. 'I'll shoot the bugger,' said

Ned, ramming his revolver against the man's forehead. There were cries of alarm and shock from the other prisoners, and one man, somewhat braver than his fellows, stepped forward, 'You've had it all your own way so far,' he said. 'And no one has interfered. But if you shoot Rankin, you'll have to shoot the lot of us.'

Ned's revolver was still pressed against Rankin's head. 'Who was the other one?' he repeated.

Someone called out, 'It was Gill, the newspaper proprietor,' Lowering his revolver, Ned thought quickly. It was imperative that Gill should not get to the telegraph office to send a message for help to a nearby town. He sent Joe Byrne to the telegraph office to take care of things there, and, leaving Steve and Dan to continue looking after the prisoners, he himself set off for Gill's house, accompanied by Constable Richards and Lyving, the bank clerk.

At the telegraph office, Joe held up the postmaster and his assistant, rendered the switchboard useless, and checked through the copies of all telegrams sent that day, to satisfy himself that Gill had not got any message out.

Meanwhile, Lyving and Constable Richards had conducted Ned to Gill's home which was next door to his newspaper and printing office. The door was opened by Mrs Gill to whom Richards introduced Kelly.

'Don't be frightened,' said Kelly. 'I'm not going to hurt you or your husband. He shouldn't have run away, though.'

'I'm not afraid,' Mrs Gill replied, 'but he hasn't come back here. If you were to shoot me now, I still couldn't tell you where he is. I dare say you gave him such a fright that he's probably collapsed somewhere.'

This was actually close to the truth. At that moment the newspaper proprietor was lying hidden in Billabong Creek, not far behind his office. And there he stayed until he was certain the Kellys had left town.

'You can see the woman is telling the truth, Kelly,' said Lyving.

Kelly addressed himself to Mrs Gill. 'What I want your husband to do is print some copies of a statement I've written, about certain things I've done. I'll pay for them when I come back to collect them later. I wanted to explain to him how I wanted it done.'

'Well, I can't help it. He's not here,' said Mrs Gill, and refused to accept the statement which Kelly wanted to leave with her. Lyving, however, offered to take care of it and give it to Gill as soon as possible, so Ned handed it over to him. The three men then left the Gill house, and made their way to the telegraph office to join Joe Byrne. On the way, they called in at another of Jerilderie's hotels, McDougall's. Ned slapped his revolver down on the bar, paid for drinks for everyone present, and informed the landlord he was taking a mare from the stable and would return it in three weeks' time. He and his party then proceeded to the telegraph office, where Joe had everything under control. As a final precaution, Ned broke the insulators with the butt of his revolver and led his little company, including the postmaster and his assistant, back to the Royal Mail Hotel.

On Kelly's instructions, Joe Byrne loaded the money from the bank on to one of the police horses, and rode out of town. Ned himself was in no hurry to leave. After buying more drinks for the crowd in the dining-room, he went next door to the bank, and returned with a pair of riding breeches, and a gold watch and chain belonging to Tarleton. He also took Lyving's saddle with which he saddled the mare he had taken from McDougall's Hotel. By now, the crowd in the hotel had been drinking for several hours, and had grown so noisy that Dan and Steve, who were themselves not drinking, had given up trying to keep them in order. Passers-by were even beginning to collect outside the front door. Calling on everyone to keep quiet, Ned stood on a chair and addressed the gathering. 'I want to say a few words,' he announced, 'about why I'm an outlaw, and what I'm doing here today.' He then proceeded to give his account of the events which had led to his being declared an outlaw. He described the visit of Constable Fitzpatrick to Eleven Mile Creek, and the arrest of his mother. He talked of his encounter with the police search party at Stringybark Creek and reminisced about the 'bloody old crooked musket' with which he had shot Lonigan. 'It was so crooked, it could shoot round corners.' He boasted of the two hundred and eighty horses he had stolen, and insisted that horse-stealing was his only crime.

Next, Ned's manner became heavily playful. 'I really came here today,' he said, 'to kill your two policemen. They're worse than the bloody black-trackers – especially that bloke Richards there. I've got a particular down on him, and I'm going to shoot him in a minute.'

Constable Richards seemed unperturbed by this remark which was greeted with laughter by the somewhat drunken crowd. 'I must also say,' continued Kelly, 'that I am very much obliged to the Victorian police for the way in which they're acting. If they go on as they are doing, I shall never have any cause to complain. It must be very pleasant for them to roam about the country on double pay, and they're not causing us any worry.'

After the cheers with which this was received, Kelly ended on a more serious note. 'If your postmaster tries to mend his wires before tomorrow, I'll come back and shoot him. In fact, to make sure he doesn't, I think I'll take him with me into the bush for a few miles, and let him walk home. We're going off to Urana now, to rob the coach, and if anyone tries to give an alarm, they'll be shot.'

Ned walked out into the street where he was immediately approached by a Presbyterian clergyman, the Reverend Mr Gribble, who asked him to return the mare he had taken from McDougall's, as Miss McDougall was particularly fond of it. At the same time, Lyving rushed out after him to beg him not to take his saddle, as he couldn't afford to buy another one. Ned agreed to both these requests, and took the mare back to McDougall's himself.

When he returned to the pub, Ned received another complaint from Mr Gribble. One of Kelly's gang had taken his watch. It was of sentimental value to him, and he could not bear to lose it.

'Show me who took it,' said Ned, and Gribble pointed out Steve Hart.

'Steve, did you take this man's watch?'

'Sure, I took the bloody thing.'

'Then give it back to him.'

Steve handed the watch to Ned who, after examining it, said, 'It's not bloody-well worth a chew of tobacco,' and passed it back to Steve. 'Here, you took it. You give it back.' And, before an amused crowd, Steve had to return the watch to Gribble.

As he, Dan and Ned walked down the road to the police station with Constable Richards, the disgruntled Steve told Ned he was a fool to return a mare simply because a girl was fond of it. Eventually, Ned became so annoyed he almost started a fight with Steve, reminding him that it wouldn't be the first time he had had to teach him a lesson. Steve continued to grumble sulkily, and Ned exclaimed, 'Shut your mouth. You're nothing but a bloody cunt.'

A few minutes' later, when they were in the paddock behind the police station catching Devine's mare, Steve muttered to Richards, 'Kelly's a fine man and I like him. But he shouldn't have called me that.'

In the police station, Ned and Dan took off their uniforms, and dressed in their own clothes. After locking Richards up with Devine the three outlaws rode back to the Royal Mail Hotel to take a final farewell of their audience there. Steve took another watch and chain, this time from Cox, the landlord of the hotel, and warned him not to tell the others. Cox immediately sought out Ned and complained to him, and again Steve was made to return the stolen property. Ned noticed that, while he and his companions had been changing their clothes at the police station, the bank clerk Lyving had taken the opportunity to escape, and was probably on his way to a neighbouring town. Uttering a final warning to those present not to leave the town before four o'clock, and not to free the police before seven o'clock, Ned left with Dan and Steve. They leapt on to their horses and, amid cheers from a section of the crowd who had rushed out into the street, galloped out of the town. The three appeared to ride off in different directions, but they met again, as arranged, at Wunnamurra Station, a few miles along the road to the Murray River and Victoria. At the homestead at Wunnamurra, Ned enquired if anyone had seen the bank clerk, Lyving.

'I'll shoot Lyving when I see him,' he declared. 'I gave that bastard everything of his back that he asked for. He almost begged me at the bank not to destroy his life policy, and when I was taking his saddle he begged for that back too. Seeing he was a poor man, I gave it back, and now, as soon as he gets a chance, the bastard rushes off to betray me.'

He drank a glass of water, and rode off towards the Murray.

SEVEN

Here is the complete text of the statement Kelly attempted to have printed at Jerilderie. It is written in the form of a letter addressed, presumably, to the editor of the local newspaper. The bank clerk, Lyving, who took it from Kelly, handed it over to the authorities.

Dear Sir,
I wish to acquaint you with some of the occurrences of the present past and future.
In or about the spring of 1870 the ground was very soft a hawker named Mr. Gould got his waggon bogged between Greta and my mother's house on the eleven miles creek, the ground was that rotten it would bog a duck in places so Mr. Gould had abandon his waggon for fear of loosing his horses in the spewy ground he was stopping at my mothers awaiting finer or dryer weather Mr. McCormack and his wife hawkers also were camped in Greta the mosquitoes were very bad which they generally are in wet spring and to help them Mr. Johns had a horse called ruila cruta although a gelding was as clever as old Wombat or any other stallion at running horses away and taking them on his beat which was from Greta swamp to the seven mile creek consequently he enticed McCormacks horse away from Greta.
Mr. Gould was up early feeding his horses heard a bell and seen McCormack horse for he knew the horse well he sent his boy to take him back to Greta.
When McCormack's got the horse they came straight out to Goold and accused him of working the horse; this was false and Goold was amazed at the idea I could not help laughing to hear Mrs. McCormack accusing him of using the horse after him being so kind as to send his boy to take him from the ruta cruta and take him back to them.
I pleaded Goulds innocence and Mrs. McCormack turned on me and accused me of bringing the horse from Greta to Goold's waggon to pull him out of the bog I did not say

much to the woman as my mother was present but the same day me and my uncle was cutting calves Gould wrapped up a note and a pair of the calves testicles and gave them to me to give them to Mrs. McCormack. I did not see her and gave the parcel to a boy to give to her when she would come instead of giving it to her he gave it to her husband consequently McCormack said he would summons me I told him neither me nor Goold used their horse.

he said I was a liar and he could welt me or any of my breed I was about 14 years of age but accepted the challenge and dismounting when Mrs. McCormack struck my horse in the flank with a bullocks skin it jumped forward and my fist came in collision with McCormack's nose and cause him to loose his equillibrium and fall postrate I tied up my horse to finish the battle but McCormack got up and ran to the Police camp.

Constable Hall asked me what the row was about. I told him they accused me and Gould of using their horse and I hit him and would do the same to him if he challenged me McCormack pulled me and swore their lies against me.

I was sentenced to three months for hitting him and three months for the parcel and bound to keep the peace for 12 months.

Mrs. McCormack gave good substantial evidence as she is well acquainted with that place called Tasmania better known as the Dervon or Vandiemans land and McCormack being a Police man over the convicts and women being scarce released from that land of bondage and tyranny, and they came to Victoria and are at present residents of Greta and on the 29th of March I was released from prison and came home Wild Wright came to the eleven mile to see Mr. Gunn stopped all night and lost his mare both him and me looked all day for her and could not get her Wright who was a stranger to me was in a hurry to get back to Mansfield and I gave him another mare and he told me if I found his mare to keep her until he brought mine back.

I was going to Wangaratta and saw the mare and I caught her and took her with me all the Police and Detective Berrill seen her as Martins girls used to ride her about the town during several days that I stopped at Petre Martains Star Hotel in Wangaratta, she was a chestnut mare white face

Jerilderie Police Station, 8th February 1879: as a preliminary to the bank raid, Kelly lured Constables Devine and Richards out of the station, then handcuffed them and locked them up in their own cells.

'Blood Money': after the raids on Jerilderie and the Bank of New South Wales the reward was raised to £8,000.

The Kelly Gang: after 1880 they were popular heroes and 'original photographs' of doubtful authenticity sold in thousands.

Black-trackers and police photographed together at Benalla Police Station in 1879. The police pictured here are, l. to r., Senior Constable King of Queensland, Sub-Inspector O'Connor, Area Superintendent J. Sadler and the Police Commissioner, Captain Standish.

(above) Joe Byrne found that the Kelly's suspicions of Sherritt were true and on Saturday, 26th June 1880, he killed him.

(left) Aaron Sherritt, the lifelong friend of Joe Byrne and police informer on the Kellys.

docked tail very remarkable branded (M) as plain as the hands on a town clock, the property of a Telegraph Master in Mansfield, he lost her on the 6th gazetted her o the 12th of March and I was a prisoner in Beechworth Gaol until the 29 of March therefore I could not have stole the mare.

I was riding the mare through Greta Constable Hall came to me and said he wanted me to sign some papers that I did not sign at Beechworth concerning my bail bonds I thought it was the truth he said the papers was at the Barracks and I had no idea he wanted to arrest me or I would have quietly rode away instead of going to the Barracks.

I was getting off when Hall caught hold of me and thought to throw me but made a mistake and came on the broad of his back himself in the dust the mare galloped away and instead of me putting my foot on Halls neck and taking his revolver and putting him in the lock up. I tried to catch the mare. Hall got up and snapped three or four caps at me and would have shot me but the colts patent refused.

This is well known in Greta Hall never told me he wanted to arrest me until after he tried to shoot me when I heard the caps snapping I stood until Hall came close he had me covered and was shaking with fear and I knew he would pull the trigger before he would be game to put his hand on me so I duped and jumped at him caught the revolver with one hand and Hall by the collar with the other.

I dare not strike him or my sureties would loose the bond money I used to trip him and let him take a mouth ful of dust now and again as he was as helpless as a big guano after leaving a dead bullock or horse.

I kept throwing him in the dust until I got him across the street the very spot where Mrs. O'Briens Hotel stands now the cellar was just dug then there was some brush fencing where the post and rail was taking down and on this I threw the big cowardly Hall on his belly I straddled him and rooted both spurs into his thighs he roared like a big calf attacked by dogs and shifted several yards of fence I got his hands at the back of his neck and tried to make him let the revolver go but he stuck to it like grim death to a dead volunteer he called for assistance to a man named Cohen and Barnett, Lewis, Thompson, Jewitt two blacksmiths who was looking on I dare not strike any of them as I was bound to keep the peace or I could have spread those curs like dung in a paddock.

they got ropes tied my hands and feet and Hall beat me over the head with his six chambered colts revolver nine stitches were put in some of the cuts by Dr. Hastings And when Wild Wright and my mother came they could trace us across the street by the blood in the dust and which spoiled the lustre of the paint on the gate-post of the Barracks Hall sent for more Police and Doctor Hastings Next morning I was handcuffed a rope tied from them to my legs and to the seat of the cart and taken to Wangaratta Hall was frightened I would throw him out of the cart so he tied me whilst Constable Arthur laughed at his cowardice for it was he who escorted me and Hall to Wangaratta.

I was tried and committed as Hall swore I claimed the mare the Doctor died or he would have proved Hall a perjurer Hall has been tried several times for perjury but got clear as this is no crime in the Police force it is a credit to a Policeman to convict an innocent man but any mutt can pot a guilty one Halls character is well known about El Dorado and Snowy Creek and Hall was considerably in debt to Mr. L. O'Brien and he was going to leave Greta Mr. O'Brien seen no other chance of getting his money so there was a subscription collected for Hall and with the aid of this money he got James Murdock who was recently hung in Wagga Wagga to give false evidence against me but I was acquitted on the charge of horsestealing and on Hall and Murdocks evidence I was found guilty of receiving and got 3 years experience in Beechworth Pentridges dungeons. this is the only charge ever proved against me Therefore I can say I never was convicted of horse or cattle stealing.

My Brother Dan was never charged with assaulting a woman but he was sentenced to three months without the option of a fine and one month and two pound fine for damaging property by Mr. Butler P.M. a sentence that there is no law to uphold therefore the minister of Justice neglected his duty in that case, but there never was such a thing as justice in the English laws but any amount of injustice to be had. Out of over thirty head of the very best horses and land could produce I could only find one when I got my liberty.

Constable Flood stole and sold the most of them to the navvies on the railway line one bay cob he stole and sold four different times the line was completed and the men all gone when I came out and Flood was shifted to Oxley.

he carried on the same game there all the stray horses that was any time without an owner and not in the Police Gazette Flood used to claim He was doing a good trade at Oxley until Mr. Brown of the Laceby Station got him shifted as he always running his horses about.

Flood is different to Sergeant Steel, Strachan, Hall and the most of Police as they have got to hire cads and if they fail the police are quite helpless. But Flood can make a cheque single-handed he is the greatest horsestealer with the exception of myself and George King I know of.

I never worked on a farm a horse and saddle was never traced to me after leaving employment since February 1873 I worked as a faller at Mr. J. Saunders and R Rules sawmills then for Heach and Dockendorf I never worked for less than two pound ten a week since I left Pentridge and in 1875 or 1876 I was overseer for Saunders and Rule. Bourkes waterholes sawmills in Victoria since then I was on the King river. during my stay there I ran a wild bull which I gave to Lydicher a farmer he sold him to Carr a Publican and Butcher who killed him for beef, sometime afterwards I was blamed for stealing this bull from James Whitty Boggy Creek I asked Whitty Oxley racecourse why he blamed me for stealing his bull.

he said he had found his bull and never blamed me but his son-in-law Farrell told him he heard I sold the bull to Carr not long afterwards I heard again I was blamed for stealing a mob of calves from Whitty and Farrell which I know nothing about. I began to think they wanted me to give them something to talk about. Therefore I started wholesale and retail horse and cattle dealing Whitty and Burns not being satisfied with all the picked land on the Boggy Creek and King River and the run of their stock on certificate ground free and no one interfering with them paid heavy rent to the banks for all the open ground so as a poor man could keep no stock, and impounded every beast they could get, even off Government roads.

If a poor man happened to leave his horse or a bit of a poddy calf outside his paddock they would be impounded.

I have known over 60 head of horses impounded in one day by Whitty and Burns all belonging to poor farmers they would have to leave their ploughing or harvest or other employment to go to Oxley.

when they would get there perhaps not have money enough to release them and have to give a bill of sale or borrow money which is no easy matter and along with this sort of work, Farrell the Policeman stole a horse from George King and had him in Whitty and Farrell's Paddocks until he left the force

and all this was the cause of me and my step-father George King taking their horses and selling them to Baumgarten and Kennedy.

the pick of them was taken to a good market and the culls were kept in Petersons paddock and their brands altered by me two was sold to Kennedy and the rest to Baumgarten who were strangers to me and I believe honest men.

They paid me full value for the horses and could not have known they were stolen.

no person had anything to do with the stealing and selling of the horses but me and George King.

William Cooke who was convicted for Whitty's horses was innocent he was not in my company at Petersons. But it is not the place of the Police to convict guilty men as it is by them they get their living had the right parties been convicted it would have been a bad job for the Police as Berry would have sacked a great many of them only I came to their aid and kept them in their bilits and good employment and got them double pay and yet the ungrateful articles convicted my mother and an infant my brother-in-law and another man who was innocent and still annoy my brothers and sisters and the ignorant unicorns even threaten to shoot myself But as soon as I am dead they will be heels up in the muroo. there will be no more police required they will be sacked and supplanted by soldiers on low pay in the towns and special constables made of some of the farmers to make up for this double pay and expense.

It will pay Government to give those people who are suffering innocence, justice and liberty. if not I will be compelled to show some colonial strategm which will open the eyes of not only the Victoria Police and inhabitants but also the whole British army and now doubt they will acknowledge their hounds were barking at the wrong stump and that Fitzpatrick will be the cause of greater slaughter to the Union Jack than Saint Patrick was to the snakes and toads in Ireland.

The Queen of England was as guilty as Baumgarten and Kennedy Williamson and Skillion of what they were convicted for when the horses were found on the Murray River I wrote a latter to Mr. Swanhill of Lake Rowan to acquaint the Auctioneer and to advertize my horses for sale I brought some of them to that place but did not sell I sold some of them in Benalla Melbourne and other places and left the colony and became a rambling gambler soon after I left there was a warrant for me and the Police searched the place and watched night and day for two or three weeks and when they could not snare me they got a warrant against my brother Dan And on the 15th of April Fitzpatrick came to the eleven mile creek to arrest him he had some conversation with a horse dealer whom he swore was William Skillion this man was not called in Beechworth besides several other witnesses, who alone could have proved Fitzpatricks falsehood after leaving this man he went to the house asked was dan in Dan came out I hear previous to this Fitzpatrick had some conversation with Williamson on the hill. he asked Dan to come to Greta with him as he had a warrant for him for stealing Whitty's horses Dan said all right they both went inside Dan was having something to eat his mother asked Fitzpatrick what he wanted Dan for the trooper said he had a warrant for him Dan then asked him to produce it he said it was only a telegram sent from Chiltern but Sergeant Whelan ordered him to relieve Steel at Greta and call and arrest Dan and take him in to Wangaratta next morning and get him remanded Dans mother said Dan need not go without a warrant unless he liked and that the trooper had no business on her premises without some authority besides his own word.

The trooper pulled out his revolver and said he would

blow her brains out if she interfered in the arrest she told him it was a good job for him Ned was not there or he would ram his revolver down his throat Dan looked out and said Ned is coming now, the trooper being off his guard looked out and when Dan got his attention drawn he dropped the knife and fork which showed he had no murderous intent and slapped Heenan's hug on him took his revolver and kept him there until Skillion and Ryan came with horses which Dan sold that night.

The trooper left and invented some scheme to say that he got shot which any man can see is false, he told Dan to clear out that Seargeant Steel and Detective Brown and Strachan would be there before morning Strachan had been over the Murray trying to get up a case against him and they would convict him if they caught him as the stock society offored an enticement for witnesses to swear anything and the germans over the Murray would swear to the wrong man as well as the right.

Next day Williamson and my mother was arrested and Skillion the day after who was not there at all at the time of the row which can be proved by 8 or 9 witnesses and the Police got great credit and praise in the papers for arresting the mother of 12 children one an infant on her breast and those two quiet hard working innocent men who would not know the difference between a revolver and a saucepan handle and kept them six months awaiting trial and then convicted them on the evidence of the meanest article that ever the sun shone on it seems that the jury was well chosen by the Police as there was a discharged Sergenat amongst them which is contrary to law they thought it impossible for a Policeman to swear a lie but I can assure them it was by that means and hiring cads they get promoted I have heard from a trooper that he never knew Fitzpatrick to be one night sober and that he sold his sister to a chinaman but he looks a young strapping rather genteel more fit to be a starcher to a laundress than a policeman For to a keen observer he has the wrong appearance for a manly heart the deceit and cowardice is too plain to be seen in the puny cabbage hearted looking face.

I heard nothing of this transaction until very close on the trial I being than over 400 miles from Greta when I heard

I was outlawed and a hundred pound reward for me for shooting a trooper in Victoria and a hundred pound for any man that could prove a conviction of horse-stealing against me so I came back to Victoria knew I would get no justice if I gave myself up I enquired after my brother Dan and found him digging on Bullock Creek heard how the Police used to be blowing that they would not ask me to stand they would shoot me first and then cry surrender and how they used to rush into the house upset all the milk dishes break tins of eggs empty the flour out of bags onto the ground and even the meat out of the cask and destroy all the provisions and shove the girls in front of them into the rooms like dogs so as if anyone was there they would shoot the girls first but they knew well I was not there or I would have scattered their blood and brains like rain I would manure the Eleven Mile with their bloated carcasses and yet remember there is not one drop of murderous blood in my veins

Superintendent Smith used to say to my sisters see all the men all I have out today I will have as many more tomorrow and we will blow him into pieces as small as paper that is in our guns Detective Ward and Constable Hayes took out their revolvers and threatened to shoot the girls and children in Mrs. Skillions absence the greatest ruffians and murderers no matter how deprived would not be guilty of such a cowardly action, and this sort of cruelty and disgraceful and cowardly conduct to my brothers and sisters who had no protection coupled with the conviction of my mother and those men certainly made my blood boil and I don't thing there is a man born could have the patience to suffer it as long as I did or ever allow his blood to get cold while such insults as these were unavenged and yet in every paper that is printed I am called the blackest and coldest blooded murderer ever on record But if I hear any more of it I will not exactly show them what cold blooded murder is but wholesale and retail slaughter something different to shooting three troopers in self defence and robbing a bank. I would have been rather hot blooded to throw down my rifle and let them shoot me and my innocent brother. they were not satisfied with frightening my sisters night and day and destroying their provisions and lagging my mother and infant and those innocent men but should follow me and my brother into the wilds where he had been quietly digging neither molesting or interfering with anyone he was making good wages as the creek is very rish within half a mile from where I shot Kennedy. I was not there long and on the 25th of October I came on Police tracks between Table top and the bogs. I crossed them and returning in the evening I came on a different lot of tracks making for the shingle hut I went to our camp and told my brother and his two mates. me and my brother went and found their camp at the shingle hut about a mile from my brother's house. We saw they carried long firearms and we knew our doom was sealed if we could not beat those before the others would come as I knew the other party of Police would soon join them and if they came on us at our camp they would shoot us down like dogs at our work as we had only two guns we thought it best to try and bail those up, take their firearms and ammunition and horses and we could stand a chance with the rest We approached the spring as close as we could get to the camp as the intervening space being clear ground and no battery we saw two men at the logs they got up and one took a double barreled fowling piece and fetched a horse down and hobbled him at the tent we thought there were more men in the tent asleep those outside being on sentry we could have shot those two men without speaking but not wishing to take their lives we waited McIntyre laid his gun against a stump and Lonigan sat on the logs I advanced, my brother Dan keeping McIntyre covered which he took to be Constable Flood and had he not obeyed my orders, or attempted to reach for the gun or draw his revolver he would have been shot dead. but when I called on them to throw up their hands McIntyre obeyed and Lonigan ran some six or seven yards to a battery of logs instead of dropping behind the one he was sitting on, he had just got to the logs and put his head up to take aim when I shot him that instant or he would have shot me as I took him for Strachan the man who said he would not ask me to stand he would shoot me first like a dog. But it happened to be Lonigan the man who in company with Sergeant Whelan Fitzpatrick and King the Bootmaker and Constable O'Day that tried to put a pair of handcuffs on me in Benalla but could not and had to allow McInnis the miller to put them on, previous to Fitzpatrick swearing he

84

was shot, I was fined two pounds for hitting Fitzpatrick and two pounds for not allowing five curs like Sergeant Whelan O'Day Fitzpatrick King and Lonigan who caught me by the privates and would have sent me to Kingdom come only I was not ready and he is the man that blowed before he left Violet Town if Ned Kelly was to be shot he was the man would shoot him and no doubt he would shoot me even if I threw up my arms and laid down as he knew four of them could not arrest me single handed not to talk of the rest of my mates, also either he or me would have to die, this he knew well therefore he had a right to keep out my road, Fitzpatrick is the only one I hit out of the five in Benalla, this shows my feeling towards him as he said we were good friends and even swore it but he was the biggest enemy I had in the country with the exception of Lonigan and he can be thankful I was not there when he took a revolver and threatened to shoot my mother in her own house it is not true I fired three shots and missed him at a yard and a half I don't think I would use a revolver to shoot a man like him when I was within a yard and a half of him or attempt to fire into a house where my mother brothers and sisters was and according to Fitzpatricks statement all around him a man that is such a bad shot as to miss a man three time at a yard and a half would never attempt to fire into house among a house full of women and children while I had a pair of arms and bunch of fives at the end of them they never failed to peg out anything they came in contact with and Fitzpatrick knew the weight of one of them only too well as it run up against him once in Benalla and cost me two pound odd as he is very subject to fainting. As soon as I shot Lonigan he jumped up and staggered some distance from the logs with his hands raised and then fell he surrendered but too late I asked McIntyre who was in the tent he replied no one. I advanced and took possession of their two revolvers and fowling piece which I loaded with bullets instead of shot.

I asked McIntyre where his mates was he said they had gone down the creek and he did not expect them that night he asked me was I going to shoot him and his mates. I told him no I would shoot no man if he gave up his arms and leave the force he said the police all knew Fitzpatrick had wronged us and he intended to leave the force as he had bad health and his life was insured he told me he intended going home and that Kennedy and Scanlon were out looking for our camp and also about the other Police he told me the N.S.W. Police had shot a man for shooting Sergeant Walling I told him if they did they had shot the wrong man and I expect your gang came to do that same with me he said no they did not come to shoot me they came to apprehend me I asked him what they carried spencer rifles and breech loading fowling pieces and so much ammunition for as the Police was only supposed to carry one revolver and 6 cartridges in the revolver but they had eighteen rounds of revolver cartridges each three dozen for the fowling piece and twenty one spencer rifle cartridges and God knows how many they had away with the rifle this looked as if they meant not only to shoot me but to riddle me but I don't know either Kennedy, Scanlon or him and had nothing against them, he said he would get them to give up their arms if I would not shoot them as I could not blame them, they had to do their duty I said I did not blame them for doing honest duty but I could not suffer them blowing me to pieces in my own native land and they knew Fitzpatrick wronged us and why not make it public and convict him but no they would rather riddle poor unfortunate creoles. but they will rue the day ever Fitzpatrick got among them. Our two mates came over when they heard the shot fired but went back again for fear the Police might come to our camp while we were all away and manure bullock flat with us on our arrival I stopped at the logs and Dan went back to the spring for fear the troopers would come in that way but I soon heard them coming up the creek I told McIntyre to tell them to give up their arms, he spoke to Kennedy who was some distance in front of Scanlon he reached for his revolver and jumped off, on the offside of his horse and got behind a tree when I called on them to throw up their arms and Scanlon who carried the rifle slewed his horse around to gallop away but the horse would not go and as quick as thought fired at me with the rifle without unslinging it and was in the act of firing again when I had to shoot him and he fell from his horse.

    I could have shot them without speaking but their lives was no good to me. McIntyre jumped on Kennedys horse and I allowed him to go as I did not like to shoot him after he surrendered or I would have shot him as he was between me and Kennedy therefore I could not shoot Kennedy without shooting him first. Kennedy kept firing from behind the tree my brother Dan advanced and Kennedy ran I followed him he stopped behind another tree and fired again. I shot him in the arm pit and he dropped his revolver and ran I fired again with the gun as he slewed around to surrender. I did not know he had dropped his revolver, the bullet passed through the right side of his chest and he could not live or I would have let him go had they been my own brothers I could not help shooting them or else let them shoot me which they would have done had their bullets been directed as they intended them. But as for handcuffing Kennedy to a tree or cutting his ear off or brutally treating any of them is a falsehood if Kennedy's ear was cut off it was not done by me and none of my mates was near him after he was shot I put his cloak over him and left him as well as I could and were they my own brothers I could not have been more sorry for them this cannot be called wilful murder for I was compelled to shoot them, or lie down and let them shoot me it would not be wilful murder if they packed our remains in, shattered into a mass of animated gore to Mansfield, they would have got great praise and credit as well as promotion but I am reconed a horrid brute because I had not been cowardly enough to lie down for them under such trying circumstances and insults to my people certainly their wives and children are to be pitied but they must remember those men came into the bush with the intention of scattering pieces of me and my brother all over the bush and yet they know and acknowledge I have been wronged and my mother and four or five men lagged innocent and is my brothers and sisters and my mother not to be pitied also who has no alternative only to put up with the brutal and cowardly conduct of a parcel of big ugly fat-necked wombat headed big bellied magpie legged narrow hipped splay-footed sons of Irish Bailiffs or english landlords which is better known as officers of Justice or Victorian Police who some calls honest gentlemen but I would like to know what business an honest man would have in the Police as it is an old saying it takes a rogue to catch a rogue and a man that knows nothing about roguery would never enter the force and take an oath to arrest brother sister father or mother if required and to have a case and conviction if possible any man knows it is possible to swear a lie and if a policeman looses a conviction for the sake of swearing a lie he has broke his oath therefore he is a perjuror either ways, a Policeman is a disgrace to his country not alone to the mother that suckled him, in the first place he is a rogue in his heart but too cowardly to follow it up without having the force to disguise it. Next he is a traitor to his country ancestors and religion as they were all catholics before the Saxons and Cranmore yoke held sway since then they were persecuted massacred thrown into martyrdom and tortured beyond the ideas of the present generation. What would people say if they saw a strapping big lump of an Irishman shepherding sheep for fifteen bob a week or tailing turkeys in Tallarook ranges for a smile from Julia or even begging his tucker, they would say he ought to be ashamed of himself and tar-and-feather him. But he would be a king to a policeman who for a lazy loafing cowardly bilit left the ash corner deserted the shamrock, the emblem of true wit and beauty to serve under a flag and nation that has destroyed massacred and murdered their fore-fathers by the greatest of torture as rolling them down hill in spiked barrels pulling their toe and finger nails and on the wheel and every torture imaginable more was transported to Van Diemand's Land to pine their young lives away in starvation and misery among tyrants worse than the promised hell itself all of true blood bone and beauty, that was not murdered on their own soil, or had fled to America or other countries to bloom again another day were doomed to Port McQuarie, Toweringabbie, Norfolk island and Emu plains and in those places of tyrany and condemnation many a blooming Irishman rather than subdue to the Saxon yoke were flogged to death and bravely died in servile chains but true to the shamrock and a credit to Paddys land What would people say if I became a policeman and took an oath to arrest my brothers and sisters and relations and convict them by fair or foul means after the conviction of my mother and the persecutions and insults offered to myself and people Would they say I was a decent gentleman and yet a policeman is still in worse and guilty of meaner actions than that The Queen must surely be proud of such heroic men as the Police and Irish soldiers as It takes eight or eleven of the biggest mud crushers in Melbourne to take one poor little half starved larrakin to a watchhouse. I have seen as many as eleven, big and ugly enough to lift Mount Macedon out of a crab hole more like the species of a baboon or Guerilla than a man actually come into a court house and swear they could not arrest one eight stone larrakin and then armed with battens and niddies without some civilians assistance and some of them going to the hospital from the effects of hits from the fists of the larrakin and the Magistrate would send the poor little larrakin into a dungeon for being a better man than such a parcel of armed curs. What would England do if America declared war and hoisted a green flag as it is all Irishman that has got command of her armies forts and batteries even her very life guards and beef tasters are Irish would they not slew around and fight her with their own arms for the sake of the colour they dare not wear for years and to reinstate it and rise old Erins isle once more from the pressure and tyrannism of the English yoke which has kept it in proverty and starvation and caused them to wear the enemy's coat. What else can England expect.

Is there not big fat-necked Unicorns enough paid to torment and drive me to do thing which I don't wish to do, without the public assisting them I have never interfered with any person unless they deserved it and yet there are civilians who take fire-arms against me, for what reason I do not know unless they want me to turn on them and exterminate them with out medicine. I shall be compelled to make an example of some of them if they cannot find no other employment if I had robbed and plundered ravished and murdered everything I met young and old rich and poor the public could not do any more than take firearms and assisting the police as they have done, but by the light that shines pegged on an ant-bed with their bellies opened their fat taken out rendered and poured down their throat boiling hot will be cool to what pleasure I will give some of them and any person aiding or harbouring or assisting the Police in any way whatever or employing any person whom they know to be a detective or cad or those who would be so deprived as to take blood money will be outlawed and declared unfit to be allowed human buriel their property either consumed or confiscated and them theirs and all belonging to them exterminated off the face of the earth, the enemy I cannot catch myself I shall give a payable reward for, I would like to know who put that article that reminds me of a poodle dog half clipped in the lion fashion called Brooke E. Smith Superintendent of Police he knows as much about commanding Police as Captain Standish does about mustering mosquitoes and boiling them down for the fat on the back blocks of the Lachlan for he had a head like a turnip a stiff-neck as big as his shoulders narrow hipped and pointed towards the feet like a vine stake and if there is any one to be called a murderer regarding Kennedy, Scanlon and Lonigan it is that misplaced poodle he gets as much pay as a dozen good troopers if there is any *good* in them, and what does he do for it he cannot look behind him without turning his whole frame it takes three or four police to keep sentry while he sleeps in Wangaratta, for fear of body snatchers do they think he is a superior animal to the men that has to guard him if so why not send the men that gets big pay and reconed superior to the common police after me and you shall soon save the country of high salaries to men that is fit for nothing else but getting better men than himself shot and sending orphan children to the industrial school to make prostitutes and cads of them for the Detectives and other evil disposed persons send the high paid and men that received big salaries for year in a gang by themselves after me, As it makes no difference to them but it will give them a chance of showing whether they are worth more pay than a common trooper or not and I think the Public will soon find they are only in the road of good men and obtaining money under false pretences. I do not call McIntyre a coward for I reckon he is as game a man as wears the Jacket as he had the presence of mind to know his position, directly as he was spoken to, and only foolishness to disobey, it was cowardice that made Lonigan and the others fight it is only foolhardiness to disobey an outlaw as any Policeman or other man who do not throw up their arms directly as I call on them knows the consequence which is a speedy dispatch to Kingdom come I wish those men who joined the stock protection society to withdraw their money and give it and as much more the widows and orphans and poor of Greta district where I spent and will again spend many a happy day fearless free and bold as it only aids the police to procure false witnesses and go whacks with men to steal horses and lag innocent men it would suit them far better to subscribe a sum and give it to the poor of their district and there is no fear of anyone stealing their property for no man could steal their horses without the knowledge of the poor if any man was mean enough to steal their property the poor would rise out to a man and find them if they were on the face of the earth it will always pay a rish man to be liberal with the poor and make as little enemies as he can as he shall find if the poor is on his side he shall loose nothing by it. If they depend on the police they shall be drove to destruction. as they can not and will not protect them if duffing and bushranging were abolished the police would have to cadge for living I speak from experience as I have sold horses and cattle innumerable and yet eight head of the culls is all ever was found I never was interfered with whilst I kept up this successful trade. I give fair warning to all those who has reason to fear me to sell out and give £10 out of every hundred towards the widow and orphan fund and do not attempt to reside in Victoria but as short a time as possible after reading this notice, neglect this and abide by the consequences, which shall be worse than the rust in the wheat in Victoria or the druth of a dry season to the grasshoppers in New South Wales I do not wish to give the order full force without giving timely warning, but I am a widows son outlawed and my orders *must be obeyed*.

Edward Kelly.

EIGHT

When the Kellys left Jerilderie, they had no intention of robbing the coach at the nearby town of Urana. That boast had been made at Jerilderie in order to give themselves a better start back to Victoria. But by nine o'clock that evening the telegraph service was in operation again, and several New South Wales towns in the vicinity were fearful of being visited by the Kellys. The New South Wales Government decided to take the Gang seriously, and agreed to match the reward offered by Victoria for their capture. This had by now risen to £4,000, so the total reward claimable was £8,000. Still, no one came forward to claim it. In the Kelly Country, it was noticed that there were suddenly a large number of Bank of New South Wales banknotes in circulation. There was also a new song about the Kellys which the police, to their extreme annoyance, heard sung everywhere:

> It's when they robbed the Euroa bank,
> You said they'd be run down,
> But now they've robbed another
> That's in Jerilderie town.
> That's in Jerilderie town, boys,
> And we'll always take their part,
> And shout again: 'Long may they reign,
> The Kellys, Byrne and Hart.'

The police continued to receive information about the movements of the Kelly Gang, but all of it proved incorrect. That a gang of four young ruffians could kidnap the police, parade about in their uniforms throughout a leisurely week-end, coolly rob the bank on Monday while holding a large number of prisoners in a local pub, and then just ride off and not be traced, hardly seemed credible. The stories of Kelly's style and his courage ('as game as Ned Kelly' and 'as cool as Ned Kelly' are still frequently heard expressions in Australia) multiplied after the Jerilderie affair. His courtesy to women was also remarked upon: this, of course, was well in the bushranger-highwayman tradition. To more and more people, not only in Victoria, but in the other Australian colonies, Ned Kelly became a hero, while the police were thought of as comic and incompetent villains.

After the Jerilderie raid in February the Gang was inactive for the remainder of 1879. The police continued to search for their hideout, and must, inadvertently, have passed within a mile or two of it on occasion. Reports came in of Ned or Joe Byrne being seen here or there, but the trail was always cold by the time the police acted. Joe even spent nights at home with his family, now and then, without the police hearing of it. A letter of his to his closest friend Aaron Sherritt, dated 26th June, 1879, mentions one such occasion, and also reveals that, at this late stage, Ned would still have liked Aaron to join the Gang:

Dear Aaron,
I write these few stolen lines to let you know I am still living. I'm not the least afraid of being captured, dear Aaron. Meet me, you and Jack [Aaron's brother], this side of Puzzle Ranges. Neddy and I have come to the conclusion to get you to join us. I was advised to turn traitor, but I said I would die at Ned's side first.

Dear Aaron, it is best for you to join us, Aaron. A short life and a jolly one. The Lloyds and Quinns want you shot, but I say no you are on our side. If it is nothing only the sake of your mother and sisters. We sent that bloody Hart to your place twice. Did my mother tell you the message that I left for you. I slept at home three days on the 24th May. Did Patsy [Joe's brother, 'Paddy' Byrne] give you the booty I left for you. I intend to pay old Sunday Dodg and old Mullane. O, that bloody snob, where is he? I will make a target of him. Meet me on next Thursday, you and Jack, and we will have another bank quite handy. I told Hart to call last Thursday evening. I would like to know if he obeyed us or not. If not, we will shoot him.

If you come on our tracks, close your puss. We know you were at Kate's several times. You had just gone one night as we came. We followed you four miles, but returned without success. If you do not meet me where I ask you, meet me under London you know [London Rock, a large rock in the

gully behind the Byrne homestead]. I will riddle that bloody Mullane if I catch him. No more from the enforced outlaw, until I see yourself.
I remain,
Yours truly
You know

Joe Byrne had a gift for writing doggerel. While the Gang were taking it easy after the Jerilderie raid, he produced a rough and ready ballad about the Euroa and Jerilderie exploits, which, sung to the tune of 'The Wearin' of the Green', was soon plaguing the ears of the police in the Kelly Country and across the border in New South Wales (see Appendix II). It ends:

Where they have gone's a mystery, the police they cannot tell,
So until we hear from them again, I'll bid you all farewell.

Where they had gone was indeed a mystery to the police. The day after Joe Byrne and Dan Kelly tried to persuade him to join them in robbing a bank in New South Wales, Aaron Sherritt had visited Benalla Police Station and talked to Superintendent Hare. He had told Hare the Gang were planning a hold-up across the border, suppressing only the fact that he had been asked to join them. He even described the brands of the horses Joe and Dan were riding. The Superintendent handed him £2 for his trouble, and telegraphed warnings to the police stations on the way to Goulburn.

Although, on this occasion, Aaron's information had proved too generalized to be of any use, Hare realized that Aaron, who was obviously in close, if intermittent, contact with the Gang, might one day lead him to the Kellys. The following account by Hare of his dealings with Aaron comes from the Superintendent's memoirs:

Directly the bank was stuck up at Jerilderie I started off to Beechworth, and sent for Aaron Sherritt. His first words to me were, 'Did I not tell you they would stick up a bank in New South Wales?' I replied, 'Yes, but you told me they were going to Goulburn.' I said, 'Well, what is to be done now?' He replied, 'They will be back probably tonight to

Woolshed.' He told me to meet him that night at a place indicated by him in the ranges (known to the detective [Ward]), he would then show me where they tied up their horses, whilst they went into Mrs Byrne's house for supper. I agreed to his suggestion, and told the detective what I had done. His reply was, 'I have known Sherritt for years, and if he likes he can put you in the position to capture the Kellys, but I doubt his doing so.' I told him Aaron felt sure they would return from Jerilderie that night, and I had arranged to go with him, and meet him at eight o'clock that night at a certain spot in the ranges, which I described, a party of police accompanying us. Having no men at Beechworth, I drove the detective to Eldorado, which was beyond Woolshed, where I had a party of police stationed. As the detective was well known in the locality, and I was not, I put him in the boot of the buggy under the seat, and he remained in that position nearly all the way. I merely state this to show how cautious we had to be in all our movements. Had he been recognized driving in a buggy, the friends of the outlaws would soon have heard of it. I had to take him because he had to direct the party where to meet us that night, and I have not been in the district for very many years, and knew little of it.

At eight o'clock that night the detective and I met Aaron at the appointed spot in the ranges. We waited anxiously for the men from Eldorado to turn up. After waiting for an hour, Aaron said to me, 'You will be late, Mr Hare. We should have been nearly three miles from this by this time.' I was very much annoyed at the men not keeping their appointment; and I turned to the detective and said to him: 'Will you stick to me, as it will never do to lose this chance of getting the outlaws?' His reply was: 'Yes, Mr Hare, I will stick to you and do whatever you tell me to do.' I turned to Aaron and said: 'All right; we are ready to go with you now.' He turned towards me to see if I meant it, I said, 'Come on.'

We mounted our horses. I followed Aaron, the detective following me. The night was terribly dark, and Aaron took us at a good pace. The country was rugged and broken, but he rode ahead just as if he was in his own garden. He appeared to trust to his horse, and I trusted to him. We rode along without a word being spoken by any of us. He might have taken me over a precipice, as I could see nothing before me. Suddenly Aaron stopped, and in a whisper said to me, 'This is the bushrangers' country; no one ever comes in here but them.' We were then about ten miles from Beechworth on the ranges at the back of Woolshed, and so we rode along, winding round a drain one minute, and over logs and rocks the next, trusting entirely to our horses. Suddenly Aaron pulled up, and I went up beside him, the detective doing likewise. Aaron said, 'They are back from Jerilderie. Do you see that fire in the distance?' I replied, 'Yes.' He said, 'The bushrangers are there; I have never before seen a fire in this place, and for some reason they have lighted one, and there they are.' We all three dismounted from our horses and sat down on the ground to decide what was to be done. Aaron said, 'What do you wish me to do? I will do whatever you like.' I thought 'nothing venture nothing have,' so I questioned him as to the fire being made by the outlaws, but he was perfectly convinced of it. I then told him that first thing I wanted to be sure of was whether the bush-rangers were sitting or sleeping near the fire, and he had better take off his boots, leave his horse with me, and crawl along the ground as close to the fire as he could get, and see if he could recognize the voices if he could hear any, if not, to get as close up as he could and find out whether the outlaws were there. He never hesitated for a moment, and did exactly what I told him to do, and the detective and myself were left alone. We both were fully convinced we should have to 'do or die' that night, and we were quite prepared to take the risk. We stayed in the same spot for about ten minutes, deciding how we were to make the attack, when we heard footsteps coming towards us at a quick pace. The detective said, 'He has sold us; who is this coming towards us?' I said, 'Keep quiet.' We both, with revolvers in our hands, remained perfectly still until the footsteps came within a yard of us, and a voice we recognized as Aaron's said, 'Mr Hare, we have been deceived, that fire is on the opposite range and some miles away.' My first thought was that Aaron had gone up to the fire and started the bushrangers off, or else had given them notice he would bring us up to them. I questioned him and he appeared perfectly honest, and said, 'If you will come with me I will convince you that what I am saying is the truth.'

We mounted our horses and found that what he had stated was perfectly correct. Aaron then said, 'We are awfully late, we must hurry on to Mrs Byrne's house,' and we again followed him in the same order as before. He commenced to go down a fearfully steep range. I said not a word but followed him, until he pulled up and said, 'I am afraid to go down here tonight, it is so very dark.' I said, 'Is there no other way you can get down?' He replied, 'Only by going a mile round.' He said, 'Be careful not to move from your saddle, for this is a terribly steep range, and if you attempt to get off you will roll down some hundreds of feet.' He told me to get off the horse on the off side, he doing the same himself, and the detective also. We then led our horses round and got down another gap in the mountains. After riding about a mile Aaron told us that we had better dismount and tie our horses to a tree, and walk down to the spot he would take us to.

We did so, and we followed him down the ranges until we came to a house, which turned out to be Mrs Byrne's, the mother of the outlaw Joe Byrne. Here also, as in Power's case, we met some watch-dogs in the shape of a flock of geese, and they did give the alarm, and no mistake. However, after a short time, Aaron crawled up to the house, so as to ascertain if there was any one talking inside. Everything was quiet, there was a candle burning. He returned and said, 'They expect them tonight. You see, they have left the candle burning, and some supper ready on the table.' He then said, 'Let us go up to a clump of trees at the back of the house, where they generally tie up their horses.' I had previously been told by another agent of this clump of trees, where marks of horses having been tied up were to be seen. Aaron said to me, 'Go into that clump. They often tie up their horses there, and lay down beside them and have a sleep, after having their supper at Mrs Byrne's.' I walked into the clump, but found no horses there, and returned to Aaron. Aaron then said, 'We must now wait in this stock-yard, which leads up to the clump. If they come they will come through here.' It was then about two o'clock in the morning. We sat down and waited until daylight, and then, nothing happening, we started back to our horses, reaching Beechworth at eight o'clock.

Aaron suggested to me that I should bring a party of men and come and live in the mountains at the back of Mrs Byrne's house. He told me he could put me in a spot which was unknown to any one except the bushrangers, and the only danger of my being discovered was by them. He said I could stay in the mountains by day, and take up my position in the stock-yard behind Mrs Byrne's at night, and that if I had patience I was certain to get them. I complied with his suggestion, and that evening I brought a party to the spot indicated by him. We brought our blankets and some provisions, intending to stay there until we caught the Kellys, watching by night, and laying in our camp all day. In camp I arranged that no two men should be together throughout the day, whether sleeping or at meals, so that if we were attacked by the outlaws, and some of us were shot, the others could fight.

The life was extremely monotonous, for me especially; but the excitement kept us up, and we always expected that sooner or later we should come across the outlaws.

Our daily life was as follows: At dusk in the evening, one at a time, we used to leave our camp and make down to the stock-yard, I always leading the way, and the other men following. We had to be most careful where we trod, for fear of our tracks being seen on the following day. We each took up positions behind trees outside the stock-yard, I taking the opening into the yard myself. I had given orders to the men not to move from their positions until I called to them, no matter what happened. We were all lying about ten or fifteen yards apart. The nights were bitterly cold.

Aaron used to spend his evenings at Mrs Byrne's with his young woman, and he obtained all the information they were possessed of, and when he left their house between twelve and one o'clock he used to lie down and watch with us. He always took up his position beside me, and used to relate all kinds of encouraging reports that he had obtained during the day as to the prospect of the Kellys turning up. Hardly a night that we took up our positions but we thought we should have some luck. As day broke in the morning we used to make back to our camp in the mountains in a very disappointed mood, walking singly, and avoiding the paths or soft places, so as not to leave any tracks behind us.

The great danger I felt was a surprise when getting into the camp of a morning and taking up our positions in the evening. I felt sure that some morning or evening when we took up our post the Kellys would find out our camps and take possession of them, so therefore I always went into camp first in the morning and left it first in the evening, and felt a relief when we all got into our places without being fired on. We dared not make a fire for fear of the smoke being noticed, so we had to live on water, preserved beef, and bread. I stayed in this camp for twenty-five days, and during that time, although we used to see some members of the Byrne family passing to and fro, they never discovered our whereabouts. I always kept a sentry by day over the camp, and the sentry's position was behind a rock near the spot I had made my resting-place, which was the highest, above all the men.

Night after night Aaron used to go and see his young woman, and bring back hopes of success. This used to keep up the spirits of the men, and we all felt sure if we could keep watching without our whereabouts being discovered we would eventually be successful.

I should have stated before this, that when I went with my party into the mountains, I also placed four men in a spot pointed out to me by Sherritt, which was one of the camps used by the Kellys. It was here they stayed for two days after the murders, while Aaron supplied them with food. It was a wonderfully romantic spot, on the edge of a precipice, and only approachable on one side. Two men could keep off a dozen. This camp was placed under Senior Constable Mayes, a bold, trustworthy, well-tried man, in whom I had the utmost confidence. He had a difficulty in getting water for his men, and had to send two miles for it. Sometimes the men were sent by day, but generally by night, and through an indiscretion on the part of one of these men, our whereabouts was discovered. Old Mrs Byrne was a most active old party. She was constantly looking about for the tracks of police, horses, and men. She was walking along the bank of a creek where the men at the upper camp were in the habit of getting their water, when she discovered a spot where a man had been sitting and amusing himself with a stick – as it is called 'whittling' it. She immediately came to the conclusion that some police were camped close by, and that night she confided her fears to Aaron, and told him he must have a good look in the ranges next day. He promised to make every effort to find out if her surmise was correct, and he came straight to the stock-yard where I was watching, and informed me of the discovery the old woman had made. Aaron next day got his horse and pretended to make a search, returning next night and telling Mrs Byrne he could find no trace of anybody. The old lady was convinced there must have been some police about, because she said the footmarks were evidently those of a policeman. These people appear to know the difference between the footprints of police and other persons. However, the old woman could not be convinced she was wrong, and up to that time had perfect faith in Aaron, and so also had his young woman, her daughter.

Generally when we left the stock-yard in the morning, Sherritt would leave us and go to his own hut on the ranges, or else to his father's place, which was between our camp and Beechworth; but sometimes he would come into our camp and get his breakfast, and perhaps stop a part of the day. Very often he had to carry provisions for us from Beechworth during the night. He was always ready to do anything for me, and yet many of the men distrusted him. I never did from the first moment I took up with him, and his end showed I was right in my opinion of him. Of a night, whilst I was watching with him, he would sit beside me and tell me the adventures of his life, and give me information of many things that were formerly unexplained. He told me how he, Joe Byrne, and Ned Kelly used to steal horses wholesale, and how they used to dispose of them, and the way they changed the brands of the horses so that the most experienced hand would not discover the trick. It was as follows: Supposing a horse was branded H on the near shoulder, they would turn the H into H B (conjoined) by getting a pair of tweezers, pulling out the hairs to make a B, and then prick the skin with a needle dipped in iodine. This burns up the skin, and for about a month afterwards it looks like an old brand; new brands were also put on in this fashion, and they never could be detected. After branding the horses they had collected, they would make for some squatter's station where they were unknown, ask permission to put their horses into his stock-yard, on the pretence that they had met a stranger who wanted to purchase the mob of horses, this stranger being one of their own party. Generally speaking, the squatter or some one belonging to the station would walk down to look at the horses, and he would hear them making bargains about the price of each animal, so as to lead the people of the station to believe that it was a genuine sale. At last they would agree to a price, and then would ask the squatter to allow them to go into his office to draw up a receipt, in which all the brands would be entered, both old and manufactured ones. After the receipt had been drawn up the squatter would be asked to witness it, and the supposed buyers would start off towards Melbourne, and the seller appear to return back to New South Wales. If by chance any of the horses were claimed by their owners, the receipt would be produced, and they would so avoid being arrested.

Aaron used to tell me they made raids on horses from about Wagga to Albury, took them a back track to Melbourne, and on their return would pick up a number of horses in Victoria and take them over to Wagga or Albury for sale. One of the party used to act as the master, and the others as his servants; the master always going ahead and making arrangements where the horses were to be paddocked for the night.

For hours did Aaron relate anecdotes to me of the same description as the above, and he enlightened me greatly into the ways and the life of horse-stealers. I cannot refrain from telling another of his stories. I was sitting beside him one night, when he had brought us some very hopeful information, and we were all very elated at our prospect of success. I said, 'Well, Aaron, I feel sure you will get the reward offered for the Kellys.' (I had promised him he should have the whole sum of £8,000 if it was upon his information that the Kellys were captured.) At this time his young woman was getting rather suspicious that he was working for the police, although she used to meet him of an evening very near our camp and walk with him. I asked him how he would like the reward disposed of, supposing he got it? He said, 'I should like to have a few mares and an entire horse, and get a nice farm.' I told him he should get a respectable girl, marry her, leave all his old associates, and begin life again amongst new people. He agreed with all I said, and turned round and said to me, 'Mr Hare, do you think, if you got me the best mares you could buy, and got me the best entire horse you could purchase, that I could withstand the temptation of taking my neighbour's horses and selling them? No, I could not, no more than fly.'

On another occasion we were expecting the outlaws to bring some money they had stolen from the bank to Mrs Byrne's. Amongst my men I had one who was a thorough larrakin, and Aaron took a great fancy to him. I sent him to Beechworth for some supplies, and Aaron met him on the way, and they both rode into Beechworth together. My man was taken for one of the Kelly spies, especially as he was in Aaron's company. The people of Beechworth at once became alarmed, seeing Aaron and his companion riding about the streets – no one knowing the companion was a policeman. Numbers of people went at once to the police station and reported that Aaron and another suspicious person, riding good horses, were seen in the outskirts of the town. The constable was delighted to have a chance of being seen with Aaron, and made the most of his opportunity.

On the way back to my camp Aaron took the constable into his confidence; he told him that he felt certain that the bushrangers would return from Jerilderie after they had stuck up the bank there, and the first place they would come to was Mrs Byrne's. Aaron said to him, 'I want you to join me in a scheme, and if it comes off we shall have the best of the arrangement.' The constable said, 'What is it?' He replied, 'I feel sure the Kelly gang will return from Jerilderie either tonight or during the course of this week. Joe Byrne will be leading a pack-horse, with the gold and notes fastened up in a brown cloth coat. Directly Mr Hare opens fire on the men, the pack-horse will, in all probability, break away with the treasure. You and I can go after the horse, catch him, and take his pack off in the bush, hide it, and let the horse go; and next day, in the excitement, we can slip away and divide the cash. It can do no harm to any one, because some one will get it, and we might just as well have it as anybody else.' The constable appeared to agree to Aaron's suggestion, and told me what had passed between them. I told him not to tell any one else in camp about the arrangement, and to lead Aaron to believe that he would assist him in the matter. Unfortunately the Kellys did not put in an appearance, and so the matter fell through.

I must give one more narrative about Aaron, just to show the peculiar kind of man he was, even on the chance of being thought tedious. He came to me one morning and said, 'Mr Hare, I want to go away for a couple of days to look after some cattle of mine. I will be back within two days.' I questioned him closely, what cattle he was going after, and asked him if he wanted any money. I had not engaged him at any fixed salary, but whilst he was watching with me he used to ask me for a pound or two, and I gave it to him. He often refused to take money from me, as he thought I was paying him out of my own pocket, whereas the Government refunded me all I paid him, and he only took sufficient to pay his expenses. Before he started off after his cattle, I said to him, 'Are you sure you have got enough money to pay your way?' He replied, 'I have a pound of the money you gave me last time;' and away he started, and returned according to his promise.

Aaron Sherritt's 'young woman', with whom he used to spend nights at the Byrne homestead, was Joe Byrne's sister. Her mother, the crafty old bushwoman Mrs Byrne, had begun to have serious doubts about where Aaron's sympathies really lay, and on one of her early morning explorations in the hills surrounding her property, she was to have her doubts confirmed. Unconvinced by Aaron's assurance that there was no police camp in the vicinity, she was prowling about on the hillside to the west of the Byrne homestead when she came upon the police, asleep in their blankets amongst the huge rocks near the entrance to the caves. The sentry awakened Hare who watched as the old woman crept quietly about. She approached one of the sleeping men, looked down at him, and then turned about and made her way out of the camp. Waiting until she was some distance away, Hare then went over to find out who it was she had seen. It was Aaron Sherritt. He was lying on his side, his face shielded by a hat, but as usual he was not covered by a blanket, and his clothes were distinctive: white flannel shirt and dark trousers tucked into high Wellington boots.

When Hare awakened Aaron and told him what had happened, Aaron turned pale with fear. 'Now I'm as good as dead,' was all he could say. But Hare roused him to activity, persuading him to ride off immediately and show himself to friends somewhere else, in order to establish an alibi. Meanwhile, the police kept a watch on Mrs Byrne as she slowly made her way towards a nearby hill from which she could look down on the police camp. She obviously was intent on finding out how many police there were. Hare instructed a constable to intercept the old woman and give her a fright. But, when the Constable suddenly sprang at her from behind a rock, her initial fright soon gave way to fury, and she screamed, 'I'll get my son and the Kellys to shoot the whole bloody lot of you, just like they did Kennedy.'

Aaron paid his usual visit to the Byrnes that evening, and was greatly relieved to discover that Mrs Byrne had apparently not recognized him. She at first accused him of having shown the police where to camp, and then was sceptical about his failure to find the police when he had searched for them, but she mentioned having seen one policeman asleep, and continued: 'If I could only find out how many there are altogether, I'd get Joe to shoot them.'

The police party, except for Hare who returned to Benalla, spent another four months in the hills waiting in vain for the Kellys to show themselves. During this time, Aaron's relationship with the Byrne family continued to deteriorate. Miss Byrne broke off her engagement with him, Aaron in a fit of pique stole a horse from her and sold it for £3, and Mrs Byrne had a warrant issued for his arrest. The police managed to have the case rigged so that Aaron would not have to spend a term in gaol.

One day, Ned Kelly turned up at the home of Aaron's parents. Mrs Sherritt was out, and two of Aaron's teenage sisters were looking after the newest addition to the family, a five-months old baby. Ned nursed the baby, said he was hungry and ate some bread which was baking in the oven, and asked one of the girls to make tea so that he could take some out to his comrades. He left a message for Aaron asking him again to come and join them.

The winter wore on, and the press took to wondering whether the outlaws would be captured before they died of old age.

The Ovens and Murray Advertizer satirized the pompous incompetence of police procedure:

> The arrangements made for the final 'bursting-up' of the outlaws are very complete. The programme is this: When the Kellys are confronted with a reasonable number – say 200 – of troopers, the Chief Commissioner is to be sent for. He is to proceed to the spot by special train and drag, both of which are kept in constant readiness. When he arrives near the scene of operations, he is met by the artillery band, which, playing 'See the Conquering Hero Comes', will precede him to where the main body of troopers is stationed. Then, bowing to the outlaw chief in the fascinating manner which has rendered him invincible on the shady side of Collins Street, he is to fire the first shot out of a silver mounted pistol. Then the fight is to proceed to Wagner's music of the future.

But, if the police were having a difficult time, so were the Kellys. Ned's sister, Mrs Skillion, continued to organize supplies, but money was running out. Though the Gang were relatively safe as long as they remained in hiding, to emerge and undertake another bank raid would be much more dangerous now than it had been fifteen months previously at Jerilderie. Now the Queensland Government had sent six black trackers under the command of an Inspector O'Connor, and Kelly knew that, given time, the 'black devils', as he called them, would find him.

The Gang had now been in hiding for fifteen months. As the autumn of 1880 moved towards winter, there were some who thought the last had been heard of the Kellys. A famous bushranger, Andrew George Scott, known as Captain Moonlite, sent an offer to Ned to join forces with him, but Kelly indignantly rejected the offer, threatening to shoot down Moonlite and his gang if they attempted to approach the hideout. Ned made one of his rare appearances in the bar of a hotel near Oxley where, in reply to a Mrs Woods who told him she thought it a great pity he had become an outlaw, he said: 'Madam, what is a man's lot can't be blotted out.'

In the highest ranks of the police force, dissension was rife. Chief Commissioner Standish attempted to remove Assistant Chief Commissioner Nicolson from the Kelly case. Nicolson, who had but recently replaced Hare at Benalla, appealed to

Chief Secretary Ramsay and was given a month's grace to effect the Gang's capture. The month passed, and Hare was asked by the Chief Secretary to take charge again, and was given *carte blanche*. He arrived in Benalla on June 2nd, 1880, to hear that some mould-boards of ploughs had been stolen from farms in the Oxley and Greta districts, and that the Kellys were suspected. It was thought that the outlaws might be making armour out of the iron moulds. 'Rubbish,' said Superintendent Hare.

The police agent who made the first shrewd guess about armour was perfectly correct. The Kellys had indeed stolen the mould-boards and were busy fashioning them into primitive suits of armour, each consisting of a front and back plate, with side pieces for the shoulders, and a smaller plate to protect the stomach and thighs. Ned's suit, which had a helmet as well, weighed 97 pounds. The armour was to be used in the Gang's first offensive against the police, Kelly's idea being to create some kind of diversion that would bring a special train of police and black-trackers to a particular spot, derail the train, and ambush and shoot any survivors. The Gang could then immediately rob any one of half-a-dozen banks before police reinforcements could be brought in.

Aaron Sherritt, having quickly recovered from being jilted by Miss Byrne, took up with a fifteen-year-old girl named Mary Barry. After living with her in her parents' hut in the Woolshed ranges for some months, he married her, and they moved into an unoccupied house at the foot of the Sugarloaf, not more than a mile and half from Mrs Byrne's house. Joe Byrne, no longer considering himself Aaron's best friend, approached old Mrs Sherritt in a paddock one day. 'I'm going to kill Aaron,' he told her. 'And that Dectective Ward. Between them they've got us nearly starved to death.'

Horrified, Mrs Sherritt said, 'But Aaron would never harm you.'

'You needn't try to tell me that,' replied Joe, 'When he and Ward and Mr Hare very nearly caught us twice.'

Four constables lived secretly in Aaron's house by day, and kept a watch on Mrs Byrne's place at night. But Joe's young brother Danny peered through a back window of Aaron's house one evening, and saw the police: within a few hours the information had been conveyed to the Kellys. Ned suddenly decided on the nature of the diversion which was to bring the police and the trackers out to the Woolshed by train. He gave detailed and careful instructions to Joe Byrne.

On Saturday, June 26, 1880, as the night drew on in the valley, Aaron Sherritt, his young wife and the four constables sat down to their evening meal by the light of candles and an oil-lamp. After they had eaten, Aaron's mother-in-law, Mrs Barry, arrived to spend the evening with her daughter, and three of the four policemen retired to rest in the bedroom on the other side of the wooden partition which separated the only two rooms in the house. When, suddenly, there was a knock at the door, Mrs Sherritt called out, 'Who's there?'

'It's me. I've lost my way.'

Aaron recognized the voice of Anton Wicks, a German who lived in the valley, and who always lost his way home when he got drunk. 'You'd better go and put him on the right road, Aaron,' said his wife, and Aaron went to the door and opened it. He began to speak to Wicks, and then noticed that the frightened German was handcuffed and that two men were standing behind him. One of the men, Joe Byrne, lifted his double-barrelled shotgun and fired, shooting Aaron in the chest. As he fell back into the hut, Joe stepped forward and fired again, this time killing him with a shot in the stomach. The second man, Dan Kelly, came in from outside.

'Joe, why did you do it? Don't shoot me,' screamed Mrs Barry.

'That bastard will never give me away again,' said Joe. 'I'm not going to hurt you, Mrs Barry, but who's the man in the next room.' He had caught a glimpse of Constable Duross going into the bedroom just as Aaron had come to the door.

'It's a man by the name of Duross,' said Mrs Barry.

'Tell him to come out here.'

A terrified Mrs Sherritt was sent in to bring him out, but all four policemen remained where they were. Two of them were, by this time, hiding under the bed. 'You must be a bloody cunt to guard yourself with a woman,' Joe shouted. But Duross and his fellow constables were immune to taunts. Mrs Sherritt was sent in a second time, after Mrs Barry had admitted there were two men in there. The police refused to let her out again. Eventually, shots were fired into the room, and Joe yelled 'Come out, or I'll shoot you down like bloody dogs. I've got plenty of ammunition.' The police continued to whisper together in the next room, while Joe unlocked Anton Wicks's handcuffs and allowed him to run home. Mrs Barry went into the next room at Joe's command, to entice the men out, and she, too, was dragged to the floor by one of the constables, and made to remain there.

Apparently losing interest in the proceedings, Joe and Dan left at about nine o'clock, and rode off across the valley. The police and the two women stayed under cover until dawn, fearful that the outlaws were still nearby waiting for them to emerge. It was past midday on Sunday when one of the constables reported in Beechworth, and the news of Aaron's murder was telegraphed on to Superintendent Hare in Benalla. Hare had, a few days previously, been informed that Joe Byrne's mother was announcing to all who would listen, 'Joe and his mates are about to do something that will not only astonish Australia, but the whole world.' Was this, Hare wondered, the prelude to it?

A 'Bird's Eye View of Glenrowan', as printed in the *Illustrated Sydney News*, 5th August 1880.

1. Jones' Hotel;
2. Out house;
3. Railway Station;
4. Station Master's House;
5. McDonald's Hotel;
6. Platelayers' Tents;
7. Positions taken by Police;
8. Trench: Lieutenant O'Connor and Black Trackers' Post;
9. Spot where Mr. Hare was shot;
10. Paddock where horses were shot;
11. Tree where Ned Kelly was captured;
12. Road to Bracken's Station;
13. Half a mile from here the rails were taken up.

Glenrowan

The Last Stand: 'a strange apparition. His head, chest and sides were all protected with heavy plates of quarter-inch iron. Many shots hit him, yet he always recovered himself, and tapping his breast laughed derisively as he coolly returned their fire. It appeared as if he were a fiend with a charmed life.'

The man was captured, but the myth continued, as the size of Ned Kelly in relation to his captors suggests.

The police party from Wangaratta with the double-barrelled shotguns that finally brought down Ned Kelly.

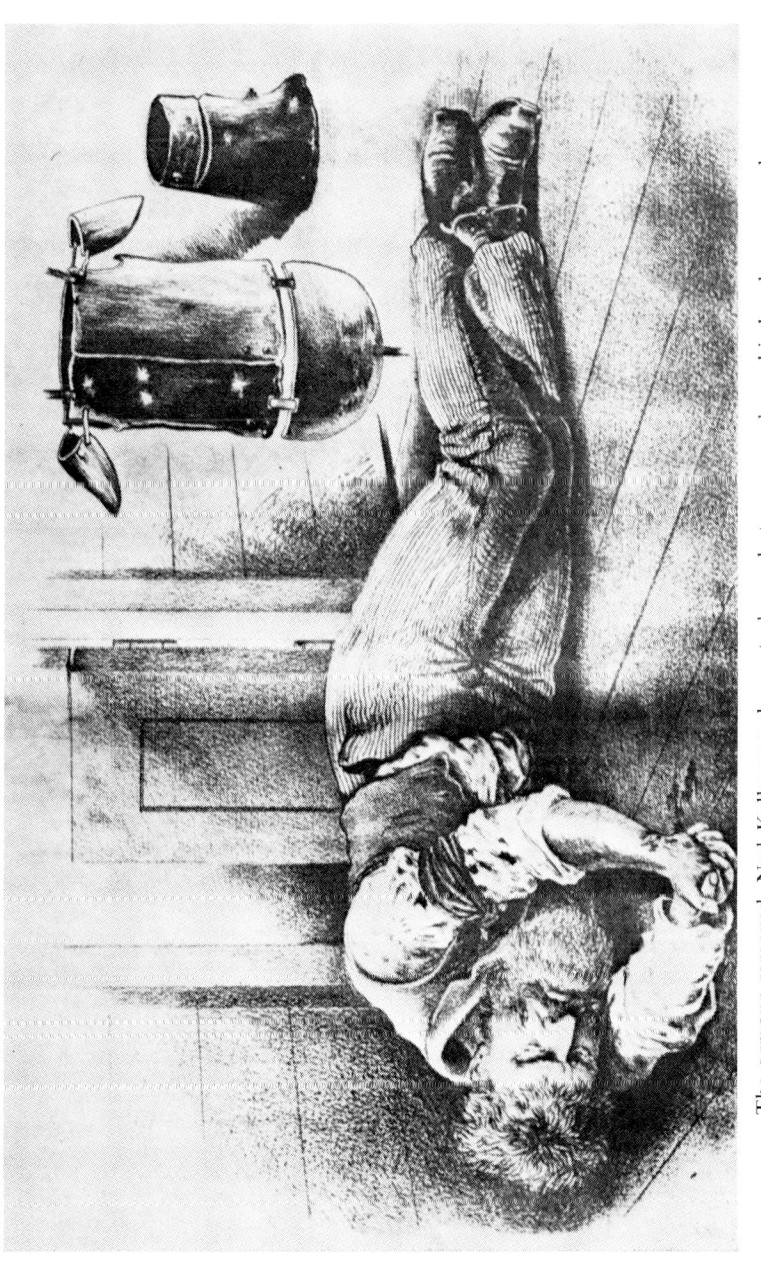

The armour removed. Ned Kelly was shown to have shotgun wounds on his hands, arms and legs, and bruises on his face, chest and groin.

Burnt body lying on a sheet of bark.

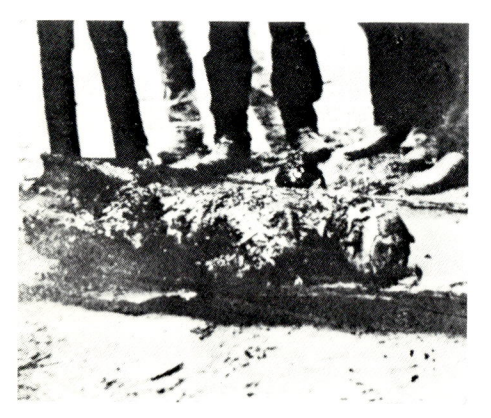

The burned bodies of Dan Kelly and Steve Hart were raked from the remains of the Glenrowan Inn and exhibited to police and eager sightseers.

29th June 1880. Joe Byrne's body was strung up puppet-like outside the police station at Benalla, and the photographers stepped in.

Close-up photographs were sold as souvenir post cards.

The Honourable Mr Justice Barry

Mr. Justice Redmond Barry presided at the trial of Ned Kelly. At Ellen Kelly's trial he had threatened Ned with a fifteen-year sentence. Now he sentenced him to death.

NINE

Ned Kelly's plan involved wrecking the trainload of police at Glenrowan, a small country town between Benalla and Wangaratta. By dawn on Sunday morning, June 27th, Joe and Dan had ridden the forty miles from Sherritt's house to Glenrowan. Ned Kelly and Steve Hart had been there since midnight. The town was what other countries call a village, consisting merely of a handful of impermanent shacks, a general store, blacksmith's shop, and two single-storied hotels, or inns, one on either side of the railway line. Other essential services such as police and school were outside the township, about a mile away in the direction of Benalla. Of the two pubs, McDonald's Hotel was known to be frequented by Kelly sympathizers, while the Glenrowan Inn, run by its English landlady, Ann Jones, was a quieter place. A wooden building, made of stringybark boards and fronted by a verandah, its bar and parlour were separated by a passage which led to the guest rooms at the back of the house. The Glenrowan Inn had come into being at the height of the gold rush. Its roof was of corrugated iron, and it sat, squat but inviting, about a hundred yards from the railway line, and less than a hundred yards from the railway station itself. It was here, at the Glenrowan Inn, that the Kellys were to make their last stand, but when Ned Kelly and Steve Hart rode into Glenrowan late on that Saturday evening, only a couple of hours after Joe Byrne had murdered Aaron Sherritt, they naturally made for McDonald's Hotel where they were sure to meet friends. It was shortly after midnight when Ned and Dan approached the house of the stationmaster, John Stanistreet. On the way they passed tents occupied by labourers employed on the railway line, and, suspecting that detectives might have been planted among the workers, Ned burst in and questioned one or two of them at revolver point. Having satisfied himself that such was not the case, he continued to the stationmaster's house, awakened Stanistreet, introduced himself and told the astonished stationmaster that he required him to stop a special train which would be passing through in a few hours. The stationmaster replied that he had no means of ensuring that a special train would stop, and Kelly asked who was capable of tearing up the rails. The answer, of course, was the platelayers whose tents Ned and Steve had visited on their way to the house.

Several platelayers and their families were rounded up, and, while the wives and children were taken off by Steve to Stanistreet's house, Ned forced the railway workers to march ahead of him down the line towards Wangaratta, stopping at a toolbox beside the line to extract the necessary implements. Ned was in a manic mood. He informed the linesmen that he had shot several policemen in Beechworth the previous evening, which was untrue, and that he now expected a special train from Benalla, carrying police and black-trackers. 'I'm going to shoot every one of the bastards,' he promised.

About five or six hundred yards from the station they stopped, at a point where the line curved sharply to cross over a steep ravine. It was here that Ned made them begin tearing up the tracks, threatening them with his revolver when they hesitated. It took the men two hours to remove two sizeable lengths of track, after which they were marched back to join their families at Stanistreet's house.

There was nothing to do now but await the arrival of the special train which Ned was so confidently expecting. His plan of action had, in fact, been perfectly timed: if the police had taken action speedily, they would surely have fallen into his trap. It was, ironically, their cowardice and procrastination which gave them their victory over the Kelly Gang. Aaron, Ned was certain, would have been killed early the previous evening. The news would have been quickly conveyed to the police at Beechworth, and thence to Benalla and Melbourne. Alerted to the presence of the Kellys in the district, the police would send in the black-trackers and all available reinforcements.

This is precisely what happened. Unfortunately for the Kellys, however, it happened much more slowly. Before Constable Armstrong finally plucked up sufficient courage to leave Sherritt's house and report the shooting in Beechworth, he had tried to persuade two passing civilians to do the job for him. Both were too terrified of the Kellys to undertake the commission. It was only in the broad daylight of mid-morning that the constable himself ventured out on the road.

It was not until after lunch on Sunday afternoon that the news of Aaron's murder reached Superintendent Hare in the smoking room of the Commercial Hotel, Benalla, where he was enjoying a post-prandial Havana. He lost no time in telegraphing the information on to Chief Commissioner Standish in Melbourne, but that gentleman was out when the telegram was delivered, and did not return home until four-thirty. It was evening before he had obtained an order for a special train to proceed to Beechworth, and had persuaded Inspector O'Connor from Queensland and his black-trackers to board it. O'Connor and his blacks had by this time been withdrawn from the Kelly search. They were on the eve of their departure for Queensland, and were staying at Essendon, a suburb of Melbourne. Standish arranged for the special train to leave from the central station at Spencer Street, and to stop at Essendon to pick up the Queensland party. Or, in the colourful and portentous language of *The Age,* on June 29th, 1880: 'Captain Standish ordered the special train to convey the blacks to the scene of the outrage, so that they might there pick up the tracks of the dreaded gang; but no one at that time imagined that the expedition would have such a speedy and sensational termination; that, in fact, it would end in the annihilation of the band in a manner that must strike terror into the hearts of all sympathizers and men inclined to imitate the doings of the gang.'

But, when the news arrived at Spencer Street Station that a special train was required, all the engines were cold, and it was not until after ten o'clock that evening that a start was made. At 10.15 the train steamed out of the station carrying five newspaper reporters, one of them armed. At Essendon, Inspector O'Connor and his five black-trackers were picked up, one of the original complement of six having died. Two ladies joined the train here as well. They were Inspector O'Connor's wife and her sister, a Miss Smith. ('Those ladies,' wrote Superintendent Hare in his memoirs, 'intended to proceed to Beechworth and remain there whilst we went in pursuit of the gang.') The men all seemed in excellent spirits at the prospect of an encounter, and the train proceeded rapidly on its way. At Craigieburn, it crashed through the gates at a crossing, and one of its brakes was torn off. This necessitated a stoppage of nearly half an hour. After that, fair progress was made to Benalla where the train arrived at 1.30 a.m. and where Superintendent Hare and his contingent of eight policemen and seventeen horses joined the party. A Mr Charles C. Rawlings, according to *The Age*, also added himself to the number here. While the horses were being boxed, a long consultation was held and thus more time was lost.

The night was a splendid one, the moon shining with unusual brightness, whilst the sharp, frosty air caused the slightest noise in the bush beyond to be distinctly heard. It was suspected that the Kellys or some of their friends might try to obstruct the train, perhaps by dynamiting the line, and, in order to avoid danger, Hare suggested that one of the police be strapped to the front of the engine to keep a look-out, but this plan was not carried out. There was a spare engine at Benalla station, which Hare had been holding in readiness in case the special from Melbourne failed to arrive, and it was decided to send this on ahead as a pilot. Accordingly, it started about a hundred yards ahead of the special train which it was intended should proceed to Wangaratta twenty-three miles further on, and there turn off to Beechworth, twenty-six miles to the east. Inspector O'Connor, Superintendent Hare and the two ladies occupied one compartment, the gentlemen of the press a second, and the police and black-trackers a third. The train finally moved out of Benalla. The first station it would have to pass en route to Wangaratta was Glenrowan, about fourteen miles distant.

Meanwhile, almost a full twenty-four hours earlier, before dawn on the Sunday morning, Dan Kelly and Joe Byrne arrived in Glenrowan, having ridden over the Oxley Plains from the Woolshed, and gave Ned and Steve their account of the murder of Aaron Sherritt. Ned had commandeered a backroom of the Glenrowan Inn as an armoury, and as day dawned he and the Gang indulged their habit of holding up passers-by, taking them prisoner and shepherding them into the pub. Mrs Jones was delighted at the extra trade this provided. Her sixteen-year-old daughter prepared breakfast for the outlaws, and flirted with them as she served it. The day advanced, there was no sign of the special train, and many more inhabitants of Glenrowan were rounded up and invited to join the prisoners at the Inn. During this time the stationmaster and his family were still confined to their house, while a number of Kelly sympathizers had congregated at McDonald's Hotel on the other side of the railway tracks. Among the prisoners at the Glenrowan Inn was the local schoolmaster, Thomas Curnow. He, his wife, his sister, his child and his brother-in-law had all been accosted by Kelly as they were settting off for a ride in their buggy. The women were sent to the stationmaster's house. (See Curnow's narrative, Appendix I (b)). The crowd at the Inn numbered about fifty, happily drinking and chatting and, as usual, being alternately harangued by Ned or entertained by his colleagues. Much of the fantasy-life of the Australian male centres around the pub: it is where he recounts to his mates how he told the boss to get off, what he retorted to the constable on duty, or how frequently he cheated his wife. The Kellys carried this public-bar 'skiting', as it is called in Australia, to absurd heights, and, in a sense, their exploits were an acting-out in real life of Australian pub fantasies. They certainly loved nothing better than to lean on a bar, and boast to a crowd of listeners about their latest raid.

The schoolmaster appears to have been one of the very few citizens in the pub possessed of a social conscience. He was a sufficiently educated man both to understand how the Kelly Gang had been forced into existence by social and economic conditions in the colony, and to realize that their anarchic and murderous exploits must not be allowed to continue. Cleverly, Curnow set about ingratiating himself with Ned, in the hope that at some stage he might be allowed to leave the pub and raise an alarm. The Kellys were openly boasting that the railway tracks had been ripped up, and that the special train would crash into the ravine shortly after it had passed Glenrowan station.

Afternoon wore on, and the party became jollier and noisier. A jumping competition was held in the hotel yard. Inside, there was dancing: Curnow found himself obliged to dance with Dan Kelly, to concertina accompaniment. Ned himself joined in a hop step and jump, and was disgruntled to find himself outdistanced by one of the prisoners. 'You seem a bit off today, Ned,' said Joe Byrne.

During the afternoon, as the Glenrowan prisoners became merrier, and the Kellys more confident as they were surrounded by friends and well-wishers, there was a certain amount of to-ing and fro-ing in the town. Several of the prisoners were allowed to go home during the afternoon, and they all eventually returned to the pub. Curnow asked Kelly's permission to go across to Stanistreet's to visit his wife and his sister. Permission was granted, and at the stationmaster's Curnow advised Steve Hart, who was complaining of sore and swollen feet, to bathe his feet in hot water. While Steve was doing this, Curnow conversed with the stationmaster: a scheme was forming in his mind, an idea suggested by the red Llama-wool scarf he had noticed his sister wearing.

Curnow returned to the Inn. As night fell, Kelly announced he was going down to the police station to bring the local constable, Bracken, back to the pub. He needed a local person to call the policeman out, and Curnow suggested his brother-in-law, Dave Mortimer, who boarded next door to the police station and knew Bracken well. Kelly agreed, and Curnow seized the opportunity to ask if, at the same time, he might collect his own family and take them home for the night. He assured Ned he was with him heart and soul. 'I know that; I can see it,' replied Kelly, and acceded to the schoolmaster's request.

Two or three hours later, having brought his wife, child and sister over from Stanistreet's, Curnow set out in his buggy, accompanied on horseback by his brother-in-law Dave Mortimer, Ned Kelly and Joe Byrne, and two young men, one of them the postmaster's son. When they arrived at the police station, Mortimer's knocking failed to arouse Constable Bracken, and eventually the postmaster's brother had to be awakened in the house next door, and sent to bring Bracken out. Finally a sullen Constable Bracken, his wife persuaded to silence by the fact of her husband's being held as hostage, was pressed into the party which then separated: the Curnow family was sent home and advised to go quietly to bed, while the others returned to the Glenrowan Inn with the unwilling constable.

By this time, Ned was considerably perplexed at the failure of the police train to put in an appearance. It was now quite late on Sunday evening, and his three colleagues were becoming distinctly anxious. 'Something's gone wrong,' said Dan, and he suggested they should clear out while they could. But Ned's reply was, 'I'm tired of running. We'll stand and fight.' The twenty-five year old leader glanced around at his 'band of brothers': Joe Byrne, aged twenty-three; Steve Hart, twenty-one; Dan Kelly, nineteen. 'We won't give in,' he said, as though to himself.

As the night lengthened a mood of enforced gaiety spread among outlaws and prisoners alike. The Gang displayed their improvised armour to be admired by the crowd, the concertina struck up again and soon there was renewed dancing, singing of songs about the Kellys and other bold colonial spirits, and a great deal more drinking. Mrs Jones was heard to exclaim that she hoped the Kellys would stay for a week. Sunday night eased into the early hours of Monday morning. The chairs were cleared away for everyone to dance a quadrille.

By two o'clock on Monday morning Ned had been persuaded by his brother that it would be dangerous to wait any longer. 'All right,' he said to one of the crowd. 'We're off soon, and then you can clear out whenever you like.' Dan, greatly relieved, ran amongst the prisoners, calling 'Now you can all go home.' But Ned had been conferring with Mrs Jones, and, before anyone could get to the door, the landlady cried out. 'You're not to go yet. Mr Kelly's going to give you a lecture.'

Amidst cheering, Mr Kelly climbed on to a chair, and began to speak:

'First, I want to tell you that if I ever hear that anyone here tonight tells the police about anything we've said or done, I shall make it my duty to visit them some day and settle up with them. So you know what to expect. I'm not a bit afraid of the police, and if it was only them hunting for me I'd never be taken. But it's those damned black-trackers I'm really afraid of. I'm really scared of them because I know what they can do. They could track me over bare stones. A white man doesn't stand a chance with them at all, and it was mainly to kill those black bastards that I tore up those rails down the line. In fact, that's what brought me here. I knew that when they heard we'd been at Beechworth on Saturday night, they'd pack those bloody devils after us, and I was going to be ready for them.

I can't make out what's delayed that train. They must have taken a different route or something. Perhaps they've got information about where we are now, I don't know. Well, anyhow, let them come when they like. We'll be ready for them.

I suppose some of you people would like to know what I've been up to lately, and how I've managed to escape capture so long. Well, I don't mind telling you a bit. It'll pass the time, and it can't do any harm. A lot of people think that we had to stick up the bank at Jerilderie because we were running short of money. Well, that's not true. When we went to Jerilderie, we had no idea of robbing the bank. I wanted to catch that bloody scoundrel Sullivan that turned Queen's evidence in New Zealand [Sullivan, a murderer who had been active in New Zealand in the 1860s, was pardoned and came to live in Victoria. But he had left the colony six years earlier, in 1874.] I heard that he was at Rutherglen, and I followed him, but by that time he'd gone on to Uralla. We went up to Uralla, and then on to Wagga, but we lost track of him. We were making our way back home through Jerilderie when we decided to stick up the bank, which we did, as you all know.

I don't know how much money we took, but it was a lot more than they said in the papers. Anyway, we didn't catch Sullivan, and I'd rather have caught him than robbed a dozen banks. I consider him one of the greatest villains unhung, and if I ever come across him, then God help him. I won't shoot the bastard, that'd be too good for him. I'll hang, draw and quarter him. I'll hunt the bastard till I die. I tell you, I'll give five hundred quid to the man who can lead me to him. I'd follow him to England if I thought he was there, because—'

Ned's audience never learned why he felt so strongly about Sullivan as to speak of him so vehemently, for at that moment he broke off, interrupted by the shrill warning blast of a train whistle not far down the line. Kelly thought quickly. 'By Christ,' he exclaimed, 'that bastard Curnow has tricked us.' He rushed outside, leaped on his mare, and galloped off. Within a few moments he had returned. 'The bastard's stopped the train, and they're coming up here. We'll have to stand and fight.' Followed by Dan, Steve and Joe, he raced off to the back room they had set aside for their private use. When the four of them returned to the front parlour two or three minutes later, minutes during which the sound of the police train slowly steaming in to Glenrowan Station could be heard, they were wearing their strange, unwieldy armour.

The time was just after three o'clock on the morning of Monday, June 28th.

The special train had come to a sudden halt less than a mile from Glenrowan. Danger signals from the pilot engine were the cause, and in a few seconds the driver of the pilot came back to the train to say that a man, in a state of great excitement, had stopped the engine by waving a red light. This was Curnow with his sister's red scarf held in front of a candle. The man had stated that Glenrowan was stuck up by the Kellys, who had torn up the lines just beyond the station in order to destroy the party which they knew would pass along the line in the special. The news and the stated intentions of the gang dismayed the party somewhat, but the police nevertheless seemed eager for action. The members of the press barricaded their windows with the cushions upon which they had previously sat, and in response to the request which some of the number made, the lights in the train were extinguished. It was then ten minutes to three. Once he had given the alarm, Curnow disappeared in the forest and his story was accepted with caution; but it was soon made apparent that he had saved the lives of those in the train, which to a certainty would, along with the pilot engine, have been hurled into a deep gully just below the Glenrowan Station, and behind a curve in the line which would have prevented the second driver from seeing the pilot go over the embankment where the rails had been torn up. Superintendent Hare, with one or two of the police, proceeded in the pilot engine to the railway station, closely followed by the special. On arriving at the station the horses were quickly got out of the trucks by the men, whilst Hare, with one or two men and the civilian volunteer, Rawlings, proceeded towards the Glenrowan Inn to seek information. When they were within sixteen yards of the Inn, one of the Gang fired at them. The police abandoned the horses and rushed to their arms. The black-trackers sprang forward with their leader, and soon took up a position in front of the house. Hare, according to the journalist from *The Age* upon whose report this account of the siege is based, could be plainly seen by the light of the moon. He walked towards the hotel. He was within about twenty-five yards of the verandah when the tall figure of a man came round the corner, and fired. The shot caught Hare in the wrist. Senior Constable Kelly and Mr Rawlings were close to him, and the former promptly returned the fire, which was also taken up by Hare, despite his wound.

Just before Superintendent Hare was wounded, Constable Bracken, the local policeman who had been made prisoner in the hotel, made his escape, and running towards the railway station, quickly spread the information that the Kellys, with about forty prisoners, were inmates of the hotel. Behind the building there was a kitchen, the walls of which were constructed of slabs. Into this the police fired. When about sixty shots had been sent into the walls of the building, the clear voice of Hare was distinguished above the screams of the terrified women and children who were in the hotel, giving the order to stop firing. This was now repeated by Senior Constable Kelly to the men who, under cover, were surrounding the house at the back. The Kellys fired three or four more shots, after which one of them called to the police, 'Come on, you fucking wretches. You can fire away; you'll never harm us.' A few straggling shots were then fired, the sharp sounds of the rifle echoing from the hill called Morgan's Lookout, at the foot of which the fight took place.

Then all was silent again, and after the lapse of about a quarter of an hour Superintendent Hare approached the station and stated that he had been wounded in the wrist. The wound was a very bad one, and was bleeding heavily. There was no doctor present, but the representatives of the press succeeded in stopping the rapid loss of blood. Hare's re-appearance in the trenches was the signal for renewed firing, and the valley was soon filled with smoke. Hare then became faint from loss of blood, and was compelled to leave the field. He went back to Benalla on an engine in order to have his injury attended to, and to send more men to the front.

A long and tedious interval followed, during which time Stanistreet, the stationmaster, suddenly left the Inn, where he had been kept prisoner with the other residents of Glenrowan. He walked boldly away, and narrowly escaped being shot by the police, saving himself by proclaiming he was the station-master. He reported that the gang were still in the Inn, and that the shots of the police had struck the daughter of Mrs Jones, a girl fifteen years of age, on the head, whilst the son, John Jones, a boy of nine, was wounded in the hip. Very soon after this, hysterical screams of terror were heard from Mrs Jones and a Mrs Reardon, both of whom were walking about the place, disregarding the danger to be feared from the volleys which the police, at short intervals, poured into the hotel. Mrs Jones's grief took the form of vindictiveness towards the police, whom she called murderers. The police frequently called upon the women to come away, but they hesitated. Mrs Reardon was carrying a baby only a few months old in her arms.

Inside the Inn, Dan Kelly had said to her, 'Put your kids outside and tell them to scream, and scream yourself. If you get clear, tell the police to stop shooting until daybreak, to give all these people a chance to get out. We'll fight for ourselves.'

Mrs Reardon rushed out with her children, screaming, 'I'm a woman. Let me escape with my children.'

Sergeant Steele called from behind a tree, 'Put your hands up and come over here, or I'll shoot you like bloody dogs.'

Mrs Reardon ran forward with her baby, and Steele began firing at her. A fellow constable cried, 'Don't shoot. Can't you see it's a woman with a child?' But Steele, apparently convinced the woman was the innkeeper, replied excitedly, 'I've shot Mother Jones in the tits.' He fired again, and shot Mrs Reardon's nineteen-year-old son in the shoulder. 'I've wounded Dan Kelly,' he shouted. The boy, who had been following his mother, was dragged back into the safety of the Inn by his father. Mrs Jones renewed her abuse of the police. 'Murderers!' she yelled. 'Ned Kelly is better than any of you!' Inside, Reardon, the father of the wounded boy, could hear Dan Kelly and Steve Hart talking in the back room. One of them called out for Ned, whom they imagined was outside, nearby. But there was no answer. 'What shall we do?' said the other.

Questioned by a reporter as soon as she was clear of the firing, Mrs Reardon made a statement which reached print in this form:

'My husband is a plate-layer employed on the railway, and we live about a mile from the station, on the Benalla side. At three o'clock on Sunday morning we were all in bed. We were aroused by Ned Kelly, who knocked at the door, and told my husband, when he opened it, to surrender. He advised us to dress, and I did so. They had also made a prisoner of Sullivan, another plate-layer, and Kelly brought us to the station, where I was kept for some hours. Kelly took my husband and Sullivan down the line, in order to tear up the line and destroy the train with the police. He was afterwards taken to the hotel. There are a lot of innocent people in there now, and they are frightened to come out for fear the police will kill them. Amongst the people who are in there are James and Michael Reardon, my husband and son, Catherine and William Rennison, John and Patrick Delaney (who are here coursing), **W. S. Cooke** (a labourer), Martin Sherry (a plate-layer), John Larkins (a farmer), Edward Reynolds (the brother of the postmaster), Robert Gibbons, the brothers Meanliffe, and other strangers I do not know.'

While the woman was telling her story, the firing of the police became very brisk, and it was replied to by the outlaws in the Inn. Senior Constable Kelly at that juncture found a rifle stained with blood lying on the side of the hill, and this led to the supposition that one of the gang had been wounded, and had escaped through the forest towards Morgan's Lookout. Just then nine police under Superintendent Sadleir, accompanied by a Dr Hutchinson, arrived from Benalla. Almost immediately after, seven policemen under Sergeant Steele rode in from Wangaratta. The alarm had been given there by Bracken, who had caught a horse and ridden the ten miles in a surprisingly short space of time. Just before their arrival a heavy volley was poured into the Inn by the police.

According to statements made later by some of the prisoners, that volley proved fatal to Joe Byrne, who was drinking a nobbler of whisky at the bar, when he was shot in the groin. He was then carried to the back of the building, where he died slowly, and in great pain. This fact was, at the time, unknown to the police.

The morning broke beautiful and clear. The police were disposed all round the Inn, when they were beset by a danger from the rear. Ned Kelly was the cause. He, it appears, was the man who had shot at Hare, and he himself was wounded by the fire which was returned. He could not, without danger, get back into the hotel, so he attempted to escape. Being wounded in the foot, he could not get very far, and hid in a gully for most of the night. Kelly himself, after his capture, claimed that he could have got away then. As he left the Glenrowan Inn, one of the prisoners claimed to have heard him cry, 'Come on, boys, follow me!' Whether he hoped then that they might all escape is by no means certain. It was shortly after Kelly left the Inn that his friends in McDonald's Hotel fired off two rockets apparently as a signal to Kelly sympathizers to rally to Glenrowan from the surrounding countryside. There was, no doubt, real danger that several of them might have joined the Kellys in attacking the police. But, in fact, they did not. There is no way of telling now how many of them there were: perhaps a handful, perhaps a hundred.

It was nearly eight o'clock when Kelly's tall figure was seen close behind the line of police. At first it was thought he was an aborigine. He wore a grey coat over his armour, and walked coolly and slowly towards the police. His head, chest, back and sides were all protected with heavy plates of quarter-inch iron. When he had got to within easy distance of Senior Constable Kelly, who was watching him, he fired. Sergeant Steele, Senior Constable Kelly and a railway guard returned fire on him. Nine police joined in and fired point-blank at Kelly; but although, in consequence of the way in which he staggered, it was apparent that many of the shots hit him, yet he always recovered himself, and tapping his breast, laughed derisively at his opponents as he coolly returned the fire, fighting only with a revolver. It appeared as if he was a fiend with a charmed life. Senior Constable Kelly cried out, 'Look out, boys. It's the bunyip!' A railwayman shouted, 'It's old Nick himself.'

The police continued to rain bullets upon him. It was Steele who finally brought him down by firing at his legs which were unprotected by the armour. Kelly fell. 'I'm done,' he muttered as the police rushed at him. But, as he fell, he tried to raise his revolver against Steele, who seized his hand as the bullet shot harmlessly into the air. 'Steady, don't break my fingers,' said Ned. It was only when they had wrenched off his helmet that the police realized who it was. 'You bloody wretch,' cried Steele, who had to be restrained by Constable Bracken from shooting Kelly on the spot. 'Let me live as long as I can,' Kelly gasped. When he was stripped of his armour, it was found that, under it, he wore the sash he had been awarded as a child for bravery. He became quite submissive, and was taken to the railway station by Sergeant Steele, Constable Dwyer, and two representatives of the Melbourne press.

At the railway station Kelly appeared to be very weak from the loss of blood, and some brandy was given him. He was examined in the guard's van by Dr Nicholson and Dr Hutchinson, who found that he was suffering from two bullet wounds in the left arm, a bullet in the right foot near the right toe, and two wounds in the right leg, those inflicted by Sergeant Steele. (In most accounts of the capture of Kelly, the number of bullet wounds he suffered has risen to twenty-eight.) By now, Kelly seemed quite composed, and made the following statement to the press:

'What I intended to do, and in fact was just about doing, was to go down with some of my mates and meet the special train and rake it with shot. The train, however, came before I expected, and I had to return to the hotel. I thought the train would go on, and on that account I had the rails pulled up, so that these bloody black-trackers might be settled. It does not much matter what brought me to Glenrowan. I do not know, or I'm not saying. It doesn't matter much, any way. If I liked, I could have got away last night. I got into the bush with my grey mare, and laid there all night. I had a good chance, but I wanted to see the thing end.

'When the police fired the first round I got wounded in the left foot. Shortly afterwards I was shot through the left arm. It was in the front of the house where I received these injuries. At the commencement of the affair this morning I fired three or four shots from the front of Jones's Hotel, but I do not know who I was firing at. I only fired when I saw flashes. I then cleared for the bush, but remained there near the hotel all night. Two constables passed close by me talking, and I could have shot them before I had time to shout, if I liked. I could have shot several constables at one time. I was a good distance away, but I came back again. I have got a charge of duck-shot in my leg. Why don't the police use bullets instead of duck-shot?

'One of the policemen that was firing at me was a splendid shot. I don't know his name. Perhaps I would have done better if I had cleared away on my grey mare. It was just like blows from a man's fist receiving the bullets on my armour. I wanted to fire into the carriages, only the police started on us too quickly. I knew the police would come, and I expected them.'

Inspector Sadleir here remarked, 'You wanted then to kill the people in the train?' Kelly replied, 'Yes; of course I did. God help them, they would have got shot all the same. Wouldn't they have tried to kill me? When I saw my best friend Joe Byrne fall, from my place in the bushes up there, the heart went out of me.'

'Ned,' said Sadleir, 'the fate of the other two is certain. Do you think, if you sent a message to them, they would surrender?'

'No, they're only boys. They won't come out fighting like men,' replied Kelly. 'They'll stay in there until they're finished.'

'Why did you come back when you saw all the police?' someone asked. 'You must have known you didn't have a chance.'

'A man would be a nice sort of dingo to walk out on his mates,' said Kelly.

At various times during the morning more police arrived, but the bushrangers could not be dislodged; nor, which was more perplexing still, could the prisoners inside be persuaded to leave, although the police repeatedly called upon them to come out. At twelve o'clock, however, the people inside, consisting of about thirty men and youths, suddenly rushed out of the front door, holding their hands aloft. The police told them to advance towards where they were located, but many were so terror-stricken that they ran hither and thither screaming for mercy. One by one they were minutely searched, and despatched to the railway station.

The police after this kept up a constant fire on the pub. It was noticed that the fire from the besieged bushrangers was not returned after one o'clock, but it was believed that Dan Kelly and Hart intended to lie quiet until night, and under cover of the darkness make their escape. The police for a time also ceased firing. A consultation was held amongst the officers to decide what was to be done next. At one moment it was decided to telegraph for a field-gun from Melbourne, but fearing it would not arrive in time to be of any use the police determined to adopt another mode of dislodging the remaining outlaws.

Just as they were about to put their newly conceived plan into operation, Ned's sister Mrs Skillian, dressed in a dark riding-habit trimmed with scarlet, and wearing a jaunty hat adorned with a conspicuous white feather, appeared on the scene. Dean Gibney earnestly requested her to go to the hotel and ask her brother and Hart to surrender. She said she would like to see her brother before he died, but she would sooner see him burned in the house than ask him to surrender. This, in fact, was the procedure which the police had decided upon in order to bring the outlaws from their cover. Some 200 people by this time had arrived on the station platform.

The police opened up a heavy fire on the hotel from the front and rear. This was done in order to cover the operations of Senior Constable Johnstone, who rapidly approached the house on the north side with a bundle of straw, which he placed against the weather-boards and set on fire. It was known that Martin Sherry, an old man, was still in the house. When the last prisoners had escaped he was still alive, though badly wounded. The thought that the unfortunate man would be sacrificed, and perish in the flames with the Kellys, gave rise to strong expressions of anti-police feeling from the crowd.

Kate Kelly now came upon the scene, but the only expression which escaped her lips was, 'My poor, poor brother.' Mrs Skillian exclaimed, 'I must see Dan before he dies,' and then sped towards the hotel, from the roof of which by this time tongues of flame were beginning to ascend. The police ordered her to go back, and she hesitated. Dean Gibney emerged from the crowd, saying he would save Sherry, and was encouraged on his mission by a cheer from the spectators. He walked boldly to the front door, and was lost to view amongst the smoke. Directly afterwards a mass of flames burst from the walls and roof of the dwelling at the same instant. A shout of terror from the crowd announced the fear that was felt for the safety of the priest. Constable Armstrong, with some other policemen, rushed into the building from the rear and, a few seconds afterwards, they and Dean Gibney were seen to emerge, carrying with them Sherry, who was dying, and the dead body of Joe Byrne.

On reaching safety they stated that Dan Kelly and Hart were lying upon the floor apparently dead. Nothing, however, could be done to rescue their remains from the fire. Soon afterwards the building was completely demolished, and on a search being made amongst the ruins, two charred skeletons were raked out from the smouldering debris. The two young men had been lying stretched out side by side on the floor in the back room, with bags under their heads for pillows, and their armour laid aside. Father Gibney concluded that they had killed themselves rather than be taken or killed by the police. The wounded Ned, when told his mates would be burned to death, had replied, 'No fear. They'd finish one another when they found the game was up. We all swore to shoot one another rather than surrender to the police.' Poison was, in fact, found in the possession of Joe Byrne, though he had had no chance to make use of it.

Sherry died soon after being rescued from the burning building. Ned Kelly was brought on to Benalla by the evening train, and lodged in the lock-up, to await the inquest to be held in the morning. But first his sisters came in to see him, to kiss him and to say goodbye. Then they returned to the Inn, in time to see the charred remains of Dan and Steve being carried out. Joe Byrne's body had already been taken away by the police, but an attempt to bring the bodies of Dan Kelly and Steve Hart to the station aroused such resentment among the onlookers, many of whom were armed, that the police decided not to risk it. Steve's brother Dick said, 'If you want the bodies, you'll have to fight for them.' He and the Kelly relatives were allowed to depart, taking the bodies with them, back to Kelly Country.

The enthusiastic representative of *The Age* interviewed several people that evening. Among the statements printed in his newspaper on June 30th were the following:

John Stanistreet, stationmaster at Glenrowan: 'About three o'clock on Sunday morning a knock came to my door, at the gatehouse, within one hundred yards of the station on the Melbourne side. I jumped up, and thinking it was someone wanting to get through the gates in a hurry, I commenced to dress as soon as possible. I half dressed, and went to the door. Just when I got there it was burst in, but previous to that there was some impatient talk, which caused me to dress quickly. When the door was burst in I asked, "What is that for?" or "Who are you?" The answer was, "I am Ned Kelly." I then saw a man, clad in an overcoat, standing in the doorway. He pushed me into my bedroom, where my wife and some of the children were in bed. There were two girls and one infant besides my wife. Then he said to me, "You have to come with me and take up the rails." "Wait," said I, "until I dress." He said, "Yes," and I completed my dressing and followed him out of the house.

'On the line there were seven or eight men standing at the gate which crosses the line to Mrs Jones's hotel, the Glenrowan Inn. He said, "You direct those men how to raise some of the rails, as we expect a special train very soon." I objected, saying, "I know nothing about lifting rails off the line; the only persons who understand it are the repairers; they live outside and along the line." Ned Kelly then went into Reardon the platelayer's house. Reardon lives outside the line on the Greta side, about a quarter of a mile away. Steve Hart was present, and Kelly left us in his charge. When Kelly went away Hart gave me a prod with his rifle in the side, saying, "You get the tools out that are necessary to raise those rails." I said, "I have not the key of the chest;" and he said, "Break the lock." He told one of the men to do so, and on arriving at the station he got one of the men to do it. This was in the little back shed used as a store-room, between the station and the gatehouse. The tools were thrown out, and in the meantime Reardon and Sullivan, the line-repairers, arrived with Ned Kelly. These two men and Ned proceeded down the line towards Wangaratta to lift the rails. We were still under Steve Hart, and we remained where we were over two hours, and then Ned Kelly and the repairers returned. Ned then inquired about the signalling of trains, as to how I stopped a train with the signal-lights. I said, "'White is right, red is wrong, and green is gently, come along.'" He said, "There is a special train coming; you give no signals." Speaking to Hart he said, "Watch his countenance, and if he gives any signal, shoot him." He then marched us into my residence, and left us there under Steve Hart. There were then about seventeen altogether, other persons subsequently being placed in my house also. There were present Reardon's family, the Ryan family, Cameron (son of the gatekeeper on the other line), Sullivan, line-repairer, and others whom I do not remember. We were locked up all day on Sunday, and were only allowed out under surveillance. The women were permitted to go to Jones's Hotel about five o'clock, and shortly afterwards all the men but me and my family went away. Steve Hart stopped with us, and during the night Dan Kelly relieved Hart, and he was afterwards relieved by Byrne.

'Just before the special train arrived I was ordered to the hotel by Hart, who was on and off duty all the time, to follow him to Jones's, and not signal the train. I went into the back kitchen, where Mrs Jones and daughter, aged about fourteen, and two younger children were. There was also a man there named Neil M'Kew. By this time the train had arrived, and firing was going on furiously. I did not see Ned Kelly in the room. I with others stood in the chimney. I did not hear any remark passed by any of the gang, and they disappeared. A ball passed through the hut, and grazed Miss Jane Jones, fourteen years of age, on the forehead. The girl said, "I'm shot," and turned to me. I saw the blood and told her it was nothing. The mother commenced to cry, and soon afterwards I left the kitchen, and went into the back-yard. I then saw three of the gang there standing behind the chimney. They had their rifles in their hands. One of them said, I don't know which, "If you go out you'll be shot." I walked straight down the path towards the house. The firing was then going on all round me, but I was uninjured. One of the police very nearly shot me, but I said "Station master" when he challenged me. I forgot to mention that during Sunday afternoon Steve Hart demanded and received my revolver.'

Mr Robert Gibbons: 'I am a farmer, and have recently been stopping at Glenrowan with Mr Reynolds. I came to the railway station about eight o'clock on Sunday night with Mr Reynolds to ask about his little boy, who had not been home. When we knocked at the door, Mrs Stanistreet told us that Mr Hart was inside, and that they had been stuck up ever since three o'clock on Sunday morning. We followed her in, and saw Steve Hart. She told him who we were, and he then put his fire-arms down, giving us to understand that we were not to go out. We remained there about two hours, when Ned Kelly came, and Hart ordered us to come out of the room. Ned Kelly then told us that we would all have to go down to the police-barracks with him. He kept us waiting there for about two hours, he having gone for Bracken. He returned to us with Bracken. He kept us waiting there about an hour and a half. Byrne at that time was with us. There he told me and Mr Reynolds we would have to go to Jones's Hotel. We went to the hotel, and he told us to get into the bar parlour. It was then about ten o'clock Sunday night, and we remained there until the train came. During that time the Kellys were going about the place making themselves quite jolly. Byrne was in charge of the back-door, the other door being locked. A little after three o'clock the train came. Prior to that the gang drank quite freely with the others. When the train arrived Ned came and said, "You are not to whisper a word that has been said here about me. If I hear of anyone doing so I will shoot you." He went to the door of the room and said, "Here she comes," and then the gang busied themselves in making preparations, but for what I did not know. They came back and said the first man who left the room in which we were would be shot. Two of them then mounted their horses, and rode away, but I could not tell which two. They came back in about ten minutes' time. When they came back, I saw that Dan was one of the two who had gone away. Dan went into a back room. All four in turn went into the same room. Very soon afterwards a hurried move was made, and firing commenced. There must have been about forty men, women and children in the house then. The women and children commenced to shriek, and Mrs Jones's eldest daughter was wounded in the side of the head, and the eldest boy shot in the thigh. The bullets rattled through the side of the house, and we laid down. We were packed so close that we had to lie on our sides. It was those who laid next to the door who prompted us to come out, and we did so because we feared that the bullets would come through faster than ever. We also feared a cannon would be used, and about ten o'clock we ran out. I heard some of them say that Byrne, or one of the gang, was lying dead in the back. I know that Dan was alive when I left.'

Sergeant Steele: 'I am a sergeant of police at Wangaratta. I arrived here with five men about five a.m. We were at once challenged by police, and answered, "Wangaratta police." My men were then distributed around the hut, and I got to the tree near the back door of the hut. There was no firing then. A woman and child came to the back-door screaming, and I told the woman if she ran in quick she would not be molested. A man then came to the back-door, and I asked him to throw up his arms or I would fire on him. He was only about twenty-five yards distant. The man stooped and ran towards the stables and I fired. He then turned and ran back to the house, and I fired again. I am certain I hit him with the second shot, as he screamed and fell against the door. There was some hot firing, and the bullets whistled all around me. The firing was kept up for some time, and some of the men behind me called out. It was then breaking day. I looked round, and saw a man stalking down. I thought he was a black-fellow, and called on the others to be careful. I then saw him present a revolver and fire at the police. I could see the bullets hitting him, and staggering him for a moment, with no further effect. I therefore thought he had armour on, and determined to have a close shot at him. I ran towards him, and when within ten yards of him he saw me, and turned round to fire at me. I then aimed at his legs, and he staggered, but he still tried to aim at me. I then fired the second barrel on the legs. We were then in the open. He fell, and cried, "I'm done, I'm done." I ran up to him then, and he again tried to shoot me, but I caught the revolver and pushed it down. I was behind him, and he could not turn on me quick enough to shoot me. Whilst I held the revolver away from me he fired the revolver. Senior Constable Kelly then came up and assisted me to secure him. So did O'Dwyer, and a host of others at once followed. We only found one revolver on him, and a bag of ammunition. We divested him of his armour. I was strained after the scuffle which ensured.'

Senior Constable Kelly: 'When we started from the platform we ran down towards the railway-gates, hearing that the gang were in Jones's public-house. The men at that time had not sufficient time to scatter, and all made towards the hotel. As we approached, someone came out on the verandah and fired on us. Mr Superintendent Hare, with Mr Rawlings, a volunteer from Benalla, was close to me. Mr Hare said, "I am shot in the wrist," but he continued to fire. We sought cover, and Hare said to me, "For God's sake, surround the house, and don't let them escape." He then fired again, and gave the gun to Rawlings. He then left saying, "Kelly, place the men under cover," and I placed the men around the house. Mr O'Connor and his trackers took up a position in front of the hotel. I then went round towards the back of the premises. Constable Arthur was with me, and we crawled about 400 yards. In this way we got to within about fifty yards of the hut, at the back of a tree. We kept strict watch, and fired upon anyone who attempted to leave the hut. There were four horses saddled and tied up to the back-door. These we shot in order to prevent the sudden escape of the gang. When we left the station we met Constable Bracken, who told us that the gang were at Jones's. He, I believe, jumped on one of our horses, and rode off to Benalla to get further assistance, and at half past six o'clock he returned with the Wangaratta police, Sergeant Steele being at their head. We continued to fire, and at about eight o'clock, so far as I can remember, Ned Kelly made his appearance under the brow of the hill, 300 yards from the hut. He deliberately fired at me. I returned the fire, and my men closed around him, Sergeant Steele being behind him, myself on one side, and Dowsett, the railway-guard, on the other. About ten rifles were brought to bear on him, and we hit him several times. His heavy armour, however, protected him, and he walked boldly to and fro. Near a fallen tree he fell, and we rushed forward. I caught him by the head as Steele grasped his hand, in which he still held his revolver. He fired it, but did no damage. His armour was taken off, and he was carried to the railway station, where he was searched, but only threepence was found on him, a silver Geneva watch, and a lot of ammunition. I asked him to tell me where Sergeant Kennedy's watch was, and he said, "I cannot tell you; I would not like to tell you about it." He also said, "I had to shoot Sergeant Kennedy and Scanlan for my own safety. I cannot tell you any more." '

TEN

The charred bodies of Dan Kelly and Steve Hart, taken back to Greta by the relatives of the outlaws, were placed on display in Dan's sister's house. According to the Melbourne *Herald* reporter:

'The scene at Greta was indescribable. The people seemed to flock from the gum-trees. There were some of the worst looking people there I ever saw in my life. The two bodies were carried into Mrs Skillion's hut, amid the wailing and groaning of over 200 people. They were laid down on the table side by side – a dreadful sight. Their friends rushed to the hut to get a glimpse of them, but Mrs Skillion took down a gun, and threatened to blow out the brains of the first person that entered the house without her permission. She then allowed only three at a time to enter. The first who went in were two girls and an old man, a relative of the Harts. He cried like a child. Then Tom Lloyd and Quinn went in. They looked at the bodies for a moment, and then Tom Lloyd took hold of Kate Kelly's hand and, lifting his right hand to heaven, swore a most dreadful oath that he would never leave their deaths unavenged.'

The mourners stayed all day, many of them drinking heavily, and at one moment it seemed likely that their passion would erupt in an immediate riot against the police. In a situation which, in fact, remained potentially explosive for some days, the authorities acted with restraint, and a squad of sixteen police detailed to retrieve the bodies of Dan and Steve was, at the last moment, recalled. The two men were buried by their relatives in Greta cemetery, in the presence of a large crowd. Tom Lloyd, he of the 'most dreadful oath', applied for Joe Byrne's body to be handed over to his family, but this the police refused. On the Tuesday morning, the day after the Glenrowan siege, they allowed his body to be strung up outside the police station at Benalla in order to be photographed, and later in the day he was buried quickly in Benalla cemetery.

Ned, meanwhile, had been taken to Benalla where he spent the night under guard in the police barracks. Next morning, carried on a stretcher, he was put on a train to Melbourne, guarded by a dozen constables. A cousin of Ned's, one of the Lloyd girls, came to see him leave. She was allowed to speak to him, and wept uncontrollably as the train moved out. Kelly's stretcher was placed on the floor of the luggage van; a reporter who was on the train wrote that Kelly looked terribly emaciated and that his face was covered in bruises where police bullets had struck his helmet. He remained silent and sullen throughout the journey, but appeared not to mind when, at every stop, people leaped on to the train to peer in at him. The doctor who accompanied him noted that he seemed like a man in a trance, and glared at strangers. 'Most men wounded and lacking sleep as he was would have been far more prostrated, but he has a splendid constitution. His body looked as if it was well nourished. His skin was clean as if he had just come out of a Turkish bath. I attended to his wounds, and now and then gave him some brandy and water. He seemed grateful, but gave the idea he wished to die.'

One of the policemen guarding Kelly was Senior Constable Armstrong who had been one of the four police in Sherritt's hut when he was killed. He spoke to Kelly about this, and Ned observed, 'You would have been foolhardy to leave the hut that night. You would have been all shot but one. It was not our game to shoot you all. We wanted one of you to go in and draw the police out.'

At Spencer Street railway station in Melbourne, a huge crowd had assembled, anxious to catch a glimpse of Kelly. But they were cheated out of this enjoyment, for he was taken off the train at North Melbourne and conveyed to Melbourne Gaol where, again, there was a tremendous crowd waiting, many of whom ambiguously cheered as the waggon clattered through the prison gateway. The prison doctor examined Kelly immediately on his arrival in the gaol hospital, and recorded:

'Healthy and exceptionally clean. Most serious wound in left arm. Ball struck when arm was bent, entering mid-way between wrist and elbow, passing through arm and piercing it again above the elbow. Four slug wounds in right thigh and leg. Slugs in right hand near thumb prevented him from using rifle. Shot in left foot near big toe, bullet passing through instep. Kelly suffering from mental depression.'

Ned Kelly's mother was, at this time, still serving her three years' sentence in the same gaol. After a few days, when Ned had become strong enough to receive visitors, she was allowed to see him for half an hour. Five weeks later, Kelly was considered well enough to stand trial, and was taken by train back to Beechworth, to the Court of Petty Sessions, where a preliminary examination was conducted before W. H. Foster, a police magistrate. He was charged with the murder of Constable Lonigan, whose shooting had been witnessed by Constable McIntyre. McIntyre's deposition read as follows:

> The information and complaint of Thomas McIntyre of Melbourne in the Colony of Victoria, Constable, taken this thirtieth day of July in the year of our Lord One thousand eight hundred and eighty, before the undersigned, one of Her Majesty's Justices of the Peace in and for the said Bailiwick [Central, Melbourne] who saith that Edward Kelly, on the twenty-sixth day of October in the year one thousand eight hundred and seventy-eight at Springy Bark Creek in the Northern Bailiwick, feloniously, wilfully, and of his malice aforethought did kill and murder one Thomas Lonigan.

Kelly was represented by Mr David Gaunson, a Melbourne solicitor, member of the Legislative Assembly, and a leading member of the Society for the Abolition of Capital Punishment. At this preliminary hearing, Kelly was committed to stand trial in October. On the way up to Beechworth in the train, he had occasionally talked to the police who accompanied him. When a discussion arose about the numbers of Chinese in Australia, and the police displayed a colour prejudice, Ned exclaimed, 'One Chinaman is worth all the bloody Europeans living. If I had a pig-tail, I'd go to China.' When the train passed the hills where he had spent much of his life in hiding, he looked out of the window and said, 'There they are. Will I ever be there again?'

After the preliminary hearing Kelly was returned to gaol in Melbourne. Fear of rioting in the Kelly Country caused the authorities to transfer the trial itself from Beechworth to Melbourne, and the trial of Edward Kelly for the murder of Constables Lonigan and Scanlan began in the Court House in Russell Street, Melbourne, on Monday, October 18th. The presiding judge was Sir Redmond Barry, who had earlier sentenced Ned's mother and who, at that time, had uttered from the bench a most improper threat to Ned. The Prosecutor for the Queen was one Charles Alexander Smyth, and Kelly's attorney, David Gaunson, had briefed Henry Massy Bindon, to appear for the defence. Kelly's defence had been paid for by the Crown.

On October 18th, Bindon successfully applied to have the trial postponed, in the hope that a more experienced Counsel could be briefed to appear for Kelly, and Sir Redmond Barry agreed to a postponement until October 28th. On the 28th, Bindon asked for a further adjournment which was refused, and the trial of Kelly, on the first charge of murdering Constable Lonigan, began on that day.

Eight witnesses for the prosecution were called on the first day. These included Detective Ward, Constable Patrick Day of Benalla, Constable McIntyre, the only eye-witness, and five men to whom, at the time of the Euroa bank hold-up, Kelly had boasted of the Stringybark Creek murders: George Stephens, a groom at Younghusband's Station; William Fitzgerald, a labourer; Henry Dudley and Robert McDougall, visitors at Younghusband's; and the drapery hawker, James Gloster.

The first day's hearing adjourned shortly after 6 p.m. Sir Redmond Barry announced that he would be prepared to sit very late the following day, if necessary, as he was unwilling to have the jury confined during the racing week. The Crown called several more witnesses the following day, including Mr Robert Scott, manager of the National Bank at Euroa; Lyving, the accountant from the Bank of New South Wales at Jerilderie, and John Tarleton, the manager of that branch. There was little that the defence lawyer could do for his client: he was unable to call any witnesses of his own, and could only attempt to chip away at the prosecution's evidence during cross-examination. The law at that time forbade the prisoner giving evidence on his own behalf, on the somewhat curious ground that any such statement might be against the prisoner's own interest. Bindon attempted to discredit the Crown's only eye-witness, Constable McIntyre, the survivor of the Stringybark encounter.

At 5.10 p.m. on the second day of the trial, Sir Redmond Barry concluded his charge to the jury, instructing them that they would not deliver a verdict of manslaughter, and that their verdict must be either guilty or not guilty of murder. The jury retired for half an hour, and returned to deliver a unanimous verdict of guilty. 'What have you to say,' Sir Redmond Barry asked Kelly, 'why the Court should not pass sentence of death upon you?'

Kelly replied: 'Well, it is rather late for me to speak now. I tried to do so this morning, but I thought afterwards that I had better not. No one understands my case as I do, and I almost wish now that I had spoken; not that I fear death. On the evidence that has been given, no doubt, the jury or any other jury could not give any other verdict. But it is on account of the witnesses, and with their evidence, no different verdict could be given. No one knows anything about my case but myself. Mr Bindon knows nothing about it at all, and Mr Gaunson knows nothing, though they have tried to do their best for me. I'm sorry I did not ask my counsel to sit down, and examine the witnesses myself. I could have made things look different, I'm sure. No one understands my case.'

At the conclusion of Kelly's statement, the court crier proclaimed, 'Oyez, oyez, oyez. All manner of persons are commanded to keep silence whilst sentence of death is passed upon the prisoner at the bar, upon pain of imprisonment.'

Judge Barry began what was doubtless intended as a short homily to the prisoner before sentencing him, but found himself interrupted by Kelly with whom he was forced to indulge in a somewhat undignified slanging match. The encounter was reported in *The Argus* of October 30th, 1880:

His Honour: Edward Kelly, the verdict is one which you must have fully expected.
Prisoner: Under the circumstances, I did expect this verdict.
His Honour: No circumstances that I can conceive could here control the verdict.
Prisoner: Perhaps if you had heard me examine the witnesses, you might understand. I could do it.
His Honour: I will even give you credit for the skill which you desire to show you possess.
Prisoner: I don't say this out of flashness. I do not recognize

myself as a great man; but it is quite possible for me to clear myself of this charge if I liked to do so. If I desired to do it, I could have done so in spite of anything attempted against me.

His Honour: The facts against you are so numerous and so conclusive, not only as regards the offence which you are now charged with, but also for the long series of criminal acts which you have committed during the last eighteen months, that I do not think any rational person could have arrived at any other conclusion. The verdict of the jury was irresistible, and there could not be any doubt about its being a right verdict. I have no right or wish to inflict upon you any personal remarks. It is painful in the extreme to perform the duty which I have now to discharge, and I will confine myself strictly to do it. I do not think that anything I could say would aggravate the pain you must now be suffering.

Prisoner: No; I declare before you and my God that my mind is as easy and clear as it possibly can be. (Sensation.)

His Honour: It is blasphemous of you to say so.

Prisoner: I do not fear death, and I am the last man in the world to take a man's life away. I believe that two years ago, before this thing happened, if a man pointed a gun at me to shoot me, I should not have stopped him, so careful was I of taking life. I am not a murderer, but if there is innocent life at stake, then I say I must take some action. If I see innocent life taken, I should certainly shoot if I was forced to do so, but I should first want to know whether this could not be prevented, but I should have to do it if it could not be stopped in any other way.

His Honour: Your statement involves wicked and criminal reflection of untruth upon the witnesses who have given evidence.

Prisoner: I dare say the day will come when we shall all have to go to a bigger court than this. Then we will see who is right and who is wrong. As regards anything about myself, all I care for is that my mother, who is now in prison, shall not have it to say that she reared a son who could not have altered this charge if he had liked to do so.

His Honour: An offence of the kind which you stand accused of is not of an ordinary character. There are many murders which have been discovered and committed in this colony under different circumstances, but none show greater atrocity than those you committed. These crimes proceed from different motives. Some arise from a sordid desire to take from others the property which they acquired or inherited, some from jealousy, some from a base desire to thieve, but this crime was an enormity out of all proportion. A party of men took up arms against society, organized as it was for mutual protection and regard for the law.

Prisoner: Yes, that is the way the evidence brought it out.

His Honour: Unfortunately, in a new community, where society was not bound together so closely as it should be, there was a class which looked upon the perpetrators of these crimes as heroes. But these unfortunate, ill-educated, ill-prompted youths must be taught to consider the value of human life. It could hardly be believed that a man would sacrifice the life of his fellow creatures in this wild manner. The idea was enough to make one shudder in thinking of it. The end of your companions was comparatively a better termination than the miserable death which awaits you. It is remarkable that although New South Wales had joined Victoria in offering a large reward for the detection of the gang, no person was found to discover it. There seemed to be a spell cast over the people of this particular district, which I can only attribute either to sympathy with crime or dread of the consequences of doing their duty. For months the country has been disturbed by you and your associates, and you have actually had the hardihood to confess to having stolen two hundred horses.

Prisoner: Who proves this?

His Honour: That is your own statement.

Prisoner: You have not heard me, if I had examined the witnesses, I could have brought it out differently.

His Honour: I am not accusing you. This statement has been made several times by the witnesses. You confessed it to them and you stand self-accused. It is also proved that you committed several attacks upon the banks, and you seem to have appropriated large sums of money – several thousands of pounds. It has also come within my knowledge that the country has expended about £50,000 in consequence of the acts of which you and your party have been guilty. Although we have had such examples as Clarke, Gardiner, Melville,

Morgan and Scott, who have all met ignominious deaths, still the effect has, apparently, not been to hinder others from following in their footsteps. I think that this is much to be deplored, and some steps must be taken to have society protected. Your unfortunate and miserable associates have met with deaths which you might envy. I will forward to the Executive the notes of the evidence which I have taken and all circumstances connected with your case, but I cannot hold out any hope to you that the sentence which I am now about to pass will be remitted. I desire not to give you any further pain or to aggravate the distressing feelings which you must be enduring.

Judge Barry then passed sentence of death, ending with the formula: 'May the Lord have mercy on your soul.' The prisoner replied, 'Yes, I will meet you there.'

On the way back to Melbourne gaol, Ned reminded the policemen that there were other Kellys alive, and ready to fight, 'It will take forty thousand police to get rid of them,' he boasted. 'I'll come back from the grave to fight with them.'

Kelly's counsel, Gaunson, naturally sought a reprieve, and, with the aid of his younger brother William Gaunson, organized a public demonstration, and even managed to collect sixty thousand signatures from throughout the colony. The Executive Council, however, determined that Kelly should be executed on Thursday, November 11th. A personal appeal to the Governor by a deputation consisting of the Gaunson brothers, two others and Kate Kelly, was unsuccessful, even though a mass meeting of over 4,000 people in Melbourne the previous evening, chaired by the President of the Society for the Abolition of Capital Punishment, had asked for the exercise of the royal prerogative of mercy.

Signatures continued to pour in, and a further unavailing approach was made to the Governor, three days before the date of execution. Who were these thousands who begged clemency for Kelly? Presumably the majority of them were humanists rather than active supporters of the Kelly Gang. One newspaper, reporting the mass meeting at the Hippodrome, was appalled by the sight of 'so many respectably dressed citizens, women in particular,' associating themselves with Kelly's cause. The conservative *Age*, however, called it 'a meeting of thieves, prostitutes and foolish persons', and thought it dangerous to the Commonwealth.

Kelly's judge, Sir Redmond Barry had written to the Governor of Victoria the day after the conclusion of the trial:

> Sir,
> I have the honour to report for the information of your Excellency and the Executive Council that the Prisoner was tried before me on Thursday and Friday in this week for the Wilful murder of Thomas Lonigan a constable at the Wombat ranges creek on Saturday, the 26th of October.
> He was found Guilty and sentenced to death.
> The History of the prisoner during the last two years and the numerous criminal acts with which he admitted on several occasions to different people he was connected are sufficiently well known to render it unnecessary for me to say more than that the case was amply proved and that I see no reason whatever to recommend that the sentence should not be carried into execution.
> My notes of the evidence will be forwarded without delay.
> I have the honour to be,
>   Your Excellency's most obedient servant,
>   Sgd Redmond Barry
>   Senior puisne judge of the Colony of Victoria
>   Supreme Court Oct 30th 1880.

Barry, whom Ned had promised to meet after death, collapsed two days after Kelly's execution, and died ten days later.

Ned, in his last days, dictated a final appeal for mercy to the Governor. After a renewed justification of his acts, and an oath that it was never his intention to take anyone's life, he concluded:

> I know it is useless me trespassing on your valuable time. Because of the expense the government has been put to, which is not my fault, they will only be satisfied with my life, although I have been found guilty and condemned to death on a charge of all men in the world I should be the last one to be guilty of. There is one wish in conclusion I would like you to grant me – that is the release of my mother before my execution, as detaining her in prison could not make any

difference to the government now. For the day will come when all men will be judged by their mercy and their deeds.'

Kelly's request concerning his mother was refused. He dictated another statement to his solicitor, hoping it would be published and perhaps, at the last moment, lead to a reprieve. But it remained unpublished. It read:

I don't pretend that I have lived a blameless life, or that one fault justifies another. But the public judging a case like mine should remember that the darkest life may have a bright side. After the worst has been said against a man, he may, if he's heard, tell a story in his own rough way that will lead them to soften their harshest thoughts against him and find as many excuses for him as he would plead for himself.

For my own part, I don't care one straw about my life nor the result of the trial, and I know very well from the stories I've been told how I am spoken of; that the public at large execrate my name. The newspapers have not spoken of me with that patient tolerance generally extended to men awaiting trial and are assumed according to the boast of British Justice to be innocent until they are proved to be guilty. But I don't mind, for I am the last that curries public favour or dreads the public frown. Let the hand of the law strike me down if it will, but I ask that my story may be heard and considered, not that I wish to avert any decree the law may deem necessary to vindicate justice or win a word of pity from anyone.

If my lips teach the public that men are made mad by bad treatment, and if the police are taught that they may exasperate to madness men they persecute and ill-treat, my life will not be entirely thrown away. People who live in large towns have no idea of the tyrannical conduct of police far removed from court. They have no idea of the harsh overbearing manner in which they execute their duties, of how they neglect their duties and abuse their powers.

On November 10th, the eve of his execution, Kelly was allowed to see his mother, whose last words to him were, 'Mind you die like a Kelly, Ned.' He ate his last meal, consisting of roast lamb with green peas, and a bottle of claret, and was

Ned Kelly posed for this photograph at the old Melbourne Gaol on 10th November 1880, the day before he was hanged. This is the way he chose to be remembered.

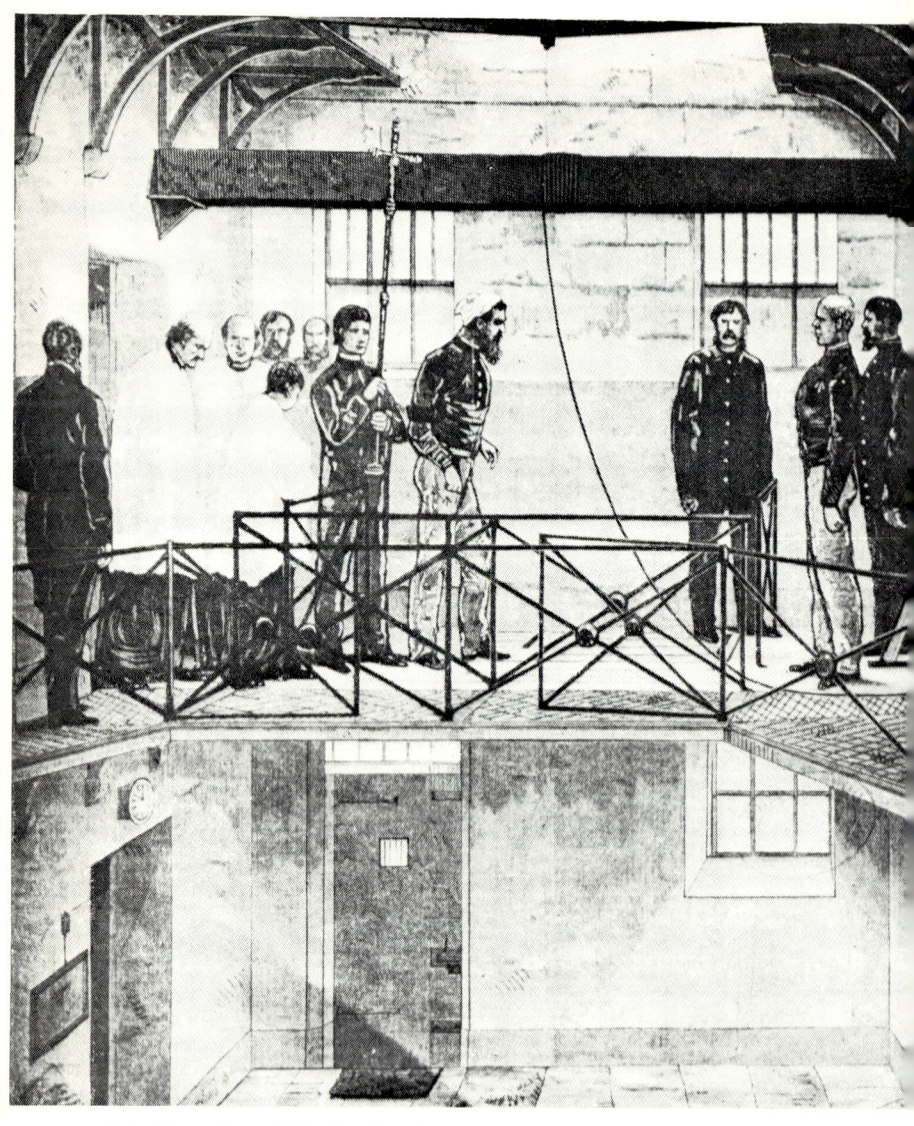

11th November 1880, the hanging of Edward Kelly 'until his body was dead'.

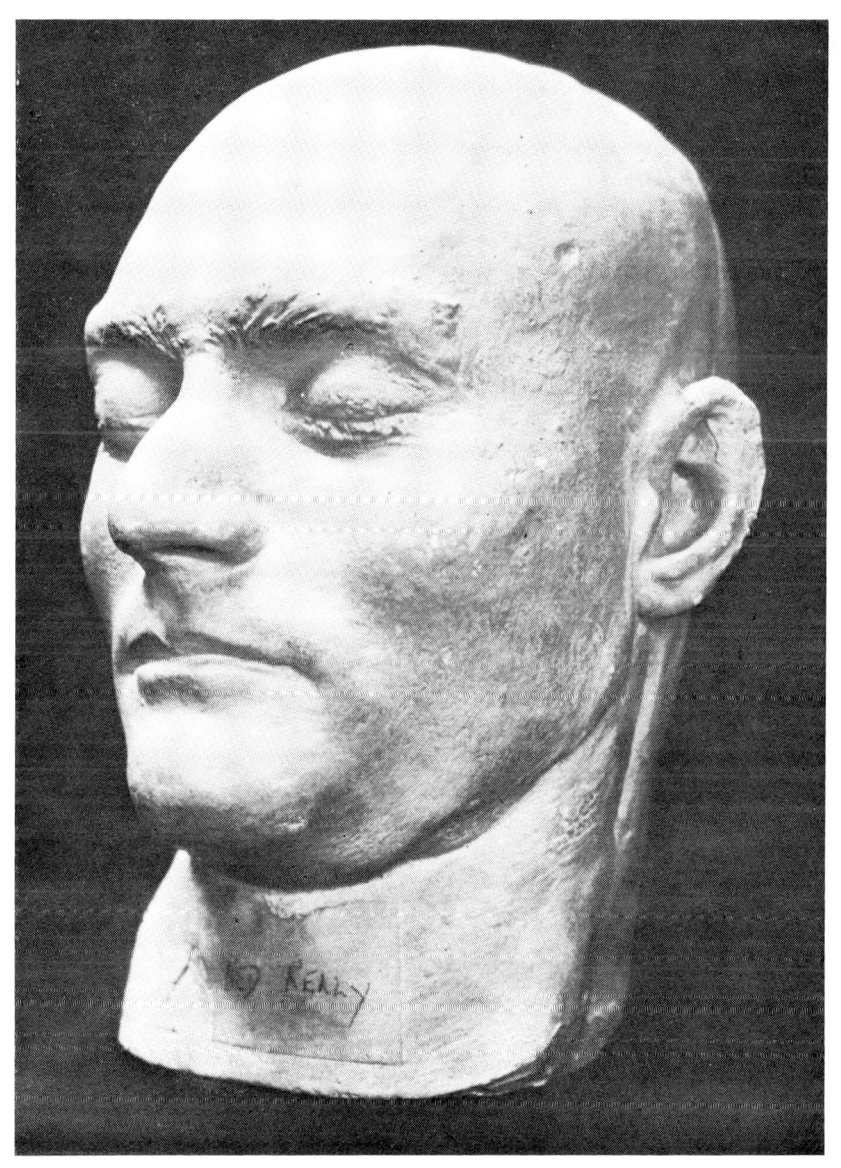

Death mask: after the execution, Ned Kelly's head was severed from his body for closer inspection. The headless body was buried in an unmarked grave in the condemned criminals' section of the old Melbourne Gaol.

visited by his sisters and his cousins Tom and Kate Lloyd. That night, his cell was closely guarded to ensure that he should not escape the gallows by committing suicide. It is said that, before he went to sleep, Kelly sang to himself some of the songs about the Gang, and other bush ballads. At last, he retired for the night, fell asleep about half past two, and awakened again at five a.m. when he spent twenty minutes at prayer. After this, he appeared to be quite calm, and even began to sing again. 'Although the songs which he sang were not sacred,' wrote a reporter who had stayed at the gaol overnight, 'they were of the better class of secular composition, and contained nothing in themselves offensive.'

At nine o'clock on the morning of Thursday, November 11th, 1880, the chaplain arrived to administer the last rites of the Church, and to spend Kelly's last moments of life with him. At half past nine, they were joined by Dean O'Hea who had known Kelly as a child, and is said to have baptized him. The two reverend gentlemen remained with Kelly until it was time for Colonel Rede, the Sherriff, and Mr Ellis, the Under-Sherriff, to present themselves at the door of the condemned cell and demand the body of the prisoner. The hangman followed, and proceeded to pinion Kelly's arms. The prisoner remarked, 'There's no need to do that,' but submitted quietly enough.

He walked to the scaffold calmly, and murmured, 'Ah, well, it has come to this,' as the noose was placed over his head. 'The prisoner,' said a press report, 'winced slightly at the first touch of the rope, but quickly recovered himself and moved his head in order to facilitate the work of Upjohn [the hangman] in fixing the knot properly.'

'Such is life,' said Kelly, as the signal was given. A bolt was withdrawn, and he fell to his death, a death not exactly instantaneous. A reporter who witnessed the event wrote, 'There was, for a second or two, only the usual shudder which passes through the frame of hanged men. But then the legs were drawn up for some distance and fell suddenly again. This movement was repeated several times. But finally all motion ceased, and, at the end of four minutes, all was over and Edward Kelly had gone to a higher tribunal to answer for his faults and crimes.'

Kelly's relatives asked for permission to bury his body. This was refused, and he was buried within the Gaol precincts. He had lived just over twenty-five years.

The fame of the Kelly Gang did not subside with the death of Ned: in fact, public agitation increased for a time, and led, the following year, to a Royal Commission to enquire into the circumstances of the Kelly Gang's activities and, indeed, the structure and organization of the Victorian Police Force. A number of prominent police officers concerned with the handling of the Kelly case were forced to retire, among them Commissioner Standish, and Superintendents Nicholson and Hare. Others were down-graded, and the Police Force underwent a gradual process of liberalization.

Ninety people, police and civilians, claimed a share of the £8,000 reward money, and sixty-six of the claims were allowed: Superintendent Hare was given £800, and the Glenrowan schoolmaster, Thomas Curnow, £550. The four policemen who hid in another room of Sherritt's hut while he was murdered received £42 5s. 9d. each, and were dismissed from the force.

One of Ned's sisters, Kate, took to the stage in Melbourne, and appeared in a lurid melodrama about the exploits of the Gang, to the extreme anger of other members of the family. A few years later, in her middle thirties, Kate drowned herself at Forbes, in New South Wales. Ned's mother, Mrs Kelly, lived to be eight-five, and died in Greta in March, 1923. During the later years of her life, she was looked after by Ned's young brother Jim. He, too, lived to old age, and was pointed out to the writer of this book in Euroa in 1946.

The legend of Ned Kelly had already begun in his lifetime, and during the present century it has continued to be kept alive in Australia. Of the two Appendices which follow, the first, consisting of contemporary documents, throws some light on the official background from which the myth emerged, while the poems and songs in the second Appendix reveal the beginnings of the mythologizing process while the Gang was still active.

APPENDIX I

CONTEMPORARY DOCUMENTS

(a) Superintendent Hare's report to the Chief Commissioner of Police

'Sir,   'Rupertswood, Sunbury, 2nd July 1880.

'I have the honour to inform you that I deem it my duty to give you a full report of all the circumstances from the commencement of the time I was directed to proceed to Benalla up to the period of the Kelly gang being surrounded by the Police at Glenrowan on the 27th June.

'You may remember, on the 30th April last, when visiting the depôt, you informed me that I was to proceed to Benalla to relieve Mr Nicolson, and to take charge of the whole of the proceedings in connection with the capture of the Kellys. I protested in the strongest manner possible at the injustice of my being sent up there again. I pointed out that there were three officers senior to me – viz., Mr Winch, Mr Chomley, and Mr Chambers – none of whom had been called upon to undertake the hardships that I had to undergo during the seven months that I was with you in that district. I also pointed out that the responsibility should be thrown on the senior officers. I stated that a promise was made to me when I was sent for previous to the capture of Power, the bushranger; that Mr Nicolson and Mr Montford had reaped the benefit of that capture; and that I, who was directed to organize the whole affair, am still in the same position as I was then, notwithstanding the promise made by the Chief Secretary, Sir James McCulloch. Ten years having elapsed since then, and my position in the police force being still the same, I did not see any advantage to be gained by being told off on this special duty. Your reply to this was, "It's no use saying anything about it; you'll have to go." I then requested that I might be allowed to see the Hon. the Chief Secretary on the subject, as I wished to enter my protest to him against being sent up to Benalla. You agreed to make an appointment for me, and at two o'clock that day I saw Mr Ramsay in his office. I then pointed out to him the disadvantage to me of sending me up there. Mr Ramsay replied, "Mr Hare, this Kelly business has been discussed by the Cabinet; and it is their unanimous decision that you should be sent up to take charge of affairs. I give you *carte blanche* to do whatevery you think proper, and I leave you entirely untrammelled. The Government have such entire confidence in you that they will bear you out in whatever you deem it advisable to do." I replied, "Very well, Mr Ramsay; when do you wish me to go?" He said, "As soon as possible." I told him that I would leave in two or three days' time. On Monday the 3rd May I received a note from you informing me that the Hon. the Chief Secretary, at the earnest request of Mr Nicolson, had consented to allow him to remain at Benalla for one month longer, and that my orders for transfer were cancelled for the present.

'I received orders from you at the end of May that I was to proceed at once to Benalla to relieve Mr Nicolson. I accordingly, on the 2nd June, went up there. I arrived at Benalla at about 11 o'clock that day. I saw Messrs Nicolson, Sadleir, and O'Connor in the office. After some conversation on general subjects, Mr Nicolson produced a letter he had received from you, directing him to give me all the information he had obtained concerning the Kelly gang during his stay at Benalla. He showed me the state of his financial account with one of his agents, and said there was nothing owing to any of the others. He opened a drawer and showed me a number of papers and the correspondence which had taken place during his stay at Benalla, and said, "You can get all the information from these papers." He gave me no verbal information whatever, but said, "Mr Sadleir can tell you all I know concerning the movements of the outlaws." He left the office, and I never spoke to him again, and he went to Melbourne by the evening train. The principal agent employed by Mr Nicolson I had appointed to meet me that evening. He was one who was considered the best man they had. After talking with him a few minutes, he positively refused to work for me or have anything to do with me, although he had accompanied the police from Beechworth the previous day for the purpose of having an interview with me.

'That evening I telegraphed to Detective Ward to come down

to Benalla the next morning by train. He did so, and, after some conversation, he informed me that on the previous evening the senior constable in charge of Beechworth had received a telegram from Mr Nicolson to pay off all the agents he had employed.

'I at once endeavored to obtain a copy of this telegram in the office, but there was no record kept of it, nor did the clerks know anything about it, so I presume it must have been sent from the railway telegraph office, as Mr Sadleir knew nothing whatever about it.

'I directed Detective Ward to return to Beechworth at once and order the senior constable to allow matters to continue as they had been previous to my taking charge, as I did not wish to make an alteration in anything until I was in a position to judge what was best to be done.

'For the first two or three days of my stay at Benalla I occupied my time in reading up the papers in the office, and obtaining all the information I possibly could on the subject. I had a long conversation with Mr Sadleir, who assisted me in every possible way, and gave me all the information in his power. I conversed with the different non-commissioned officers and constables I came across, and obtained their views on the duty upon which I was engaged. Most of Mr Nicolson's communications with his agents were by word of mouth and not in writing, and the information I obtained from documents in the office was very scant and not of much service to me. I then started round the district to see the non-commissioned officers in charge of the principal stations. I had long talks with them and their men on the state of affairs, and informed them that I intended stationing black trackers, whom I expected from Queensland, at Benalla, Wangaratta, and Beechworth. I also told them that at each of these towns I would have a full party of men stationed, so that, if any information was received about the Kellys, they would be in a position to go in pursuit at once; and all I wished them to do was to communicate by telegraph with me previous to their starting off, so that I might know in which direction they had gone.

'After a few days I returned to Benalla, and started off two or three parties of men who had been specially taken on in the police force, in consequence of their knowledge of the country and the outlaws, and directed them to obtain private horses, and go into the country they knew best, and knock about amongst their friends and relatives, in order to see if they could get any information concerning the outlaws. They might go where they liked, and remain out as long at they thought fit. I also made up three watch parties, consisting of four men each, and directed them to watch certain places by night and remain concealed all day. I made sundry other arrangements, which it will not be advisable for me to fully enter into.

'From the date of my arrival at Benalla up to Sunday the 27th June I heard nothing positive concerning the movements of the outlaws, although their agents and sympathizers were particularly active, and I was privately informed that the outlaws were about to commence some outrages which would not only astonish Australia but the whole world.

'On the 24th I received a communication from you that Mr O'Connor and his black trackers were to be sent back to Queensland. I informed Mr O'Connor accordingly. The next morning he started away from Benalla with his "boys". I had but one Queensland black of our own at Benalla, and there was another at Mansfield. I telegraphed for the one at Mansfield to be sent down to Benalla at once, so that I might have two trackers in case anything happened before Mr Chomley, who had gone to Queensland for a fresh supply of trackers for our own force, returned, as I did not expect him back for eight or ten days.

'On Sunday the 27th ultimo I was at the telegraph office at Benalla, at ten o'clock a.m. I received telegrams from all the stations in the district that all was quiet. I made an appointment with the telegraph master to be at the office again at 9 p.m. About half-past two o'clock that day I received a memo from the railway telegraph office to go to the general telegraph office, as there was important information for me there, and a memo to the same effect had been sent to the telegraph master. I lost no time in going there, and received a message from Beechworth that Aaron Sherritt, in whose house I had a watch party, had been shot the previous evening at six o'clock. I immediately sent for Mr Sadleir, and we consulted together as to the best course to adopt. First of all we decided to give you all the information in our possession, and ask you to request Mr O'Connor to return without loss of time to Benalla, with his "boys", as we considered they might have a good chance of tracking the outlaws from Sherritt's house.

'About eight o'clock that evening I received a telegram from you informing me that Mr O'Connor would be sent up by special train, leaving town at ten o'clock. I also telegraphed to you asking authority to send on a pilot engine in front of our train. Your reply to me was, "A good idea; there's no knowing what desperate deed the outlaws may now be guilty of. Have the pilot."

'The whole afternoon Mr Sadleir and myself were engaged in the telegraph office, warning all stations to be on the alert, and at places where there were no telegraph offices private messengers were employed, and sent out to convey the information of the outrage at Beechworth, and to be on the alert also.

'I started off then for the railway station, having previously sent word to the station master to have an engine ready to go to Beechworth as soon as possible, as it was my intention to take up my party and the two trackers, in the event of Mr O'Connor not consenting to return. I told Mr Stephens, stationmaster, that a special was to leave town at ten o'clock, and that I wished the engine that I had ordered to act as pilot to the train to Beechworth, which would reach Benalla about two a.m.

'He informed me that he had no engine there which could run to Beechworth, that line requiring peculiar engines. I requested him to get the engine which was to come down to Wangaratta from Beechworth the following morning to get up steam at once, run down to Wangaratta, and wait there till my arrival, so that it could act as pilot thence to Beechworth. He consented to do this, and also to have trucks ready to convey the horses and men from Benalla to Beechworth.

'I then returned to the telegraph office, where Mr Sadleir had remained during my absence. We made arrangements for horses and provisions to be ready for the trackers, and told off the following men to accompany me to Beechworth: – Senior Constable Kelly, Constables Arthur, Barry, Gascoigne, Canny, Kirkham, and Phillips, leaving a party behind us all ready equipped, with two black trackers, for Mr Sadleir, in case anything occurred while I was away. I remained in the telegraph office until 10 o'clock p.m. Having completed all arrangements I went to lie down for two or three hours, as I expected to reach Sherritt's house by daybreak the next morning to commence tracking from there.

'At one o'clock I went to the railway station, had the horses put in the trucks, and waited the arrival of the special, which reached Benalla, I think, about half past 1. Mr Rawlings, a gentleman residing at Winton, asked me to allow him to travel in the special to Beechworth from Benalla, as he had a pass on all the railways. I told him I had no objection to his doing so. The engineer in charge of the Benalla station suggested that I should put a constable in front of the engine, to keep a look-out along the line. I accordingly told off Constable Barry for this duty, and saw him securely fastened on the engine. I afterwards ascertained that the engine that brought the train from town had become disabled on the way up, and it was decided to send it as the pilot, and send the Benalla engine to Wangaratta with the train. The engine-drivers refused to allow Barry to go on their engine, so I recalled him. The occupants of the train from Melbourne was as follows: – Mr O'Connor, his wife and sister, five Queensland trackers, and six gentlemen connected with the press.

'My party, already mentioned, joined the train here. Previous to starting I asked the stationmaster to give me the key of the railway carriages, as the guard insisted on locking us in. He complied with my request. The pilot engine started about five minutes before our train. We went along at a rapid pace without interruption until within two or three miles of Glenrowan station I heard our engine whistle. I put my head out of the carriage, looked ahead, and saw the pilot pulled up within 300 yards of us. I immediately unlocked my carriage, jumped out of the train, and walked towards the pilot. When about a few yards beyond our engine, I met a man walking towards me from the pilot with a lamp. He came from the pilot engine, and told me that he had been stopped by a red handkerchief being held up, and lighted by a match held behind it. When he pulled up he saw a man without coat or hat approaching, who appeared greatly excited, and told him that the line had been broken up either this side or the other of Glenrowan. He said the man told him the Kellys had taken possession of everybody in Glenrowan, and that they said they were going to attack the police on their arrival. I asked him where the man was. He said after giving the information he ran away into the bush, as he had left his wife and family at home, and that he was a schoolmaster at Glenrowan. He said, "I invited him to go on the engine, but he declined." I then ordered all the carriages to be unlocked, lights extinguished, and gave the occupants the information that had been given to me, and to be ready for any emergency. I at once walked towards the pilot, taking with me three men, leaving Mr O'Connor and his men with Senior Constable Kelly and the remainder of my men. I walked along the line myself, and distributed the men on each side, telling them to separate and keep a sharp look-out. When I reached the pilot the engine-driver repeated the story about the schoolmaster, and I told the driver to go on quietly in front of the train. He declined doing so until I jumped on the engine myself and brought up the three men with me. I placed the men in the best position, and told them to keep a sharp look-out and be ready for anything that might occur. I took up my position at the opening of the engine, and then told the driver to go ahead cautiously, and be ready to go ahead or backwards at any moment in the event of my directing him to do so. He said his engine was in a very disabled state, having lost its brake, and could not be depended on. He advised that he should shunt back to the train, and that the two engines should be hitched on together, and so take on the train. I consented to this, and we shunted back. I then directed Senior Constable Kelly to jump on the other engine with three men, and to put them in the most secure places, prepared for any emergency. I gave information to Mr O'Connor of what I had ascertained and done, and we started off at a slow pace towards Glenrowan. When we reached the station everything was in darkness, not a soul moving anywhere. I got off the engine and told every man to jump out of the train and keep a sharp look-out. I then started off in company with Mr Rawlings to the stationmaster's house, which was about 70 or 80 yards from the station, where I saw a light in the window. I knocked at the window, and looking through saw a woman and children. She asked, "Who's there?" I answered, "Police; open the window." I asked her where her husband was. She replied, "They have taken him away into the bush." She was greatly excited, and for some time could scarcely answer me. I begged her to be calm and tell me who had taken her husband away. She said, "The Kellys." I asked in which direction they had gone, and she pointed in the direction of Warby's ranges.

'I immediately hastened back to the station with Mr Rawlings, who told me he was thoroughly acquainted with the country, and would gladly render me all the assistance he could. He told me he was unarmed, and asked me if I had any spare arms. I told him "No," but that I would give him my revolver and stick to the double-barrelled gun myself. On reaching the station I told the men what I had been informed by the stationmaster's wife, and to lose no time in getting the horses out of the train and saddling them. Whilst the men were so engaged, Constable Bracken appeared on the platform in a very excited state. He said, "Mr Hare, I have just escaped from Jones's Hotel, where the Kellys have a large number of prisoners confined. For God's sake go as quickly as possible, otherwise they will escape." I called on the men to follow me with their arms as quickly as they could. Many of them were holding horses. I told them to let go the horses, as the Kellys were in the house, and follow me, running off towards Jones's Hotel. Some six or seven men followed me, amongst them were some of the black trackers, but I cannot say who any of them were. When approaching the hotel the place was quite silent and dark, and when within about twenty yards of the verandah I saw a flash of fire, but could not distinguish any figures. Instantly three persons also commenced firing from the verandah, which was in total darkness – the moonbeams at the back of the house caused our men to be plainly seen – a continuous fire was kept up on both sides. I was struck by the first shot, and my left arm dropped helpless beside me. The firing was continued on both sides with great determination for about five minutes, when it ceased from the verandah, and screams from men, women, and children came from the inside of the house. I at once called on my men to cease firing, which they did. When the firing commenced I called upon the men to be steady, and I cannot speak too highly of the conduct of the men on this occasion, as they stood with firmness, receiving volley after volley from the verandah, and replying to it. The men were all on my right, and the fire seemed to come in a line, as if the men were on parade. I kept using my gun with my right hand, and I think I fired six shots. I had great difficulty in loading, having but the use of one arm. I had to put the stock of the gun between my legs in order to reload. I cannot remember any of the men who were with me during the firing except Senior Constable Kelly. I told him I was badly wounded, and directed him to take all the men and surround Jones's Hotel, so as to prevent the escape of the outlaws, and saw this was being done. During the firing there were shouts from the outlaws calling on us to fire away – we could do them no harm.

'Feeling that I was losing large quantities of blood, I returned towards the railway platform. On my way thither I saw Mr O'Connor running up a drain with some of his boys. As I passed him I called out to him I was hit. Senior Constable Kelly called out to me to send some more ammunition at once from the train. I did so directly I arrived at the platform, and Mr Rawlings volunteered to take the ammunition round, and distribute it amongst the men, which he did. There were a number of gentlemen of the press on the platform when I arrived there, and they very kindly took a handkerchief, and bound up my arm. I then returned to the front, intending to go round the men posted, but after visiting two or three of them I felt myself getting very weak and faint from loss of blood. When I again reached the platform I was staggering, and the gentlemen of the press assisted me into a railway carriage. I intended to run down to Benalla to have my arm dressed, and to return immediately it was done. After getting into the carriage I was given a little sherry, which rallied me considerably, but the blood was still flowing from my arm. I started an engine away to inform Mr Sadleir of what had occurred, requesting him to come as soon as possible with every available man on the station, and bring up a supply of ammunition, and shortly after that I followed on another engine to Benalla. Owing to my great loss of blood, I had great difficulty in keeping myself from fainting on my way down. We reached Benalla in about ten minutes. On my arrival there I asked the stationmaster to telegraph to Wangaratta, and direct Sergeant Steele to bring every available man he had on the station by the pilot engine, which was waiting for me there, to Glenrowan, as we had the Kellys surrounded in a house; but to be careful not to let the engine come within a mile and a half of Glenrowan, as the rails had been torn up. I then started off to the Benalla Telegraph Office, which was about a mile and a quarter distant from the station. Being afraid to walk that distance by myself, feeling so faint, I asked a Mr Lewis, school inspector from Wangaratta, whom I met, to accompany me, which he did.

'On the way we called at Dr Nicholson's – this was about 4 a.m. I told the doctor I was shot by the Kellys, and I wished him to dress my arm, as the blood was still flowing freely. I told him I could not wait to have it done then, but to follow me to the telegraph office, as I wished him to return to Glenrowan with me, and to lose no time about it. I then started off with Mr Lewis, leaving Dr Nicholson to dress. On reaching the telegraph office I could barely stagger in. I found the office open, and dictated a telegram to the stationmaster to send to you. I also sent a telegram to the police at Beechworth and Violet Town, directing them to proceed with all available force to Glenrowan, as the Kellys were surrounded in a house, and as I did not know how much assistance might be required to secure them. I then laid down on a mattrass, and Mr Sadleir came into the office. I told him what had occurred, and to hasten back as quickly as possible, and I would follow him. His reply was—"Don't be such a fool. You are a regular glutton. You have one bullet through you now, and I suppose you want more." He then left the office, and hastened away. Just then Dr Nicholson entered. He examined my wound, and told me I had sustained a very bad fracture of the wrist, and that it would be madness for me to return. He procured an impromptu splint and lint, and, with the assistance of Mr Lewis and Mr Saxe (telegraph-master), dressed the wound. During the dressing I fainted. How long I remained in that state I do not know, but when I came to myself both the doctor and Mr Lewis had gone, and Mr Saxe gave me some strong spirits, and with his assistance, and that of one of his clerks, I walked to my lodgings, about a quarter of a mile away. I was unable to proceed, and was confined to bed all day, suffering great pain.

'At about 3 o'clock, Dr Charles Ryan arrived from Melbourne, and dressed my hand, and Dr Nicholson, returning just then, assisted in the operation.

'In conclusion, I wish to place on record the very great assistance rendered to me by Mr Sadleir from the time I arrived at Benalla up to the eventful day. He spared neither time nor trouble, and I would desire strongly to urge upon you the necessity of suitably acknowledging his services.

'Whilst mentioning the assistance rendered to me by Mr Sadleir, I would also desire to place on record my high appreciation of the conduct and services of the police force, both of Queensland and Victoria, who by their steadiness and courage seconded my efforts and contributed to the successful termination of the duties they were especially called upon to perform.

'I would also bring under your notice the great services rendered by Mr Saxe, telegraph-master at Benalla. The police in the district found him always ready to assist them at any moment, day or night (Sundays inclusive), and he complied with everything he was asked to do most readily and cheerfully. I would therefore urge upon you the desirability of bringing his conduct under the notice of the Hon. the Postmaster-General, with a view to his promotion in the service, as you are well aware, from your own personal knowledge, of the many services rendered to us by him.

'With regard to the reward offered for the apprehension of the offenders, both by this Government and that of New South Wales, I trust that a board will be appointed to decide to whom it is to be paid, and that the constables and trackers who were engaged at the destruction of the gang will be allowed to partake of a portion, especially those who accompanied me from Benalla. I need hardly say that I decline to participate in any of the rewards already offered for the capture of these outlaws.

'I cannot bring my report to a close without strongly drawing the attention of the Government to the praiseworthy and plucky conduct of Mr Curnow, who in my opinion was mainly instrumental in saving the lives of the whole party in giving the information of the lines being destroyed, and of the Kellys being at Glenrowan.

'Constable Bracken showed great presence of mind, and deserves much credit for his conduct on the occasion, and I think he has a claim to a good share of the reward.

'I think, also, that the thanks of the Government are due to Mr Rawlings, who ably assisted me throughout the firing. He had previously offered me the benefit of his knowledge and experience of that part of the country. He ran considerable risk in serving out the ammunition to the police, and I feel very grateful to him for his personal service to me.

'Since writing the above I have seen a statement made by Mr O'Connor to the press, and after reading it I can have no doubt his statement is perfectly correct, but in my report I have merely stated facts that are within my remembrance, and no doubt in the darkness of the morning, and the excitement of the time, I may have omitted many incidents that occurred.

'When I took charge of the district from the 2nd of June

last, as far as I was able to ascertain, no more was known of the outlaws or their movements than when I left Benalla twelve months ago. The statements that have appeared in the public press for some weeks past, to the effect that the outlaws were surrounded by a cordon of the police and their agents, had not the slightest foundation. I do not take any special credit to myself and men in being able to surround them in Jones's Hotel on 28th June. The chance occurred; we took advantage of it, and success attended us. You may recollect that at my interview with the Chief Secretary I objected to having a large party of trackers kept at Benalla, and as Mr O'Connor objected to divide his men, I suggested that some native trackers should be provided from Queensland for our own force. I said also it was a general belief that the outlaws were afraid to show out because of the trackers, and in my opinion, if such was the case, the sooner Mr O'Connor and men were removed the better, because, should the gang make a raid, there would be a probability of capturing them, but as long as they remained in the mountains we had little chance of finding them. Mr Ramsay agreed with me in this opinion. I frequently expressed the same opinion to you in the last few months. The trackers were removed on the 25th June; the outlaws believing they had left for Queensland, showed out on the 26th. On the 28th the gang was destroyed, and its leader captured.

'I have the honour to be, Sir,
'Your most obedient servant,
'FRANCIS HARE,
'Superintendent of Police.

(b) Statement written by Thomas Curnow and read by him to the Royal Commission on the Victorian Police.

'On Sunday morning, 27th June 1880, I determined to take my wife, sister, and child out for a drive along the road from Glenrowan to Greta. We left the school in a buggy at about eleven o'clock in the morning, accompanied by David Mortimer, my brother-in-law, who rode on horseback. When we got in sight of Mrs Jones's hotel, and opposite the railway crossing, through which we intended to pass, we noticed a number of people about Jones's hotel, and at the crossing. I said, "Mrs Jones must be dead; she has been very ill." As we got near the hotel, a man ran out of it towards Mrs Jones's stable, distant about twenty yards from the hotel. I drove past the hotel to the crossing, and, seeing Mr Stanistreet asked him, "What's the matter?" He replied, "The Kellys are here; you can't go through." I thought he was joking, and made a motion to drive through the gates, when a man on horseback, who blocked up the crossing and was talking to a young man whom I knew to be named Delaney, wheeled round his horse and said to me, "Who are you?" I saw then that he had revolvers in his belt, and was convinced of the truth of Mr Stanistreet's statement that the Kellys were there. I replied that I was the teacher at Glenrowan. He said, "Oh! you are the schoolmaster here, are you, and who are those?" pointing to my wife, sister, and brother-in-law. I told him. He then said, "Where are you going?" I answered, "Out for a drive." He then said, "I am sorry, but I must detain you," and directed us to get out of the buggy, which we did. He then turned again to Delaney and resumed his conversation with him. I afterwards found that the man who had addressed me was Ned Kelly, the outlaw. I noticed another armed man near Ned Kelly, and I afterwards found that he was Byrne. When we got out of the buggy I led the horse off from the crossing and tied him to the railway fence alongside, directing Mrs and Miss Curnow to go into Mr Stanistreet's house, which they did. As soon as I had fastened the horse, I joined Mr and Mrs Stanistreet and others, who I was told had been taken prisoners by the gang, and was informed by them that Glenrowan had been stuck up since three o'clock that morning, and that the gang had forced Reardon and others to tear up part of the railway line beyond the station, with the purpose of wrecking a special train of police and black trackers, which the outlaws said would pass through Glenrowan. Some person then – I believe it was one of the boys who had been hailed up by the gang – told me that the Kellys had been at Beechworth during the previous night, and had shot several police. After some further conversation, we all listened to what Ned Kelly was saying to Delaney. The outlaw was accusing Delaney of having some short time previous ridden a horse from near Greta into Wangaratta to oblige a policeman, and of having sought admission into the police force. He threatened to shoot Delaney for this, and pointed a revolver at him several times. Ned Kelly declared to all of us who were listening to him that he would have the life of any one who aided the police in any way, or who even showed a friendly feeling for them, and declared that he could and would find them out. He said that a law was made rendering it a crime for any one to help them (the outlaws), and that he would make it a crime against the Kelly gang for any one to aid the police. The women, who were listening to what Kelly was saying, asked him to let Delaney off. After keeping Delaney in a state of extreme terror for about half an hour the outlaw made him promise never again to seek admission into the police force, and finally said, "I forgive you this time; but mind you be careful for the future." Byrne then produced a bottle of brandy, and offered some in a tumbler to all adults there. Some accepted it. Byrne drank some himself, and gave Delaney two-thirds of a tumbler, which he drank. Ned Kelly refused to take any, and directed some of his boy prisoners to take my horse and buggy into Mrs Jones's yard, which they did. Ned Kelly and Byrne then went from the railway crossing to Mrs Jones's hotel, preceded by the majority of their male prisoners, and I was with them. When we reached Mrs Jones's there were, including those who had just been taken over, about fifty persons in and about the hotel, all of whom appeared to be prisoners of the gang. We were allowed to go about in the hotel, excepting one room, which the outlaws used, and of which they kept the key, and we were allowed outside, but were forbidden to leave the premises. Dan Kelly, a short time after I entered the hotel, asked me to have a drink, and I drank with him at the bar. I said to him that I had been told that they had been at Beechworth during the previous night, and had shot several police. I asked him whether it was true. He replied that they had been near Beechworth last night, and had done "some shooting", and that they had burned the "b——s out", alluding to police. Byrne came in the bar, and, looking at Dan Kelly's glass, said, "Be careful, old man." Dan Kelly replied, "All right," and poured water into his brandy. While talking with Byrne and Dan Kelly, I expressed surprise at Glenrowan being struck up by them, and they said that they had come to Glenrowan in order to wreck a special train of inspectors, police, and black trackers, which would pass through Glenrowan for Beechworth, to take up their trail from there. They said that they had ridden hard across country, often being up to the saddle-girths in water, to get to Glenrowan, and that they had

had the line torn up at a dangerous part, and were going to send the train and its occupants to h—l. About one o'clock I was standing in the yard of Jones's hotel, thinking of the intentions of the gang, and I keenly felt that it was my duty to do anything that I could to prevent the outrage which the outlaws had planned from being accomplished, and I determined that I would try to do so. While standing in the yard Dan Kelly came out of the hotel and asked me to go inside and have a dance. I said that I could not dance in the boots which I had on. Ned Kelly then came out of the hotel, and hearing me object to dance because of my boots, said, "Come on; never mind your boots." I said to him that it was awkward to me to dance in those boots, as I was lame, but that I would dance with pleasure if he would go to the school with me to get a pair of dancing boots. It flashed across my mind that, in passing the Glenrowan police barracks to reach my house, Bracken, the trooper stationed there, might see us and would be able to give an alarm. I knew that Bracken had been stationed at Greta, and felt sure that he would recognize Ned Kelly. He (Ned Kelly) said he would go, and we were getting ready, when Dan Kelly interfered, and said that Ned had better stay behind, and let him or Byrne go with me. Some one else also urged Ned Kelly not to go away, and said that my house was near the police barracks. Ned Kelly turned to me, and asked if it was. I said, "Yes; we shall have to pass the barracks. I had forgotten that." He then said that we would not go, and I went into the hotel, and danced with Dan Kelly. After we had finished dancing, Ned Kelly said that he would go down to the police barracks and bring Bracken and Reynolds, the postmaster, up to Jones's. I laughed and said to him that I would rather than a hundred pounds that he would, and asked to be allowed to accompany him when he went, and to take home my wife, sister, and child. He gave me no reply. The intention to do something to baffle the murderous designs of the gang grew on me, and I resolved to do my utmost to gain the confidence of the outlaws, and to make them believe me to be a sympathizer with them. I saw clearly that unless I succeeded in doing this I should not be able to get their permission to go home with my wife, child, and sister, and consequently should not be able to do anything to prevent the destruction of the special train and its occupants by giving information to the police in Benalla, which I purposed doing if I could induce the outlaws to allow me and mine to go home. The outlaws kept a very sharp watch on their prisoners without seeming to do so. About three o'clock in the afternoon Ned and Dan Kelly caused several of their prisoners to engage in jumping, and in the hop, step, and jump. Ned Kelly joined with them, and used a revolver in each hand as weights. After the jumping was concluded, I left Jones's and went to Mr Stanistreet's house to see my wife and sister. They came out to meet me, and noticing the red lama scarf wrapped round my sister caused me to think, "What a splendid danger signal that would make." The idea of stopping the train by means of it then entered my mind, and made me still more anxious for liberty. I went with my wife and sister into Mr Stanistreet's house, and saw Hart lying down on a sofa. He had three loaded guns by his side. He complained to me of having swollen and painful feet, caused, he said, by not having had his boots off for several days and nights. I advised him to bathe them in hot water, and requested it for him. It was brought, and he did so. Shortly after Mr Stanistreet and I were walking about at the back of his house, and Mr Stanistreet expressed a wish that an alarm could be given. Mrs Stanistreet came out to us, and I asked them if they thought it would be wrong to break a promise given to the outlaws. They said that it would not. I then asked Mr Stanistreet had the outlaws taken his revolver from him. He said they had not. I saw what use this fact could be made of by me in my efforts to gain the confidence of the outlaws, and to make them believe that they could safely allow me to go home. I said to Mr and Mrs Stanistreet that we had better go inside, for I was afraid of being suspected by the gang if they saw us in private conversation, and we did so. I do not know whether Mr or Mrs Stanistreet suspected the use I intended making of my liberty if I got it; but afterwards I heard Mrs Stanistreet saying to Ned Kelly that he ought to allow me to take my sister, who was in delicate health, home. I was sitting in Mr Stanistreet's when Dan Kelly came in enquiring for a parcel in a small bag which he had lost. He seemed very anxious about it, and examined the house throughout in search of it. He could not find it, and went to McDonald's hotel to see if it was there. He came back unsuccessful, and I went to Jones's with him, and he searched there, but failed to find it. When he gave up searching for it, I requested him to tell Ned that I wanted to speak to him. I was near the door of Jones's kitchen then. He went into the hotel and brought Ned Kelly out, and I told him that Mr Stanistreet possessed a loaded revolver from the Railway department, and advised them for their safety to obtain it, as some one might get it and do them an injury. They thanked me, and I perceived that I had in a great measure obtained their confidence by telling them this. About dusk I heard Ned Kelly saying to Mrs Jones (they were standing between the hotel and the kitchen, which was a detached building) that he was going down soon to the police barracks to capture Bracken, and that he was going to take her daughter down to call Bracken out. Mrs Jones asked him not to take her. Ned Kelly said that he did not intend to shoot Bracken, and that her daughter must go. I advanced to them, and said to Ned Kelly that I thought it would be better for him to take Dave Mortimer, my brother-in-law, to call Bracken out, because Bracken knew his voice well, and by hearing it would suspect nothing. Ned Kelly, after a pause, said that he would do so. He then went to Mrs Jones's stable, and I followed him, and asked would he allow me to take my party home when he went down for Bracken; and I assured him that he had no cause for fearing me, as I was with him heart and soul. He replied, "I know that, and can see it," and he acceded to my request. I went over to Mrs Stanistreet's and brought my wife and sister to Mrs Jones's, and took them into the kitchen. Ned Kelly said that we must wait till he was ready to go. I found, on going back to Jones's, that a log fire had been made on the Wangaratta side of the hotel yard, and that many of the prisoners of the gang were standing around it. It was then dark. Other prisoners were in the hotel, and the outlaws encouraged them to amuse themselves by playing cards. I waited with my wife and sister in Jones's kitchen for, I believe, two or three hours before Ned Kelly directed me to put my horse into the buggy. He and Byrne then went into the room which they had reserved for their own use. I drove to the front of Jones's hotel, and put my wife and sister and Alec Reynolds, who was about seven years of age, the son of the postmaster at Glenrowan, into the buggy. Ned Kelly directed me to take the little boy with us. We were kept waiting in front of the hotel about an hour. Ned Kelly then came to us on horseback, and told me to drive on. It was then, I believe, about ten o'clock. As we got into the road, I found that we were accompanied by Ned Kelly, Byrne, and my brother-in-law, each on horseback, and by a Mr E. Reynolds and R. Gibbins on foot, both of whom resided with Mr Reynolds, the Glenrowan postmaster. On the road down, Ned Kelly said that he was going to fill the ruts around with the fat carcasses of the police. The outlaws each had a light-coloured overcoat on, and I was amazed at the bulky appearance which they presented. I had then no knowledge that the outlaws possessed iron armour. Each one carried a bundle in front of him, and in one hand a gun or a rifle. We reached the barracks, and were directed by Ned Kelly to halt about twenty yards distant from the front door of the barracks. Ned Kelly got off his horse and fastened him to a fence near, ordering my brother-in-law to do the same, and he did so. Kelly then ordered him to advance to the barracks door and knock, which he did. Ned Kelly got behind an angle of the walls, and levelled his rifle either at Dave Mortimer or at the door. No reply came to the knocking or calling, though they were often and loudly repeated at Ned Kelly's whispered command. When I saw Kelly level his rifle, I told my party to get out of the buggy, which they did, and I advanced to my horse's head, for I thought Kelly might fire. I was then about seven or eight yards from Kelly. No result being produced by either knocking or calling, Ned Kelly left his position and advanced to Byrne, directing me, in an undertone, to call Mortimer away, which I did, and he came. Byrne, who had remained near us, and Ned Kelly then spoke to one another, and Kelly took Alec Reynolds, the postmaster's son, and Mr E. Reynolds, and passed with them into Reynolds's yard. We neither saw nor heard anything for, I think, more than an hour, when Ned Kelly appeared, having Bracken, E. Reynolds, and Bracken's horse with him. Kelly stopped when he reached us, and ordered Bracken to mount the horse brought round, and Bracken did so. Ned Kelly put a halter on the horse, which he kept hold of, saying – "I can't trust you with the bridle, Bracken.' Bracken said to Ned Kelly that had he not been ill in bed all day he (Kelly) would not have taken him easily, and that if the horse he was on was what it used to be it would take more than Ned Kelly to keep him a prisoner. Ned Kelly and Byrne mounted their horses, and I and my party got into the buggy. It was then, I believe, between eleven and twelve o'clock. Ned Kelly then said that I could go home and take my party with me. He directed us to "go quietly to bed, and not to dream too loud", and intimated that if I acted otherwise we would get shot, as one of them would be down to our place during the night to see that we were all right. I then left them and drove home, distant from the barracks one or two hundred yards, leaving the outlaws and their captives ready to start back to the railway station. As soon as we were out of hearing of the outlaws, I announced to my wife and sister my intention to go to Benalla and give information as to the intentions and whereabouts of the outlaws. They both anxiously and earnestly opposed my purpose, saying that it was not at all likely that we should be allowed to come home unless some of the agents of the gang were watching; that I should not be able to reach Benalla, as I should be shot on the road by spies, and that, even if I succeeded, we should be hunted out and shot. While the discussion was going on, and supper was being got ready, I quietly prepared everything, including the red lama scarf, candle, and matches, to go to Benalla, intending to keep as close to the railway line as I could, in case of the special coming before I could reach there. I declared to my wife that I did not intend to go by the road – that I meant to keep as close to the line as possible in order to be safer. At last, my sister gave way, but my wife worked herself in such an excited and hysterical state that she declared that she would not leave the house – that if I would go she would stay there, and she, baby, and my sister would be murdered. I wanted to take them to my mother-in-law's farm, about one-third of a mile from our place, for safety while I was away. At length, Mrs Curnow consented to go to her mother's to obtain advice, and, as we were momentarily expecting the promised visit from one of the gang, I left the doors unlocked, and wrote a note, leaving it on the table, stating that we were gone to Mrs Mortimer's to obtain medicine, as Miss Curnow was taken ill. My sister wore her red lama scarf, at my request. When we got there Mrs Curnow was exceedingly anxious to get home again and would not stay there, and we went back. I succeeded in persuading Mrs Curnow to go to bed; and my sister and I told her I had given up my project. My sister engaged my wife's attention while I went out to harness my horse to go, for I could not rest, and felt that I must perform what was clearly my duty. I heard the train coming in the distance as I was harnessing the horse, and I immediately caught up the candle, scarf, and matches, and ran down the line to meet the train. I ran on until I got to where I could see straight before me along the line, and where those in the train would be able to see the danger signal for some distance. I then lit the candle and held it behind the red scarf. As the guard's van got opposite me I caught sight of the guard, who shouted "What's the matter?" I yelled "The Kellys," and the pilot engine then stopped a little past me, and the guard jumped down. I told the guard of the line being torn up just beyond the station, and of the Kelly gang lying in wait at the station for the special train of police. He said a special train was behind him, and he would go on to the station and then pull up. I cried, "No, no! don't you do that or you will get shot." He then said that he would go back and stop the special which was coming on. He asked me who I was, and I told him I was the school teacher there, and requested him not to divulge who it was that stopped and warned him, as I was doing it at the risk of my life. He promised to keep my name secret. He asked me to jump in the van, but I declined, as my wife and sister were without protection. The pilot engine whistled several times while I was talking with the guard. The pilot went back, and I hastened home and found Mrs Curnow had been almost insane while I was stopping the train, and had been made worse by the whistling of the pilot engine. She would not leave the house after I had stopped the train, and we blew out the lights to seem to be in bed. My sister hid the red scarf and my wet clothes, and we were going to deny that it was I who had stopped the train, if one of the outlaws came down to us. After the first volleys had been fired, I, with an old man who lived opposite me, went up to Jones's to ascertain who were victorious; but we were ordered back by the police, and we returned home. While I was away my sister and wife had a terrible fright through Mr Rawlings, who had accompanied the police, coming down to the school. They thought that he was Ned Kelly when he asked for the door to be opened. When I reached home I found Mr Rawlings there. He asked me to draw a plan of Mrs Jones's house, which I partly did; but, on hearing the train returning from Benalla, he hurried out, and stopping it, he got into it. During the Sunday afternoon I heard Mr Stanistreet ask Ned Kelly to allow the rails torn up to be replaced, and he pointed out to Ned Kelly the sacrifice of innocent lives which would ensue if the Monday morning's passenger train were wrecked. The outlaw refused to allow it to be done. In speaking of and to one another the outlaws had assumed names. In the *Argus* report, May 16th, of James Reardon's evidence, given before the Police Commission at Glenrowan, it is stated that James Reardon said he told me that "the line was broken", and that he told me "how the train could be stopped". Mr Reardon is labouring under a wrong impression. I am positive that he did not tell me how the train could be stopped. Stopping the train, nor how to stop it, was not mentioned to me by any one. Of this I am absolutely certain. I have been informed that an impression prevails that it was in my power, before the outlaws stuck up Glenrowan, to have furnished information to the authorities relating to the Kelly gang or their friends. Others assert that I was employed by the authorities to obtain information. I desire to emphatically state that this impression and assertion are both false.'

(c) Editorial article in *Melbourne Punch*, 1st July 1880

THE KELLY GANG

The complete extermination of this band of cowardly murderers which was accomplished last Monday, is a matter of sincere congratulations amongst all classes, and we hasten to offer our hearty thanks to those concerned in the annihilation of a national evil. To the prompt and decisive action of Mr Ramsay, and to the pluck and determination of Superintendent Hare and his brave associates, is due the fact that the country has been rid of the Kelly nightmare.

Since the first outbreak of the murderers in 1878, there have not been wanting persons – some of whom at any rate should have known better – who regarded the outlaws as brave, although lawless and misguided men. The career of the gang is now fortunately at an end, and upon looking back through the whole bloody page, we fail to perceive one single act of even criminal bravery, much less of manly courage. There was not the making of one soldier in the whole of their four worthless carcasses.

We are aware that this opinion will seem strange to many who still hold to the belief that under other circumstances Ned

Kelly would have been a hero. Under no circumstances could the wretch's nature have been altered. He murdered with the ferocity of a wild beast, when there was no chance of retaliation. He swaggered with the bravado of a bully before powerless men when he himself was armed to the teeth, but he displayed no bravery. He was at heart a thorough coward, whose hand shook so when he was menaced with real danger, that he was unable to take an aim at one of his myriad pursuers.

Lying and cowardice are usually close companions, and a perusal of his 'statement' leads us to the belief that in this last adventure both these elements of his nature were strongly exhibited.

He – the man who betrayed Power years before – says as an instance of his bravery that he could have got away; but he does not tell us how it was that he did get away. The fact, we have no doubt, is that, like a coward and a traitor, he sneaked off leaving his brother and Hart and Byrne to their fate. During the night he lay afraid to move for fear of being arrested. His statement that he could have shot several policemen who passed near him, may be true, but he knew well that the first shot would have been his last, for it would have betrayed his whereabouts at once.

Frightened to death by the fear of the gallows if arrested, and of Byrne's bullet if he deserted his mates, and knowing that he was cased in iron, he determined to get back to the shelter of the hotel. So terrified was the wretch that, though he took deliberate aim, and had the security of knowing that he wore armour, his coward hand was not steady enough to hit the mark. Compare this with the bravery of Sergeant Steele.

He was not fighting to save his neck from the gallows – he wore no armour – his hand never shook as he sent bullet after bullet true to its mark – and when he found that they fell harmless from the iron-plated breast and head, he, still cool of brain, sure of eye and steady of hand, aimed at the ruffian's legs and brought down his man at the first shot. Rushing upon him, fearless of his boasted skill, and his loaded revolver, Steele disarmed and secured the desperado. Then Ned Kelly, like a beaten dog, roared most bravely, the sole performance of his life to which the term could be applied.

To the clergyman who, believing him to be dying, endeavoured to comfort him, he snivelled out something about his previous acquaintance with religion, as if to prove to the world that in his thoroughly base character not even the vice of hypocrisy was wanting. Why this very priest himself, when boldly daring death in the flames to rescue the unfortunate platelayer, displayed a bravery that cowards like the Kellys would have shrunk from in terror.

When they were four to one, they shot down innocent and unarmed men, they brutally murdered Kennedy, when he lay dying and begged that his life might be allowed the bare chance of recovery. They affected to be brave when they knew that their security lay in their bullet-proof armour. And with all their baptism of blood, all their boasting, all their bravado, all their bravery (?), the incontrovertible fact remains – *they did not kill a single man in fair fight!* Most brave heroes!

Nemesis has overtaken the gang. Dan Kelly, Hart and Byrne, who were always loud in their determination to 'roast all the —— policemen', have been present at the burnt offering as victims, not as sacrificers. No doubt they fought after a manner, like a parcel of rats at bay. They died like rats in a hole – burnt out like vermin.

And Ned, the leader, the man who would never be taken alive – is captured roaring with physical pain like a wounded bull, and the hero straightway commences with lying statements to pose as a brave fellow, when every act of his lawless career, from the brutal ending of Kennedy to his attempt to leave his comrades in the lurch, shows unmistakable signs of his being a white-livered, even if a bloody, poltroon.

The grave yawns for him. His hemp is spun and twisted. If his life hold out long enough to enable him to reach the gallows, it will be found that he met his fate with abject terror, or with unseemly bravado put on to hide the inward quaking. The nation clamours eagerly for the life so long and bloodily forfeited to its outraged laws, and all those of the community who have a proper detestation of a cowardly murderer, must contemplate without pity, the ultimate fate of a wretch without one redeeming point, that of Edward Kelly, Murderer, Traitor, Hypocrite, Liar and Coward!

(d) REPORTED APPEARANCES OF THE KELLY OUTLAWS

The portion of the return within square brackets is that furnished by Superintendent Sadleir. The other portion contains additions to Mr Sadleir's return, remarks thereon, and the particulars of some cases not noted by him.

Date Report Received	Date of Appearance	Where Seen, &c.	Steps Taken by Police
1878	1878	*Mr Nicolson in charge*	
November 2	October 31	At Margery and Peterson's, near Bungowannah	Search by Detective Kennedy, and subsequently by Mr Nicolson, to November 5th.
,, 4 or 5	November 4	Wangaratta Bridge and crossings at railway	Inspector Brooke Smith making inquiry. In the meantime search started at Sheep Station Creek. Later tracks taken up by Mr Smith, which led to police horses being found on Warby's Ranges. The identity of offenders only conjectured by informants.
,, 6	,, 3	At Sheep Station Creek, by bark stripper	Search party, under Captain Standish, Mr Nicolson, and Mr Sadleir, at daybreak on 7th.
,, 6	October 29	Pioneer Bridge	No search, later information having been received.
,, 11	November 11	Crossing railway near Glenrowan; reported by platelayer, who did not identify offender	Search by Messrs Nicolson, Sadleir, and Smith, with party, on 12th, at daybreak; unable to follow tracks.
December 6	Not given	Near Gaffney's Creek	Search and inquiry by local police, and not traced.
,, 10	December 9 and 10	Faithfull's Creek and Euroa ...	This was the date when Euroa bank was stuck up. Search by police, under Mr Nicolson.
,, 13	December 12	Near Violet Town	Rumour unfounded.
		Captain Standish and Mr Hare in charge.	
December 18	November 24	Violet Town	Rumour unfounded.
,, 19	December 8	At Chappell's, Woolshed Creek, near Beechworth	No steps taken; later appearance at Euroa on 10th instant.

166

Reported Appearances of the Kelly Outlaws—*continued*

Date Report Received	Date of Appearance	Where Seen, &c.	Steps Taken by Police
1878	1878	*Captain Standish and Mr Hare in charge*—continued	
December 21	Not given	Strathbogie	Report unfounded.
,, 23	Not given	Kialla	Report unfounded.
,, 26	Not given; a few days previous	At Yarck, twelve miles from Alexandra, by a man named Ware	Inquiry by Alexandra police. Report found to be untrue.
,, 27	December 26	Seven miles from Lake Rowan (Steve Hart only seen), by Joseph Coombes	Inquiry by Lake Rowan police. Report found to be untrue.
,, 28	About December 13	Near Doon	Rumour unfounded.
,, 30	December 22	At Mrs Byrne's, Sebastopol (Joe Byrne only)	Report too old to be acted on. Reported by Detective Ward.
,, 30		Near Moyhu	Report unfounded.
,, 31	December 21	Ned Kelly only. At Mrs Byrne's	No steps. Reported by Detective Ward, who recommends Mrs Byrne's house to be watched.
1879 January 3	,, 1879 30	Wallan Wallan	Local police searched. Found to be untrue.
,, 7	January 5	Four men, supposed Kellys, at Green Hills, near Wodonga	Place searched by Sergeant Harkin and party, but no trace.
,, 7	,, 5	Near Cotter's, Broken River	Inquiry by Mansfield police; the informant, Eyres, not reliable. No trace.
,, 7	,, 5	Four men, supposed outlaws, on Chiltern road	Reported by Sergeant Harkin, who made search, but could not trace these persons; not supposed to be the outlaws.

REPORTED APPEARANCES OF THE KELLY OUTLAWS—*continued*

Date Report Received	Date of Appearance	Where Seen, &c.	Steps Taken by Police

Captain Standish and Mr Hare in charge—continued

Date Report Received	Date of Appearance	Where Seen, &c.	Steps Taken by Police
1879 January 8	1879 ,, 4	Pat. Quinn's, near Moyhu (all the outlaws). N. Kelly dressed as a woman	No steps. The informant, George Cherry, to inquire of his informant, and report further. No further report from Cherry.
,, 9	,, 1	Tarnagulla (Steve Hart only)	Inquiry by local police. Story unfounded.
,, 10	,, 6	Three miles from Kilfera to Greta	Gang inquired about Harty's arrest, and threatened police. No steps, as information did not indicate particular locality, and was too stale.
,, 13	,, 7	McIvor's hut, four miles from last locality	Information too stale; Senior-Constable Strahan, with watch party, placed at crossings in vicinity.
,, 13	,, 9 and 10	At Wright's mail station, Wodonga and Chiltern road	Inquiry by Sergeant Harkin and police, who report matter doubtful. Detective Eason, by telegrams on 17th, thinks report not reliable.
,, 16	About 10 days before	Stony Creek, near Violet Town	Search by police, without result.
,, 17	1878 January 4	Barwidgee	Report too stale.
,, 18	December 25	Near Winton	Reported by Acting Chief Secretary, who directed search to be made in locality indicated for proceeds of bank robbery. Search by Senior-Constable Strahan and party, who could not find the 'plant'.
,, 17 & 19	1879 January 4	Barwidgee, by Chinese Ah Maw (all the outlaws seen)	Party sent on 20th, accompanied by informant. No trace, and report considered doubtful. Banks in neighbourhood warned.

REPORTED APPEARANCES OF THE KELLY OUTLAWS—*continued*

Date Report Received	Date of Appearance	Where Seen, &c.	Steps Taken by Police
1879	1879	*Captain Standish and Mr Hare in charge—continued*	
January 21	,, 21	Muddy Creek, Euroa, and Murchison road	Reported by Patrick Moffat (constable on leave). Superintendent Sadleir and party, by special train, searched and found report untrue. Informant mistook others for outlaws.
,, 21	,, 15	Dry Creek, near Doon (Steve Hart only)	Inquiry by Mansfield police. Report traced to Absalom James, who afterwards denied the affair.
,, 25	,, 22	Near Winton railway gates	No record of action taken.
,, 27	,, 27	On Strathbogie, over Violet Town (Ned Kelly and Steve Hart only)	Reported by *elias* Sherrington to Assistant Commissioner of Police that he had seen offenders same day, and spoken to them. Four parties of police sent out on 29th. Report believed to be wholly unreliable.
,, 27	About 17th January	Strathbogie	A mere suspicion.
,, 31	January 29	Sheep Station Creek, near Beechworth	A. Sherritt reported seeing D. Kelly and Joe Byrne, and other information.
February 2	,, 21	Tom Lloyd's, near Greta	Too stale to act upon.
,, 3	February 1	Lancashire Lead, near Chiltern. J. Byrne and (supposed) Dan Kelly	Party, under Senior-Constable Strahan, on foot, sent to inquire; Superintendent Sadleir also followed. Traces could not be followed.
,, 8	No date	Gang supposed near Talangatta getting horses to cross river	Superintendent Sadleir to Albury to inform and act with police there on same day. Senior-Constable Mullane and parties also in search near Talangatta.

169

Reported Appearances of the Kelly Outlaws—*continued*

Date Report Received	Date of Appearance	Where Seen, &c.	Steps Taken by Police
1879	1879	*Captain Standish and Mr Hare in charge—continued*	
February 10	February 10	Jerilderie, New South Wales ...	Jerilderie bank stuck up. Four parties to watch crossings to Victoria, and all police warned.
,, 11	,, 10	Near Cashel	Report unfounded. Kellys at Jerilderie this day. *See* B 154.
,, 12	,, 12	Urana, New South Wales (all the outlaws)	Reported by Albury police.
,, 12	,, 12	Taylor's Gap, near Beechworth (Dan Kelly only)	Detective Ward and two constables sent to search; no result; report believed to be doubtful. Party watching Tom Lloyd's from 16th, and party from Kilfera in ranges to Ryan's Creek.
,, 20	,, 15 & 16	Urana, New South Wales ...	Reported by Albury police.
,, 20	,, 22	Rutherglen and Wahgunyah ...	Report was to effect that attack by outlaws was imminent. Two parties of police, two in each, secretly lodged in each township.
,, 23	,, 23	Howlong, New South Wales. Outlaws not seen, but telegraph wires cut that morning each side of town	Party of police sent with Albury police from Wodonga. No appearance of outlaws.
,, 25	Not given	Near Barnawartha	The gang were said to be drinking; Ned Kelly suffering from blight. Wodonga police in search, but no trace. Report believed untrue.
,, 28	February 28 2 p.m.	Whorouly	Search by police. A case of mistaken identity.
March 2	March 1	Doctor's Point, near Wodonga	Four armed men seen, not traced; but circumstances showed report to be unreliable.

170

REPORTED APPEARANCES OF THE KELLY OUTLAWS—*continued*

Date Report Received	Date of Appearance	Where Seen, &c.	Steps Taken by Police
1879	1879		
March 2	February 22	Near Greta	Too stale to use.
„ 30	Not given	Sebastopol, near Beechworth	Detective Ward reported Byrne somewhere in neighbourhood; place not directly indicated. Superintendent Hare to Beechworth to make inquiry.

Captain Standish and Mr Hare in charge—continued

April 6	Not given	Reported by Mr Graves, M.L.A., that Ned Kelly seen near Melbourne	No steps taken.
„ 9	Not given	Tumut, New South Wales	Man, named Coller, reports Kellys in neighbourhood. An idle tale.
„ 11	April 11	Bowman's Forest, near Beechworth	Inquiries made. Statement believed to be untrue.
„ 25	Previous evening	Sheep Station Creek, near Beechworth (Joe Byrne only, supposed)	(?) *See* Detective Ward's ten telegrams, May 25th, 1879.
May 29	April 20	Caniambo, near Mooroopna	Mooroopna police searched. No result.
June 14	June 14	Lime Kilns, near Devenish	The outlaw Dan Kelly supposed to be hiding here. Cashel police searched. Report untrue.
„ 26	„ 26	Near Corowa	Search by Inspector Brooke Smith, Detective Ward, and others. Story found untrue.
July 2	...	Puzzle Ranges, near Woolshed	The information was received through A. Sherritt, who was asked by letter from Joe Byrne to meet him. Sherritt went, but reported that he failed to meet Byrne.

171

Reported Appearances of the Kelly Outlaws—*continued*

Date Report Received	Date of Appearance	Where Seen, &c.	Steps Taken by Police
1879	1879	*Captain Standish and Mr Hare in charge*—continued	
July 5	July 2	Lake Rowan to Yarrawonga road	Ned Kelly, and three others not known, armed. Reported by Kennealy. Not credited; heavy rains also prevented tracking. Inquiries by Lake Rowan police, without result.
		Mr Nicolson in charge	
July 11	July 10	At Mrs Jones's, near Beechworth	[Reported by Mrs Jones, 3 p.m. on 11th. After consultation with local police, it was considered not to be desirable to attempt tracking and so compromise the Jones family in case of failure. The outlaws were seen by children only, and were on foot. It was further said that the supposed appearance of the outlaws was to make a raid on the Beechworth banks; provision made accordingly.] Instructions issued. Yackandandah bank insecure. Approachable through Commissioner's Creek. Strength increased 1879. Enquiries made. Report denied. Telegraphic communication established between banks, telegraph office, and police station, Beechworth, with a view to signals being given all round on slightest alarm.
,, 11	,, 10 4 p.m.	Sheepstation Creek. The outlaw Byrne and his younger brother were seen together on horseback at Reed's Creek Ranges	
,, 12	,, 9	Near Doon	[Search and enquiry by Mansfield police. Statement found untrue.]

REPORTED APPEARANCES OF THE KELLY OUTLAWS—*continued*

Date Report Received	Date of Appearance	Where Seen, &c.	Steps Taken by Police
		Mr Nicolson in charge—continued	
1879	1879		
July 14	,, 11	Mrs Byrne, Sebastopol	[Reported by Chinaman; did not state which of outlaws were seen. No action taken; report too stale.]
,, 23	,, ...	...	About this time it was ascertained that some of the haunts of the gang were Hedi Ranges, Gum Flat, Hurdle Creek Ranges. Woolshed, Barrambogie, Pilot Ranges and vicinity, Rats' Castle, Wooragee, and Hurdle Creek.
,, 31	,, 30	Mrs Jones's, near Beechworth	[Reported by Moses. Action taken.] From 13th to 23rd August 1879, Carrington and Baron search on foot to Table Top, Drum Top, ranges head of Boggy and Fifteen-Mile Creeks, Myrtree and Greta Ranges, but found no trace. They heard that Ned Kelly paid imprisoned sympathizers' legal expenses. Foote often leaves home for three or four days. Sometimes he takes a parcel with him. When he returns fresh news oozes out of him, and has money.—C. 26. August 26th, Baron employed about Sebastopol
August 9	August 5	Near Violet Town	[Four men, one supposed to be Ned Kelly. Benalla and local police searched. Report seems to have arisen from a scare.]
,, 17	,, 14	Ranges near Sebastopol (Joe Byrne only)	[Report received from two boys by Moses and Detective Ward, who disbelieved statement. No search.]
,, 27	Not given	Near Boweya	[Reported by anonymous letter. Constable McGuirk went out to watch.]

173

Reported Appearances of the Kelly Outlaws—*continued*

Date Report Received	Date of Appearance	Where Seen, &c.	Steps Taken by Police
1879	1879	*Mr Nicolson in charge*—continued	
August 28	...	...	A threatening letter received from Joe Byrne to Moses by post.—C. 118. At Moses's request he proceeds to see Bruce, but obtains no information from him as to whereabouts of outlaws.
,, 29	Not given	Near Glenrowan	[Scout Carrington reports gang likely to be in vicinity of Bryan Orangery. Scouts employed in that neighbourhood watching for several weeks.]
September 1	...	...	A threatening letter from Joe Byrne to Moses, Senior-Constable Mullane, and Detective Ward, warning them of mischief before that day month. This letter was given by the outlaws to an agent to be posted to the police. It was posted, and every precaution taken to increase the confidence of the outlaws in their fancied security and their belief in the ignorance of the police.—C. 124. A notice of this letter was published in one of the local newspapers, in compliance with request of outlaws.—C. 118. [This report was three (3) weeks old.]
,, 3	August 3 (about)	Wilson's paddock, near Greta	
,, 2	September 1	Near Sebastopol (Joe Byrne only)	[Agent Moses only employed to watch, on the recommendation of Detective Ward.]
,, 6	July 9 (about)	In a paddock near Greta	Information to Superintendent Sadleir of the four outlaws having been seen two months previously in a paddock near Greta. Information too stale.

174

Reported Appearances of the Kelly Outlaws—*continued*

Date Report Received	Date of Appearance	Where Seen, &c.	Steps Taken by Police
1879 September 9	1879 ,, ,,	*Mr Nicolson in charge*—continued Dan Kelly at Mrs Skillian's stable door	Information too stale. Informant promised to watch, and communicate sooner next time. The other outlaws were probably present, as Mrs Skillian was seen carrying a bucket supposed filled with tea, and a parcel supposed to have been bread.
,, 12	September 10	Dan Kelly alleged to have been seen in Crawford's paddock	Arrangements made to watch. Jones to meet Mr Nicolson at Beechworth on 15th. He met Mr Nicolson for first time at Wangaratta with Bruce.
,, 12	August 29	Ned Kelly alleged to have been seen at Goorambat, seven miles from Benalla	[Too stale to use, but informant undertook to watch and report any re-appearance.] Was seen several times by Mr Nicolson and Sergeant Whelan. Ned Kelly about this time was reported as suffering from sciatica.
,, 24	September 15	Mrs Byrne's ...	Moses gives the information. It is too stale. The Jones's instructed to watch and secure tracks.
,, 16	,, 6	... ...	Mr Nicolson had a private interview with Moses in Beechworth this 16th September, and Moses admitted having seen Byrne on 6th, and that Jones received from Byrne *the threatening letter to Detective Ward*.—C. 124.
,, 22	...	... ...	Examined a camp 23rd August on Porcupine Creek, in a gully leading between Sebastopol and the Pilot Range. Found traces of three or four horses. Evidently a place of concealment. Byrne passed this way on return from Jerilderie into Victoria. But this camp is more recent, horses and men believed to have been the outlaws having been seen on the 23rd August. This is of value, as indicating one of the outlaws' routes.

175

Reported Appearances of the Kelly Outlaws—*continued*

Date Report Received	Date of Appearance	Where Seen, &c.	Steps Taken by Police
1879	1879	*Mr Nicolson in charge*—continued	
September 24	August 31	Mr Crawford's paddock	El Dorado police put on alert. Information sent through agent to outlaw's brother Patsy for Byrne that even £20 would not at any time be found in the El Dorado or any other small post office. Jones was working, and Byrne asked him to ascertain amount of money in El Dorado Savings Bank.
,, 24	September 19	Mrs Byrne's	Joe Byrne left £2 in silver for Jones for posting a threatening letter to Detective Ward.
,, 29	,, 28	Near Greta	[This is the report mentioned in evidence of Captain Standish, Mr Nicolson, and Mr Sadleir. Informant *alias* 'Foote'.] Mr Sadleir did not know the place indicated by the informant, therefore his services as guide could not be relied upon.—*Vide* memo. to Chief Commissioner of Police in Mr Nicolson's evidence. The informant was willing, and intended to come; and Mr Nicolson telegraphed to Mr Sadleir to bring him, which he did not do. Mr O'Connor did not consider Mr Sadleir's guidance sufficiently good under the circumstances.
October 4	Week previous	Near Hollow station	[Enquiry by police.] No truth in rumour.
,, 9	May previous	Near Lake Rowan and Taminick road	[Agent placed to watch locality.] Five men seen at Ryan's door, Lake Rowan.—C. 59. Horsemen pass through informant's paddock at night occasionally. Informant called at Benalla office. Arrangements made.

REPORTED APPEARANCES OF THE KELLY OUTLAWS—*continued*

Date Report Received	Date of Appearance	Where Seen, &c.	Steps Taken by Police
1879	1879	*Mr Nicolson in charge*—continued	
October 16	Not given	Between Greta and Oxley	[This report was only general as to haunts of gang. Renwick (*alias*) employed as scout in this locality.] Renwick employed on 17th. Rain set in, and portion of country indicated flooded. One of the McAuliffes purchased four well-bred horses, supposed for the outlaws, and hired Wilson's paddock, opposite Bowdren's.
,, 23	September 22	Sloan's paddock, near Wangaratta	[A man named Smith reported that he had been made prisoner by gang. *See* last item for steps taken. Diseased Stock agent also employed in these localities.] Edward Smith, farmer, Sloan's paddock, reported that he and young Morgan had been made prisoners by the gang on the night of the 22nd September, and kept in Hart's (senior) house for several hours before being released. He had to swear that he would not divulge anything for one month. The police ascertained that young Morgan would not corroborate Smith. Morgan would only reply that he knew nothing about it. Morgan is connected with the sympathizers From Wangaratta police.—Richard Hart would have been prosecuted if Morgan had consented to give evidence.
,, 29	,, 13	Near Greta	[Reported by Denny, who also conveyed warning *re* Jamieson bank and escort. Banks in neighbourhood and police specially warned.] Mr Nicolson was informed that

177

Reported Appearances of the Kelly Outlaws—*continued*

Date Report Received	Date of Appearance	Where Seen, &c.	Steps Taken by Police
1879	1879	*Mr Nicolson in charge*—continued	
October 29	…	…	the outlaws' knowledge of vigilance of the local police, and the defection of a scout of the gang, caused them to abandon this project.
,, 30, 31	…	…	Joe Byrne, outlaw, writes several letters to the Jones's. Replies dictated by police. Requests in Byrne's letters acceded to as far as possible, with the view of the Jones's securing his confidence. Arrangements made by Mr Nicolson with Detective Ward and Senior-Constable Mullane.
November 7	November 6	Near Peechelba	[Reported by Jones, who met Joe Byrne by appointment.] Under direction of police, Jones succeeds in making an arrangement, through one of brothers of outlaw Byrne, to meet the gang at Thompson's, near to Peechelba. On arriving finds Thompson gone twelve months, and no signs of the gang; but on his return home next day, on a scrubby track through the ranges, Byrne the outlaw suddenly appeared and signed to him to follow into the bush. When out of sight of the track they had a long conversation together, Byrne wanting Jones to join them as a scout. Byrne's mind appeared burdened about the murder of Sergeant Kennedy, and revealed several ideas and plans they had in view, which enabled Mr Nicolson to take precautions against them. Byrne's spurs were bloody, and

178

Reported Appearances of the Kelly Outlaws—continued

Date Report Received	Date of Appearance	Where Seen, &c.	Steps Taken by Police
1879 November 7	1879 7	*Mr Nicolson in charge*—continued	he had the appearance of having ridden hard. Jones believed he was under the eyes of the gang both going to and returning from Thompson's, to test his good faith. No police were sent, as this extraordinary appointment of Byrne was evidently taken with such precautions as to baffle any pursuit that might be instituted. (*See* Foote, September 29.) The object of this interview was to obtain more knowledge of the men and their plans. The outlaw Byrne made another appointment to meet him again at Evans's Gap.
,, 7	,, 7	Coloopna, near Shepparton ...	[Report that nine armed men seen. Turned out to be cricketers.]
,, 7	,, 23	Nerandera, New South Wales...	Action taken by New South Wales police.
,, 13	,, 13	Jones's house, near Beechworth	Detective Ward sent to make enquiries. No tracks. Dan Kelly appeared at hut this afternoon, with revolver in hand, and asked for Jones, and searched each room for him. Jones was working in a paddock, but, on hearing of Dan Kelly's visit, he hid himself until dark, and rode into Beechworth, frightened lest the gang had come to carry him off. Mr Nicolson arrived accidentally at 12 p.m. Jones instructed to conceal his fear from the gang by going to Julien's to amuse himself, and thereby account for his absence from home.

REPORTED APPEARANCES OF THE KELLY OUTLAWS—*continued*

Date Report Received	Date of Appearance	Where Seen, &c.	Steps Taken by Police
1879	1879	*Mr Nicolson in charge—continued*	
November 17	September 14	Murphy's hut ...	No steps. Too stale. Outlaw Byrne said to have visited Murphy's empty hut on 14th September.
,, 20	July 1	Near Nilacoota, Mansfield road, (supposed Ned Kelly only)	Further special steps taken to protect banks, and warning given. Beechworth reinforced. Cave party being formed. [No action. Report too stale.]
,, 27	November 23	Mrs Jones's, near Beechworth...	On November 23rd Byrne visited Jones's hut about 8 p.m. Other members of the gang evidently outside. Dogs barked for two hours before he entered. He was well dressed. Shook hands with all, including Moses. Complimented Jones upon the work he had done for them about posting letters and caricatures during past month. Said that Dan had been sent on the 13th to tell him not to meet him at Evans's Gap. That he and Ned had two separate plans for doing one of the Beechworth banks. His own plan was to get into a bank quietly at night, stick up the manager in or out of bed. If he had not all the keys, one of the gang and one of the brothers S. were to accompany Byrne to the person who had the keys, and get them, even if blood was shed over it. Two of the party were then to remain with the bankers until the money was got out of the safe, and then Byrne was to carry off the swag. Byrne said their horses were bad.

180

REPORTED APPEARANCES OF THE KELLY OUTLAWS—*continued*

Date Report Received	Date of Appearance	Where Seen, &c.	Steps Taken by Police
1879 November 27	1879	*Mr Nicolson in charge*—continued	His grey horse was still the best. A female present suggested if he would tell where the others were and give himself up he might get his pardon. He replied that the people would say he was worse than Sullivan, and hunt him out of the colony. He remarked that the police were tired of watching his mother's place. He looked as if fretting. Now looks under 10 stone weight. He left about 12 p.m., saying he would come again on Sunday the 30th. Information four days old. Offender on foot. No tracks left. Moses to watch Mrs Byrne's. Jones to sleep in his garden, outside his hut Cave party established on 3rd December.
1880 January 31	Some days previous	Shear's Gully, near Euroa (Steve Hart only)	[Report enquired into and found untrue.]
February 6	December	Eleven-Mile Creek	[Report nearly two months old.] Carrington reports young Tom Lloyd and the McAuliffes about Greta and Fifteen-Mile Creek Swamp. They appear to have money. Gallop about at night shouting and noisy. Smith, who had been despatched by Detective Ward to El Dorado, Woolshed, Sebastopol, and Reid's Creek, returned, and reports nothing known of police movements (cave party).

Reported Appearances of the Kelly Outlaws—*continued*

Date Report Received	Date of Appearance	Where Seen, &c.	Steps Taken by Police
1880	1879	*Mr Nicolson in charge*—continued	
February 10	December 19 (about)	Mrs Skillian's, Greta ...	Agent at present watching. Reported that Ned and Dan were seen rushing into Mrs Skillian's, and a third man on horseback rode off at the sight of the stranger. The latter overtook the man on horseback, a relative of the outlaws. The latter admitted that the other two were the outlaws – the Kellys. Denny also reports Ned Kelly and Byrne about Fifteen-Mile Creek.
,, 11	...	...	Visit from Denny. Gang about Greta Ranges. Portion of Greta Swamp burned from stone crossing nearly to township. Expect to ascertain outlaws' exact locality soon.
,, 23	...	...	17th April 1880. – Renwick reports Eth. Hart still at Glenrowan. McAuliffes, Lloyd, and other sympathizers at Mrs Jones's, and rowdy, especially to strangers. Was of opinion that outlaws cross railway line on foot, horses through gates, thus no traces, and that they are using their friends' horses. The above corroborated by Denny about 4th March.
,, 21	1880 February 19	Mrs Byrne's, Sebastopol (Joe Byrne only)	[Watch maintained. Report believed unfounded. *See* G. 169.] Patsy Byrne says Joe slept at his mother's hut on this date. Untrue, Patsy evidently sounding. Denny says gang at present about Greta Swamp and ranges, hiding in long grass and bulrushes by day, on the prowl by night. Seldom carry their rifles on foot. Cross railway on

Reported Appearances of the Kelly Outlaws—*continued*

Date Report Received	Date of Appearance	Where Seen, &c.	Steps Taken by Police
1880	1880	*Mr Nicolson in charge*—continued	
			foot. Their horses taken to meet them when they shift. Requested police to be kept quiet. No action at present. Would soon furnish definite information. 1st March 1880. From Greta. Quiet. 12th March 1880 – Horses stolen at Greta from a drover Gallagher. N.B. – The first plough mould boards stolen were Mr Sinclair's, Glenrowan. Missed on 22nd March 1880.
,, 27	,, 23	Myrtleford ...	[Report too stale, and arrangements made to watch for any further appearance.]
,, 27	Two days previous	Near Baumgarten's ...	[Enquiries by police. Report found untrue.]
March 11	Not given ...	Mount Typo ...	[Reported by Mr Graves, M.L.A. Report indefinite.] Smith, 22nd March, works at Glenrowan railway station on watch. Reports Ettie Hart, at Mrs Jones's, visited by sympathizers, but no sign of outlaws. 24th – McAuliffes and Lloyds cease visiting Mrs Jones's. McDonnell tells him outlaws not far off.
,, 4	...	...	5th March – Mrs Skillian purchased stores in Benalla; old Tom Lloyd also. Communicated to Wangaratta police with other information from Denny. Renwick instructed by Sergeant Steele, C. 177. Country indicated searched twice recently. Smith and Gallagher did not report to police until at Broken River station.

Reported Appearances of the Kelly Outlaws—*continued*

Date Report Received	Date of Appearance	Where Seen, &c.	Steps Taken by Police
		Mr Nicolson in charge—continued	
1880 April 1	1880	… …	Detective Ward instructed to withdraw the cave party.
,, 21	…	… …	Denny reports that up to early last winter the outlaws camped frequently in Wilson's paddock, but their absences were frequent and irregular, from nine days to one month. They now put up a small low tent at night. They have recently removed. Exact locality unknown, but believed to be in one of the gullies of the ranges about. Very suspicious and wary, yet exhibiting a certain degree of carelessness. Further definite information will be furnished. Ned Kelly trusts much in Byrne. They often ride together at night, leaving Steve Hart with Dan Kelly following, one or more of the Lloyds or McAuliffes with them, the latter giving signals if anyone appears, whom the gang then avoids. Denny will furnish further definite information as to their action, whether they settle down again, or plan a raid. They are very short of money, and becoming suspicious of their friends.
,, 24	…	…	Agents on the alert keenly. Winton, Glenrowan, and Lake Rowan agent, Smith, informed on good authority, that the outlaws have been seen about lately by one or two persons who dared not tell. Further reported that gang said to be reduced to the last straits, and without means of carrying on longer. Movements circumscribed, and unable to find an unguarded bank to rob.

Reported Appearances of the Kelly Outlaws—*continued*

Date Report Received	Date of Appearance	Where Seen, &c.	Steps Taken by Police
1880	1880	*Mr Nicolson in charge*—continued	
April 27	April 23	Eleven-Mile Creek	Enquiries by the police. Mrs Skillian's hut watched. Upon April 23rc (afternoon) Dan Kelly is said, upon fair authority, to have been seen near the Eleven-Mile Creek, galloping towards Mrs Skillian's place. C. 215. By Smith and Sergeant Whelan.
,, 29	March 27	Broken Creek	Communicated to Glenrowan police. On the 27th March, four horsemen, believed to be the gang, called at a hut, Broken Creek, Lake Rowan, and enquired for a well-known resident of Lake Rowan. They were informed that the person they enquired for was inside. They replied that the man they wanted was another of same name, who lived at Glenrowan, and they rode away. C.215
,, 30	April 7	In Greta	[Reported by a woman, who says she saw the outlaws D. and E. Kelly in daylight, riding through township. Not credited.]
May 1	Not stated	Mrs Byrne's, Sebastopol	[Reported by anonymous letter. No action.] 8th May 1880. Examined with Renwick maps of roads Moyhu, Greta, and Lake Rowan district, prior to another tour.
,, 11	...	...	Constable Bracken stationed at Glenrowan for police duty, but really to assist Smith in watching Mrs Skillian's at night, anc any other work. Communicated to Sergeant Steele, Wangaratta. Watch party formed upon Warby Ranges. Suspicious movements of Dick Hart, elder brother of outlaw Steve Hart. He has returned to Mrs Jones's, Glen-

185

REPORTED APPEARANCES OF THE KELLY OUTLAWS—*continued*

Date Report Received	Date of Appearance	Where Seen, &c.	Steps Taken by Police
1880	1880		
May 11		*Mr Nicolson in charge*—continued	rowan. On night of 14th Dick went up behind the hotel; absent two hours. Next night he came out in front of house, and cracked a stockwhip three times, like a signal.
,, 15	...	...	A party of horsemen passed through Glenrowan, going north. Two returned, one missing. The rest overhauled at Yarrawonga by police. Proved to be John, Dan, and Mick Nolan, Renwick, watching Ryan's, Lake Rowan, discovering that some one was hiding in a hut, Senior-Constable Kelly and Lake Rowan police searched the hut, and found young Tom Lloyd to be the occupant and the missing man of the band of sympathizers above referred to.
,, 17	May 10	Near Chiltern	Mrs Jones, of near Beechworth, reports visit of Byrne and Dan Kelly to B——n's.
,, 18	,, 10	Near Chiltern	This information tested further, and found correct. Moses on watch. Beechworth police discovered B——n had visited Sebastopol, and conveyed a letter from outlaw Byrne to his mother. Detective Ward also reports message sent by Mrs Byrne to Mrs Jones, near Beechworth, not to let Moses know, nor to allow Joe or Dan to visit her house, lest Moses should betray them.
,, 21	...	...	Sergeant Steele instructed to have Hart's house, near Wangaratta, watched at night. Denny reports that the plough mould boards recently stolen had been fitted into jackets for outlaws to wear.

186

REPORTED APPEARANCES OF THE KELLY OUTLAWS—*continued*

Date Report Received	Date of Appearance	Where Seen, &c.	Steps Taken by Police
1880 May 22	1880 ...	...	*Mr Nicolson in charge*—continued Smith on watch. McAuliffe has given notice to the outlaw Ned Kelly that he must get some money. He must do another bank, as he, McAuliffe, was unable to continue aiding him longer.
,, 25 & 26	May 24 and 26	At Mrs Sherritt's and Mrs Byrne's, Sebastopol	[Search party started, but withdrawn on account of rain, by recommendation of local police and Moses.]
,, 29	26	Sebastopol	Mr Nicolson despatched Renwick by night train to Beechworth, to reconnoitre, &c. Arranged for party of police to watch Mrs Byrne's temporarily while other steps were being taken. Mr Nicolson interviewed one person at Beechworth, who alleged she saw the outlaw Byrne at Murphy's empty hut, and that another person saw the four outlaws at Mrs Byrne's hut. Mr Nicolson informed Detective Ward and Senior-Constable Mullane of his leaving North-Eastern District, and explained to them the necessity for their obtaining Superintendent Hare's authority to continue employment of Moses after Mr N. leaves, as no authority existed from Chief Commissioner of Police to employ him. Mr N. had done so latterly at his own risk.
,, 30	30	Sebastopol (Joe Byrne only supposed)	[Reported by Scout Renwick. Search party, under Mr Nicolson, with trackers, with result that tracks seen were not those of outlaws.] Searched place of alleged appearance, and found information to be incorrect.
,, 31	Previous week	Woolshed Creek	Scout informed. Report too stale.

187

REPORTED APPEARANCES OF THE KELLY OUTLAWS—*continued*

Date Report Received		Date of Appearance	Where Seen, &c.	Steps Taken by Police
1880		1880		
			Mr Hare in charge	
June	19	Various within last nine months	Fifteen-mile Creek and neighbourhood	No action by police. *See* D 7.
,,	14	Three weeks previous	Near Greta	Report indefinite. No action. *See* D 10.

C. H. NICOLSON,
Acting Commisssioner of Police
J. SADLEIR,
Superintendent of Police.

(e) ARRESTS AND CONVICTIONS OF THE QUINNS, KELLYS, AND LLOYDS

Name	Offence	Where Tried	Date	How disposed of
James Quinn, jun.	Having stolen cattle	Kilmore	2.12.56	Discharged.
,,	Violent assault	,,	30.9.60	6 weeks.
,,	Horse stealing	Melbourne	18.10.60	Discharged.
,,	,,	,,	5.2.61	4 months (illegally using).
,,	Assaulting police	Donnybrook	23.8.61	£10, or 6 weeks (paid).
,,	Horse stealing	Clunes	30.8.61	Discharged.
,,	Violent assault	Kilmore	29.3.62	,,
,,	Horse stealing	Beechworth	1.2.64	12 months.
,,	Threatening	Wangaratta	3.8.71	£5, or six weeks.
,,	Assault	,,	,,	3 months.
,,	Bodily harm	Beechworth	2.2.72	3 years
,,	,,	,,	16.4.72	18 months } Cumulative.
,,	,,	,,	17.4.73	2 years
,,	Assault	Benalla G.S.	15.7.78	Discharged.
,,	Kelly sympathizer	Benalla	16.9.78	3 months.
John Quinn	Horse stealing	Beechworth	1.79	Discharged.
,,	Cattle stealing	Melbourne	4.60	,,
,,	,,	Gisborne	27.6.60	,,
Patk. Quinn	Robbery under arms	Donnybrook	23.11.61	,,
,,	Grievous bodily harm	Beechworth	10.70	4 years, Son-in-law of James Quinn, sen.
John Kelly (Red)	...	Tipperary	...	To Tasmania.
,,	Unlawful possession of a hide	Avenel	5.65	6 months.
James Kelly, sen.	Cattle stealing	Kilmore	12.5.62	Discharged ⎫
,,	,,	,,	21.10.62	3 years ⎬ Brother of Red Kelly.
,,	Arson	,,	22.4.63	15 years ⎭
James Kelly, jun.	Illegally using a horse	Wangaratta	.71	Discharged.
,,	Cattle stealing	Beechworth	17.4.73	2½ years } Cumulative.
,,	,,	,,	,,	2½ years

189

Arrests and Convictions of the Quinns, Kellys, and Lloyds—*continued*

Name	Offence	Where Tried	Date	How disposed of
James Kelly, Jim.	Horse stealing	Wagga, N.S.W.	27.6.77	3 years.
Edward Kelly	Assault and robbery	Benalla	26.10.69	Discharged.
,,	Obscene language	Wangaratta	10.11.70	3 months ⎫ Cumulative.
,,	Assault	,,	,,	3 months ⎭
,,	,,	,,	,,	12 months in default of sureties to keep the peace. Sureties found.
,,	Horse stealing	Beechworth	2.8.71	3 years.
,,	Drunk and assaulting police	Benalla	18.9.77	£3 1s., or 3 months.
,,	Robbery under arms	Kyneton	5.70	Discharged.
,,	Murder and outlawry	Melbourne	11.11.80	*Executed.*
Daniel Kelly	Illegally using a horse	Wangaratta	.71	Discharged.
,,	Wilful damage	Benalla	19.10.77	3 months.
,,	Stealing a saddle	Beechworth	13.10.76	Discharged.
,,	Murder and outlawry	...	28.6.70	*Shot at Glenrowan.*
Ellen Kelly	Abetting shooting	Beechworth	10.78	3 years.
John Lloyd, sen.	Assault	Donnybrook	5.10.60	Discharged.
,,	Drunk and disorderly	Kilmore	21.3.62	,,
,,	Larceny	,,	22.4.62	,,
,,	Cattle stealing	Beechworth	19.10.65	5 years.
,,	Maliciously killing a horse	,,	3.2.73	4 years.
Thomas Lloyd, sen.	Cattle stealing	,,	19.10.65	5 years.
,,	Kelly sympathizer	,,	1.79	Discharged.
Thomas Lloyd, jun.	Wilful damage	Benalla	19.10.77	3 months.
,,	Indecent assault	Beechworth	28.2.78	3 months.
,,	Assaulting police	Benalla	11.3.79	7 days.
,,	Kelly sympathizer	Beechworth	.79	Discharged.
,,	Manslaughter	,,	.79	,,
John Lloyd, jun.	Wilful damage	Benalla	19.10.77	3 months.
,,	Kelly sympathizer	Beechworth	1.79	Discharged.

APPENDIX II

SOME KELLY BALLADS

All but the final one of the following ballads and songs are known to have been sung in Victoria during the lifetime of the Kelly Gang. The author of this book has made his own editions from the varying extant texts.

The Bold Kelly Gang

Oh, there's not a dodge worth knowing,
Or showing, that's going,
But you'll learn – and we're not blowing –
From the bold Kelly Gang.

We have mates where e'er we go
That somehow let us know
The approach of every foe
To the bold Kelly Gang.

There's not a peeler riding
Wombat ranges, hill or siding,
But would rather be in hiding
Though he'd like to see us hang.

We thin their ranks,
We rob the banks,
And don't say thanks,
That's what we do.

Oh, the terror of the camp is the bold Kelly Gang.
So, if you want a spree,
Come with me, and you'll see
How grand it is to be
In the bold Kelly Gang.

Stringybark Creek

A sergeant and three constables set out from Mansfield town,
Near the end of last October for to hunt the Kellys down.
They travelled to the Wombat Hills, and thought it quite a lark
When they camped upon the borders of a creek called Stringybark.

They had grub and ammunition there to last them many a week;
Next morning two of them rode out to search all round the creek,
Leaving McIntyre behind them in the camp to cook the grub,
And Lonigan to sweep the floor, and boss the washing tub.

It was shortly after breakfast that Mac thought he heard a noise,
So, gun in hand, he sallied forth to try and find the cause.
But he never saw the Kellys planted safe behind a log,
So he sauntered back to smoke and yarn, and have a sip of grog.

But Ned Kelly and his comrades thought they'd take a closer look,
For, being short of grub, they wished to interview the cook.
And of fire-arms and cartridges they found they had too few,
So they longed to grab the pistols, guns, and ammunition too.

The troopers at the stump alone they then were pleased to see,
Both watching while their billy boiled to make a cup of tea.
They smoked and chatted gaily, never thinking of alarms,
Till they heard the fearful cry behind: 'Bail up! Throw up your arms!'

The traps, they started wildly, but Mac he firmly stood
With arms thrown up, while Lonigan made tracks to gain the wood
And pull out his revolver; but, before he touched the stock,
Ned Kelly drew his trigger, fired, and dropped him like a rock.

Then after searching McIntyre all through the camp they went,
And cleared the guns and cartridges and pistols from the tent.
But brave Kelly murmured sadly, as he loaded up his gun,
'Oh, what a bloody pity that the bastard tried to run.'

'Twas later in the afternoon the sergeant and his mate
Came riding blithely through the bush to meet a cruel fate.
The Kellys have the drop on you! cried McIntyre aloud,
But the troopers took it as a joke and sat their horses proud.

Then trooper Scanlan made a move his rifle to unsling,
But to his heart a bullet sped and death was in the sting;
Then Kennedy leapt from his mount and ran for cover near,
And fought, a game man to the last, for all that life held dear.

The sergeant's horse raced from the camp alike from friend and foe,
And McIntyre, his life at stake, sprang to the saddle-bow
And galloped far into the night, a haunted, harassed soul,
Then like a hunted bandicoot hid in a wombat hole.

At dawn of day he hastened forth and made for Mansfield town
To break the news that made men vow to shoot the bandits down,
So from that hour the Kelly gang was hunted far and wide,
Like outlawed dingoes of the wild until the day they died.

Stringybark
(a fragment)

>Four of them rode away, that day,
>under a summer sky,
>carrying rifles on their backs.
>'Kelly', they said, 'must die'.
>
>Ned and his three mates kept alert,
>eager to join the fight.
>Dan, Joey Byrne and young Steve Hart
>knew all the police by sight.

Evening it was, at Stringybark,
light faded from the sky.
Lonigan, drowsing by the fire,
yawned, while the Gang passed by.

The Ballad of Kelly's Gang
by Joe Byrne

[Part i was probably written by Joe Byrne. Part ii is more likely pastiche.]

i

Oh, Paddy dear, and did you hear the news that's going 'round?
On the head of bold Ned Kelly they have placed two thousand pound,
And on Steve Hart, Joe Byrne and Dan two thousand more they'd give;
But if the price was doubled, boys, the Kelly Gang would live.
'Tis hard to think such plucky hearts in crime should be employed,
'Tis by police persecution they have all been much annoyed.
Revenge is sweet, and in the bush they can defy the law:
Such bailing-up and plundering you never saw before.

'Twas in November, seventy-eight, the Kelly Gang came down,
Just after shooting Kennedy in famed Euroa town.
Blood horses they all rode upon, revolvers in their hand,
They took the township by surprise, and gold was their demand.
Ned Kelly walked into the bank, a cheque held in his hand,
And to have it changed for money, of Scott he did demand.
And when that Scott refused him, he looked at him dead straight
And said, 'My name's Ned Kelly, and this here man's my mate.'

With pistols pointing at his nut poor Scott just stood amazed,
His stick he would have liked to cut, but was with funk half-crazed.
The poor cashier in dread and fear stood trembling at the knees,
At last they saw it was no use, and handed out the keys.
The safe was quickly gutted then, the drawers turned out as well,
The Kellys being quite polite, like any noble swell.
With flimsies, gold and silver coin, the threepennies and all,
Amounting to two thousand pounds, they made a glorious haul.

'Now hand out all your fire-arms,' the robber boldly said,
'And all your ammunition – or a bullet through your head.
Then jump into this buggy and we'll take you for a drive;
Your wife and family too must come, so make them look alive.'
They drove them to a station about five miles away,
Where twenty other people had been bailed up all the day.
The owner of the station and the men in his employ
And a few unwary travellers their company did enjoy.

An Indian hawker fell in, too, as everybody knows;
He came in handy to the gang by fitting them with clothes.
Then with their worn-out clothing they made a few bonfires,
And next destroyed the telegraph by cutting down the wires.
Throughout the whole affair, my boys, they never fired a shot;
The way they worked was splendid and shall never be forgot.
Where they have gone's a mystery, the troopers cannot tell;
Until I hear from them again, I'll bid yous all farewell.

ii

Oh, Paddy dear, to shed a tear, I can't but sympathise
Those Kellys are the devils, for they made another rise,
This time across the Billabong, where Morgan had his beat,
They've robbed the banks of thousands and in safety did retreat.
The matter may be serious, Pat, but still I can't but laugh,
To think the tales the bobbies told must all amount to chaff.
They said they had them all hemmed in, they could not get
  away,
But they turned up in New South Wales, and made the journey
  pay.

They rode into Jerilderie town at twelve o'clock at night,
Aroused the troopers from their beds and gave them such a
  fright;
They took them in their nightshirts, ashamed I am to tell,
They covered them with guns and then they locked them in a
  cell.
They next informed the women-folk that they were going to
  stay,
And take possession of the camp until the following day.
They fed their horses in the stalls, without the slightest fear,
Then went to rest their weary limbs till daylight did appear.

Next morning being Sunday morn, of course they must be good;
They dressed themselves in troopers' clothes, and Ned he chopped some wood.
No one at all suspected them, for troopers they did pass,
And Dan, the most religious, took the trooper's wife to mass.
They spent the day most pleasantly, had plenty of good cheer,
With fried beef steak and onions, tomato sauce and beer.
The ladies in attendance they indulged in pleasant talk,
And just to ease the troopers' minds, they took them for a walk.

On Monday morning early, still the masters of the ground,
They took their horses to the forge and had them shod all round.
Then back they came and mounted, their plans all laid so well,
In company with the troopers they stuck up the Royal Hotel.
They bailed up all the occupants and placed them in a room,
Saying, 'Do as we command you, or death will be your doom.'
A Chinese cook 'No savvee' cried, not knowing what to fear,
But they brought him to his senses with a blow beneath the ear.

All who approached the house just shared a similar kind of fate,
And in a very little while they numbered twenty-eight.
They shouted freely for all hands and paid for all they drank,
And two of them remained in charge, while two went to the bank.
The farce was here repeated, as I've already told;
They bailed up all the banker's clerks, and robbed them of their gold.
The manager could not be found, and Kelly in great wrath
Searched high and low, and luckily he found him in the bath.

Now when they robbed Euroa bank you said they'd be run down,
But now they've robbed another one that's in Jerilderie town.
That's in Jerilderie town, my boys, and we shall take their part,
And shout again, 'Long may they reign – the Kellys, Byrne and Hart.'
As high above the mountain-tops so beautiful and grand,
Our young Australian heroes in bold defiance stand,
In bold defiance stand, my boys, the heroes of today,
So let us stand together, boys, and shout again, 'Hurray!'

Come All You Wild Colonial Boys

Come all you wild colonial boys, attention to me pay,
For in my song I will unfold the truth without delay.
'Twas of a famous outlawed band that roamed this country round—
Ned Kelly was their captain, and no better could be found.

The Governor of Victoria was a most unpleasant man,
And a warrant he likewise put out to take his brother Dan.
But when one day some troopers came, young Dan to apprehend,
He like a tiger stood at bay, his mother to defend.

Five hundred pounds reward was made for Ned, if he were found,
From place to place they hunted him as if he was a hound.
Now driven to desperation to the bush brave Ned did take,
With Dan, Steve Hart and brave Joe Byrne, all for his mother's sake.

And although they deemed them outlaws, yet brave men they proved to be,
And vengeance ranked in every breast for Kelly's misery.
They burnt his mother's vine-clad hut, which caused his heart to yearn,
And angered his companions, Dan, Steve Hart and brave Joe Byrne.

One day as Ned and his three mates in ambush were concealed,
They spied three mounted troopers and their presence did reveal.
They called to them. 'Surrender!' These words Ned to them said—
'Resist, a man amongst you, and I'll surely shoot you dead.'

Now Kennedy, Scanlon, Lonigan, in fear were lying low,
When Ned amongst them recognised his old and vicious foe;
Then thoughts came of his mother with a baby at her breast,
And it filled Ned's heart with anger, and the country knows the rest.

Up in the Wombat Ranges brave Ned Kelly made his haunt,
And all Victoria's troopers at his name would truly daunt.
For months they lay in ambush till at last they were betrayed
By traitor Aaron Sherritt, and his life the treachery paid.

It was at the Glenrowan station where the conflict raged severe,
When more than fifty policemen at the scene then did appear.
No credit to their bravery, no credit to their name,
Ned Kelly terrified them all and put their blood to shame.

Farewell to Greta

Farewell to my home in Greta, my sister Kate, farewell.
It grieves my heart to leave you, but here I cannot dwell.
They've placed a price upon my head, my hands they've stained with gore,
And I must roam the forest wild, within Australia's shore.

But should they cross my chequered path, by all I hold on earth,
I'll give them cause to rue the day their mothers gave them birth.
I'll shoot them down like kangaroos that roam the forests wide,
And leave their bodies bleaching upon some woodland side.

Oh, Ned, my dearest brother, you know you cannot go
And risk to be encountered by such a mighty foe!
It's duly north lies Morgan's Tower, and pointing to the sky
South-east and East the mighty range of Gippsland mountains lie.

You know the country well, dear Ned, so take your comrades there
Where you may live as freely as the wombat and the bear.
But, quick, here come four troopers; one kiss before we part,
Now haste and join your brother Dan, Joe Byrne and Stevie Hart.

Come All Young Men With Feeling

Come all young men with feeling,
With regret I must unfold;
I have a tale to tell of men
Whose hearts are stout and bold.

The odds against the Kelly gang
Were fifty if not more,
And yet there was not courage
For to face but only four.

Long life unto Kate Kelly,
She was a noble girl;
She appeared upon the scene
In spite of all the world.

For true she loved her brothers,
Likewise the other two;
And so she proved to all the world
Her heart was fair and true.

If any praise be due at all,
Then let the praise be gave
To those four young unfortunates
Who now lie in the grave.

The Ned Kelly Song
(a fragment)

Ned Kelly was born in a ramshackle hut,
   He'd battled since he was a kid:
He grew up with bad men and duffers and thieves,
   And learnt all the bad things they did.

Now down at Glenrowan they held up the pub,
   And were having a drink and a song,
When the troopers rushed up and surrounded the place;
   The Kellys had waited too long.

Some say he's a hero and gave to the poor,
  While others, 'A Killer' they say;
To me it just proves the old saying is true,
  The saying that crime doesn't pay.

Yet when I look round at some people I know,
  And the prices of things that we buy,
I just think to myself, well perhaps, after all,
  Old Ned wasn't such a bad guy.

BIBLIOGRAPHY

Brown, M. *Australian Son* (Melbourne, 1948).
Cave, C. F. and others. *Ned Kelly: Man and Myth* (A Symposium) (Melbourne, 1968).
Clune, F. (Ed) *A Noose for Ned* (Sydney, 1949).
Hare, F. A. *The Last of the Bushrangers* (London, 1892).
Jennings, M. J. *Ned Kelly: The Legend and the Man* (Melbourne, 1968).
Kenneally, J. J. *The Complete Inner History of the Kelly Gang and Their Pursuers* (Melbourne, 1942).
Melville, R. and Nolan, S. *Ned Kelly: 27 Paintings by Sidney Nolan* (London, 1964).
Meredith, J. (Ed.) *Six Authentic Songs from the Kelly Country* (Sydney, 1955).
Stewart, D. *Ned Kelly* (A play) (Sydney, 1946).

GW01339515

מסורה

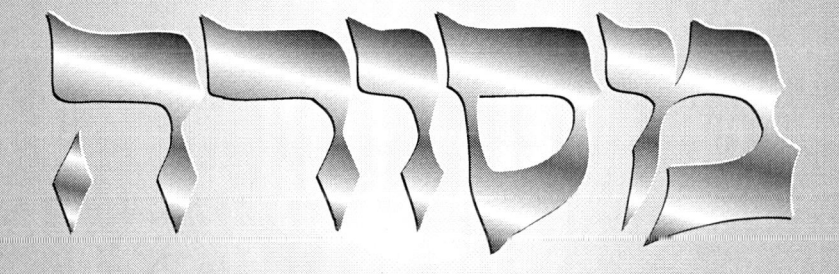

ArtScroll® Series

Rabbi Nosson Scherman / Rabbi Meir Zlotowitz
General Editors

The Answer Is...

Over **1,000** answers to **300** questions

PESACH HAGGADAH
הגדה של פסח

by
Rabbi Chagai Vilosky

Adapted and translated from the
Hebrew *"Haggadah Ki Yish'alcha"* by

Malky Heimowitz and Libby Lazewnik

Published by

ARTSCROLL®
Mesorah Publications, ltd

FIRST EDITION
First Impression ... March 2014

Published and Distributed by
MESORAH PUBLICATIONS, LTD.
4401 Second Avenue / Brooklyn, N.Y 11232

Distributed in Europe by
LEHMANNS
Unit E, Viking Business Park
Rolling Mill Road
Jarow, Tyne & Wear, NE32 3DP
England

Distributed in Australia and New Zealand
by **GOLDS WORLDS OF JUDAICA**
3-13 William Street
Balaclava, Melbourne 3183
Victoria, Australia

Distributed in Israel by
SIFRIATI / A. GITLER — BOOKS
Moshav Magshimim
Israel

Distributed in South Africa by
KOLLEL BOOKSHOP
Northfield Centre, 17 Northfield Avenue
Glenhazel 2192, Johannesburg, South Africa

ARTSCROLL® SERIES
HAGGADAH: THE ANSWER IS...
© Copyright 2014, by MESORAH PUBLICATIONS, Ltd.
4401 Second Avenue / Brooklyn, N.Y. 11232 / (718) 921-9000 / www.artscroll.com

---

ALL RIGHTS RESERVED
The text, prefatory and associated textual contents and introductions
— including the typographic layout, cover artwork and ornamental graphics —
have been designed, edited and revised as to content, form and style.

No part of this book may be reproduced
IN ANY FORM, PHOTOCOPYING, OR COMPUTER RETRIEVAL SYSTEMS
— even for personal use without written permission from
the copyright holder, Mesorah Publications Ltd.
except by a reviewer who wishes to quote brief passages
in connection with a review written for inclusion in magazines or newspapers.

THE RIGHTS OF THE COPYRIGHT HOLDER WILL BE STRICTLY ENFORCED.

ISBN 10: 1-4226-1483-2 / ISBN 13: 978-1-4226-1483-9

Typography by CompuScribe at ArtScroll Studios, Ltd.
Printed in the United States of America by Noble Book Press Corp.
Bound by Sefercraft, Quality Bookbinders, Ltd., Brooklyn N.Y. 11232

Rabbi CHAIM P. SCHEINBERG	**הרב חיים פינחס שיינברג**
Rosh Hayeshiva "TORAH ORE"	ראש ישיבת "תורה אור"
and Morah Hora'ah of Kiryat Mattersdorf	ומורה הוראה דקרית מטרסדורף

בס"ד, חודש אדר ראשון, תשס"ח

מכתב ברכה

הנה הביאו לפני תכריך כתבים גדול על הגדה של פסח, אשר בשם "כי ישאלך" תכונה, וכשמו כן הוא ביאור כל עניני ההגדה בדרך של שאלה ותשובה, אשר חיברו וליקטו הרה"ג ר' חגי וולוסקי שליט"א, וערך את כל עניני הסדר בצורה של שאלה ותשובה וסיכום העניינים, כך שכל עניני ההגדה מבוארים באר היטב ובו דבור על אופניו, ואין ספק שברכה גדולה תהיה בחיבור זה בהבנת עניני ליל הסדר.

וע"כ אמרתי לברכו שחפץ ה' בידו יצלח, ויתקבלו הדברים בלב המעיינים בהגדה זאת, ותרבה הדעת את השם, ויזכה לחבר חיבורים נוספים בתוה"ק ולשבת באהלה של תורה כל ימי חייו.

רחוב פנים מאירות 2, ירושלים, ת.ד. 6979, טל. 537-1513 (02), ישראל
2 Panim Meirot St., Jerusalem, P.O.B. 6979, Tel. (02) 537-1513, Israel

Haskamah to the original Hebrew edition

אשר זעליג וייס
כגן 8
פעיה"ק ירושלם ת"ו

בס"ד   תאריך

Haskamah to the original Hebrew edition

יוסף יחיאל הלוי במרגי
רב הקהילה החרדית חיפה

בס"ד, חיפה ‏‎_____‎

בואו שמעו אגד לרועת ידידי הרב
הג' ולו"מ שלום, אשר התאמץ זרך לפני
האלות שאול הדורש השתמש זהן דבור ההלכה
וז"יש כר שגיש ידנ הדקדק מילי תשורה
הלכה נורה תרה לכל מדיין לכאורה של הלא
כאמור של הסבר אך כי אחתים זאת אמר וגו

יעץ שרכו שיסף להפיק מעניני חידה
ולזכר גדות ולמדיריה

כהפני מונה

הסכמה שניתנה למהדורה הראשונה - תשס"ח

Haskamah to the original Hebrew edition

✥ Introduction

I am grateful to Hashem for granting me the merit of compiling a Haggadah containing questions and answers gleaned from the words of Sages, commentators, and Torah leaders throughout the generations.

A primary objective of the Seder night is for a person to "see himself as though he left Egypt." We achieve this by fulfilling one of the central mitzvos of the Seder night: *sippur Yetzias Mitzrayim*, relating the story of the Exodus.

The mitzvah of *sippur Yetzias Mitzrayim* is incumbent on every Jew, the unlearned and the scholar alike. Even one who is already well versed in the story of the Exodus is obligated to relate and reexperience it, as the Haggadah itself tells us: *Even if we were all men of wisdom, understanding, experience, and knowledge of the Torah — it would still be an obligation upon us to tell about the Exodus from Egypt.*

Chazal instructed that the story of the Exodus be told in question-and-answer style, reflecting the wording of the Torah's commandment to relate this story: וְהָיָה כִּי יִשְׁאָלְךָ בִנְךָ, *And it shall be when your son will ask you* (Exodus 13:14). When a person inquires about something, it generally indicates his interest in the topic, and the answer he receives has a greater influence than his simply hearing a speech. The questioner also becomes an engaged participant in the discussion rather than a dispassionate observer. This is why we go out of our way on the Seder night to pique the children's curiosity with many unique practices designed to prompt them to ask questions.

In keeping with the question-and-answer style of the Seder night, this Haggadah is structured as a compendium of hundreds of questions and answers. This format also allows the leader of the Seder to involve the participants in the mitzvah of *sippur Yetzias Mitzrayim*. (Answers that are not attributed to a source are insights whose source I have not been able to locate.)

Seder night is an auspicious time for strengthening our own *emunah* (faith), and instilling that *emunah* in the hearts of our children. On this night, we have the potential to attain great spiritual heights that we can carry with us through the rest of the year.

May we merit eating of the Pesach sacrifices, and may we sing a song of praise to Hashem to celebrate our final redemption.

ערב פסח / EREV PESACH

בדיקת חמץ

Some say this declaration of intent before searching for chametz:

הִנְנִי מוּכָן וּמְזוּמָן לְקַיֵּם מִצְוַת עֲשֵׂה וְלֹא תַעֲשֶׂה שֶׁל בְּדִיקַת חָמֵץ. לְשֵׁם יִחוּד קוּדְשָׁא בְּרִיךְ הוּא וּשְׁכִינְתֵּיהּ, עַל יְדֵי הַהוּא טָמִיר וְנֶעְלָם, בְּשֵׁם כָּל יִשְׂרָאֵל: וִיהִי נֹעַם אֲדֹנָי אֱלֹהֵינוּ עָלֵינוּ, וּמַעֲשֵׂה יָדֵינוּ כּוֹנְנָה עָלֵינוּ, וּמַעֲשֵׂה יָדֵינוּ כּוֹנְנֵהוּ:

The chametz search is initiated with the recitation of the following blessing:

בָּרוּךְ אַתָּה יהוה אֱלֹהֵינוּ מֶלֶךְ הָעוֹלָם, אֲשֶׁר קִדְּשָׁנוּ בְּמִצְוֹתָיו, וְצִוָּנוּ עַל בִּעוּר חָמֵץ.

Upon completion of the chametz search, the chametz is wrapped well and set aside to be burned the next morning and the following declaration is made. The declaration must be understood in order to take effect; one who does not understand the Aramaic text may recite it in English, Yiddish, or any other language. Any chametz that will be used for that evening's supper or the next day's breakfast or for any other purpose prior to the final removal of chametz the next morning is not included in this declaration.

כָּל חֲמִירָא וַחֲמִיעָא דְּאִכָּא בִרְשׁוּתִי, דְּלָא חֲמִתֵּהּ וּדְלָא בִעַרְתֵּהּ וּדְלָא יְדַעְנָא לֵהּ, לִבָּטֵל וְלֶהֱוֵי הֶפְקֵר כְּעַפְרָא דְאַרְעָא.

ביעור חמץ

The following declaration, which includes all chametz without exception, is to be made after the burning of leftover chametz. It should be recited in a language which one understands. When Passover begins on Saturday night, this declaration is made on Saturday morning. Any chametz remaining from the Saturday morning meal is flushed down the drain before the declaration is made.

Some have the custom to recite the following declaration of intent:

הִנְנִי מוּכָן וּמְזוּמָן לְקַיֵּם מִצְוַת עֲשֵׂה וְלֹא תַעֲשֶׂה שֶׁל שְׂרֵיפַת חָמֵץ, לְשֵׁם יִחוּד קוּדְשָׁא בְּרִיךְ הוּא וּשְׁכִינְתֵּיהּ עַל יְדֵי הַהוּא טָמִיר וְנֶעְלָם בְּשֵׁם כָּל יִשְׂרָאֵל: וִיהִי נֹעַם אֲדֹנָי אֱלֹהֵינוּ עָלֵינוּ, וּמַעֲשֵׂה יָדֵינוּ כּוֹנְנָה עָלֵינוּ, וּמַעֲשֵׂה יָדֵינוּ כּוֹנְנֵהוּ:

THE SEARCH FOR CHAMETZ

Some say this declaration of intent before searching for chametz:

Behold, I am prepared and ready to fulfill the positive and prohibitive mitzvos of searching for *chametz*. For the sake of the unification of the Holy One, Blessed is He, and His presence, through Him Who is hidden and inscrutable — [I pray] in the name of all Israel. May the pleasantness of the Lord, our God, be upon us, and may He establish our handiwork for us; our handiwork may He establish.

The chametz *search is initiated with the recitation of the following blessing:*

Blessed are You, HASHEM, our God, King of the universe, Who has sanctified us with His commandments, and commanded us concerning the removal of *chametz*.

Upon completion of the *chametz* search, the *chametz* is wrapped well and set aside to be burned the next morning and the following declaration is made. The declaration must be understood in order to take effect; one who does not understand the Aramaic text may recite it in English, Yiddish, or any other language. Any *chametz* that will be used for that evening's supper or the next day's breakfast or for any other purpose prior to the final removal of *chametz* the next morning is not included in this declaration.

Any *chametz* which is in my possession which I did not see, and remove, nor know about, shall be nullified and become ownerless, like the dust of the earth.

BURNING THE CHAMETZ

The following declaration, which includes all chametz *without exception, is to be made after the burning of leftover* chametz. *It should be recited in a language which one understands. When Passover begins on Saturday night, this declaration is made on Saturday morning. Any* chametz *remaining from the Saturday morning meal is flushed down the drain before the declaration is made.*

Some have the custom to recite the following declaration of intent:

Behold, I am prepared and ready to fulfill the positive and prohibitive mitzvos of burning *chametz*. For the sake of the unification of the Holy One, Blessed is He, and His presence, through Him Who is hidden and inscrutable — [I pray] in the name of all Israel. May the pleasantness of the Lord, our God, be upon us, and may He establish our handiwork for us; our handiwork may He establish.

כָּל חֲמִירָא וַחֲמִיעָא דְּאִכָּא בִרְשׁוּתִי, דַּחֲזִתֵּהּ וּדְלָא חֲזִתֵּהּ, דַּחֲמִתֵּהּ וּדְלָא חֲמִתֵּהּ, דְּבִעַרְתֵּהּ וּדְלָא בִעַרְתֵּהּ, לִבָּטֵל וְלֶהֱוֵי הֶפְקֵר כְּעַפְרָא דְאַרְעָא.

עירוב תבשילין

It is forbidden to prepare on Yom Tov for the next day even if that day is the Sabbath. If, however, Sabbath preparations were started before Yom Tov began, they may be continued on Yom Tov. The *eruv tavshilin* constitutes this preparation. A matzah and any cooked food (such as fish, meat, or an egg) are set aside on the day before Yom Tov to be used on Sabbath and the blessing is recited followed by the declaration [made in a language understood by the one making the *eruv*]. If the first days of Passover fall on Thursday and Friday, an *eruv tavshilin* must be made on Wednesday.

In Eretz Yisrael, where only one day Yom Tov is in effect, the *eruv* is omitted.

בָּרוּךְ אַתָּה יהוה אֱלֹהֵינוּ מֶלֶךְ הָעוֹלָם, אֲשֶׁר קִדְּשָׁנוּ בְּמִצְוֹתָיו, וְצִוָּנוּ עַל מִצְוַת עֵרוּב.

בַּהֲדֵין עֵרוּבָא יְהֵא שָׁרֵא לָנָא לַאֲפוּיֵי לְבַשּׁוּלֵי וּלְאַצְלוּיֵי וּלְאַטְמוּנֵי וּלְאַדְלוּקֵי שְׁרָגָא וּלְתַקָּנָא וּלְמֶעְבַּד כָּל צָרְכָּנָא, מִיּוֹמָא טָבָא לְשַׁבַּתָּא לָנָא וּלְכָל יִשְׂרָאֵל הַדָּרִים בָּעִיר הַזֹּאת.

סדר אמירת קרבן פסח

After *Minchah*, many customarily recite the following passages that describe the קָרְבַּן פֶּסַח, *pesach*-offering.

רִבּוֹן הָעוֹלָמִים, אַתָּה צִוִּיתָנוּ לְהַקְרִיב קָרְבַּן הַפֶּסַח בְּמוֹעֲדוֹ בְּאַרְבָּעָה עָשָׂר יוֹם לַחֹדֶשׁ הָרִאשׁוֹן, וְלִהְיוֹת כֹּהֲנִים בַּעֲבוֹדָתָם וּלְוִיִּים בְּדוּכָנָם וְיִשְׂרָאֵל בְּמַעֲמָדָם קוֹרְאִים אֶת הַהַלֵּל.

Any *chametz* which is in my possession which I did or did not see, which I did or did not remove, shall be nullified and become ownerless, like the dust of the earth.

THE ERUV TAVSHILIN

It is forbidden to prepare on Yom Tov for the next day even if that day is the Sabbath. If, however, Sabbath preparations were started before Yom Tov began, they may be continued on Yom Tov. The *eruv tavshilin* constitutes this preparation. A matzah and any cooked food (such as fish, meat, or an egg) are set aside on the day before Yom Tov to be used on Sabbath and the blessing is recited followed by the declaration [made in a language understood by the one making the *eruv*]. If the first days of Passover fall on Thursday and Friday, an *eruv tavshilin* must be made on Wednesday.

In Eretz Yisrael, where only one day Yom Tov is in effect, the *eruv* is omitted.

Blessed are You, HASHEM, our God, King of the universe, Who sanctified us by His commandments and commanded us concerning the commandment of *Eruv*.

Through this *Eruv* may we be permitted to bake, cook, fry, insulate, kindle flame, prepare for, and do anything necessary on the Festival for the sake of the Shabbos — for ourselves and for all Jews who live in this city.

KORBAN PESACH

After *Minchah*, many customarily recite the following passages that describe the קָרְבַּן פֶּסַח, *pesach*-offering.

Master of the universe, You commanded us to bring the *pesach*-offering at its set time, on the fourteenth day of the first month; and that the Kohanim be at their assigned service, the Levites on their platform, and the Israelites at their station reciting the *Hallel*.

וְעַתָּה בַּעֲוֹנוֹתֵינוּ חָרַב בֵּית הַמִּקְדָּשׁ וּבָטֵל קָרְבַּן הַפֶּסַח, וְאֵין לָנוּ לֹא כֹהֵן בַּעֲבוֹדָתוֹ וְלֹא לֵוִי בְּדוּכָנוֹ וְלֹא יִשְׂרָאֵל בְּמַעֲמָדוֹ, וְלֹא נוּכַל לְהַקְרִיב הַיּוֹם קָרְבַּן פֶּסַח. אֲבָל אַתָּה אָמַרְתָּ וּנְשַׁלְּמָה פָרִים שְׂפָתֵינוּ. לָכֵן יְהִי רָצוֹן מִלְּפָנֶיךָ יְהֹוָה אֱלֹהֵינוּ וֵאלֹהֵי אֲבוֹתֵינוּ שֶׁיִּהְיֶה שִׂיחַ שְׂפָתוֹתֵינוּ חָשׁוּב לְפָנֶיךָ כְּאִלּוּ הִקְרַבְנוּ אֶת הַפֶּסַח בְּמוֹעֲדוֹ וְעָמַדְנוּ עַל מַעֲמָדוֹ, וְדִבְּרוּ הַלְוִיִּים בְּשִׁיר וְהַלֵּל לְהוֹדוֹת לַיהוָֹה. וְאַתָּה תְּכוֹנֵן מִקְדָּשְׁךָ עַל מְכוֹנוֹ, וְנַעֲשֶׂה וְנַקְרִיב לְפָנֶיךָ אֶת הַפֶּסַח בְּמוֹעֲדוֹ, כְּמוֹ שֶׁכָּתַבְתָּ עָלֵינוּ בְּתוֹרָתֶךָ עַל יְדֵי מֹשֶׁה עַבְדְּךָ כָּאָמוּר:

שמות יב:א-יא

וַיֹּאמֶר יְהֹוָה אֶל מֹשֶׁה וְאֶל אַהֲרֹן בְּאֶרֶץ מִצְרַיִם לֵאמֹר. הַחֹדֶשׁ הַזֶּה לָכֶם רֹאשׁ חֳדָשִׁים רִאשׁוֹן הוּא לָכֶם לְחָדְשֵׁי הַשָּׁנָה. דַּבְּרוּ אֶל כָּל עֲדַת יִשְׂרָאֵל לֵאמֹר בֶּעָשֹׂר לַחֹדֶשׁ הַזֶּה וְיִקְחוּ לָהֶם אִישׁ שֶׂה לְבֵית אָבֹת שֶׂה לַבָּיִת. וְאִם יִמְעַט הַבַּיִת מִהְיוֹת מִשֶּׂה וְלָקַח הוּא וּשְׁכֵנוֹ הַקָּרֹב אֶל בֵּיתוֹ בְּמִכְסַת נְפָשֹׁת אִישׁ לְפִי אָכְלוֹ תָּכֹסּוּ עַל הַשֶּׂה. שֶׂה תָמִים זָכָר בֶּן שָׁנָה יִהְיֶה לָכֶם מִן הַכְּבָשִׂים וּמִן הָעִזִּים תִּקָּחוּ. וְהָיָה לָכֶם לְמִשְׁמֶרֶת עַד אַרְבָּעָה עָשָׂר יוֹם לַחֹדֶשׁ הַזֶּה וְשָׁחֲטוּ אֹתוֹ כֹּל קְהַל עֲדַת יִשְׂרָאֵל בֵּין הָעַרְבָּיִם. וְלָקְחוּ מִן הַדָּם וְנָתְנוּ עַל שְׁתֵּי הַמְּזוּזֹת וְעַל הַמַּשְׁקוֹף עַל הַבָּתִּים אֲשֶׁר יֹאכְלוּ אֹתוֹ בָּהֶם. וְאָכְלוּ אֶת הַבָּשָׂר בַּלַּיְלָה הַזֶּה צְלִי אֵשׁ וּמַצּוֹת עַל מְרֹרִים יֹאכְלֻהוּ. אַל תֹּאכְלוּ מִמֶּנּוּ נָא וּבָשֵׁל מְבֻשָּׁל בַּמָּיִם כִּי אִם צְלִי אֵשׁ רֹאשׁוֹ עַל כְּרָעָיו וְעַל קִרְבּוֹ. וְלֹא תוֹתִירוּ מִמֶּנּוּ עַד בֹּקֶר וְהַנֹּתָר מִמֶּנּוּ עַד בֹּקֶר בָּאֵשׁ תִּשְׂרֹפוּ. וְכָכָה תֹּאכְלוּ

But now, through our sins, the Holy Temple is destroyed, the *pesach*-offering is discontinued, and we have neither Kohen at his service, nor Levite on his platform, nor Israelite at his station. So we are unable to bring the *pesach*-offering today. But You said: "Let our lips compensate for the bulls" — therefore, may it be Your will, HASHEM, our God and the God of our forefathers, that the prayer of our lips be considered by You as if we had brought the *pesach*- offering at its set time, had stood at its station, and the Levites had uttered song and *Hallel*, to thank HASHEM. And may You establish Your sanctuary on its prepared site, that we may ascend and bring the *pesach*-offering before You at its set time — as You have prescribed for us in Your Torah, through Moshe, Your servant, as it is said:

Exodus 12:1-11

And HASHEM said to Moshe and Aharon in the land of Egypt, saying: This month shall be for you the beginning of the months, it shall be for you the first of the months of the year. Speak to the entire assembly of Israel saying: On the tenth of this month, they shall take for themselves — each man — a lamb or kid for each father's house, a lamb or kid for the household. But if the household will be too small for a lamb or kid, then he and his neighbor who is near his house shall take according to the number of people; everyone according to what he eats shall be counted a lamb/kid. An unblemished lamb or kid, a male, within its first year shall it be for you; from the sheep or goats shall you take it. It shall be yours for examination until the fourteenth day of this month; the entire congregation of the assembly of Israel shall slaughter it in the afternoon. They shall take some of its blood and they shall place it on the two doorposts and on the lintel of the houses in which they will eat it. They shall eat the meat on that night — roasted over the fire — and matzos; with bitter herbs shall they eat it. You shall not eat it partially roasted or cooked in water, only roasted over fire — its head, its legs, with its innards. You shall not leave any of it until morning; any of it that is left until morning you shall burn in the fire. So shall you eat

אֹתוֹ מָתְנֵיכֶם חֲגֻרִים נַעֲלֵיכֶם בְּרַגְלֵיכֶם וּמַקֶּלְכֶם בְּיֶדְכֶם וַאֲכַלְתֶּם אֹתוֹ בְּחִפָּזוֹן פֶּסַח הוּא לַיהוה.

Some recite the following ten Scriptural passages as part of the recital of the *korban Pesach*. Others continue on p. 18.

שמות יב:כא-כח

וַיִּקְרָא מֹשֶׁה לְכָל זִקְנֵי יִשְׂרָאֵל וַיֹּאמֶר אֲלֵהֶם מִשְׁכוּ וּקְחוּ לָכֶם צֹאן לְמִשְׁפְּחֹתֵיכֶם וְשַׁחֲטוּ הַפָּסַח. וּלְקַחְתֶּם אֲגֻדַּת אֵזוֹב וּטְבַלְתֶּם בַּדָּם אֲשֶׁר בַּסַּף וְהִגַּעְתֶּם אֶל הַמַּשְׁקוֹף וְאֶל שְׁתֵּי הַמְּזוּזֹת מִן הַדָּם אֲשֶׁר בַּסָּף וְאַתֶּם לֹא תֵצְאוּ אִישׁ מִפֶּתַח בֵּיתוֹ עַד בֹּקֶר. וְעָבַר יהוה לִנְגֹּף אֶת מִצְרַיִם וְרָאָה אֶת הַדָּם עַל הַמַּשְׁקוֹף וְעַל שְׁתֵּי הַמְּזוּזֹת וּפָסַח יהוה עַל הַפֶּתַח וְלֹא יִתֵּן הַמַּשְׁחִית לָבֹא אֶל בָּתֵּיכֶם לִנְגֹּף. וּשְׁמַרְתֶּם אֶת הַדָּבָר הַזֶּה לְחָק לְךָ וּלְבָנֶיךָ עַד עוֹלָם.

וְהָיָה כִּי תָבֹאוּ אֶל הָאָרֶץ אֲשֶׁר יִתֵּן יהוה לָכֶם כַּאֲשֶׁר דִּבֵּר וּשְׁמַרְתֶּם אֶת הָעֲבֹדָה הַזֹּאת. וְהָיָה כִּי יֹאמְרוּ אֲלֵיכֶם בְּנֵיכֶם מָה הָעֲבֹדָה הַזֹּאת לָכֶם. וַאֲמַרְתֶּם זֶבַח פֶּסַח הוּא לַיהוה אֲשֶׁר פָּסַח עַל בָּתֵּי בְנֵי יִשְׂרָאֵל בְּמִצְרַיִם בְּנָגְפּוֹ אֶת מִצְרַיִם וְאֶת בָּתֵּינוּ הִצִּיל וַיִּקֹּד הָעָם וַיִּשְׁתַּחֲווּ. וַיֵּלְכוּ וַיַּעֲשׂוּ בְּנֵי יִשְׂרָאֵל כַּאֲשֶׁר צִוָּה יהוה אֶת מֹשֶׁה וְאַהֲרֹן כֵּן עָשׂוּ.

שמות יב:מג-נ

וַיֹּאמֶר יהוה אֶל מֹשֶׁה וְאַהֲרֹן זֹאת חֻקַּת הַפָּסַח כָּל בֶּן נֵכָר לֹא יֹאכַל בּוֹ. וְכָל עֶבֶד אִישׁ מִקְנַת כָּסֶף וּמַלְתָּה אֹתוֹ אָז יֹאכַל בּוֹ. תּוֹשָׁב וְשָׂכִיר לֹא יֹאכַל בּוֹ. בְּבַיִת אֶחָד יֵאָכֵל לֹא תוֹצִיא מִן הַבַּיִת מִן הַבָּשָׂר חוּצָה וְעֶצֶם לֹא תִשְׁבְּרוּ בוֹ. כָּל עֲדַת יִשְׂרָאֵל יַעֲשׂוּ אֹתוֹ.

וְכִי יָגוּר אִתְּךָ גֵּר וְעָשָׂה פֶסַח לַיהוה הִמּוֹל לוֹ כָל זָכָר וְאָז יִקְרַב לַעֲשֹׂתוֹ וְהָיָה כְּאֶזְרַח הָאָרֶץ וְכָל עָרֵל לֹא יֹאכַל בּוֹ. תּוֹרָה אַחַת יִהְיֶה לָאֶזְרָח וְלַגֵּר הַגָּר בְּתוֹכְכֶם. וַיַּעֲשׂוּ כָּל בְּנֵי יִשְׂרָאֵל כַּאֲשֶׁר צִוָּה יהוה אֶת מֹשֶׁה וְאֶת אַהֲרֹן כֵּן עָשׂוּ.

הגדה של פסח [8]

it: your loins girded, your shoes on your feet, and your staff in your hand; you shall eat it in haste — it is a *pesach*-offering to HASHEM.

Some recite the following ten Scriptural passages as part of the recital of the *korban Pesach*. Others continue on p. 18.

Exodus 12:21-28

Moshe called to all the elders of Israel and said to them, "Draw forth or buy yourselves one of the flock for your families, and slaughter the *pesach*-offering. You shall take a bundle of hyssop and dip it into the blood that is in the basin, and touch the lintel and the two doorposts with some of the blood that is in the basin, and as for you, you shall not leave the entrance of your house until morning. HASHEM will pass through to smite Egypt, and He will see the blood that is on the lintel and the two doorposts; and HASHEM will pass over the entrance and He will not permit the destroyer to enter your homes to smite. You shall observe this matter as a decree for yourself and for your children forever.

"It shall be that when you come to the land that HASHEM will give you, as He has spoken, you shall observe this service. And it shall be that when your children say to you, 'What is this service to you?' You shall say, 'It is a *pesach* feast-offering to HASHEM, Who passed over the houses of the Children of Israel in Egypt when He smote the Egyptians, but He saved our households,'" and the people bowed their heads and prostrated themselves. The Children of Israel went and did as HASHEM commanded Moshe and Aharon, so did they do.

Exodus 12:43-50

HASHEM said to Moshe and Aharon, "This is the decree of the *pesach*-offering: no alienated person may eat of it. Every slave of a man, who was bought for money, you shall circumcise him; then he may eat of it. A sojourner and a hired laborer may not eat of it. In one house shall it be eaten; you shall not remove any of the meat [of the *korban Pesach*] from the house to the outside, and you shall not break a bone in it. The entire assembly of Israel shall perform it.

"When a proselyte sojourns among you he shall make the *pesach*-offering for HASHEM; each of his males shall be circumcised, and then he may draw near to perform it and he shall be like the native of the land; no uncircumcised male may eat from it. One law shall there be for the native and the proselyte who lives among you." All the Children of Israel did as HASHEM had commanded Moshe and Aharon, so did they do.

HAGGADAH: THE ANSWER IS . . .

ויקרא כג:ד-ה

אֵלֶּה מוֹעֲדֵי יהוה מִקְרָאֵי קֹדֶשׁ אֲשֶׁר תִּקְרְאוּ אֹתָם בְּמוֹעֲדָם. בַּחֹדֶשׁ הָרִאשׁוֹן בְּאַרְבָּעָה עָשָׂר לַחֹדֶשׁ בֵּין הָעַרְבָּיִם פֶּסַח לַיהוה.

במדבר ט:א-יד

וַיְדַבֵּר יהוה אֶל מֹשֶׁה בְמִדְבַּר סִינַי בַּשָּׁנָה הַשֵּׁנִית לְצֵאתָם מֵאֶרֶץ מִצְרַיִם בַּחֹדֶשׁ הָרִאשׁוֹן לֵאמֹר. וְיַעֲשׂוּ בְנֵי יִשְׂרָאֵל אֶת הַפָּסַח בְּמוֹעֲדוֹ. בְּאַרְבָּעָה עָשָׂר יוֹם בַּחֹדֶשׁ הַזֶּה בֵּין הָעַרְבַּיִם תַּעֲשׂוּ אֹתוֹ בְּמֹעֲדוֹ כְּכָל חֻקֹּתָיו וּכְכָל מִשְׁפָּטָיו תַּעֲשׂוּ אֹתוֹ. וַיְדַבֵּר מֹשֶׁה אֶל בְּנֵי יִשְׂרָאֵל לַעֲשֹׂת הַפָּסַח. וַיַּעֲשׂוּ אֶת הַפֶּסַח בָּרִאשׁוֹן בְּאַרְבָּעָה עָשָׂר יוֹם לַחֹדֶשׁ בֵּין הָעַרְבַּיִם בְּמִדְבַּר סִינָי כְּכֹל אֲשֶׁר צִוָּה יהוה אֶת מֹשֶׁה כֵּן עָשׂוּ בְּנֵי יִשְׂרָאֵל. וַיְהִי אֲנָשִׁים אֲשֶׁר הָיוּ טְמֵאִים לְנֶפֶשׁ אָדָם וְלֹא יָכְלוּ לַעֲשֹׂת הַפֶּסַח בַּיּוֹם הַהוּא וַיִּקְרְבוּ לִפְנֵי מֹשֶׁה וְלִפְנֵי אַהֲרֹן בַּיּוֹם הַהוּא. וַיֹּאמְרוּ הָאֲנָשִׁים הָהֵמָּה אֵלָיו אֲנַחְנוּ טְמֵאִים לְנֶפֶשׁ אָדָם לָמָּה נִגָּרַע לְבִלְתִּי הַקְרִיב אֶת קָרְבַּן יהוה בְּמֹעֲדוֹ בְּתוֹךְ בְּנֵי יִשְׂרָאֵל.

וַיֹּאמֶר אֲלֵהֶם מֹשֶׁה עִמְדוּ וְאֶשְׁמְעָה מַה יְצַוֶּה יהוה לָכֶם. וַיְדַבֵּר יהוה אֶל מֹשֶׁה לֵּאמֹר. דַּבֵּר אֶל בְּנֵי יִשְׂרָאֵל לֵאמֹר אִישׁ אִישׁ כִּי יִהְיֶה טָמֵא לָנֶפֶשׁ אוֹ בְדֶרֶךְ רְחֹקָה לָכֶם אוֹ לְדֹרֹתֵיכֶם וְעָשָׂה פֶסַח לַיהוה. בַּחֹדֶשׁ הַשֵּׁנִי בְּאַרְבָּעָה עָשָׂר יוֹם בֵּין הָעַרְבַּיִם יַעֲשׂוּ אֹתוֹ עַל מַצּוֹת וּמְרֹרִים יֹאכְלֻהוּ. לֹא יַשְׁאִירוּ מִמֶּנּוּ עַד בֹּקֶר וְעֶצֶם לֹא יִשְׁבְּרוּ בוֹ כְּכָל חֻקַּת הַפֶּסַח יַעֲשׂוּ אֹתוֹ: וְהָאִישׁ אֲשֶׁר הוּא טָהוֹר וּבְדֶרֶךְ לֹא הָיָה וְחָדַל לַעֲשׂוֹת הַפֶּסַח וְנִכְרְתָה הַנֶּפֶשׁ הַהִוא מֵעַמֶּיהָ כִּי קָרְבַּן יהוה לֹא הִקְרִיב בְּמֹעֲדוֹ חֶטְאוֹ יִשָּׂא הָאִישׁ הַהוּא. וְכִי יָגוּר אִתְּכֶם גֵּר וְעָשָׂה פֶסַח לַיהוה כְּחֻקַּת הַפֶּסַח וּכְמִשְׁפָּטוֹ כֵּן יַעֲשֶׂה חֻקָּה אַחַת יִהְיֶה לָכֶם וְלַגֵּר וּלְאֶזְרַח הָאָרֶץ.

Leviticus 23:4-5

These are the appointed Festivals of HASHEM, the holy convocations, which you shall designate in their appropriate time. In the first month on the fourteenth of the month in the afternoon is the time of the *pesach*-offering to HASHEM.

Numbers 9:1-14

HASHEM spoke to Moshe, in the Wilderness of Sinai, in the second year from their exodus from the land of Egypt, in the first month, saying: "The Children of Israel shall make the *pesach*-offering in its appointed time. On the fourteenth day of this month in the afternoon shall you make it, in its appointed time; according to all its decrees and laws shall you make it."

Moshe spoke to the Children of Israel to make the *pesach*-offering. They made the *pesach*-offering in the first [month], on the fourteenth day of the month, in the afternoon, in the Wilderness of Sinai; according to everything that HASHEM had commanded Moshe, so the Children of Israel did.

There were men who had been contaminated by a human corpse and could not make the *pesach*-offering on that day; so they approached Moshe and Aharon on that day. And those men said to him, "We are unclean through contact with a dead person; why should we be deprived of offering HASHEM's sacrifice in its time among the Children of Israel?"

Moshe said to them, "Stand and I will hear what HASHEM will command you."

HASHEM spoke to Moshe, saying, "Speak to the Children of Israel, saying: If any man will become contaminated through a human corpse or on a distant road, whether you or your generations, he shall make the *pesach*-offering for HASHEM, in the second month, on the fourteenth day, in the afternoon, shall they make it; with matzos and bitter herbs shall they eat it. They shall not leave over from it until morning nor shall they break a bone of it; like all the decrees of the *pesach*-offering shall they make it. But a man who is pure and was not on the road and had refrained from making the *pesach*-offering, that soul shall be cut off from its people, for he had not offered HASHEM's offering in its appointed time; that man will bear his sin. When a convert shall dwell with you, and he shall make a *pesach*-offering to HASHEM, according to the decree of the *pesach*-offering and its law, so shall he do; one decree shall be for you, for the proselyte and the native of the Land."

[11] **HAGGADAH: THE ANSWER IS . . .**

במדבר כח:טז

וּבַחֹדֶשׁ הָרִאשׁוֹן בְּאַרְבָּעָה עָשָׂר יוֹם לַחֹדֶשׁ פֶּסַח לַיהוה.

דברים טז:א-ח

שָׁמוֹר אֶת חֹדֶשׁ הָאָבִיב וְעָשִׂיתָ פֶּסַח לַיהוה אֱלֹהֶיךָ כִּי בְּחֹדֶשׁ הָאָבִיב הוֹצִיאֲךָ יהוה אֱלֹהֶיךָ מִמִּצְרַיִם לָיְלָה. וְזָבַחְתָּ פֶּסַח לַיהוה אֱלֹהֶיךָ צֹאן וּבָקָר בַּמָּקוֹם אֲשֶׁר יִבְחַר יהוה לְשַׁכֵּן שְׁמוֹ שָׁם. לֹא תֹאכַל עָלָיו חָמֵץ שִׁבְעַת יָמִים תֹּאכַל עָלָיו מַצּוֹת לֶחֶם עֹנִי כִּי בְחִפָּזוֹן יָצָאתָ מֵאֶרֶץ מִצְרַיִם לְמַעַן תִּזְכֹּר אֶת יוֹם צֵאתְךָ מֵאֶרֶץ מִצְרַיִם כֹּל יְמֵי חַיֶּיךָ. וְלֹא יֵרָאֶה לְךָ שְׂאֹר בְּכָל גְּבֻלְךָ שִׁבְעַת יָמִים וְלֹא יָלִין מִן הַבָּשָׂר אֲשֶׁר תִּזְבַּח בָּעֶרֶב בַּיּוֹם הָרִאשׁוֹן לַבֹּקֶר. לֹא תוּכַל לִזְבֹּחַ אֶת הַפָּסַח בְּאַחַד שְׁעָרֶיךָ אֲשֶׁר יהוה אֱלֹהֶיךָ נֹתֵן לָךְ. כִּי אִם אֶל הַמָּקוֹם אֲשֶׁר יִבְחַר יהוה אֱלֹהֶיךָ לְשַׁכֵּן שְׁמוֹ שָׁם תִּזְבַּח אֶת הַפֶּסַח בָּעָרֶב כְּבוֹא הַשֶּׁמֶשׁ מוֹעֵד צֵאתְךָ מִמִּצְרָיִם. וּבִשַּׁלְתָּ וְאָכַלְתָּ בַּמָּקוֹם אֲשֶׁר יִבְחַר יהוה אֱלֹהֶיךָ בּוֹ וּפָנִיתָ בַבֹּקֶר וְהָלַכְתָּ לְאֹהָלֶיךָ. שֵׁשֶׁת יָמִים תֹּאכַל מַצּוֹת וּבַיּוֹם הַשְּׁבִיעִי עֲצֶרֶת לַיהוה אֱלֹהֶיךָ לֹא תַעֲשֶׂה מְלָאכָה.

יהושע ה:י-יא

וַיַּחֲנוּ בְנֵי יִשְׂרָאֵל בַּגִּלְגָּל וַיַּעֲשׂוּ אֶת הַפֶּסַח בְּאַרְבָּעָה עָשָׂר יוֹם לַחֹדֶשׁ בָּעֶרֶב בְּעַרְבוֹת יְרִיחוֹ. וַיֹּאכְלוּ מֵעֲבוּר הָאָרֶץ מִמָּחֳרַת הַפֶּסַח מַצּוֹת וְקָלוּי בְּעֶצֶם הַיּוֹם הַזֶּה.

מלכים ב כג:כא-כב

וַיְצַו הַמֶּלֶךְ אֶת כָּל הָעָם לֵאמֹר עֲשׂוּ פֶסַח לַיהוה אֱלֹהֵיכֶם כַּכָּתוּב עַל סֵפֶר הַבְּרִית הַזֶּה. כִּי לֹא נַעֲשָׂה כַּפֶּסַח הַזֶּה מִימֵי הַשֹּׁפְטִים אֲשֶׁר שָׁפְטוּ אֶת יִשְׂרָאֵל וְכֹל יְמֵי מַלְכֵי יִשְׂרָאֵל וּמַלְכֵי יְהוּדָה: כִּי אִם בִּשְׁמֹנֶה עֶשְׂרֵה שָׁנָה לַמֶּלֶךְ יֹאשִׁיָּהוּ נַעֲשָׂה הַפֶּסַח הַזֶּה לַיהוה בִּירוּשָׁלָםִ:

Numbers 28:16

In the first month, on the fourteenth day of the month, shall be a *pesach*-offering to HASHEM.

Deuteronomy 16:1-8

You shall observe the month of springtime and perform the *pesach*-offering for HASHEM, your God, for in the month of springtime HASHEM, your God, took you out of Egypt at night. You shall slaughter the *pesach*-offering to HASHEM, your God, from the flock, and [also offer] cattle, in the place where HASHEM will choose to rest His Name. You shall not eat leavened bread with it, for seven days you shall eat matzos because of it, bread of affliction, for you departed from the land of Egypt in haste — so that you will remember the day of your departure from the land of Egypt all the days of your life.

No leaven of yours shall be seen throughout your boundary for seven days, nor shall any of the flesh that you offer on the afternoon before the first day remain overnight until morning. You may not slaughter the *pesach*-offering in one of your cities that HASHEM, your God, gives you; except at the place that HASHEM, your God, will choose to rest His Name, there shall you slaughter the *pesach*- offering in the afternoon, when the sun descends, the appointed time of your departure from Egypt. You shall roast it and eat it in the place that HASHEM, your God, will choose, and in the morning you may turn back and go to your tents. For a six-day period you shall eat matzos and on the seventh day shall be an assembly to HASHEM, your God; you shall not perform any labor.

Joshua 5:10-11

The Children of Israel encamped at Gilgal and performed the *pesach*-offering on the fourteenth day of the month in the evening, in the plains of Jericho. They ate from the grain of the land on the day after the *pesach*-offering, matzos and roasted grain, on this very day.

II Kings 23:21-22

The king then commanded the people, saying, "Perform the *pesach*-offering unto HASHEM your God, as written in this Book of the Covenant." For such a *pesach*-offering had not been celebrated since the days of the Judges who judged Israel, and all the days of the kings of Israel and the kings of Judah; but in the eighteenth year of King Yoshiyahu this Pesach was celebrated unto HASHEM in Jerusalem.

[13] **HAGGADAH: THE ANSWER IS . . .**

דברי הימים ב ל:א-כ

וַיִּשְׁלַח יְחִזְקִיָּהוּ עַל כָּל יִשְׂרָאֵל וִיהוּדָה וְגַם אִגְּרוֹת כָּתַב עַל אֶפְרַיִם וּמְנַשֶּׁה לָבוֹא לְבֵית יְהֹוָה בִּירוּשָׁלָם לַעֲשׂוֹת פֶּסַח לַיהֹוָה אֱלֹהֵי יִשְׂרָאֵל. וַיִּוָּעַץ הַמֶּלֶךְ וְשָׂרָיו וְכָל הַקָּהָל בִּירוּשָׁלָם לַעֲשׂוֹת הַפֶּסַח בַּחֹדֶשׁ הַשֵּׁנִי. כִּי לֹא יָכְלוּ לַעֲשֹׂתוֹ בָּעֵת הַהִיא כִּי הַכֹּהֲנִים לֹא הִתְקַדְּשׁוּ לְמַדַּי וְהָעָם לֹא נֶאֶסְפוּ לִירוּשָׁלָם. וַיִּישַׁר הַדָּבָר בְּעֵינֵי הַמֶּלֶךְ וּבְעֵינֵי כָּל הַקָּהָל: וַיַּעֲמִידוּ דָבָר לְהַעֲבִיר קוֹל בְּכָל יִשְׂרָאֵל מִבְּאֵר שֶׁבַע וְעַד דָּן לָבוֹא לַעֲשׂוֹת פֶּסַח לַיהֹוָה אֱלֹהֵי יִשְׂרָאֵל בִּירוּשָׁלָם כִּי לֹא לָרֹב עָשׂוּ כַּכָּתוּב: וַיֵּלְכוּ הָרָצִים בָּאִגְּרוֹת מִיַּד הַמֶּלֶךְ וְשָׂרָיו בְּכָל יִשְׂרָאֵל וִיהוּדָה וּכְמִצְוַת הַמֶּלֶךְ לֵאמֹר בְּנֵי יִשְׂרָאֵל שׁוּבוּ אֶל יְהֹוָה אֱלֹהֵי אַבְרָהָם יִצְחָק וְיִשְׂרָאֵל וְיָשֹׁב אֶל הַפְּלֵיטָה הַנִּשְׁאֶרֶת לָכֶם מִכַּף מַלְכֵי אַשּׁוּר. וְאַל תִּהְיוּ כַּאֲבוֹתֵיכֶם וְכַאֲחֵיכֶם אֲשֶׁר מָעֲלוּ בַּיהֹוָה אֱלֹהֵי אֲבוֹתֵיהֶם וַיִּתְּנֵם לְשַׁמָּה כַּאֲשֶׁר אַתֶּם רֹאִים: עַתָּה אַל תַּקְשׁוּ עָרְפְּכֶם כַּאֲבוֹתֵיכֶם תְּנוּ יָד לַיהֹוָה וּבֹאוּ לְמִקְדָּשׁוֹ אֲשֶׁר הִקְדִּישׁ לְעוֹלָם וְעִבְדוּ אֶת יְהֹוָה אֱלֹהֵיכֶם וְיָשֹׁב מִכֶּם חֲרוֹן אַפּוֹ: כִּי בְשׁוּבְכֶם עַל יְהֹוָה אֲחֵיכֶם וּבְנֵיכֶם לְרַחֲמִים לִפְנֵי שׁוֹבֵיהֶם וְלָשׁוּב לָאָרֶץ הַזֹּאת כִּי חַנּוּן וְרַחוּם יְהֹוָה אֱלֹהֵיכֶם וְלֹא יָסִיר פָּנִים מִכֶּם אִם תָּשׁוּבוּ אֵלָיו: וַיִּהְיוּ הָרָצִים עֹבְרִים מֵעִיר לָעִיר בְּאֶרֶץ אֶפְרַיִם וּמְנַשֶּׁה וְעַד זְבֻלוּן וַיִּהְיוּ מַשְׂחִיקִים עֲלֵיהֶם וּמַלְעִגִים בָּם. אַךְ אֲנָשִׁים מֵאָשֵׁר וּמְנַשֶּׁה וּמִזְּבֻלוּן נִכְנְעוּ וַיָּבֹאוּ לִירוּשָׁלָם. גַּם בִּיהוּדָה הָיְתָה יַד הָאֱלֹהִים לָתֵת לָהֶם לֵב אֶחָד לַעֲשׂוֹת מִצְוַת הַמֶּלֶךְ וְהַשָּׂרִים בִּדְבַר יְהֹוָה. וַיֵּאָסְפוּ יְרוּשָׁלַם עַם רָב לַעֲשׂוֹת אֶת חַג הַמַּצּוֹת בַּחֹדֶשׁ הַשֵּׁנִי קָהָל לָרֹב מְאֹד. וַיָּקֻמוּ וַיָּסִירוּ אֶת הַמִּזְבְּחוֹת אֲשֶׁר בִּירוּשָׁלָם וְאֵת כָּל הַמְקַטְּרוֹת הֵסִירוּ וַיַּשְׁלִיכוּ לְנַחַל קִדְרוֹן. וַיִּשְׁחֲטוּ הַפֶּסַח בְּאַרְבָּעָה עָשָׂר לַחֹדֶשׁ הַשֵּׁנִי וְהַכֹּהֲנִים וְהַלְוִיִּם נִכְלְמוּ וַיִּתְקַדְּשׁוּ וַיָּבִיאוּ עֹלוֹת

הגדה של פסח [14]

II Chronicles 30:1-20

Chizkiyahu then sent word to all of Israel and Judah, and also wrote letters to Ephraim and Menasheh to come to the Temple of HASHEM in Jerusalem to perform the *pesach*-offering to HASHEM, God of Israel. For the king and his officers and all the congregation had conferred and decided to perform the *pesach*-offering in the second month, for they had not been able to perform it at its [proper] time, for the Kohanim had not yet sanctified themselves in sufficient numbers, and the people had not been gathered to Jerusalem by then. The matter was deemed proper by the king and all of the congregation. They established the matter to make an announcement throughout all of Israel, from Beer-sheva to Dan, to come and perform the *pesach*-offering unto HASHEM, God of Israel, in Jerusalem, because for a long time they had not done in accordance with what was written.

The runners went throughout all of Israel and Judah with the letters from the hand of the king and his leaders, and by order of the king, saying, "Return to HASHEM, the God of Avraham, Yitzchak, and Yisrael, and He will return to the remnant of you that still remains from the hands of the kings of Ashur. Do not be like your fathers and brothers who betrayed HASHEM, the God of their forefathers, so that He made them into a desolation, as you see. Do not stiffen your necks now as your fathers did! Reach out to HASHEM and come to His Sanctuary, which He has sanctified forever, and worship HASHEM, your God, so that His burning wrath may turn away from you! For when you return to HASHEM, your brothers and sons will be regarded with mercy by their captors, and [will be allowed] to return to this land, for HASHEM your God is gracious and merciful, and He will not turn His face away from you if you return to Him!"

The runners passed from city to city in the land of Ephraim and Menasheh up to Zevulun but people laughed at them and mocked them. However, some people from Asher, Menasheh, and Zevulun humbled themselves and came to Jerusalem. Also in Judah the hand of God was upon them, instilling them all with a united heart to follow the commandment of the king and the leaders regarding the word of HASHEM.

So a great crowd assembled in Jerusalem to observe the Festival of Matzos in the second month — a very large congregation. They got up and removed the altars that were in Jerusalem, they also removed all the incense altars and threw them into the Kidron Ravine. They slaughtered the *pesach*-offering on the fourteenth of the second month, and the Kohanim and Levites felt humiliated and sanctified themselves and brought burnt-offerings

[15] **HAGGADAH: THE ANSWER IS . . .**

בֵּית יְהוָה: וַיַּעַמְדוּ עַל עָמְדָם כְּמִשְׁפָּטָם כְּתוֹרַת מֹשֶׁה אִישׁ הָאֱלֹהִים הַכֹּהֲנִים זֹרְקִים אֶת הַדָּם מִיַּד הַלְוִיִּם. כִּי רַבַּת בַּקָּהָל אֲשֶׁר לֹא הִתְקַדָּשׁוּ וְהַלְוִיִּם עַל שְׁחִיטַת הַפְּסָחִים לְכֹל לֹא טָהוֹר לְהַקְדִּישׁ לַיהוָה. כִּי מַרְבִּית הָעָם רַבַּת מֵאֶפְרַיִם וּמְנַשֶּׁה יִשָּׂשכָר וּזְבֻלוּן לֹא הִטֶּהָרוּ כִּי אָכְלוּ אֶת הַפֶּסַח בְּלֹא כַכָּתוּב כִּי הִתְפַּלֵּל יְחִזְקִיָּהוּ עֲלֵיהֶם לֵאמֹר יְהוָה הַטּוֹב יְכַפֵּר בְּעַד. כָּל לְבָבוֹ הֵכִין לִדְרוֹשׁ הָאֱלֹהִים יְהוָה אֱלֹהֵי אֲבוֹתָיו וְלֹא כְּטָהֳרַת הַקֹּדֶשׁ. וַיִּשְׁמַע יְהוָה אֶל יְחִזְקִיָּהוּ וַיִּרְפָּא אֶת הָעָם.

דברי הימים ב לה:א-יט

וַיַּעַשׂ יֹאשִׁיָּהוּ בִירוּשָׁלִַם פֶּסַח לַיהוָה וַיִּשְׁחֲטוּ הַפֶּסַח בְּאַרְבָּעָה עָשָׂר לַחֹדֶשׁ הָרִאשׁוֹן. וַיַּעֲמֵד הַכֹּהֲנִים עַל מִשְׁמְרוֹתָם וַיְחַזְּקֵם לַעֲבוֹדַת בֵּית יְהוָה. וַיֹּאמֶר לַלְוִיִּם הַמְּבִינִים לְכָל יִשְׂרָאֵל הַקְּדוֹשִׁים לַיהוָה תְּנוּ אֶת אֲרוֹן הַקֹּדֶשׁ בַּבַּיִת אֲשֶׁר בָּנָה שְׁלֹמֹה בֶן דָּוִיד מֶלֶךְ יִשְׂרָאֵל אֵין לָכֶם מַשָּׂא בַּכָּתֵף עַתָּה עִבְדוּ אֶת יְהוָה אֱלֹהֵיכֶם וְאֵת עַמּוֹ יִשְׂרָאֵל. וְהָכִינוּ לְבֵית אֲבוֹתֵיכֶם בְּמַחְלְקוֹתֵיכֶם בִּכְתָב דָּוִיד מֶלֶךְ יִשְׂרָאֵל וּבְמִכְתַּב שְׁלֹמֹה בְנוֹ. וְעִמְדוּ בַקֹּדֶשׁ לִפְלֻגּוֹת בֵּית הָאָבוֹת לַאֲחֵיכֶם בְּנֵי הָעָם וַחֲלֻקַּת בֵּית אָב לַלְוִיִּם. וְשַׁחֲטוּ הַפָּסַח וְהִתְקַדְּשׁוּ וְהָכִינוּ לַאֲחֵיכֶם לַעֲשׂוֹת כִּדְבַר יְהוָה בְּיַד מֹשֶׁה. וַיָּרֶם יֹאשִׁיָּהוּ לִבְנֵי הָעָם צֹאן כְּבָשִׂים וּבְנֵי עִזִּים הַכֹּל לַפְּסָחִים לְכָל הַנִּמְצָא לְמִסְפַּר שְׁלֹשִׁים אֶלֶף וּבָקָר שְׁלֹשֶׁת אֲלָפִים אֵלֶּה מֵרְכוּשׁ הַמֶּלֶךְ. וְשָׂרָיו לִנְדָבָה לָעָם לַכֹּהֲנִים וְלַלְוִיִּם הֵרִימוּ חִלְקִיָּה וּזְכַרְיָהוּ וִיחִיאֵל נְגִידֵי בֵּית הָאֱלֹהִים לַכֹּהֲנִים נָתְנוּ לַפְּסָחִים אַלְפַּיִם וְשֵׁשׁ מֵאוֹת וּבָקָר שְׁלֹשׁ מֵאוֹת. וְכָנַנְיָהוּ וּשְׁמַעְיָהוּ וּנְתַנְאֵל אֶחָיו וַחֲשַׁבְיָהוּ וִיעִיאֵל וְיוֹזָבָד שָׂרֵי הַלְוִיִּם הֵרִימוּ לַלְוִיִּם לַפְּסָחִים חֲמֵשֶׁת אֲלָפִים וּבָקָר חֲמֵשׁ מֵאוֹת.

to the Temple of HASHEM. They stood at their ordained positions, in accordance with the Torah of Moshe, the man of God — the Kohanim threw the blood [on the Altar], [taking it] from the hands of the Levites. For there were many in the congregation who had not sanctified themselves, and the Levites took charge of slaughtering the *pesach*-offering for anyone who was not pure, to sanctify it to HASHEM. For many of the people — many from Ephraim, Menasheh, Yissachar, and Zevulun — had not purified themselves, and they ate the *pesach*-offering not in accordance with that which is written; but Chizkiyahu prayed for them, saying, "May the benevolent HASHEM grant atonement for whoever sets his heart to seek out God, HASHEM, the God of his forefathers, though without the purity required for the sacred." HASHEM listened to Chizkiyahu and absolved the people.

II Chronicles 35:1-19

Yoshiyahu made the *pesach*-offering to HASHEM. They slaughtered the *pesach*-offering on the fourteenth day of the first month.

He set up the Kohanim according to their divisions, and he encouraged them in the service of the Temple of HASHEM. He then said to the Levites, who taught all of Israel, who were consecrated to HASHEM, "Place the Holy Ark in the Temple that Shlomo son of David, the king of Israel, built. Then you will no longer have any carrying on your shoulder; so now serve HASHEM your God and His people Israel. Organize yourselves by your fathers' families, according to your divisions, in accordance with the written instructions of David king of Israel and the written instructions of his son Shlomo. Stand in the Sanctuary according to the groupings of your fathers' families near your kinsmen, the populace, and the Levites' fathers' family division. Slaughter the *pesach*-offering; sanctify yourselves and prepare your kinsmen to act in accordance with the word of HASHEM, through Moshe."

Yoshiyahu donated animals of the flock — sheep and goats — to the populace, all of them for *pesach*-offerings for those who were present, in the amount of thirty thousand, in addition to three thousand [head of] cattle; all this was from the personal property of the king. His officers also contributed voluntarily to the populace, to the Kohanim and to the Levites. Chilkiyah, Zecharyahu, and Yechiel, the managers of the Temple of God, gave two thousand six hundred [sheep] to the Kohanim for *pesach*-offerings, and three hundred [head of] cattle. Cananyahu, together with his brethren Shemaiah and Nesanel, and Chashavyahu, Yeiel, and Yozabad, officers of the Levites, donated five thousand [sheep] for *pesach*-[offerings] for the Levites, and five hundred [head of] cattle.

[17] **HAGGADAH: THE ANSWER IS . . .**

וַתִּכּוֹן הָעֲבוֹדָה וַיַּעַמְדוּ הַכֹּהֲנִים עַל עָמְדָם וְהַלְוִיִם עַל מַחְלְקוֹתָם כְּמִצְוַת הַמֶּלֶךְ. וַיִּשְׁחֲטוּ הַפֶּסַח וַיִּזְרְקוּ הַכֹּהֲנִים מִיָּדָם וְהַלְוִיִם מַפְשִׁיטִים. וַיָּסִירוּ הָעֹלָה לְתִתָּם לְמִפְלַגּוֹת לְבֵית אָבוֹת לִבְנֵי הָעָם לְהַקְרִיב לַיהוה כַּכָּתוּב בְּסֵפֶר מֹשֶׁה וְכֵן לַבָּקָר. וַיְבַשְּׁלוּ הַפֶּסַח בָּאֵשׁ כַּמִּשְׁפָּט וְהַקֳּדָשִׁים בִּשְּׁלוּ בַּסִּירוֹת וּבַדְּוָדִים וּבַצֵּלָחוֹת וַיָּרִיצוּ לְכָל בְּנֵי הָעָם. וְאַחַר הֵכִינוּ לָהֶם וְלַכֹּהֲנִים כִּי הַכֹּהֲנִים בְּנֵי אַהֲרֹן בְּהַעֲלוֹת הָעוֹלָה וְהַחֲלָבִים עַד לָיְלָה וְהַלְוִיִם הֵכִינוּ לָהֶם וְלַכֹּהֲנִים בְּנֵי אַהֲרֹן. וְהַמְשֹׁרְרִים בְּנֵי אָסָף עַל מַעֲמָדָם כְּמִצְוַת דָּוִיד וְאָסָף וְהֵימָן וִידֻתוּן חוֹזֵה הַמֶּלֶךְ וְהַשֹּׁעֲרִים לְשַׁעַר וָשָׁעַר אֵין לָהֶם לָסוּר מֵעַל עֲבֹדָתָם כִּי אֲחֵיהֶם הַלְוִיִם הֵכִינוּ לָהֶם. וַתִּכּוֹן כָּל עֲבוֹדַת יהוה בַּיּוֹם הַהוּא לַעֲשׂוֹת הַפֶּסַח וְהַעֲלוֹת עֹלוֹת עַל מִזְבַּח יהוה כְּמִצְוַת הַמֶּלֶךְ יֹאשִׁיָּהוּ. וַיַּעֲשׂוּ בְנֵי יִשְׂרָאֵל הַנִּמְצְאִים אֶת הַפֶּסַח בָּעֵת הַהִיא וְאֶת חַג הַמַּצּוֹת שִׁבְעַת יָמִים. וְלֹא נַעֲשָׂה פֶסַח כָּמֹהוּ בְּיִשְׂרָאֵל מִימֵי שְׁמוּאֵל הַנָּבִיא וְכָל מַלְכֵי יִשְׂרָאֵל לֹא עָשׂוּ כַּפֶּסַח אֲשֶׁר עָשָׂה יֹאשִׁיָּהוּ וְהַכֹּהֲנִים וְהַלְוִיִם וְכָל יְהוּדָה וְיִשְׂרָאֵל הַנִּמְצָא וְיוֹשְׁבֵי יְרוּשָׁלָ͏ִם. בִּשְׁמוֹנֶה עֶשְׂרֵה שָׁנָה לְמַלְכוּת יֹאשִׁיָּהוּ נַעֲשָׂה הַפֶּסַח הַזֶּה.

All continue here:

כָּךְ הָיְתָה עֲבוֹדַת קָרְבַּן הַפֶּסַח בְּבֵית אֱלֹהֵינוּ בְּיוֹם אַרְבָּעָה עָשָׂר בְּנִיסָן:

אֵין שׁוֹחֲטִין אוֹתוֹ אֶלָּא אַחַר תָּמִיד שֶׁל בֵּין הָעַרְבָּיִם. עֶרֶב פֶּסַח, בֵּין בְּחֹל בֵּין בְּשַׁבָּת, הָיָה הַתָּמִיד נִשְׁחַט בְּשֶׁבַע וּמֶחֱצָה וְקָרֵב בִּשְׁמוֹנָה וּמֶחֱצָה. וְאִם חָל עֶרֶב פֶּסַח לִהְיוֹת עֶרֶב שַׁבָּת הָיוּ שׁוֹחֲטִין אוֹתוֹ בְּשֵׁשׁ וּמֶחֱצָה וְקָרֵב בְּשֶׁבַע וּמֶחֱצָה. וְהַפֶּסַח אַחֲרָיו.

Thus the service was in order. The Kohanim were stationed at their positions and the Levites in their divisions, in accordance with the king's orders. They slaughtered the *pesach*-offering, and the Kohanim threw [the blood, which they had taken] from their hands, while the Levites were flaying. They removed the parts that were to be offered up — in order to give [flesh of the *pesach*-offering] to the family groups of the populace — to offer them up before HASHEM, as is written in the Book of Moshe; and similarly for the cattle. They cooked the *pesach*-offering over the fire according to the law, and they cooked the [other] sacrificial meat in pots and cauldrons and pans, and distributed it quickly to all the populace. Afterward they prepared [the *pesach*-offering] for themselves and for the Kohanim, because the Kohanim — the descendants of Aharon — were busy burning burnt-offerings and fats until nighttime, so now the Levites prepared for themselves and for the Kohanim, the descendants of Aharon.

The singers, the descendants of Asaf, stood at their positions — according to the decree of David, Asaf, Heiman, and Yedusun the king's seer — with the gatekeepers at every gate; they did not have to leave their own tasks, for their brother Levites had prepared for them. The entire service of HASHEM was thus well organized on that day, to perform the *pesach*-offering and to bring up burnt-offerings upon the Altar of HASHEM, in accordance with the command of King Yoshiyahu. So the Children of Israel who were present performed the *pesach*-offering at that time, and then the Festival of Unleavened Bread for seven days. Such a *pesach*-offering had not been celebrated since the days of Shmuel the Prophet. None of the kings of Israel performed like the *pesach*-offering that Yoshiyahu did with the Kohanim, the Levites, all of Judah and Israel who were present, and the inhabitants of Jerusalem. It was in the eighteenth year of Yoshiyahu's reign that this *pesach*-offering was performed.

All continue here:

This was the service of the *pesach*-offering on the fourteenth of Nisan:

We may not slaughter it until after the afternoon *tamid*-offering. On the eve of Pesach, whether on a weekday or on Shabbos, the *tamid*-offering would be slaughtered at seven and a half hours [after daybreak], and offered at eight and a half hours. But when Erev Pesach fell on Friday, they would slaughter it at six and a half hours, and offer it at seven and a half. [In either case] the *pesach*-offering [was slaughtered] after it.

[19] **HAGGADAH: THE ANSWER IS . . .**

כָּל אָדָם מִיִּשְׂרָאֵל, אֶחָד הָאִישׁ וְאֶחָד הָאִשָּׁה, כָּל שֶׁיָּכוֹל לְהַגִּיעַ לִירוּשָׁלַיִם בִּשְׁעַת שְׁחִיטַת הַפֶּסַח הַיָּב בְּקָרְבַּן פֶּסַח.

מְבִיאוּ מִן הַכְּבָשִׂים אוֹ מִן הָעִזִּים, זָכָר תָּמִים בֶּן שָׁנָה, וְשׁוֹחֲטוֹ בְּכָל מָקוֹם בָּעֲזָרָה, אַחַר גְּמַר עֲבוֹדַת תָּמִיד הָעֶרֶב וְאַחַר הֲטָבַת הַנֵּרוֹת.

וְאֵין שׁוֹחֲטִין הַפֶּסַח, וְלֹא זוֹרְקִין הַדָּם, וְלֹא מַקְטִירִין הַחֵלֶב, עַל הֶחָמֵץ.

שָׁחַט הַשּׁוֹחֵט, וְקִבֵּל דָּמוֹ הַכֹּהֵן שֶׁבְּרֹאשׁ הַשּׁוּרָה בִּכְלִי שָׁרֵת, וְנוֹתֵן לַחֲבֵרוֹ, וַחֲבֵרוֹ לַחֲבֵרוֹ. כֹּהֵן הַקָּרוֹב אֵצֶל הַמִּזְבֵּחַ זוֹרְקוֹ זְרִיקָה אַחַת כְּנֶגֶד הַיְסוֹד, וְחוֹזֵר הַכְּלִי רֵיקָן לַחֲבֵרוֹ, וַחֲבֵרוֹ לַחֲבֵרוֹ. מְקַבֵּל אֶת הַמָּלֵא וּמַחֲזִיר אֶת הָרֵיקָן. וְהָיוּ הַכֹּהֲנִים עוֹמְדִים שׁוּרוֹת וּבִידֵיהֶם בָּזִיכִין שֶׁכֻּלָּן כֶּסֶף אוֹ כֻלָּן זָהָב. וְלֹא הָיוּ מְעֹרָבִים. וְלֹא הָיוּ לַבָּזִיכִין שׁוּלַיִם, שֶׁלֹּא יַנִּיחוּם וְיִקְרֹשׁ הַדָּם.

אַחַר כָּךְ תּוֹלִין אֶת הַפֶּסַח בְּאֻנְקְלָיוֹת, וּמַפְשִׁיט אוֹתוֹ כֻּלּוֹ, וְקוֹרְעִין בִּטְנוֹ וּמוֹצִיאִין אֵמוּרָיו — הַחֵלֶב שֶׁעַל הַקֶּרֶב, וְיוֹתֶרֶת הַכָּבֵד, וּשְׁתֵּי הַכְּלָיוֹת, וְהַחֵלֶב שֶׁעֲלֵיהֶן, וְהָאַלְיָה לְעֻמַּת הֶעָצֶה. נוֹתְנָן בִּכְלִי שָׁרֵת וּמוֹלְחָן וּמַקְטִירָן הַכֹּהֵן עַל הַמַּעֲרָכָה, חֶלְבֵי כָּל זֶבַח וָזֶבַח לְבַדּוֹ. בַּחֹל, בַּיּוֹם וְלֹא בַּלַּיְלָה שֶׁהוּא יוֹם טוֹב. אֲבָל אִם חָל עֶרֶב פֶּסַח בַּשַּׁבָּת, מַקְטִירִין וְהוֹלְכִין כָּל הַלַּיְלָה. וּמוֹצִיא קְרָבָיו וּמְמַחֶה אוֹתָן עַד שֶׁמֵּסִיר מֵהֶן הַפֶּרֶשׁ.

שְׁחִיטָתוֹ וּזְרִיקַת דָּמוֹ וּמִחוּי קְרָבָיו וְהֶקְטֵר חֲלָבָיו דּוֹחִין אֶת הַשַּׁבָּת, וּשְׁאָר עִנְיָנָיו אֵין דּוֹחִין.

Every Jew, male or female, whoever is able to reach Jerusalem in time to slaughter the *pesach*, is obligated to bring the *pesach*-offering.

It may be brought from sheep or from goats, an unblemished male in its first year. It may be slaughtered anywhere in the Temple Courtyard, after the completion of the afternoon *tamid*-offering, and after the kindling of the Menorah's lamps.

We may not slaughter the *pesach*, nor throw its blood [onto the Altar], nor burn its fats [on the Altar], if *chametz* is in our possession.

Someone [even a non-Kohen] would slaughter [the animal]. The Kohen at the head of the line [closest to the animal] would receive its blood in a sanctified vessel and pass it to his colleague, and he to his colleague. The Kohen closest to the Altar would throw it, with one throwing, at the base [of the Altar], then return the vessel to his colleague, and he to his colleague. He would first accept the full one, then return the empty one. The Kohanim would stand in lines, [all the Kohanim of each line] holding either silver or golden vessels. But they would not mix [two types of vessels in one line]. The vessels did not have flat bottoms, lest one would put down a vessel [and forget it], thus causing the blood to congeal.

Following this, they would suspend the *pesach* from hooks. They would skin it completely, tear open its stomach, and remove the organs ordained for the Altar — the suet covering the stomach, the diaphragm with the liver, the two kidneys and the suet upon them, and [in the case of a lamb] the tail opposite the kidneys. They would place [these organs] in a sanctified vessel and salt them, then a Kohen would burn them on the Altar fire. The portions of each offering [would be placed on the fire] separately. On a weekday, [this would be done] by day and not at night when the festival had already begun. But when Erev Pesach fell on Shabbos, they would burn [the organs] during the entire night. They would remove the innards and squeeze them until all their wastes were removed.

Slaughtering it, throwing its blood, squeezing out its innards, and burning its fats [on the Altar] supersede Shabbos; but its other requirements do not supersede [Shabbos]

HAGGADAH: THE ANSWER IS . . .

בְּשָׁלֹשׁ כִּתּוֹת הַפֶּסַח נִשְׁחָט. וְאֵין כַּת פְּחוּתָה מִשְּׁלֹשִׁים אֲנָשִׁים. נִכְנְסָה כַּת אַחַת, נִתְמַלְאָה הָעֲזָרָה, נוֹעֲלִין אוֹתָהּ. וּבְעוֹד שֶׁהֵם שׁוֹחֲטִין וּמַקְרִיבִין, הַכֹּהֲנִים תּוֹקְעִין, הֶחָלִיל מַכֶּה לִפְנֵי הַמִּזְבֵּחַ, וְהַלְוִיִּים קוֹרְאִין אֶת הַהַלֵּל. אִם גָּמְרוּ קֹדֶם שֶׁיַּקְרִיבוּ כֻּלָּם, שָׁנוּ; אִם שָׁנוּ, שִׁלְּשׁוּ. עַל כָּל קְרִיאָה תָּקְעוּ הֵרִיעוּ וְתָקְעוּ. גָּמְרָה כַּת אַחַת לְהַקְרִיב, פּוֹתְחִין הָעֲזָרָה, יָצְאָה כַּת רִאשׁוֹנָה, נִכְנְסָה כַּת שְׁנִיָּה, נָעֲלוּ דַּלְתוֹת הָעֲזָרָה. גָּמְרָה, יָצְאָה שְׁנִיָּה וְנִכְנְסָה שְׁלִישִׁית. כְּמַעֲשֵׂה הָרִאשׁוֹנָה כָּךְ מַעֲשֵׂה הַשְּׁנִיָּה וְהַשְּׁלִישִׁית.

אַחַר שֶׁיָּצְאוּ כֻּלָּן רוֹחֲצִין הָעֲזָרָה מִלִּכְלוּכֵי הַדָּם, וַאֲפִלּוּ בַּשַּׁבָּת. אַמַּת הַמַּיִם הָיְתָה עוֹבֶרֶת בָּעֲזָרָה, שֶׁכְּשֶׁרוֹצִין לְהָדִיחַ הָרִצְפָּה סוֹתְמִין מְקוֹם יְצִיאַת הַמַּיִם וְהִיא מִתְמַלֵּאת עַל כָּל גְּדוֹתֶיהָ, עַד שֶׁהַמַּיִם עוֹלִין וְצָפִין וּמְקַבְּצִין אֲלֵיהֶם כָּל דָּם וְלִכְלוּךְ שֶׁבָּעֲזָרָה. אַחַר כָּךְ פּוֹתְחִין הַסְּתִימָה וְיוֹצְאִין הַמַּיִם עִם הַלִּכְלוּךְ, נִמְצֵאת הָרִצְפָּה מְנֻקָּה, זֶהוּ כְּבוֹד הַבַּיִת.

יָצְאוּ כָּל אֶחָד עִם פִּסְחוֹ וְצָלוּ אוֹתָם. כֵּיצַד צוֹלִין אוֹתוֹ? מְבִיאִין שַׁפּוּד שֶׁל רִמּוֹן, תּוֹחֲבוֹ מִתּוֹךְ פִּיו עַד בֵּית נְקוּבָתוֹ, וְתוֹלֵהוּ לְתוֹךְ הַתַּנּוּר וְהָאֵשׁ לְמַטָּה, וְתוֹלֶה כְּרָעָיו וּבְנֵי מֵעָיו חוּצָה לוֹ, וְאֵין מְנַקְּרִין אֶת הַפֶּסַח כִּשְׁאָר בָּשָׂר.

בְּשַׁבָּת אֵינָן מוֹלִיכִין אֶת הַפֶּסַח לְבֵיתָם, אֶלָּא כַּת הָרִאשׁוֹנָה יוֹצְאִין בְּפִסְחֵיהֶן וְיוֹשְׁבִין בְּהַר הַבַּיִת, הַשְּׁנִיָּה יוֹצְאִין עִם פִּסְחֵיהֶן וְיוֹשְׁבִין בַּחֵיל, וְהַשְּׁלִישִׁית בִּמְקוֹמָהּ עוֹמֶדֶת. חֲשֵׁכָה, יָצְאוּ וְצָלוּ אֶת פִּסְחֵיהֶן.

The *pesach* is slaughtered in three groups, no group comprising less than thirty men. The first entered, filling the Courtyard; then they closed the gates. For as long as they slaughtered and offered [the *pesach*], the Kohanim would blow the shofar, the flute would play before the Altar, and the Levites would recite *Hallel*. If they completed [*Hallel*] before all had brought their offerings, they repeated it. If they completed [*Hallel*] a second time, they would recite it a third time. For each recitation, they blew *tekiah, teruah, tekiah*. When the first group was done offering, they opened the Courtyard [gates]. The first group left, the second group entered, and the Courtyard gates were closed. When they were done, the second group left, and the third group entered. Like the procedure of the first, so was the procedure of the second and third.

After all [three groups] had left, they [the Kohanim] would wash the [stone] Courtyard [floor] of the blood, even on Shabbos. A channel of water passed through the Courtyard. When they wished to wash the floor, they would block the outlet, causing the water to overflow and gather all the bloods and other waste matter in the Courtyard. Then they would remove the blockage and the water with the waste would run out. Thus, the floor would be clean. And this is the manner of cleansing the Temple.

They left, each with his *pesach*, and roasted them. In what manner was it roasted? They would bring a pomegranate wood spit, thrust it through its mouth to its anus and suspend it inside the oven with the fire below it. Its legs and innards were suspended outside [its body cavity]. They would not purge the *pesach* in the same manner as other meat.

On Shabbos they would not carry the *pesach* [meat] to their homes. Rather, the first group would go out [of the Courtyard] with their *pesach*-offerings and remain on the Temple Mount. The second group would go out and remain within the Cheil [a ten cubit wide area, just outside the Courtyard walls]. The third group would remain where they were. When it became dark, they would leave [for their homes] and roast their *pesach*-offerings.

כְּשֶׁמַּקְרִיבִין אֶת הַפֶּסַח בָּרִאשׁוֹן מַקְרִיבִין עִמּוֹ בַּיּוֹם אַרְבָּעָה עָשָׂר זֶבַח שְׁלָמִים, מִן הַבָּקָר אוֹ מִן הַצֹּאן, גְּדוֹלִים אוֹ קְטַנִּים, זְכָרִים אוֹ נְקֵבוֹת, וְהִיא נִקְרֵאת חֲגִיגַת אַרְבָּעָה עָשָׂר, עַל זֶה נֶאֱמַר בַּתּוֹרָה, וְזָבַחְתָּ פֶּסַח לַיהוה אֱלֹהֶיךָ צֹאן וּבָקָר. וְלֹא קְבָעָהּ הַכָּתוּב חוֹבָה אֶלָּא רְשׁוּת בִּלְבַד, מִכָּל מָקוֹם הִיא כְחוֹבָה מִדִּבְרֵי סוֹפְרִים, כְּדֵי שֶׁיְּהֵא הַפֶּסַח נֶאֱכָל עַל הַשֹּׂבַע. אֵימָתַי מְבִיאִין עִמּוֹ חֲגִיגָה? בִּזְמַן שֶׁהוּא בָא בְחֹל, בְּטָהֳרָה וּבַמּוֹעֵט. וְנֶאֱכֶלֶת לִשְׁנֵי יָמִים וְלַיְלָה אֶחָד, וְדִינָהּ כְּכָל תּוֹרַת זִבְחֵי שְׁלָמִים, טְעוּנָה סְמִיכָה וּנְסָכִים וּמַתַּן דָּמִים שְׁתַּיִם שֶׁהֵן אַרְבַּע וּשְׁפִיכַת שְׁיָרִים לַיְסוֹד.

זֶהוּ סֵדֶר עֲבוֹדַת קָרְבַּן פֶּסַח וַחֲגִיגָה שֶׁעָמְּוֹ בְּבֵית אֱלֹהֵינוּ שֶׁיִּבָּנֶה בִּמְהֵרָה בְיָמֵינוּ, אָמֵן. אַשְׁרֵי הָעָם שֶׁכָּכָה לּוֹ, אַשְׁרֵי הָעָם שֶׁיהוה אֱלֹהָיו.

אֱלֹהֵינוּ וֵאלֹהֵי אֲבוֹתֵינוּ, מֶלֶךְ רַחֲמָן רַחֵם עָלֵינוּ, טוֹב וּמֵטִיב הִדָּרֶשׁ לָנוּ. שׁוּבָה אֵלֵינוּ בַּהֲמוֹן רַחֲמֶיךָ בִּגְלַל אָבוֹת שֶׁעָשׂוּ רְצוֹנֶךָ. בְּנֵה בֵיתְךָ כְּבַתְּחִלָּה וְכוֹנֵן מִקְדָּשְׁךָ עַל מְכוֹנוֹ. וְהַרְאֵנוּ בְּבִנְיָנוֹ וְשַׂמְּחֵנוּ בְּתִקּוּנוֹ. וְהָשֵׁב שְׁכִינָתְךָ לְתוֹכוֹ, וְהָשֵׁב כֹּהֲנִים לַעֲבוֹדָתָם וּלְוִיִּים לְשִׁירָם וּלְזִמְרָם, וְהָשֵׁב יִשְׂרָאֵל לִנְוֵיהֶם. וְשָׁם נַעֲלֶה וְנֵרָאֶה וְנִשְׁתַּחֲוֶה לְפָנֶיךָ. וְנֹאכַל שָׁם מִן הַזְּבָחִים וּמִן הַפְּסָחִים אֲשֶׁר יַגִּיעַ דָּמָם עַל קִיר מִזְבַּחֲךָ לְרָצוֹן. יִהְיוּ לְרָצוֹן אִמְרֵי פִי וְהֶגְיוֹן לִבִּי לְפָנֶיךָ, יהוה צוּרִי וְגוֹאֲלִי.

When they would bring the *pesach*-offering, they would bring with it — on the fourteenth of Nisan — a peace-offering, either from the cattle herd or from the flock, old or young, male or female. This is called "the festive offering of the fourteenth." Regarding this the Torah states: "And you shall slaughter the *pesach*-offering to HASHEM, your God, from the flock and cattle." Yet the Torah did not establish this as an obligation, but only as a voluntary offering. Nevertheless, it was made obligatory by the Rabbis, in order that the *pesach*-offering be eaten in satiety. When may the festive-offering be brought with it [the *pesach*]? When it [the *pesach*] is brought on a weekday, in purity and there are few. It may be eaten for two days and the included night, its laws being the same as the laws of other peace-offerings. It requires *semichah*, libations, two [Altar] applications of blood that are equivalent to four, and pouring the remainder [of the blood] at the [Altar's] base.

This is the order of the *pesach*-offering and the festive-offering brought with it in the Temple of our God — may it be rebuilt speedily, in our days — Amen. Praiseworthy is the people for whom this is so; praiseworthy is the people whose God is HASHEM.

Our God and the God of our forefathers, O merciful King, have mercy on us; O good and beneficent One, let Yourself be sought out by us; return to us in Your yearning mercy for the sake of the forefathers who did Your will. Rebuild Your House as it was at first, and establish Your Sanctuary on its prepared site; show us its rebuilding and gladden us in its perfection. Return Your *Shechinah* to it; restore the Kohanim to their service, the Levites to their song and music; and restore Israel to their dwellings. And there may we ascend and appear and prostrate ourselves before You. There we shall eat of the peace-offerings and *pesach*-offerings whose blood will gain the sides of Your Altar for favorable acceptance. May the expressions of my mouth and the thoughts of my heart find favor before You, HASHEM, my Rock and my Redeemer.

[25] **HAGGADAH: THE ANSWER IS . . .**

הדלקת נרות

The candles are lit and the following blessings are recited. When Yom Tov falls on the Sabbath, the words in parentheses are added.

בָּרוּךְ אַתָּה יהוה אֱלֹהֵינוּ מֶלֶךְ הָעוֹלָם, אֲשֶׁר קִדְּשָׁנוּ בְּמִצְוֹתָיו, וְצִוָּנוּ לְהַדְלִיק נֵר שֶׁל (שַׁבָּת וְשֶׁל) יוֹם טוֹב.

בָּרוּךְ אַתָּה יהוה אֱלֹהֵינוּ מֶלֶךְ הָעוֹלָם, שֶׁהֶחֱיָנוּ וְקִיְּמָנוּ וְהִגִּיעָנוּ לַזְּמַן הַזֶּה.

It is customary to recite the following prayer after the kindling. The words in brackets are included as they apply.

יְהִי רָצוֹן לְפָנֶיךָ, יהוה אֱלֹהַי וֵאלֹהֵי אֲבוֹתַי, שֶׁתְּחוֹנֵן אוֹתִי [וְאֶת אִישִׁי, וְאֶת בָּנַי, וְאֶת בְּנוֹתַי, וְאֶת אָבִי, וְאֶת אִמִּי] וְאֶת כָּל קְרוֹבַי; וְתִתֵּן לָנוּ וּלְכָל יִשְׂרָאֵל חַיִּים טוֹבִים וַאֲרוּכִים; וְתִזְכְּרֵנוּ בְּזִכְרוֹן טוֹבָה וּבְרָכָה; וְתִפְקְדֵנוּ בִּפְקֻדַּת יְשׁוּעָה וְרַחֲמִים; וּתְבָרְכֵנוּ בְּרָכוֹת גְּדוֹלוֹת; וְתַשְׁלִים בָּתֵּינוּ; וְתַשְׁכֵּן שְׁכִינָתְךָ בֵּינֵינוּ. וְזַכֵּנִי לְגַדֵּל בָּנִים וּבְנֵי בָנִים חֲכָמִים וּנְבוֹנִים, אוֹהֲבֵי יהוה, יִרְאֵי אֱלֹהִים, אַנְשֵׁי אֱמֶת, זֶרַע קֹדֶשׁ, בַּיהוה דְּבֵקִים, וּמְאִירִים אֶת הָעוֹלָם בַּתּוֹרָה וּבְמַעֲשִׂים טוֹבִים, וּבְכָל מְלֶאכֶת עֲבוֹדַת הַבּוֹרֵא. אָנָּא שְׁמַע אֶת תְּחִנָּתִי בָּעֵת הַזֹּאת, בִּזְכוּת שָׂרָה וְרִבְקָה וְרָחֵל וְלֵאָה אִמּוֹתֵינוּ, וְהָאֵר נֵרֵנוּ שֶׁלֹּא יִכְבֶּה לְעוֹלָם וָעֶד, וְהָאֵר פָּנֶיךָ וְנִוָּשֵׁעָה. אָמֵן.

LIGHTING THE CANDLES

The candles are lit and the following blessings are recited. When Yom Tov falls on the Sabbath, the words in parentheses are added.

Blessed are You, HASHEM, our God, King of the universe, Who has sanctified us through His commandments, and commanded us to kindle the flame of the (Sabbath and the) Festival.

Blessed are You, HASHEM, our God, King of the universe, Who has kept us alive, sustained us, and brought us to this season.

It is customary to recite the following prayer after the kindling. The words in brackets are included as they apply.

May it be Your will, HASHEM, my God and God of my forefathers, that You show favor to me [my husband, my sons, my daughters, my father, my mother] and all my relatives; and that You grant us and all Israel a good and long life; that You remember us with a beneficent memory and blessing; that You consider us with a consideration of salvation and compassion; that You bless us with great blessings; that You make our households complete; that You cause Your Presence to dwell among us. Privilege me to raise children and grandchildren who are wise and understanding, who love HASHEM and fear God, people of truth, holy offspring, attached to HASHEM, who illuminate the world with Torah and good deeds and with every labor in the service of the Creator. Please, hear my plea at this time, in the merit of Sarah, Rivkah, Rachel, and Leah, our mothers, and cause our light to illuminate that it not be extinguished forever, and let Your countenance shine so that we are saved. Amen.

הסדר / THE SEDER

✑ Why Is the Holiday Called "Pesach"?

Q *Why is it that the Torah refers to the holiday of Pesach as "Chag HaMatzos," [it refers to the pesach-offering as Pesach], while Chazal refer to it as "Pesach"?*

A ☐ **KEDUSHAS LEVI**: The tefillin we wear contain the verse שְׁמַע יִשְׂרָאֵל ה' אֱלֹהֵינוּ ה' **אֶחָד**, *Hear O Israel: HASHEM is our God, HASHEM is the One and Only* (Deuteronomy 6:4), while the "tefillin" of Hashem contain the verse וּמִי כְעַמְּךָ יִשְׂרָאֵל גּוֹי **אֶחָד** בָּאָרֶץ, *And who is like Your people Israel, a unique nation on earth* (Divrei HaYamim I 17:21). We proclaim Hashem's uniqueness, while He proclaims our uniqueness (Berachos 6a).

Similarly, the Torah refers to this holiday as "Chag HaMatzos," invoking praise of the Jews who ate matzah when they left Egypt. We, on the other hand, refer to the holiday as "Pesach," invoking praise of Hashem Who miraculously skipped (*pasach*) over the homes of the Jews in Egypt during the plague of the firstborn.

☐ **EIL MILUIM**: This can be explained by means of a parable: A king went out hunting in the field and met a shepherd playing a flute. The king took a liking to the shepherd and appointed him as one of his attendants. With time, this attendant rose through the ranks, eventually becoming the king's finance minister.

The young minister was very popular among the king's subjects, but the other ministers, envying him for his meteoric rise to power, spread a slanderous rumor that he had stolen from the king's treasury. A surprise search was conducted in the shepherd's home to inspect his private wealth, but the investigators discovered only a modest home with no stores of gold or silver.

They did, however, come across a locked room. The king ordered that it be opened, but all that was found there was a stick, a sack, and a flute. Asked what the purpose of these hidden objects was, the minister replied, "My master the king, every day I go into this room to remember my previous status, in order to prevent myself from becoming haughty. Every day, I remember how God was kind enough to allow me to find favor in the eyes of the king and reach the point I am at today. It was not by virtue of my own merit that I attained such heights of success, but rather by the grace of God."

The name Pesach represents the great miracle that Hashem performed for us by skipping over the homes of our ancestors in Egypt and redeeming us from slavery. In order that we not become haughty, however, we also refer to the holiday — in our prayers and in *Bircas HaMazon* (Grace After Meals) — as Chag HaMatzos, which reminds us of the poor man's bread we ate during our enslavement in Egypt. Remembering our modest beginnings ensures that we remain humble and subservient, like the shepherd in the parable.

◆§ The Uniqueness of the Seder Night

Q *Why is there a widespread custom to wear a kittel (a simple white garment) at the Seder?*

A
- **MAHARAL:** On the Seder night, every Jew rises to a lofty spiritual level, just as the Kohen Gadol rose to a lofty level when he entered the Holy of Holies on Yom Kippur wearing white garments.
- **TAZ (472:3):** A white garment is suggestive of freedom and joy, and on the Seder night we rejoice over our freedom from the Egyptian bondage.
- **SHULCHAN ARUCH HARAV:** The *kittel* is reminiscent of burial shrouds. Wearing it prevents us from becoming haughty as a result of the joy we feel at the Seder.
- **BRISKER RAV:** We wear the *kittel* as a deviation from the usual practice, to prompt the children to ask questions.
- **A WHITE GARMENT** is reminiscent of angels. When the father performs the mitzvah of relating the story of the Exodus on Seder night, he strives to resemble an angel, in keeping with Chazal's exhortation to learn Torah from a rebbi who resembles an angel.

הגדה של פסח [32]

Q Why do we call this night "Seder" night?

A
- **MAHARIL:** The name Seder, which means "order," implies that all of the events that occurred to the Jews from the time of the Exodus have followed a particular order. The course of history is not coincidental or random but is guided by Divine Providence.
- **RAV AHARON OF KARLIN:** The Seder night begins the "order" of the entire year: Pesach begins the annual cycle of the holidays, and all of the mitzvos are shaped by the Exodus.
- **TIFERES SHLOMO:** The Seder night is a night of special protection — "leil shimurim" — and it also confers protection on all other nights of the year, depending on our behavior on this night. In order to merit this protection, we have to make sure that we conduct ourselves according to the proper protocol ("Seder") of this night.

Q Why do we recline at the Seder?

A
- **RAMBAM:** On this night, every person is supposed to feel as though he himself left the enslavement of Egypt. By reclining in the manner of free men, we experience that feeling of freedom.
- **ARUCH HASHULCHAN:** This is done as a deviation from the usual practice, to prompt the children to notice and ask questions.
- *Heseibah* (הסיבה), reclining, commemorates the manner in which Hashem led us out of Egypt to the wilderness: וַיַּסֵּב אֱלֹהִים אֶת הָעָם דֶּרֶךְ הַמִּדְבָּר יַם סוּף, *So God **turned** the people toward the way of the Wilderness to the Sea of Reeds* (Exodus 13:18). Based on this verse, Chazal (*Shemos Rabbah* 20:18) teach that even a pauper is obligated to recline at the Seder, in order to publicize how Hashem led the Jews out of Egypt in a roundabout manner.

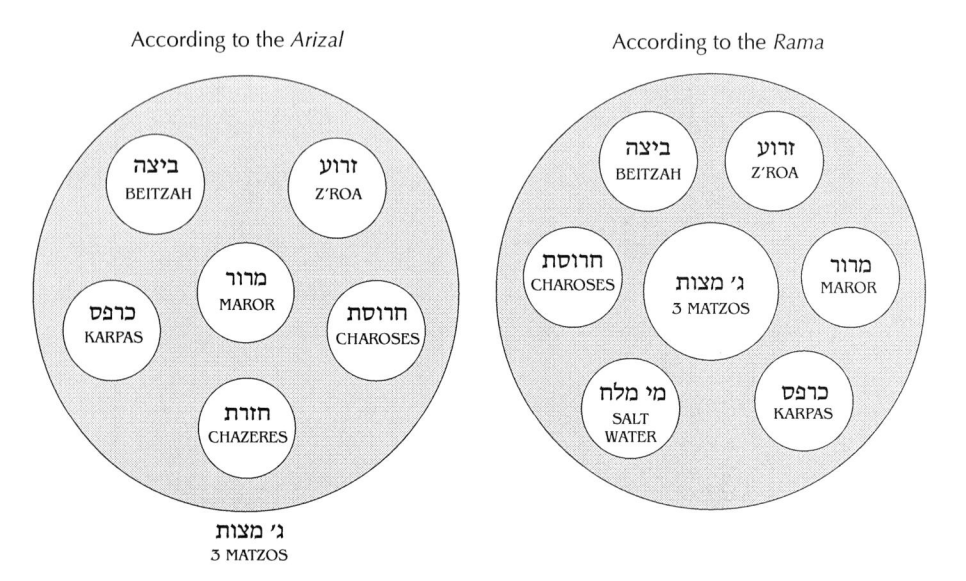

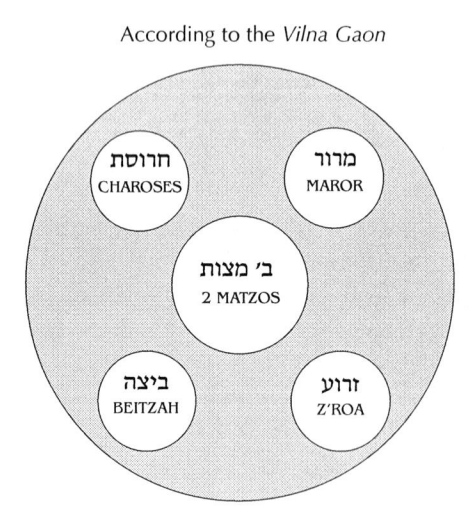

הקערה
The Seder Plate

According to the *Arizal*

- ביצה / BEITZAH
- זרוע / Z'ROA
- מרור / MAROR
- כרפס / KARPAS
- חרוסת / CHAROSES
- חזרת / CHAZERES

ג׳ מצות / 3 MATZOS

According to the *Rama*

- ביצה / BEITZAH
- זרוע / Z'ROA
- חרוסת / CHAROSES
- ג׳ מצות / 3 MATZOS
- מרור / MAROR
- מי מלח / SALT WATER
- כרפס / KARPAS

According to the *Vilna Gaon*

- חרוסת / CHAROSES
- מרור / MAROR
- ב׳ מצות / 2 MATZOS
- ביצה / BEITZAH
- זרוע / Z'ROA

הגדה של פסח [34]

~§ The Seder Plate

Q *Why is an egg, which symbolizes mourning for the destruction of the Beis HaMikdash, eaten at the Seder, when we are supposed to be joyous?*

A
- ☐ **KOL BO:** In the month of Nissan, when we celebrate Pesach, we anticipate the future redemption. On the Seder night, when we see that Mashiach has not yet arrived, it is proper to mourn.

- ☐ **REMA** (476:2): The first day of Pesach always falls on the same day of the week as Tishah B'Av of that year (for example, if the first day of Pesach is Tuesday, Tishah B'Av also falls on Tuesday later that year). To symbolize this, we eat an egg, which is a food given to mourners.

- ☐ **CHASAM SOFER:** Eggs, unlike other foods, become harder the longer they are cooked. Similarly, the more a Jew is afflicted, the more firmly he clings to his faith, as the verse states, וְכַאֲשֶׁר יְעַנּוּ אֹתוֹ כֵּן יִרְבֶּה וְכֵן יִפְרֹץ, *But as much as they would afflict it* [the nation], *so it would increase* (Exodus 1:12).

- ☐ **TORAS EMES:** Every creature in the world is born complete, except those that hatch from an egg. Although from the outside an egg appears complete, this is not the case inside the egg when it is first laid. Similarly, when the Jews left Egypt, the redemption seemed to be complete, but in reality it was not so; the redemption happened fifty days later, when we received the Torah.

סימני הסדר
The Order of the Seder

Kaddesh	**Sanctify** the day with the recitation of Kiddush.	קדש
Urechatz	**Wash** the hands before eating Karpas.	ורחץ
Karpas	Eat a **vegetable** dipped in salt water.	כרפס
Yachatz	**Break** the middle matzah. Put away larger half for Afikoman.	יחץ
Maggid	**Narrate** the story of Yetzias Mitzrayim.	מגיד
Rachtzah	**Wash** the hands prior to the meal.	רחצה
Motzi	Recite the blessing, **Who brings forth,** over matzah as a food.	מוציא
Matzah	Recite the blessing over **matzah.**	מצה
Maror	Recite the blessing for the eating of the **bitter herbs.**	מרור
Korech	Eat the **sandwich** of matzah and bitter herbs.	כורך
Shulchan Orech	The **table prepared** with the festive meal.	שלחן עורך
Tzafun	Eat the Afikoman which had been **hidden** all during the Seder.	צפון
Barech	Recite Bircas HaMazon, the **blessings** after the meal.	ברך
Hallel	Recite the **Hallel** Psalms of praise.	הלל
Nirtzah	Pray that God **accept** our observance and speedily send the Messiah.	נרצה

הגדה של פסח

❧ The Fifteen Steps of the Seder

The fifteen steps of the Seder are made up of three segments:

1. *Kaddesh* to *Maggid*:
   This segment is devoted to the Exodus from Egypt.
2. *Rachtzah* to *Korech*:
   This segment is devoted to the special foods we eat on Seder night over which special blessings are recited, in addition to the usual blessings said over the food.
3. *Shulchan Orech* to *Nirtzah*:
   This segment is devoted to the future redemption.

Q: Why do we recite the names of the fifteen steps of the Seder — Kaddesh, Urechatz, etc.?

A:
- ☐ **YESOD V'SHORESH HAAVODAH:** The names of these fifteen steps allude to deep mystical secrets, and it is therefore an auspicious omen to recite them.

- ☐ **REBBE OF MINSK:** The fifteen steps of the Seder are known as "*simanei haSeder*" — literally, "signs of the Seder." The halachah is that a lost object is claimed by means of identifying signs. During the year, as the Jew languishes in exile, he loses some of his spiritual identity and holiness. The *simanim* of the Seder — the "signs" of the Seder — allude to the fact that on the Seder night a Jew can "find" himself and reawaken himself to serve Hashem. By invoking the *simanei haSeder*, a person is naming the "signs" by which he can reclaim the spiritual heritage that he has lost.

- ☐ It is to apprise the young children of what will be happening on the Seder night and prompt them to ask the four questions of *Mah Nishtanah*.

- ☐ The names of the fifteen steps are recited to ensure that the Seder will be conducted properly, without any mistakes or deviations.

Q: Why are the four cups of wine not included in the list of the fifteen steps?

A:
- ☐ **RAV ZELAZNIK:** The first step, *Kaddesh*, includes all four of the cups.

HAGGADAH: THE ANSWER IS . . .

- The cups of wine are each part of another mitzvah of the Seder night: the first cup, in Kiddush; the second cup, in the recitation of the Haggadah; the third cup, in Bickas HaMazon; and the fourth cup, in Hallel.

◈§ The Haggadah

Q *Why is it called a "Haggadah"?*

A
- **AVUDRAHAM:** The name Haggadah is derived from the verse where we are commanded to tell the story of the Exodus: וְהִגַּדְתָּ לְבִנְךָ, *And you shall tell your son* (Exodus 13:8).
- The Haggadah contains praise and thanks to Hashem for taking us out of Egypt, in keeping with the *Targum Yerushalmi*'s interpretation of the word הִגַּדְתִּי in the verse הִגַּדְתִּי הַיּוֹם לַה' אֱלֹהֶיךָ, *I declare today to HASHEM, your God* (Deuteronomy 26:3). *Targum Yerushalmi* renders הִגַּדְתִּי as "*shabchis*," a term of praise.

Q *Why does Moshe Rabbeinu's name not appear in the Haggadah (with the exception of an incidental mention in the verse וַיַּאֲמִינוּ בַּה' וּבְמֹשֶׁה עַבְדּוֹ, And they had faith in HASHEM and in Moshe, His servant)?*

A
- **KLI CHEMDAH:** The spiritual redemption from Egypt was effected directly by Hashem, while the physical redemption was effected through Moshe Rabbeinu. The fact that Moshe's name is not mentioned in the Haggadah teaches us that the primary aspect of the redemption was spiritual.
- **RAV REUVEN MARGALIOS:** This is in order to stress that the redemption was not brought about by an angel or a messenger, but only by Hashem Himself.
- **SIFSEI CHAIM:** On the Seder night, we emphasize that Hashem redeemed us from Egypt, without the involvement of any other force.

❧ The Four Cups

Q: Why do we drink four cups of wine?

A: ☐ **MIDRASH** (*Shemos Rabbah*): The four cups of wine correspond to the four expressions of redemption: **וְהוֹצֵאתִי** אֶתְכֶם מִתַּחַת סִבְלֹת מִצְרַיִם **וְהִצַּלְתִּי** אֶתְכֶם מֵעֲבֹדָתָם **וְגָאַלְתִּי** אֶתְכֶם בִּזְרוֹעַ נְטוּיָה וּבִשְׁפָטִים גְּדֹלִים **וְלָקַחְתִּי** אֶתְכֶם לִי לְעָם, *I shall take you out* from under the burdens of Egypt; *I shall rescue you* from their service; *I shall redeem you* with an outstretched arm and with great judgments; *I shall take you to Me* for a people (*Exodus* 6:6-7). The four cups also correspond to the four edicts enacted by the evil Pharaoh: (1) the edict of slavery, to build treasure houses for the king, (2) the edict to gather the straw with which to make bricks for the building, (3) the edict to kill every baby boy, and (4) the edict to throw all the babies into the river. By drinking these four cups, we fulfill the verse כּוֹס יְשׁוּעוֹת אֶשָּׂא, *I will raise the cup of salvations* (*Psalms* 116:13).

☐ **MIDRASH** (*Bereishis Rabbah*): The four cups correspond to the four times the word "cup" is used in the description of the wine steward's dream: **וְכוֹס** פַּרְעֹה בְּיָדִי וָאֶקַּח אֶת הָעֲנָבִים וָאֶשְׂחַט אֹתָם אֶל **כּוֹס** פַּרְעֹה וָאֶתֵּן אֶת **הַכּוֹס** עַל כַּף פַּרְעֹה... וְנָתַתָּ **כוֹס** פַּרְעֹה בְּיָדוֹ, *And Pharaoh's cup was in my hand and I took the grapes, pressed them into Pharaoh's cup, and I placed the cup on Pharaoh's palm... And you will place Pharaoh's cup in his hand* (*Genesis* 40:11,13). This presaged the redemption of the Jews.

☐ **YERUSHALMI** (*Pesachim* 10:1): The four cups correspond to the four "cups of retribution" that Hashem will mete out to the nations that enslaved the Jewish people.

☐ **VILNA GAON**: The four cups correspond to four eras: this world, the days of Mashiach, the revival of the dead, and the World to Come. The first cup, that of Kiddush, corresponds to this world, signifying that a person has to sanctify himself in this world. The second cup, which accompanies the performance of the mitzvah of relating the story of the Exodus, corresponds to the days of Mashiach, about which the verse states, כִּימֵי צֵאתְךָ מֵאֶרֶץ מִצְרָיִם אַרְאֶנּוּ נִפְלָאוֹת, *As in the days when you left the land of Egypt, I will show it [the nation]* wonders (*Michah* 7:15). The third cup, that of the Grace After Meals, corresponds to the revival of the dead, when we will partake of the feast of the Leviathan. And the fourth cup, that of Hallel, corresponds to the World to Come, when we will praise Hashem.

- ☐ **SHELAH:** The four cups correspond to the four Matriarchs: Sarah, Rivkah, Rachel, and Leah. Over the first cup, that of Kiddush, we recite the words אֲשֶׁר בָּחַר בָּנוּ מִכָּל עָם, *Who has chosen us from all nations*, corresponding to Sarah, who converted the women. The second cup, for Rivkah, accompanies *Maggid*, in which we tell the story of the struggle between Yaakov and Lavan, who was Rivkah's brother. The third cup, that of Bircas HaMazon, said after a meal, corresponds to Rachel, whose son Yosef provided food for Egypt. And the fourth cup, that of Hallel, the songs of praise, corresponds to Leah, who was the first one to give thanks to Hashem (when her son Yehudah was born — see *Berachos* 7b).

- ☐ **ABARBANEL:** The four cups correspond to four distinct redemptions of the Jewish people: (1) when Hashem chose Avraham and his descendants to be His special people, (2) the redemption from Egypt, (3) our redemption from the hands of our oppressors throughout the various exiles, and (4) the future redemption.

Q *Why do we drink specifically four cups of wine rather than using a different drink or eating four servings of a particular food?*

A
- ☐ **MATTEH MOSHE:** The Jewish people are compared to a grapevine. Just as a grapevine cannot be grafted with any other tree, so too the Jewish people maintain their uniqueness and cannot meld with other nations. By drinking four cups of wine, we highlight the uniqueness of the Jewish people, who did not assimilate into Egyptian society.

- ☐ **RAV AHARON OF KARLIN:** The numerical value of the words *kos yayin*, cup of wine, is 156. The numerical value of *cheirus*, freedom, is 624, which is equivalent to 156 multiplied by four. We therefore drink four cups of wine to commemorate our freedom from Egypt.

- ☐ **SHEM MISHMUEL:** The four cups of wine allude to the praiseworthy actions of the Jewish people. Just as wine clouds a person's judgment, the Jews suspended their judgment, as it were, and followed Moshe into the wilderness with complete faith despite having no provisions.

- ☐ **HAGGADAH CHODESH HAAVIV:** Wine is unique in that if it is left inside the grape, it spoils, but if it is separated from the grape, it improves. Similarly, when the Jewish people were in Egypt, they descended to the forty-ninth level of impurity, but when they left Egypt, they abandoned impurity and idol worship and embraced Torah and holiness.

Q: Why do we not recite a blessing over the mitzvah of drinking four cups of wine?

A:
- ☐ **ROKEACH:** We recite blessings only over mitzvos that are performed without interruption. Since the four cups are drunk at intervals, no special blessing is recited over them.

- ☐ **AVUDRAHAM:** The time to recite a blessing over the four cups is before we drink the first cup, but because that is the cup used for Kiddush, as on every Shabbos and Yom Tov, we do not say a separate blessing over it. Once we have not recited a special blessing over the first cup, we no longer recite one over the subsequent three cups. They are all part of one mitzvah and we do not wish to make a separation between the first cup and the other three.

It was late afternoon on Erev Pesach when a visitor came to see Rav Yoshe Ber of Brisk. "Rebbe," he asked, "am I allowed to fulfill the mitzvah to drink the four cups with milk?"

"Why?" asked the rav. "Are you ill?"

"I am perfectly healthy, thank God," the Jew answered. "But wine is expensive. I can't afford it this year."

The rav ruled that he could fulfill his obligation with milk, and when the Jew took leave of him, the rav handed him twenty-five rubles.

At first the Jew was reluctant to take the money. He had not come to ask for a donation, but to ask a question of halachah. After much persuading, the Jew agreed to take the money as a loan.

After the Jew left, the rebbetzin, who had observed the exchange, asked, "Why did you give him so much? If you were giving him money to buy wine, two or three rubles would have been enough."

"By the man's question," answered Rav Yoshe Ber, "I realized that he not only lacked wine, but also other necessities for the holiday, such as chicken and meat. Otherwise, how could he drink four cups of milk?"

קדש

Kiddush should be recited and the Seder begun as soon after synagogue services as possible — however, not before nightfall. Each participant's cup should be poured by someone else to symbolize the majesty of the evening, as though each participant had a servant.

Some have a custom to say the following declaration of intent:

הִנְנִי מוּכָן וּמְזוּמָּן לְקַדֵּשׁ עַל הַיַּיִן וּלְקַיֵּם מִצְוַת כּוֹס רִאשׁוֹן מֵאַרְבַּע כּוֹסוֹת. לְשֵׁם יִחוּד קֻדְשָׁא בְּרִיךְ הוּא וּשְׁכִינְתֵּיהּ, עַל יְדֵי הַהוּא טָמִיר וְנֶעְלָם, בְּשֵׁם כָּל יִשְׂרָאֵל. וִיהִי נֹעַם אֲדֹנָי אֱלֹהֵינוּ עָלֵינוּ, וּמַעֲשֵׂה יָדֵינוּ כּוֹנְנָה עָלֵינוּ, וּמַעֲשֵׂה יָדֵינוּ כּוֹנְנֵהוּ.

On Friday night begin here:

(וַיְהִי עֶרֶב וַיְהִי בֹקֶר)

יוֹם הַשִּׁשִּׁי וַיְכֻלּוּ הַשָּׁמַיִם וְהָאָרֶץ וְכָל צְבָאָם. וַיְכַל אֱלֹהִים בַּיּוֹם הַשְּׁבִיעִי מְלַאכְתּוֹ אֲשֶׁר עָשָׂה, וַיִּשְׁבֹּת בַּיּוֹם הַשְּׁבִיעִי מִכָּל מְלַאכְתּוֹ אֲשֶׁר עָשָׂה. וַיְבָרֶךְ אֱלֹהִים אֶת יוֹם הַשְּׁבִיעִי וַיְקַדֵּשׁ אֹתוֹ, כִּי בוֹ שָׁבַת מִכָּל מְלַאכְתּוֹ אֲשֶׁר בָּרָא אֱלֹהִים לַעֲשׂוֹת.[1]

□ **MA'ASEH NISSIM:** The Ashkenazi custom is to recite the blessing of *hagafen* on each cup. We do not recite an additional blessing over the mitzvah, just as we do not recite a separate blessing over the mitzvah of Bircas HaMazon.

קדש / Kaddesh

Q *Why are women obligated to drink the four cups of wine when they are generally exempt from time-bound commandments?*

A □ **MIDRASH:** Although women were not directly threatened by Pharaoh's decree to annihilate the baby boys, this decree had serious implications for them as well; in order for the women to survive and flourish, the males had to live, too. Women drink four cups of wine to give thanks that the males were saved from this decree.

הגדה של פסח [42]

KADDESH

Kiddush should be recited and the Seder begun as soon after synagogue services as possible — however, not before nightfall. Each participant's cup should be poured by someone else to symbolize the majesty of the evening, as though each participant had a servant.

Some have a custom to say the following declaration of intent:

Behold, I am prepared and ready to recite the Kiddush over wine, and to fulfill the mitzvah of the first of the Four Cups. For the sake of the unification of the Holy One, Blessed is He, and His Presence, through Him Who is hidden and inscrutable — [I pray] in the name of all Israel. May the pleasantness of the Lord, our God, be upon us, and may He establish our handiwork for us; our handiwork may He establish.

On Friday night begin here:

(And there was evening and there was morning)

The sixth day. Thus the heaven and the earth were finished, and all their array. On the seventh day God completed His work which He had done, and He abstained on the seventh day from all His work which He had done. God blessed the seventh day and hallowed it, because on it He abstained from all His work which God created to make.[1]

---

1. *Genesis* 1:31-2:3.

☐ **SDEI CHEMED:** Women were also included in the miracle of the redemption from Egypt..

Q *How does the Kiddush on the Seder night differ from the Kiddush of Shabbos and the holidays?*

A ☐ On Shabbos and the holidays, we wash and eat the meal immediately after Kiddush. On the Seder night, we wash and eat the meal later, after Maggid.

☐ During the rest of the year, the person making Kiddush pours his own cup of wine. At the Seder, as a symbol of freedom, someone else pours the Kiddush wine for the head of the household (and for some, the custom is that none of the participants of the Seder pours his own cup).

[43] **HAGGADAH: THE ANSWER IS . . .**

*On all nights other than Friday, begin here;
on Friday night include all passages in parentheses.*

סַבְרִי מָרָנָן וְרַבָּנָן וְרַבּוֹתַי:

בָּרוּךְ אַתָּה יהוה אֱלֹהֵינוּ מֶלֶךְ הָעוֹלָם, בּוֹרֵא פְּרִי הַגָּפֶן.

בָּרוּךְ אַתָּה יהוה אֱלֹהֵינוּ מֶלֶךְ הָעוֹלָם, אֲשֶׁר בָּחַר בָּנוּ מִכָּל עָם, וְרוֹמְמָנוּ מִכָּל לָשׁוֹן, וְקִדְּשָׁנוּ בְּמִצְוֹתָיו. וַתִּתֶּן לָנוּ יהוה אֱלֹהֵינוּ בְּאַהֲבָה (שַׁבָּתוֹת לִמְנוּחָה וּ)מוֹעֲדִים לְשִׂמְחָה חַגִּים וּזְמַנִּים לְשָׂשׂוֹן אֶת יוֹם (הַשַּׁבָּת הַזֶּה וְאֶת יוֹם) חַג הַמַּצּוֹת הַזֶּה, זְמַן חֵרוּתֵנוּ (בְּאַהֲבָה) מִקְרָא קֹדֶשׁ, זֵכֶר לִיצִיאַת מִצְרָיִם. כִּי בָנוּ בָחַרְתָּ וְאוֹתָנוּ קִדַּשְׁתָּ מִכָּל הָעַמִּים, (וְשַׁבָּת) וּמוֹעֲדֵי קָדְשֶׁךָ (בְּאַהֲבָה וּבְרָצוֹן) בְּשִׂמְחָה וּבְשָׂשׂוֹן הִנְחַלְתָּנוּ. בָּרוּךְ אַתָּה יהוה, מְקַדֵּשׁ (הַשַּׁבָּת וְ)יִשְׂרָאֵל וְהַזְּמַנִּים.

*On Saturday night, add the following two paragraphs.
Two candles or wicks with flames touching are held and the following blessings are recited. After the first blessing, hold the fingers up to the flame to see the reflected light.*

בָּרוּךְ אַתָּה יהוה אֱלֹהֵינוּ מֶלֶךְ הָעוֹלָם, בּוֹרֵא מְאוֹרֵי הָאֵשׁ.

בָּרוּךְ אַתָּה יהוה אֱלֹהֵינוּ מֶלֶךְ הָעוֹלָם, הַמַּבְדִּיל בֵּין קֹדֶשׁ לְחוֹל, בֵּין אוֹר לְחֹשֶׁךְ, בֵּין יִשְׂרָאֵל לָעַמִּים, בֵּין יוֹם הַשְּׁבִיעִי לְשֵׁשֶׁת יְמֵי הַמַּעֲשֶׂה. בֵּין קְדֻשַּׁת שַׁבָּת לִקְדֻשַּׁת יוֹם טוֹב הִבְדַּלְתָּ, וְאֶת יוֹם הַשְּׁבִיעִי מִשֵּׁשֶׁת יְמֵי הַמַּעֲשֶׂה קִדַּשְׁתָּ, הִבְדַּלְתָּ וְקִדַּשְׁתָּ אֶת עַמְּךָ יִשְׂרָאֵל בִּקְדֻשָּׁתֶךָ. בָּרוּךְ אַתָּה יהוה, הַמַּבְדִּיל בֵּין קֹדֶשׁ לְקֹדֶשׁ.

הגדה של פסח [44]

On all nights other than Friday, begin here;
on Friday night include all passages in parentheses.

By your leave, my masters and teachers:

Blessed are You, HASHEM, our God, King of the universe, Who creates the fruit of the vine.

Blessed are You, HASHEM, our God, King of the universe, Who has chosen us from all nations, exalted us above all tongues, and sanctified us with His commandments. And You, HASHEM, our God, have lovingly given us (Sabbaths for rest,) appointed times for gladness, feasts and seasons for joy, (this Sabbath and) this Feast of Matzos, the season of our freedom (in love), a holy convocation in commemoration of the Exodus from Egypt. For You have chosen and sanctified us above all peoples, (and the Sabbath) and Your holy festivals (in love and favor), in gladness and joy have You granted us as a heritage. Blessed are You, HASHEM, Who sanctifies (the Sabbath,) Israel, and the festive seasons.

On Saturday night, add the following two paragraphs.
Two candles or wicks with flames touching are held and the following blessings are recited. After the first blessing, hold the fingers up to the flame to see the reflected light.

Blessed are You, HASHEM, our God, King of the universe, Who creates the illumination of the fire.

Blessed are You, HASHEM, our God, King of the universe, Who distinguishes between sacred and secular, between light and darkness, between Israel and the nations, between the seventh day and the six days of activity. You have distinguished between the holiness of the Sabbath and the holiness of a Festival, and have sanctified the seventh day above the six days of activity. You distinguished and sanctified Your nation, Israel, with Your holiness. Blessed are You, HASHEM, Who distinguishes between holiness and holiness.

[45] **HAGGADAH: THE ANSWER IS . . .**

On all nights conclude here:

בָּרוּךְ אַתָּה יהוה אֱלֹהֵינוּ מֶלֶךְ הָעוֹלָם, שֶׁהֶחֱיָנוּ וְקִיְּמָנוּ וְהִגִּיעָנוּ לַזְּמַן הַזֶּה.

The wine should be drunk without delay while reclining on the left side. It is preferable to drink the entire cup, but at the very least, most of the cup should be drained.

ורחץ

The head of the household — according to many opinions, all participants in the Seder — washes his hands as if to eat bread [pouring water from a cup, twice on the right hand and twice on the left], but without reciting a blessing.

- ☐ Kiddush on the Seder night must be made on wine, while on Shabbos or the holidays it is permissible, *b'dieved*, to make Kiddush on bread.
- ☐ Kiddush on the Seder night may be recited only at night, after dark, while Shabbos and most holidays may be ushered in earlier, and Kiddush may be recited even while it is still day.

ורחץ / Urechatz

The source for this hand-washing is the halachah in the Talmud (*Pesachim* 115a) that states that a food that was dipped in a liquid requires *netilas yadayim*, ritual hand-washing. Since we are about to dip a vegetable in salt water and eat it (*Karpas*), we are required to wash. No blessing is recited over this hand-washing (*Shulchan Aruch* 158:4).

Q. Why do we wash our hands after Kaddesh?

A.
- ☐ **CHIDDUSHEI HARIM:** At times, עֲשֵׂה טוֹב, *Do good*, comes before סוּר מֵרָע, *Turn from evil*. The Seder night is one of these times.

- ☐ **AVNEI NEZER:** *Urechatz*, which represents purification from evil (as it states, סוּר מֵרָע, *Turn from evil*), is done after *Kaddesh*, which represents sanctification (עֲשֵׂה טוֹב, *Do good*).

[46] הגדה של פסח

On all nights conclude here:

Blessed are You, HASHEM, our God, King of the universe, Who has kept us alive, sustained us, and brought us to this season.

The wine should be drunk without delay while reclining on the left side. It is preferable to drink the entire cup, but at the very least, most of the cup should be drained.

URECHATZ

The head of the household — according to many opinions, all participants in the Seder — washes his hands as if to eat bread [pouring water from a cup, twice on the right hand and twice on the left], but without reciting a blessing.

Although the usual spiritual progression is the reverse — first eliminate evil and then do good — this holy night is unique, and a person is able to become sanctified even if he has not yet drawn himself away from evil.

☐ All year, *netilas yadayim* confers purity on a person. The hand-washing of the Seder night confers an additional purity: the pure *chinuch* of the Jewish child.

☐ The word "*urechatz*" begins with the letter *vav* because it is connected to *Kaddesh*, which precedes it. In *Kaddesh*, we declare that the Jewish people are sanctified to Hashem. As part of the sanctification of this night, it is proper for us to wash away impurity.

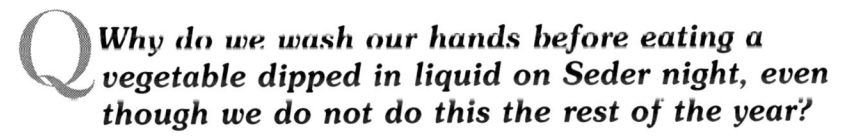

Q *Why do we wash our hands before eating a vegetable dipped in liquid on Seder night, even though we do not do this the rest of the year?*

A ☐ **PELE YO'ETZ:** On the Seder night, we meticulously observe every mitzvah and stringency, even the most minor, just as we are meticulous on Pesach regarding the tiniest amount of *chametz* (leaven).

☐ **CHAYEI ADAM:** This hand-washing is one of the unusual practices of the Seder night whose goal is to prompt the children to ask questions.

[47] **HAGGADAH: THE ANSWER IS . . .**

כרפס

All participants take a vegetable other than maror and dip it into salt water. A piece smaller in volume than half an egg should be used. The following blessing is recited [with the intention that it also applies to the maror which will be eaten during the meal] before the vegetable is eaten.

בָּרוּךְ אַתָּה יהוה אֱלֹהֵינוּ מֶלֶךְ הָעוֹלָם, בּוֹרֵא פְּרִי הָאֲדָמָה.

יחץ

The head of the household breaks the middle matzah in two. He puts the smaller part back between the two whole matzos, and wraps up the larger part for later use as the Afikoman. Some briefly place the Afikoman portion on their shoulders, in accordance with the Biblical verse recounting that Israel left Egypt carrying their matzos on their shoulders, and say בְּבֶהָלוּ יָצָאנוּ מִמִּצְרָיִם, *"In haste we went out of Egypt."*

☐ We are meticulous to observe this hand-washing on the Seder night to accustom ourselves to the higher level of purity that will be required of us when the Beis HaMikdash is rebuilt.

❧ כרפס / Karpas

The blessing we say before we eat the *karpas* includes the *maror* that we will eat later (*Tosafos*). This is why we do not say *borei pri ha'adamah* before we eat the *maror*, but only recite the special blessing of *al achilas maror*.

Q Why do we call it karpas?

A ☐ **AVUDRAHAM:** The letters of the word "*karpas*" (כַּרְפַּס) can be rearranged to read ס׳ פרך; the letter *samech*, whose numerical value is 60, represents the 600,000 Jews (60 multiplied by 10,000) who performed *avodas perech*, hard labor, in Egypt.

Q Why do we eat karpas?

A ☐ **MAHARIL:** Eating a vegetable at the beginning of the meal stimulates the appetite. This is a practice of free men.

הגדה של פסח [48]

KARPAS

All participants take a vegetable other than maror and dip it into salt water. A piece smaller in volume than half an egg should be used. The following blessing is recited [with the intention that it also applies to the maror which will be eaten during the meal] before the vegetable is eaten.

Blessed are You, HASHEM, our God, King of the universe, Who creates the fruits of the earth.

YACHATZ

The head of the household breaks the middle matzah in two. He puts the smaller part back between the two whole matzos, and wraps up the larger part for later use as the Afikoman. Some briefly place the Afikoman portion on their shoulders, in accordance with the Biblical verse recounting that Israel left Egypt carrying their matzos on their shoulders, and say בְּבְחִלוּ יָצָאנוּ מִמִּצְרָיִם, "*In haste we went out of Egypt.*"

- ☐ **YISMACH YISRAEL:** *Karpas* follows the sanctification of *Kaddesh* and the ritual purification of *Urechatz*. This hints at the Jew's obligation to uncover the hidden spark of holiness that is buried deep inside him, just as the vegetable eaten for *Karpas* grows buried in the earth, yet merits having a blessing made over it at the Seder. Seeing how a lowly vegetable can be elevated to such a sanctified status can inspire a person to rise from a lowly level and reach heights of holiness.
- ☐ We eat the *Karpas* as a deviation from the normal practice, to prompt the children to ask why we are dipping a vegetable in salt water and eating it before the meal begins.
- ☐ The vegetable used for *Karpas* grows in the earth, alluding to the lowly status of the Jews in Egypt, where they were trampled upon like earth.

◆§ יחץ / Yachatz

Q *Why does Yachatz follow Karpas?*

A ☐ **ALSHICH:** The word "*yachatz*" means "break in half." Here we break the middle matzah in half and hide the larger piece as the *Afikoman*. *Yachatz* follows *Karpas* to teach that if a

מגיד

Some recite the following declaration of intent before Maggid:

הִנְנִי מוּכָן וּמְזוּמָן לְקַיֵּם הַמִּצְוָה לְסַפֵּר בִּיצִיאַת מִצְרָיִם. לְשֵׁם יִחוּד קֻדְשָׁא בְּרִיךְ הוּא וּשְׁכִינְתֵּיהּ, עַל יְדֵי הַהוּא טָמִיר וְנֶעְלָם, בְּשֵׁם כָּל יִשְׂרָאֵל. וִיהִי נֹעַם אֲדֹנָי אֱלֹהֵינוּ עָלֵינוּ, וּמַעֲשֵׂה יָדֵינוּ כּוֹנְנָה עָלֵינוּ, וּמַעֲשֵׂה יָדֵינוּ כּוֹנְנֵהוּ:

person contents himself with *Karpas* (i.e., vegetables, simple foods) and does not pursue luxury, he will be able to "break bread" (*Yachatz*) and share his food with the poor.

Q: Why do we hide the Afikoman?

A:
- ☐ **KOL BO:** This prompts the children to ask questions: why is the matzah being hidden, even though it has not even been eaten yet?
- ☐ **SFAS EMES:** The matzah reminds us of the redemption from Egypt. We hide it in order to express our belief that at the time of the future redemption, we will see great miracles again, even though right now Hashem's ways are hidden from us.
- ☐ **DIVREI YOEL:** We are embarrassed that our sins have prevented the Beis HaMikdash from being rebuilt and therefore we cannot bring the *korban Pesach*, so we hide the *Afikoman*, which commemorates the *korban Pesach*.
- ☐ We hide the *Afikoman* so that it will not be seen during the meal and accidentally eaten.

Q: Why do we break the matzah in half?

A:
- ☐ **ROKEACH:** Breaking the matzah commemorates the splitting of the sea.
- ☐ **RAN:** The Torah calls matzah לֶחֶם עֹנִי, *bread of affliction* (*Deuteronomy* 16:3). The word "*oni*" is written *chaser*, without a *vav*. Chazal derive from this that the matzah should be broken, in the manner of a pauper, who does not have a whole loaf of bread, but only pieces of bread. For this reason, both times that matzah is eaten for the sake of a mitzvah, we use a broken piece.

MAGGID

Some recite the following declaration of intent before Maggid:

Behold, I am prepared and ready to fulfill the mitzvah of telling of the Exodus from Egypt. For the sake of the unification of the Holy One, Blessed is He, and His presence, through Him Who is hidden and inscrutable — [I pray] in the name of all Israel. May the pleasantness of the Lord, our God, be upon us, and may He establish our handiwork for us; our handiwork may He establish.

- ☐ **MAHARIL:** Matzah is poor man's bread. When we eat matzah on the Seder night, we eat it in the manner of a pauper, who does not know whether he will have bread the next day and therefore saves half of his bread for tomorrow.

- ☐ **RAV AHARON OF KARLIN:** During the *Bris Bein Habesarim* (Covenant Between the Parts), when Hashem informed Avraham that there would be an Egyptian exile, Avraham took animals and cut them in half. In commemoration of this, we break the middle matzah.

- ☐ **CHASAM SOFER:** We break the matzah in half to hint that the Seder night is divided into two portions: the first half relates to the exile in Egypt, while the second half relates to the redemption.

מגיד / Maggid

Q *Why is no blessing recited over the mitzvah of sippur Yetzias Mitzrayim (retelling the story of the Exodus)?*

A
- ☐ **SHIBBOLEI HALEKET:** The selection that begins with the words בָּרוּךְ הַמָּקוֹם, *Blessed is the Omnipresent*, and ends with the blessing אֲשֶׁר גְּאָלָנוּ, *Who has redeemed us*, is considered the blessing for this mitzvah.

- ☐ **RASHBA:** Telling the story of the Exodus is a mitzvah that has no fixed amount, since we can discharge our obligation even with casual talk about the Exodus. Since we do not recite a blessing over a mitzvah that has no fixed amount, we do not say a blessing over this mitzvah.

- ☐ **MEIRI:** This mitzvah is covered by Shema and its blessings, which mention the Exodus.

- ☐ **PRI MEGADIM:** The obligation to relate the story of the Exodus may be discharged just by thinking about it, and no blessing is recited over a mitzvah that does not require action.

- ☐ **CHASAM SOFER:** When a gentile converts, he recites the blessing over his immersion *after* the immersion. Prior to immersing, he is not yet Jewish and may not say the words "Who has sanctified us with His mitzvos and commanded us...." On the Seder night, we are required to view ourselves as if we have left Egypt, so at the beginning of the Seder, we are still "gentiles," so to speak. Consequently, we cannot recite a blessing before the mitzvah of *sippur Yetzias Mitzrayim*.

- ☐ **BIRKAS HASHIR:** The mitzvah of *sippur Yetzias Mitzrayim* is included in the blessing of Kiddush, where we mention the Exodus.

- ☐ **SFAS EMES:** We do not recite blessings over interpersonal mitzvos, such as doing *chesed* or visiting the sick, since these mitzvos are intuitive and would be self-evident even without a Divine commandment. Likewise, it should be obvious to every Jew that he has to thank Hashem for the miracle of the Exodus, in accordance with the Talmud's teaching in the name of Rav Nachman, "A slave who is set free must thank and praise his master for freeing him" (*Pesachim* 119). Even if Hashem had not commanded us to remember the Exodus, simple logic would have dictated that we were duty-bound to thank Him for it.

- ☐ The mitzvah of *sippur Yetzias Mitzrayim* requires the presence of a listener, and we do not recite a blessing over a mitzvah that is dependent on another person. For instance, we do not recite a blessing over the mitzvah of *tzedakah* (giving charity), because we are concerned that the intended recipient might not receive or accept the money and the blessing will have been in vain (see *She'eilos U'Teshuvos Rashba* 1:254).

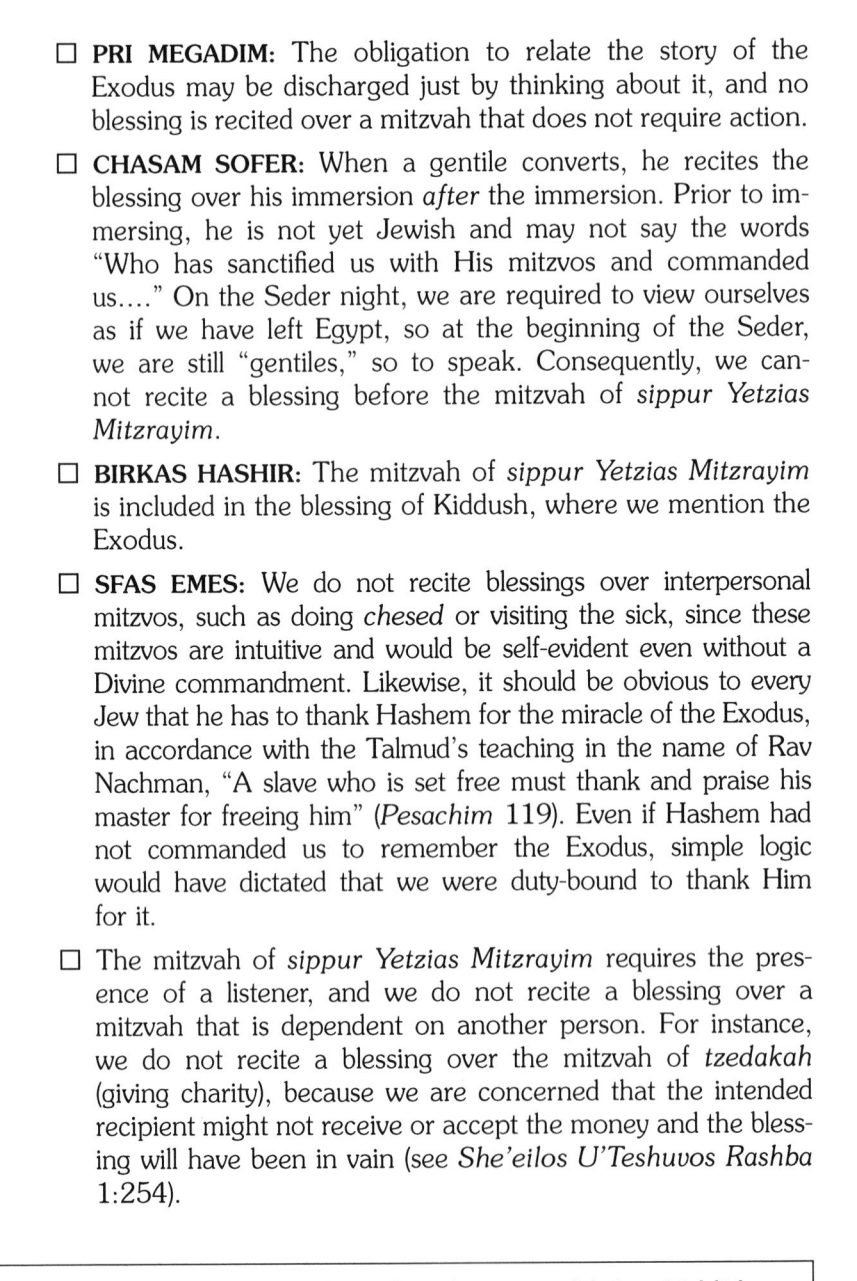

The Chafetz Chaim would translate the Haggadah into Yiddish on the Seder night so that everyone would understand what was being said and thank Hashem for all the miracles. Thus they could fulfill the mitzvah to relate the story of the Exodus properly (Rav Leib HaKohen, the son of the Chafetz Chaim).

Q *Why does the mitzvah of וְהִגַּדְתָּ לְבִנְךָ,*
And you shall tell your son,
apply specifically on the Seder night?

A ☐ **RAV BETZALEL ZOLTY:** On the Seder night, the focus is on the children. We derive this from a fundamental dispute between Pharaoh and the leaders of the Jewish nation, Moshe and Aharon. Moshe and Aharon asked Pharaoh to let the entire Jewish people leave Egypt, as the verse states, בִּנְעָרֵינוּ וּבִזְקֵנֵינוּ נֵלֵךְ, *With our youngsters and with our elders shall we go* (Exodus 10:9). Pharaoh realized that the redemption of the Jewish people had to include the children, and he therefore insisted that only the men be allowed to leave. Children will also play a fundamental role in the future redemption, as the verse states: וְהֵשִׁיב לֵב אָבוֹת עַל בָּנִים וְלֵב בָּנִים עַל אֲבוֹתָם, *And he will turn back [to God] the hearts of fathers with [their] sons and the hearts of sons with their fathers* (Malachi 3:24). For this reason, on the Seder night, when we tell the story of the redemption from Egypt, we stress that the children were integral participants, and the mitzvah to relate the story to the children applies specifically now.

☐ **NESIVOS SHALOM:** With the fulfillment of the mitzvah of וְהִגַּדְתָּ לְבִנְךָ, *And you shall tell your son*, a father instills in his children belief in Hashem. There is no more suitable time to impart this important principle than Pesach, the holiday of faith.

Q *The mitzvah of remembering the Exodus applies every day of the year. How is our recalling the Exodus on the Seder night different?*

A ☐ **MAHARAL:** Every day of the year the obligation is to *mention* that Hashem redeemed our ancestors from Egypt. The obligation on the Seder night is to *demonstrate* that we ourselves left Egypt: חַיָּב אָדָם לִרְאוֹת אֶת עַצְמוֹ כְּאִלּוּ הוּא יָצָא מִמִּצְרַיִם, *It is one's duty to regard himself as though he personally had gone out of Egypt* (Pesachim 116b). During the rest of the year, recalling the Exodus is enough. On this night, we

---

The Chasam Sofer used to translate every word of the Haggadah for his children, without any commentaries or lengthy explanations (*Minhagei HaChasam Sofer*).

The broken matzah is lifted for all to see as the head of the household begins with the following brief explanation of the proceedings.

הָא לַחְמָא עַנְיָא דִּי אֲכָלוּ אַבְהָתָנָא בְּאַרְעָא דְמִצְרָיִם. כָּל דִּכְפִין יֵיתֵי וְיֵכוֹל, כָּל דִּצְרִיךְ יֵיתֵי וְיִפְסַח. הָשַּׁתָּא הָכָא, לְשָׁנָה הַבָּאָה בְּאַרְעָא דְיִשְׂרָאֵל. הָשַּׁתָּא עַבְדֵי, לְשָׁנָה הַבָּאָה בְּנֵי חוֹרִין.

fulfill the mitzvah of *sippur Yetzias Mitzrayim* in a manner that highlights our personal involvement in the redemption.

□ **RAV CHAIM SOLOVEITCHIK:** There are three differences between the mitzvah of *zechiras Yetzias Mitzrayim*, remembering the Exodus, which applies all year round, and the mitzvah of *sippur Yetzias Mitzrayim*, telling the story of the Exodus, which applies only on the Seder night:

1. *Zechiras Yetzias Mitzrayim* involves only oneself, while *sippur Yetzias Mitzrayim* involves others, in the form of question-and-answer dialogue.

2. *Zechiras Yetzias Mitzrayim* requires only the mention of the Exodus, while *sippur Yetzias Mitzrayim* follows the specific sequence ordained by Chazal that we carry out on the Seder night: opening with a description of our people's lowly beginnings and concluding with glorious descriptions of the redemption.

3. *Sippur Yetzias Mitzrayim* includes all the reasons for the Exodus, to the extent that Rabban Gamliel said that one who does not mention Pesach, matzah, and *maror* has not fulfilled his obligation. It also involves an entire Seder, replete with unusual practices aimed at prompting the children to ask questions. *Zechiras Yetzias Mitzrayim* includes none of this.

□ **BRISKER RAV:** *Sippur Yetzias Mitzrayim* on the Seder night includes the study of the laws of Pesach. These are not included in *zechiras Yetzias Mitzrayim*.

◈§ הָא לַחְמָא עַנְיָא / **This is the bread of affliction**

According to *Ra'avyah* and *Malbim*, the recitation of *Ha Lachma Anya* was instituted in Bavel; according to *Shibbolei HaLeket*, it was instituted in Eretz Yisrael.

The broken matzah is lifted for all to see as the head of the household begins with the following brief explanation of the proceedings.

This is the bread of affliction that our fathers ate in the land of Egypt. Whoever is hungry — let him come and eat! Whoever is needy — let him come and celebrate Passover! Now, we are here; next year may we be in the Land of Israel! Now, we are slaves; next year may we be free men!

According to *Ma'aseh Nissim*, the recitation of *Ha Lachma Anya* was instituted after the destruction of the second Beis HaMikdash. *Ha Lachma Anya* was not said while the Beis HaMikdash was standing (according to the Rambam's text).

The *Yaavetz* points out that the paragraph of *Ha Lachma Anya* contains twenty-eight words, the numerical equivalent of the word כֹּחַ, *power*, as in the verse אֲשֶׁר הוֹצֵאתָ מֵאֶרֶץ מִצְרַיִם **בְּכֹחַ** גָּדוֹל וּבְיָד חֲזָקָה..., *...whom You have taken out of the land of Egypt, with great **power** and a strong hand* (Exodus 32:11).

According to the *Abarbanel*, *Ha Lachma Anya* should be recited at the entrance to the house, with the door open, so that paupers can hear the invitation and enter.

Ha Lachma Anya speaks of the matzah that the Jews ate in Egypt. This paragraph marks the beginning of the Haggadah, indicating that this "bread of affliction" will be the subject of our forthcoming discussion.

Ha Lachma Anya contains three statements, referring to the past, the present, and the future respectively. The first sentence is a reference to the past, referring to the Jews' suffering in Egypt. The second sentence is about the present, inviting the poor to partake of our meal. This demonstrates that it is the Jewish people's unity that protected them from destruction throughout history. The final sentence gives us hope that we will soon experience the future final redemption.

Q: Why does the Haggadah begin with Ha Lachma Anya?

A: ❑ **KOL BO:** It is an explanation to the children of why we break the matzah in half in *Yachatz*. We break the matzah and put away half of it in the manner of paupers, who leave over half of their food for the next day. Since the topic of *Ha Lachma*

Anya is inviting the poor, it hints that we break the matzah because we ourselves are like paupers.

- ☐ **ABARBANEL:** We wish to ensure, at the beginning of the Seder, that every needy person is provided for.
- ☐ **MAHARAL:** We want to make it clear that the story we are about to tell relates to the matzah, the "bread of affliction."
- ☐ **SIACH YITZCHAK:** Before we begin the mitzvah of telling the story of the Exodus, we involve ourselves in the mitzvah of *tzedakah*. This is in the spirit of the Talmud's teaching that Rabbi Elazar would give charity before beginning to pray (*Bava Basra* 10a).
- ☐ **RAV URI KELLERMAN:** Humility is a fundamental trait in the service of Hashem and allows us to become close to Him. We begin the Haggadah with a dose of humility, discussing the "bread of affliction" and welcoming the needy, in order to draw ourselves nearer to Hashem and strengthen our faith.

Q Why is this passage written in Aramaic?

A
- ☐ **AVUDRAHAM:** The angels do not understand Aramaic (see *Shabbos* 12b). Therefore, the author of the Haggadah chose to use Aramaic for this section so that the angels will not attempt to prosecute us and mention the sins that make us unworthy of redemption.
- ☐ **RASHBATZ; KOL BO:** During the Second Temple era, the women and children understood only Aramaic. In order to ensure their participation in the Seder, this paragraph is said in the vernacular.
- ☐ **RA'AVAN:** Only this paragraph was instituted in Bavel, where Aramaic was spoken; that is why the rest of the Haggadah is not in Aramaic.
- ☐ **MA'ASEH NISSIM:** *Ha Lachma Anya* is said in Aramaic to set it apart from the rest of the Haggadah, with which we fulfill the obligation to relate the story of the Exodus.
- ☐ **ORCHOS CHAIM:** It is said in Aramaic so that the gentiles will not understand what is being said and think that the Jews are plotting a rebellion when they say that next year they will be free men.

- ☐ **MALBIM:** It is said in the vernacular so that the children will understand what is being said.
- ☐ **BELZER REBBE:** When the Jews left Egypt, they were elevated to the level of angels, and the matzah they ate had the taste of manna, the "food of angels." On the Seder night too we are elevated to the level of angels by eating matzah. When we introduce this "food of angels," we do so in Aramaic so as not to incur the angels' jealousy.
- ☐ On the Seder night, the Shechinah reveals itself. By reciting this section in Aramaic, we are declaring that Hashem is with us and we can make requests of Him directly, without requiring the angels to act as intermediaries.
- ☐ The Haggadah begins and ends with Aramaic; its opening paragraph is *Ha Lachma Anya*, and it closes with *Chad Gadya*. The Maharal teaches that the Aramaic language contains a level of holiness that indicates a world beyond this temporal one. The use of Aramaic at the opening and closing of the Haggadah shows that the Jewish people transcend this world and belong to a higher realm.
- ☐ It is said in the vernacular so that the poor will understand it and accept the invitation to come and eat.

Q: Why is matzah called "lachma anya," bread of affliction?

A:
- ☐ **TALMUD** (*Pesachim* 115): The word *anya* is related to the verb *la'anos*, "to say" or "to answer," since much of what is said when retelling the story of the Exodus revolves around the matzah.
- ☐ **TALMUD** (*Pesachim* 36): Matzah has no flavoring, and is therefore "poor" in taste (*ani*, poor, is related to the word *anya*).
- ☐ **RAMBAN:** *Anya*, affliction, is a reference to the Jews' affliction in Egypt, where they received scant rations of bread and water.
- ☐ **AVUDRAHAM:** Because matzah is more difficult to digest than regular bread, it is typically given to prisoners so that they will not eat much. This was the food given to the Jewish slaves in Egypt.
- ☐ **DOVER SHALOM:** The word *anya* is related to the word *anah*, answer. The Seder night is an auspicious time for Hashem to respond to our requests. At a time when we eat matzah, we are "answered."

The Seder plate is removed and the second of the four cups of wine is poured. The youngest present asks the reasons for the unusual proceedings of the evening.

מַה נִּשְׁתַּנָּה הַלַּיְלָה הַזֶּה מִכָּל הַלֵּילוֹת?

Q *What is so special about Pesach that specifically on this holiday we extend a special invitation to the needy?*

A ☐ **RID:** There are several mitzvos on Pesach night that relate to eating. We invite those who lack food in order to enable them to fulfill these mitzvos.

☐ **AVUDRAHAM:** It is very costly to buy matzah and other food for the Seder night. Since the poor cannot afford these high costs, we invite them to partake with us.

☐ **BINAH L'ITIM:** The needy are generally embarrassed to be hosted by others, but on the Seder night, we assure them that they need not be ashamed, for our ancestors were paupers in Egypt. Just as Hashem redeemed our ancestors, He will aid the needy in our time.

☐ **VILNA GAON:** On every other holiday, there is a general obligation to be happy, and we invite needy guests to share in our joy. On the Seder night, however, our invitation to the needy comes from our desire to enable them to fulfill the special obligation for each person to feel as though he was freed from Egypt.

☐ **BEIS HALEVI:** We refer to the mitzvah of *tzedakah* at the opening of the Seder to emphasize our fervent hope that through *tzedakah* we will merit the future redemption, as Chazal teach, "Great is charity, for it brings the redemption closer" (*Bava Basra* 10a).

☐ **SHA'AR HATZIYUN** (*Mishnah Berurah* 429:1): Seder night is a time of freedom, when we recline in regal fashion. It is not respectful to Hashem that some of His people go hungry at this time.

☐ **HASHIR V'HASHEVACH:** Remembering the slavery and suffering in Egypt is a crucial part of the mitzvah of the Seder night. When we invite the poor in, we acutely feel how we, too, were once indigent.

The Seder plate is removed and the second of the four cups of wine is poured. The youngest present asks the reasons for the unusual proceedings of the evening.

W hy is this night different from all other nights?

- ☐ The Beis HaMikdash was destroyed because of disharmony; the redemption will come about as a result of unity. On Pesach, the holiday of redemption, the entire Jewish people reclines as one and thus hastens the redemption.

Q What is the point of inviting the needy to the meal after everyone has been seated at the Seder table and the door is already closed?

A
- ☐ **RA'AVAN:** The invitation is not directed at the needy, but rather at the members of the household, who are now enjoined to begin the Seder and fulfill the mitzvos of the night.

- ☐ **CHASAM SOFER:** *Ha Lachma Anya* is not an invitation, but a proclamation. Some people believe that it is preferable to serve Hashem in solitude, but we proclaim that the ideal form of service is in the company of other people. Therefore we invite others to come and join us in performing the mitzvos of the Seder.

- ☐ **DIVREI YOEL:** *Ha Lachma Anya* is not an invitation to paupers, but a prayer that the holiness of the Seder night prompt Hashem to shower goodness on all of the Jewish people.

- ☐ **MINCHAS ASHER:** In ancient times, *Ha Lachma Anya* was said as an invitation to the needy during the day, before the *korban Pesach* was slaughtered. This was well before the Seder had started, when paupers were looking for a place to eat and it was still possible to invite them.

⋄§ מַה נִּשְׁתַּנָּה / *Why is this night different?*

Mah Nishtanah consists of four questions that draw attention to the unusual practices of the Seder night. The answers to these questions constitute the basis of *sippur Yetzias Mitzrayim*, telling the story of the Exodus. The origin of this section is in the Mishnah (*Pesachim* 116a): "The second cup is poured for him, and here the son asks his father... 'Why is this night different from all other nights?'"

As the Mishnah informs us, the Four Questions are asked after the

שֶׁבְּכָל הַלֵּילוֹת אָנוּ אוֹכְלִין חָמֵץ וּמַצָּה, הַלַּיְלָה הַזֶּה כֻּלּוֹ מַצָּה.

second cup of wine is poured. After the first cup, the child is not yet puzzled. He knows that we recite Kiddush on every Shabbos and holiday. When we pour the second cup, however, he begins to wonder why this night is different from other nights.

During the Talmudic era, a standard text was instituted for *Mah Nishtanah*. After the destruction of the Second Beis HaMikdash, the fourth question was altered. The original question, "On all other nights we eat meat that is roasted, boiled, or cooked, but this night we eat only roasted," was replaced with the question about reclining, since we no longer offer the *korban Pesach*.

Abarbanel explains that these particular questions were chosen for *Mah Nishtanah* because they highlight contradictory actions performed during the Seder. On one hand, we eat matzah and *maror*, which represent slavery (as discussed in the first two questions of *Mah Nishtanah*). On the other hand, we dip our food and recline, in the manner of free men (as discussed in the last two questions).

Q *Why do we tell the story of the Exodus by way of question and answer?*

A
- **MALBIM:** The style of question and answer arouses a person's excitement and piques his interest at the very beginning of the Seder. (For this reason, a person must ask the questions even if he is having the Seder alone.)

- **GA'AL YISRAEL HAGGADAH:** The Torah commands us to learn about the Exodus in the manner of question and answer, as the verse states, וְהָיָה כִּי יִשְׁאָלְךָ בִנְךָ, *And it will be when your son asks you* (*Exodus* 13:14).

- **KSAV SOFER:** The foundation of the Exodus was faith, and on the Seder night a special holiness is manifest that enables parents to implant pure faith in the hearts of their children. When a person is interested in knowing the reason for something, the explanation he receives makes a far bigger impression than if he was simply told the facts. For this reason, we deviate from our usual practices in order to intrigue the children. This prompts them to ask questions and to be interested in hearing the answers.

1. On all other nights we may eat *chametz* and matzah, but on this night — only matzah.

- ☐ **RAV YECHEZKEL ABRAMSKY:** Ideas conveyed in question-and-answer style have a particular appeal.
- ☐ A question-and-answer discussion turns the questioner into an involved participant rather than a passive listener.

Q *What if there are no children at the Seder table to ask the Four Questions?*

A ☐ If a person has no son, his wife asks him the Four Questions, and if she is unable to ask, or the person is alone, he asks the Four Questions himself.

Q *Why is Mah Nishtanah said after Ha Lachma Anya?*

A ☐ **RASHI:** After *Ha Lachma Anya*, we pour the second cup of wine. The child is used to seeing one cup of wine poured for Kiddush, and he wonders why a second cup is poured, prompting him to ask questions.

☐ At the beginning of the Seder, just as we begin saying the Haggadah, we present a triumphant response to Pharaoh, who displayed total disregard for the children — beginning with the decree that every baby boy be killed and continuing with his insistence that the children not be allowed to leave Egypt and serve Hashem in the wilderness. By saying *Mah Nishtanah* at the beginning of the Seder, we show Pharaoh and his ilk how much we value children. On this night, children take center stage, for the mitzvah of telling the story of the Exodus cannot be performed without the children's involvement.

Q *Why do we say, "On this night, [we eat] only matzah?" We eat many other things on the Seder night.*

A ☐ **CHASAM SOFER:** The question being asked is not *Why do we eat only matzah*, but *Why are we forbidden to eat chametz?* In other words, why couldn't we eat a piece of matzah

[61] HAGGADAH: THE ANSWER IS . . .

שֶׁבְּכָל הַלֵּילוֹת אָנוּ אוֹכְלִין שְׁאָר יְרָקוֹת, הַלַּיְלָה הַזֶּה מָרוֹר.

שֶׁבְּכָל הַלֵּילוֹת אֵין אָנוּ מַטְבִּילִין אֲפִילוּ פַּעַם אֶחָת, הַלַּיְלָה הַזֶּה שְׁתֵּי פְעָמִים.

שֶׁבְּכָל הַלֵּילוֹת אָנוּ אוֹכְלִין בֵּין יוֹשְׁבִין וּבֵין מְסֻבִּין, הַלַּיְלָה הַזֶּה כֻּלָּנוּ מְסֻבִּין.

The Seder plate is returned. The matzos are kept uncovered as the Haggadah is recited in unison. The Haggadah should be translated, if necessary, and the story of the Exodus should be amplified upon.

עֲבָדִים הָיִינוּ לְפַרְעֹה בְּמִצְרָיִם, וַיּוֹצִיאֵנוּ יהוה אֱלֹהֵינוּ מִשָּׁם בְּיָד חֲזָקָה

---

in order to remember the matzah that the Jews ate in Egypt, and then eat *chametz* as well? Why do we eat *only* matzah?

☐ **BIRKAS HASHIR:** The question is, *Why must the matzah be eaten alone, with no condiments?*

☐ **V'ZOS LIYEHUDAH:** The question is, *Why are we* **obligated** *to eat matzah?* The foods we eat during a meal are foods that we *choose* to eat, so why are we being told that we *must* eat a specific food?

Q *What is so unusual about eating maror that it deserves a question? We eat these types of vegetables on other nights of the year as well.*

A ☐ **AVUDRAHAM:** On other nights of the year we eat a variety of vegetables, some of which are tasty and some of which are bitter. On this night, we specifically eat a bitter vegetable.

Q *Why do we dip food twice on the Seder night?*

A ☐ **TALMUD** (*Pesachim* 110): We dip food twice to prompt the children to ask about the unusual practices of the Seder night, such as dipping two vegetables.

☐ **BEN ISH CHAI:** The Egyptian exile began with "dipping,"

[62] הגדה של פסח

2. **On all other nights** we eat many vegetables, but on this night [we eat] *maror*.

3. **On all other nights** we do not dip even once, but on this night, twice.

4. **On all other nights** we eat either sitting or reclining, but on this night we all recline.

<small>The Seder plate is returned. The matzos are kept uncovered as the Haggadah is recited in unison. The Haggadah should be translated, if necessary, and the story of the Exodus should be amplified upon.</small>

We were slaves to Pharaoh in Egypt, but HASHEM, our God, took us out from there with a mighty

---

when Yosef's tunic was dipped in blood after his brothers sold him into slavery. The redemption also began with "dipping," when the Jews dipped a bundle of hyssop into the blood of the *korban Pesach* and smeared the blood on their doorposts (*Exodus* 12:22). We dip twice to commemorate the beginning of the exile and its end.

☐ The first dipping — *karpas* in salt water — is done to stimulate the appetite, in the manner of free men. The second dipping — *maror* in *charoses* — is done to remember the cement with which our ancestors performed hard labor.

Q *Why do we question the fact that we dip our food on the Seder night? It is normal to dip food all year round.*

A ☐ RA'AVAN: On the Seder night we say a blessing (on the *maror*) before we dip. The rest of the year, we dip without saying a special blessing.

☐ TZUF AMARIM: The rest of the year, dipping is optional; on the Seder night, it is a requirement.

⚜ עֲבָדִים הָיִינוּ / We were slaves

Chazal instructed that the story of the Exodus follow a specific sequence: of *beginning with disgrace and ending with praise* (*Pesachim* 116). There is a dispute between Rav and Shmuel over what constitutes the "disgrace" and the "praise." Rav says that the disgrace is מִתְּחִלָּה עוֹבְדֵי

וּבִזְרוֹעַ נְטוּיָה. וְאִלּוּ לֹא הוֹצִיא הַקָּדוֹשׁ בָּרוּךְ הוּא אֶת אֲבוֹתֵינוּ מִמִּצְרַיִם, הֲרֵי אָנוּ וּבָנֵינוּ וּבְנֵי בָנֵינוּ מְשֻׁעְבָּדִים הָיִינוּ לְפַרְעֹה בְּמִצְרָיִם.

עֲבוֹדָה זָרָה הָיוּ אֲבוֹתֵינוּ, *Originally our ancestors were idol worshipers*, and the praise is וְעַכְשָׁו קֵרְבָנוּ הַמָּקוֹם לַעֲבוֹדָתוֹ, *And now the Omnipresent has brought us near to His service.* Shmuel says that the disgrace is עֲבָדִים הָיִינוּ לְפַרְעֹה בְּמִצְרַיִם, *We were slaves to Pharaoh in Egypt*, and the praise is וַיּוֹצִיאֵנוּ ה', *But HASHEM, our God, took us out from there.*

Q *Why is it necessary to "begin with disgrace and end with praise"?*

A
- **VILNA GAON:** The Jews in Egypt did not conduct themselves with holiness and purity and were not deserving of redemption, yet Hashem still redeemed them. By describing the disgrace of the Jews in Egypt, we highlight the kindness of Hashem in redeeming them.

- **MAHARAL:** One can learn about something from understanding its opposite. In order to appreciate the significance of the Exodus from Egypt, and the lofty level the Jewish people then achieved, we need to first understand how lowly the Jews' status was prior to the redemption.

- **KSAV SOFER:** The praise of Hashem is heightened by describing the depths from which the Jewish people were redeemed.

- **RAV AVRAHAM JOFFEN:** By describing the Jews' disgrace, we uncover the root cause of the exile, just as a doctor needs to know the underlying cause of an illness in order to heal a patient.

- **NESIVOS SHALOM:** The Egyptian exile differed from all the other exiles in the sense that Egypt was a "house of slavery," a place where people lost their identity and their power of independent thought. By describing the condition of the Jews prior to the redemption, we magnify the miracle that Hashem did for us when He freed us from Egypt.

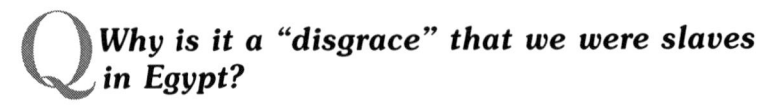

Q *Why is it a "disgrace" that we were slaves in Egypt?*

hand and an outstretched arm. Had not the Holy One, Blessed is He, taken our fathers out from Egypt, then we, our children, and our children's children would have remained subservient to Pharaoh in Egypt.

A ☐ **RAV YOSEF KORNITZER:** The disgrace was that we saw ourselves as slaves to Pharaoh, and not to Hashem. A person who believes in Divine Providence understands that every decree comes from Hashem. When the Jews were in Egypt, their faith was lacking, and that was a disgrace.

Q **Why should we praise Hashem for redeeming us from Egypt; He was the One Who brought us there in the first place?**

A ☐ **KSAV SOFER:** Hashem brought the Jewish people to Egypt because they needed to be refined and purified. Just as a launderer is paid to clean a soiled garment, we thank Hashem for purifying us in Egypt and then redeeming us.

☐ **RAV AHARON KOTLER:** We thank Hashem for taking us down to the Egyptian "refinery," where the Jewish nation was born.

Q **At the beginning of Avadim Hayinu, we say** עֲבָדִים הָיִינוּ לְפַרְעֹה, **We were slaves to Pharaoh, but at the end we say that had Hashem not taken us out,** מְשֻׁעְבָּדִים הָיִינוּ לְפַרְעֹה, **We would have remained subservient to Pharaoh. What is the difference?**

A ☐ **MA'ASEH NISSIM:** The word *eved* implies a temporary enslavement, for a set period of time, while *shibud* implies total, permanent enslavement. At first, we were עֲבָדִים, *slaves*, for a certain period of time. But had Hashem not redeemed us from Egypt, we would have descended into the state of מְשֻׁעְבָּדִים, and we would have remained there in total enslavement.

☐ **CHEMDAS SHLOMO:** In the early stage of our enslavement, when we were עֲבָדִים, we had hopes of redemption. With time, however, we became מְשֻׁעְבָּדִים, hopelessly enslaved. This made Hashem's kindness in redeeming us that much greater

וַאֲפִילוּ כֻּלָּנוּ חֲכָמִים, כֻּלָּנוּ נְבוֹנִים, כֻּלָּנוּ זְקֵנִים, כֻּלָּנוּ יוֹדְעִים אֶת הַתּוֹרָה, מִצְוָה עָלֵינוּ לְסַפֵּר בִּיצִיאַת מִצְרָיִם. וְכָל הַמַּרְבֶּה לְסַפֵּר בִּיצִיאַת מִצְרַיִם, הֲרֵי זֶה מְשֻׁבָּח.

- ☐ **SHO'EL U'MEISHIV:** An *eved* is forcibly enslaved, while a *meshubad* can be enslaved of his own will. Initially, we were forcibly enslaved, but had Hashem not taken us out of Egypt, we would have eventually become מְשֻׁעְבָּדִים, willingly enslaved.

- ☐ **NETZIV:** The word מְשֻׁעְבָּדִים means "beholden." Had we remained in Egypt until the end of the 400-year exile (and not experienced the miracles that accompanied the accelerated redemption after 210 years), we would have felt indebted to Pharaoh for freeing us out of his own goodwill.

- ☐ **HASHIR V'HASHEVACH:** Had we escaped from Egypt through natural means — by running away or rebelling — we would have been freed in body, but our minds would still have been enslaved to Egyptian culture. We would have remained slaves to Pharaoh in the spiritual sense. We therefore say that had Hashem not taken us out of Egypt, we would still be *subservient to Pharaoh*.

Q *How does this passage answer the questions asked in Mah Nishtanah?*

A ☐ **ABARBANEL:** In *Mah Nishtanah*, we ask about the contradictory practices of the Seder night, some of which are indicative of slavery and some of which are reminiscent of freedom. *Avadim Hayinu* answers the questions by describing how we went from being slaves to being free men. This explains why we act like paupers at the beginning of the Seder, and by the end of the night we act like free men.

Q *What is the difference between "a mighty hand" and "an outstretched arm?"*

A ☐ **MALBIM:** *A mighty hand* conveys that Hashem took us out of Egypt against the will of the Egyptians. *An outstretched arm* means He took us out with an open revelation of His

Even if we were all men of wisdom, understanding, experience, and knowledge of the Torah — it would still be an obligation upon us to tell about the Exodus from Egypt. The more one tells about the discussion of the Exodus, the more he is praiseworthy.

---

might, leaving no room for anyone to think that the Exodus was a natural phenomenon.

- **RE'ACH DUDA'IM:** *A mighty hand* refers to the great power with which Hashem took the Jews out of Egypt, while *an outstretched arm* implies that although the attribute of justice was prosecuting against the Jews, Hashem redeemed them with love and mercy.

- **MARBEH LESAPER HAGGADAH:** *A mighty hand* refers to the physical salvation from Pharaoh and slavery. *An outstretched arm* refers to the spiritual redemption from the forty-nine levels of impurity.

Q: Why would we think that "men of wisdom" would be exempt from the mitzvah of telling the story of the Exodus?

A:
- **RAV CHAIM PALAGI:** Mordechai writes (*Berachos* 1:16) that *sippur*, telling the story, is done in a loud voice, but Rambam rules (*Hilchos Dei'os* 5:7) that a Torah scholar should not shout or raise his voice, but should rather speak softly to everyone. Although we are generally supposed to conduct ourselves in the manner of *talmidei chachamim*, who do not raise their voices, on the Seder night we are supposed to veer from our usual practice, for it is a mitzvah *l'saper* — to tell the story in a loud voice.

- **RAV YECHEZKEL LEVENSTEIN:** Even if one does not think that scholars are exempt from the mitzvah of recounting the story of the Exodus, one might think that it is preferable that they study more esoteric Torah subjects. The Haggadah is telling us that even a scholar has to focus on the story of the Exodus.

- **SIFSEI CHAIM:** One might have thought that the mitzvah to recount the Exodus is incumbent only on those who are not

מַעֲשֶׂה בְּרַבִּי אֱלִיעֶזֶר וְרַבִּי יְהוֹשֻׁעַ וְרַבִּי אֶלְעָזָר בֶּן עֲזַרְיָה וְרַבִּי עֲקִיבָא וְרַבִּי טַרְפוֹן שֶׁהָיוּ מְסֻבִּין בִּבְנֵי בְרַק, וְהָיוּ מְסַפְּרִים בִּיצִיאַת מִצְרַיִם כָּל אוֹתוֹ הַלַּיְלָה. עַד

familiar with the story, and that scholars would be exempt. The Haggadah therefore informs us that even scholars are obligated.

Q *The more one tells about the Exodus, the more he is praiseworthy. How should one "tell more about the Exodus"?*

A ☐ **AVUDRAHAM:** One should add to the story while speaking about the Exodus.

☐ **KOL BO; RASHBATZ:** One should tell more of the story even *after* the time of the obligation to recount the Exodus (which is *chatzos*, midnight).

☐ One should "tell more" in the qualitative sense, by delving into the subject in depth.

☐ One should have more people to whom to tell the story.

The more one tells about the discussion of the Exodus, the more he is praiseworthy.

This can be compared to a group of merchants sailing the ocean along with their cargo. Suddenly, a big storm erupts and the ship begins to rock. All the merchants fear for the safety of their merchandise.

Obviously, it would not enter their minds at that perilous moment to start calculating which of them is more or less prosperous, or who has the most merchandise on board. An observer, standing and watching, would not be able to tell which of them owns merchandise of great value and which merchant is the wealthiest of them all.

When the storm abates and they continue their journey to dry land, the merchants sing in praise and thanksgiving to Hashem. At this stage, it becomes apparent which of them is wealthier — based on the degree of their joy.

Similarly, by recounting the miracles and wonders that were performed for our forefathers at the Exodus, one can recognize which of them is more joyous over the redemption...

הגדה של פסח

It happened that Rabbi Eliezer, Rabbi Yehoshua, Rabbi Elazar ben Azaryah, Rabbi Akiva, and Rabbi Tarfon were gathered (at the Seder) in Bnei Brak. They discussed the Exodus from Egypt all that night until their

---

Q *Why is the miracle of the Exodus emphasized so much more than other miracles that happened to the Jewish people?*

A ☐ RAV YECHEZKEL LEVENSTEIN: The Exodus transformed the Jews from Pharaoh's slaves to servants of Hashem.

☐ RE'ACH DUDA'IM: The Exodus is the foundation of all the mitzvos of the Torah, since all of the fundamentals of our faith were established then.

מַעֲשֶׂה בְּרַבִּי אֱלִיעֶזֶר / It happened that Rabbi Eliezer

This story about five Sages who gathered in Bnei Brak to discuss the Exodus proves that every person is obligated in this mitzvah, even great scholars. This story highlights the great love these Sages had for the mitzvah of relating the story of the Exodus (*Maharal*).

The Beis HaLevi points out that the Talmud (*Berachos* 9) records a dispute regarding the time by which the *korban Pesach* must be eaten: May it be eaten all night or only until midnight? This story teaches us that the halachah was established in accordance with the view that one may eat the *korban Pesach* all night. The mitzvah of recounting the Exodus is fulfilled while eating the *korban Pesach*, as the Haggadah states, "*You shall tell your son*" applies only at the time when matzah and maror lie before you. The five Sages stayed up all that night relating the story of the Exodus. They could only tell the story while the *korban Pesach* was in front of them, so it must be that the *korban Pesach* may be eaten the entire night.

Q *Why does this passage follow Avadim Hayinu?*

A ☐ *Avadim Hayinu* ended with the statement *The more one tells about the Exodus, the more he is praiseworthy.* This paragraph illustrates to what lengths these Sages went to fulfill the mitzvah. They spent the entire night discussing the

שֶׁבָּאוּ תַלְמִידֵיהֶם וְאָמְרוּ לָהֶם, רַבּוֹתֵינוּ הִגִּיעַ זְמַן קְרִיאַת שְׁמַע שֶׁל שַׁחֲרִית.

Exodus in detail, even though they were well versed in the story of the Exodus.

Q *Who are the Sages in this story?*

A ☐ ***Rabbi Eliezer*** is Rabbi Eliezer ben Horkanus, a second-generation *Tanna* and a student of Rabban Yochanan ben Zakkai. In his youth, he worked the fields for his father, but he wished to learn Torah, so he fled to the *beis midrash* of Rabban Yochanan ben Zakkai. After the destruction of the Beis HaMikdash, he relocated to Yavneh and served as a judge on the Sanhedrin. He later moved to Lod.

Rabbi Yehoshua, another second-generation *Tanna*, was one of the leading students of Rabban Yochanan ben Zakkai.

Rabbi Elazar ben Azaryah, a third-generation *Tanna*, was one of the leading scholars of Yavneh and served as the head of the rabbinical court. He was appointed *nasi* (head of the Sanhedrin) after Rabban Gamliel was removed from the position.

Rabbi Akiva was one of the greatest of the *Tannaim*. Originally, he worked as a shepherd for the wealthy Kalba Savua of Yerushalayim, whose daughter he married. At the age of forty, he began to study Torah, and he studied under Rabbi Eliezer, Rabbi Yehoshua, and Rabbi Tarfon.

Rabbi Tarfon was a second-generation *Tanna*, a student of Rabban Gamliel and Rabban Yochanan ben Zakkai.

Q *Why is the participation of these particular Sages in the Seder significant?*

A ☐ The participation of these Sages demonstrates that every Jew is obligated in the mitzvah of telling the story of the Exodus, including:

Converts — Rabbi Akiva was descended from converts (*Sanhedrin* 96);

Kohanim — Rabbi Elazar ben Azaryah and Rabbi Tarfon were Kohanim (*Bava Metzia* 11); and students came and said to them: "Our teachers, the time has come for the reading of the morning Shema."

***

Levi'im — Rabbi Yehoshua and Rabbi Eliezer were Levi'im. (The tribe of Levi, which includes Kohanim, was not enslaved in Egypt.)

☐ Each of these *Tannaim* was unique in some way with regard to his Torah study:
Rabbi Eliezer abandoned his father's wealth and learned Torah amid great personal sacrifice.
Rabbi Yehoshua was placed in the *beis midrash* while yet in his cradle, for his mother wanted him to hear the sound of Torah from infancy.
Rabbi Elazar ben Azaryah became a *nasi* at the young age of eighteen.
Rabbi Akiva expounded the meaning of even the crowns on the letters of the Torah (*Menachos* 29b).

Q: What is the significance of the fact that this Seder was held in Bnei Brak?

A: ☐ **ABARBANEL:** Bnei Brak is not the name of the location of their Seder, but rather an allusion to beautiful, shiny utensils used at this Seder. The word *bnei* is a reference to students, since a student is like a son to his teacher, and *brak* means shiny. This tells us that these Sages were not holding their Seder in the city of Bnei Brak. Rather, they were sitting and eating with the *nasi*, Rabbi Elazar ben Azaryah, who was very wealthy.

☐ **MA'ASEI HASHEM:** Bnei Brak was the city where Rabbi Akiva lived. He was the rav of the city, and his *beis din* was located there.

☐ **SHIVCHA D'MARA:** "Brak" is related to "*barkai*," the first light of dawn, implying that these Sages engaged in discussing the Exodus until dawn.

Q: Why did the students interrupt these Sages when the time arrived to say Shema?

A: ☐ **BRISKER RAV:** These Sages were involved in Torah study, and the halachah is that Torah study is interrupted only for

אָמַר רַבִּי אֶלְעָזָר בֶּן עֲזַרְיָה, הֲרֵי אֲנִי כְּבֶן שִׁבְעִים שָׁנָה, וְלֹא זָכִיתִי שֶׁתֵּאָמֵר יְצִיאַת מִצְרַיִם בַּלֵּילוֹת, עַד שֶׁדְּרָשָׁהּ בֶּן זוֹמָא, שֶׁנֶּאֱמַר,

---

Krias Shema (Shulchan Aruch, Orach Chaim 687:2).

☐ The students had come to inform them that the night was over, and there was no longer an obligation to tell the story of the Exodus, which applies only at night.

☐ One of the Sages was Rabbi Eliezer, who held that *Krias Shema* should be concluded by sunrise. The students came to these Sages at dawn, rather than waiting until the end of the third halachic hour of the day (which is the generally accepted deadline for reciting *Krias Shema*), in keeping with the opinion of Rabbi Eliezer.

◆§ אָמַר רַבִּי אֶלְעָזָר בֶּן עֲזַרְיָה /
Rabbi Elazar ben Azaryah said

The source of this passage is the *mishnah* that begins, *The Exodus from Egypt should be mentioned at nighttime* (*Berachos* 12b). After reading about the gathering of the five Sages, among them Rabbi Elazar ben Azaryah, the Haggadah quotes Rabbi Elazar ben Azaryah's teaching regarding the mitzvah of remembering the Exodus.

Q *What is the connection between this passage and the previous one about the Seder of the five Sages?*

A ☐ SHIBBOLEI HALEKET: This passage is a continuation of the previous one. When the five Sages were about to recite the morning Shema after their Seder in Bnei Brak, Rabbi Elazar ben Azaryah told them about the dispute described in this passage. Indeed, in the Rambam's text, this passage begins, אָמַר **לָהֶם** רַבִּי אֶלְעָזָר בֶּן עֲזַרְיָה..., *Rabbi Elazar ben Azaryah said* **to them**..., indicating that this paragraph continues the story of the five Sages in Bnei Brak.

☐ MAHARAL: The juxtaposition of these two passages teaches that just as one is obligated to recite *Krias Shema* (mentioned in the first passage about the five Sages) every night, he is also obligated to tell of the miracles of the Exodus every

Rabbi Elazar ben Azaryah said: I am like a seventy-year-old man, but I could not succeed in having the Exodus from Egypt mentioned every night, until Ben Zoma expounded it, as it is stated:

---

night (indicated in the second passage about Rabbi Elazar ben Azaryah), particularly on Seder night.

- ☐ **RAV BETZALEL HAKOHEN OF VILNA:** Although the subject of this *mishnah* about Rabbi Elazar ben Azaryah is the requirement to remember the Exodus every day of the year, it is written here because of its ending, which informs us that the Exodus will still be remembered even during the days of Mashiach.

Q: Why did Rabbi Elazar ben Azaryah say that he was "like" a seventy-year-old man?

A: ☐ He was not actually seventy years old. Opinions as to his real age vary:

- ☐ **TALMUD** (*Berachos* 27): He was eighteen years old, and on the day he was appointed to the position of *nasi*, his hair turned white like a man of seventy, so that he would look more distinguished.
- ☐ **RAMBAM:** He learned Torah so diligently that his strength was sapped, and he looked like a seventy-year-old man.
- ☐ **RITVA:** He was sixteen years old.
- ☐ **AVUDRAHAM:** He was thirteen years old.
- ☐ **BIRKAS HASHIR:** The Talmud (*Berachos* 27) teaches that Rabbi Elazar ben Azaryah was eighteen at the time of his appointment as *nasi*. The Arizal teaches that his soul was an incarnation of the prophet Shmuel, who lived fifty-two years. Eighteen and fifty-two equal seventy; thus Rabbi Elazar ben Azaryah was "like" a seventy-year-old man.

Q: What was the nature of the dispute between Ben Zoma and the Sages?

A: ☐ **RAMBAM:** The dispute was whether there is a Scriptural basis for the obligation to recall the Exodus every night. Rabbi Elazar ben Azaryah could not find a Scriptural basis, until

לְמַעַן תִּזְכֹּר אֶת יוֹם צֵאתְךָ מֵאֶרֶץ מִצְרַיִם כֹּל יְמֵי חַיֶּיךָ.[1] יְמֵי חַיֶּיךָ הַיָּמִים, כֹּל יְמֵי חַיֶּיךָ הַלֵּילוֹת. וַחֲכָמִים אוֹמְרִים, יְמֵי חַיֶּיךָ הָעוֹלָם הַזֶּה, כֹּל יְמֵי חַיֶּיךָ לְהָבִיא לִימוֹת הַמָּשִׁיחַ.

בָּרוּךְ הַמָּקוֹם, בָּרוּךְ הוּא. בָּרוּךְ שֶׁנָּתַן תּוֹרָה

Ben Zoma expounded the verse לְמַעַן תִּזְכֹּר אֶת יוֹם צֵאתְךָ מֵאֶרֶץ מִצְרַיִם כֹּל יְמֵי חַיֶּיךָ, *In order that you may remember the day you left Egypt all the days of your life* (Deuteronomy 16:3). The Sages disagreed, however, and expounded this verse as a reference to the days of Mashiach.

- **ABARBANEL:** Ben Zoma held that the words יְמֵי חַיֶּיךָ, *the days of your life*, indicate that the Exodus should be mentioned during the day, and the added word כֹּל, *all*, indicates that it should be mentioned at night as well. The Sages disagreed. They held that daytime and nighttime are part of the same twenty-four-hour unit and expounded the additional word in a different manner.

- **MAHARAL:** Ben Zoma held that the Exodus has to be mentioned at night, because the plague of the firstborn happened at night, and it should be mentioned also during the day, because the Exodus happened by day. The Sages, however, held that the nighttime plague of the firstborn was merely a preparation for the Exodus, and since the actual redemption took place by day, the obligation is to mention the Exodus only during the day.

- **VILNA GAON:** The words כֹּל יְמֵי, *all the days*, can mean either (1) the entire day or (2) every day. Ben Zoma held that the meaning is "the entire day," including the night. The Sages held that the meaning is "every day," including the days of Mashiach.

Q: Why was Rabbi Elazar's opinion not accepted until Ben Zoma supported it?

A:
- **SHIBBOLEI HALEKET; AVUDRAHAM:** Initially, Rabbi Elazar was alone in his opinion, so the majority opinion outweighed his. However, when Ben Zoma expressed the same view as

"In order that you may remember the day you left Egypt all the days of your life."[1] The phrase "the days of your life" would have indicated only the days; the addition of the word "all" includes the nights as well. But the Sages declare that "the days of your life" would mean only the present world; the addition of "all" includes the era of the Messiah.

Blessed is the Omnipresent; blessed is He. Blessed is the One Who has given the Torah

---

1. *Deuteronomy* 16:3.

Rabbi Elazar, his was no longer an individual opinion, and it was accepted.

□ **SHA'AR BAS RABBIM:** Rabbi Elazar's opinion was not accepted due to his youth — until Ben Zoma taught the famous mishnah *Who is wise? He who learns from every person* (*Avos* 4:1). As a result of this teaching, Rabbi Elazar's words were accepted.

בָּרוּךְ הַמָּקוֹם / Blessed is the Omnipresent

This passage praises the Torah, which was given to the entire Jewish people. It goes on to list the four sons representing four types of Jews, indicating that the Torah speaks to every individual on his level. There is hope that even the wicked son will mend his ways by studying the Torah (*Rav Chaim Soloveitchik*).

Q *Why does this passage follow the previous ones about the five Sages and the dispute of Rabbi Elazar ben Azaryah?*

A □ **PEIRUSH KADMON:** The passage is the blessing on the Haggadah, similar to the blessings recited over the Torah before its reading.

□ **ABARBANEL:** The Haggadah first presented the specifics of the mitzvah of telling the story of the Exodus. Then it explained how the story should be told, bringing the example of the *Tannaim* in Bnei Brak, who spent the entire night discussing the Exodus. Now the Haggadah is indicating that one should not delve into complex explanations of the mitzvos, but should rather explain the story as a narrative, in a way that all four sons will understand.

- **MALBIM:** Up to this point in the Haggadah, we have been discussing the rational basis for the mitzvah of telling the story of the Exodus. From here on, the Haggadah elaborates on the Scriptural basis for the mitzvah.

Q: Why is Hashem called הַמָּקוֹם, the Omnipresent?

A:
- **SHIBBOLEI HALEKET:** The *Midrash Tanchuma* teaches that the verse הִנֵּה מָקוֹם אִתִּי, *Behold! There is a place near Me*, (*Exodus* 33:21), is a reference to Hashem, because He is the "place" of the world. Therefore He is called "*HaMakom*."
- **MAGGID OF PLOTZK:** Hashem is called the "place of the world," in much the same way that a place surrounds and sets a location for a person. Since Hashem is the place of the world, without Him the world could not exist. The miracles of the Exodus and the subsequent giving of the Torah caused Hashem's Name to spread throughout the world, making everyone understand that it is impossible to exist without Him. Therefore He is called "*HaMakom*" here in relation to the giving of the Torah.
- **RAV CHAIM VOLOZHINER:** *Midrash Rabbah* teaches that Hashem is the "place" of the world, based on the verse וַיִּפְגַּע בַּמָּקוֹם, *He encountered the place* (*Genesis* 28:11). Just as a place contains an object, so too Hashem contains and sustains the entire world. This is a fundamental principle of faith, appropriate for the Seder night, when we strengthen our *emunah*.

Q: Why is the word בָּרוּךְ, blessed, repeated four times in this passage?

A:
- **TALMUD** (*Berachos* 54b): Four types of people are obligated to give thanks to Hashem: a prisoner who has been freed, a sick person who has been healed, a person who has crossed a sea, and a person who has traveled through a desert. The Jewish people underwent all of these experiences. They

הגדה של פסח [76]

were imprisoned in Egypt, they experienced terrible afflictions, they crossed a sea, and they traveled through a desert — and they therefore are required to give thanks. The four repetitions of בָּרוּךְ, *blessed*, correspond to these four categories of miracles.

- **SHIBBOLEI HALEKET:** There is no blessing over the recitation of the Haggadah; one of the reasons for this is that the Shema blessings of the *Maariv* prayers before the Seder cover the recitation of the Haggadah. The four-time repetition of the word בָּרוּךְ, *blessed*, corresponds to the four blessings of the evening Shema (two before Shema and two after).

- **MAGGID OF PLOTZK:** We are thanking Hashem for the miracles that happened during the four exiles that the Jewish people experienced.

- **MALBIM:** This passage was intended as a dialogue. The leader of the Seder says, בָּרוּךְ הַמָּקוֹם, *Blessed is the Omnipresent*, and the other participants respond, בָּרוּךְ הוּא, *Blessed is He*. Then the leader of the Seder continues, בָּרוּךְ שֶׁנָּתַן תּוֹרָה לְעַמּוֹ יִשְׂרָאֵל, *Blessed is the One Who has given the Torah to His people Israel*, and the participants respond again, בָּרוּךְ הוּא, *Blessed is He*.

- **ESHEL B'RAMAH:** The four phrases that begin with בָּרוּךְ correspond to the four sons:

  The first phrase:
  בָּרוּךְ הַמָּקוֹם, *Blessed is the Omnipresent*, corresponds to the wise son, who blesses Hashem.

  The second phrase:
  בָּרוּךְ הוּא, *Blessed is He*, corresponds to the wicked son, who does not believe in Divine Providence and thus uses the third-person pronoun "He."

  The third phrase:
  בָּרוּךְ שֶׁנָּתַן תּוֹרָה לְעַמּוֹ יִשְׂרָאֵל, *Blessed is the One Who has given the Torah to His people Israel*, corresponds to the simple son, who learns Torah and sees in it the greatness of Hashem.

  The fourth phrase:
  בָּרוּךְ הוּא, *Blessed is He*, corresponds to the son who is unable to ask. He does not understand the greatness of the Creator and therefore also speaks in the third person.

לְעַמּוֹ יִשְׂרָאֵל, בָּרוּךְ הוּא. כְּנֶגֶד אַרְבָּעָה בָנִים דִּבְּרָה תוֹרָה. אֶחָד חָכָם. וְאֶחָד רָשָׁע. וְאֶחָד תָּם. וְאֶחָד שֶׁאֵינוֹ יוֹדֵעַ לִשְׁאוֹל:

◈§ כְּנֶגֶד אַרְבָּעָה בָנִים דִּבְּרָה תוֹרָה /
Concerning four sons does the Torah speak

This passage is from a *baraisa* whose source is *Mechilta* in *Parashas Bo* and the *Yerushalmi*, *Pesachim* 10:4, which quote the Torah, where the questions and answers of these four sons appear. The answers to the four sons appear in the Torah in the following order:

1. the answer to the wicked son (*Exodus* 12:26).
2. the answer to the son who is unable to ask (ibid. 13:8).
3. the answer to the simple son (ibid. 13:14).
4. the answer to the wise son (*Deuteronomy* 6:20).

Q *Why do we praise Hashem for giving us the Torah specifically in the context of the four sons?*

A ☐ **ABARBANEL:** The Torah can be explained to each child according to his level of comprehension.

☐ **RAV CHAIM SOLOVEITCHIK:** The Torah is unique among all other fields of study in that it can be studied and understood by anyone according to his level of intelligence and comprehension. A great scholar and a young child can learn the same Torah. When listing the four sons, we thank Hashem for giving us a Torah that is relevant to each of them on his level.

Q *Why does the Haggadah list the sons in a different order from that in the Torah?*

A ☐ **RITVA:** The Haggadah lists the sons in order of their intelligence: first the wise son; then the wicked son, who is also intelligent, but whose heart is evil; then the simple son, who is not very clever but possesses enough intelligence to ask; and finally the son who is unable to ask, who is the least intelligent of all.

☐ **ARIZAL:** The sons are listed in pairs, or "*chavrusas*." The wise son is capable of helping the wicked son learn without harming himself; this pair is listed first because of their superior to His people Israel; Blessed is He. Concerning four sons does the Torah speak — a **wise** one, a **wicked** one, a **simple** one, and **one who is unable to ask.**

---

intellectual ability. The simple son is the partner of the son who is unable to ask; for this pair, simple explanations are sufficient.

☐ **RAV AVRAHAM ADLER:** The sons are listed according to their closeness to Judaism. First is the wise son, who fulfills the mitzvos. Next is the wicked son, who has abandoned Judaism, but nevertheless knows the Torah. After that is the simple son, who has not tasted the Torah's wisdom, and last is the son who is unable to ask because he is assimilated into secular society.

Q What do the four sons symbolize?

A ☐ **VILNA GAON:** The mitzvah of telling the story of the Exodus is written four times in the Torah, three times in *Parashas Bo*, and once in *Parashas Va'eschanan*. The four sons correspond to those four mentions of this mitzvah.

☐ **MA'ASEH NISSIM:** The four sons correspond to the four merits by which the Jews were redeemed from Egypt:
1. The merit of the korban Pesach and circumcision — this is represented by the wise son, who fulfills the mitzvos even at the cost of personal sacrifice.
2. The covenant between Hashem and the Jewish people — this is represented by the wicked son, who eschews

---

A wise one, a wicked one, a simple one, and one who is unable to ask...

Before beginning his own Seder, Rav Tzvi Elimelech of Dinov, author of *Bnei Yissaschar*, would walk through the streets to see how the laypeople were conducting their Sedarim. As he passed by a particular home, Rav Tzvi Elimelech heard a Jew reading the Haggadah and reciting the words *A wise one, a wicked one, a simple one, and one who is unable to ask*. Each time this Jew reached the word "echad," one, he shouted the word loudly, as though he were reciting the Shema.

Later, the Bnei Yissaschar remarked that this simple Jew turned each of the sons — including the wicked son — into a holy prayer akin to *Krias Shema*.

---

[79] **HAGGADAH: THE ANSWER IS . . .**

חָכָם מָה הוּא אוֹמֵר? מָה הָעֵדֹת וְהַחֻקִּים וְהַמִּשְׁפָּטִים אֲשֶׁר צִוָּה יהוה אֱלֹהֵינוּ אֶתְכֶם?[1] וְאַף אַתָּה אֱמָר לוֹ כְּהִלְכוֹת הַפֶּסַח, אֵין מַפְטִירִין אַחַר הַפֶּסַח אֲפִיקוֹמָן.

Judaism, but is nevertheless included in Hashem's covenant with the Jewish people.

3. *The merit of receiving the Torah* — this is represented by the simple son, who believes in the Torah and obeys its laws.

4. *The merit of the Patriarchs* — this is represented by the son who is unable to ask, yet is nevertheless linked to our ancestors.

☐ **IMREI EMES:** The four sons correspond to the four questions of *Mah Nishtanah*. The wise son corresponds to the first question, regarding the matzah, which is a testimony to the mitzvos that Hashem commanded (as the wise son asks, *What are the testimonies...*). The wicked son corresponds to the second question, regarding the *maror*, because the wicked son spurns "*merirus*," the bitter, sorrowful feeling a person has when he regrets his sins and wants to repent. The simple son corresponds to the fourth question, regarding reclining, for he asks, *What is this?* when he sees everyone acting differently: reclining rather than sitting at the table. The son who is unable to ask corresponds to the third question, regarding the two dippings, for we dip in order to prompt him to ask.

Q *Why does the word echad, "one," appear in connection with each of the sons in this passage?*

A ☐ **HASHIR V'HASHEVACH:** The repetition of the word *echad* in this instance connotes *bein ... u'bein*, "whether...or..." The Haggadah is stressing that the mitzvah of telling the story of the Exodus relates to every type of child, "whether he is wise or wicked, whether simple or unable to ask," and it does not apply only to the wise one.

☐ **RAV CHAIM SHMULEVITZ:** The Haggadah is intimating that every single person ("*every one*") has the potential to become any one of the four sons.

הגדה של פסח [80]

The wise son — what does he say? "What are the testimonies, decrees, and ordinances which HASHEM, our God, has commanded you?"[1] Therefore explain to him the laws of the Passover offering: that one may not eat dessert after the final taste of the Passover offering.

---
1. *Deuteronomy 6:20.*

- ☐ **MARBEH LESAPER HAGGADAH:** We are obligated to delve into the concept of Hashem's Oneness (*Chovos HaLevavos, Sha'ar HaYichud*, Ch. 3), and this obligation applies to each person on his level. That is why we stress the word *echad*, one, in relation to each of the sons. Each one should understand that Hashem is *Echad*, One, according to his ability to grasp this concept.
- ☐ The Haggadah is advising parents to treat each child as though he were an only child.
- ☐ The word *echad*, one, appears four times in this passage. The numerical value of *echad* is 13, which, multiplied by four, equals 52, the numerical value of *ben*, son, and Eliyahu. The theme of the Seder night is redemption. We not only relate the story of the redemption from Egypt, but also our hope that the future redemption will come speedily. In the future, the prophet Eliyahu will herald the final redemption, as the verse states, וְהֵשִׁיב לֵב אָבוֹת עַל בָּנִים וְלֵב בָּנִים עַל אֲבוֹתָם, *And he will turn back [to God] the hearts of fathers with [their] sons and the hearts of sons with their fathers* (*Malachi* 3:24).

חָכָם / The Wise Son

Q Who is the wise son?

A
- ☐ **RAV SHLOMO ALKABETZ:** He is one who is scrupulous in mitzvah observance
- ☐ **VILNA GAON:** He is the opposite of the son who is unable to ask.
- ☐ **KSAV SOFER:** He is the son who learned Torah and imbibed *mussar, derech eretz*, and fear of Heaven in his upbringing.

- **RAV CHAIM BERLIN:** He is a child who has not yet reached bar-mitzvah age. That is why he asks about the mitzvos that "Hashem has commanded *you*."
- **OHR YAHEL:** He is a child who wants to learn, as the Mishnah teaches, "Who is wise? He who learns from every person" (*Avos* 4:1).
- **DIVREI YOEL:** He is the opposite of the wicked son. In the battle against the wicked, it is not enough to be righteous; one must be wise as well.

Q: Why is the wise son, whose answer appears last in the Torah, discussed first?

A:
- **AVUDRAHAM:** The wise son is first because he is the most distinguished of the four sons.
- **MAHARAL:** He is first in order to begin with words of wisdom.
- He is discussed first in order to present an example and role model for the other sons.

Q: Why does the question of the wise son not directly relate to Pesach?

A:
- **HASHIR V'HASHEVACH:** The wise son asks this question all year round — not only on the Seder night, and not only in connection with Pesach.

Q: The wise son and the wicked son both refer to the laws of Pesach in second person. The wise son asks, "What are the testimonies, decrees, and ordinances which HASHEM, our God, has commanded 'you'?" The wicked son asks, "Of what purpose is this work to 'you'?" Why do we regard the wise son's question positively and the wicked son's question negatively?

A:
- **KOL BO:** The wise son considers himself part of the community, as evidenced by the fact that he says אֱלֹהֵינוּ, *our God*, in his question. The wicked son, however, seeks to exclude himself from the community.
- **CHIDA:** The wise son is regarded positively because he

הגדה של פסח

mentions Hashem, while the wicked son avoids any mention of Him.

- **OZHEROVER REBBE:** The wise son does not expect to receive an answer to his question immediately. In the Torah, his question is prefaced with the words כִּי יִשְׁאָלְךָ בִנְךָ מָחָר לֵאמֹר, *If your child asks you **tomorrow**, saying* (Deuteronomy 6:20). First, he fulfills the mitzvah of the *korban Pesach*, and only then does he request an explanation. The wicked son, however, demands an answer on the spot: מָה הָעֲבֹדָה הַזֹּאת, *Of what purpose is **this** work*. The word זֹאת, *this*, implies that he points to the proceedings and expects an immediate response.

Q Why does the wise son specify three types of commandments: testimonies, decrees, and ordinances?

A
- **RASHBATZ:** The wise son has a different question about each of these three types of commandments:

עֵדֹת, *testimonies*, are commandments that relate to a particular historical event (e.g., Shabbos). Regarding this category of mitzvos, the wise son asks, On what basis do we believe? What events do these mitzvos attest to?

חֻקִּים, *decrees*, are commandments whose reason is not given (e.g., the red heifer and the prohibition of eating meat and milk together). Regarding this category of mitzvos, the wise son asks, What is the purpose of mitzvos whose reason we do not understand?

מִשְׁפָּטִים, *ordinances*, are commandments that have a logical basis (e.g., the prohibition against murder and theft). Regarding this category of mitzvos, the wise son asks, Why does the Torah give us these mitzvos, which are intuitive and do not require an explicit commandment?

The Torah tells us to answer the wise son's questions with the statement עֲבָדִים הָיִינוּ לְפַרְעֹה בְּמִצְרַיִם וַיּוֹצִיאֵנוּ ה' אֱלֹהֵינוּ מִשָּׁם, *We were slaves to Pharaoh in Egypt, but HASHEM, our God, took us out from there* (Deuteronomy 6:21). This statement explains what the *testimonies* of the Seder night attest to — the Exodus — and also establishes the basis of our belief in Hashem.

In addition, we tell him, וַיְצַוֵּנוּ ה' לַעֲשׂוֹת אֶת כָּל הַחֻקִּים הָאֵלֶּה, *HASHEM commanded us to perform all these decrees* (ibid. 6:24). We are now obligated to fulfill Hashem's *decrees*

— even the ones we do not understand — since we became His servants when He took us out of Egypt. A servant follows the orders of his master, whether or not he understands why he is commanded to do them.

As for the *ordinances*, we say to the wise son, וּצְדָקָה תִּהְיֶה לָּנוּ כִּי נִשְׁמֹר לַעֲשׂוֹת אֶת כָּל הַמִּצְוָה הַזֹּאת, *And it will be a merit for us if we are careful to perform this entire commandment* (Deuteronomy 6:25). The reason the Torah gives us these logical commandments is in order to bestow on us greater reward, in accordance with the principle that "One who is commanded and fulfills [the commandment] is greater than one who is not commanded yet fulfills."

Q **How does the response regarding not eating and following the pesach-offering answer the question of the wise son?**

A ☐ **RID:** According to this, the wise son's question is, Why do we eat the *korban chagigah* before the *korban Pesach*, if the *korban Pesach* is the main offering of the Seder night? We answer that the *korban Pesach* is eaten at the end of the Seder, because we are not allowed to eat anything else after it, as its flavor is meant to remain in our mouths.

☐ **RAV TZVI PESACH FRANK:** The wise son is asking about the source of the additional customs we perform at the Seder that are not mentioned explicitly in the Torah, such as the four cups of wine and the *Afikoman*. We answer that all of these laws are from Hashem, and just as we must meticulously fulfill the laws of Pesach that are written in the Torah, so too must we carefully fulfill the laws that are not explicitly written, such as *One may not eat dessert after the final taste of the Passover offering.*

Q **Of all the laws of Pesach, why does the Haggadah tell us to answer the wise son specifically with the halachah "One may not eat dessert after the final taste of the Passover offering"?**

A ☐ **MALBIM:** This is to convey that we should not omit any of the laws of Pesach when we teach our children about the Exodus. We should even teach him the laws that apply after the Seder meal.

- **MA'ASEI HASHEM:** It is in order to teach that just as the taste of the *Afikoman* (which today represents the *korban Pesach* at the Seder) is meant to remain in our mouth at the end of the Seder, so too the answers and explanations we give at the Seder should remain with our children even after the Seder.
- **KSAV SOFER:** This halachah relates to the *korban Pesach* (or *Afikoman*, today), which is eaten in satiety. A hungry person eats to quiet his hunger pangs and therefore cannot eat entirely for the sake of the mitzvah. A satiated person, on the other hand, can eat with the intention of fulfilling the mitzvah. By teaching him this particular halachah, we are telling the wise son that when he fulfills mitzvos, he should always do so for the sake of Heaven, and not for his own enjoyment or benefit.
- **ALTER OF NOVARDOK:** This halachah serves as an example to the wise son: Just as we do not eat anything else after the *korban Pesach*, nothing can "come after" the Torah. Nothing compares to the Torah, for everything else is meaningless in comparison.
- **SIFSEI CHAIM:** By teaching the wise son this halachah, we are conveying to him that we do mitzvos not only because we are obligated, but also out of love. Because we love to fulfill Hashem's commandments, we want the taste of the *Afikoman* to remain in our mouths.

Q *Why does the Haggadah give a different answer from the answer the Torah gives to the wise son?*

A
- **MAHARAL:** The wise son already knows the answer given in the Torah, which talks about how we were slaves in Egypt. The Haggadah therefore chooses to answer the wise son by familiarizing him with the laws of Pesach and the reasons for the related commandments.
- **MALBIM:** The wicked son, the simple son, and the son who is unable to ask all require proof from explicit verses in the Torah, since their faith is incomplete. The wise son, on the other hand, believes fully and does not require Scriptural proof. We therefore address the substance of his question rather than quoting a verse from the Torah.

רָשָׁע מָה הוּא אוֹמֵר? מָה הָעֲבֹדָה הַזֹּאת לָכֶם?¹ לָכֶם וְלֹא לוֹ, וּלְפִי שֶׁהוֹצִיא אֶת עַצְמוֹ מִן הַכְּלָל, כָּפַר בְּעִקָּר — וְאַף אַתָּה

רָשָׁע / The Wicked Son

Q Who is the wicked son?

A
- ☐ **MAHARAL:** He is the opposite of the wise son.

- ☐ **VILNA GAON:** He is the opposite of the simple son, who follows obediently. This is reflected in the juxtaposition of the simple person and the wicked in the verse אַחַת הִיא עַל כֵּן אָמַרְתִּי תָּם וְרָשָׁע הוּא מְכַלֶּה, *It is all the same; therefore I say, "He destroys the blameless with the wicked"* (Job 9:22).

- ☐ **BEIS HALEVI:** The wicked son denies the existence of Hashem. This is reflected in the words שֶׁהוֹצִיא אֶת עַצְמוֹ, *by excluding himself*, which can be interpreted to mean that he excludes Hashem from his life.

- ☐ **RAV AVRAHAM JOFFEN:** He is not a heretic; we should not give answers to heretics. The wicked son does believe in the Exodus and its related miracles, but he complains that the commandment of *korban Pesach* is burdensome.

- ☐ **DIVREI YOEL:** He is someone who is known as a wicked person, has adopted the practices of non-Jews, and does not wish to change his ways. On the contrary, he becomes angry when he is chastised.

- ☐ **NESIVOS SHALOM:** The wicked son is not evil at his core; he is simply someone whose evil inclination overtakes him at times.

- ☐ **RAV AVRAHAM ADLER:** He is someone who studied Torah in his youth but embraced heresy and now mocks the Torah. This person has hopes of returning in the merit of the Torah he learned and the good deeds he performed in his father's home.

Q What is the wicked son asking?

The wicked son — what does he say? "Of what purpose is this work to you?"[1] He says, "To you," thereby excluding himself. By excluding himself from the community of believers, he denies the basic principle of Judaism. Therefore,

---
1. *Exodus* 12:26.

A
- □ **RITVA; AVUDRAHAM** (based on the *Yerushalmi*): He is asking why we bother to recite the Haggadah, which delays the meal.
- □ **KSAV SOFER**: The wicked son sees his father doing the menial work of preparing the *korban Pesach* — which includes cleaning it, roasting it, and removing its wastes — and he questions why his father must do this work himself. Why not assign the task to a servant? That is the meaning of the question *Of what purpose is this work to you?*
- □ **BEN ISH CHAI**: The wicked son questions the need to go through the motions of observing the mitzvos. Instead of doing "this work" — the actions — why can't we just think about and discuss the commandments?
- □ **ALTER OF NOVARDOK**: The wicked son is questioning the need for the meticulousness with which we fulfill the mitzvos.
- □ **OZHEROVER REBBE**: The wicked son is questioning why we have to commemorate an event that took place thousands of years ago: *Of what purpose is this work to you?*
- □ He is asking why we must work so hard to prepare an entire Seder in commemoration of the Exodus. We could relive the experience some other, easier way.

Q *Which basic principle of Judaism does the wicked son deny?*

A
- □ **ROKEACH**: He does not believe in the mitzvos of Hashem, Who is the "*ikar*," the foundation of the world's existence. In other words, he denies Hashem's authority.
- □ **ORCHOS CHAIM; KOL BO**: He does not accept upon himself the yoke of Heaven and does not even mention Hashem's Name.
- □ **ALTER OF KELM**: He denies the principle of Divine Providence, a basic principle of Judaism.

הַקְהֵה אֶת שִׁנָּיו וֶאֱמָר לוֹ, בַּעֲבוּר זֶה עָשָׂה יהוה לִי בְּצֵאתִי מִמִּצְרָיִם.¹ לִי וְלֹא לוֹ, אִלּוּ הָיָה שָׁם לֹא הָיָה נִגְאָל.

- ☐ Excluding himself from the community of Torah-observant Jews is considered a denial of the basic principle of Judaism.

Q The wicked son seems to reject only the mitzvah of the korban Pesach, and a person who rejects one commandment is not considered a heretic. Why then does the Haggadah say that the wicked son denies the basic principle of Judaism?

A ☐ **HAFLA'AH:** Hashem commanded us to sacrifice a lamb for the korban Pesach, which was the Egyptian deity. (The lamb is also the zodiac sign of the month of Nissan.) By not offering the korban Pesach, the wicked son effectively classifies himself as one who believes in idolatry, and he is therefore considered a full-fledged heretic.

Q What is the meaning of the instruction to blunt his teeth?

A ☐ **RASHI:** Show anger toward the wicked son, in keeping with the verse וְשִׁנֵּי בָנִים תִּקְהֶינָה, *But the teeth of the sons are set on edge* (Jeremiah 31:28), indicating that they are angry.
- ☐ **RA'AVAN:** Answer him in kind, responding to his scornful question with a similarly sharp answer.
- ☐ The numerical value of the word *rasha*, wicked one, is 570. The numerical value of the word *tzaddik*, righteous one, is 204. The difference between these two values is 366, which is the value of the word *shinav*, his teeth. Our job is to try to remove the venom in the wicked son's words and turn him into a righteous person.

Q Why do we answer both the wicked son and the son who is unable to ask with the same verse: "It is because of this that HASHEM did so for me when I went out of Egypt"?

blunt his teeth and tell him: "It is because of this that HASHEM did so for me when I went out of Egypt."[1] "For me," but not for him — had he been there, he would not have been redeemed.

---

1. *Exodus* 13:8.

- **ORCHOS CHAIM:** The redemption from Egypt involved supernatural miracles, which are performed only for people who follow Hashem faithfully, like the wise son and the simple son. The wicked son is not worthy of having miracles performed for him, for obvious reasons, but neither is the son who is unable to ask, since he lacks the ability to appreciate the miracles that Hashem performs. We therefore answer both of these sons that the redemption was not in their merit, but in the merit of others.

- **KLI YAKAR:** The silence of the son who is unable to ask is not as innocuous as it seems. Perhaps the underlying reason that he does not ask questions is not an inability to ask, but a lack of interest. Even so, we do not add the words *for me, but not for him* to our answer to the son who is unable to ask, as we do in our answer to the wicked son, since the interest of the son who is unable to ask is piqued after we tell him about the Exodus. We are confident that his conduct will be different from that of the wicked son — that he will accept what we tell him and become worthy of redemption.

- **VILNA GAON:** We do not answer the wicked son directly. Instead, the answer is given to those around him, such as to the son who is unable to ask. The wicked son will be able to listen and hear the answer as well.

- **KSAV SOFER:** The Haggadah is cautioning parents that if their young son is unable to ask, they should work on strengthening his faith. If they do not do this, they might eventually find that this son has deteriorated and turned into a wicked son.

- **IR DAVID:** The verse used in the answer to these two sons states, וְהִגַּדְתָּ לְבִנְךָ בַּיּוֹם הַהוּא **לֵאמֹר** בַּעֲבוּר זֶה עָשָׂה ה' לִי בְּצֵאתִי מִמִּצְרָיִם, *You shall tell your son on that day, saying*, "It is because of this that HASHEM did so for me when I went out of Egypt" (*Exodus* 13:8). The word לֵאמֹר, *saying*, implies that these sons should repeat the remainder of the verse after us so that they themselves will fulfill the mitzvah of retelling the story of the Exodus. Both these sons need to hear this answer, because if they do not say the words of this verse, they have not discharged their obligation to recount the Exodus (according to the view of Rabban Gamliel, as expressed later in the Haggadah).

☐ The common denominator between the wicked son and the son who is unable to ask is their distance from Judaism. The son who is unable to ask is so far from Judaism that he does not even know to ask. We give the same answer to both of them, exhorting them not to lose their connection to God, because in the Egyptian exile (as in subsequent exiles and the Holocaust as well), there was no distinction made between a believing Jew and a nonbelieving Jew; both were equally persecuted. We remind the wicked son and the son who is unable to ask, who have abandoned Judaism, that a Jew can never detach himself from his roots.

Q In the Torah, we are told to answer the wicked son with the words ... וַאֲמַרְתֶּם זֶבַח פֶּסַח, You shall say, "It is a Pesach feast offering..." (Exodus 12:27), while the Haggadah says, ... אֱמֹר לוֹ בַּעֲבוּר זֶה, Tell him, "It is because of this..." Why does the Haggadah use a different verse than the Torah to answer this son?

A ☐ **RASHBAM:** Chazal wished to make the point that Hashem performed the miracles of the Exodus לִי וְלֹא לוֹ, for me but not for him. This point is derived from the verse that the Haggadah cites, בַּעֲבוּר זֶה עָשָׂה ה' לִי, It is because of this that HASHEM did so for me, but cannot be learned from the answer that the Torah provides for the wicked son.

☐ **SHIBBOLEI HALEKET:** The wicked son asked, מָה הָעֲבֹדָה הַזֹּאת לָכֶם, Of what purpose is **this work** to you? In response, the author of the Haggadah wished to address the matter of the work. We therefore quote from a verse (Exodus 13:8) that is preceded with the words וְעָבַדְתָּ אֶת הָעֲבֹדָה הַזֹּאת, You shall perform **this work** (ibid. 5), and say, בַּעֲבוּר זֶה עָשָׂה ה' לִי, It is because of **this [work]** that HASHEM did so for me.

☐ **OZHEROVER REBBE:** The wicked son questions why we are celebrating an event that happened thousands of years ago.

In answer, we explain why the whole premise of the question is wrong: although the Exodus took place thousands of years ago, it still has a direct impact on us as individuals. This is expressed with the verse that the Haggadah uses: בַּעֲבוּר זֶה עָשָׂה ה' **לִי** בְּצֵאתִי מִמִּצְרָיִם, *It is because of this that* HASHEM *did so **for me** when **I** went out of Egypt.*

☐ **MINCHAS YITZCHAK:** The answer to the wicked son must be a harsh one, since we are talking to a heretic. We therefore must use a verse that begins with the word וְהִגַּדְתָּ, *You shall tell,* which implies a harsh tone, rather than with a verse that begins with the word וַאֲמַרְתֶּם, *You shall say,* which conveys a soft tone.

Q: *Shouldn't we answer the wicked son directly, by telling him that Hashem did miracles "for me, but not for you"? Why is this phrased in the third person?*

A: ☐ **RID; SHIBBOLEI HALEKET:** We answer the wicked son in the same manner that he asked. He excluded himself from the community by saying, *Of what purpose is this work to* **you**, so we answer him in kind — in the third person, excluding him.

☐ **MALBIM:** The answer we give is not for the wicked son, but for the others who were present when he asked his disparaging question. This is compared to firefighters who were summoned to extinguish a fire in a burning house. When they arrived at the scene of the fire, they sprayed water on the surrounding houses rather than on the burning structure. "The fire has already devastated that house," the firefighters explained to the surprised neighbors, "and it is doubtful it can be salvaged. But the surrounding houses need to be protected from the raging fire. That is why we are focusing our efforts on them first."

Similarly, when the wicked son utters words of blasphemy and ridicule, we have to "spray water" on the other people present — water symbolizing Torah — to make them immune to the wicked son's words, before we can attempt to save the wicked son.

☐ **DOVER SHALOM:** We do not want any of the participants at the Seder to think that we are singling him out as wicked. We therefore refer to the wicked son in the third person.

Q *How can we be so confident that the wicked son would not have been redeemed? Many wicked people left Egypt!*

A
☐ **MA'ASEH NISSIM:** The Haggadah does not say that he would not have left Egypt, but rather that he would not have been redeemed. The word *geulah*, redemption, can refer to acquisition. This implies that Hashem would not have been willing to "acquire" the wicked son as a servant even if he would have left Egypt.

☐ **BIRKAS HASHIR:** In Egypt, even the wicked people circumcised themselves and partook of the *korban Pesach* (after their initial refusal to do so). This wicked son, on the other hand, would not have been willing to participate in the *korban Pesach* or the mitzvah of circumcision, and therefore he would not have been redeemed.

☐ **KSAV SOFER:** Even though the Jews had fallen to the forty-ninth level of impurity, they still had respect for their elders and would not have dared to be insolent to their leaders. They were therefore worthy of redemption. Had this wicked son been there, however, and displayed the same insolence that he shows at the Seder, he would not have been worthy of redemption.

☐ **ALTER OF KELM:** The wicked son might think that he could have simply followed the masses and been redeemed along with the Jews when they left Egypt despite his wickedness. We therefore tell him that Hashem watches over each individual and knows every person's thoughts. Had the wicked son been in Egypt, Hashem would have distinguished him from the masses and he would not have been redeemed.

☐ **SHA'AR BAS RABBIM:** Hashem commanded the Jews to mark the entrances to their homes, so that the Angel of Death would skip over their houses. The wicked son, who excludes himself from the community and does not believe in Hashem or His commandments, would not have marked the entrance to his home and so would have fallen prey to the Angel of Death.

☐ **ALTER OF NOVARDOK:** Had the Jews not trusted Hashem and followed Him into the wilderness, they would have remained in Egypt, enslaved to Pharaoh. From the wicked son's questions, it is clear that he would not have had the necessary faith to embark on the journey through the desert and would have opted to remain behind in Egypt.

- ☐ **RAV REUVEN KATZ:** The wicked son has no interest in the redemption of the Jewish people. He would rather be enslaved to the depravity of Egypt. Had he been in Egypt, he would not have left, but would have chosen to adopt the Egyptian culture.
- ☐ **HASHIR V'HASHEVACH:** The *korban Pesach* is a communal offering. The wicked son excludes himself from the community and therefore cannot be part of the communal redemption.
- ☐ **RAV YECHEZKEL LEVENSTEIN:** The purpose of the redemption was to transform us into servants of Hashem. If someone rejects this service, as the wicked son does, he proves himself unfit for redemption.

Q *Why do we answer the wicked son in such a harsh manner, rather than drawing him close or at least employing the strategy of "the left hand pushes away, and the right hand draws near"?*

A
- ☐ **MALBIM:** We answer the question in the manner in which it was asked. Just as a person's teeth are blunted if he eats hard foods, so the wicked son gets the answer he deserves in response to his own insolent words.
- ☐ **KSAV SOFER:** The wicked son is insolent to the extent that he mocks his father for fulfilling the Torah's commandments. He has no hope of improvement, and we therefore answer him harshly.
- ☐ **RAV YERUCHAM LEVOVITZ:** It *is* appropriate to answer the wicked son in a way that draws him closer, but in this passage we are not giving him an answer. We are trying to induce him to be open to hearing an answer.
- ☐ **RAV MENACHEM ZIEMBA:** The wicked son's arguments do not stem from his inner being, but rather from the poison he has imbibed from the outside world and that has become stuck "in his teeth." The remedy for this is to "blunt his teeth" and remove the poison by displaying love to him. (Blunting his teeth, in this sense, is not harsh, but rather reflects a gentle approach that "defangs" the wicked son.)
- ☐ **RAV REUVEN KATZ:** No answer that we can give will satisfy the wicked son, so there is no point in answering him. Instead, we "blunt his teeth" so that he will not be able to "bite" others and inject them with his venom.

[93] **HAGGADAH: THE ANSWER IS . . .**

תָּם מָה הוּא אוֹמֵר? מַה זֹּאת? וְאָמַרְתָּ אֵלָיו, בְּחֹזֶק יָד הוֹצִיאָנוּ יהוה מִמִּצְרַיִם מִבֵּית עֲבָדִים.[1]

וְשֶׁאֵינוֹ יוֹדֵעַ לִשְׁאוֹל, אַתְּ פְּתַח לוֹ. שֶׁנֶּאֱמַר,

---

☐ **CHOMAS HADAS V'HA'EMUNAH:** The wicked son's question is, *Of what purpose is this work to you?* If we tell him that we receive reward in the Next World for fulfilling the commandments and the punishment of Gehinnom for violating those commandments, he will be scornful of such intangible consequences. Therefore, we answer that we are punished immediately for transgressions — which is represented by the words *blunt his teeth* — and we are rewarded with redemption for doing mitzvos. Hearing this answer might persuade him to mend his ways.

◆§ תָּם / The Simple Son

Q *Who is the simple son?*

A ☐ **YERUSHALMI** (*Pesachim* 10:4): He is a fool.

☐ **RASHI** (*Genesis* 25:27): He is someone who is not cunning enough to easily deceive others. Yaakov was described as a *tam*, a simple man.

☐ **VILNA GAON:** He is the opposite of the wicked son, as reflected in the verse אַחַת הִיא עַל כֵּן אָמַרְתִּי תָּם וְרָשָׁע הוּא מְכַלֶּה, *It is all the same; therefore I say, "He destroys the blameless with the wicked"* (Job 9:22).

☐ **KSAV SOFER:** He is a Jew who never learned Torah and knows nothing about the mitzvos.

☐ He is one whose intelligence is limited, as reflected in the simplicity of his question: מַה זֹּאת, *What is this?*

Q *What is the simple son asking?*

A ☐ **RAV EZRA TRAUB:** The Torah is called *zos*, this, as in the verse ... וְזֹאת הַתּוֹרָה, *This is the teaching...* (Deuteronomy

The simple son — what does he say? "What is this?" Tell him: "With a strong hand did HASHEM take us out of Egypt, from the house of bondage."[1]

As for **the son who is unable to ask**, you must initiate the subject for him, as it is stated:

---

1. *Exodus* 13:14.

4:44). The simple son is asking, Why did *we* merit receiving the Torah, while the angels did not?

☐ The simple son is asking, Why did Hashem redeem the Jewish people from Egypt Himself and not through a messenger? We answer him, בְּחֹזֶק יָד הוֹצִיאָנוּ ה' מִמִּצְרַיִם מִבֵּית עֲבָדִים, *With a strong hand did HASHEM take us out of Egypt, from the house of bondage.* We were taken out of a "house of bondage." This redemption had two aspects: physical and spiritual. Such a redemption can be accomplished only by Hashem, not by any angel.

◈§ שֶׁאֵינוֹ יוֹדֵעַ לִשְׁאוֹל / The son who is unable to ask

Q Who is the son who is unable to ask?

A ☐ ORCHOS CHAIM: He is a child who lacks the discernment to be able to ask.

☐ RAV SHLOMO ALKABETZ: He is a child who is not a fool, but is fearful of making a mistake and is therefore too shy to ask.

☐ VILNA GAON: He is the opposite of a *talmid chacham*.

☐ RAV AVRAHAM ADLER: He is a Jew who has assimilated into secular culture and knows nothing of Judaism.

Q Why is the word אַתְּ, *you*, in the feminine, used here?

A ☐ DIVREI CHAIM: The word אַתְּ contains the first and last letters of the Hebrew alphabet. The Haggadah is instructing us to teach him everything from *alef* to *tav*.

וְהִגַּדְתָּ לְבִנְךָ בַּיּוֹם הַהוּא לֵאמֹר, בַּעֲבוּר זֶה עָשָׂה יהוה לִי בְּצֵאתִי מִמִּצְרָיִם.[1]

יָכוֹל מֵרֹאשׁ חֹדֶשׁ, תַּלְמוּד לוֹמַר בַּיּוֹם הַהוּא. אִי בַּיּוֹם הַהוּא, יָכוֹל מִבְּעוֹד יוֹם, תַּלְמוּד לוֹמַר בַּעֲבוּר זֶה.

- ☐ **AVNEI NEZER**: As a general rule, masculine terminology is used to refer to a giver, while feminine terminology is used to refer to a receiver. The Haggadah is teaching us that a true educator allows the student's own abilities to flower so that he can understand and give of himself. In acting in this capacity, the teacher reverts to the feminine role of receiver.

- ☐ **BE'ER SHMUEL**: A mother has the power to imbue the fear of Heaven in her children as she nurtures them. These words are therefore directed at the mother, urging her to open the heart of her young child to learning, since he is not yet mature enough to understand his father's words of Torah.

- ☐ **RAV ARYEH LEIB GURWICZ**: A father educates his child through logic, while a mother teaches through emotion. The child who is unable to ask cannot be taught through logic; he must be reached through emotion, in the way of a mother.

- ☐ **RAV SHLOMO ZALMAN AUERBACH**: The use of the feminine pronoun teaches that women are also obligated in the mitzvah of telling the story of the Exodus, even though it is a time-bound mitzvah, because they too were included in the miracle.

∞§ יָכוֹל מֵרֹאשׁ חֹדֶשׁ / *From the first day of the month*

In the answer to the son who is unable to ask, the Haggadah quoted the verse וְהִגַּדְתָּ לְבִנְךָ **בַּיּוֹם הַהוּא** לֵאמֹר בַּעֲבוּר זֶה עָשָׂה ה' לִי בְּצֵאתִי מִמִּצְרָיִם, *You shall tell your son* **on that day** *saying, "It is because of this that* HASHEM *did so for me when I went out of Egypt."* Now we go on to explain when "that day" is.

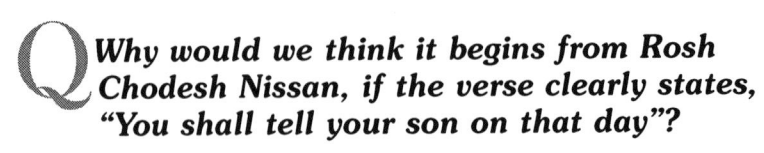

Q *Why would we think it begins from Rosh Chodesh Nissan, if the verse clearly states, "You shall tell your son on that day"?*

הגדה של פסח [96]

You shall tell your son on that day: "It is because of this that HASHEM did so for me when I went out of Egypt."[1]

One might think that the obligation to discuss the Exodus commences from the first day of the month of Nissan, but the Torah says: "You shall tell your son on that day." But the expression "on that day" could be understood to mean only during the daytime; therefore the Torah adds: "It is because of this [that HASHEM did so for me when I went out of Egypt]."

---

1. *Exodus* 13:8.

A
- ☐ **PEIRUSH KADMON:** We might think so because there is a special mitzvah to study the laws of Pesach thirty days before the holiday, a mitzvah that does not apply to any other holiday. (Although some apply this halachah to the other festivals, the halachah only mentions Pesach.)
- ☐ **SHIBBOLEI HALEKET:** One could think so because Hashem commanded the Jews regarding the *korban Pesach* on the first day of Nissan.
- ☐ **RITVA:** The zodiac sign of the month of Nissan is a lamb. Therefore this passage is saying, יָכוֹל מֵרֹאשׁ חֹדֶשׁ — *one might think* that the *korban Pesach*, which was the sacrifice of a lamb, could be brought any time from the first of the month.
- ☐ **MALBIM:** Since the Torah states, several verses earlier, וְעָבַדְתָּ אֶת הָעֲבֹדָה הַזֹּאת בַּחֹדֶשׁ הַזֶּה, *You shall perform this service in this month* (*Exodus* 13:5), and it does not specify a date, we might think it begins from Rosh Chodesh.
- ☐ **RAV CHAIM SOLOVEITCHIK:** There is a mitzvah to usher in every holiday early, just as we usher in Shabbos early (*Orach Chaim* 261). One might think that this law of adding to a holiday applies also to Pesach. Therefore, the Haggadah teaches that the mitzvah of telling the story of the Exodus applies only *on that day* — at the prescribed time, and not before.

Q *"It is because of this." What is "this"?*

A
- ☐ **RASHI:** *Zeh*, this, refers to the fulfillment of the mitzvos of the Seder — *korban Pesach*, *matzah*, and *maror*.

בַּעֲבוּר זֶה לֹא אָמַרְתִּי אֶלָּא בְּשָׁעָה שֶׁיֵּשׁ מַצָּה וּמָרוֹר מֻנָּחִים לְפָנֶיךָ.

מִתְּחִלָּה עוֹבְדֵי עֲבוֹדָה זָרָה הָיוּ אֲבוֹתֵינוּ, וְעַכְשָׁו קֵרְבָנוּ הַמָּקוֹם לַעֲבוֹדָתוֹ. שֶׁנֶּאֱמַר, וַיֹּאמֶר יְהוֹשֻׁעַ אֶל כָּל הָעָם, כֹּה אָמַר יהוה אֱלֹהֵי יִשְׂרָאֵל, בְּעֵבֶר הַנָּהָר יָשְׁבוּ אֲבוֹתֵיכֶם מֵעוֹלָם, תֶּרַח אֲבִי אַבְרָהָם וַאֲבִי נָחוֹר, וַיַּעַבְדוּ

- □ **AVUDRAHAM:** The word *zeh*, this, has the numerical equivalent of 12, corresponding to the twelve mitzvos of the Seder night: the four cups of wine, *charoses*, *karpas*, two handwashings, *hamotzi*, matzah, *maror*, and *korech*.

- □ **OHR HACHAIM:** The word *zeh*, this, has the numerical equivalent of 12, corresponding to the twelve mitzvos of Pesach: *korban Pesach*, matzah, *maror*, reciting the Haggadah, the seven days of the holiday, and Kiddush of the first day.

- □ The word *zeh*, this, is an acronym for זֹאת הַתּוֹרָה, *this is the Torah*, implying that we left Egypt for the purpose of receiving the Torah and fulfilling its precepts.

◈§ מִתְּחִלָּה עוֹבְדֵי עֲבוֹדָה זָרָה / Originally they were idol worshipers

After establishing when we are obligated to fulfill the mitzvah of telling about the Exodus (as the previous passage concludes, *Only at the time when matzah and maror lie before you*), we now begin relating the story itself.

Q *Why does the passage of Avadim Hayinu (We were slaves to Pharaoh) come before this passage, MiTechilah Ovdei Avodah Zarah (Originally our ancestors were idol worshipers), when chronologically the events were reversed?*

A □ **HASHIR V'HASHEVACH:** The passage of *Avadim Hayinu* discusses the miracles of the Exodus that Hashem performed for us, while the passage of *MiTechilah Ovdei Avodah Zarah* does not mention any miracles. We choose to open with a passage

The pronoun "this" implies something tangible, thus, "You shall tell your son" applies only at the time when matzah and *maror* lie before you — at the Seder.

Originally our ancestors were idol worshipers, but now the Omnipresent has brought us near to His service, as it is written: Yehoshua said to all the people, "So says HASHEM, God of Israel: Your fathers always lived beyond the Euphrates River, Terach the father of Avraham and Nachor, and they served

---

that includes praises of Hashem for the miracles He did, even if this does not follow the chronological order of events.

☐ **RAV AVIGDOR NEBENZAHL:** There is a dispute between Rav and Shmuel over whether the Talmudic precept *We begin with disgrace and end with praise* (Pesachim 116) is fulfilled with the passage of *Avadim Hayinu* (as per Shmuel) or with the passage of *MiTechilah Ovdei Avodah Zarah* (as per Rav).

Had we begun the Haggadah with *MiTechilah* and continued chronologically to *Avadim Hayinu*, it would not have been clear that the story of the enslavement — as described in *Avadim Hayinu* — was in itself a disgrace. Then we would not have fulfilled the precept of beginning with disgrace and ending with praise according to Shmuel's view. *Avadim Hayinu* would have seemed simply like a natural continuation of the story. The Haggadah therefore begins with *Avadim Hayinu* and only then continues with *MiTechilah*, in order to highlight the disgrace and satisfy both opinions.

Q: *What does the fact that Terach, the father of Avraham, worshiped idols have to do with the story of the Exodus?*

A: ☐ **RID:** We thank Hashem for redeeming us from Egypt even though our ancestors worshiped idols when they were free men — in the times of Terach, before the Egyptian exile, and even persisted in worshiping idols in Egypt until they reached the forty-ninth level of impurity — and still Hashem redeemed us.

HAGGADAH: THE ANSWER IS . . .

אֱלֹהִים אֲחֵרִים. וָאֶקַּח אֶת אֲבִיכֶם אֶת אַבְרָהָם מֵעֵבֶר הַנָּהָר, וָאוֹלֵךְ אוֹתוֹ בְּכָל אֶרֶץ כְּנָעַן, וָאַרְבֶּה אֶת זַרְעוֹ, וָאֶתֶּן לוֹ אֶת יִצְחָק. וָאֶתֵּן לְיִצְחָק אֶת יַעֲקֹב וְאֶת עֵשָׂו, וָאֶתֵּן לְעֵשָׂו אֶת הַר שֵׂעִיר לָרֶשֶׁת אוֹתוֹ, וְיַעֲקֹב וּבָנָיו יָרְדוּ מִצְרָיִם.[1]

- **RITVA:** We say these words in an attempt to win over the wicked son by telling him the historical background of the Jewish people: originally our ancestors worshiped idols, but after Avraham recognized his Creator, the Jewish people began to follow Hashem's ways. We hope that after hearing this, the wicked son will change his ways.

- **MICHTAV MEELIYAHU:** This teaches us how courageous Avraham was in standing up to his own family and society. For this, Avraham was called "Avraham HaIvri" — Avraham who stood "on the other side" — because he stood on one side, while the rest of the world stood on the other side. The Haggadah is emphasizing that the recognition of Hashem as the Creator began with Avraham, not with Terach or his predecessors.

- These words are aimed at encouraging the son who is unable to ask. "Don't give up even if it's difficult," we tell him. "Avraham Avinu also encountered many difficulties along his journey to coming close to his Creator. Even if you find yourself in hostile surroundings, you can still prevail spiritually, just as Avraham did."

Q: Why is it significant that Hashem led Avraham through the entire land?

A:
- **RAV YECHEZKEL LEVENSTEIN:** This emphasizes that no person leads himself through life; Hashem leads him.

- **SIFSEI CHAIM:** Avraham's traveling through the entire land enabled his descendants to conquer the land miraculously, since every place he passed through was later conquered by the Jewish people (*Ramban, Genesis 12:10*).

other gods. Then I took your father Avraham from beyond the river and I led him through all the land of Canaan. I multiplied his offspring and gave him Yitzchak. To Yitzchak I gave Yaakov and Esav; to Esav I gave Mount Seir to inherit, but Yaakov and his children went down to Egypt."[1]

---

1. *Joshua* 24:2-4.

- **HASHIR V'HASHEVACH:** This is a praise of Avraham Avinu, who labored to spread recognition of Hashem as the Creator and inspire others to believe in Him.

Q *Why is it significant that Mount Seir was given to Esav?*

A
- **ABARBANEL:** It emphasizes that Esav was not included in the category of Avraham's heirs.
- **VILNA GAON:** We thank Hashem for giving Mount Seir to Esav. Because he received this territory, he no longer contested Yaakov's right to the Land of Israel.
- **DOVER SHALOM:** The Haggadah is informing us that Esav has no connection whatsoever to the Land of Israel, just as our idolatrous ancestors who lived *beyond the Euphrates* had no connection to the Land of Israel.
- **RAV AHARON BAKST:** The Haggadah's comparison between the Jewish people's receiving the Land of Israel and Esav's receiving Mount Seir is like comparing a human child to a young animal. An animal is born able to walk, and within a short time is able to find its own food. In contrast, a newborn baby has to pass through many stages of development before he is able to walk and fend for itself.

  Similarly, Esav's descendants received their territorial inheritance immediately with no suffering. In contrast, the Jewish people had to endure many stages of development, suffering through the Egyptian exile. Since the Jewish people experienced such hardships, they were elevated to a higher spiritual level and merited to live an exalted spiritual existence.

בָּרוּךְ שׁוֹמֵר הַבְטָחָתוֹ לְיִשְׂרָאֵל, בָּרוּךְ הוּא. שֶׁהַקָּדוֹשׁ בָּרוּךְ הוּא חִשַּׁב אֶת הַקֵּץ, לַעֲשׂוֹת כְּמָה שֶׁאָמַר לְאַבְרָהָם אָבִינוּ בִּבְרִית בֵּין הַבְּתָרִים, שֶׁנֶּאֱמַר, וַיֹּאמֶר לְאַבְרָם, יָדֹעַ תֵּדַע כִּי גֵר יִהְיֶה זַרְעֲךָ בְּאֶרֶץ לֹא לָהֶם, וַעֲבָדוּם וְעִנּוּ אֹתָם, אַרְבַּע מֵאוֹת שָׁנָה. וְגַם אֶת הַגּוֹי אֲשֶׁר יַעֲבֹדוּ דָּן אָנֹכִי, וְאַחֲרֵי כֵן יֵצְאוּ בִּרְכֻשׁ גָּדוֹל.[1]

◆§ בָּרוּךְ שׁוֹמֵר הַבְטָחָתוֹ / **Blessed is He Who keeps His pledge**

This passage is a continuation of the previous one, which ended with the mention of Esav's inheriting Mount Seir while Yaakov and his children went down to Egypt. One might think that Esav was more fortunate than Yaakov, since he received his inheritance without suffering, while Yaakov's children were enslaved in Egypt. We therefore go on to say, בָּרוּךְ שׁוֹמֵר הַבְטָחָתוֹ לְיִשְׂרָאֵל, *Blessed is He Who keeps His pledge to Israel*, praising Hashem for the process we underwent. Although the beginning of this process was difficult and painful, in the end it was for our benefit (*Chayei Adam*).

Q *Why do we praise Hashem for keeping His pledge? Every decent person keeps his word!*

A ☐ **RASHBAM:** Hashem could have calculated the beginning of the exile from the time that Yaakov went down to Egypt, but in His great kindness He calculated it instead from the time Yitzchak was born, even before the Egyptian bondage began. We thank Him for reducing the exile by 190 years (the numerical value of the word "*keitz*," end, which appears in this passage, in the phrase שֶׁהַקָּדוֹשׁ בָּרוּךְ הוּא חִשַּׁב אֶת הַקֵּץ, *For the Holy One, Blessed is He, calculated the end of the bondage*), allowing us to leave after only 210 years instead of after 400.

☐ **MA'ASEH NISSIM:** The wording here is בָּרוּךְ **שׁוֹמֵר** הַבְטָחָתוֹ לְיִשְׂרָאֵל, *Blessed is He Who **keeps** His pledge to Israel*. The word "*shomer*" can also mean "watches" or "waits," as in the verse וְאָבִיו שָׁמַר אֶת הַדָּבָר, *But his father kept the matter in mind* (Genesis 37:11) — i.e., his father "anticipated" or

Blessed is He Who keeps His pledge to Israel; Blessed is He! For the Holy One, Blessed is He, calculated the end of the bondage in order to do as He said to our father Avraham at the Covenant between the Parts, as it is stated: He said to Avram, "Know with certainty that your offspring will be aliens in a land not their own, they will serve them, and they will oppress them four hundred years; but also upon the nation which they shall serve will I execute judgment, and afterward they shall leave with great possessions."[1]

---

1. Genesis 15:13-14.

"kept watch" over the matter. Not only did Hashem keep His pledge, He also waited with longing to fulfill it.

☐ **DUBNO MAGGID:** Although Hashem promised Avraham that He would give the land of Canaan to his descendants, Avraham was concerned that his descendants might sin and forfeit their claim to the land. We thank Hashem for fulfilling His pledge even though Avraham's descendants *did* sin.

☐ **RAV YITZCHAK ISAAC CHAVER:** Hashem promised Avraham גֵּר יִהְיֶה זַרְעֲךָ..., *Your offspring will be aliens*... (Genesis 15:13), but He did not specify which descendants. We thank Hashem for keeping His pledge *to Israel*, rather than fulfilling His promise through Avraham's other descendants.

Q Which pledge are we referring to?

A ☐ **RITVA:** It refers to the promise Hashem gave to Avraham in the covenant between the parts: כִּי גֵר יִהְיֶה זַרְעֲךָ בְּאֶרֶץ לֹא לָהֶם...וְאַחֲרֵי כֵן יֵצְאוּ בִּרְכֻשׁ גָּדוֹל, *Your offspring will be aliens in a land not their own...and afterward they shall leave with great possessions* (Genesis 15:13–14).

☐ **MAHARAL:** We are speaking of the promise that our enemies will not succeed in annihilating us, as we mention in the next passage of *V'Hi Sho'amdah*.

☐ **IYUN TEFILLAH:** It is the promise that Hashem will always be with the Jewish people, even in exile, as we see in the next passage: *In every generation they rise against us to* annihilate us. But the Holy One, Blessed is He, rescues us from their hand.

Q: Why do we repeat the word בָּרוּךְ, Blessed?

- **SHIBBOLEI HALEKET:** We are mentioning two blessings here: we bless Hashem first for the redemption from Egypt, and then we bless Him for the enslavement, in keeping with the precept *A person is required to recite a blessing over the bad just as he recites a blessing over the good* (Berachos 60).
- **IYUN TEFILLAH:** We bless Hashem first for watching over the Jewish people in exile, and then for having *calculated the end of the bondage*.
- **MALBIM:** This phrase is meant to be said responsively. The leader of the Seder says, בָּרוּךְ שׁוֹמֵר הַבְטָחָתוֹ לְיִשְׂרָאֵל, *Blessed is He Who keeps His pledge to Israel*, and the other participants respond, בָּרוּךְ הוּא, *Blessed is He*.
- **OHR HACHAMAH:** This is a complete blessing, beginning and ending with בָּרוּךְ, *blessed*.

Q: Why did Hashem decree that the Jews had to be exiled in Egypt?

A:
- **TALMUD** (Nedarim 32): It was decreed because Avraham sent Torah scholars out to war against the four kings, and because he questioned Hashem's promise by saying, בַּמָּה אֵדַע כִּי אִירָשֶׁנָּה, *Whereby shall I know that I am to inherit it?* (Genesis 15:8).
- **RALBAG:** The exile was a preparation for receiving the Torah.
- **ABARBANEL:** The decree came about because of the sin of selling Yosef.

Q: How long did the enslavement in Egypt actually last?

A:
- There are varying opinions regarding the length of the enslavement:
  1. **116 years**, from the time Levi, the last surviving son of Yaakov, passed away, as the Torah tells us וַיָּמָת יוֹסֵף וְכָל אֶחָיו...וַיָּקָם מֶלֶךְ חָדָשׁ, *Yosef died, and all his brothers...A*

new king arose over Egypt (*Exodus* 1:6,8). It was only after Yosef and all his siblings died that a new king arose and began the subjugation.

2. **210 years**, which is the length of time the Jews were actually in Egypt. It is also the numerical equivalent of the word *redu* in the verse, וַיֹּאמֶר הִנֵּה שָׁמַעְתִּי כִּי יֶשׁ שֶׁבֶר בְּמִצְרָיִם **רְדוּ** שָׁמָּה וְשִׁבְרוּ לָנוּ מִשָּׁם וְנִחְיֶה וְלֹא נָמוּת, *And he said*, *"Behold, I have heard that there are provisions in Egypt; go down there and purchase for us from there, that we may live and not die"* (*Genesis* 42:2; see *Rashi* there).

3. **400 years**, from the time of Yitzchak's birth.

4. **430 years**, from the time of the Covenant Between the Parts, when Hashem informed Avraham of the impending exile and enslavement.

Q If Hashem promised that the Jews would be enslaved for 400 years, why did the exile end when they were in Egypt for only 210 years?

A
☐ **PIRKEI D'RABBI ELIEZER:** The original decree was that they would have to work only during the daytime for 400 years. But the Egyptians forced them to work at night as well, so the total length of the exile was shortened accordingly.

☐ **MECHILTA:** Hashem redeemed the Jewish people earlier than planned, but the remaining years were added to the later exiles.

☐ **ARIZAL:** Hashem saw that if the Jews would not be redeemed from Egypt at that juncture, they would fall to the fiftieth level of impurity. If that happened, it would no longer be possible for them to be redeemed at all, and His promise to Avraham would remain unfulfilled. In order to fulfill that promise, He hastened the redemption.

☐ **ANAF YOSEF:** Hashem originally decreed that the exile would last 400 years, but He reduced the length of the exile in reward for the Jewish people's good deeds (namely, the four areas in which they were scrupulous: not changing their names, not changing their language, etc.).

☐ **MICHTAV MEELIYAHU:** The Jews were in Egypt for 400 years in the spiritual sense, for their ministering angel was subjugated to the ministering angel of Egypt from the time of the Covenant Between the Parts.

- Hashem calculated the beginning of the exile from the time of Yitzchak's birth. This is hinted at in the verse אֲשֶׁר כָּרַת אֶת אַבְרָהָם וּשְׁבוּעָתוֹ לְיִשְׂחָק, *That He made with Avraham and His vow to Yitzchak* (*Psalms* 105:9). The name Yitzchak is spelled in an unusual way in this verse, with a *shin* substituted for the *tzaddi*. The numerical value of *shin* is 300, the numerical value of *tzaddi* is 90, and the difference between the two is 210, corresponding to the 210 years the Jews were in Egypt.
- The enslavement was so severe that it was as if they had been exiled for 400 years. The time span of the exile was therefore shortened.

Q *Why were the Egyptians punished if they were simply fulfilling Hashem's instructions in the Covenant Between the Parts?*

A
- **RABBEINU BACHYA:** The Egyptians were given permission to enslave the Jews, but they abused this right by imposing excessive harshness and cruelty. They went beyond the directive by embittering the lives of the Jews and enacting such decrees as throwing all baby boys into the river.
- **RAMBAM:** Hashem decreed that the Jewish people would be enslaved in a land that was not theirs, but He did not specify which land that would be, nor did He command the Egyptians to be the ones to carry out this prophecy. The Egyptians *chose* to enslave the Jews, and they were therefore punished.
- **RAMBAN:** Hashem decreed that the Jews would be enslaved, but the Egyptians did not do so with the intention of fulfilling Hashem's command; their intentions were purely evil.
- **VILNA GAON:** The Egyptians were punished for denying Hashem's existence, as Pharaoh stated, לֹא יָדַעְתִּי אֶת ה', *I do not know HASHEM* (*Exodus* 5:2).
- **KEDUSHAS LEVI:** By going far and beyond Hashem's command in their cruelty toward the Jewish people, the Egyptians demonstrated clearly that their intention was not to fulfill Hashem's will. They were therefore punished not only for going beyond the parameters of the Covenant Between the Parts, but for *everything* they did to the Jewish people.
- **MESHECH CHOCHMAH:** The Egyptians were punished for their lack of gratitude toward the Jewish people after Yosef

had so greatly enriched their country. They were also punished for throwing the Jewish babies into the river, a transgression of the Noachide law against murder.

- **RAV REUVEN BENGIS:** The Covenant Between the Parts stated clearly that the nation that enslaved the Jews would be punished: *Upon the nation which they shall serve will I execute judgment*. In deciding to enslave the Jewish people, the Egyptians effectively agreed to suffer the consequences.

Q: What does the word וְגַם, but also, come to add?

A:
- **RASHI:** The word וְגַם, *but also*, is an allusion to the four other kingdoms that would later subjugate the Jewish people. They *also* will be punished.

Q: Hashem asked the Jewish people to take the possessions of the Egyptians: דַּבֶּר נָא בְּאָזְנֵי הָעָם וְיִשְׁאֲלוּ אִישׁ מֵאֵת רֵעֵהוּ וְאִשָּׁה מֵאֵת רְעוּתָהּ כְּלֵי כֶסֶף וּכְלֵי זָהָב, *Please speak in the ears of the people: Let each man request of his fellow and each woman from her fellow silver vessels and gold vessels* (Exodus 11:2). Why did Hashem have to request that they do this, if it was for their own benefit?

A:
- **MAHARSHA:** If not for Hashem's request, the Jews might have opted to forgo the opportunity to take the Egyptians' valuables. Hashem wanted to ensure that they would take these possessions.
- **SIFSEI CHACHAMIM:** If Hashem had not specifically instructed them to take the Egyptians' wealth, the Jews might have been afraid to do so.
- **DUBNO MAGGID:** This can be explained by means of a parable. A wrestling match was held between two combatants. It was determined that the winner would be the one who pushed the other into a pit some distance away from where the match began. When the match started, one of the combatants lifted his competitor into the air and ran in the direction of the pit. As they approached the pit, the second combatant recovered, jumping off the shoulders of the first and throwing him into the pit. After this comeback victory,

the winner was asked why he had allowed the other wrestler to carry him until the pit. "Am I a porter?" he retorted. "Why should I drag him all the way to the pit? Instead, I let him drag *me* there, and that was when I started to fight him."

Similarly, the Jewish people knew that they would receive the Egyptians' wealth at the Sea of Reeds. Rather than carry the Egyptians' possessions with them to the sea, they preferred to allow the Egyptians to be their "porters." But Hashem requested that they take the wealth of the Egyptians while still in Egypt, in order to fulfill the promise of *And afterward they shall leave with great possessions*.

- **KSAV SOFER:** "Borrowing" the Egyptians' silver and gold seemed like a conniving scheme, and Moshe would have considered such a plan improper. Hashem therefore had to give an explicit command that the Jews take the Egyptians' wealth so they would know the plan had His full approval.

- **RAV SAMSON RAPHAEL HIRSCH:** The Egyptians admired the Jews for not looting any of their possessions during the plague of darkness, as the verse states, וַיִּתֵּן ה' אֶת חֵן הָעָם בְּעֵינֵי מִצְרָיִם, *HASHEM granted the people favor in the eyes of Egypt* (Exodus 11:3). Wishing to maintain this favorable impression, the Jews did not want to take anything from the Egyptians. Nevertheless, Hashem instructed that they take the Egyptians' wealth, in order that the Egyptians would be compelled to chase after them and would ultimately drown in the Sea of Reeds.

- **HASHIR V'HASHEVACH:** Hashem had to command the Jews to take this wealth, because the Jews did not want to benefit from the Egyptians' money (just as many Holocaust survivors did not want to accept reparations from Germany).

Q *The Talmud (Berachos 9) teaches that Hashem told the Jewish people to take the wealth of Egypt so that Avraham would not complain that Hashem only kept the first part of the Covenant Between the Parts ("They will serve them and they will oppress them"), but did not keep the second part of the covenant ("And afterward they shall leave with great possessions). Is concern about Avraham's potential complaint the only reason that Hashem should fulfill His promise?*

A ☐ **RAV ITZELE OF VOLOZHIN:** The Midrash teaches that the promise that *they shall leave with great possessions* refers to the Torah, the spiritual treasure that the Jews received after leaving Egypt. Hashem could have fulfilled His promise by giving the Jews the Torah and nothing else, but then Avraham might have complained that the prophecy of *They will serve them and they will oppress them* was only fulfilled in the literal sense, while the prophecy of *Afterward they shall leave with great possessions* was fulfilled in a more abstract sense. Hashem therefore ensured that the second part of the promise was also fulfilled literally.

☐ **MINCHAS ASHER:** The promise was fulfilled when the Jewish people received the wealth of Egypt after the Egyptians drowned at the Sea of Reeds, a week after the Exodus. But Avraham could have argued that this was not the true fulfillment of the verse *They shall leave with great possessions*, since they did not receive the wealth of Egypt immediately upon leaving. To ensure that Avraham would not be upset that the Jewish people received nothing until the splitting of the sea, Hashem instructed the Jews to take the Egyptians' possessions when they left.

☐ The Jewish people were at the forty-ninth level of impurity at the time of the redemption and were "full of sin," as the Midrash teaches. In this state, they were unworthy of the fulfillment of Hashem's promise that they would leave with great wealth. But Avraham, who saw the good in people and always tried to judge them favorably, would not have agreed to condemn his descendants. Knowing that Avraham would invariably argue in his descendants' favor and insist that they were worthy of receiving the great wealth they had been promised, Hashem made sure that this promise was fulfilled.

Q **Why did Hashem command the Jews to borrow the valuables of the Egyptians, rather than instructing the Egyptians to give the Jews their valuables?**

A ☐ **RAN:** Had the Egyptians given the Jews their valuables as a gift, rather than as a loan, the Egyptians might not have chased after them when they saw that the Jews did not return after three days. The miracle of the sea splitting would never have happened.

The matzos are covered and the cups lifted as the following paragraph is proclaimed joyously. Upon its conclusion, the cups are put down and the matzos are uncovered.

וְהִיא שֶׁעָמְדָה לַאֲבוֹתֵינוּ וְלָנוּ, שֶׁלֹּא אֶחָד בִּלְבָד עָמַד עָלֵינוּ לְכַלּוֹתֵנוּ. אֶלָּא שֶׁבְּכָל דּוֹר וָדוֹר עוֹמְדִים עָלֵינוּ לְכַלּוֹתֵנוּ, וְהַקָּדוֹשׁ בָּרוּךְ הוּא מַצִּילֵנוּ מִיָּדָם.

- **RABBEINU BACHYA:** The verse that describes Hashem's command to "borrow" the Egyptians' possessions says, וְיִשְׁאֲלוּ אִישׁ מֵאֵת רֵעֵהוּ וְאִשָּׁה מֵאֵת רְעוּתָהּ כְּלֵי כֶסֶף וּכְלֵי זָהָב, *Let each man request of his fellow and each woman from her fellow silver vessels and gold vessels* (*Exodus* 11:2). Here the word "*vayishalu*" does not mean "they shall borrow," but rather "they shall request" or "they shall demand" the possessions as a payment for their work. There was no deception here, merely a demand that the Egyptians pay the departing Jews for their labor.

- **VILNA GAON:** Hashem punished Pharaoh measure for measure. At the beginning of the enslavement, Pharaoh himself worked alongside the Jews, displaying friendship and camaraderie, to dupe them into agreeing to work for him. Even afterward, he continued to deceive them, instructing the midwives to kill all Jewish newborn males and inform the mothers that their babies had died naturally in childbirth. In retribution for this deception, Hashem commanded the Jews to "borrow" the Egyptians' possessions before they left Egypt. This would induce Pharaoh to chase the Jews into the Sea of Reeds, where the Egyptians would drown.

- **SIFSEI CHAIM:** Had the Egyptians given the Jews their valuables as a gift, the Jews would have been beholden to them, and Hashem did not want them to feel any gratitude toward the Egyptians.

It is said that the Brisker Rav asked his son, "Why don't we commemorate the great wealth with which the Jewish people left Egypt, just as we use *maror* to commemorate the slavery?"

"The *maror* and other tribulations have remained with us until today," his son replied, "while there is nothing left of the great wealth."

The matzos are covered and the cups lifted as the following paragraph is proclaimed joyously. Upon its conclusion, the cups are put down and the matzos are uncovered.

It is this that has stood by our fathers and us. For not only one has risen against us to annihilate us, but in every generation they rise against us to annihilate us. But the Holy One, Blessed is He, rescues us from their hand.

- **RAV AVIGDOR NEBENZAHL:** The Egyptians had used their vessels for idolatry and had idolatrous images engraved on them. Had the Egyptians given these vessels to the Jews as a gift, the Jews would not have been permitted to use them, since a Jew cannot own anything that was used for idolatry. Therefore Hashem, instructed the Jews to *borrow* the vessels so that they would still be considered the possession of the Egyptians. This would allow the Jews to use these vessels, since they did not really belong to them but to the Egyptians.

וְהִיא שֶׁעָמְדָה / *It is this that has stood*

Q *Why do we raise the cup of wine when we recite V'Hi She'amdah?*

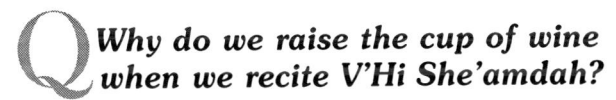

A
- **LEKET YOSHER:** We raise the cup as we thank Hashem and publicize the miracles He has performed for us, in fulfillment of the verse כּוֹס יְשׁוּעוֹת אֶשָּׂא וּבְשֵׁם ה' אֶקְרָא, *I will raise the cup of salvations and the Name of HASHEM I will invoke* (Psalms 116:13).

- **RAV MEIR LEHMANN:** We raise the cup to publicly proclaim that the Jewish people were saved from assimilation in the merit of maintaining their uniqueness. This avoidance of assimilation is symbolized by the cup of wine, which represents our adherence to the prohibition of drinking *yayin nesech* (wine that has been touched by a non-Jew).

- **KLAUSENBERGER REBBE:** We raise the cup to proclaim, and beseech Hashem, that the merit of our affliction in exile should stand us in good stead. It should release us from the prosecution of the attribute of judgment and earn us deliverance from all of our trials through the attribute of mercy

צֵא וּלְמַד מַה בִּקֵּשׁ לָבָן הָאֲרַמִּי לַעֲשׂוֹת לְיַעֲקֹב אָבִינוּ, שֶׁפַּרְעֹה לֹא גָזַר

Q What is it that we refer to as וְהִיא, "this"?

A
- **SHIBBOLEI HALEKET:** Hashem's promise to Avraham in the Covenant Between the Parts that He would redeem us.
- **ARIZAL:** The Shechinah, as Chazal teach, *Wherever they were exiled, the Shechinah was with them* (Megillah 29).
- **ABARBANEL:** The word "v'hi," it is this, is an acronym for those things that have *stood by our fathers and us*. The *vav* represents the six orders of the Mishnah; the *hei* represents the five *Chumashim* of the Torah; the *yud* represents the Ten Commandments; and the *alef* represents Hashem, Who is One. In the merit of Torah study and our service to Hashem, we survived.
- **MAHARAL:** The promise that Hashem would exact retribution from our enemies: *But also upon the nation which they shall serve will I execute judgment.*
- **VILNA GAON:** The promise that Hashem would be always with us and save us from the nations that wished to destroy us.
- **KORBAN PESACH:** Our adherence to the prohibition of *yayin nesech* (wine that has been touched by a non-Jew) — represented by the cup of wine that we raise when we recite this passage — has kept us separate from the nations of the world.
- **RAV MEIR LEHMANN:** The Torah, which elevates us and endows us with eternal life.
- **RAV REUVEN BENGIS:** The promise that Hashem would one day gather in all the exiles of the Jewish people.
- **DIVREI YOEL:** The promise of *And afterward they shall leave with great possessions.*

Q Why is the word דּוֹר, generation, repeated twice in this phrase?

A
- **RAV CHAIM BERLIN:** The attempt to annihilate the Jewish people was not identical in every generation. In some generations, our enemies sought to exterminate us or force us to

> Go and learn what Lavan the Aramean attempted to do to our father Yaakov! For Pharaoh decreed

renounce our faith. In others, they employed friendly means to persuade us to join them and abandon our heritage. But whether the method was violent or gentle, the goal was the same: to destroy us.

Q *How can we say that there are those who rise up to annihilate us in every generation? Weren't there generations in which the gentile nations treated the Jews well?*

A ☐ In every generation, the nations wish to annihilate us, even if it appears otherwise and the gentiles seem to be our friends. The Haggadah goes on to illustrate this point in the following passage: *Go and learn what Lavan the Aramean attempted to do to our father Yaakov!*

Lavan is the prototype of an enemy who appears to be friendly but is in truth dangerous and scheming. Lavan was Yaakov's father-in-law, the grandfather of his children, and by rights he should have been genuinely caring and affectionate toward Yaakov and his family. Nevertheless, Lavan sought to kill him and was eventually exposed as a mortal enemy. We thank Hashem for saving us not only from our self-proclaimed enemies, but also from our hidden enemies, like Lavan.

◆§ צֵא וּלְמַד / *Go and learn* §◆

This passage is a continuation of the previous one, which ends with the words *But the Holy One, Blessed is He, rescues us from their hand.* Hashem watches over us in every generation, as illustrated by the example of Yaakov's deliverance from Lavan's hands: *Go out and learn what Lavan the Aramean attempted to do to our father Yaakov!*

Q *What is meant by* צֵא, *go out?*

A ☐ **CHIDA:** *Go out* of the discussion of Egypt (which has been the subject until now) *and learn* about the other enemies of the Jewish people, such as Lavan.

☐ **ACHARIS L'SHALOM:** Like Lavan, many of the gentile

אֶלָּא עַל הַזְּכָרִים, וְלָבָן בִּקֵּשׁ לַעֲקוֹר אֶת הַכֹּל. שֶׁנֶּאֱמַר:

nations hide their true intentions toward the Jews. To expose their intentions, we must *go out and learn* what is truly motivating them.

☐ **MALBIM:** *Go out and learn* from the example of Lavan and apply it to another historical figure: Pharaoh.

Q: Why does Lavan's treatment of Yaakov serve as the prototype for the gentile nations' hatred toward the Jewish people?

A: ☐ **SHIBBOLEI HALEKET:** Lavan serves as an example of an evildoer who plotted to harm the Jewish people. Although Hashem prevented him from carrying out his scheme, He considered it as though Lavan had carried out his intentions and punished him accordingly.

☐ **VILNA GAON:** There have been periods in the history of the Jewish people that seemed to be idyllic, such as the period in which Yaakov lived with Lavan. During that time he married, had children, and earned a good livelihood. Yet beneath the image that Lavan presented of a caring family man lurked a conniving swindler who wanted to destroy Yaakov. Hashem teaches us that even when the gentiles present a favorable façade to us, we should not be lulled into thinking they love us.

☐ **MAHARAL:** Lavan's hatred toward Yaakov is the prototype of baseless hatred and anti-Semitism. Some nations at least justify their hatred toward us with an ostensible reason — even if that reason is laughable — just as Esav justified his hatred of Yaakov with the fact that Yaakov "stole" the blessings. But Lavan's hatred had no rhyme or reason.

☐ **SHO'EL U'MEISHIV:** Lavan serves as evidence of the intensity of the gentiles' hatred toward the Jews. Lavan was both Yaakov's uncle and his father-in-law, yet despite these strong family ties, he wanted to wipe out Yaakov and his children.

☐ Yaakov's escape from the house of Lavan served as a prototype for the redemption from Egypt in many respects, as Chazal teach, *The actions of the forefathers served as a sign for their children*:

only against the males, and Lavan attempted to uproot everything, as it is said:

- Yaakov left Lavan's house with great wealth, and the Jews left Egypt with great wealth.
- Yaakov's staff was instrumental in earning his wealth (when he increased his flock), and Moshe's staff was instrumental in the process of the Egyptian redemption.
- Lavan discovered Yaakov's departure on the third day after he had left, and the Egyptians decided to chase the Jews on the third day after their departure, when it became clear that the Jews were not returning from their purported three-day journey.
- Lavan overtook Yaakov on the seventh day after his departure, and the Egyptians overtook the Jews at the Sea of Reeds on the seventh day after the Jewish people left Egypt.

Q *Where do we find that Lavan tried to "uproot everything"?*

A
- **RASHI** (*Deuteronomy* 26:5): Lavan sought to uproot everything when he chased after Yaakov. Because he contemplated doing this — that is, eradicating Yaakov and his descendants — Hashem considered it as if he actually did it. Regarding the nations of the world, the Holy One considers a wicked thought to be the same as carrying out the action.
- **PRI CHAIM**: When he was chasing Yaakov, Lavan caught up to him and said, יֶשׁ לְאֵל יָדִי לַעֲשׂוֹת עִמָּכֶם רָע, *It is in my power to do you all harm* (*Genesis* 31:29). Lavan did not say, לַעֲשׂוֹת לָכֶם רָע, *to do harm to you*, but rather עִמָּכֶם לַעֲשׂוֹת רָע, *to do harm with you* — i.e., to do evil together with you. This implies that Lavan wished to contaminate Yaakov spiritually.
- **RAV YOSEF SHIMANOWITZ**: The Midrash teaches that Rivkah became barren because of Lavan's blessing to her. Were it not for this, Rivkah would have been the mother of the twelve tribes. Therefore "*la'akor*" can mean "to render them infertile" ("*akarah*," infertile, comes from the word "*akar*," uproot).

אֲרַמִּי אֹבֵד אָבִי, וַיֵּרֶד מִצְרַיְמָה וַיָּגָר שָׁם בִּמְתֵי מְעָט, וַיְהִי שָׁם לְגוֹי, גָּדוֹל עָצוּם וָרָב.¹

- **RAV YOSEF OF SLUTZK:** The Talmud in *Gittin* teaches that if someone sends an emissary to designate a woman as his betrothed, and the emissary dies before returning, the sender is forbidden to marry any woman in the world. Since he does not know which woman the agent designated for him, the second woman might be a close relative of the first, and it is forbidden to marry two women who are close relatives (such as sisters). Thus he may not marry anyone, because he has no way to know if he is marrying a close relative of the first woman he married.

    Lavan wished to kill Eliezer, who had been sent as an emissary to find a wife for Yitzchak and betroth Yitzchak to her. Had Lavan managed to kill Eliezer, Yitzchak would not have been allowed to marry any woman in the world. Had that happened, Yaakov could not have been born, the Jewish people could not have been created, and Lavan's wish would have been fulfilled.

- **RAV REUVEN BENGIS:** Hashem told Avraham to leave Lot, since the Shechinah could not dwell with him as long as he was connected to an impure person (see *Rashi, Genesis* 13:14). For this reason, Lavan did not want Yaakov to leave him — because he did not want the Shechinah to dwell with Yaakov. He wanted to distance Yaakov from Hashem and destroy him spiritually.

- **RAV SHLOMO ZALMAN AUERBACH:** In explaining the verse הַלְלוּ אֶת ה' כָּל גּוֹיִם, *Praise HASHEM, all you nations* (*Psalms* 117:1), the Chafetz Chaim says that the gentile nations must praise Hashem because only they know all the nefarious plots they aimed to carry out against the Jewish people — plots that were foiled by Hashem. Similarly, only Lavan knew what he intended to do to Yaakov. The Torah testifies to this when it says אֲרַמִּי אֹבֵד אָבִי, *An Aramean attempted to destroy my father* (*Deuteronomy* 26:5).

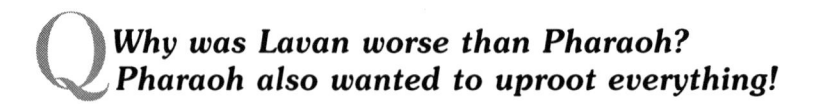

Q *Why was Lavan worse than Pharaoh? Pharaoh also wanted to uproot everything!*

> An Aramean attempted to destroy my father. Then he descended to Egypt and sojourned there, with few people; and there he became a nation — great, mighty, and numerous.[1]

1. *Deuteronomy* 26:5.

A
- **MAHARAL:** Pharaoh chased after the Jews in order to bring them back to Egypt, not in order to kill them. Lavan, on the other hand, sought to harm Yaakov.
- **VILNA GAON:** Pharaoh openly displayed his hatred toward the Jews, while Lavan pretended to be Yaakov's friend.
- **MALBIM:** Lavan wanted to destroy everyone, while Pharaoh decreed that only the baby boys be killed.
- **HAGGADAH SHELEIMAH:** Chazal teach, *One who causes another to sin is worse than one who kills another* (see Rashi, *Deuteronomy* 23:9). Pharaoh decreed the physical annihilation of the Jews, but did not force them to worship idols. Lavan, in contrast, wished to destroy Yaakov spiritually by getting him to assimilate.

❧ אֲרַמִּי אֹבֵד אָבִי / *An Aramean attempted to destroy my father*

This is the first verse of the passage in *Parashas Ki Savo* known as *Mikra Bikkurim* (*Deuteronomy* 26:5-8), which was recited when a person brought the first fruits to Jerusalem. This passage briefly summarizes our nation's early history, beginning with Yaakov's stay in Lavan's house and concluding with the Exodus.

The Haggadah quotes each of the four verses of *Mikra Bikkurim* and expounds on them in detail, phrase by phrase.

Q *Why does the Haggadah quote these four verses from Deuteronomy rather than the detailed account of the Exodus found in the Torah portions of Shemos through Beshalach?*

A
- The description in *Deuteronomy* does not include Moshes' name, and the Haggadah does not want to mention Moshes' name. (See p. 38 for why the Haggadah does not mention Moshe's name.)

[117] **HAGGADAH: THE ANSWER IS . . .**

- **ABARBANEL:** On the Seder night, we follow Chazal's instruction to *begin with disgrace and end with praise*. The Haggadah cites these verses of *Mikra Bikkurim* because they follow this structure, beginning with the "disgrace" of Yaakov's experience with Lavan and ending with praise of Hashem.

- **SIFSEI CHAIM:** There is a parallel between the Jewish people at the Seder and the person bringing *bikkurim*. When a farmer sees the fruits of his labor, he naturally feels satisfaction at his handiwork. In order to prevent him from attributing his success only to his own efforts, the Torah commands him to bring *bikkurim*, the first fruits of his produce, as an expression of gratitude to Hashem for the crops He blessed him with. Similarly, on the Seder night, we thank Hashem for taking us out of Egypt, because we are fully aware that it was not our own power that brought about the redemption.

Q Who is the "Aramean"?

- **PEIRUSH KADMON:** It refers to Lavan the Aramean, who wished to destroy Yaakov.

- **RASHBAM:** The "Aramean" is Avraham Avinu, who was from Aram and who was exiled (*oveid* can mean either "destroy" or "exiled," so the verse can be translated, *My father, the Aramean, was exiled*).

- **SEFORNO:** The verse is speaking of Yaakov, who was called *oveid* because at one point he was poor and homeless, and *oveid* can mean "poor," as in the verse תְּנוּ שֵׁכָר לְאוֹבֵד, *Give strong drink to the woebegone* (Proverbs 31:6). Therefore the verse can be translated, *My father was a poor Aramean*.

- **OHR HACHAIM:** It refers to the evil inclination, which is called a *ramai*, trickster (the Hebrew words *ramai* and *Arami* have the same letters), because it deceives people in order to destroy them. *Avi*, my father, refers to Adam HaRishon, who was duped to sin by the evil inclination.

- **SHELAH:** It is Bilam, who descended to Egypt in order to advise Pharaoh how to destroy the Jewish people.

Q Why is the word אוֹבֵד, which literally means "destroys," written in the present tense rather than in the past tense?

A ☐ **MAHARAL:** The word *oveid* here is a noun, not a verb. The Haggadah refers to Yaakov as an *oveid* because Lavan wished to destroy him.

☐ **DIVREI CHAIM:** The gentile nations' hatred toward the Jewish people persists in every generation, including our own. The Haggadah is stressing here that Lavan's attempt to destroy us was not an isolated historical incident. It is an ongoing campaign, for the Lavans of each generation are constantly trying to break the chain of our heritage.

☐ **HASHIR V'HASHEVACH:** Lavan's hatred toward Yaakov was continuous and unremitting. Even when Lavan acted friendly toward Yaakov and begged him to stay with him, he was out to trick him and ultimately cheated him out of his wages.

Q *Why does the Haggadah record only Yaakov's struggle with Lavan but not his flight from Esav?*

A ☐ **MAHARAL:** The Haggadah records only those enemies who pursued us for no reason. Esav had a purported reason for pursuing Yaakov: he was angry that Yaakov had "stolen" his blessings.

☐ **BEIS HALEVI:** The Haggadah records only those exiles from which we have been redeemed, but we have not yet been redeemed from the exile of Esav (also known as Edom). That will happen only when Mashiach comes.

Q *What does Lavan's attempt to destroy Yaakov have to do with Yaakov's descent to Egypt many years later?*

A ☐ **CHUKAS HAPESACH HAGGADAH:** Lavan indirectly caused Yaakov and his family to descend to Egypt by tricking Yaakov into marrying Lavan's eldest daughter, Leah, first. The sons Yaakov had with Leah harbored jealousy toward Rachel's son Yosef, who acted like a leader even though he was not the firstborn. This jealousy spurred them into selling Yosef into slavery, which resulted in the descent of Yaakov and his family to Egypt. Had Lavan allowed Yaakov to marry Rachel first, instead of tricking him into marrying Leah first, Yosef would rightfully have been the firstborn, and there would have been no jealousy, no sale, and no descent to Egypt.

[119] **HAGGADAH: THE ANSWER IS . . .**

וַיֵּרֶד מִצְרַיְמָה: אָנוּס עַל פִּי הַדִּבּוּר.
וַיָּגָר שָׁם. מְלַמֵּד שֶׁלֹּא יָרַד יַעֲקֹב אָבִינוּ לְהִשְׁתַּקֵּעַ בְּמִצְרַיִם, אֶלָּא לָגוּר שָׁם. שֶׁנֶּאֱמַר, וַיֹּאמְרוּ אֶל פַּרְעֹה, לָגוּר בָּאָרֶץ בָּאנוּ, כִּי אֵין מִרְעֶה לַצֹּאן אֲשֶׁר לַעֲבָדֶיךָ, כִּי כָבֵד הָרָעָב בְּאֶרֶץ כְּנָעַן, וְעַתָּה יֵשְׁבוּ נָא עֲבָדֶיךָ בְּאֶרֶץ גֹּשֶׁן.[1]

- **TZITZ ELIEZER:** Rabbi Yonasan ben Uziel teaches that Lavan and Bilam were one and the same person. Lavan did not content himself with pursuing Yaakov. He continued to harbor hatred toward him and his descendants even much later. He went down to Egypt in the guise of Bilam to continue his mission of destroying Yaakov. (Bilam became one of Pharaoh's most respected advisers and encouraged Pharaoh to destroy the Jews.)

Q *Which decree (literally, the word דִּיבּוּר means "statement") compelled Yaakov to descend to Egypt?*

A
- **RASHI; PEIRUSH KADMON; RASHBAM:** This refers to Hashem's statement to Yaakov before he descended to Egypt: ...אַל תִּירָא מֵרְדָה מִצְרַיְמָה, *Have no fear of descending to Egypt...* (Genesis 46:3).
- **RA'AVAN; RASHBATZ; MACHZOR VITRI:** It was Hashem's statement to Avraham in the Covenant Between the Parts: ...גֵּר יִהְיֶה זַרְעֲךָ בְּאֶרֶץ לֹא לָהֶם, *Your offspring will be aliens in a land not their own...* (Genesis 15:13).
- **MAGGID OF PLOTZK:** This statement was Yosef's derogatory words about his brothers, which resulted in his being sold and the family's subsequent descent to Egypt.
- **SHE'EIRIS MENACHEM:** It was Avraham's question בַּמָּה אֵדַע כִּי אִירָשֶׁנָּה, *Whereby shall I know that I am to inherit it?* (Genesis 15:8), which resulted in his descendants being exiled to Egypt (see *Nedarim* 32).

Q *Why do we say that Yaakov was "compelled" to descend to Egypt? He descended of his own volition, in order to see Yosef.*

Then he descended to Egypt — compelled by Divine decree.

He sojourned there — this teaches that our father Yaakov did not descend to Egypt to settle, but only to sojourn temporarily, as it says: They (the sons of Yaakov) said to Pharaoh: "We have come to sojourn in this land because there is no pasture for the flocks of your servants, because the famine is severe in the Land of Canaan. And now, please let your servants dwell in the land of Goshen."[1]

---

1. *Genesis* 47:4.

A
- **PEIRUSH KADMON:** Chazal teach that in truth Yaakov should have descended to Egypt in iron chains (*Shabbos* 89b). The Haggadah is pointing out that it was a kindness that he was compelled to go down to Egypt as a result of the *Divine decree* and not by physical force.
- **TOLDOS ADAM:** Although Yaakov descended to Egypt of his own will, it was the famine in Eretz Yisrael that made this descent necessary and compelled him to go.
- **NETZIV:** Yaakov was afraid to go to Egypt, lest his descendants assimilate. The actual descent was of his own volition, but it involved an element of coercion, because he feared assimilation and did not want to go.

Q **Why did Yaakov's sons attribute their stay in Egypt to the lack of pasture for their sheep, rather than cite their own need for food during the famine?**

A
- **RABBEINU BACHYA:** Yaakov's sons wanted to apprise Pharaoh of the severity of the famine in Canaan, which had reached the point where people were eating grass, leaving no pasture for the animals.
- **GA'AL YISRAEL HAGGADAH:** Yaakov's sons followed the halachah that it is forbidden to eat anything before feeding one's animals. They therefore attributed the reason for their descent to Egypt to the animals rather than to themselves.

בִּמְתֵי מְעָט. כְּמָה שֶׁנֶּאֱמַר, בְּשִׁבְעִים נֶפֶשׁ יָרְדוּ אֲבֹתֶיךָ מִצְרָיְמָה, וְעַתָּה שָׂמְךָ יהוה אֱלֹהֶיךָ כְּכוֹכְבֵי הַשָּׁמַיִם לָרֹב.[1]
וַיְהִי שָׁם לְגוֹי. מְלַמֵּד שֶׁהָיוּ יִשְׂרָאֵל מְצֻיָּנִים שָׁם.

- **HASHIR V'HASHEVACH:** Were it not for the need for pasture for the animals, Yaakov's family could have bought food in Egypt, gone home, and then returned to Egypt for food when necessary. They stayed in Egypt only because the animals needed land for grazing.

- People have the capacity to act cruelly to other human beings while displaying compassion to animals (as in the Holocaust, when the Nazis brutally murdered millions of people while at the same time rescuing and nurturing animals). Yaakov's sons mentioned the animals to Pharaoh in order to present a rationale that he would find more convincing.

Q *What did Yaakov's family accomplish by remaining in Egypt, if the famine had struck Egypt as well?*

A - **RAMBAN:** In other famine-afflicted lands, people were reduced to eating grass, and there was no pasture left for the animals. In Egypt, however, where food had been stored and was available for purchase, grazing land still remained for animals to eat.

- **RITVA:** The Nile River in Egypt sustained large areas of land for pasture.

Q *Why does the verse say נֶפֶשׁ, soul, in the singular rather than the plural נְפָשׁוֹת, souls?*

A - **RASHI** (*Genesis* 46:26): With regard to Esav's family — which numbered only six — the Torah uses the plural term "*nefashos*," since they worshiped numerous deities. Yaakov's family, however, is referred to in the singular, "*nefesh*," since they all worshiped one God.

- **KLI YAKAR:** They are referred to in the singular because they were unified and at peace with each other.

With few people — as it is written: With seventy persons, your forefathers descended to Egypt, and now HASHEM, your God, has made you as numerous as the stars of heaven.[1]

There he became a nation — this teaches that the Israelites were distinctive there.

---
1. *Deuteronomy* 10:22.

- ☐ **OHR HACHAIM:** The Torah is emphasizing that they were all uniformly righteous.
- ☐ The word "*nefesh*" has the numerical value of 430, which alludes to the 430-year period that elapsed from the Covenant Between the Parts until the redemption.

Q *In what way are the Jewish people similar to stars?*

A
- ☐ **KLI YAKAR:** Just as the stars become visible only after dark, a person's reputation is cemented only after his death. Until a person's death, it is impossible to know whether his righteousness will endure.
- ☐ **BAAL SHEM TOV:** Every star looks tiny; only when one draws closer to the stars can one perceive how massive they are. Similarly, even if a Jew appears to be simple, when one gets to know him and discovers his strengths, one will realize his greatness.
- ☐ **DIVREI SHAUL:** Despite their size and power, stars appear to be tiny due to their distance from Earth. Similarly, Hashem promised Avraham that He would consider the Jewish people great even though the nations of the world consider them insignificant.
- ☐ **SFAS EMES:** Just as the function of the stars is to illuminate the darkness of night, so too the function of the Jewish people is to illuminate the darkness of this world.

Q *What is the meaning of this description of* מְצֻיָּנִים, *distinctive?*

A
- ☐ **RI BEN YAKAR:** The Jews were distinctive in their height and countenance.

גָּדוֹל עָצוּם. כְּמָה שֶׁנֶּאֱמַר, וּבְנֵי יִשְׂרָאֵל פָּרוּ וַיִּשְׁרְצוּ וַיִּרְבּוּ וַיַּעַצְמוּ בִּמְאֹד מְאֹד, וַתִּמָּלֵא הָאָרֶץ אֹתָם.[1]

- ☐ **RASHI:** They segregated themselves in one city and did not spread out among the Egyptians.
- ☐ **RASHBAM:** They wore distinctive clothing, so as not to mix with the Egyptians.
- ☐ **RA'AVAN:** They were outstanding people.
- ☐ **MACHZOR VITRI:** They were distinctive in their fertility — they bore six babies at a time.

Q *What is the unusual word וַיִּשְׁרְצוּ, increased greatly, meant to convey?*

A
- ☐ **RASHI:** The word *vayishretzu*, increased greatly, is related to the word *sheretz*, vermin. Just as vermin give birth to many offspring at once, so too did the Jewish mothers have six babies at a time.
- ☐ **SEFORNO:** After the death of Yosef and his brothers, the Jews adopted lowly practices and descended to the level of *sheratzim*, insects.
- ☐ **KLI YAKAR:** After Yosef died and the generation who had descended to Egypt was gone, the Jews lost their special protection. The Egyptians began to view them as lowly, like *sheratzim*, insects.
- ☐ **MALBIM:** The word implies unnatural fertility, like that of insects, which breed rapidly.

Q *What is the difference between גָּדוֹל, great, and עָצוּם, mighty?*

A
- ☐ **ABARBANEL:** The term גָּדוֹל, great, refers to the Jews' outward appearance, while עָצוּם, mighty, refers to their strength. The Torah is telling us that the Jewish children were miraculously strong, even though they were born as multiples, which are generally weaker than single births.
- ☐ **MALBIM:** The term גָּדוֹל, great, refers to their number, while עָצוּם, mighty, refers to their strength.

הגדה של פסח

Great, mighty — as it says: *And the Children of Israel were fruitful, increased greatly, multiplied, and became very, very mighty; and the land was filled with them.*[1]

1. *Exodus* 1:7.

☐ The words גָּדוֹל עָצוּם וָרָב, *great, mighty, and numerous*, allude to the three Patriarchs:

גָּדוֹל, *great*, is a reference to Avraham, about whom the Torah says, וְאֶעֶשְׂךָ לְגוֹי גָּדוֹל, *And I will make of you a **great** nation* (*Genesis* 12:2).

עָצוּם, *mighty*, is a reference to Yitzchak, to whom it was said, לֵךְ מֵעִמָּנוּ כִּי עָצַמְתָּ מִמֶּנּוּ מְאֹד, *Go away from us for you have become much **mightier** than we!* (*Genesis* 26:16).

וָרָב, *numerous*, is a reference to Yaakov, who was blessed with the words וְיַפְרְךָ וְיַרְבֶּךָ, *May [HASHEM] make you fruitful and make you **numerous*** (*Genesis* 28:3).

Q *Why does this verse use so many terms — "fruitful, increased greatly, multiplied, and became very, very mighty" — to say the same thing?*

A ☐ **RASHI:** This teaches that each Jewish woman gave birth to six babies at a time (as indicated by the six words פָּרוּ וַיִּשְׁרְצוּ וַיִּרְבּוּ וַיַּעַצְמוּ בִּמְאֹד מְאֹד — *Mizrachi*).

☐ **BARUCH SHE'AMAR:** Each term tells us something new. The word פָּרוּ, *were fruitful*, indicates that there were no barren men or women among the Jews. The word וַיִּשְׁרְצוּ, *increased greatly*, implies that they gave birth to sextuplets. The word וַיִּרְבּוּ, *multiplied*, tells us that none of their babies died. The

---

They increased greatly...
The verse says וְכַאֲשֶׁר יְעַנּוּ אֹתוֹ כֵּן יִרְבֶּה וְכֵן יִפְרֹץ, *But as much as they would afflict it, so it would increase* (*Exodus* 1:12). The verse does not say וְכַאֲשֶׁר יְעַנּוּ אֹתוֹ כֵּן רָבָה וְכֵן פָּרַץ, *But as much as they would afflict it, so it increased* (in the past tense).

The verse is phrased in the future tense because the Torah is not only describing the Egyptian exile; it is promising that in every generation, the Jewish people need not fear their enemies. The more their enemies plot against them and persecute them, the more the Jewish people will thrive.

וָרָב. כְּמָה שֶׁנֶּאֱמַר, רְבָבָה כְּצֶמַח הַשָּׂדֶה נְתַתִּיךְ, וַתִּרְבִּי וַתִּגְדְּלִי וַתָּבֹאִי בַּעֲדִי עֲדָיִים, שָׁדַיִם נָכֹנוּ וּשְׂעָרֵךְ צִמֵּחַ, וְאַתְּ עֵרֹם וְעֶרְיָה; וָאֶעֱבֹר עָלַיִךְ וָאֶרְאֵךְ מִתְבּוֹסֶסֶת בְּדָמָיִךְ, וָאֹמַר לָךְ, בְּדָמַיִךְ חֲיִי, וָאֹמַר לָךְ, בְּדָמַיִךְ חֲיִי.[1]

וַיָּרֵעוּ אֹתָנוּ הַמִּצְרִים, וַיְעַנּוּנוּ, וַיִּתְּנוּ עָלֵינוּ עֲבֹדָה קָשָׁה.[2]

---

word וַיַּעַצְמוּ, *became mighty*, conveys that the Jewish children were strong even though they were born in multiples.

Q *In what way were the Jewish people similar to the plants of the field?*

A ☐ **TALMUD** (*Sotah* 11): The women gave birth in the fields, and the Jewish babies were swallowed up by the ground after birth to prevent them from being snatched by the Egyptian taskmasters. After these taskmasters left, the babies would sprout from the ground like grass.

☐ **RITVA**: They grew like the plants of the field, painlessly and without effort.

☐ **MA'ASEI HASHEM**: The procreation and growth of the Jewish people in Egypt occurred primarily in the fields.

☐ **YAAVETZ**: Just as a plant grows better the more it is cut and pruned, so too, the more the Jewish people were trampled and enslaved, the more they grew and flourished.

☐ **MA'ASEH NISSIM**: Plants of the field require cultivation, as opposed to plants that grow in the wild. The Jewish people are worthy of dwelling with the Shechinah and achieving holiness when their growth is carefully cultivated, like plants of the field.

Q *The repetition of the phrase בְּדָמַיִךְ חֲיִי alludes to the two mitzvos involving blood that the Jews performed prior to leaving Egypt: korban Pesach and circumcision. What is the significance of these two mitzvos?*

הגדה של פסח [126]

Numerous — as it says: I made you as numerous as the plants of the field; you grew and developed, and became charming, beautiful of figure; your hair grown long; but you were naked and bare. And I passed over you and saw you downtrodden in your blood and I said to you: "Through your blood shall you live!" And I said to you: "Through your blood shall you live!"[1]

The Egyptians did evil to us and afflicted us; and imposed hard labor upon us.[2]

---

1. *Ezekiel* 16:7,6. 2. *Deuteronomy* 26:6.

A
- □ **RAV CHAIM SOFER:** The blood of the *korban Pesach* indicates redemption and freedom, while the blood of circumcision symbolizes self-sacrifice in the performance of God's commandments.
- □ **RAV SHLOMO ZALMAN AUERBACH:** The Jews required miraculous intervention to leave Egypt. In order to merit that intervention, they had to demonstrate *mesirus nefesh*, self-sacrifice for God. Both of these mitzvos required *mesirus nefesh*. The mitzvah of circumcision involved physical affliction, while the mitzvah of *korban Pesach* involved personal risk, since the Jews were sacrificing the Egyptian deity.

פּ וַיָּרֵעוּ אֹתָנוּ הַמִּצְרִים / *The Egyptians did evil to us*

Q *To which specific evil are we referring here?*

A
- □ **RITVA:** At the beginning, the Egyptians did evil *to* the Jewish people by enacting harsh decrees against them. Later, they tortured the Jews physically.
- □ **RASHBATZ:** They considered *us* evil. This is alluded to by the use of the word אֹתָנוּ as opposed to לָנוּ: "they made *us* evil."
- □ **ABARBANEL:** They considered the Jews evil people, accusing them of being spies and branding them as ingrates. Thus, "they made *us* evil."
- □ **ALSHICH:** The Egyptians "made us evil" by preventing the Jews from praying to Hashem.

וַיָּרֵעוּ אֹתָנוּ הַמִּצְרִים. כְּמָה שֶׁנֶּאֱמַר, הָבָה נִתְחַכְּמָה לוֹ, פֶּן יִרְבֶּה, וְהָיָה כִּי תִקְרֶאנָה מִלְחָמָה, וְנוֹסַף גַּם הוּא עַל שֹׂנְאֵינוּ, וְנִלְחַם בָּנוּ, וְעָלָה מִן הָאָרֶץ.[1] וַיְעַנּוּנוּ. כְּמָה שֶׁנֶּאֱמַר, וַיָּשִׂימוּ עָלָיו שָׂרֵי מִסִּים, לְמַעַן עַנֹּתוֹ בְּסִבְלֹתָם, וַיִּבֶן עָרֵי מִסְכְּנוֹת לְפַרְעֹה, אֶת פִּתֹם וְאֶת רַעַמְסֵס.[2]

- YAAVETZ: They "made us evil" by forcing the Jews to serve them and not allowing them to serve Hashem.

- RAV MORDECHAI GIFTER: The Egyptian leaders were concerned that their decrees would not meet with the approval of the Egyptian populace. They therefore embarked on a smear campaign against the Jews to turn the Egyptians against us. After *making us evil*, they were able to torture us, as the verse continues, *And they afflicted us*. This has been the pattern of anti-Semitism throughout history. First Jew-haters tell the masses how evil the Jews are, and then the general population is incited to kill the Jews.

- The words וַיָּרֵעוּ אֹתָנוּ can be interpreted to mean *They befriended us*, from the root word "rei'a," friend. Initially the Egyptians treated the Jews cordially, giving them reasonable employment terms, in order to trick them into working. Later, the Egyptians imposed slave labor on the Jews and tortured them.

Q *"Let us deal with them wisely."* To whom is this referring?

A
- RASHI: This refers to the Jewish people.

- TARGUM YONASAN BEN UZIEL: The word "*lo*" in this phrase is singular; the verse can be translated, *Let us deal with Him wisely*. This refers to Hashem, the One Who saves the Jewish people (see *Sotah* 11).

Q Why did Pharaoh think that he had to outsmart the Jewish people rather than persecute them openly?

The Egyptians did evil to us — as it says: Let us deal with them wisely lest they multiply and, if we happen to be at war, they may join our enemies and fight against us and then leave the country.[1]

And they afflicted us — as it says: They set taskmasters over them in order to oppress them with their burdens; and they built Pithom and Raamses as treasure cities for Pharaoh.[2]

---

1. *Exodus* 1:10. 2. Ibid. 1:11.

A
- □ **MIDRASH RABBAH:** Pharaoh understood that attacking the Jews openly would be too great a betrayal after the previous king of Egypt had invited Yaakov and his sons to live in Egypt. He therefore devised a scheme for persecuting them so that at first they would not realize what was happening.
- □ **RAMBAN:** Pharaoh was concerned that his own people would not take kindly to a campaign of annihilation against the Jews. He therefore developed a strategy for gradually intensifying the persecution so that Egyptians would not have reason to protest.
- □ **RABBEINU BACHYA:** Originally, Pharaoh did not intend to carry out mass extermination. His goal was to weaken the Jews through hard labor and prevent them from procreating. Later, when he saw that their number was increasing despite his efforts, he embarked on a campaign of annihilation.

Q **We are told that Pharaoh sent "sarei misim" which literally means "tax masters" over the Jews. Why did he impose taxes on the Jews in addition to enslaving them with hard labor?**

A
- □ **RAV MEIR LEHMANN:** The Egyptians claimed that the Jews were getting rich at their expense. They imposed taxes on them in order to strip the Jews of their wealth and reclaim what they thought was rightfully theirs.
- □ **HASHIR V'HASHEVACH:** This was one of the tactics of the enslavement. Pharaoh imposed taxes on the Jews, in addition to the hard labor, simply to add to the Jews' hardships.

וַיִּתְּנוּ עָלֵינוּ עֲבֹדָה קָשָׁה. וַיַּעַבְדוּ,וַיֹּאמַר שֶׁנֶּאֱמַר כְּמָה קָשָׁה. עֲבֹדָה עָלֵינוּ וַיִּתְּנוּ
מִצְרַיִם אֶת בְּנֵי יִשְׂרָאֵל בְּפָרֶךְ.[1]
וַנִּצְעַק אֶל יהוה אֱלֹהֵי אֲבֹתֵינוּ, וַיִּשְׁמַע יהוה
אֶת קֹלֵנוּ, וַיַּרְא אֶת עָנְיֵנוּ, וְאֶת עֲמָלֵנוּ,
וְאֶת לַחֲצֵנוּ.[2]

- □ **RAV MOSHE STERNBUCH:** Pharaoh imposed taxes on the Jews as a pretext to oppress them. The taxes were the first step in the enslavement to turn them into a downtrodden people.
- □ The Egyptians hated the Jews so much that they made the tax collectors into taskmasters to enslave the Jews. As a result, they lost tax revenue since the tax collectors were no longer collecting taxes, but the Egyptians preferred to have the Jews tortured.

Q *What is the difference between* וַיְעַנּוּנוּ, *and they afflicted us, and* וַיִּתְּנוּ עָלֵינוּ עֲבֹדָה קָשָׁה, *imposed hard labor upon us?*

A □ **ABARBANEL:** *They afflicted us* refers to the work the Jews performed for Pharaoh with bricks and mortar. *They imposed hard labor upon us* refers to fact that every Egyptian was able to treat a Jew like his own personal slave.
- □ **MALBIM:** *They afflicted us* implies that they tortured the Jews for no purpose, in addition to the *hard labor* they imposed on them.
- □ **HASHIR V'HASHEVACH:** *They afflicted us* implies that they

---

I shall take you out from under the burdens of Egypt (Exodus 6:6)
The first step in the redemption was making the exile intolerable to the Jews, since the redemption could not come as long as they were able to cope with the travails of exile. The verse וְהוֹצֵאתִי אֶתְכֶם מִתַּחַת סִבְלֹת מִצְרָיִם, *I shall take you out from under the burdens of Egypt*, can be interpreted to mean, *I will take you out of your ability to tolerate the Egyptians, and I will make the exile unbearable to you* (since the word *"sovel"* means both "burden" and "tolerate").
In this vein, Rav Shimshon of Shpitovka, a disciple of the Mezritcher Maggid, used to say, "It is easier to take the Jews out of the exile than to take the exile out of the Jews."

They imposed hard labor upon us — as it says: The Egyptians subjugated the Children of Israel with hard labor.¹

We cried out to HASHEM, the God of our fathers; and HASHEM heard our cry and saw our affliction, our burden, and our oppression.²

---

1. *Exodus* 1:13. 1. *Deuteronomy* 26:7.

---

tortured us for no purpose, while *They imposed hard labor upon us* means that they assigned men the work of women and women the work of men.

Q *What does the unusual word פָּרֶךְ, hard labor, signify?*

A
- **YALKUT SHIMONI:** The word "*parech*" is a compound of "*peh rach*," a soft mouth. This indicates that at first the Egyptians used gentle words of persuasion to convince the Jews to work: at the beginning, they promised to pay the Jews for each brick they laid, so the Jews hurried to build as many bricks as they could each day. Then the Egyptians forced them to complete the same quota of bricks each day without pay.
- **MIDRASH RABBAH:** The Egyptians assigned men the work of women and women the work of men.
- **RASHI:** "*Parech*" implies hard labor that destroys the body.
- **RASHBATZ:** The word "*parech*" is related to the word "*paroches*," curtain; just as a curtain separates two rooms, the Egyptians separated the Jews from their spouses.
- **VILNA GAON:** The work the Egyptians imposed described as "*parech*" was not necessarily physically grueling, but it is difficult to perform any labor to which one is unaccustomed.
- **NETZIV:** "*Parech*" is pointless labor, work that a master imposes purely to torture his servant.

◈§ וַנִּצְעַק אֶל ה׳ / **We cried out to HASHEM**

Q *What was the nature of the cry referred to in this verse?*

[131] **HAGGADAH: THE ANSWER IS . . .**

וַנִּצְעַק אֶל יהוה אֱלֹהֵי אֲבֹתֵינוּ. כְּמָה שֶׁנֶּאֱמַר, וַיְהִי בַיָּמִים הָרַבִּים הָהֵם, וַיָּמָת מֶלֶךְ מִצְרַיִם, וַיֵּאָנְחוּ בְנֵי יִשְׂרָאֵל מִן הָעֲבֹדָה, וַיִּזְעָקוּ, וַתַּעַל שַׁוְעָתָם אֶל הָאֱלֹהִים מִן הָעֲבֹדָה.[1]

A
- ☐ **ABARBANEL:** It was a cry of repentance and prayer to Hashem to redeem us.
- ☐ **SEFORNO:** The cry was a shriek of heartache over the slave labor.
- ☐ **YITAV PANIM:** The *Zohar* teaches that the Jews in Egypt lacked wisdom. They were like a young child who cannot speak and cries out wordlessly when he wants something.

Q *Why did the Jews groan and cry only after Pharaoh's death?*

A
- ☐ **RASHI:** While Pharaoh was alive, he did not force the Jews to worship idols because of his affection for Yosef. After he died, the Egyptians began to force the Jews to worship idols. That was why the Jews groaned and cried only after Pharaoh's death.
- ☐ **BA'ALEI HATOSAFOS:** When Pharaoh was alive, the Jews waited for him to die so his decrees would be rescinded. Once he died and they saw that the decrees remained in effect, they groaned and cried.
- ☐ **RAMBAN:** After Pharaoh died, the Jews were afraid that the new king would be even worse.
- ☐ **BARTENURA:** One opinion in Chazal says that Pharaoh did not actually die. He was struck with *tzara'as*, and a person who has *tzara'as* is considered dead. To alleviate his symptoms, Pharaoh washed himself in the blood of the Jewish babies that he slaughtered. This is why the Jewish people groaned and cried.
- ☐ **MA'ASEI HASHEM:** While Pharaoh was alive, the Jews were kept busy building him treasure houses. When he died, they had a slight respite. Now that they took a break from their hard labor and were able to focus on their miserable plight, they groaned and cried.

הגדה של פסח [132]

We cried out to HASHEM, the God of our fathers
— as it says: It happened in the course of those many days that the king of Egypt died; and the Children of Israel groaned because of the servitude and cried; their cry because of the servitude rose up to God.[1]

---

1. *Exodus* 2:23.

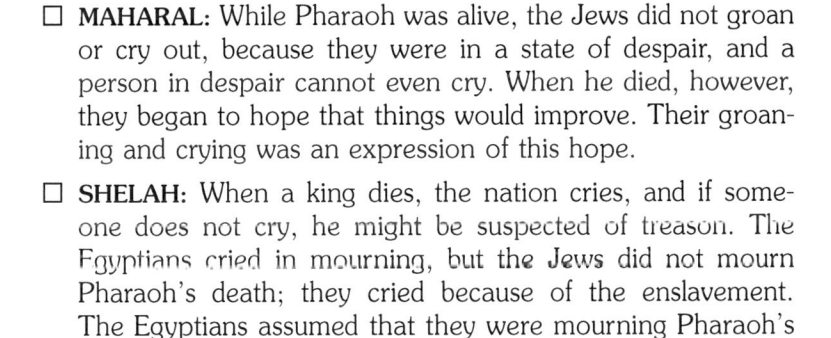

- ☐ **MAHARAL:** While Pharaoh was alive, the Jews did not groan or cry out, because they were in a state of despair, and a person in despair cannot even cry. When he died, however, they began to hope that things would improve. Their groaning and crying was an expression of this hope.

- ☐ **SHELAH:** When a king dies, the nation cries, and if someone does not cry, he might be suspected of treason. The Egyptians cried in mourning, but the Jews did not mourn Pharaoh's death; they cried because of the enslavement. The Egyptians assumed that they were mourning Pharaoh's death, but Hashem knew the truth.

- ☐ **VILNA GAON:** As long as Pharaoh was alive, the Jews were slaves only to him, but when he died, they were enslaved by all of the Egyptians.

A leading merchant in Pressburg once came to the Chasam Sofer seeking his blessing and encouragement after his business took a downturn.

"I heard that your brother is poverty stricken and has a large family to care for," the Chasam Sofer replied, "but you don't help him at all."

The merchant was taken aback at the rav's words and tried to excuse his behavior. "I just explained to the rav that my business has been floundering recently. How can I support anyone else?"

The Chasam Sofer responded by quoting a verse in *Parashas Va'eira*:
וְגַם אֲנִי שָׁמַעְתִּי אֶת נַאֲקַת בְּנֵי יִשְׂרָאֵל אֲשֶׁר מִצְרַיִם מַעֲבִדִים אֹתָם וָאֶזְכֹּר אֶת בְּרִיתִי,
Moreover, I have heard the groan of the Children of Israel whom Egypt enslaves and I have remembered My covenant (Exodus 6:5).

"What is the function of the seemingly superfluous words *v'gam* and *es* in this verse?" the Chasam Sofer asked. "The answer is that when the Jews were crying out because of the burden of the Egyptian enslavement, each one heard the groans of the other and felt his pain. In reward for their empathy and caring, Hashem also heard their cries and redeemed them from their plight."

וַיִּשְׁמַע יהוה אֶת קֹלֵנוּ. כְּמָה שֶׁנֶּאֱמַר, וַיִּשְׁמַע אֱלֹהִים אֶת נַאֲקָתָם, וַיִּזְכֹּר אֱלֹהִים אֶת בְּרִיתוֹ אֶת אַבְרָהָם, אֶת יִצְחָק, וְאֶת יַעֲקֹב.[1]
וַיַּרְא אֶת עָנְיֵנוּ. זוֹ פְּרִישׁוּת דֶּרֶךְ אֶרֶץ, כְּמָה שֶׁנֶּאֱמַר וַיַּרְא אֱלֹהִים אֶת בְּנֵי יִשְׂרָאֵל, וַיֵּדַע אֱלֹהִים.[2]
וְאֶת עֲמָלֵנוּ. אֵלוּ הַבָּנִים, כְּמָה שֶׁנֶּאֱמַר, כָּל הַבֵּן הַיִּלּוֹד הַיְאֹרָה תַּשְׁלִיכֻהוּ, וְכָל הַבַּת תְּחַיּוּן.[3]

- ☐ **DUBNO MAGGID:** Pharaoh forbade the Jews from emitting a groan or cry. When he died, they were finally able to cry out.
- ☐ **TZUF AMARIM:** According to *Targum Yonasan ben Uziel*, the Egyptian necromancers advised Pharaoh to slaughter only the firstborn Jewish children, in order to prevent them from performing the service of the Mishkan later on. The Jews cried because they did not know who would perform this service if the firstborn were killed.
- ☐ It is customary that prisoners are freed when a king dies. The Jews hoped that they would be freed when Pharaoh died, and when that did not happen, they groaned and cried.

Q *How do the words "And He saw our affliction" indicate a disruption of family life?*

A ☐ **RAV YEHOSHUA LEIB DISKIN:** Hashem calculated the number of children that should have been born had the Egyptians not prevented the Jews from maintaining normal family life. This is something only Hashem could have known.
- ☐ **RAV MEIR LEHMANN:** It is obvious that Hashem could see that the Jews were being tortured, because that was clearly evident to everyone. If the verse states that Hashem *saw our affliction*, it must be referring to an affliction that only He could see; namely, *the disruption of family life*.

Q *Why is it necessary to say that God saw and God knew? Is this not redundant? It would be enough to say either God saw or God knew.*

HASHEM heard our cry — as it says: God heard their groaning, and God recalled His covenant with Avraham, with Yitzchak, and with Yaakov.[1]

And He saw our affliction — that is the disruption of family life, as it says: God saw the Children of Israel and God knew.[2]

Our burden — refers to the children, as it says: Every son that is born you shall cast into the river, but every daughter you shall let live.[3]

---

1. *Exodus* 2:24. 2. ibid. 2:25. 3. Ibid. 1:22.

A
- **MIDRASH RABBAH:** Each phrase in the verse implies something else. Hashem *saw* that the Jews did not possess the merit of good deeds that would earn them redemption, yet He *knew* that He had to redeem them.
- **RABBEINU BACHYA:** Hashem *saw* the way the Egyptians tortured the Jews openly, and He *knew* of the tortures the Egyptians inflicted on them surreptitiously.
- **MALBIM:** Hashem *saw* the outer, physical condition of the Jews, and He *knew* of their inner, spiritual condition.
- **BEIS HALEVI:** Hashem *saw* the actions of the Jews during the enslavement, yet He judged them favorably, *knowing* that their actions were a consequence of their enslavement and not a function of their own will.

Q *How do the words "our burden" indicate the children?*

A
- **RAV SHLOMO ZALMAN AUERBACH:** The word *amal*, burden, refers to toil that a person willingly imposes on himself for his own benefit. The Jews' labor in Egypt was not performed willingly, and therefore the word "*amal*" cannot be a reference to the slave labor. It must be referring to the labor involved in bearing and raising children, which a person undertakes willingly.

Q *Why was it necessary to stipulate that the girls be allowed to live, if the decree already stated that only the boys be cast into the river?*

וְאֶת לַחֲצֵנוּ. זוֹ הַדְּחַק, כְּמָה שֶׁנֶּאֱמַר, וְגַם רָאִיתִי אֶת הַלַּחַץ אֲשֶׁר מִצְרַיִם לֹחֲצִים אֹתָם.[1]

וַיּוֹצִאֵנוּ יהוה מִמִּצְרַיִם בְּיָד חֲזָקָה, וּבִזְרֹעַ נְטוּיָה, וּבְמֹרָא גָּדֹל, וּבְאֹתוֹת וּבְמֹפְתִים.[2]

A ☐ **RITVA:** The extent of Pharaoh's evil is reflected not only in the decree to murder the baby boys, but also in the statement that the girls be allowed to live. His intention was to take the Jewish girls and defile them, in keeping with the Egyptian penchant for promiscuity.

☐ **VILNA GAON:** Allowing the girls to live was part of Pharaoh's plan for destroying the Jewish people. He realized that some mothers would manage to conceal their baby boys and prevent them from being killed. This would lead to a situation where there would be many more Jewish girls than boys, resulting in each man having several wives. In consequence, there would be a great deal of fighting and disharmony. This was Pharaoh's intention — to destroy the peace in Jewish homes — and he therefore specified that the girls be allowed to live.

☐ **HASHIR V'HASHEVACH:** Pharaoh and his people envied the Jewish women's fertility and ease in childbearing. They spared the Jewish girls so they would marry Egyptian men and help propagate the Egyptian people.

☐ **RAV MORDECHAI GIFTER:** Pharaoh wanted the midwives to keep the girls alive, because he saw that the Jewish babies

---

Our burden—this refers to the children
The Yid HaKadosh of Peshischa said, "It is natural that people are so busy with their day-to-day responsibilities and livelihood that they have no time for Torah study and prayer. They say, 'I'm working so that I'll be able to raise my son to learn Torah and do mitzvos.'

"But when the son grows older, he too has no time for Torah and prayer, because he has to raise his own son to learn Torah. I wish I could finally see that son at the end of the generations for whom all of his ancestors labored!"

הגדה של פסח

Our oppression — refers to the pressure expressed in the words: I have also seen how the Egyptians are oppressing them.[1]

Hashem took us out of Egypt with a mighty hand and with an outstretched arm, with great awe, with signs and with wonders.[2]

---

1. *Exodus* 3:9. 2. *Deuteronomy* 26:8.

---

were strong and robust and did not die in childhood. His plan was that the Jewish girls would marry Egyptians and bear children who were similarly strong and robust.

Q What is the pressure referred to in this passage?

A
- ☐ **RABBEINU BACHYA:** The pressure was the crowding of the Jews in Goshen.
- ☐ **KOL BO:** "The pressure" refers to the Egyptian taskmasters prodding the Jews to fill their daily quota of labor.
- ☐ **PIDYON SHEVUYIM:** The Egyptians constantly pressured the Jews to work so that they would not be able to pray.
- ☐ **RAV MEIR LEHMANN:** The pressure was the emotional distress that the Egyptians caused with their decrees.

וַיּוֹצִיאֵנוּ ה' / *Hashem took us out*

Q What is the distinction between "a mighty hand" and "an outstretched arm"?

A
- ☐ **GA'AL YISRAEL HAGGADAH:** These two phrases, *a mighty hand* and *an outstretched arm*, symbolize the bond between the Jewish people and Hashem. This can be illustrated by a parable: A child stumbled into a pit, and his father extricated him with a rope. The child held on to the rope with his hands from below, while the father pulled with his arms from above. Similarly, the *mighty hand* refers to the Jews "holding on" to Hashem from below, while the *outstretched arm* represents Hashem "holding out an arm" to us from above.

[137] **HAGGADAH: THE ANSWER IS . . .**

וַיּוֹצִאֵנוּ יהוה מִמִּצְרַיִם. לֹא עַל יְדֵי מַלְאָךְ, וְלֹא עַל יְדֵי שָׂרָף, וְלֹא עַל יְדֵי שָׁלִיחַ, אֶלָּא הַקָּדוֹשׁ בָּרוּךְ הוּא בִּכְבוֹדוֹ וּבְעַצְמוֹ. שֶׁנֶּאֱמַר, וְעָבַרְתִּי בְאֶרֶץ מִצְרַיִם בַּלַּיְלָה הַזֶּה, וְהִכֵּיתִי כָל בְּכוֹר בְּאֶרֶץ מִצְרַיִם מֵאָדָם וְעַד בְּהֵמָה, וּבְכָל אֱלֹהֵי מִצְרַיִם אֶעֱשֶׂה שְׁפָטִים, אֲנִי יהוה.[1]

Q: What is the difference between "signs" and "wonders"?

A:
- **ABARBANEL:** A "sign" is a small miracle, and a "wonder" is a major, powerful miracle.
- **VILNA GAON:** An "os," sign, is a natural phenomenon, while a "mofeis," wonder, is a change in nature.

Q: What is the significance of the seemingly repetitive description "in His glory, Himself"?

A:
- **RAV MEIR LEHMANN:** Hashem conducted Himself in two distinct manners:

  בִּכְבוֹדוֹ, *in His glory* — Hashem acted toward the Egyptians with a mighty hand and with an outstretched arm.

  בְּעַצְמוֹ, *Himself* — Hashem acted toward the Jewish people with kindness, like a shepherd who personally guides his sheep.

Q: Why are the words "I will pass through the land of Egypt on that night" necessary? It is obvious from the words "I will slay all the firstborn in the land of Egypt" that Hashem passed through Egypt.

A:
- **CHOZEH OF LUBLIN:** The Midrash teaches that the attribute of judgment went before Hashem and argued that the Jews worshiped idols just as the Egyptians did and therefore did not deserve to be redeemed. But Hashem averted His attention from the Jews' misdeeds and redeemed

HASHEM took us out of Egypt — not through an angel, not through a seraph, not through a messenger, but the Holy One, Blessed is He, in His glory, Himself, as it says: *I will pass through the land of Egypt on that night; I will slay all the firstborn in the land of Egypt from man to beast; and upon all the gods of Egypt will I execute judgments; I, HASHEM.*[1]

1. *Exodus* 12:12.

---

them. In this sense, the word וְעָבַרְתִּי, *I will pass through*, can be interpreted to mean *I will overlook [the Jews' misdeeds] in the land of Egypt*. Hashem would slay the Egyptian firstborn despite this so that the Jewish people would be freed.

Q *Why did Hashem redeem the Jewish people specifically at midnight?*

A ☐ **NESIVOS SHALOM:** This showed that the redemption of the Jewish people happens in the darkest time of the night, at the climax of the exile. This symbolizes the triumph of holiness and light over impurity and darkness.

Q *What was the great benefit of Hashem slaying the Egyptian firstborn Himself, and not via an angel or messenger?*

A ☐ **TALMUD** (*Sanhedrin* 94a): Hashem wanted to personally punish Pharaoh measure for measure: In the case of Pharaoh, he himself blasphemed, so he was punished by Hashem Himself. Sancheirev, who blasphemed through a messenger, was punished by Hashem via a messenger.

☐ **RABBEINU BACHYA:** The attribute of justice was prosecuting the Jewish people and claiming that they were undeserving of salvation. Had the redemption been assigned to a messenger, the Jews might not have been redeemed. This is why Hashem Himself redeemed them.

☐ **ABARBANEL:** Because the Egyptian women were promiscuous, it was impossible to know which child of theirs was in fact a firstborn. Hashem had to wreak the Plague of the Firstborn Himself because only He was able to identify all of the Egyptian firstborn.

☐ **YAAVETZ; ARIZAL:** Before they left Egypt, the Jews had fallen to the forty-ninth level of impurity. Their spiritual state was such that an angel could not have differentiated between them and the Egyptians, and therefore could not have rescued them. Only Hashem was able to distinguish between Jew and Egyptian and spare the Jewish firstborn.

☐ **OHR HACHAIM:** Hashem struck the Egyptians Himself out of His love for the Jewish people. When one cares about someone, he exerts extra effort for him; he would not merely send someone to do it for him.

☐ **HAFLA'AH:** An angel's mission is temporary, while Hashem's actions are eternal. Hashem redeemed us Himself so that the miracle of the Exodus would remain forever, as the verse states, אֵל מוֹצִיאָם מִמִּצְרָיִם, *It is God Who **brings them out** of Egypt* (Numbers 23:22) — in the present tense.

☐ **TOLDOS ADAM:** The set time of the redemption had not yet arrived. In order to cut the exile short and redeem the Jewish people early, Hashem Himself had to intervene.

☐ **GA'AL YISRAEL HAGGADAH:** The redemption had two aspects: physical and spiritual. The Jews' bodies could have been redeemed by a messenger, but in order to redeem their souls and rescue the Jews from spiritual impurity, it was necessary to first defeat the ministering angel of Egypt. This was something only Hashem Himself could do.

☐ **BEIS HALEVI:** Two miracles occurred on the night of Pesach: (1) the punishment of the Egyptians through the tenth plague and (2) the redemption of the Jews. An angel could have carried out the Egyptians' punishment, but could not have brought about the Jews' redemption. Since the angels claimed that the Jews had no merit and did not deserve to be redeemed, Hashem had to redeem them Himself.

☐ **RAV YEHOSHUA LEIB DISKIN:** The Plague of the Firstborn took place at midnight, and the exact timing of midnight differs from place to place. Hashem Himself passed through the land of Egypt Himself to slay the firstborn at precisely midnight in each place, something an angel could not have done.

- **SFAS EMES:** There was no angel who was willing to speak favorably of the Jewish people, so Hashem had to redeem them Himself.
- **MAHARSHAM:** Pharaoh believed that there were two gods: one responsible for good and the other for bad. Had the Egyptian firstborn been struck by an angel, people might have thought that Pharaoh was correct: that one angel metes out punishment while another does good. To uproot this belief, Hashem Himself punished the Egyptian firstborn and also redeemed the Jews, showing that there is one God Who does everything.
- **MICHTAV MEELIYAHU:** The impurity of Egypt was so intense that an angel could not have entered the land without its holiness being damaged.
- **SIFSEI CHAIM:** Hashem did so because He wanted the Jews to connect with Him, as we find in the verse עַם זוּ יָצַרְתִּי לִי תְּהִלָּתִי יְסַפֵּרוּ, *This people I fashioned for Myself that they might declare My praise* (Yeshayahu 43:21).
- **RAV SHLOMO ZALMAN AUERBACH:** The Exodus was not an ordinary release of slaves, but rather the birth of a people. This required that the Jews be elevated from their low level of impurity to a lofty level of holiness. Only Hashem Himself could have accomplished this.

Q *The Jews were commanded to smear blood on their doorframes to prevent the Angel of Death from entering their homes during the Plague of the Firstborn. This seems to indicate that there was an angel responsible for this plague. On the other hand, we just said that Hashem, Himself, carried it out. Did the angel carry out the slaying of the firstborn or not?*

A
- **BA'ALEI HATOSAFOS:** Hashem, together with an angel, killed the firstborn.
- **VILNA GAON:** On any given night, some people die at the hands of the Angel of Death. But on Pesach night, Hashem saw to it that no Jew died of natural causes.
- **RAV AKIVA EIGER:** During the plague of the firstborn, all firstborn sons died, both the firstborns of the mothers and

וְעָבַרְתִּי בְאֶרֶץ מִצְרַיִם בַּלַּיְלָה הַזֶּה — אֲנִי וְלֹא מַלְאָךְ. וְהִכֵּיתִי כָל בְּכוֹר בְּאֶרֶץ מִצְרַיִם — אֲנִי וְלֹא שָׂרָף. וּבְכָל אֱלֹהֵי מִצְרַיִם אֶעֱשֶׂה שְׁפָטִים — אֲנִי וְלֹא הַשָּׁלִיחַ. אֲנִי יהוה. אֲנִי הוּא, וְלֹא אַחֵר.

בְּיָד חֲזָקָה. זוֹ הַדֶּבֶר, כְּמָה שֶׁנֶּאֱמַר, הִנֵּה יַד יהוה הוֹיָה בְּמִקְנְךָ אֲשֶׁר בַּשָּׂדֶה, בַּסּוּסִים בַּחֲמֹרִים בַּגְּמַלִּים בַּבָּקָר וּבַצֹּאן, דֶּבֶר כָּבֵד מְאֹד.[1]

the firstborns of the fathers. It is much easier to identify a maternal firstborn than a paternal firstborn. Therefore the Angel of Death killed the maternal firstborns, while Hashem killed the paternal firstborns. Since the Angel of Death does not differentiate between good and evil, the Jewish firstborn were also in danger, and they had to place blood on their doorframes to ward him off.

☐ **RAV CHAIM BERLIN:** The Angel of Death killed the Egyptian firstborn, but if an Egyptian firstborn happened to be in a Jewish home at that time, Hashem Himself killed him. The Angel of Death was unable to enter the Jewish homes and differentiate between Jew and Egyptian.

☐ **RAV AHARON KOTLER:** Each plague was a composite of five plagues. Four of these five plagues were brought by an angel; the fifth, which included the Plague of the Firstborn, was brought by Hashem.

Q *Was not Moshe the messenger sent to free the Jews from Egypt, as the verse states,* וְאֶשְׁלָחֲךָ אֶל פַּרְעֹה וְהוֹצֵא אֶת עַמִּי בְנֵי יִשְׂרָאֵל מִמִּצְרָיִם, *I shall dispatch you to Pharaoh and you shall take My people the Children of Israel out of Egypt (Exodus 3:10)?*

A ☐ **RID:** Moshe was sent only to *speak* to Pharaoh, not to actually take the Jews out of Egypt. Hashem took the Jews out Himself.

"I will pass through the land of Egypt on that night" — I and no angel; **"I will slay all the firstborn in the land of Egypt"** — I and no seraph; **"And upon all the gods of Egypt will I execute judgments"** — I and no messenger; **"I, HASHEM"** — it is I and no other.

With a mighty hand — refers to the pestilence, as it says: Behold, the hand of HASHEM shall strike your cattle which are in the field, the horses, the donkeys, the camels, the herds, and the flocks — a very severe pestilence.[1]

---

1. *Exodus* 9:3.

☐ **SHIBBOLEI HALEKET:** The first nine plagues were effected by Moshe and Aharon, but the tenth, the Plague of the Firstborn, was brought by Hashem. The words *I and no messenger* refer to the tenth plague.

☐ **BRISKER RAV:** When Moshe was sent to speak to Pharaoh, the Shechinah spoke directly from his throat. Although he was Hashem's messenger, it was Hashem Who redeemed the Jewish people, not Moshe.

Q *Why does this verse make reference only to the plagues of Blood and Pestilence?*

A ☐ **SHIBBOLEI HALEKET:** The combined numerical value of the Hebrew words *dam*, blood, and *dever*, pestilence, is 250 (44 + 206 = 250). This corresponds to the total number of plagues that the Egyptians suffered, as the Haggadah explains.

☐ **ORCHOS CHAIM:** Chazal teach that each plague also contained an element of the plague of Pestilence, so the verse highlights this plague.

☐ **MA'ASEH NISSIM:** The five fingers of each "mighty hand" represent five plagues. Pestilence was the fifth plague — that is, it was the completion of one "hand" of plagues that started with the plague of Blood.

☐ **NETZIV:** The reference to pestilence here is not to the actual plague of Pestilence that affected the Egyptians' livestock. Rather, it refers to the elimination of the Jewish evildoers during the plague of Darkness, which was also a form of pestilence.

וּבִזְרֹעַ נְטוּיָה. זוֹ הַחֶרֶב, כְּמָה שֶׁנֶּאֱמַר, וְחַרְבּוֹ שְׁלוּפָה בְּיָדוֹ, נְטוּיָה עַל יְרוּשָׁלָיִם.[1]

וּבְמֹרָא גָּדֹל. זוֹ גִּלּוּי שְׁכִינָה, כְּמָה שֶׁנֶּאֱמַר, אוֹ הֲנִסָּה אֱלֹהִים לָבוֹא לָקַחַת לוֹ גוֹי מִקֶּרֶב גּוֹי, בְּמַסֹּת, בְּאֹתֹת, וּבְמוֹפְתִים, וּבְמִלְחָמָה, וּבְיָד

Q *Why is the plague of Pestilence specifically considered a function of "a mighty hand"?*

A ☐ **RAV SHLOMO ALKABETZ:** The plague of Pestilence should have been the final plague by virtue of its intensity; it was *a mighty hand*, powerful enough to free the Jews from Egypt. However, Hashem postponed the Exodus and brought another five plagues in order to engender greater recognition of His Name, as the verse states, וְאַךְ אוֹתְךָ וְאֶת עַמְּךָ בַּדָּבֶר... וְאוּלָם בַּעֲבוּר זֹאת הֶעֱמַדְתִּיךָ בַּעֲבוּר הַרְאֹתְךָ אֶת כֹּחִי וּלְמַעַן סַפֵּר שְׁמִי בְּכָל הָאָרֶץ, *I could have stricken you and your people with the pestilence... However, for this have I let you endure, in order to show you My strength and so that My Name may be declared throughout the world* (Exodus 9:15–16).

☐ **ABARBANEL:** The plague of Pestilence is referred to explicitly as "the hand of Hashem," as the verse states, הִנֵּה יַד ה' הוֹיָה בְּמִקְנְךָ, *Behold, the hand of HASHEM is on your livestock* (Exodus 9:3).

☐ **RAV AVIGDOR NEBENZAHL:** The plague of Pestilence was akin to five plagues, since it struck five types of animals: horses, donkeys, camels, cattle, and sheep (as stated in the verse that the Haggadah quotes here). Each of these species was struck with a different plague, for a total of five, corresponding to the five fingers of a hand.

Q *To which sword does the "outstretched arm" refer?*

A ☐ **SHIBBOLEI HALEKET:** It refers to the sword of Moshe.

☐ **RITVA:** "Sword" is a general term for Hashem's retribution against the Egyptians.

With an outstretched arm — refers to the sword, as it says: His drawn sword in His hand, outstretched over Jerusalem.[1]

With great awe — alludes to the revelation of the Shechinah, as it says: Has God ever attempted to take unto Himself a nation from the midst of another nation by trials, miraculous signs, and wonders, by war and

---

1. *I Chronicles* 21:16.

- **RASHBATZ:** It is the sword with which Pharaoh was threatened, in the verse פֶּן יִפְגָּעֵנוּ בַּדֶּבֶר אוֹ בֶחָרֶב, *Lest He strike us dead with the plague or the sword* (*Exodus* 5:3). In truth Moshe and Aharon should have said *lest He strike you*, but they changed the subject from second person to first person out of deference to Pharaoh.
- **AKEIDAS YITZCHAK:** It means the sword brandished by the Egyptian firstborn against their parents in an effort to convince Pharaoh to free the Jews and avert the Plague of the Firstborn.
- **ETZ CHAIM:** It is Hashem's sword. This is what the verse means by *HASHEM took us out of Egypt...with an outstretched arm*. The Exodus was conditional upon the Jews' subsequent acceptance of the Torah; had they not accepted the Torah, Hashem would have killed them in the wilderness, as it says, בַּמִּדְבָּר הַזֶּה יִתַּמּוּ וְשָׁם יָמֻתוּ, *In this wilderness shall they cease to be, and there shall they die!* (*Numbers* 14:35). Thus He was, so to speak, holding a sword over their heads.
- **SFAS HAYAM:** The intent is the sword of the Angel of Death.
- **NETZIV:** Chazal teach that in between each of the plagues, many Egyptians died by the sword to prevent them from banding together and killing the Jews.

Q *Which war took place during the Exodus?*

A
- **IBN EZRA:** This refers to when the firstborn were slain and the Egyptian deities were cut down.
- **DA'AS ZEKEINIM:** This refers to when the Egyptians drowned in the Sea of Reeds, as it states, ה' יִלָּחֵם לָכֶם, *HASHEM shall make war for you* (*Exodus* 14:14).

חֲזָקָה, וּבִזְרוֹעַ נְטוּיָה, וּבְמוֹרָאִים גְּדֹלִים, בְּכֹל אֲשֶׁר עָשָׂה לָכֶם יהוה אֱלֹהֵיכֶם בְּמִצְרַיִם לְעֵינֶיךָ.[1] **וּבְאֹתוֹת.** זֶה הַמַּטֶּה, כְּמָה שֶׁנֶּאֱמַר, וְאֶת הַמַּטֶּה הַזֶּה תִּקַּח בְּיָדֶךָ, אֲשֶׁר תַּעֲשֶׂה בּוֹ אֶת הָאֹתֹת.[2] **וּבְמֹפְתִים.** זֶה הַדָּם, כְּמָה שֶׁנֶּאֱמַר, וְנָתַתִּי מוֹפְתִים בַּשָּׁמַיִם וּבָאָרֶץ:[3]

As each of the words דָּם, blood, אֵשׁ, fire, and עָשָׁן, smoke, is said, a bit of wine is removed from the cup, with the finger or by pouring.

דָּם וָאֵשׁ וְתִימְרוֹת עָשָׁן.

דָּבָר אַחֵר בְּיָד חֲזָקָה, שְׁתַּיִם. וּבִזְרוֹעַ נְטוּיָה, שְׁתַּיִם. וּבְמוֹרָא גָּדֹל, שְׁתַּיִם. וּבְאֹתוֹת, שְׁתַּיִם. וּבְמֹפְתִים, שְׁתַּיִם: אֵלּוּ עֶשֶׂר מַכּוֹת שֶׁהֵבִיא הַקָּדוֹשׁ בָּרוּךְ הוּא עַל הַמִּצְרִים בְּמִצְרַיִם, וְאֵלּוּ הֵן:

Q Why is the plague of Blood referred to with the plural מֹפְתִים, wonders?

A
□ **RITVA:** The plague of Blood involved *two* wondrous aspects:
1. The water turned into blood.
2. If an Egyptian and Jew shared a cup, the Egyptian drank blood while the Jew drank water.

□ **VILNA GAON:** The plague of Blood involved two wondrous aspects:
1. It became clear that Hashem was Master over Pharaoh and the Nile, which was the Egyptian deity.
2. Pharaoh and the Egyptians were punished.

Q Why do we remove drops of wine from our goblets when we say דָּם וָאֵשׁ וְתִימְרוֹת עָשָׁן, Blood, fire, and columns of smoke?

A
□ **HASHIR V'HASHEVACH:** When the Jews roasted the *korban Pesach*, the smoke rose into the air. Seeing this, the

with a mighty hand and outstretched arm and by awesome revelations, as all that HASHEM your God did for you in Egypt, before your eyes?¹

With signs — refers to the miracles performed with the staff as it says: Take this staff in your hand, that you may perform the miraculous signs with it.²

With wonders — alludes to the blood, as it says: I will show wonders in the heavens and on the earth:³

<small>As each of the words דָּם, blood, אֵשׁ, fire, and עָשָׁן, smoke, is said, a bit of wine is removed from the cup, with the finger or by pouring.</small>

Blood, fire, and columns of smoke.

Another explanation of the preceding verse: [Each phrase represents two plagues,] hence: **mighty hand** — two; **outstretched arm** — two; **great awe** — two; **signs** — two; **wonders** — two. These are the Ten Plagues which the Holy One, Blessed is He, brought upon the Egyptians in Egypt, namely:

---

1. *Deuteronomy* 4:34. 2. *Exodus* 4:17. 3. *Joel* 3:3.

Egyptians ground their teeth at this dishonor to their gods, but were helpless to do anything about it. In the memory of their suffering, we spill a bit of wine.

☐ **BE'ER MAYIM:** It is a hint that these are like drops from the cup of bitterness that Hashem fed the Egyptians.

☐ **VAYAGED L'AVRAHAM:** We do this to make our children wonder and ask why. It is yet another unusual thing we do on the Seder night!

עֶשֶׂר מַכּוֹת / *The Ten Plagues*

The Ten Plagues are divided into two sets of five. The first set of five ends with the plague of Pestilence, and the second five end with the Plague of the Firstborn. The plague of Pestilence is described as the "hand of Hashem," as represented by the words *with a mighty hand* in the verse HASHEM *took us out of Egypt with a mighty hand* ... The Plague of the Firstborn is represented by the words *with an outstretched arm*, which refer to the sword that felled the Egyptian firstborn.

[147] **HAGGADAH: THE ANSWER IS . . .**

Q: Why do we remove wine from our goblets with the recitation of each plague?

A:
- **REMA (473:7):** It is written in the Maharil's name that a person must use his finger to remove a bit of wine from his goblet sixteen times: three times when saying דָּם וָאֵשׁ וְתִמְרוֹת עָשָׁן, *Blood, fire, and columns of smoke*; ten times when reciting the Ten Plagues; and three additional times when saying דְּצַ"ךְ עֲדַ"שׁ בְּאַחַ"ב, *D'TZACH, ADASH, B'ACHAB* — for a total of sixteen times. The sixteen times correspond to the letters *yud* and *vav* from the Four-Letter Name of Hashem, Who struck Pharaoh.

- **VILNA GAON:** With each drop that is spilled, the amount of wine in the cup decreases. This hints at the fact that with each plague, the Egyptians became diminished and decreased in number.

- **MISHNAH BERURAH:** We spill the wine with a finger in accordance with the verse אֶצְבַּע אֱלֹהִים הוּא, *It is a finger of God (Exodus 8:15)*.

- **RAV YECHEZKEL ABRAMSKY:** When the Egyptians drowned, the angels wanted to sing, but Hashem stopped them. "My creatures are drowning," He said, "and you want to sing?" The Jewish people, in contrast, recited a *shirah* (song of praise) over their rescue and redemption (and not in joy over the Egyptians' downfall). Our joy in our redemption is one of the reasons that we drink the four cups of wine. Removing a bit of wine symbolizes that there is a small flaw in our happiness, which is not complete because the Egyptians had to drown.

- **MO'ADEI TZVI:** Removing drops of wine from our goblets hints that each of the Ten Plagues that afflicted the Egyptians was only a "drop" in the cup of their punishment. Most of the "cup of bitterness" still remains, to be fed to the rest of the Jewish people's enemies in the future.

- **HASHIR V'HASHEVACH:** The majority of the Haggadah and praise on the Seder night is recited over the second cup, and among the praises we insert the punishments that Hashem brought on the Egyptians. Thus, there is an intermingling of praise on the one hand and punishment on the other — both recited over the second cup.

    How do we demonstrate the difference? By removing

a bit of wine from our goblets, we indicate that the small amount of spilled wine corresponds to the punishment, while the rest of the wine in our goblets is used to say Hallel and sing Hashem's praises.

Q: Why did Hashem bring about the Exodus through the Ten Plagues?

A:
- **SEFORNO:** Seeing how Hashem controlled nature through the Ten Plagues served to strengthen the faith of the Jewish people.
- **MA'ASEH NISSIM:** Hashem brought the Ten Plagues in order to benefit the Jewish people. In the wake of the plagues, the entire world saw that the Jewish people are Hashem's children. At a later date, Hashem would refrain from venting His anger on the Jewish people — as it says regarding the sin of the golden calf, לָמָּה יֹאמְרוּ מִצְרַיִם לֵאמֹר בְּרָעָה הוֹצִיאָם לַהֲרֹג אֹתָם בֶּהָרִים, *Why should Egypt say the following: "With evil intent did He take them out, to kill them in the mountains"?* (Exodus 32:12). Hashem knew that His children would later sin and would need to be punished for

---

A *talmid chacham* who was present at the Alter of Slabodka's Seder related that when they reached the part of the Haggadah that mentions the Ten Plagues, the Alter asked, "Why do we spill wine from our cups in memory of each individual plague? The Egyptians deserved the plagues, and they served as a spiritual medicine for them, so why the need to spill wine to commemorate their suffering?"

The Alter answered his own question. "We have an obligation to participate in their great suffering and mortification: the mortification of human beings who were created *b'tzelem Elokim*, in the image of God.

"As we sit on the Seder night in an expansive, exalted state of mind, rejoicing over our redemption and our freedom and reciting blessings over the four cups of wine, we must remember that 'beloved is man, who was created in the image of God.' We feel the pain of every person without distinction, even if he is an Egyptian who hates and oppresses us. Therefore, we must remove a bit of the wine in our full goblets with each plague."

Rav Yosef Shalom Elyashiv *zt"l* explained the reason for the custom of spilling a bit of wine: While the Egyptians were being punished, Hashem's joy could not be complete—as Chazal say, "Hashem told the angels, 'My handiwork is drowning in the sea and you are singing?'" Therefore, we remove a little of the wine that symbolizes our happiness.

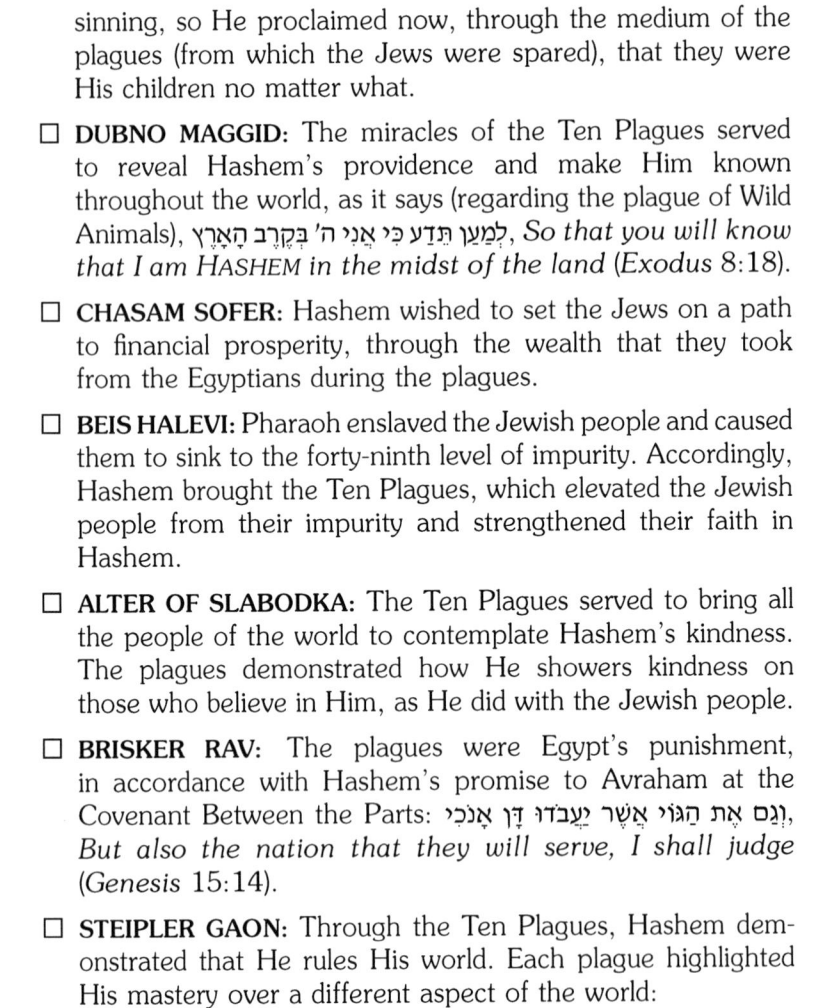

sinning, so He proclaimed now, through the medium of the plagues (from which the Jews were spared), that they were His children no matter what.

- **DUBNO MAGGID:** The miracles of the Ten Plagues served to reveal Hashem's providence and make Him known throughout the world, as it says (regarding the plague of Wild Animals), לְמַעַן תֵּדַע כִּי אֲנִי ה' בְּקֶרֶב הָאָרֶץ, *So that you will know that I am HASHEM in the midst of the land* (Exodus 8:18).

- **CHASAM SOFER:** Hashem wished to set the Jews on a path to financial prosperity, through the wealth that they took from the Egyptians during the plagues.

- **BEIS HALEVI:** Pharaoh enslaved the Jewish people and caused them to sink to the forty-ninth level of impurity. Accordingly, Hashem brought the Ten Plagues, which elevated the Jewish people from their impurity and strengthened their faith in Hashem.

- **ALTER OF SLABODKA:** The Ten Plagues served to bring all the people of the world to contemplate Hashem's kindness. The plagues demonstrated how He showers kindness on those who believe in Him, as He did with the Jewish people.

- **BRISKER RAV:** The plagues were Egypt's punishment, in accordance with Hashem's promise to Avraham at the Covenant Between the Parts: וְגַם אֶת הַגּוֹי אֲשֶׁר יַעֲבֹדוּ דָּן אָנֹכִי, *But also the nation that they will serve, I shall judge* (Genesis 15:14).

- **STEIPLER GAON:** Through the Ten Plagues, Hashem demonstrated that He rules His world. Each plague highlighted His mastery over a different aspect of the world:

    The plague of Blood demonstrated that Hashem's control extends to the water.

    The Frogs showed that Hashem controls insects and creatures that live in the water.

    The Lice showed that Hashem rules the earth as well (the lice came from the dust of the earth).

    The Wild Beasts demonstrated that Hashem rules over the animal kingdom.

    The Pestilence showed that He wields control over life.

    The Boils demonstrated that a person's health is in Hashem's hands.

The Locusts demonstrated that Hashem rules over the creatures that fly, for they did not come to Goshen.

The plague of Darkness showed that Hashem lights up the world.

The Plague of the Firstborn demonstrated that Hashem controls human life.

- ☐ It was necessary to temporarily suspend the laws of nature in order for everyone to comprehend that there exists a Supreme Power that activates nature's laws at His will. The Ten Plagues served this goal. They affected every aspect of the world — beginning with the Nile and ending with the Egyptian firstborn.

Q *Why were there exactly ten plagues, not more and not less?*

A
- ☐ **MIDRASH** (*Shemos Rabbah*): The Ten Plagues correspond to the ten trials by which Avraham was tested and over which he triumphed.

- ☐ **ZOHAR:** With each plague, the Jewish people were purified. HaKadosh Baruch Hu extracted them from one of the negative attributes of the ten *klippos* (shells of impurity) and introduced them to one of the ten holy *sefiros* (Divine attributes).

- ☐ **MA'ASEI HASHEM:** The Ten Plagues correspond to the ten utterances with which the world was created. Pharaoh denied the existence of Hashem, saying, לֹא יָדַעְתִּי אֶת ה', *I do not know* HASHEM (*Exodus* 5:2). In response to the words of heresy that he spoke, he was afflicted with the Ten Plagues, demonstrating that there is, indeed, a Creator.

- ☐ The Ten Plagues correspond to the Ten Commandments. In the merit of the Jews fulfilling these commandments, the world, whose nature was changed during the plagues, continues to exist.

Q *Why did the plagues not help Pharaoh repent?*

A
- ☐ **ALTER OF SLABODKA:** Plagues do not bring about repentance, but rather a contemplation of the way Hashem runs the world. Pharaoh was so immersed in impurity that he could not arrive at a place where such contemplation was possible.

[151] **HAGGADAH: THE ANSWER IS . . .**

As each of the plagues is mentioned, a bit of wine is removed from the cup. The same is done by each word of Rabbi Yehudah's mnemonic.

דָם. צְפַרְדֵּעַ. כִּנִּים. עָרוֹב. דֶּבֶר. שְׁחִין.
בָּרָד. אַרְבֶּה. חֹשֶׁךְ. מַכַּת בְּכוֹרוֹת.

Q *Why were the Egyptians punished with these specific plagues?*

A ☐ **RABBEINU BACHYA:** They were inflicted on the Egyptians *middah keneged middah*, measure for measure, for the suffering that the Egyptians inflicted on the Jews. For example, since the Egyptians forced the Jewish slaves to draw water from the Nile, the river was turned into blood.

Q *Why does the Haggadah repeat itself:* אֵלּוּ עֶשֶׂר מַכּוֹת ... וְאֵלּוּ הֵן, *These are the Ten Plagues...and these are they?*

A ☐ **MA'ASEI HASHEM:** Some of the plagues caused more than one type of damage. In order that we do not err in our calculation of the number of plagues, the Haggadah repeats that the total number of plagues was "these" ten.

☐ **CHASAM SOFER:** The numerical values of the letters of the word הֵן, *they*, in this passage are 5 and 50. The repetition of *These are they* hints that each of the Ten Plagues that Hashem visited upon the Egyptians was a composite of five plagues, so that the sum total of plagues that beset the Egyptians was fifty.

◈ דָּם / *Blood*

The plague of Blood harmed the Egyptians in several ways:
- The Egyptians could not drink water.
- The fish in the Nile died.
- The Nile dried up.

Q *Which miracles took place during the plague of Blood?*

A ☐ **MIDRASH RABBAH:** Blood flowed from the trees and stones, and even their saliva turned into blood. Also, the Jewish

As each of the plagues is mentioned, a bit of wine is removed from the cup. The same is done by each word of Rabbi Yehudah's mnemonic.

1. Blood 2. Frogs 3. Lice 4. Wild Beasts
5. Pestilence 6. Boils 7. Hail 8. Locusts
9. Darkness 10. Plague of the Firstborn.

---

people became wealthy because the Egyptians paid them for water.

- **YALKUT SHIMONI:** If a Jew and an Egyptian drank from the same vessel, the Jew drank his drink, while the Egyptian drank blood.

- During the plague of Blood, the Egyptians experienced the plague with the three senses of sight, taste, and smell:

  With sight, as the verse says, וַיַּךְ אֶת הַמַּיִם אֲשֶׁר בַּיְאֹר לְעֵינֵי פַרְעֹה וּלְעֵינֵי עֲבָדָיו, *He struck the water in the presence of Pharaoh and in the presence of his servants [literally, "before the eyes of Pharaoh and his servants"]* (Exodus 7:20). They saw the Nile turn into blood.

  With taste, as it says, וְהַדָּגָה אֲשֶׁר בַּיְאֹר מֵתָה...וְלֹא יָכְלוּ מִצְרַיִם לִשְׁתּוֹת מַיִם מִן הַיְאֹר, *The fish-life that was in the river died...; Egypt could not drink water from the river* (Exodus 7:21). They tasted the blood.

  With smell, as it says, וַיִּבְאַשׁ הַיְאֹר, *And the river became foul* (ibid. 7:21). The Nile had a foul smell.

Q: Why was this the first plague?

A:
- **MIDRASH RABBAH:** Hashem told Moshe, "Because Pharaoh was haughty and said, לִי יְאֹרִי וַאֲנִי עֲשִׂיתִנִי, *Mine is my river, and I have made myself [powerful]* (Ezekiel 29:3), I will begin the punishment there."

- **MIDRASH HAGADOL:** This plague was first in order to embarrass the Egyptians by punishing their god first.

- **ABARBANEL:** This plague was a punishment for the Egyptians, because they worshiped the Nile. Hashem said, "I will strike their god first," and He turned the Nile's water into blood.

- **RAV MOSHE FEINSTEIN:** The Egyptians performed all sorts of harsh and shocking acts, such as slaughtering Jewish babies and bathing in their blood and placing the babies in the walls instead of bricks. They displayed full corruption and evil at every stage. The first plague exposed this truth when their water turned into blood.

Q Why were the Egyptians punished with the plague of Blood?

A
- **MIDRASH HAGADOL:** The Egyptians were punished with blood because they spilled the blood of Jewish children when they tossed them into the Nile.

- **MIDRASH TANCHUMA:** The Egyptians were punished measure for measure, because they did not permit the Jewish women to immerse themselves from their impurity (blood).

- **RABBEINU BACHYA:** The Egyptians' primary source of security was the Nile, and they forced the Jewish slaves to draw water from that river. Therefore they were struck through the Nile.

- **KLI YAKAR:** As part of the plague, the fish in the Nile died. This is because the Egyptians wished to nullify Yaakov's blessing וְיִדְגּוּ לָרֹב בְּקֶרֶב הָאָרֶץ, *May they proliferate abundantly like fish within the land* (Genesis 48:16).

- **MALBIM:** With this plague, Hashem showed that from the first He would be striking the Egyptian god: the Nile River.

- **OZNAYIM LATORAH:** The blood that flowed from the trees and stones during this plague corresponded to the blood of the Jewish children that were placed inside Egyptian structures in place of bricks.

- **STEIPLER GAON:** Hashem wanted to make His Name famous throughout the world. With the plague of Blood, He afflicted the Egyptians through water, showing the whole world that He rules over water.

צְפַרְדֵּעַ / Frogs

The plague of Frogs harmed the Egyptians in several ways:
- The frogs infested every Egyptian home.
- The frogs infested every Egyptian body.
- The frogs would jump into the Egyptians' ovens and their food.

- All of Egypt was filled with a foul odor from the smell of the frogs.
- The frogs emasculated the Egyptian men (*Shemos Rabbah* 10:4).

Q: What miracles took place during the plague of Frogs?

A:
- ☐ **YALKUT SHIMONI:** The plague began with a single frog, which came from outside of Egypt and multiplied in the Nile, producing many frogs.
- ☐ **MIDRASH RABBAH:** It was impossible to eat hot food in Egypt, because the frogs would leap into the cooking fires and put them out.
- ☐ **MIDRASH RABBAH:** Wherever there was mud, it was immediately filled with frogs.
- ☐ **MAHARSHA:** Frogs usually keep away from fire and live in the water, but here, where there was a special Divine command to go into the ovens and cooking fires, the frogs obeyed in order to sanctify Hashem's Name.

Q: Why did the plague of Frogs begin with just one frog?

A:
- ☐ **OZNAYIM LATORAH:** Hashem, in His compassion, gives the sinner time to repent. The plague started with one frog that rose from the Nile. Had the Egyptians repented, Hashem would have returned the frog to the river, and that would have been the end of the plague.

Q: Why were the Egyptians punished with the plague of Frogs?

A:
- ☐ **MIDRASH RABBAH:** Hashem told Pharaoh, "You said, לִי יְאֹרִי וַאֲנִי עֲשִׂיתִנִי, *Mine is my river, and I have made myself [powerful]* (Ezekiel 29:3). I will show you if the river is Mine or yours, for My plagues will strike it, and at My decree it will give forth frogs. As I have decreed on the water, so the river will do."
- ☐ **MIDRASH RABBAH:** The Egyptians were punished with the plague of Frogs measure for measure. Because the Egyptians

befouled the the Jewish people, forcing them to do evil things, the frogs befouled them.

☐ **MIDRASH TANCHUMA:** Because the Egyptian overseers would wake up the Jews for work early in the morning by croaking at their windows like frogs, the frogs harassed the Egyptians with their croaking, day and night. Also, because the Egyptians forced the Jewish people to be porters and carry their goods, the frogs came and ruined their goods.

☐ **MIDRASH YELAMDEINU:** Hashem said, "Let the frogs, which grow in the water, come and harass the Egyptians, who wanted to destroy a nation that was destined to receive the Torah, which is compared to water."

☐ **KLI YAKAR:** Pharaoh desecrated Heaven's Name when he said, לֹא יָדַעְתִּי אֶת ה׳, *I do not know HASHEM* (*Exodus* 5:2). Accordingly, Hashem afflicted the Egyptians with frogs, who publicly sanctified Heaven's name through their tremendous self-sacrifice (for example, by entering the hot ovens).

☐ **RABBEINU BACHYA:** The frogs would croak in the people's innards, giving them no rest — just as the Egyptians gave the Jewish people no rest when they forced them into back-breaking labor.

☐ **SEFORNO:** The frogs showed the whole world that Hashem rules over everything. Hashem determined the plague's starting time and its ending time. In addition, the frogs, unlike other living beings, lived in the Nile according to the timetable that had been decreed for them, despite the fact that every other creature in the river died in the plague of blood.

☐ **ABARBANEL:** The parents of the boys who were drowned in the Nile screamed at the Egyptian murderers to stop, but the Egyptians ignored their cries. Accordingly, the frogs croaked in their stomachs; this time, the noise could not be ignored.

☐ **VILNA GAON:** The Egyptians were punished with frogs because they played with them for entertainment and forced the Jews to catch the creatures for them. They would tell the Jews, "Go out and bring us [impure] creeping and crawling creatures so that we may play."

☐ **RAV SAMSON RAPHAEL HIRSCH:** The frog is a small creature that generally fears humans and hides from them. In Egypt, however, the frogs were brazen, to show the Egyptian overseers what it is like to be treated badly and teach them a lesson in human relations.

- **HASHIR V'HASHEVACH:** The Egyptians drowned Jewish children in the Nile. Accordingly, they were plagued with frogs, which croaked with their throats. The croaking was the blood of the children crying out; the blood of those Jewish children cried out from the frogs' throats.
- **STEIPLER GAON:** Hashem wanted to publicize His Name in the world. With the plague of Frogs, He showed the whole world that He rules over the creatures in the water.

Q *The Talmud teaches (Pesachim 53) that Chananyah, Mishael, and Azaryah learned from the frogs' self-sacrifice and entered a fiery furnace rather than worship idols. Why did they learn this from the frogs and not from Avraham Avinu, who entered a fiery furnace rather than giving up his faith in Hashem?*

A
- **MAHARSHA:** There was a special innovation in the plague of Frogs. Hashem decreed that frogs would enter everywhere, including places where it is against the frogs' nature to go, in order that they would sanctify Heaven's Name. Frogs usually distance themselves from fire and live in the water, yet many of them willingly entered hot ovens and jumped into the cooking fires. Thus, the lesson of the frogs was distinct from that learned from Avraham.
- **RAV YONASAN EIBESHITZ:** Every individual frog could have used evasion tactics and remained in cooler areas while allowing other frogs to enter the flames, but the frogs in Egypt did not do that. They did not try to evade the fire, but instead sanctified Hashem. This is the unique behavior that Chananyah, Mishael, and Azaryah learned from. They too did not try to hide even though their defiant behavior would make them liable to punishment in a furnace.
- **RAV YEHOSHUA LEIB DISKIN:** The frogs in Egypt suffered greatly, both in the fires they jumped into and when inside the Egyptians, and they did so with enormous self-sacrifice. This lesson about the readiness to give up one's life for the sanctification of Hashem's Name through great pain and suffering is what Chananyah, Mishael, and Azaryah learned from the frogs. They could not learn it from Avraham, because he

[157] **HAGGADAH: THE ANSWER IS . . .**

did not suffer greatly in the fiery furnace: he was willing to sacrifice himself, but a miracle occurred to save him.

☐ **RAV YERUCHAM LEVOVITZ:** Frogs have no free will. When Hashem decided to strike Pharaoh with a plague of Frogs, the frogs did as they were ordered without hesitation or doubt, even when they had to give up their lives by jumping into hot ovens. Chananyah, Mishael, and Azaryah learned from them. Drawing a parallel to their own situation, they understood that they were obligated to sanctify Heaven's Name and sacrifice their lives without question.

Q *The verses tell us that the necromancers of Egypt duplicated the plague of Frogs that Hashem brought upon Egypt:* וַתַּעַל הַצְּפַרְדֵּעַ וַתְּכַס אֶת אֶרֶץ מִצְרָיִם וַיַּעֲשׂוּ כֵן הַחַרְטֻמִּים בְּלָטֵיהֶם וַיַּעֲלוּ אֶת הַצְפַרְדְּעִים עַל אֶרֶץ מִצְרָיִם, *The frog-infestation ascended and covered the land of Egypt. The necromancers did the same through their incantations, and they brought up the frogs upon the land of Egypt (Exodus 8:2-3). Why the duplication?*

A ☐ **MIDRASH RABBAH:** The Egyptians had a quarrel with their neighbors over the borders between their countries. The plague of Frogs settled the argument, since it took place only in Egypt and not outside her borders. Wherever the frogs did not go was clearly not considered part of Egypt. The necromancers, in an effort to appease Pharaoh, attempted to increase the plague's range, but the frogs refused to extend past Egypt's borders. They did not spread to any countries apart from Egypt, as our verse indicates — *The frog-infestation covered the land of Egypt* — demonstrating to her neighbors exactly where the true borders were.

◈§ כִּנִּים / Lice

The plague of Lice harmed the Egyptians in several ways:
- According to the Ralbag, the dust of the earth became filled with lice, and the necromancers were unable to stand on the ground. A magician whose feet are not touching the ground cannot wield his magic, as it says, וַיַּעֲשׂוּ כֵן הַחַרְטֻמִּים בְּלָטֵיהֶם לְהוֹצִיא אֶת הַכִּנִּים וְלֹא יָכֹלוּ, *The sorcerers did the same with their incantations to draw forth the lice, but they could not (Exodus 8:14).*

- There were lice on the people.
- There were lice on the animals.
- The lice entered their bodies like arrows.

Q What miracles took place during the plague of Lice?

A ☐ **RAMBAM:** The lice also infested the land of Goshen, but did not bother the Jewish people.

☐ The size of a single louse was somewhere between the size of a chicken egg and a goose egg.

☐ The dust of Egypt was covered in lice, to a height of two *amos* (approximately 1.2 meters, or 4 feet).

Q Why were the Egyptians punished with the plague of Lice?

A ☐ **MIDRASH RABBAH:** Hashem afflicted the Egyptians, who had denied His existence, with lice, a plague they were unable to remove from their bodies. When they failed, they were forced to acknowledge Hashem's existence.

☐ **RABBEINU BACHYA:** The Egyptians caused the Jews great suffering by preventing them from washing themselves. Accordingly, their bodies were afflicted with lice that they could not get rid of.

☐ **KLI YAKAR:** The Egyptians oppressed the Jewish people, forcing them to toil and perspire heavily. Accordingly, the Egyptians were punished with the plague of Lice, which brought on heavy perspiration and high fever.

☐ **ABARBANEL:** The Egyptians were punished with lice — which were present throughout Egypt and forced them to stop working the land — because they robbed the Jews of their land.

☐ **VILNA GAON:** The Egyptians forced the Jews to clean the streets, so Hashem turned their dust into lice.

עָרוֹב / Wild Beasts

Q What miracles took place during the plague of Wild Beasts?

A ☐ **MIDRASH RABBAH:** Pharaoh's home was in the center of the city. The animals entered from the edges of the city and passed by all the houses on the way, aiming directly for the palace in order to begin the plague with Pharaoh, who had been the one to come up with the idea of enslaving the Jews.

☐ **KLI YAKAR:** Hashem's promise when He warned Pharaoh about His plague — וְשַׂמְתִּי פְדֻת בֵּין עַמִּי וּבֵין עַמֶּךָ, *I shall make a distinction between My people and your people* (Exodus 8:19) — came to fruition: when a wild beast would encounter a Jew in Egypt, it did not harm him.

☐ **RABBEINU BACHYA:** The first plagues took place in a circumscribed area and did not move from place to place, but the beasts were sent in from the desert and roamed the land. Hashem performed a miracle, and the animals did not enter the land of Goshen.

☐ **RAV ITZELE OF VOLOZHIN:** According to the Midrash, the wild beasts came along with the natural soil on which they were accustomed to living. When animals are in their natural habitat, they are dangerous and capable of inflicting harm. When they are not in their own habitats, however, they are not as dangerous. Hashem brought the beasts to Egypt together with their natural soil, so that they would feel as confident as they were in their usual habitats and inflict greater damage.

Q *Why were the Egyptians punished with the plague of Wild Beasts?*

A ☐ **MIDRASH** (*Shemos Rabbah*): Hashem said, "You placed throngs of people over My children, as it is written, וַיָּשִׂימוּ עָלָיו שָׂרֵי מִסִּים לְמַעַן עַנֹּתוֹ בְּסִבְלֹתָם, *So they appointed taskmasters over it [the Jewish people] in order to afflict it with their burdens* (Exodus 1:11). I, too, will place the birds of the sky and the beasts of the earth in throngs over you, as it says, הִנְנִי מַשְׁלִיחַ בְּךָ וּבַעֲבָדֶיךָ וּבְעַמְּךָ וּבְבָתֶּיךָ אֶת הֶעָרֹב, *I shall incite against you, your servants, your people, and your houses the* **swarm** *of wild beasts* (Exodus 8:17).

☐ **KLI YAKAR:** The Egyptians were punished with the plague of Wild Beasts measure for measure — because they enslaved the Jewish people, who were compared to animals, as the verse says, כִּי חָיוֹת הֵנָּה, *For they are [like] animals* (Exodus 1:19).

- **ABARBANEL:** Hashem brought wild animals to devour the Egyptian children, because the Egyptians entered the Jewish homes and stole away the children to do their work.
- **VILNA GAON:** The Egyptians goaded the Jews and told them, "Hunt wild animals for us." Their aim was to have the Jews fail at the hunt and remain in the desert instead of returning home — to prevent them from procreating. Therefore, measure for measure, Hashem sent wild beasts to hunt them.
- **STEIPLER GAON:** Through the plagues in Egypt, Hashem demonstrated that He rules over the world. With the plague of Wild Beasts, He showed that He rules over all living creatures.
- The Egyptians denied the principle of reward and punishment, claiming that everything exists in a random chaos for both the righteous and the wicked. Therefore they were punished with *arov* (ערוב), wild beasts, which comes from the word *irbuvyah* (ערבוביה), mixture. In this plague, everyone saw that there *is* a difference between the righteous and the wicked, that Hashem does make distinctions, as the verse says regarding this plague, וְהִפְלֵיתִי בַיּוֹם הַהוּא אֶת אֶרֶץ גֹּשֶׁן, *And on that day I shall set apart the land of Goshen* (Exodus 8:18).

Q *The verse that describes this plague says,*
וּמָלְאוּ בָּתֵּי מִצְרַיִם אֶת הֶעָרֹב וְגַם הָאֲדָמָה אֲשֶׁר הֵם עָלֶיהָ,
The houses of Egypt shall be filled with the swarm, and even the ground upon which they are (Exodus 8:17). If the houses were filled, then certainly the ground upon which the houses sat were filled with the wild beasts. Why the redundant language?

A
- **SEFORNO:** The word "ground" teaches that even when the houses were locked up, the Egyptians did not feel secure. The ground on which the homes rested became filled with snakes, so the snakes entered the Egyptians' homes through the floor.
- **CHANUKAS HATORAH:** Chazal tell us that there is a creature that lives among the flora on the ground that bears the form of a man. These creatures are known as *"avnei hasadeh"* (stones of the field) or *"adonei hasadeh"* (masters of the

field). It attaches itself to the ground and nourishes itself from the soil like any other plant, and when detached from the ground it perishes. Among the beasts that came to Egypt was this creature, and it had to bring along the earth underneath it in order to remain alive. The word "*adamah*," ground, teaches that even this creature's special soil was filled with wild beasts.

☐ **RAV YEHOSHUA LEIB DISKIN:** In order for the animals to "feel at home" and inflict maximum damage, Hashem had them bring along the earth that they were used to living on so that they would think they were back in the forest. *And the houses of Egypt shall be filled* tells of the animals' arrival. *The ground upon which they are* teaches that Hashem brought them to Egypt along with the ground they lived on, so that they would prey on the Egyptians without fear or timidity.

Q **Why did Moshe ask Pharaoh to allow the Jews to take a three-day journey to the wilderness, rather than ask that they be freed unconditionally?**

A ☐ **REMA:** Had Moshe requested that Pharaoh free the Jews completely, Pharaoh might have protested that freeing the Jews would incur a tremendous financial loss for Egypt. He would have claimed that the subsequent plagues and punishments were unjustified, for how could he be expected to simply release six hundred thousand slaves?

Moshe therefore made a more reasonable request: דֶּרֶךְ שְׁלֹשֶׁת יָמִים נֵלֵךְ בַּמִּדְבָּר, *We will go on a three-day journey in the wilderness* (Exodus 8:23). When Pharaoh did not accede even to this request, he demonstrated that he was a cruel, tyrannical ruler and that he and his people were deserving of the heavy punishments they experienced.

Q **וְהִפְלֵיתִי בַיּוֹם הַהוּא אֶת אֶרֶץ גֹּשֶׁן, *And on that day I shall set apart the land of Goshen* (Exodus 8:18) — why does the verse tell us that specifically during this plague Hashem separated Goshen? After all, Hashem spared Goshen during the other plagues as well.**

הגדה של פסח [162]

A ☐ **RAMBAN:** All the other plagues remained in a confined area, but when Hashem sent in wild animals from the wilderness, He allowed them to rampage throughout the land without limiting them to any specific region inside Egypt. The Torah is telling us that even so, these beasts did not enter the boundaries of Goshen.

☐ **ARUCH HASHULCHAN:** The goal of this plague was to demonstrate the principles of reward and punishment, which Pharaoh denied. When Pharaoh and the Egyptians saw that this plague took place only in Egypt and not in nearby Goshen, they understood in the clearest possible way that there was Someone orchestrating these events in retribution for their treatment of the Jews.

☐ **RAV YEHOSHUA LEIB DISKIN:** During this plague, Hashem brought to Egypt wild animals from every country. The beasts that lived near Goshen had to reach Egypt through Goshen, but even though the wild animals passed through Goshen, they did not harm the Jewish people. By telling us *I shall set apart the land of Goshen*, the Torah is letting us know that even though the animals passed through Goshen, Hashem *set apart the land of Goshen* and did not let them prey on the Jews.

Q *The psalm that describes the Exodus says, וַיָּבֹא עָרֹב כִּנִּים בְּכָל גְּבוּלָם, Hordes of beasts arrived and lice throughout their borders (Psalms 105:31). The plague of Lice came before the plague of Wild Beasts. Why is the plague of Wild Beasts listed before the plague of Lice in this verse?*

A ☐ **DUBNO MAGGID:** This can be compared to a wealthy man who hosted a wedding. Each night during the week of *sheva berachos*, he invited a group of guests from a certain population. On the first day, he invited his friends; on the second day — relatives; on the third day — business colleagues, and so on. On the fourth day, when he saw a guest who had also been present on the first day, he asked what he was doing there. The man replied, "I was invited twice: on the first day as a friend, and on the fourth day, you invited the city's Torah scholars."

Such was the case with the lice. They came once during the plague of Lice, and then they came a second time during the plague of Wild Beasts, along with the other wild creatures. The verse in *Tehillim* refers to the lice that arrived during the plague of Wild Beasts.

❧ דֶּבֶר / *Pestilence*

Q *What miracles took place during the plague of Pestilence?*

A
- **MIDRASH** (*Shemos Rabbah*): Any animal jointly owned by an Egyptian and a Jew was spared.
- **RAV YEHOSHUA LEIB DISKIN:** Animals belonging to the Jews did not die — not even those animals that were old or sick and about to die.

Q *Why were the Egyptians punished with this plague?*

A
- **KLI YAKAR:** When they went down to Egypt, Yaakov and his family were shepherds. The Egyptians forced them to become construction workers, and the Jews' sheep died for lack of care. The Egyptians were punished measure for measure, and their own flocks were decimated.
- **VILNA GAON:** The Egyptians were punished with pestilence because they wanted to steal the Jews' cattle, and also because they forced the Jewish people to shepherd the Egyptians' sheep and cattle to prevent them from going home and procreating so that their numbers would not increase.
- **STEIPLER GAON:** Hashem wanted to show the whole world that He runs the world. During the plague of Pestilence, He demonstrated that He is master over all living creatures — as only the animals of the Egyptians died, while not a single one of the Jews' animals was harmed.
- To inflict damage on a national symbol of Egypt — their horses were a symbol of Egypt's strength.
- To undermine the Egyptian economy, through killing off the livestock: the donkeys and camels that were used to carry their merchandise and property.
- The Egyptians forced the Jews to do the work of their animals, such as plowing or bearing burdens. Hashem therefore killed off their livestock, measure for measure.

Q וְהִנֵּה לֹא מֵת מִמִּקְנֵה יִשְׂרָאֵל עַד אֶחָד וַיִּכְבַּד לֵב פַּרְעֹה, And behold, of the livestock of Israel not even one had died — yet Pharaoh's heart became stubborn (Exodus 9:7) — why did Pharaoh not repent when he witnessed this wonder?

A
- **OHR YAHEL:** It is in man's nature not to admit his mistakes, but rather to seek excuses and justifications. This was Pharaoh's approach.

- **IMREI EMES:** Pharaoh stole thousands of animals from the Jews. When he realized that there was a plague decimating the livestock in his land, he sent people to find out what had been done to his animals. When he was told that the animals had not died after all (because they were the property of the Jews), he hardened his heart.

- **NETZIV:** When the results of the plague, which did not afflict the Jews, were reported to Pharaoh, this should have spurred him to contemplation; he should have realized that Moshe's words had indeed come true. But when he saw that some of the Egyptians' livestock also remained alive (those that were owned jointly with Jews), his heart hardened.

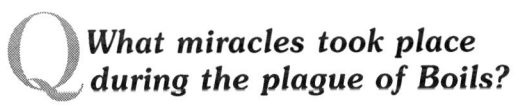

שְׁחִין / Boils

Q What miracles took place during the plague of Boils?

A
- **MIDRASH** (*Shemos Rabbah*): When one hurls an arrow upward, the arrow travels a short distance. To bring this plague, Moshe threw a handful of furnace soot and it reached the Throne of Glory. Similarly, when one scatters a tiny amount, it spreads over a limited area. But Moshe took just a handful of soot and managed to scatter it over the entire land of Egypt.

- **KLI YAKAR:** In contrast to the other plagues, the boils did not afflict all the Egyptians at once. Rather, it targeted the necromancers first, and only then the other Egyptians.

Q Why were the Egyptians punished with this plague?

A
- ☐ **MIDRASH** (*Tanna D'Vei Eliyahu*): The Egyptians treated the Jews as their personal servants and made them heat and cool water for them. What did the Egyptians do then? They would bathe in the water and then go home happy. Therefore, Hashem brought the plague of Boils, so that they were not able to touch any water, either hot or cold.

- ☐ **MIDRASH AGGADAH:** The Egyptians enslaved the Jews and did not allow them time to even scratch themselves or relieve their aches. Therefore they were stricken with boils and experienced constant discomfort from which they could not find relief.

- ☐ **KLI YAKAR:** The Egyptians separated the Jewish men from their wives. They were punished, measure for measure, with boils, which caused them to limit contact with their wives.

- ☐ **HASHIR V'HASHEVACH:** The Egyptians slaughtered Jewish children and drained their blood for Pharaoh — who had *tzara'as* — to bathe in. In response to this terrible deed, the Egyptians were afflicted with boils, which caused *tzara'as*.

- ☐ **RABBEINU BACHYA:** The Egyptians were initially afflicted through their property and their money — with the plague of Wild Beasts — and then they were afflicted physically in the plague of Boils. Then, finally, the firstborn sons were killed in the Plague of the Firstborn. All this was measure for measure: at first, the Egyptians beat and oppressed the Jews, afflicting their bodies and taking their possessions, and in the end they decreed death and destruction upon the Jews: כָּל הַבֵּן הַיִּלּוֹד הַיְאֹרָה תַּשְׁלִיכֻהוּ, *Every son that will be born — into the river shall you throw him!* (Exodus 1:22).

- ☐ The Egyptians beat the Jews until their bodies were covered with sores. Measure for measure, Hashem sent the plague of Boils and afflicted the Egyptians the same way.

Q *Why was it only in the plague of Boils that it says,* וַיְחַזֵּק ה' אֶת לֵב פַּרְעֹה, *HASHEM strengthened the heart of Pharaoh (Exodus 9:12)?*

A
- ☐ **RAMBAN:** During the other plagues, the necromancers strengthened Pharaoh's heart so that he would stubbornly refuse to acknowledge God's power. In this plague, however, the necromancers were not able to stand before him, since

הגדה של פסח [166]

their bodies were wracked with boils, so it was Hashem who hardened his heart.

- ☐ **MIDRASH** (*Shemos Rabbah*): This plague was the first of the second set of plagues. In the first five plagues, Hashem gave Pharaoh the possibility of repenting. When he did not do so, Hashem hardened Pharaoh's heart and did not allow him to repent, to repay him for his sins.

בָּרָד / Hail

The plague of Hail harmed the Egyptians in several ways:
- The hail struck both people and animals.
- The grass was struck with hail.
- The trees were struck.

Q: What miracles took place during the plague of Hail?

A: ☐ **MIDRASH** (*Shemos Rabbah*): There were many miracles that occurred in this plague:

1. No hail fell in the land of Goshen. Only the Egyptians experienced stormy weather.
2. Hashem performed wonders: only the wheat and buckwheat were not afflicted.
3. Large lumps of ice fell and sealed the Egyptians in, like the walls of a prison.
4. When the Egyptians sat down, they were burned with ice; when they stood, they were burned with fire.

☐ **YALKUT SHIMONI**: The rain fell, and the wind entered it and turned it into hail.

☐ **YALKUT REUVENI**: By nature, water and fire hate one another and cannot co-exist. When they saw the war that Hashem was waging, they made peace between themselves and mingled with each other.

☐ **BRISKER RAV**: The hail fell only where there were people or animals or grass in the field.

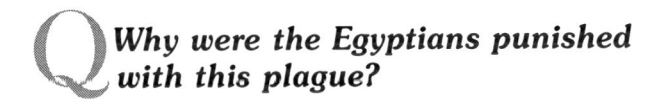

Q: Why were the Egyptians punished with this plague?

[167] HAGGADAH: THE ANSWER IS . . .

A
- ☐ **MIDRASH** (*Shemos Rabbah*): The Egyptians had put the Jewish people in charge of planting gardens and orchards to prevent them from procreating and increasing in number. Therefore, measure for measure, Hashem brought the hail and destroyed what the Jews had planted.
- ☐ **KLI YAKAR:** The loud noise of the hail came in reaction to Pharaoh's derision, when he refused to listen to Hashem and said out loud, ...מִי ה' אֲשֶׁר אֶשְׁמַע בְּקֹלוֹ, *Who is HASHEM, that I should heed His voice...?* (Exodus 5:2).
- ☐ **VILNA GAON:** They were punished with hail because they pelted the Jews with stones.

Q *Why was it only before the plague of Hail that Hashem warned, "For this time I shall send all My plagues against your heart"?*

A
- ☐ **OHR HACHAIM:** Until this plague, Pharaoh believed that each plague was an act of sorcery. Even when his necromancers told him, during the previous plague, אֶצְבַּע אֱלֹהִים הִוא, *It is the finger of God!* (Exodus 8:15), he still believed that the source of the plagues was magic. He assumed that his own sorcerers were simply incapable of achieving Moshe and Aharon's level and were unable to match their feats. Now, however, Hashem told him regarding this plague that *this time* He was sending all His plagues against him. When he saw the plague of hail — a miraculous mixture of fire and ice, which no human being could possibly conjure — Pharaoh finally came to the correct conclusion: that it was Hashem Himself Who had brought all the plagues.
- ☐ **ABARBANEL:** The plague of hail begins the third set of plagues when they are grouped into three sets: דְּצַ״ךְ עֲדַ״שׁ בְּאַחַ״ב, *D'TZACH, ADASH, B'ACHAB.* The aim of the third set of plagues was to demonstrate Hashem's ability to perform unique wonders. In saying, *For this time...*, Hashem was referring to all the plagues in this group: *barad*, Hail, which killed both people and animals in the field; *arbeh*, Locusts, in which the locusts devoured all the grass in the land; *choshech*, Darkness, in which Hashem punished the Egyptians in secret — in darkness; and *bechoros*, the Plague of the Firstborn, in which He struck down the Egyptians' firstborn sons.

הגדה של פסח [168]

Q *Regarding this plague, the verse says,* הַיָּרֵא אֶת דְּבַר ה' מֵעַבְדֵי פַּרְעֹה הֵנִיס אֶת עֲבָדָיו וְאֶת מִקְנֵהוּ אֶל הַבָּתִּים, *Whoever among the servants of Pharaoh feared the word of* HASHEM *chased his servants and his livestock into the houses (Exodus 9:20) — why did only those Egyptians who feared Hashem's word take these precautionary measures? Would this not have been the sensible thing for anyone to do?*

A ☐ B'CHIPAZON PESACH: *Those with fear of Heaven* refers to Egyptians who had not committed the sin of improper breeding of animals. Therefore, Hashem gave them the wisdom and desire to bring their animals inside, where they were spared.

☐ STEIPLER GAON: Heresy is not the result of a lack of wisdom, but a function of a person's will. A person who does not wish to believe in something will dismiss it in his heart and decide not to be afraid of it. A spirit of impurity and foolishness drove the Egyptians and distorted their thinking.

☐ These were not truly God-fearing people, as it does not say, *Whoever feared* HASHEM, but rather, *Whoever feared the word of* HASHEM. This kind of fearful person is afraid of everything. At Moshe's warning, some Egyptians were anxious that there might be truth to his words, and they decided to bring their servants and animals inside — just in case.

Q *Why did Moshe respond to Pharaoh's request that he pray for him only now, during the plague of Hail, saying,* כְּצֵאתִי אֶת הָעִיר אֶפְרֹשׂ אֶת כַּפַּי אֶל ה', *When I leave the city, I shall spread out my hands to* HASHEM *(Exodus 9:29)? Why did Moshe not pray after the other six plagues?*

A ☐ KLI YAKAR: Moshe said these words — *When I leave the city...* — to emphasize the magnitude of the miracle: that after Moshe requested that the plague cease, wherever Pharaoh would find himself, even outside the city, there would be no hail.

☐ RAMBAN: Pharaoh demanded that the hail cease immediately. Moshe replied that the hail would not stop at once, but only after he prayed to Hashem — and that his prayer would take place only after he had left the city.

☐ **RAV YONASAN EIBESHITZ:** During the plague of Hail, the city was filled with animals that the Egyptians worshiped as gods, since they had taken their animals inside the city limits to protect them. Moshe did not want to pray in a city full of idols, and therefore he left in order to pray. During the other plagues, on the other hand, the sheep remained outside the city and Moshe was able to pray there.

☐ **RAV SHLOMO KLUGER:** It was during the plague of Hail that Pharaoh first said, הַ׳ הַצַּדִּיק, *HASHEM is the Righteous One* (*Exodus* 9:27). In saying so, he dismissed idol worship and desired Moshe to pray in the city, which, in Pharaoh's opinion, was now free of idol worship. Moshe replied, וְאַתָּה וַעֲבָדֶיךָ יָדַעְתִּי כִּי טֶרֶם תִּירְאוּן מִפְּנֵי ה׳ אֱלֹהִים, *And as for you and your servants, I know that you are not yet afraid of HASHEM, God* (*Exodus* 9:30). In other words: "I know that your intentions are not authentic. When the pressure is gone, you will return to your old ways." Therefore, the dismissal of idol worship was ineffective, and it was necessary for Moshe to leave the city.

☐ **CHASAM SOFER:** The *Shulchan Aruch* (*Orach Chaim* 94:9) states that if a person wishes to pray in an open field, but is afraid that passersby may interrupt him, it is preferable that he pray in a place where it is clear to him that he will not be disturbed, even if there may be idols present. During all the other plagues, Moshe prayed inside the city despite the fact that it was full of idols, for fear that he would be disturbed by passersby if he prayed out in the field. After Egypt was beset with hail, however, there were no passersby in the fields and no one to interrupt him. Therefore, he prayed in the field to avoid praying in a city full of idols.

אַרְבֶּה / Locusts

The plague of Locusts harmed the Egyptians in several ways:
- The locusts entered the warehouses and decimated sacks of wheat. They entered homes and ate jewelry, clothing, and other property (*Midrash HaGadol*).
- Hashem brought blind locusts, which could not see the food they were eating. Because of their blindness, the locusts never

felt satisfied with what they had eaten, and kept eating more and more — until they had eaten every last remnant of food and nothing was left (*Rav Yehoshua Leib Diskin*).
- The land became dark.
- The locusts ate the trees.

Q What miracles took place during the plague of Locusts?

A ☐ YALKUT REUVENI: A sorcerer was able to perform only one act of magic at a time; he could not perform several acts of magic simultaneously. In the plague of locusts, Hashem sent a mixture of several species, and the sorcerers were able to create some of them, but not all.

☐ MIDRASH (*Shemos Rabbah*): The Egyptians were happy when the locusts came because they were a delicacy. They planned to fill barrels with them and eat them later. But when the plague ceased, the locusts disappeared in a powerful wind — even those already salted for eating — leaving only the land they had devastated.

☐ MIDRASH: The locusts covered the land of Egypt so that the Egyptians could not see.

☐ BIUR HAINYANIM AL HACHUMASH: The locusts' usual nature was altered in several ways:
- Normally, there is an interval of time between the locusts' arrival and their spreading throughout the land. In this plague, the locusts came, and on the very same day they spread throughout the land.
- The locusts traveled a great distance in a single day — one that would normally have taken them four days to travel.
- The locusts ate only what was left after the devastation of the hail and did not touch the vegetation that remained to the Jews in the land of Goshen, despite the fact that Goshen bordered Egypt.
- After they finished eating everything that grew, the locusts did not move on to seek other food.

☐ Only male locusts came, so that they would eat nonstop and not have to pause to lay eggs.

[171] HAGGADAH: THE ANSWER IS . . .

Q Why were the Egyptians punished with this plague?

A ☐ **KLI YAKAR:** The Egyptians attempted to cancel the blessing that Hashem gave Avraham, וְהַרְבָּה **אַרְבֶּה** אֶת זַרְעֲךָ, *I shall greatly increase your offspring* (Genesis 22:17), and said, הָבָה נִתְחַכְּמָה לוֹ פֶּן יִרְבֶּה, *Let us outsmart it lest it become numerous* (Exodus 1:10). Therefore Hashem brought the arbeh, locusts, to swarm the land.

☐ **VILNA GAON:** The Egyptians forced the Jews to plant wheat and barley, so, measure for measure, the locusts devoured the grain they had planted.

☐ **STEIPLER GAON:** Through the plagues, Hashem showed the whole world that He is Master over everything. Here Hashem showed that He also controls the wind, since the locusts flew in on a powerful east wind and, after Moshe prayed on Pharaoh's behalf, sent them away with a powerful west wind.

☐ Because the Egyptians stole the Jews' grain, they were punished with locusts that ate the Egyptians' grain.

◆§ חֹשֶׁךְ / Darkness

Q What miracles took place during the plague of Darkness?

A ☐ **YALKUT SHIMONI:** The darkness, which is normally thin and intangible, was tangible in Egypt, as the verse says, וְיָמֵשׁ חֹשֶׁךְ, *And the darkness will be tangible* (Exodus 10:21).

☐ **MIDRASH RABBAH:** The plague was divided into two parts. During the second part — the last three days — a person who sat down was unable to stand, and a person who was standing was unable to sit.

☐ **MIDRASH RABBAH:** Wherever the Jews went, there was light, so while the Egyptians were groping around like blind men, the Jews were able to see.

☐ The Egyptians did not see the wicked Jews who died during the plague of Darkness.

Q Why were the Egyptians punished with the plague of Darkness?

הגדה של פסח

A
- ☐ **MIDRASH HAGADOL:** When an Egyptian wished to read at night, he would take his slave — a Jew — place a candle on his head to provide light, and warn him to make sure that the candle did not fall. The Egyptians were punished, measure for measure, with the plague of Darkness.
- ☐ **MIDRASH** (*Shemos Rabbah*): The Egyptians were punished with darkness so that the wicked Jews who did not wish to leave Egypt could be buried without the Egyptians' knowledge.
- ☐ **KLI YAKAR:** First, because the women were forced to give birth in darkness, and second, because the Jewish people had to hide their children in the dark, as Yocheved hid Moshe.
- ☐ **CHASAM SOFER:** The Egyptians caused the Jews to be afraid of every little thing. Accordingly, during the plague of Darkness, the Egyptians were paralyzed for three days and were afraid of everything that moved.
- ☐ **VILNA GAON:** Because the Egyptians wished to imprison the Jews, Hashem brought darkness, which made the Egyptians feel like prisoners.
- ☐ **RAV YOSEF SALANT:** Hashem decreed at the Covenant Between the Parts that the Jewish people would be enslaved in Egypt, but the Egyptians heaped on additional darkness and suffering, beyond what was called for. Therefore, they were punished with "darkness-plus": both the plague itself and an additional measure of darkness.
- ☐ The plague of Darkness gave the Jews an opportunity to mark down the Egyptians' property without their knowledge, in order to make it easy for them to acquire it from the Egyptians and take it along when they left Egypt.

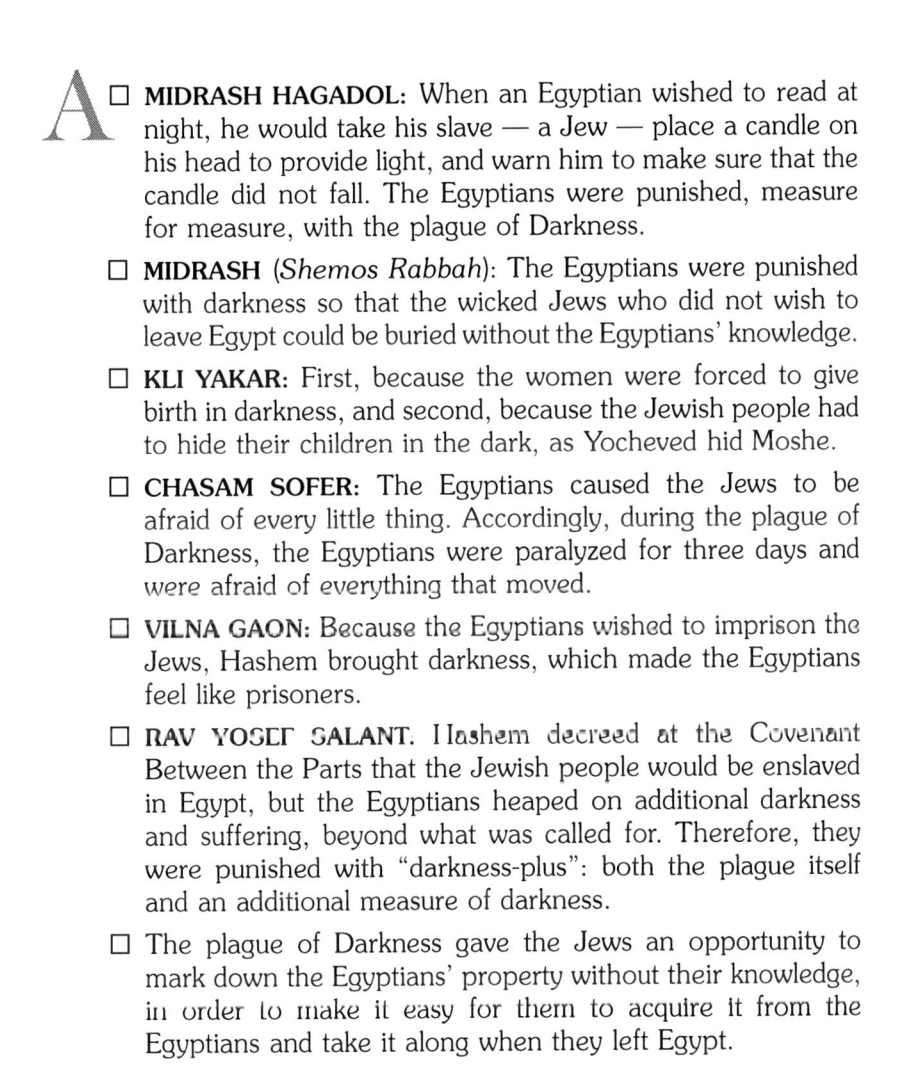

מַכַּת בְּכוֹרוֹת / *Plague of the Firstborn*

The Plague of the Firstborn harmed the Egyptians in several ways:
- Firstborn sons who were still in their mothers' wombs died, and the women miscarried.
- The firstborn of Egypt were angry over Pharaoh's refusal to free the Jews. In their fear over the coming plague, they vented their wrath by attacking their leaders and killing many of them.
- The bodies of the firstborns decayed and began spreading a great epidemic, which took a great toll on Egyptian life (*Beis HaLevi*).

רַבִּי יְהוּדָה הָיָה נוֹתֵן בָּהֶם סִמָּנִים: דְּצַ"ךְ עֲדַ"שׁ בְּאַחַ"ב.

Q *What miracles took place during the Plague of the Firstborn?*

A ☐ **MIDRASH HAGADOL:** Dogs dug up the bones of firstborn Egyptians who had died long before and brought them to their parents' homes — thus fulfilling the verse *There was no home in which there was no dead* (Exodus 12:30).
☐ Even the Egyptians who were in Jewish homes died.
☐ In a home that had no firstborn child, the oldest child died.

Q *Why were the Egyptians punished with this plague?*

A ☐ **KLI YAKAR:** The Egyptians wished to destroy the Jewish people, whom Hashem had called בְּנִי בְכֹרִי יִשְׂרָאֵל, *My firstborn son is Israel* (Exodus 4:22). Measure for measure, they were punished with the Plague of the Firstborn.

Q *Why is the tenth plague the only one with two words in its name — Makkas Bechoros — in contrast to all the other plagues, whose names do not include the word "makkas"?*

A ☐ **MIDRASH SHOCHER TOV:** When Moshe issued Hashem's warning about this impending plague, the Egyptian firstborn sons wanted to free the Jews in order to be saved. Their fathers objected, and the firstborn rebelled and killed them, as it says, לְמַכֵּה מִצְרַיִם בִּבְכוֹרֵיהֶם, *To Him Who smote Egypt through their firstborn* (Psalms 136:10). The words "*makkas bechoros*," literally, "the slaying of the firstborn," teaches that the firstborn sons themselves slayed the Egyptians.

☐ **MALBIM:** In each plague, the name alone was enough to tell us its essence. However, the word *bechoros* alone does not carry the connotation of a plague. To highlight the nature of that event, it is necessary to say *Makkas Bechoros* — the *Plague* of the Firstborn.

הגדה של פסח

Rabbi Yehudah abbreviated them by their Hebrew initials:
D'TZACH, ADASH, B'ACHAB.

☐ **BEIS HALEVI:** After the Plague of the Firstborn came an additional plague — a widespread epidemic that emanated from the rotting corpses. The two words in the name correspond to these two plagues: *makkas* — for the plague that came as a result of the slaying of the firstborn; and *bechoros* — for the slaying itself.

Q *Why did the salvation come specifically through this plague?*

A ☐ **SIFSEI CHAIM:** Hashem's salvation was particularly felt in this plague. This was the only plague in which Moshe performed no action at all. He merely sat in his house and ate of the *korban Pesach*, like the rest of the Jews. The Plague of the Firstborn was solely the result of a revelation of the Shechinah in the midst of Egypt's impurity.

৽§ רַבִּי יְהוּדָה הָיָה נוֹתֵן בָּהֶם סִמָּנִים / *Rabbi Yehudah abbreviated them by their Hebrew initials*

Q *Why did Rabbi Yehudah abbreviate the names of the plagues?*

A ☐ **RASHBATZ:** The numerical equivalent of דְּצַ"ךְ עֲדַ"שׁ בְּאַחַ"ב, D'TZACH ADASH B'ACHAB, is 501. There are several opinions cited in the Haggadah: Rabbi Yose says that the Egyptians received 50 plagues; Rabbi Eliezer, 200; and Rabbi Akiva, 250. The total of all these opinions is 500. Here, Rabbi Yehudah offers his opinion: the Egyptians were afflicted with them all, for a total of 500.

☐ **RA'AVAN:** The abbreviation is in order to teach about the plagues in a brief fashion, as Chazal say, *A person should always teach his students in a concise manner* (*Pesachim* 3b).

☐ **BARTENURA:** It was Rabbi Yehudah's way to abbreviate things. He did the same with regard to the measurements of the *lechem hapanim* (showbread) and the *shtei halechem*, the offering brought on Shavuos (*Menachos* 11:4).

- **YAAVETZ:** Because the Torah is acquired with *simanim* — abbreviations — Rabbi Yehudah saw fit to do the same here.
- **RAV YECHEZKEL ABRAMSKY:** At the Covenant Between the Parts, Hashem told Avraham that there would be three levels of exile (*Genesis* 15:13):
  1. Your offspring shall be aliens in a land not their own.
  2. They will serve them.
  3. They will oppress them.

  When the redemption came, it happened in degrees, gradually releasing the Jews from these three levels of exile. Rabbi Yehudah's abbreviations reflect this pattern:
  1. After the first three plagues, which Rabbi Yehudah refers to as *D'TZACH*, the degrading, excessive toil and oppression ceased.
  2. After the three plagues referred to as *ADASH*, the work ceased altogether.
  3. After *B'ACHAB*, the Jews left Egypt, and no longer were they aliens in a strange land.

Q. Why are the Ten Plagues divided up this way?

A.
- **SHIBBOLEI HALEKET:** In order to emphasize who brought each plague:

  D'TZACH: These plagues — Blood, Frogs, and Lice — were brought about by Aharon; these are the plagues that afflicted the land.

  ADASH: These plagues — Wild Beasts, Pestilence, and Boils — were brought about by both Moshe and Aharon; they were plagues that apparently came through nature.

  B'ACHAB: This section is divided into two parts. The first three plagues — Hail, Locusts, and Darkness — were brought about through Moshe; these are plagues that were brought by air. Then came the Plague of the Firstborn, brought by Hashem.

- **SEFORNO:** The first nine plagues were performed as signs and wonders. They are divided into three groups:

  The first group:

  D'TZACH (Blood, Frogs, Lice) — were signs that affected two of the four fundamental elements: water and earth.

[176] הגדה של פסח

The second group:

ADASH (Wild Beasts, Pestilence, Boils) — were signs using living creatures.

The third group:

B'ACH (Hail, Locusts, Darkness) — were signs that took place in the air.

☐ **RITVA:** Pharaoh denied the reality of Hashem. Rabbi Yehudah divided the plagues into groups, each of which served as a lesson for Pharaoh:

D'TZACH: These plagues (Blood, Frogs, Lice) were intended to serve as proof of Hashem's existence. That is why they each include the assertion בְּזֹאת תֵּדַע כִּי אֲנִי ה', *Through this shall you know that I am HASHEM* (Exodus 7:17).

ADASH: These plagues (Wild Beasts, Pestilence, Boils) were performed in order to prove Hashem's providence. Therefore, It says, לְמַעַן תֵּדַע כִּי אֲנִי ה' בְּקֶרֶב הָאָרֶץ, *So that you will know that I am HASHEM in the midst of the land* (Exodus 8:18).

B'ACHAB: These plagues (Hail, Locusts, Darkness, Slaying of the Firstborn) were meant to serve as proof of prophecy, as it says regarding the plague of Hail, הַיָּרֵא אֶת דְּבַר ה'...הֵנִיס אֶת עֲבָדָיו וְאֶת מִקְנֵהוּ אֶל הַבָּתִּים וַאֲשֶׁר לֹא שָׂם לִבּוֹ אֶל דְּבַר ה' יַעֲזֹב אֶת עֲבָדָיו וְאֶת מִקְנֵהוּ בַּשָּׂדֶה, *Whoever... feared the word of HASHEM chased his servants and his livestock to the houses. And whoever did not take the word of HASHEM to heart — he left his servants and his livestock in the field* (Exodus 9:20-21).

☐ **KLI YAKAR:** Hashem sent the Ten Plagues as a response to Pharaoh's denial of His existence, when he said, מִי ה' אֲשֶׁר אֶשְׁמַע בְּקֹלוֹ, *Who is HASHEM, that I should heed His voice?* (Exodus 5:2). The Ten Plagues were meant to teach Pharaoh three valuable lessons, corresponding to the three groups that Rabbi Yehudah defined with his abbreviations:

D'TZACH: In the plague of Blood, Moshe told Pharaoh, בְּזֹאת תֵּדַע כִּי אֲנִי ה', *Through this shall you know that I am HASHEM* (Exodus 7:17). In other words, Pharaoh would see that Hashem is real. He witnessed this during the plagues of Blood and Frogs, which both originated in the Nile River, the Egyptians' deity. This demonstrated that Hashem, not the Egyptian god, was in control. During the plague of Lice,

Pharaoh's necromancers acknowledged Hashem's existence, referring to the אֶצְבַּע אֱלֹהִים, *finger of God* (*Exodus* 8:15).

ADASH: Through these three plagues, in which Hashem distinguished between the Jewish people (who were not affected) and the Egyptians, Pharaoh learned that there is Divine Providence in the world. In the plague of Wild Beasts, Hashem said, וְשַׂמְתִּי פְדֻת בֵּין עַמִּי וּבֵין עַמֶּךָ, *I shall make a distinction between My people and your people* (*Exodus* 8:19). Regarding the plague of Pestilence, it says, וְהִפְלָה ה' בֵּין מִקְנֵה יִשְׂרָאֵל וּבֵין מִקְנֵה מִצְרָיִם, *HASHEM shall distinguish between the livestock of Israel and the livestock of Egypt* (*Exodus* 9:4), and in the plague of Boils — וְלֹא יָכְלוּ הַחַרְטֻמִּים לַעֲמֹד לִפְנֵי מֹשֶׁה מִפְּנֵי הַשְּׁחִין כִּי הָיָה הַשְּׁחִין בַּחַרְטֻמִּם וּבְכָל מִצְרָיִם, *The necromancers could not stand before Moshe because of the boils, because the boils were on the necromancers and on all of Egypt* (*Exodus* 9:11). Clearly, Moshe was not afflicted, while the Egyptians were.

B'ACHAB: At this stage, Pharaoh learned that Hashem rules the world by means of messengers who perform His bidding. The Egyptians, accustomed to worshiping the stars and constellations, saw that the world continued on in its usual way despite the fact that the stars were no longer visible. During the plague of Hail, the sky was covered with clouds so that the stars and constellations could not be seen. The same was true during the plague of Locusts, which *covered the surface of the entire land* (*Exodus* 10:15), and, of course, during the plague of Darkness, the sky could not be seen.

☐ **MACHZOR VITRI**: Each group of plagues was brought about in a unique way:

D'TZACH (Blood, Frogs, Lice) — by Aharon, with the staff;

ADASH (Wild Beasts, Pestilence, Boils) — by Moshe, without the staff;

B'ACHAB (Hail, Locusts, Darkness) — by Moshe, with the staff.

☐ **RAV SAMSON RAPHAEL HIRSCH**: The groupings were devised to differentiate between those plagues that came with a warning to Pharaoh from those that came without warning. In each group, the first two plagues came upon the Egyptians after a warning, while the third came with no warning, as a punishment for their not heeding the warnings of the first two plagues. Therefore:

- The plagues of Blood and Frogs came with a warning; the Lice, with no warning.
- The plagues of Wild Beasts and Pestilence came with a warning; Boils, with no warning.
- The Hail and Locusts came with a warning; the Darkness, with no warning.

☐ **BE'ER MAYIM:** Each plague that afflicted the Egyptians turned into a source of healing for the Jews. Rabbi Yehudah gave them signs in order to emphasize this point, and in each grouping the first plague provides a hint:

D'TZACH: The first plague, Blood, turned into the blood of *milah* and the *korban Pesach*.

ADASH: The first plague of this set, Wild Beasts (a mixture of wild animals), was reflected in the redemption, when the *eirev rav* (a mixture of peoples) joined the Jews in their exodus from Egypt.

B'ACHAB: The first plague in this group, Hail, turned into a great salvation during the time of Yehoshua (when Hashem rained hailstones on the Jewish people's enemies — see Yehoshua 10:11)

☐ **NESIVOS SHALOM:** The groupings teach that the plagues affected every part of creation. The first three (*D'TZACH*) were beneath the ground; they were brought through the earth itself — the dust, river, and so on. The second three (*ADASH*) affected creatures that inhabit the earth: the wild beasts that were sent to prey on the Egyptians, the cattle that contracted the pestilence, and human beings that were afflicted with the boils. The last four plagues (*B'ACHAB*) were above the ground, in the air and the sky, to proclaim that Hashem rules over the entire creation: sky, earth, and everywhere.

Q *Why did the third plague in each group (Lice, Boils, and Darkness) come with no prior warning?*

A ☐ **BA'AL HATURIM:** In each group of plagues, Hashem warned Pharaoh twice (that is, before both the first and second plagues in the set). When Pharaoh did not repent, Hashem brought a third plague without warning.

The cups are refilled. The wine that was removed is not used.

רַבִּי יוֹסֵי הַגְּלִילִי אוֹמֵר: מִנַּיִן אַתָּה אוֹמֵר שֶׁלָּקוּ הַמִּצְרִים בְּמִצְרַיִם עֶשֶׂר מַכּוֹת, וְעַל הַיָּם לָקוּ חֲמִשִּׁים מַכּוֹת? בְּמִצְרַיִם מָה הוּא אוֹמֵר, וַיֹּאמְרוּ הַחַרְטֻמִּם אֶל פַּרְעֹה, אֶצְבַּע אֱלֹהִים הִוא.[1] וְעַל הַיָּם מָה הוּא אוֹמֵר, וַיַּרְא יִשְׂרָאֵל אֶת הַיָּד הַגְּדֹלָה אֲשֶׁר עָשָׂה יהוה בְּמִצְרַיִם, וַיִּירְאוּ הָעָם אֶת יהוה, וַיַּאֲמִינוּ בַּיהוה וּבְמֹשֶׁה עַבְדּוֹ.[2] כַּמָּה לָקוּ בְאֶצְבַּע? עֶשֶׂר מַכּוֹת. אֱמוֹר מֵעַתָּה, בְּמִצְרַיִם לָקוּ עֶשֶׂר מַכּוֹת, וְעַל הַיָּם לָקוּ חֲמִשִּׁים מַכּוֹת.

רַבִּי אֱלִיעֶזֶר אוֹמֵר. מִנַּיִן שֶׁכָּל מַכָּה וּמַכָּה שֶׁהֵבִיא הַקָּדוֹשׁ בָּרוּךְ הוּא

☐ **RAMBAN:** Pharaoh received a warning only for those plagues that involved a loss of human life, because Hashem had pity on the people:

D'TZACH: During the plague of Blood, the lack of water caused Egyptians and the fish in the Nile to die. During the plague of Frogs, the frogs emasculated the Egyptians (*Shemos Rabbah* 10:4).

ADASH: The wild beasts endangered human life, and the pestilence epidemic affected the people as well.

B'ACHAB: The hail was made up of fire and water that struck the people and endangered their lives. The locusts ate whatever growing things remained after the hail wreaked its destruction, and the Egyptians and remaining livestock starved.

For the plagues that were not a threat to any creature's life, however (Lice, Boils, and Darkness), there was no prior warning.

◆§ רַבִּי יוֹסֵי הַגְּלִילִי אוֹמֵר / *Rabbi Yose the Galilean said*

This passage compares the plagues that the Egyptians received in Egypt and those that they received at the Reed Sea in accordance with

The cups are refilled. The wine that was removed is not used.

Rabbi Yose the Galilean said: How does one derive that the Egyptians were struck with ten plagues in Egypt, but with fifty plagues at the sea? — Concerning the plagues in Egypt the Torah states: The magicians said to Pharaoh, "It is the finger of God."[1] However, of those at the sea, the Torah relates: Israel saw the great "hand" which HASHEM laid upon the Egyptians, the people feared HASHEM, and they believed in HASHEM and in His servant Moshe.[2] How many plagues did they receive with the finger? Ten! Then conclude that if they suffered ten plagues in Egypt [where they were struck with a finger], they must have been made to suffer fifty plagues at the sea [where they were struck with a whole hand].

Rabbi Eliezer said: How does one derive that every plague that the Holy One, Blessed is He, inflicted

---

1. *Exodus* 8:15. 2. Ibid. 14:31.

---

the opinions of Rabbi Yose HaGlili, Rabbi Eliezer, and Rabbi Akiva. The source of these three teachings is the *Mechilta D'Rabbi Yishmael* (*Beshalach* 6).

This passage actually has no direct connection with the Seder night, since it does not deal with the Exodus from Egypt, but rather with the splitting of the Reed Sea. However, since the splitting of the sea is the direct sequel to the Exodus, we mention the punishments that the Egyptians received at the sea as well.

Since the Rambam was of the opinion that on this night the obligation is to relate only the miracles that took place in Egypt, and not the plagues that beset the Egyptians at the Reed Sea, this passage does not appear in the Rambam's Haggadah.

This is the only place in the entire Haggadah where Moshe Rabbeinu's name is mentioned — and even then, only in the form of a hint, as part of a verse in Rabbi Yose's statement. There are versions of the Haggadah that omit this paragraph entirely (the Haggadah of the *Geonim* and the Rambam's Haggadah), so that Moshe Rabbeinu's name does not appear at all. (For the reason the Haggadah leaves out Moshe's name, see page 38.)

[181] **HAGGADAH: THE ANSWER IS . . .**

עַל הַמִּצְרִים בְּמִצְרַיִם הָיְתָה שֶׁל אַרְבַּע מַכּוֹת? שֶׁנֶּאֱמַר, יְשַׁלַּח בָּם חֲרוֹן אַפּוֹ — עֶבְרָה, וָזַעַם, וְצָרָה, מִשְׁלַחַת מַלְאֲכֵי רָעִים.[1] עֶבְרָה, אַחַת. וָזַעַם, שְׁתַּיִם. וְצָרָה, שָׁלֹשׁ. מִשְׁלַחַת מַלְאֲכֵי רָעִים, אַרְבַּע. אֱמוֹר מֵעַתָּה, בְּמִצְרַיִם לָקוּ אַרְבָּעִים מַכּוֹת, וְעַל הַיָּם לָקוּ מָאתַיִם מַכּוֹת.

רַבִּי עֲקִיבָא אוֹמֵר. מִנַּיִן שֶׁכָּל מַכָּה וּמַכָּה שֶׁהֵבִיא הַקָּדוֹשׁ בָּרוּךְ הוּא עַל הַמִּצְרִים בְּמִצְרַיִם הָיְתָה שֶׁל חָמֵשׁ מַכּוֹת? שֶׁנֶּאֱמַר, יְשַׁלַּח בָּם חֲרוֹן אַפּוֹ, עֶבְרָה, וָזַעַם, וְצָרָה, מִשְׁלַחַת מַלְאֲכֵי רָעִים. חֲרוֹן אַפּוֹ, אַחַת. עֶבְרָה, שְׁתַּיִם. וָזַעַם, שָׁלֹשׁ. וְצָרָה, אַרְבַּע. מִשְׁלַחַת מַלְאֲכֵי רָעִים, חָמֵשׁ. אֱמוֹר מֵעַתָּה, בְּמִצְרַיִם לָקוּ חֲמִשִּׁים מַכּוֹת, וְעַל הַיָּם לָקוּ חֲמִשִּׁים וּמָאתַיִם מַכּוֹת.

Q Why does Rabbi Eliezer not include the words חֲרוֹן אַפּוֹ, *His fierce anger*, in his calculation?

A
- **AVUDRAHAM:** The words *charon apo* — *His anger* — are the only ones in the verse written as a possessive noun. Rabbi Eliezer counted only the words that were written as a simple noun.

- **MALBIM:** There is a difference of opinion regarding whether or not the opening phrases are included when making such calculations (*Sukkah* 6). In Rabbi Eliezer's view, the words *charon apo* should not be included; therefore, he begins his calculation with the word *evrah*, wrath. Rabbi Akiva, on the other hand, is of the view that we do begin with the opening phrase, which is why he begins counting the plagues from the words *charon apo*.

- **ALTER OF KELM:** *Charon* is a general term for anger, as we find in the episode of the sin of the golden calf: וַיִּחַר אַף מֹשֶׁה, *Moshe's anger flared up* (*Exodus* 32:19). Rabbi Eliezer is of the opinion that here too *charon* is a general term for anger, upon the Egyptians in Egypt was equal to four plagues? — for it is written: He sent upon them His fierce anger: wrath, fury, and trouble, a band of emissaries of evil.[1] [Since each plague in Egypt consisted of] 1) wrath, 2) fury, 3) trouble, and 4) a band of emissaries of evil, therefore conclude that in Egypt they were struck by forty plagues and at the sea by two hundred!

Rabbi Akiva said: How does one derive that each plague that the Holy One, Blessed is He, inflicted upon the Egyptians in Egypt was equal to five plagues? — for it is written: He sent upon them His fierce anger, wrath, fury, trouble, and a band of emissaries of evil. [Since each plague in Egypt consisted of] 1) fierce anger, 2) wrath, 3) fury, 4) trouble, and 5) a band of emissaries of evil, therefore conclude that in Egypt they were struck by fifty plagues and at the sea by two hundred and fifty!

1. *Psalms* 78:49.

---

and the rest — the *evrah*, *za'am*, and so on — describe the actual punishments that came about as a result of that anger. Therefore he counts only these four terms.

Q What is the nature of the dispute between Rabbi Yose, Rabbi Eliezer, and Rabbi Akiva in this passage?

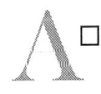

A ☐ RA'AVAN: The Sages disagree about the number of plagues that took place in Egypt and at the sea. They derive their sum totals from two verses. Regarding the plagues in Egypt it says, אֶצְבַּע אֱלֹהִים הִוא, *It is the finger of God!* (*Exodus* 8:15) and regarding the miracles at the sea, it says, וַיַּרְא יִשְׂרָאֵל אֶת הַיָּד הַגְּדֹלָה אֲשֶׁר עָשָׂה ה' בְּמִצְרַיִם, *Israel saw the great hand which HASHEM laid upon the Egyptians* (ibid. 14:31).

Rabbi Yose HaGlili expounds that in Egypt the Egyptians were struck with ten plagues, and at the sea they were struck with 50 plagues. This is because each plague in Egypt is compared to a *finger of God*, while regarding the miracle at the Sea of Reeds, the verse refers to *the great hand*. Since a hand has five fingers, we multiply the ten plagues by five to get a total of 50 plagues at the sea.

Rabbi Eliezer adds that there were four forms of punishment in each plague: עֶבְרָה אַחַת, וָזַעַם שְׁתַּיִם, וְצָרָה שָׁלֹשׁ, מִשְׁלַחַת מַלְאֲכֵי רָעִים אַרְבַּע, (1) wrath, (2) fury, (3) trouble, and (4) a band of emissaries of evil. He multiplies Rabbi Yose's total by four and concludes that the Egyptians were struck with 200 plagues (4 x 50).

Rabbi Akiva joins his own opinion to that of Rabbi Eliezer, but believes that there were five punishments instead of four. The fifth was חֲרוֹן אַפּוֹ, *His fierce anger*. According to this, the total of plagues was 250 (5 x 50).

☐ **RASHBATZ:** Rabbi Eliezer agrees with Rabbi Yose HaGlili that the Egyptians were struck with five times the number of plagues at the sea as they had received in Egypt. He adds, however, that each plague consisted of four punishments, since everything is made up of four fundamental elements. In his view, every one of these fundamental elements was afflicted and constitutes a separate plague; thus he multiplies Rabbi Yose's total of fifty by four to get a total of 200 plagues. Rabbi Akiva, on the other hand, believes that there was also a fifth fundamental element in each plague, making a total of 250 plagues.

☐ **MA'ASEH NISSIM:** The four fundamental elements dominated each plague. Rabbi Eliezer is of the opinion that only these four elements dominated, while in Rabbi Akiva's view the power of the plague itself added to the affliction, constituting a plague in itself.

Q *Why was it necessary to count — and increase — the number of plagues that the Egyptians received?*

A ☐ It says, כָּל הַמַּחֲלָה אֲשֶׁר שַׂמְתִּי בְמִצְרַיִם לֹא אָשִׂים עָלֶיךָ, *Any of the diseases that I placed in Egypt, I will not bring upon you* (Exodus 15:26). This condition demands that there be many plagues and diseases brought upon Egypt to underscore that we will not suffer from them. The more plagues we can find, the more we will not receive ourselves.

Q *On the Seder night, when the focus is the story of the Exodus, why do we recall the splitting of the sea, which took place on the seventh day of Pesach?*

A ☐ **NETZIV:** The Seder night is a pillar in the structure of our faith in Hashem. The story of the splitting of the sea is one chapter that was a part of this faith-building process. Therefore, it makes sense to include it in our retelling of the Exodus.

☐ Had the splitting of the sea been mentioned only on the seventh day of Pesach, it would have appeared as if we were joyous over the calamity that befell the Egyptians. Even though they were evil, they were still Hashem's creations, as He said to the angels when they wanted to rejoice over the Egyptians' drowning, "My creations are drowning in the sea, and you are singing?" Instead, we mention the miracles at the sea during the Seder, as part of the miracles of the Exodus. This way our joy over the Egyptians' demise does not stand out. It is clear that we are rejoicing over our salvation, and not the Egyptians' drowning.

Q *Why were the Egyptians afflicted with additional plagues at the Sea of Reeds? Why did they not receive all the plagues in Egypt?*

A ☐ **VAYAGED L'AVRAHAM:** In Egypt, the Egyptians had the merit of hosting the Jews, as it says, לֹא תְתַעֵב מִצְרִי כִּי גֵר הָיִיתָ בְאַרְצוֹ, *You shall not reject an Egyptian, for you were a sojourner in his land* (Deuteronomy 23:8). Since they had this merit, they received only ten plagues in the land. At the sea, however, after they had left their land to chase after the Jewish people, this merit could not help them.

☐ **ROKEACH:** One of the 200 punishments that the Egyptians received was for the sin of idol worship. However, the Jewish people, too, had worshiped idols in Egypt. To make sure that the Jews would not be punished as well, the Egyptians were stricken at the Sea of Reeds, when the Jewish people had repented and there was no longer a claim against them.

☐ **RAV SHLOMO BREVDA:** This was the Egyptians' punishment for the brazenness they displayed in going out in pursuit of the Jewish people to wage war with them, even after witnessing the great miracles in Egypt.

Q *Why was the Jewish people's faith in Hashem stronger at the sea than after the Ten Plagues?*

[185] **HAGGADAH: THE ANSWER IS . . .**

A ☐ **MIDRASH RABBAH:** When the Jewish people emerged from the sea, the Shechinah rested on them, and they were on a higher spiritual plane than they had been in Egypt. Thus, they were more capable of seeing the hand of God at the sea than they had been in Egypt.

☐ **MIDRASH RABBAH:** In Egypt, the Jews observed the miracles that Hashem performed during each plague — but their vision was a general one. In contrast, at the splitting of the sea, their vision was detailed and specific, as the verse says, וַיַּרְא יִשְׂרָאֵל אֶת מִצְרַיִם **מֵת** עַל שְׂפַת הַיָּם, *Israel saw the Egyptians dead on the seashore* (Exodus 14:30). The verse uses the word *meis*, dead, in the singular form, indicating that every Jew witnessed the death of the particular Egyptian who had oppressed him. This strengthened their faith.

☐ **KSAV SOFER:** At the sea, the Jewish people saw Hashem punish the Egyptians, measure for measure, for their decree to hurl the Jewish children into the river. This strengthened their faith.

☐ **CHAFETZ CHAIM:** While Egyptians throughout the land were equally afflicted with the Ten Plagues, at the sea not everyone was punished to the same degree. Each was judged according to his level of wickedness. The truly wicked were tossed about by the sea, so that it took a long time for them to drown. Those who were less wicked sank like lead and drowned immediately. The Jewish people saw the Divine Providence in this, and their faith was strengthened.

☐ **RAV MENACHEM MENDEL OF KOTZK:** During the Ten Plagues, there were those who doubted, wondering if the miracles were no more than coincidence. When they reached the sea, and were suffused with awe of Hashem, they understood that it had all come about through Divine Providence: *Israel saw...and they believed* (Exodus 14:31).

☐ **NOAM ELIMELECH:** As long as the ministering angel of Egypt was alive, a "curtain" separated the Jewish people from Hashem. But when the Egyptians died at the sea (and their angel along with them), the divider dropped away and the Jews' eyes were opened. They saw *the great hand* of Hashem and were strengthened in their faith.

☐ The purpose of the Ten Plagues that were inflicted on Egypt was primarily to remove the impurity of Egypt. The miracles at the sea, on the other hand, had a different purpose. They were aimed primarily at the Jewish people, to elevate their level of faith in order to prepare them for the revelations at Mount Sinai.

Q Why is the order not reversed, first faith and then fear of Hashem?

A ☐ **ALTER OF KELM:** At times, even a believer experiences moments of doubt. Witnessing the splitting of the sea suffused the Jewish people with awe and brought them to a higher level of faith.

☐ **RAV MOSHE STERNBUCH:** Some declare that they believe in Hashem even though they do not keep the mitzvos. This verse demonstrates that without *yiras Shamayim*, fear of Heaven, it is not truly possible to believe in Hashem.

☐ **RAV YECHEZKEL LEVENSTEIN:** The verse is telling us that the Jewish people merited seeing Hashem's conduct and the miracles He performed, so that not even a tiny whisper of doubt entered their minds. The awe they felt at seeing the miracles filled them with pure faith in Hashem.

☐ **RAV ITZELE OF VOLOZHIN:** Pharaoh consistently tried to undermine the Jews' faith in Hashem and in Moshe, His messenger. As part of this campaign, he told them that Hashem had not commanded Moshe to take them out of Egypt. This gave rise to doubts and an undermining of the Jews' faith. After the splitting of the sea, when they saw the mighty hand of God, they were filled with awe. Now, finally, the Jews believed completely in Hashem and knew that Moshe had been righteous and had not spoken on his own initiative.

Q Why did the Jews sing and praise Hashem only after the splitting of the sea, and not after they left Egypt?

A ☐ **YERUSHALMI** (*Pesachim*): The redemption was not yet complete after the Exodus from Egypt. It was only completed after the Jewish people crossed the sea and expressed their gratitude to Hashem.

☐ **RAV YISRAEL OF RUZHIN:** The Jewish people experienced other miracles in the desert, but they did not sing about them. They sang after the splitting of the sea because it was

כַּמָּה מַעֲלוֹת טוֹבוֹת לַמָּקוֹם עָלֵינוּ.
אִלּוּ הוֹצִיאָנוּ מִמִּצְרַיִם
וְלֹא עָשָׂה בָּהֶם שְׁפָטִים דַּיֵּנוּ.

only after that great milestone that they achieved a level of perfect faith.

☐ **BEN ISH CHAI:** Although the Jewish people had seen the plagues, they were afraid they might be forced to return to Egypt This fear lingered even after they left Egypt. When they saw the dead Egyptians washed up on the shores of the sea, they finally understood that the redemption was complete, and they sang out in praise and gratitude.

☐ **SIFSEI CHAIM:** The Jews also sang before the sea split, but those songs revolved around the ordinary workings of nature. At the sea, they saw extraordinary miracles that totally overturned the laws of nature and they understood Hashem's power and His rule, which rises above nature. For this reason, Hashem recorded the song that they sang at the sea for all generations.

◆§ דַּיֵּנוּ / *It would have sufficed us*

This passage lists fifteen favors that Hashem did for us in Egypt and since. It emphasizes that even had He done just one of those favors, "*dayeinu!*" — it would have sufficed. Therefore, *how much more so should we be grateful to the Omnipresent for all the numerous favors He showered upon us.* The *Rashba* points out that this list of favors that Hashem did for us, and the notion that we have not thanked Him properly, strengthens our need to thank Him as He ought to be thanked.

Rav Yechezkel Levenstein urges us not to make the error of thinking that when we say *Dayeinu,* we are saying that one miracle would have been enough and we are therefore only thanking Hashem for one of the miracles He did for us. Rather, our intention is to say that even if Hashem had performed only one miracle, that would be enough to obligate us in unending gratitude and service.

Q *Why does this passage follow the discussion of the three Sages' opinions concerning the number of plagues the Egyptians received in Egypt and at the sea?*

The Omnipresent has bestowed so many favors upon us!

Had He brought us out of Egypt,
but not executed judgments against the Egyptians,
it would have sufficed us.

A ☐ **PEIRUSH KADMON:** Both passages involve counting miracles that Hashem did for us. After discussing how the three sages calculated the number of plagues, with each of them adding more and more plagues to the count, the Haggadah begins this section by listing all the favors that Hashem does for our benefit, which is constantly multiplied, and proceeds to count them.

☐ **RASHBATZ:** This passage is a conclusion to the explanation of the four verses that begin with אֲרַמִּי אֹבֵד אָבִי, *An Aramean attempted to destroy my father*, taken from the *Mikra Bikkurim*, the declaration said upon bringing the first fruits to the Beis HaMikdash. In the Torah, this declaration concludes with the words וַיְבִאֵנוּ אֶל הַמָּקוֹם הַזֶּה וַיִּתֶּן לָנוּ אֶת הָאָרֶץ הַזֹּאת, *He brought us to this place, and He gave us this land* (Deuteronomy 26:10). Therefore, at the end of *Dayeinu*, we mention Eretz Yisrael as one of the favors that Hashem bestowed upon us.

☐ **ABARBANEL:** Some say that this passage was said by Rabbi Akiva, as a continuation of his statement, *Therefore conclude that in Egypt they were struck by fifty plagues and at the sea by 250!* By continuing with *Dayeinu*, we are reminded of the many kindnesses that Hashem did for us as a result of the Exodus.

Q *What is the meaning of the word "ma'alos" (translated here as "favors"), used in this introduction to Dayeinu?*

A ☐ **MALBIM:** The word here means praise and glory, as in *l'alei* (לְעַלֵה) *u'lekaleis*, to exalt and to sing praises — to thank Hashem for every good thing that He has done for us.

☐ **MAHARAL:** "*Ma'alos*" are advantages — referring to the benefits and advantages that are inherent in every favor that Hashem does, even more than the one that preceded it.

[189] **HAGGADAH: THE ANSWER IS . . .**

- **ABARBANEL:** It means favors — how many favors Hashem did for us in rescuing us!
- **ARUCH HASHULCHAN:** "*Ma'alos*" refers to extra things that Hashem does. Hashem promised that He would redeem the Jewish people, and He could have done just that. In His love for us, however, He did more, as we spell out in this section and for which we express our gratitude.

Q: Why do we mention specifically fifteen favors, and why these?

A:
- **RI BEN YAKAR:** It corresponds to fifteen miracles that were performed for our forefathers.
- **YAAVETZ:** The number fifteen corresponds to the fifteen steps in the Beis HaMikdash, on which the Levi'im stood when they played their instruments and sang.
- **RITVA:** It corresponds to the numerical value of Hashem's Name in the words כִּי בְּיָהּ ה' צוּר עוֹלָמִים, *For in God, HASHEM, is the strength of the worlds* (Yeshayahu 26:4). The Name is spelled with a *yud* and a *hei*, whose numerical values are 10 and 5, which total 15.
- **MAHARAL:** They are divided into three groups of five favors each:
  - The first five deal with the Exodus, when the Jews no longer suffered the Egyptians' oppression.
  - The next five deal with the miracles that were performed for the Jewish people in the desert.
  - The last five deal with the goal of our connection to Hashem.
- **VILNA GAON:** The number fifteen corresponds to the fifteen levels of Heaven, from the earth to the Throne of Glory.
- **ALTER OF KELM:** Fifteen corresponds to the fifteen attributes listed from *v'yatziv* to *v'yafeh*, after *Krias Shema* of *Shacharis*.
- **RAV CHAIM BERLIN:** It corresponds to the different ways that we see Hashem's *hashgachah*:

  He took us out of Egypt and executed judgments against [the Egyptians] — proclaiming that He controls nature, which we will relate to future generations.

And executed judgments against their gods — proclaiming that He is the mightiest of all powers.

And slayed their firstborn — one who is bereft of faith does not escape punishment.

And gave us their wealth — through Divine Providence, the Egyptians gave away their wealth and did not prevent the Jews from leaving.

And split the sea for us — an awesome miracle, revealing Hashem's providence in a situation that ran counter to nature.

And led us through [the sea] on dry land — Divine Providence was seen not only in the Jews' rescue, but also in the small details; for example, their clothes and feet did not get muddy.

And drowned our oppressors in it — the faith of the Jewish people was strengthened, as each witnessed the drowning of the particular Egyptian who had oppressed him.

And provided for our needs in the desert for forty years — counter to logic and nature, Hashem supplied the needs of the Jewish people over the course of forty years in the desert, teaching us a powerful lesson in faith.

And fed us the manna — the Jewish people saw clear evidence of Divine Providence every day, as each person received exactly as much as he needed to eat.

And gave us Shabbos — this was the fulfillment of the promise שֵׁשֶׁת יָמִים תַּעֲבֹד וְעָשִׂיתָ כָל מְלַאכְתֶּךָ, *Six days shall you... accomplish all your work* (Exodus 20:9); that is, without feeling any lack.

And brought us close to Mount Sinai — to see that there exists none but Him.

And gave us the Torah — which teaches us to believe in and trust Hashem.

And brought us into the Land of Israel — a land that Hashem watches over in a special way.

And built the Temple for us — the place that connects us to Hashem.

☐ **MA'ASEI HASHEM:** All the fundamental principles of the Torah are included in these fifteen things, according to the Rambam's approach:

אִלּוּ עָשָׂה בָהֶם שְׁפָטִים וְלֹא עָשָׂה בֵאלֹהֵיהֶם דַּיֵּנוּ.

He brought us out of Egypt teaches the existence of Hashem.
And executed judgments against [the Egyptians] shows Hashem's unity.
And led us through [the sea] on dry land teaches about reward and punishment.
And gave us the Torah emphasizes the giving of Torah from Heaven.
And executed judgments against their gods teaches that only Hashem is deserving of worship, and none other.
And gave us the Shabbos teaches that Hashem is first, before creation existed.
And brought us close to Mount Sinai shows that Hashem has no body.
And gave us their wealth demonstrates the power of prophecy — Hashem made a promise to Avraham, and He fulfilled it.
And split the sea for us teaches that there was never another prophet like Moshe, in whom the Jewish people believed.
And slayed their firstborn demonstrates Hashem's knowledge: He distinguished between the firstborn of the Jews and those of the Egyptians.
And brought us into the Land of Israel relates to the coming of Mashiach, when all of *Klal Yisrael* will reunite in Eretz Yisrael.

☐ It corresponds to the fifteen psalms beginning with the words *Shir HaMa'alos* in *sefer Tehillim* (120–134).

☐ It corresponds to the fifteen generations from Avraham Avinu to Shlomo HaMelech, who built the first Beis HaMikdash.

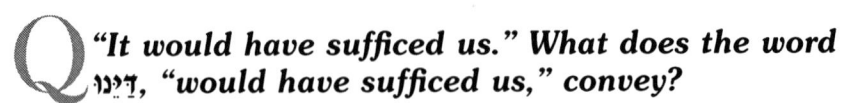

Q *"It would have sufficed us."* What does the word דַּיֵּנוּ, *"would have sufficed us,"* convey?

A ☐ **AVUDRAHAM:** It means that this favor alone would have been enough for us.

הגדה של פסח [192]

> Had He executed judgments against them,
> but not upon their gods, it would have sufficed us.

- ☐ **RITVA:** The word means we are not deserving of more than this. It is this sense of unworthiness that leads to saying, "Enough!"
- ☐ **MA'ASEI HASHEM:** The word is in fact a question: Was it possible to achieve perfection without these favors? All these things were crucial for the Jewish people to achieve perfection. Without them, we would have resembled the rest of the nations of the world. At each stage enumerated here, we gained something new that helped us achieve perfection, and so we ask, *Would it have sufficed for us?*
- ☐ **MALBIM:** The word conveys that even if there had been only one favor, it would have been reason enough to praise Hashem. How much more so should we respond with abundant praise when He has showered His many favors on us.
- ☐ **RAV YECHEZKEL LEVENSTEIN:** It tells us that had there been just one miracle, it would have been enough to strengthen our faith. How much more so when so many miracles occurred!

Q *Why do we say, Had He brought us out of Egypt, but not executed judgments against them, it would have sufficed us? Did Hashem not promise Avraham,* וְגַם אֶת הַגּוֹי אֲשֶׁר יַעֲבֹדוּ דָּן אָנֹכִי, *But also the nation that they will serve, I shall judge (Genesis 15:14)?*

A ☐ **AVUDRAHAM:** By the terms of Hashem's promise, the judgment could have been executed on only a portion of the Egyptians and not all of them. We thank Hashem for executing judgments against all of them.
- ☐ **NODA BIYEHUDAH:** The Jewish people were enslaved to Egypt for only 210 years, and not for the full 400 that Hashem had promised. Therefore, one might have thought that there was no obligation to punish the Egyptians at the earlier time that the Jews left.

אִלּוּ עָשָׂה בֵאלֹהֵיהֶם
וְלֹא הָרַג אֶת בְּכוֹרֵיהֶם — דַּיֵּנוּ.
אִלּוּ הָרַג אֶת בְּכוֹרֵיהֶם
וְלֹא נָתַן לָנוּ אֶת מָמוֹנָם — דַּיֵּנוּ.
אִלּוּ נָתַן לָנוּ אֶת מָמוֹנָם
וְלֹא קָרַע לָנוּ אֶת הַיָּם — דַּיֵּנוּ.
אִלּוּ קָרַע לָנוּ אֶת הַיָּם
וְלֹא הֶעֱבִירָנוּ בְתוֹכוֹ בֶּחָרָבָה — דַּיֵּנוּ.
אִלּוּ הֶעֱבִירָנוּ בְתוֹכוֹ בֶּחָרָבָה
וְלֹא שִׁקַּע צָרֵינוּ בְּתוֹכוֹ — דַּיֵּנוּ.

Q Why is there a special emphasis on the Plague of the Firstborn, more than for the other plagues?

A ☐ MA'ASEH NISSIM: During this plague, there was a distinction between those who were firstborn and those who were not. This distinction particularly highlighted Hashem's providence, since He — and only He — could determine who was firstborn.

☐ RAV MEIR LEHMANN: This plague encapsulates one's faith in Hashem and His conduct of the world. During this plague, the Egyptians saw without any doubt that Hashem had watched over the Jewish nation through all the previous years, even while they were in bondage.

Q To whose wealth do we refer when we say "their wealth"?

A ☐ RA'AVAN: It refers to the wealth of Egypt.

☐ RASHBAM: It means the wealth of the Egyptians at the sea, which Hashem had promised Avraham at the Covenant Between the Parts.

☐ PEIRUSH KADMON: It refers to the firstborns' money.

Had He executed judgments against their gods,
but not slain their firstborn,
it would have sufficed us.
Had He slain their firstborn,
but not given us their wealth,
it would have sufficed us.
Had He given us their wealth,
but not split the sea for us,
it would have sufficed us.
Had He split the sea for us,
but not led us through it on dry land,
it would have sufficed us.

Q *Why do we say it would have sufficed if the sea had not been split? If not for that miracle, the Egyptians would have caught up with the Jewish people and destroyed them.*

A ☐ ABARBANEL: Hashem could have caused Pharaoh not to pursue the Jews at all.

☐ KOL BO: Hashem could have rescued us in a different manner, without splitting the sea.

Q *Which miracles took place at the sea?*

A ☐ • The waters split.
- The sea became like a tent, and the Jewish people walked inside.
- The seabed became dry when the Jews passed through, while it was transformed into mud when the Egyptians came, making it hard for them to walk on the seabed.
- The water froze on the seabed like orderly rows of bricks.
- The sea split into twelve tunnels, one for each tribe.
- When the Jewish people drank from the seawater, it tasted sweet.

[195] **HAGGADAH: THE ANSWER IS . . .**

אִלּוּ שִׁקַּע צָרֵינוּ בְּתוֹכוֹ
וְלֹא סִפֵּק צָרְכֵּנוּ בַּמִּדְבָּר אַרְבָּעִים שָׁנָה דַּיֵּנוּ.
אִלּוּ סִפֵּק צָרְכֵּנוּ בַּמִּדְבָּר אַרְבָּעִים שָׁנָה
וְלֹא הֶאֱכִילָנוּ אֶת הַמָּן דַּיֵּנוּ.

Q *Which miracles took place in connection with the mann?*

A ☐ • The *mann* nourished the Jewish people for forty years in the desert. It fell continuously during all that time, without a break.

Had he led us through it [the sea] on dry land, but not drowned our oppressors in it

This can be compared to a great artist who, at the king's behest, painted a portrait of the king's horse. When the painting was done, the king hung the picture in the city square for the public to see. To his astonishment, no one paid the slightest attention to it!

The king asked a wise friend to explain this mystery to him.

"Do you know why the people are ignoring that marvelous painting?" his friend asked. "It is because it is so amazingly accurate that it appears to the people to be a real horse! It never enters their minds that the horse standing before them is nothing but a painting.

"If it is Your Majesty's wish that the people take note of the wonderful painting—cut it in half. Then everyone will understand that it is a painting and not a living horse, and they will marvel at that exquisite work of art."

The king did as his friend advised. When the people saw the cut-up "horse," they realized that it was in fact a painting, and marveled at it.

Similarly, Hashem created the world as a wondrous place. There are oceans, continents, a sun, a moon, stars, and everything else that the universe contains. Man is not moved by creation because Hashem's creativity is so much greater than that of any artist. While a human artist can fool the eye, when one feels the painting with his fingers he realizes that it is nothing but paint on canvas. Hashem, in contrast, can "fool" even our sense of touch. We see, and we touch, and we still think it is all "nature." This is how Hashem conceals His hand and His providence.

When Hashem split the sea in two, everyone saw that it was His will that made it a sea and His will that transformed the sea into dry land—and Moshe and the people sang His praises.

הגדה של פסח [196]

Had He led us through it on dry land,
but not drowned our oppressors in it,
                                                      it would have sufficed us.
Had He drowned our oppressors in it,
but not provided for our needs in the desert
for forty years,   it would have sufficed us.
Had He provided for our needs in the desert
for forty years, but not fed us the manna,
                                                      it would have sufficed us.

- It was precisely enough for each person. If someone took more than his share, the *mann* became wormy and moldy.
- On *erev Shabbos*, a double portion fell so they would have food for Shabbos. The *mann* that was saved for Shabbos did not turn wormy or moldy.
- No *mann* fell on Shabbos.
- The *mann* that was kept in a container for safekeeping for future generations did not melt in the heat of the sun.
- The *mann* did not lie on the ground, but rather at a height of two *amos*, so that the Jews did not have to bend over to pick it up.
- The *mann* was an all-encompassing food that included all the tastes in the world.

Q What were the benefits of eating the mann?

A
- ☐ **YAAVETZ:** It was entirely absorbed into the body, so there was no need for the process of excretion.
- ☐ **MA'ASEH NISSIM:** It was the food of angels. The *mann* helped the Jewish people purify themselves in advance of receiving of the Torah.
- ☐ **NETZIV:** The *mann* was a great lesson in having trust in Hashem, since the Jews went to sleep every night knowing that there was no food for tomorrow. They had to eat all of the *mann* that fell that day, without leaving any over. Despite this, they had faith in Hashem's promise that they would have food to eat the next day.

[197] **HAGGADAH: THE ANSWER IS . . .**

אִלּוּ הֶאֱכִילָנוּ אֶת הַמָּן
וְלֹא נָתַן לָנוּ אֶת הַשַּׁבָּת דַּיֵּנוּ.
אִלּוּ נָתַן לָנוּ אֶת הַשַּׁבָּת
וְלֹא קֵרְבָנוּ לִפְנֵי הַר סִינַי דַּיֵּנוּ.
אִלּוּ קֵרְבָנוּ לִפְנֵי הַר סִינַי
וְלֹא נָתַן לָנוּ אֶת הַתּוֹרָה דַּיֵּנוּ.

Q *What is the connection between eating the mann and keeping Shabbos?*

A ☐ **RASHI:** Regarding the verse וַיְבָרֶךְ אֱלֹהִים אֶת יוֹם הַשְּׁבִיעִי, *God blessed the seventh day* (Genesis 2:3), Chazal tell us, "They recited a blessing over the *mann*; they made Kiddush over the *mann*."

☐ **RAV AVIGDOR NEBENZAHL:** Though the *mann* fell every weekday, we perform certain acts in commemoration of the *mann* specifically on Shabbos — for example, saying a blessing over *lechem mishnah*, eating three *seudos*, and covering the challos. We find that the *mann* and Shabbos are linked when Moshe said to the Jewish people regarding the *mann*, רְאוּ כִּי ה' נָתַן לָכֶם הַשַּׁבָּת, *See that HASHEM has given you the Sabbath* (Exodus 16:29). Both the miracles of the *mann* and Shabbos serve as a testimony to the perfect functioning of creation.

☐ **RAV MEIR LEHMANN:** The *mann* signaled when Shabbos was coming in the desert. They knew that on the day they collected a double portion, it was time to prepare for Shabbos.

☐ **RABBI SCHORR:** On Shabbos, one can derive *ruchniyus* (spirituality) from eating physical food. In the case of the *mann* as well, the physical food turned into spiritual sustenance.

Q *Out of all of the 613 mitzvos, why is Shabbos the only mitzvah enumerated here?*

A ☐ **ORCHOS CHAIM:** The intention here is not to emphasize the qualities of Shabbos, but rather to describe the qualities of the *mann*. The special qualities of the *mann* were more easily recognizable through Shabbos, since it did not fall on

Had He fed us the manna,
but not given us the Shabbos,
> it would have sufficed us.

Had He given us the Shabbos,
but not brought us close to Mount Sinai,
> it would have sufficed us.

Had He brought us close to Mount Sinai,
but not given us the Torah,
> it would have sufficed us.

Shabbos. Instead, two portions fell on erev Shabbos, and the extra portion did not become infested with worms.

- ☐ **RA'AVAN:** Shabbos symbolizes the covenant between the Jewish people and *HaKadosh Baruch Hu*, which was made before they stood at Har Sinai — in Marah. For this reason, the Haggadah specifically mentions Shabbos as one of the favors that Hashem did for us.
- ☐ **MA'ASEH NISSIM:** Shabbos is considered the equivalent of all the mitzvos combined.
- ☐ **SHIBBOLEI HALEKET:** Shabbos is the day about which our Sages tell us, "*Me'ein Olam Haba*" — it is a taste of the World to Come. Because of this special quality, it is mentioned as one of the special favors that Hashem showed us.
- ☐ **HASHIR V'HASHEVACH:** Shabbos is the basis of our faith. Without it, we could not have received the Torah, as we say immediately afterward in this passage: *Had He given us the Sabbath, but not brought us before Mount Sinai, it would have sufficed us.*

Q *"Had He brought us before Mount Sinai, but not given us the Torah, it would have sufficed us." What would have been the purpose of standing before Mount Sinai without receiving the Torah?*

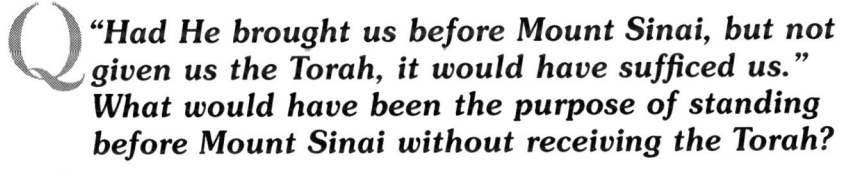

A ☐ **TALMUD** (*Eiruvin* 100b): Had the Torah not been given, we could have learned *tznius* from the cat, industriousness from the ant, and so on. In other words, even if we had not received the Torah, we would have had to observe its commandments from looking at the world around us. Still,

[199] **HAGGADAH: THE ANSWER IS . . .**

אִלּוּ נָתַן לָנוּ אֶת הַתּוֹרָה וְלֹא הִכְנִיסָנוּ לְאֶרֶץ יִשְׂרָאֵל דַּיֵּנוּ.

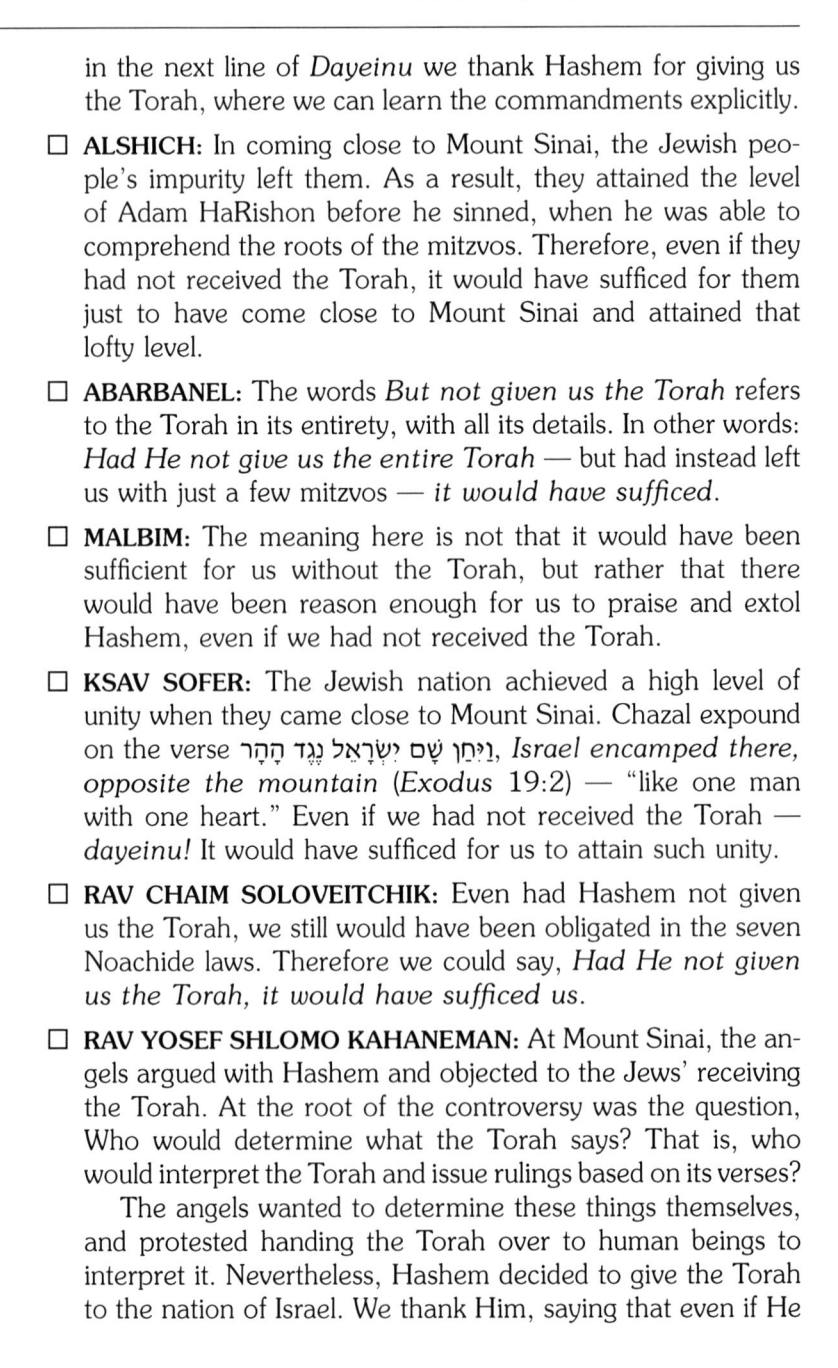

in the next line of *Dayeinu* we thank Hashem for giving us the Torah, where we can learn the commandments explicitly.

- ☐ **ALSHICH:** In coming close to Mount Sinai, the Jewish people's impurity left them. As a result, they attained the level of Adam HaRishon before he sinned, when he was able to comprehend the roots of the mitzvos. Therefore, even if they had not received the Torah, it would have sufficed for them just to have come close to Mount Sinai and attained that lofty level.

- ☐ **ABARBANEL:** The words *But not given us the Torah* refers to the Torah in its entirety, with all its details. In other words: *Had He not give us the entire Torah* — but had instead left us with just a few mitzvos — *it would have sufficed*.

- ☐ **MALBIM:** The meaning here is not that it would have been sufficient for us without the Torah, but rather that there would have been reason enough for us to praise and extol Hashem, even if we had not received the Torah.

- ☐ **KSAV SOFER:** The Jewish nation achieved a high level of unity when they came close to Mount Sinai. Chazal expound on the verse וַיִּחַן שָׁם יִשְׂרָאֵל נֶגֶד הָהָר, *Israel encamped there, opposite the mountain* (Exodus 19:2) — "like one man with one heart." Even if we had not received the Torah — *dayeinu!* It would have sufficed for us to attain such unity.

- ☐ **RAV CHAIM SOLOVEITCHIK:** Even had Hashem not given us the Torah, we still would have been obligated in the seven Noachide laws. Therefore we could say, *Had He not given us the Torah, it would have sufficed us*.

- ☐ **RAV YOSEF SHLOMO KAHANEMAN:** At Mount Sinai, the angels argued with Hashem and objected to the Jews' receiving the Torah. At the root of the controversy was the question, Who would determine what the Torah says? That is, who would interpret the Torah and issue rulings based on its verses?

  The angels wanted to determine these things themselves, and protested handing the Torah over to human beings to interpret it. Nevertheless, Hashem decided to give the Torah to the nation of Israel. We thank Him, saying that even if He

**Had He given us the Torah,
but not brought us into the Land of Israel,
it would have sufficed us.**

had not given us the Torah (i.e., the possibility of interpreting and issuing rulings on the Torah), but only the mitzvos — *dayeinu!*

☐ **RAV YECHEZKEL LEVENSTEIN:** The very fact that Hashem took us out of Egypt and freed us from Pharaoh's oppression was enough to obligate us to keep the Torah, even if it had not been given to us. After all, the *Avos* kept the Torah before it was given.

☐ **RAV YECHEZKEL SARNA:** The revelation at Mount Sinai had an exalted independent purpose. The gates of Heaven opened before the eyes of the Jewish people, and they saw, in the most tangible way, that there is nothing but Him. We therefore thank Hashem just for bringing us close to Mount Sinai — even if He had not given us the Torah, it would have been enough just to have attained such a lofty level.

☐ **OZHEROVER REBBE:** The aim of bringing us close to Mount Sinai was to teach us a lesson in humility from that humble mountain. Therefore, just coming close to the mountain and learning this lesson would have sufficed!

☐ **RAV SHLOMO ZALMAN ZELAZNIK:** Even without receiving the Torah, we would have observed the mitzvos. But Hashem brought us close to Mount Sinai and gave us the Torah, placing us in the position of a *metzuveh v'oseh* — one who does as he is commanded — of whom our Sages have said, *Greater is he who is commanded and fulfills [what he is commanded to do] than one who was not commanded and fulfills* (*Bava Kama* 87a).

☐ **SIFSEI CHAIM:** The Jewish people, on their own, were prepared to serve Hashem. Through the Torah, however, Hashem gave them the special power to repair the world spiritually.

☐ **BIRKAS HASHIR:** There are 613 mitzvos in the Torah. The numerical equivalent of the word "Torah" is 611. As we know, the first two *dibros* of the Ten Commandments were said by Hashem, and the rest were said by Moshe. We say, *Had He brought us before Mount Sinai,* so that we heard

אִלּוּ הִכְנִיסָנוּ לְאֶרֶץ יִשְׂרָאֵל
וְלֹא בָנָה לָנוּ אֶת בֵּית הַבְּחִירָה　דַּיֵּנוּ.

עַל אַחַת כַּמָּה וְכַמָּה טוֹבָה כְפוּלָה וּמְכֻפֶּלֶת לַמָּקוֹם עָלֵינוּ. שֶׁהוֹצִיאָנוּ מִמִּצְרַיִם, וְעָשָׂה בָהֶם שְׁפָטִים, וְעָשָׂה בֵאלֹהֵיהֶם, וְהָרַג אֶת בְּכוֹרֵיהֶם, וְנָתַן לָנוּ אֶת מָמוֹנָם, וְקָרַע לָנוּ אֶת הַיָּם, וְהֶעֱבִירָנוּ בְתוֹכוֹ בֶּחָרָבָה, וְשִׁקַּע צָרֵינוּ בְּתוֹכוֹ, וְסִפֵּק צָרְכֵּנוּ בַּמִּדְבָּר אַרְבָּעִים שָׁנָה, וְהֶאֱכִילָנוּ אֶת הַמָּן, וְנָתַן לָנוּ אֶת הַשַּׁבָּת, וְקֵרְבָנוּ לִפְנֵי הַר סִינַי, וְנָתַן לָנוּ אֶת הַתּוֹרָה, וְהִכְנִיסָנוּ לְאֶרֶץ יִשְׂרָאֵל, וּבָנָה לָנוּ אֶת בֵּית הַבְּחִירָה, לְכַפֵּר עַל כָּל עֲוֹנוֹתֵינוּ.

רַבָּן גַּמְלִיאֵל הָיָה אוֹמֵר. כָּל שֶׁלֹּא אָמַר שְׁלֹשָׁה דְבָרִים אֵלּוּ בַּפֶּסַח, לֹא יָצָא יְדֵי חוֹבָתוֹ, וְאֵלּוּ הֵן,

פֶּסַח. מַצָּה. וּמָרוֹר.

---

only the first two *dibros* from Hashem Himself, and He had not given us the "Torah" — that is, the other 611 mitzvos — *dayeinu*!

Q *Why do we say that it would have sufficed if Hashem had not built the Beis HaMikdash? Only when we have a Beis HaMikdash can we serve Hashem in the optimal way.*

A ☐ **ORCHOS CHAIM:** Had Hashem not built the Beis HaMikdash, the Mishkan that we had prior to it would have been enough for us.

☐ **CHAYEI ADAM:** Had Hashem not built the Beis HaMikdash, which atones for all our sins, we would at least have entered Eretz Yisrael, which also served as an atonement.

Had He brought us into the Land of Israel,
but not built the Temple for us,
it would have sufficed us.

Thus, how much more so should we be grateful to the Omnipresent for all the numerous favors He showered upon us: He brought us out of Egypt; executed judgments against the Egyptians; executed judgments against their gods; slew their firstborn; gave us their wealth; split the Sea for us; led us through it on dry land; drowned our oppressors in it; provided for our needs in the desert for forty years; fed us the manna; gave us the Sabbath; brought us close to Mount Sinai; gave us the Torah; brought us to the Land of Israel; and built us the Temple, to atone for all our sins.

Rabban Gamliel used to say: Whoever has not explained the following three things on Passover has not fulfilled his duty, namely:

Pesach — the *pesach*-offering;
Matzah — the unleavened bread;
Maror — the bitter herbs.

ئ§ רַבָּן גַּמְלִיאֵל הָיָה אוֹמֵר / *Rabban Gamliel used to say*

This paragraph was said by Rabban Gamliel II, grandson of Rabban Gamliel HaZaken (the elder), after the destruction of the first Beis HaMikdash. Its source is the Mishnah (*Pesachim* 116).

Rabban Gamliel's words, coming before Hallel, are a conclusion and summary of the Exodus story. They come to teach us that anyone who does not mention three things — the *korban Pesach*, matzah, and *maror* — does not fulfill his obligation to recount the story of the Exodus.

Rabban Gamliel does not mean that we must *say* these three words — "*pesach*," "*matzah*," and "*maror*" — but rather that we must explain their significance and their laws. In Rashi's opinion, even if a person has eaten of the *korban Pesach*, matzah, and *maror*, he has not fulfilled his obligation until he has spoken of them verbally. There is special emphasis on delving into the reasons for these mitzvos.

[203] HAGGADAH: THE ANSWER IS . . .

Q *Why does this passage follow Dayeinu in the Haggadah?*

A ☐ **MA'ASEI HASHEM:** This passage comes after the Haggadah cited the differences of opinion between Rabbi Yose, Rabbi Eliezer, and Rabbi Akiva, who spoke at length about the miracles that were performed for the Jewish people and the plagues that the Egyptians received (according to some opinions, *Dayeinu* is a continuation of that passage). Rabban Gamliel now comes to say that even if one relates the story of the Exodus with a full description of all the events, he has not fulfilled his obligation if he has not mentioned three things and elaborated on them: *korban Pesach*, matzah, and *maror*.

☐ **MALBIM:** After recounting the miracles and Hashem's kindnesses, for which we must give thanks — and before we conclude with *L'fichach* ("Therefore...") — Rabban Gamliel says that we must underscore the reasons we are obligated to praise Hashem: the oppression (represented by the matzah and *maror*) and the redemption (represented by the *korban Pesach*).

Q *Why does Rabban Gamliel make a general statement ("one who has not explained these three things ...") followed by the details? Could he not simply have said, "Whoever has not said, 'Pesach, matzah, and maror...'"?*

A ☐ **ALTER OF KELM:** Rabban Gamliel's lengthy statement is meant to pique the listener's curiosity to know the three things on which the mitzvah of the Seder night hinges. It serves as a special introduction that tells the participants at the Seder to pay close attention.

Q *Namely: Pesach — the Passover Offering; Matzah — the Unleavened Bread; Maror — the Bitter Herbs. What do the korban Pesach, matzah, and maror come to teach us?*

A ☐ **ABARBANEL:** Rabban Gamliel is telling us that on this night, there is an obligation to mention three central things. If we do not mention and expound on them (or if one of them is omitted), a person does not fulfill his obligation even if he eats of them, because they are the essence of the story of the Exodus:

Maror encompasses the story of the exile, the oppression, and the Exodus from Egypt.

Matzah includes all aspects of the redemption.

Pesach commemorates the slaying of the firstborn and the rescue of the Jewish people.

☐ **MAHARAL:** These three things correspond to the three *Avos*, in whose merit the Jewish people left Egypt:

Pesach corresponds to Yaakov, who was called *tamim*, since a *seh tamim*, unblemished lamb, was sacrificed for the *korban Pesach*.

Maror corresponds to Yitzchak, who was "bitter" because his eyes were blinded. According to the Midrash, Yitzchak requested suffering as an atonement.

Matzah corresponds to Avraham. The matzah is separated from the leaven, just as Avraham was separated from the nations of the world.

☐ **RAV MOSHE FEINSTEIN:** This teaches us about Hashem's *hashgachah*:

Pesach — even if everything seems to be functioning as usual, one must know that it is all happening by Hashem's decree and under His supervision, just as when Hashem passed over the Jewish homes on Pesach and did not strike them.

Matzah — to teach that we must not despair if we do not see the coming of the final redemption. Just as the redemption from Egypt was sudden, so too there will be no need for prior preparation before the final redemption, since it will come suddenly. We learn this from the matzah. Hashem rescued the Jewish people from Egypt in such haste that there was not even time for the dough to rise. So too the future redemption will come suddenly, in a surprising manner, with no time for prior preparation.

Maror — one must not rely on leaders and rulers. In Egypt, there seemed to be goodwill toward Yosef and his brothers, but in the end the Egyptians embittered their lives. From this we learn that one must rely only on Hashem.

☐ **RAV AVIGDOR NEBENZAHL:** When the Jewish people left Egypt, Hashem commanded them about these three fundamental mitzvos, corresponding to three bad *middos* (character traits): *kinah*, envy; *ta'avah*, lust; and *kavod*, the pursuit of honor. The three mitzvos correspond to these traits:

Pesach — the *korban Pesach* was meant to uproot the trait of *kinah*, jealousy. The lamb had to be roasted, as if to uproot the envy that burns in the bones of one who is jealous, as it says regarding this trait, רְשָׁפֶיהָ רִשְׁפֵּי אֵשׁ שַׁלְהֶבֶתְיָה, *Its flashes are flashes of fire* (*Shir HaShirim* 8:6).

Matzah — uproots the trait of seeking honor, since matzah is called *lechem oni*, poor man's bread, and a poor man is humble in demeanor. When matzah rises — symbolizing the trait of *ga'avah*, haughtiness — it becomes leavened and is forbidden. Therefore, matzah represents the opposite of *kavod*, the pursuit of honor.

Maror — uproots the trait of lust. The *maror* tastes bitter, and a person in the grip of lust does not want to experience even a little bit of suffering or hardship. He seeks only the pleasures of the present, disregarding what is truly worthwhile. The *maror* counteracts this vain pursuit.

☐ On the Seder night, we are obligated in four mitzvos commanded in the Torah: sacrificing the *korban Pesach*, eating matzah, eating *maror*, and telling the story of the Exodus. These four mitzvos are meant to rectify four grave sins:

Pesach rectifies the sin of *avodah zarah* (idolatry). We slaughter a lamb, which was worshiped as a god in Egypt.

Matzah rectifies the sin of *gilui arayos* (immorality). We are scrupulously careful not to allow even a bit of dough to rise, since the leavening in the dough is compared to the *yetzer hara*, which incites us to give in to our desires.

Maror rectifies the sin of *shefichas damim* (murder), since the numerical equivalent of *maror* is the same as that of the word *maves*, death.

Sippur Yetzias Mitzrayim, the mitzvah to recount the story of the Exodus, rectifies the sin of *lashon hara* (slander).

☐ This corresponds to the three things for which we thank Hashem that occurred on Pesach:

Pesach — corresponds to the protection that was afforded the Jewish people against the Angel of Death at the time of the Exodus, when the people were eating of the *korban Pesach*.

Matzah — the "poor man's bread," hints at the trait of being satisfied with little through the subduing of a man's haughty spirit. We thank Hashem for humbling Pharaoh's spirit until he agreed to let us leave.

Maror — reminds us of the bitterness and pain that the Jews suffered in Egypt. This prevents us from forgetting the oppression and induces us to express our gratitude to Hashem for redeeming us.

Q *Why does maror come after matzah? After all, in Egypt the order was (bitter) oppression first and only afterward the baking of the matzos.*

A ☐ **MA'ASEH NISSIM:** The primary purpose of the redemption was to transform the Jews into servants of Hashem. Rescuing us from the bitter exile was the secondary purpose. Had the *maror* come first, it would have seemed as if the primary purpose of the redemption was to free us of the bitterness and oppression.

☐ **ABARBANEL:** Rabban Gamliel lists the three things that we must mention in the order of importance of the miracle that was performed in each of these three cases. First came the miracle of passing over the homes of the Jewish people — symbolized by the *korban Pesach*. Then came the baking of the matzah, when the dough did not rise and turn into bread. This had an aspect of the supernatural, but it was a lesser miracle. And finally — the *maror*, with which no miracle occurred.

☐ **RAV YISRAEL SALANTER:** Matzah symbolizes redemption — the final outcome — while *maror* symbolizes oppression, the motive and the reason behind the redemption. In the actual sequence of events, the motive precedes the outcome. When retelling the story, however, the order is reversed: first we speak of the outcome (the matzah) and only then about the motivating factor (the *maror*).

☐ **CHIDDUSHEI HARIM:** The Jewish people had become so accustomed to slavery that they did not even complain. Furthermore, exile had become a part of who they were, to the point where they thought they could not live without it. Hashem told them, "I will take you out of a situation in which you do not even comprehend that you are suffering. After you leave and eat the matzos, you will understand how very bitter the oppression was (symbolized by the *maror*)."

☐ **BEIS HALEVI:** A person who was once a slave and is then set free can sense, as a free man, the bitterness of his previous

פֶּסַח שֶׁהָיוּ אֲבוֹתֵינוּ אוֹכְלִים בִּזְמַן שֶׁבֵּית הַמִּקְדָּשׁ הָיָה קַיָּם, עַל שׁוּם מָה? עַל שׁוּם שֶׁפָּסַח הַקָּדוֹשׁ בָּרוּךְ הוּא עַל בָּתֵּי אֲבוֹתֵינוּ בְּמִצְרַיִם. שֶׁנֶּאֱמַר, וַאֲמַרְתֶּם, זֶבַח פֶּסַח הוּא לַיהוה,

---

slave existence. The author of the Haggadah mentions the matzah first, so that those at the Seder table will feel like free men. Then, in that atmosphere, they can remember and understand the era of their slavery in Egypt, symbolized by the *maror*.

☐ **DIVREI YOEL:** This is a hint that the redemption from Egypt was not an eternal one, but would be followed by further exiles. The matzah, which is mentioned first, hints at the redemption from Egypt. The *maror*, mentioned afterward, hints at the future exiles.

☐ *Pesach*, matzah, and *maror* represent three things in a Jew's life. The *korban Pesach* symbolizes the prohibitions; sacrificing the Egyptian god was the first step in the Jews' exodus from the forty-ninth level of impurity — from refraining from doing bad. The matzah symbolizes the positive commandments, and the *maror* symbolizes suffering and hardships. When we say these three things, we must arouse ourselves first to observe the positive and negative commandments (*korban Pesach* and matzah), which are the goal of every Jewish life, and only afterward reflect on the suffering (the *maror*).

☐ These three things are listed in accordance with the order of the commandment in *Parashas Bo:* וְאָכְלוּ אֶת הַבָּשָׂר בַּלַּיְלָה הַזֶּה צְלִי אֵשׁ וּמַצּוֹת עַל מְרֹרִים יֹאכְלֻהוּ, *They shall eat the flesh on that night — roasted over the fire — and matzos; with herbs shall they eat it* (Exodus 12:8). First, Hashem commanded the Jews about the *korban Pesach*, then about the matzah, and finally about the *maror*.

☐ The author of the Haggadah puts matzah before *maror* in order to highlight the chain of events in Egypt. The start of the Jews' oppression came about through soft language (*peh rach*) symbolized by the matzah, which is also called *lechem oni* — poor man's bread. Later on, the oppression became harsher, symbolized by the *maror*.

Pesach — Why did our fathers eat a Passover offering during the period when the Temple still stood? Because the Holy One, Blessed is He, passed over the houses of our fathers in Egypt, as it is written: You shall say: "It is a Passover offering for HASHEM,

---

- ☐ Today, the mitzvah of matzah is Biblical, while *maror* is rabbinic. A *mitzvah d'Oraisa* takes precedence over a *mitzvah d'rabbanan*.

Q: Which duty has one failed to fulfill if he does not mention Pesach, Matzah, and Maror?

A:
- ☐ **RASHBATZ:** It refers to the obligation of וְהִגַּדְתָּ לְבִנְךָ, *And you shall tell your son* (Exodus 13:8) — to tell your children the story of the Exodus.

- ☐ **RASHBAM:** It is speaking of the obligation to eat the *Pesach*, matzah, and *maror*. Even if a person ate them, he has not fulfilled his obligation unless he mentions and expounds on them verbally, as there is a special emphasis on the verbal explanation in addition to the act of eating.

- ☐ **CHUKAS HAPESACH HAGGADAH:** It refers to the obligation of reciting the Haggadah. This statement is addressed to the unlettered who do not know how to read the Haggadah. For their sake, Rabban Gamliel established that they at least say these three things, along with the brief text that explains them, and thus fulfill their obligation of retelling the story of the Exodus.

- ☐ **RAN:** He has not fulfilled his obligation to tell the story of the Exodus *in the best way*. He has fulfilled the Torah obligation of telling the story through the brief explanation that he recited so far, but he has not fulfilled the rabbinical obligation until he expounds on and explains the mitzvos of the *korban Pesach*, matzah, and *maror*.

פֶּסַח / Pesach

The "*Pesach*" symbolizes the essence of the act through which the Jewish people merited to be rescued from the *maror* and attained the "matzah" — liberty and independence. As we learn from this passage,

אֲשֶׁר פָּסַח עַל בָּתֵּי בְנֵי יִשְׂרָאֵל בְּמִצְרַיִם בְּנָגְפּוֹ אֶת מִצְרַיִם, וְאֶת בָּתֵּינוּ הִצִּיל, וַיִּקֹד הָעָם וַיִּשְׁתַּחֲווּ.[1]

The middle matzah is lifted and displayed while the following paragraph is recited.

מַצָּה זוּ שֶׁאָנוּ אוֹכְלִים, עַל שׁוּם מָה? עַל שׁוּם שֶׁלֹּא הִסְפִּיק בְּצֵקָם שֶׁל אֲבוֹתֵינוּ לְהַחֲמִיץ, עַד שֶׁנִּגְלָה עֲלֵיהֶם מֶלֶךְ מַלְכֵי הַמְּלָכִים

פֶּסַח עַל בָּתֵּי the mitzvah of the *Pesach* was given to us because Hashem בְּנֵי יִשְׂרָאֵל בְּמִצְרַיִם, *passed over the houses of the Children of Israel.*

Q *Why did Hashem find it necessary to perform a special miracle in passing over the Jewish homes during the Plague of the Firstborn? After all, the Jews were not harmed in any of the other plagues.*

A ☐ MA'ASEH NISSIM: The firstborn of the Jews were also deserving of death because they, like the Egyptians, had worshiped false gods. In order to save them from being killed during this plague, Hashem performed a special miracle.

☐ MA'ASEI HASHEM: The Angel of Death was given permission to kill indiscriminately during the Plague of the Firstborn. Hashem performed a special miracle in order to save the Jewish people, including those who were not the firstborn.

Q *"Who passed over the houses of the Children of Israel in Egypt when He struck the Egyptians and spared our houses." The words "and spared our houses" seem unnecessary.*

A ☐ KSAV SOFER: We emphasize the words "*our* houses," and not the Egyptians' houses — in the same sense as the Haggadah's answer to the wicked son, *For me, but not for him.*

☐ RAV CHAIM BERLIN: The Egyptians brought their firstborn sons to the homes of the Jews in order to save them from the plague. Despite this, Hashem struck them down. Therefore,

הגדה של פסח [210]

Who passed over the houses of the Children of Israel in Egypt when He struck the Egyptians and spared our houses"; and the people bowed down and prostrated themselves.[1]

The middle matzah is lifted and displayed while the following paragraph is recited.

Matzah — Why do we eat this unleavened bread? Because the dough of our fathers did not have time to become leavened before the King of Kings,

---

1. *Exodus* 12:27.

---

the words *Who passed over the houses of the Children of Israel in Egypt* refer to the houses in which there were only Jews, and no Egyptians. *And spared our houses* refers to the Jewish homes to which the Egyptian firstborns came to be spared. Even in those houses, Hashem killed only the Egyptians and did not touch the Jewish firstborn.

☐ RAV SHMUEL WOSNER: This emphasizes the merit that brought about our rescue — the merit of our homes, which were free of any breach and which served as fortresses for us amid the darkness of Egypt.

⊷§ מַצָּה / *Matzah*

This is an answer to the first question of *Mah Nishtanah*: Why do we eat matzah and not *chametz* on the Seder night?

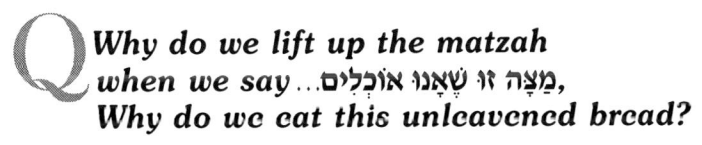

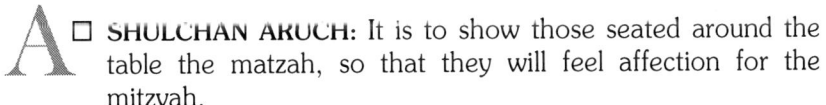

Q *Why do we lift up the matzah when we say* ...מַצָּה זוּ שֶׁאָנוּ אוֹכְלִים, *Why do we eat this unleavened bread?*

A ☐ SHULCHAN ARUCH: It is to show those seated around the table the matzah, so that they will feel affection for the mitzvah.

☐ AVUDRAHAM: This reminds us of the oppression and the freedom that the matzah represents (oppression since it was the poor man's bread that they ate as slaves in Egypt, and freedom since they baked matzah when they were freed from Egypt because there was not enough time to let the dough rise).

הַקָּדוֹשׁ בָּרוּךְ הוּא וּגְאָלָם. שֶׁנֶּאֱמַר, וַיֹּאפוּ אֶת הַבָּצֵק אֲשֶׁר הוֹצִיאוּ מִמִּצְרַיִם עֻגֹת מַצּוֹת כִּי לֹא חָמֵץ, כִּי גֹרְשׁוּ מִמִּצְרַיִם, וְלֹא יָכְלוּ לְהִתְמַהְמֵהַּ, וְגַם צֵדָה לֹא עָשׂוּ לָהֶם.[1]

☐ **SHIBBOLEI HALEKET:** We lift it up to fulfill the teaching mentioned above in *Yachol MeRosh Chodesh*, בְּשָׁעָה שֶׁיֵּשׁ מַצָּה וּמָרוֹר מֻנָּחִים לְפָנֶיךָ, *"You shall tell your son"* applies only at the time when matzah and maror lie before you — at the Seder.

Q: Why do we eat this unleavened bread? Why do we eat matzah on Pesach?

A: ☐ **AVUDRAHAM:** Already while in Egypt, the Jews were commanded, בָּרִאשֹׁן בְּאַרְבָּעָה עָשָׂר יוֹם לַחֹדֶשׁ בָּעֶרֶב תֹּאכְלוּ מַצֹּת, *In the first [month], on the fourteenth day of the month in the evening shall you eat matzos* (Exodus 12:18). This command was given for them to fulfill in the future, on the night before they left Egypt. To commemorate that first Pesach, we too eat matzos.

☐ **VILNA GAON:** We eat matzah in commemoration of the slavery, to recall the *lechem oni* — the bread of affliction — which they ate in Egypt.

☐ It is in commemoration of the exodus into freedom, when our forefathers were rescued from Egypt, as it says, וַיֹּאפוּ אֶת הַבָּצֵק אֲשֶׁר הוֹצִיאוּ מִמִּצְרַיִם עֻגֹת מַצּוֹת, *They baked the dough which they had brought out of Egypt into unleavened bread* (Exodus 12:39). They left so quickly that they did not have time to let the dough rise and it was baked as matzah.

Q: How can we say that we eat matzah because their dough did not have time to rise, when the Torah commanded the Jewish people to eat matzah even before they left Egypt?

A: ☐ **AVUDRAHAM:** The command to eat matzos for seven days was for the future, to commemorate the fact that they would leave in a hurry and their dough would not have time to rise.

the Holy One, Blessed is He, revealed Himself to them and redeemed them, as it is written: They baked the dough which they had brought out of Egypt into unleavened bread, for it had not fermented, because they were driven out of Egypt and could not delay, nor had they prepared any provisions for the way.[1]

1. *Exodus* 12:39.

☐ **MA'ASEH NISSIM:** Before the Exodus, the command was for the purpose of commemorating the *lechem oni*, poor man's bread, that they ate as slaves. On the Seder night we eat matzah in memory of the freedom — to remember that the dough did not have time to rise when the Jewish people were liberated.

☐ **BEIS HALEVI:** The Torah preceded the world, so the mitzvos of the *korban Pesach*, matzah, and *maror* were written even before the world was created. Our *Avos* observed the Torah before it was given at Mount Sinai, and they ate matzah on the night of 15 Nissan even though the Jewish people had not yet been enslaved in Egypt. Likewise, the Jews in Egypt were commanded to eat matzah even before they were redeemed, to symbolize the dough that would not rise on their departure from Egypt in the future. Like the *Avos*, they fulfilled the mitzvah before the occurrence of the events that commemorated it.

☐ **ABARBANEL:** The Jewish people were commanded to eat matzah in Egypt because it is reminiscent of suffering and oppression. The matzah that we eat today, however, is *also* in memory of the dough that did not have time to rise when the people departed from Egypt.

☐ **RAN:** The consumption of matzah in Egypt was for just one day, as the Jews could not linger. At the same time, since they had not prepared provisions for the way, they continued to eat matzos made from dough that did not rise — not in fulfillment of the command but simply out of expedience. The obligation for the generations is for all seven days of the festival of Pesach in commemoration of the hasty departure.

☐ **SFAS EMES:** The author of the Haggadah wishes to praise the Jewish people, who did not change their names, language,

The maror is lifted and displayed while the following paragraph is recited.

מָרוֹר זֶה שֶׁאָנוּ אוֹכְלִים, עַל שׁוּם מָה? עַל שׁוּם שֶׁמֵּרְרוּ הַמִּצְרִים אֶת חַיֵּי אֲבוֹתֵינוּ

or mode of dress in Egypt, despite the fact that they were in exile. The Haggadah hints at this with the words *Because the dough of the fathers did not have time to become leavened...* It is the leaven in the dough that causes matzah to change into bread. Just as the dough does not change when it remains matzah, the Jewish people did not change. This is why the Haggadah reminds us of the dough that did not rise — simply to give praise to the Jewish people.

Q *Why could the Jews not wait to leave Egypt? And what was noteworthy about their leaving in such a hurry?*

A
- **RAMBAM:** There was no advantage in it. The Haggadah is merely giving an explanation for why they did not have time to bake bread in Egypt and take it along for the way.
- **MALBIM:** Had they tarried, they would have sunk even further into the impurity of Egypt.
- **KSAV SOFER:** Up until the last moment, the Jewish people did not not believe that they were truly about to leave Egypt, as by their calculation 400 years of oppression had not yet ended. At the last minute, Hashem revealed Himself to

---

You shall safeguard the matzos...
One day, a guest came to the home of Rav Dovid of Lelov, but the Rebbe had nothing to give him to eat. All he had in his house was *shemurah matzah*, which he had been carefully saving for Pesach.

To his family's surprise, the Rebbe took the *shemurah matzah*, cooked it into a meal, and served it to his guest.

He explained to them, "We learn the obligation to eat *shemurah matzah* from the *pasuk* וּשְׁמַרְתֶּם אֶת הַמַּצּוֹת, *You shall safeguard the matzos* (*Exodus* 12:17). From the same *pasuk* we learn another halachah: 'If a mitzvah comes to your hand, do not let it slip away [*al tachmitzenah*].' By using these matzos, I am fulfilling that halachah. Hashem will provide me with other *shemurah matzos* for Pesach."

The maror is lifted and displayed while the following paragraph is recited.

Maror — Why do we eat this bitter herb? Because the Egyptians embittered the lives of our fathers

them and redeemed them, and they had no time to bake bread.

- ☐ **YITAV PANIM:** The *Chovos HaLevavos* (*Sha'ar HaKeniah*) says that *zerizus*, zealousness, prevents the entry of foreign, undesirable thoughts. The Jewish people in Egypt were sunk in impurity. Hashem made it possible for them to leave quickly so that no foreign thoughts from the powers of impurity would cling to them.

- ☐ **GA'AL YISRAEL HAGGADAH:** The hastiness came from the Shechinah, to testify to Hashem's love for the Jewish people. Despite the fact that they were spiritually empty (as hinted at by the words *nor had they prepared any provisions for the way*), Hashem redeemed them and did not wait until they were "filled" with provisions — spiritually.

- ☐ **SFAS EMES:** The Jews' hasty departure demonstrated their great faith in Hashem. Despite the fact that they had sunk to the forty-ninth level of impurity, the Jewish people believed in Him. Seeing the miracles that Hashem had performed for them and experiencing the redemption elevated them to a lofty level of *bitachon*, of trust in Hashem — the level of a person who serves Hashem out of love. They trusted in Hashem so fully that they left Egypt immediately and did not even prepare provisions for the way. Regarding this level of faith in Him, Hashem declared, זָכַרְתִּי לָךְ חֶסֶד נְעוּרַיִךְ...לֶכְתֵּךְ אַחֲרַי בַּמִּדְבָּר בְּאֶרֶץ לֹא זְרוּעָה, *I recall for you the kindness of your youth...your following Me into the wilderness* (*Yirmiyahu* 2:2).

- ☐ **RAV YERUCHAM LEVOVITZ:** The time had come for the giving of the Torah. Had they tarried, this auspicious time would have passed, and they would not, Heaven forbid, have received the Torah.

☙ מָרוֹר / *Maror*

This is a response to the second question of *Mah Nishtanah*: Why do we eat *maror* on this night?

בְּמִצְרָיִם. שֶׁנֶּאֱמַר, וַיְמָרְרוּ אֶת חַיֵּיהֶם, בַּעֲבֹדָה קָשָׁה, בְּחֹמֶר וּבִלְבֵנִים, וּבְכָל עֲבֹדָה בַּשָּׂדֶה, אֵת כָּל עֲבֹדָתָם אֲשֶׁר עָבְדוּ בָהֶם בְּפָרֶךְ.[1]

בְּכָל דּוֹר וָדוֹר חַיָּב אָדָם לִרְאוֹת אֶת עַצְמוֹ כְּאִלּוּ הוּא יָצָא מִמִּצְרָיִם. שֶׁנֶּאֱמַר, וְהִגַּדְתָּ לְבִנְךָ בַּיּוֹם הַהוּא לֵאמֹר, בַּעֲבוּר זֶה עָשָׂה יהוה לִי, בְּצֵאתִי מִמִּצְרָיִם.[2] לֹא אֶת אֲבוֹתֵינוּ בִּלְבָד גָּאַל הַקָּדוֹשׁ בָּרוּךְ הוּא, אֶלָּא אַף אוֹתָנוּ גָּאַל עִמָּהֶם. שֶׁנֶּאֱמַר, וְאוֹתָנוּ הוֹצִיא מִשָּׁם, לְמַעַן הָבִיא אֹתָנוּ לָתֶת לָנוּ אֶת הָאָרֶץ אֲשֶׁר נִשְׁבַּע לַאֲבֹתֵינוּ.[3]

Q Why the double language — בַּעֲבֹדָה קָשָׁה, with hard labor, and ...וּבְכָל עֲבֹדָה בַּשָּׂדֶה אֲשֶׁר עָבְדוּ בָהֶם בְּפָרֶךְ, with all manner of hard labor in the field...that they made them perform?

A ☐ **KSAV SOFER:** Part of the pain of the oppression that the Jewish people experienced in Egypt was the difficulty of adapting, because their work was changed every few days. The author of the Haggadah is referring to all the different kinds of hard labor. At first, they had to make bricks and mortar. After they grew accustomed to that, they were switched to another form of hard labor — working the fields. The difficulty was doubled: both the work itself, *and* the need to adapt to field labor. That is why we end with the words *Whatever service they made them perform was with hard labor.*

☐ The oppression in Egypt caused two hardships, and both of them are emphasized by the use of the double language here: (1) they were forced to do unnecessary work, and (2) they were forced to perform hard manual labor. The goal of both was to embitter their lives.

Q The Torah commanded that maror be eaten while they were still enslaved in Egypt. What purpose did this serve?

in Egypt, as it says: They embittered their lives with hard labor, with mortar and bricks, and with all manner of labor in the field: Whatever service they made them perform was with hard labor.[1]

In every generation it is one's duty to regard himself as though he personally had gone out of Egypt, as it is written: You shall tell your son on that day: "It was because of this that HASHEM did for 'me' when I went out of Egypt."[2] It was not only our fathers whom the Holy One, Blessed is He, redeemed from slavery; we, too, were redeemed with them, as it is written: He brought "us" out from there so that He might take us to the land which He had promised to our fathers.[3]

---

1. Exodus 1:14. 2. Ibid. 13:8. 3. Deuteronomy 6:23.

A ☐ Chazal tell us (Rosh Hashanah 11) that the oppression ended on Rosh Hashanah. For half a year before they departed in freedom, the Jews were not forced to work. To make sure they did not forget the taste of bitterness and the harshness of the oppression during those six months, they were commanded to eat *maror* on Pesach night while still in Egypt.

בְּכָל דּוֹר וָדוֹר / *In every generation*

This paragraph serves as the answer to the fourth question of *Mah Nishtanah*: Why do we recline? It is because, as we recite in this passage, *in every generation it is one's duty to regard himself as though he personally had gone out of Egypt*. Reclining is one of the means we have to concretize the freedom we are trying to experience on this night.

Q *Why does this passage follow Rabban Gamliel's statement about the korban Pesach, matzah, and maror?*

A ☐ This paragraph is based on the teaching of Chazal in *Pesachim* 116b. In the Gemara, these words are a continuation of Rabban Gamliel's statement. Therefore, it also follows Rabban Gamliel's statement in the Haggadah.

[217] HAGGADAH: THE ANSWER IS . . .

The matzos are covered and the cup is lifted and held until it is to be drunk. According to some customs, however, the cup is put down after the following paragraph, in which case the matzos should once more be uncovered. If this custom is followed, the matzos are to be covered and the cup raised again upon reaching the blessing אֲשֶׁר גְּאָלָנוּ, *Who has redeemed us* (p. 234).

לְפִיכָךְ אֲנַחְנוּ חַיָּבִים לְהוֹדוֹת, לְהַלֵּל, לְשַׁבֵּחַ, לְפָאֵר, לְרוֹמֵם, לְהַדֵּר, לְבָרֵךְ, לְעַלֵּה,

- ☐ **SIFSEI CHAIM:** After we have finished relating the story of the Exodus and expounding on the *korban Pesach*, matzah, and *maror*, we say this paragraph, *B'Chol Dor VaDor*, which comes to fulfill the obligation of וְהִגַּדְתָּ לְבִנְךָ בַּיּוֹם הַהוּא לֵאמֹר בַּעֲבוּר זֶה עָשָׂה ה' לִי, *You shall tell your son on that day: "It was because of this that HASHEM did for me."* We say this to concretize that obligation, as a person does when pointing at something. Through the telling of the story and this concretization, a person fulfills the obligation to regard himself as though he personally went out of Egypt.

Q *Why is there an obligation for one to see oneself as having himself left Egypt?*

A
- ☐ **RASHI'S SIDDUR:** It says, בַּעֲבוּר זֶה עָשָׂה ה' לִי בְּצֵאתִי מִמִּצְרַיִם, *It was because of this that HASHEM did for me when I went out of Egypt*, and not *when our forefathers went out of Egypt*. Every person, in every generation, is obligated to regard himself as though *he* went out of Egypt.
- ☐ **RASHBATZ:** It is an obligation because the miracle and the redemption happened to *us*. Had our forefathers not left Egypt, we would be subjugated to Pharaoh today.
- ☐ The soul of every Jew was present during the oppression in Egypt. Therefore everyone is obligated to regard himself as though he himself left the oppression of Egypt.

Q *Why the double language* — בְּכָל דּוֹר וָדוֹר, *lit., in every generation and generation?*

A
- ☐ **MA'ASEI HASHEM:** Whether in a generation where the Jewish nation was in its own land, or a generation when we are in exile, we are obligated to tell the story of the Exodus.

The matzos are covered and the cup is lifted and held until it is to be drunk. According to some customs, however, the cup is put down after the following paragraph, in which case the matzos should once more be uncovered. If this custom is followed, the matzos are to be covered and the cup raised again upon reaching the blessing אֲשֶׁר גְּאָלָנוּ, *Who has redeemed us* (p. 234).

Therefore it is our duty to thank, praise, pay tribute, glorify, exalt, honor, bless, extol, and

---

- In every generation, fathers are obligated to teach their children about the Exodus on the Seder night, even if the son is more learned than his father. One mention of "generation" refers to one in which the son is wiser than the father, and the other refers to one in which the father is wiser than the son. Either way, a father is obligated to teach his children about the Exodus.
- Rabban Gamliel says that in every generation — whether we appear to be in a state of redemption or we are in exile, whether in a generation of spiritual growth or a generation of spiritual decline — we must feel that we are a direct continuation of the miracle of the Exodus.

◈§ לְפִיכָךְ / *Therefore*

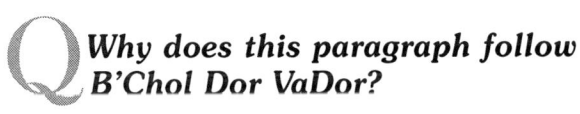

Q. Why does this paragraph follow B'Chol Dor VaDor?

A.
- **AVUDRAHAM:** This is a continuation of the preceding paragraph, in which we concretize for ourselves that *we* left Egypt. (Like the preceding paragraphs, the source of this paragraph is also the Gemara in *Pesachim* 116b.) Now we feel an obligation to thank and praise Hashem for this, which we commence to do in this passage.
- **ORCHOS CHAIM:** This passage is a blessing for Hallel, which we are about to recite.
- **MALBIM:** This is a continuation of *Dayeinu*, which we recited above. *Therefore it is our duty to thank, praise, pay tribute, glorify...*: If it is appropriate to thank Hashem for even one kindness, as we imply in *Dayeinu*, how much more so all the kindnesses taken together!

HAGGADAH: THE ANSWER IS . . .

וּלְקַלֵּס, לְמִי שֶׁעָשָׂה לַאֲבוֹתֵינוּ וְלָנוּ אֶת כָּל הַנִּסִּים הָאֵלּוּ, הוֹצִיאָנוּ מֵעַבְדוּת לְחֵרוּת, מִיָּגוֹן לְשִׂמְחָה, וּמֵאֵבֶל לְיוֹם טוֹב, וּמֵאֲפֵלָה לְאוֹר גָּדוֹל, וּמִשִּׁעְבּוּד לִגְאֻלָּה. וְנֹאמַר לְפָנָיו שִׁירָה חֲדָשָׁה, הַלְלוּיָהּ.

> **Q** To what do the different expressions of thanksgiving mentioned here correspond?

A ☐ **MACHZOR VITRI:** There are nine expressions of praise in this passage. When we add the word *"Hallelukah,"* which appears at the end of this passage, we have ten expressions, corresponding to the ten expressions with which David HaMelech composed *Tehillim: ashrei, nitzuach, niggun, shir, maskil, mizmor, tehillah, tefillah, hodayah,* and *hallelukah.*

☐ **RASHBATZ:** There are eight expressions of thanksgiving in this passage, which correspond to the four miracles that were performed on our behalf that are mentioned later in this passage:
1. He took us from slavery to freedom,
2. from grief to joy,
3. from mourning to festivity, and
4. from darkness to great light.

Just as the aforementioned kindnesses were multiple, so are we obligated to thank Hashem in multiple ways for these miracles: eight expressions of thanksgiving for four miracles.

☐ **ABARBANEL:** There are seven expressions of praise here (omitting the words לְבָרֵךְ לְעַלֵּה, *to bless, to extol*). These correspond to
- the seven levels of Heaven, and
- the seven shepherds: *l'hodos,* to thank, corresponds to Avraham, who thanked Hashem and spread His Name throughout the world; *l'hallel,* to praise, corresponds to Yitzchak, who praised Hashem; *l'shabei'ach,* to pay tribute, corresponds to Yaakov, who paid tribute to Hashem; *l'fa'eir,* to glorify, corresponds to Aharon, whom Hashem

acclaim Him Who performed all these miracles for our fathers and for us. He brought us forth from slavery to freedom, from grief to joy, from mourning to festivity, from darkness to great light, and from servitude to redemption. Let us, therefore, recite a new song before Him! Halleluyah!

glorified with the *Kehunah* (Priesthood); *l'romeim*, to exalt, corresponds to Moshe, whom Hashem exalted with prophecy; *l'hadeir*, to honor, corresponds to David HaMelech, who honored Hashem with his *Tehillim*; and *l'kaleis*, to acclaim, corresponds to Shlomo, who acclaimed *HaKadosh Baruch Hu*.

☐ **VILNA GAON:** There are nine expressions of praise in this passage, to which we add the word "*Halleluyah*," at the end of this passage, making ten expressions in all — corresponding to the Ten Plagues that were inflicted upon the Egyptians.

Q *"He brought us forth from slavery to freedom, from grief to joy, from mourning to festivity, from darkness to great light, and from servitude to redemption."* To what do these five expressions of praise for our rescue correspond?

A ☐ **MA'ASEH NISSIM:** They correspond to our rescue from the oppression of various empires:

From slavery to freedom corresponds to the Exodus from Egypt, when we were freed from slavery and oppression.

From grief to joy corresponds to our departure from the exile in Bavel. There was great anguish at the destruction of the Beis HaMikdash, and when we left Bavel, there was great joy.

From mourning to festivity corresponds to the yoke of Persia and Medea.

From darkness to great light corresponds to the Greek exile. There was darkness during the reign of Greece; as Chazal tell us, the Greeks darkened the eyes of the Jewish people with their decrees. When we were freed from this

הַלְלוּיָהּ הַלְלוּ עַבְדֵי יהוה, הַלְלוּ אֶת שֵׁם יהוה. יְהִי שֵׁם יהוה מְבֹרָךְ, מֵעַתָּה וְעַד עוֹלָם.

exile, we were redeemed from that darkness to "great light" — the miracle of Chanukah, which occurred through the lights of the Menorah.

From servitude to redemption corresponds to the fourth kingdom, Edom, from which we will experience redemption — may it be speedily in our day!

☐ **RAV SHLOMO KLUGER:** They correspond to the five merits that the Jewish people possessed in Egypt: they did not change their names, their dress, or their language, there were no slanderers (*malshinim*) among them, and there was no immorality.

◈§ הַלְלוּיָהּ / *Halleluyah*

According to the *Rashbatz*, this is an introduction to Hallel, which we will say later on. When the Jewish people left the oppression of Egypt, they did not sing songs of victory or hymns of battle and vengeance. Rather, as servants of Hashem, they thanked and praised Hashem. Similarly, on the Seder night we recite these psalms of praise from *Tehillim* (Psalms 113 and 114) to commemorate our redemption.

According to the Talmud (*Berachos* 56a), the Hallel that we say on Festivals and Rosh Chodesh, and that we are about to say now, is called *Hallel HaMitzri*, the Hallel of Egypt, since it explicitly mentions the Exodus from Egypt: ...בְּצֵאת יִשְׂרָאֵל מִמִּצְרָיִם, *When Israel went forth from Egypt*...

On the Seder night, Hallel HaMitzri is divided into two parts, with the meal and *Shefoch Chamascha* intervening: (1) Psalms 113 and 114 are said before the meal and (2) Psalms 115–118 are recited after the meal. (See p. 268 for why Hallel is divided this way.)

There are nine expressions of praise in the first paragraph of Hallel, plus a tenth — *Hallelukah*. This concludes this section of the Haggadah and completes the recounting of the Ten Plagues (*Vilna Gaon*).

Also, there are sixty words in this paragraph (counting *Hallelukah* as two words, *Hellelu Kah*), corresponding to the Jewish people who numbered six hundred thousand (60 myriads) when they left Egypt (*Bamidbar Rabbah*).

הגדה של פסח

H alleluyah! Praise, you servants of HASHEM, praise the Name of HASHEM. Blessed is the Name of HASHEM from now and forever.

Q *Here we say, "Praise, you servants of HASHEM, praise the Name of HASHEM." Psalm 135 in Tehillim, however, first says, "Praise the Name of HASHEM," and then, "Praise, you servants of HASHEM." Why is the order changed?*

A
- **ABARBANEL:** This paragraph is talking about the individual who is worthy of paying tribute to Hashem. David HaMelech is telling us that not everyone is permitted to praise Him: only the servant of Hashem who clings to Him. He therefore singles out the tribe of Levi, whom he calls *you servants of HASHEM!* Psalm 135, however, speaks in general about those who praise Hashem, and therefore it begins with *Praise the Name of HASHEM*, speaking to anyone who praises Hashem.

- **ALSHICH:** This passage refers to those servants of Hashem for whom it is most appropriate to bless Hashem for the miracles He performed for them — especially the generation of the Exodus, when they saw the Hand of God during the plagues. Therefore it addresses *you servants of HASHEM* in the first verse. Psalm 135 speaks to the world in general, throughout the generations.

- **MAHARAL:** There are two types of praise we offer to Hashem:
  1. Praise for taking us from slavery to freedom and performing miracles for us, and
  2. Praise we are His servants, just as a servant praises his master out of gratitude. (This refers to an *eved Ivri*, who became a servant because he was destitute and could not support his family, or because he could not pay his debts for civil crimes he committed. His master took him in and provided him a home and a way to redeem himself.)

  The praise in Psalm 135 is based on the first type; it is an expression of thanks and praise for the miracles that were performed for us. This psalm that appears in the Haggadah, however, also includes the second aspect — praise to Hashem because we have been chosen to be His servants. Therefore, it begins with the words *Praise, you servants of HASHEM!*

מִמִּזְרַח שֶׁמֶשׁ עַד מְבוֹאוֹ, מְהֻלָּל שֵׁם יהוה. רָם
עַל כָּל גּוֹיִם יהוה, עַל הַשָּׁמַיִם כְּבוֹדוֹ. מִי כַּיהוה
אֱלֹהֵינוּ, הַמַּגְבִּיהִי לָשָׁבֶת. הַמַּשְׁפִּילִי לִרְאוֹת,
בַּשָּׁמַיִם וּבָאָרֶץ. מְקִימִי מֵעָפָר דָּל, מֵאַשְׁפֹּת
יָרִים אֶבְיוֹן. לְהוֹשִׁיבִי עִם נְדִיבִים, עִם נְדִיבֵי
עַמּוֹ. מוֹשִׁיבִי עֲקֶרֶת הַבַּיִת, אֵם הַבָּנִים שְׂמֵחָה;
הַלְלוּיָהּ.[1]

☐ **ALTER OF KELM:** Most people are moved by something different and out of the ordinary, such as a carriage that moves without horses. We are not moved by ordinary things, such when we see an animal pulling a cart. The Sages, in contrast, were awed by the intelligence that man possesses, even though it is obvious and natural, something perfectly normal in the natural order of things.

There are two ways to serve Hashem. Psalm 135 opens with a recognition of Hashem as our Sages had — a recognition that even what most consider ordinary is out of the ordinary — and only afterward mentions the miracles that were performed for the Jewish people. Therefore it starts with *Praise the Name of HASHEM* — recognize how even the natural order is extraordinary, how Hashem runs the world with precision. Then comes the level of *Praise, you servants of HASHEM!* — the level of seeing evidence of Hashem's providence in miracles, which is clear and obvious to all.

In contrast, Hallel consists of praise to Hashem for the miracles He does and the gratitude this inspires in us. Therefore, it says first, *Praise, you servants of HASHEM.* Then, after seeing the miracles, one is also capable of discerning Hashem's conduct through the creation — even in that which seems perfectly ordinary — and reach a level of *Praise the Name of HASHEM.*

☐ **SFAS EMES:** Servitude leads to despair; a slave generally yearns to escape his master. This is in glaring contrast to servants of Hashem — we long to serve Him and do so amid great joy. David HaMelech underscored this love in the opening of his psalm: *Praise, you servants of HASHEM!* Psalm 135, on the other hand, speaks of the gratitude of

From the rising of the sun to its setting, HASHEM's Name is praised. High above all nations is HASHEM, above the heavens is His glory. Who is like HASHEM, our God, Who is enthroned on high, yet deigns to look upon heaven and earth? He raises the destitute from the dust; from the trash heaps He lifts the needy — to seat them with nobles, with nobles of His people. He transforms the barren wife into a glad mother of children. Halleluyah![1]

---

1. *Psalm* 113.

---

the general masses, not servants of Hashem. They do not appreciate the joy of servitude to Hashem, and therefore that psalm does not start with praise from Hashem's servants.

Q *Why does the verse invoke from sunrise to sunset, rather than simply say, "All day HASHEM's Name is praised?"*

A
- ☐ **MIDRASH:** This emphasizes that we literally praise Hashem from the break of day, at sunrise when He lights up the world, until the sun sets.

- ☐ **MIDRASH:** The word *shemesh*, sun, indicates that Hashem is praised and exalted not only on earth, but also by the heavenly bodies above, which includes the sun.

- ☐ **RADAK:** The verse encompasses all human beings, from east (hinted at by *the rising of the sun*) to west (hinted at by *its setting*). All of them, including idol worshipers, will praise Hashem.

- ☐ **RAV SAMSON RAPHAEL HIRSCH:** With this verse, David HaMelech is saying that knowledge of the existence of Hashem reaches every place in the world where people dwell — from east to west.

- ☐ **TZUF AMARIM:** *From the rising of the sun* implies good days, when a person can discern the positive things in his life. *To its setting* represents the times when things go badly for him. David HaMelech says that a person must praise Hashem all the time, even when things are not going well for him, as Chazal teach, *Just as one recites a blessing over the good, he must recite a blessing over the bad* (*Berachos* 60).

Q Why is the letter *yud* tacked on to the ends of the five words that tell of Hashem's actions on behalf of the needy in this passage — הַמַּגְבִּיהִי, *Who is on high;* הַמַּשְׁפִּילִי, *He deigns;* מְקִימִי, *He raises;* לְהוֹשִׁיבִי, *to seat them;* and מוֹשִׁיבִי, *He transforms?*

A ☐ **AVUDRAHAM:** *Yud* has the numerical value of 10. Five times *yud* equals 50. These five *yuds* correspond to the fifty plagues that were inflicted on the Egyptians at the sea (according to Rabbi Yose HaGlili).

☐ **TOLDOS ADAM:** The addition of the letter *yud* turns these words into a first-person conjugation — to teach us that Hashem watches over every single Jew.

☐ These five words describe five stages that the Jewish people passed through in Egypt, on their way from slavery to freedom. The letter *yud* at the end of each of these words links Hashem's kindnesses to every individual Jew:

1. הַמַּגְבִּיהִי לָשָׁבֶת, *He is enthroned on high* — Hashem raised up the Jewish people to live in the land of Goshen.
2. הַמַּשְׁפִּילִי לִרְאוֹת, *He deigns [literally, "lowers Himself"] to look* — Hashem lowered us into slavery and suffering, so that we would have an opportunity to witness the miracles that He performed for us and thus strengthen our faith in Him.
3. מְקִימִי מֵעָפָר דָּל, *He raises the destitute from the dust* — afterward, He lifted us out of degradation and oppression.
4. לְהוֹשִׁיבִי עִם נְדִיבִים, *to seat them with nobles* — in addition to the rescue, Hashem seated Moshe and Aharon *with nobles*, with Pharaoh and his officers.
5. מוֹשִׁיבִי עֲקֶרֶת הַבַּיִת, *He transforms [literally, "returns"] the barren wife* — finally, Hashem brought us to Eretz Yisrael.

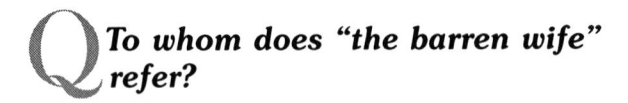

Q To whom does "the barren wife" refer?

A ☐ **PESIKTA D'RAV KAHANA:** It refers to our four Matriarchs — Sarah, Rivkah, Rachel, and Leah — who were barren.

☐ **TALMUD** (*Sotah* 12a); **ROKEACH:** The ministering angels said these words about Amram, who took back his wife, Yocheved, on the advice of their daughter, Miriam. The numerical value of Yocheved is 42 — the same as the word *eim*, mother.

☐ **RASHI:** The "barren wife" is Jerusalem — as it says regarding the Holy City that was left "barren" after the destruction, רָנִּי עֲקָרָה לֹא יָלָדָה, *Sing out, O barren one, who has not given birth* (*Yeshayahu* 54:1).

☐ **RASHBAM:** It is speaking of the women of Israel. The Egyptians wanted to keep the Jews from procreating and turn the Jewish wives into barren women, but they discovered instead that they were אֵם הַבָּנִים שְׂמֵחָה, *a glad mother of children*. For this, we thank Hashem.

☐ **METZUDAS DAVID:** It refers to a barren woman, who usually sits outside, seeking solace. Hashem watches over her and, in His kindness, gives her children to sit with at home.

☐ **MALBIM:** There were eras in which a man could marry two wives: one for bearing children and the other for pleasure. The second wife would have to drink a potion to make her barren and ensure that she would not give birth. David HaMelech is pointing to Hashem's *hashgachah*, saying that He will heal even this woman so that she will become an אֵם הַבָּנִים שְׂמֵחָה, *a glad mother of children*.

☐ **ALSHICH:** With regard to the verse וַתְּהִי שָׂרַי עֲקָרָה אֵין לָהּ וָלָד, *And Sarai was barren, she had no child* (*Genesis* 11:30), our Sages say that not only was she barren, but she did not even have a womb or "home" in which to receive and nurture an unborn child. The words *akeres habayis* therefore refer to the fact that she was barren of the "home" that is known to other women: the womb. David HaMelech tells us that Hashem can bring joy even to a barren woman who has no womb and transform her into *a glad mother of children*.

☐ **IYUN TEFILLAH:** A barren woman is afraid that her husband will divorce her. Upon giving birth to children, she is no longer afraid. Hashem has given her children and has made her into *a glad mother of children*.

[227] **HAGGADAH: THE ANSWER IS . . .**

בְּצֵאת יִשְׂרָאֵל מִמִּצְרָיִם, בֵּית יַעֲקֹב מֵעַם לֹעֵז. הָיְתָה יְהוּדָה לְקָדְשׁוֹ, יִשְׂרָאֵל מַמְשְׁלוֹתָיו. הַיָּם רָאָה וַיָּנֹס, הַיַּרְדֵּן יִסֹּב לְאָחוֹר.

ぎ בְּצֵאת יִשְׂרָאֵל / **When Israel went forth**

Q *Why repeat "when Israel went forth from Egypt" and "Yaakov" from an alien tongue?*

A ☐ **VILNA GAON:** *Israel* refers to the males and *Yaakov's household* to the females. *A people of alien tongue* (me'am lo'ez) is a reference to the la'az (slander) of the Egyptians, who claimed to have mastery over the Jewish women. Hashem disproved this when the Jewish women followed their husbands out of Egypt.

☐ **MALBIM:** *Israel* refers to the leaders, the elders — the tribe of Levi — who did not mingle with the Egyptians. *Yaakov's household* refers to the masses, who assimilated with the Egyptians and left as *a people of alien tongue*.

☐ **ALSHICH:** There are two kinds of departures. The first is when a person is attached to a community and departs from it. In addition to his physically leaving the place, he is also leaving the community on an emotional level. In the second kind of leave-taking, the person is not attached to the community; his departure involves merely leaving the place itself.

The Jewish people as a whole did not befriend the Egyptians or learn from their ways, so they are known as *Israel*. Their leaving was of the second variety: a physical departure without emotional ties. Those who did mingle with the Egyptians are called *Yaakov's household*, and their departure was of the first kind.

☐ **NETZIV:** Because of the Egyptians' influence, the Jewish people in Egypt were sunk in impurity. They were therefore called *Beis Yaakov*, Yaakov's household, when they left *a people of alien tongue* — that is, Egypt — since they were on a lowly level. When they achieved higher spiritual levels, however, they were called *Yisrael*.

☐ **MEI MEGGIDO:** There were two groups of people in the

הגדה של פסח [228]

When Israel went forth from Egypt, Yaakov's household from a people of alien tongue, Yehudah became His sanctuary, Israel His dominion. The sea saw and fled; the Jordan turned backward.

Jewish nation. The first, and better group — *Yisrael* — left Egypt and all its impurity. The second — *Beis Yaakov* — were the masses, who understood only that they were leaving an *am lo'ez*, a nation of alien tongue: the dominion of Egypt.

☐ **ALTER OF KELM:** In order to attain holiness, the Jewish people needed to cut themselves off in two ways: first, by physically leaving Egypt, which is why it says, *When Israel went forth from Egypt*. Second, *from a people of alien tongue* — by detaching themselves from the teachings of Egypt, they would become a holy people.

☐ **CHASAM SOFER:** The Jewish people were redeemed from Egypt in the merit of three things: they did not change their names, they did not change their language, and they guarded themselves against immorality. The repetitive language is used to parallel these three things:

1. Bnei Yisrael went down to Egypt as "Yisrael." In the merit of not changing that name, they were redeemed.

2. They did not change their language; therefore it says *Yaakov's household from a people of alien tongue*.

3. They did not engage in immorality; therefore it says *Yehudah became His sanctuary*. The word *l'kadsho*, His sanctuary, literally means "His holiness," implying that they remained holy.

☐ **RAV YISRAEL ZILBERMAN:** The Jewish people, forced to perform backbreaking toil, felt the oppression keenly. The tribe of Levi, who were not forced to work, sensed Egypt's impurity. *When Israel went forth from Egypt* refers to the tribe of Levi, who most strongly felt the redemption when they departed from Egypt's impurity. *Yaakov's household* refers to the rest of the Jewish people, who engaged in idolatry like their Egyptian neighbors, and only felt the redemption upon their physical departure from *a people of alien tongue*.

[229] HAGGADAH: THE ANSWER IS . . .

הֶהָרִים רָקְדוּ כְאֵילִים, גְּבָעוֹת כִּבְנֵי צֹאן. מַה
לְּךָ הַיָּם כִּי תָנוּס, הַיַּרְדֵּן תִּסֹּב לְאָחוֹר. הֶהָרִים
תִּרְקְדוּ כְאֵילִים, גְּבָעוֹת כִּבְנֵי צֹאן. מִלִּפְנֵי אָדוֹן
חוּלִי אָרֶץ, מִלִּפְנֵי אֱלוֹהַּ יַעֲקֹב. הַהֹפְכִי הַצּוּר
אֲגַם מָיִם, חַלָּמִישׁ לְמַעְיְנוֹ מָיִם.[1]

Q *To which sanctuary does the verse refer, and why does it mention specifically Yehudah?*

A ☐ **RASHI:** This refers to the *kiddush Hashem* (*kiddush* and *l'kadsho* share the same root) that Nachshon, the leader of the tribe of Yehudah, made when he leaped into the waters of the Sea of Reeds. In his merit, the sea split.

☐ **ALSHICH:** The tribe of Yehudah stood out and excelled in its faith and trust in Hashem, as we saw when they were the first to enter the sea even before it split (after Nachshon, their leader, jumped in). Therefore, the tribe merited having its descendants rule over the Jewish nation.

☐ **MAHARAL:** The tribe of Yehudah is the one from which kings descended. *L'kadsho* refers to the holiness with which the king was imbued as he was anointed with the holy oil.

☐ **ABARBANEL:** "Yehudah" refers to the group that split off from the Jewish nation and the other tribes: first, on their departure from Egypt, and later, in the days of Rechavam and Yeravam, when the kingdom was divided.

☐ **NETZIV:** "Yehudah" refers to the Jewish people as a whole. They attained lofty levels and were worthy of *ruach ha-kodesh* after they left Egypt. *L'kadsho* therefore refers to the level of holiness that they attained.

☐ **IYUN TEFILLAH:** The idea of holiness implies that the Jewish people were separated and distinguished from the nations of the world to become the children of Hashem.

Q *Why is the verb הָיְתָה, became, in the feminine form, when Yehudah is masculine?*

A ☐ **ROKEACH:** When the tribe of Yehudah leaped into the sea, following after their leader Nachshon ben Aminadav, they

The mountains skipped like rams, and the hills like young lambs. What ails you, O sea, that you flee? O Jordan, that you turn backward? O mountains, that you skip like rams? O hills, like young lambs? Before HASHEM's presence — tremble, O earth, before the presence of the God of Yaakov, Who turns the rock into a pond of water, the flint into a flowing fountain.[1]

---

1. Psalm 114.

---

became as weak as females from the roiling waves. They cried out, הוֹשִׁיעֵנִי אֱלֹהִים כִּי בָאוּ מַיִם עַד נָפֶשׁ, Save me, O God, for the waters have reached until the soul! (Psalms 69:2). The word הָיְתָה is in the feminine form to reflect this weakness.

☐ ALSHICH: This word hints at Tamar, mother of Yehudah's youngest children, who made a kiddush Hashem by her willingness to sacrifice her life rather than embarrass Yehudah. Through this act, Yehudah and Tamar imbued this important trait to their descendants: Nachshon, a descendant of theirs, also demonstrated such self-sacrifice when he sanctified Hashem's Name by jumping into the sea.

☐ MAHARAL: This teaches that the relationship between the Jewish people and Hashem is like that of a woman betrothed (from the same root as l'kadsho) to her husband.

☐ YAAVETZ: This is a reference to Elisheva, of the tribe of Yehudah, who was Aharon HaKohen's wife. L'kadsho, His sanctuary, refers to the holiness that filled the Kodesh HaKodashim — the Holy of Holies — which only Aharon, as the Kohen Gadol, was allowed to enter.

☐ RAV SAMSON RAPHAEL HIRSCH: Just as a female lacks great strength, so too does strength of the Jewish people desert them without Hashem's help. By using the feminine form, David is expressing his trust in Hashem.

Q *Why does this psalm present a question-and-answer dialogue?*

A ☐ MEIRI: It begins with a question in order to prompt a response. David wished to proclaim that the miracle of the splitting of the sea came about through Divine Providence.

[231] HAGGADAH: THE ANSWER IS . . .

☐ **RAV YECHEZKEL ABRAMSKY:** The psalm opens with four questions about phenomena in nature: the sea — which flees; the Jordan — which turns backward; the mountains — which skip like rams; and the hills — which are like young lambs. It is preferable for these ideas be presented as questions and answers, because then they are more easily understood, like the questions of *Mah Nishtanah*.

Q *What question is there as to why the Sea "fled"? Was it not a miracle that Hashem performed to allow the Jews to pass through?*

A ☐ **ALSHICH:** When Hashem created the world, He left it up to the ministering angel of the Sea of Reeds whether the sea would split; it was not something that was taken for granted. Therefore, David HaMelech asks about it in wonder, amazed at the miracle that occurred.

☐ **NETZIV:** David is asking for an explanation for the changes in nature that were wrought on behalf of the Jewish people. These miracles were seemingly unnecessary, since the Jews were on an exalted spiritual plane and did not require changes in nature to strengthen their faith.

☐ **RAV AVRAHAM GRODZINSKY:** The changes in nature were external, in order to arouse man spiritually. David's question is not about the miracles, but rather about their goal: What do they come to teach us?

☐ **RAV REUVEN GROZOVSKY:** David HaMelech is amazed that the sea "fled" and split, because there is a concept of even inanimate objects having certain traits — such as a land being holy or impure, fruit being holy, and so on — as if they have a mind of their own. Similarly, the river did not at first split for Rabbi Pinchas ben Yair, so it should not be taken for granted that the sea split.

Q *What are some differences between the splitting of the sea after the Exodus and the splitting of the Jordan River in the time of Yehoshua?*

A ☐ **MALBIM:** The sea was split forming walls of water on both sides of the Jewish people as they crossed; therefore, it says, *The sea saw and fled.* The water "fled" and the people were

הגדה של פסח [232]

able to cross on dry land. At the Jordan River, however, the water rose up in one column only on one side, as if the water turned backward on itself. Therefore it says, *The Jordan will turn backward.*

☐ **RAV YECHEZKEL ABRAMSKY:** At the sea, only after Nachshon leaped into the water with great self-sacrifice did the water divide. At the Jordan, in contrast, the water split as soon as the feet of the Kohanim stepped into it. The difference between the two is that the splitting of the sea took place before the giving of the Torah, when the Jewish people were in need of many merits and Nachshon's self-sacrifice stood them in good stead. When they crossed the Jordan, they already had the merit of the Torah. Therefore, the Jordan split when the Kohanim's feet trod on it.

Q *Isn't the rock that "turns into a pond of water" the same as the flint turning into a "flowing fountain"?*

A ☐ **ROKEACH:** *Tzur*, rock, refers to the rock at Refidim, where shortly after the Exodus the Jewish people found themselves without water. There Hashem commanded Moshe to strike the rock to get water from it. *Chalamish*, flint, refers to the stone that Moshe struck at Mei Merivah (although there Hashem had commanded him to *speak* to it).

☐ **ABARBANEL:** The verse is speaking of changes that were made in nature in relation to rocks and water. At the Sea of Reeds, Hashem turned the water into hard stones, while in the desert stones were turned into water. There, it was not just ordinary rocks (*tzur*) that were turned into water, but *chalamish*, hard, strong flint stone, also produced water.

☐ **RAV ITZELE OF VOLOZHIN:** A *tzur* is a rock in which by nature there is a bit of water. A *chalamish* is a hard, dry stone (i.e., flint) that has no water and is generally used to ignite fire. The miracle of the rock had two stages. At first, Moshe extracted a little "natural" water from the *tzur*, ordinary rock, and then the rock turned into flint — a dry rock with no water — and still water miraculously flowed from it.

According to this, the words *Who turns the rock into a pond of water* may be understood to mean that at first the waters naturally found in the rock gathered into a pond of water. And then there was an even greater miracle: Hashem

According to all customs the cup is lifted and the matzos covered during the recitation of this blessing. (On Saturday night the phrase in parentheses substitutes for the preceding phrase.)

בָּרוּךְ אַתָּה יהוה אֱלֹהֵינוּ מֶלֶךְ הָעוֹלָם, אֲשֶׁר גְּאָלָנוּ וְגָאַל אֶת אֲבוֹתֵינוּ מִמִּצְרַיִם, וְהִגִּיעָנוּ הַלַּיְלָה הַזֶּה לֶאֱכָל בּוֹ מַצָּה וּמָרוֹר. כֵּן יהוה אֱלֹהֵינוּ וֵאלֹהֵי אֲבוֹתֵינוּ, יַגִּיעֵנוּ לְמוֹעֲדִים וְלִרְגָלִים אֲחֵרִים הַבָּאִים לִקְרָאתֵנוּ לְשָׁלוֹם, שְׂמֵחִים בְּבִנְיַן עִירֶךָ וְשָׂשִׂים בַּעֲבוֹדָתֶךָ,

---

turned the stone of *flint into a flowing fountain*. The flint was transformed into a wellspring of water, a creation of *yeish me'ayin*, from nothing.

◆§ אֲשֶׁר גְּאָלָנוּ / Who redeemed us

This blessing mentions the redemption of our forefathers from Egypt, continuing the theme of the passage of *B'Chol Dor VaDor*. There it states, *It was not only our fathers whom the Holy One, Blessed is He, redeemed from slavery; we, too, were redeemed with them...* Now the blessing of *Asher Ge'alanu* goes on to say, *Blessed are You, HASHEM, our God, King of the universe, Who redeemed us and redeemed our ancestors from Egypt* (Avudraham).

Q *Our forefathers' redemption preceded our own redemption. Why then does this blessing begin with "You redeemed us" and then say "You redeemed our ancestors"? (Indeed, in L'fichach, our ancestors are mentioned before us.)*

A ☐ **CHAYEI ADAM:** Every Jewish soul was present at the oppression and the redemption. Therefore, we praise Hashem for our personal redemption first, before that of our ancestors.

☐ **DIVREI YOEL:** The oppression of the Jewish people ceased twelve months before they left Egypt. During that year, they were free men. Therefore the main thrust of the redemption from Egypt was for the benefit of future generations. Hashem took out the Jewish people so that Egypt's impurity would have no effect on future generations. Therefore, as we

[234] הגדה של פסח

According to all customs the cup is lifted and the matzos covered during the recitation of this blessing. (On Saturday night the phrase in parentheses substitutes for the preceding phrase.)

Blessed are You, HASHEM, our God, King of the universe, Who redeemed us and redeemed our ancestors from Egypt and enabled us to reach this night that we may eat on it matzah and maror. So, HASHEM, our God and God of our fathers, bring us also to future holidays and festivals in peace, gladdened in the rebuilding of Your city and joyful at Your service.

---

thank Him, we speak of ourselves — the primary goal of the Exodus — before them.

☐ **SIFSEI CHAIM:** The steps used to make the story of the Exodus come alive for us are arranged in such a way that we ultimately reach the level where we feel as though we ourselves left Egypt. Upon attaining this level, it is fitting for us to say *Who redeemed us* to thank Hashem for redeeming us, and only then thank Him for redeeming our ancestors. The blessing of *Asher Ge'alanu* expresses this feeling, which is why our gratitude for our own redemption precedes our expression of gratitude for that of our ancestors.

☐ Our personal redemption is mentioned before that of our ancestors because we — the descendants of those who left Egypt — are guarantors and living witnesses to their redemption of Egypt.

Q *The wording of this blessing sounds as if the redemption could come on other holidays. Do not Chazal say, "In Nissan they are destined to be redeemed" (Rosh Hashanah 11a)?*

A ☐ **SHIBBOLEI HALEKET:** This is not a reference to a specific holiday in which the redemption will come. Rather, we are saying that just as we are now able to eat matzah and *maror* on the Seder night without disturbance, so may we have other holidays and festivals in which we will be able to observe the mitzvos of the holiday in peace.

☐ **RID:** Word of the redemption will come on Pesach, but the redemption itself will come afterward.

[235] HAGGADAH: THE ANSWER IS . . .

וְנֹאכַל שָׁם מִן הַזְּבָחִים וּמִן הַפְּסָחִים (מִן הַפְּסָחִים וּמִן הַזְּבָחִים) אֲשֶׁר יַגִּיעַ דָּמָם עַל קִיר מִזְבַּחֲךָ לְרָצוֹן. וְנוֹדֶה לְךָ שִׁיר חָדָשׁ עַל גְּאֻלָּתֵנוּ וְעַל פְּדוּת נַפְשֵׁנוּ. בָּרוּךְ אַתָּה יהוה, גָּאַל יִשְׂרָאֵל.

Some have the custom to recite the following declaration of intent.

הִנְנִי מוּכָן וּמְזוּמָּן לְקַיֵּם מִצְוַת כּוֹס שֵׁנִי מֵאַרְבַּע כּוֹסוֹת. לְשֵׁם יִחוּד קֻדְשָׁא בְּרִיךְ הוּא וּשְׁכִינְתֵּיהּ, עַל יְדֵי הַהוּא טָמִיר וְנֶעְלָם, בְּשֵׁם כָּל יִשְׂרָאֵל. וִיהִי נֹעַם אֲדֹנָי אֱלֹהֵינוּ עָלֵינוּ, וּמַעֲשֵׂה יָדֵינוּ כּוֹנְנָה עָלֵינוּ, וּמַעֲשֵׂה יָדֵינוּ כּוֹנְנֵהוּ.

בָּרוּךְ אַתָּה יהוה אֱלֹהֵינוּ מֶלֶךְ הָעוֹלָם, בּוֹרֵא פְּרִי הַגָּפֶן.

The second cup is drunk while leaning on the left side — preferably the entire cup, but at least most of it.

☐ **DIVREI YOEL:** This is not a reference to other holidays than Pesach. Rather, it is telling us that the nature of Pesach itself will change in the future, and will be like a different holiday.

☐ Nissan is an auspicious time for redemption. However, Mashiach may come at any time of the year, as we say in *Ani Ma'amin: I believe in the coming of Mashiach...and every day, I await his coming.*

Q Why do we say שִׁיר, *song of praise*, in the masculine form, rather than שִׁירָה, in the feminine?

A ☐ **BA'ALEI HATOSAFOS** (*Pesachim* 116b): A female suffers at the time she gives birth. In the future, in the time of the Mashiach, there will be no hardships or suffering. The new song hints at a future time when there will no longer be any troubles. This is the experience of the male, and not the female.

☐ All the other songs are mentioned in the feminine form to teach us that they will have a sequel or continuation — just as the female of the species gives birth and nurtures the next generation. In the future, however, there will be a change. The redemption that will come in the future will be likened to a male who does not give birth.

There we shall eat of the offerings and Passover sacrifices (of the Passover sacrifices and offerings) whose blood will gain the sides of Your Altar for gracious acceptance. We shall then sing a new song of praise to You for our redemption and for the liberation of our souls. Blessed are You, HASHEM, Who has redeemed Israel.

Some have the custom to recite the following declaration of intent.

Behold, I am prepared and ready to fulfill the mitzvah of the second of the Four Cups. For the sake of the unification of the Holy One, Blessed is He, and His Presence, through Him Who is hidden and inscrutable — [I pray] in the name of all Israel. May the pleasantness of the Lord, our God, be upon us, and may He establish our handiwork for us; our handiwork may He establish.

Blessed are You, HASHEM, our God, King of the universe, Who creates the fruit of the vine.

The second cup is drunk while leaning on the left side — preferably the entire cup, but at least most of it.

In the coming redemption, there will be no continuation of the oppression. This song is speaking of the time after the redemption, and therefore the song is referred to in the masculine, for it will have no sequel.

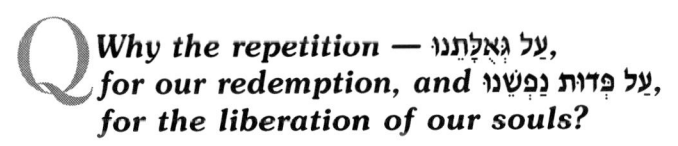

Q *Why the repetition* — עַל גְּאֻלָּתֵנוּ, *for our redemption, and* עַל פְּדוּת נַפְשֵׁנוּ, *for the liberation of our souls?*

A ☐ **KOL BO:** *Our redemption* refers to the future redemption, while *the liberation of our souls* refers specifically to the exile of Egypt.

☐ **MALBIM:** *Our redemption* refers to the redemption of the body, while *the liberation of our souls* refers to the redemption of the soul.

☐ **BRISKER RAV:** This blessing thanks Hashem for two things:
1. *for our redemption* — leaving Pharaoh's slavery;
2. *for the liberation of our souls* — our freedom and the knowledge that we will no longer be enslaved.

[237] HAGGADAH: THE ANSWER IS . . .

רחצה

The hands are washed for matzah and the following blessing is recited. It is preferable to bring water and a basin to the head of the household at the Seder table.

בָּרוּךְ אַתָּה יהוה אֱלֹהֵינוּ מֶלֶךְ הָעוֹלָם, אֲשֶׁר קִדְּשָׁנוּ בְּמִצְוֹתָיו, וְצִוָּנוּ עַל נְטִילַת יָדָיִם.

מוציא / מצה

Some recite the following before the blessing *hamotzi*.

הִנְנִי מוּכָן וּמְזוּמָּן לְקַיֵּם מִצְוַת אֲכִילַת מַצָּה. לְשֵׁם יִחוּד קֻדְשָׁא בְּרִיךְ הוּא וּשְׁכִינְתֵּיהּ, עַל יְדֵי הַהוּא טָמִיר וְנֶעְלָם, בְּשֵׁם כָּל יִשְׂרָאֵל. וִיהִי נְעַם אֲדֹנָי אֱלֹהֵינוּ עָלֵינוּ, וּמַעֲשֵׂה יָדֵינוּ כּוֹנְנָה עָלֵינוּ, וּמַעֲשֵׂה יָדֵינוּ כּוֹנְנֵהוּ.

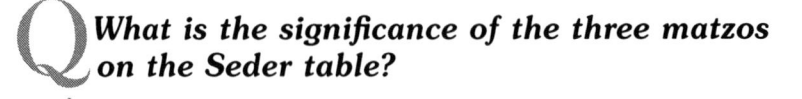

◆§ מצה / Matzah

Q *What is the significance of the three matzos on the Seder table?*

A ☐ **RAV SHERIRA GAON:** Avraham Avinu welcomed the three angels as his guests on Erev Pesach and asked Sarah to prepare three *se'ah*, measures, of flour. The three matzos at the Seder correspond to those three measures of flour.

☐ **MAHARIL:** One who is freed from prison is required to bring a *korban todah*, a thanksgiving-offering, which includes three types of matzos. To show our gratitude to Hashem for freeing the Jewish people from Egypt, we place three matzos on the table as a form of thanksgiving-offering.

☐ The three matzos correspond to the three types of Jews: Kohen, Levi, and Yisrael.

☐ After the *Bris Bein Habesarim* (Covenant Between the Parts), when Hashem informed Avraham that there would be an Egyptian exile, Avraham was told to bring three heifers, goats, and rams.

☐ At the Seder, as at every Shabbos and holiday meal, we need to have *lechem mishneh*, two whole breads. Since the middle matzah will be broken during *Yachatz*, there is a need for

הגדה של פסח

RACHTZAH

The hands are washed for matzah and the following blessing is recited. It is preferable to bring water and a basin to the head of the household at the Seder table.

Blessed are You, HASHEM, our God, King of the universe, Who has sanctified us with His commandments, and has commanded us concerning the washing of the hands.

MOTZI / MATZAH

Some recite the following before the blessing *hamotzi*.

Behold, I am prepared and ready to fulfill the mitzvah of eating matzah. For the sake of the unification of the Holy One, Blessed is He, and His Presence, through Him Who is hidden and inscrutable — [I pray] in the name of all Israel. May the pleasantness of the Lord, our God, be upon us, and may He establish our handiwork for us; our handiwork may He establish.

---

a third matzah to ensure that we will have two whole matzos for *lechem mishneh* (besides the middle, broken matzah).

☐ [It should be noted that the Vilna Gaon used only two matzos.]

Q ***What are the many spiritual properties of matzah?***

A ☐ **ZOHAR:** The matzah is called *"meichla d'asvasa,"* food of healing.

☐ **RADVAZ:** The matzah alludes to Hashem's attribute of mercy. By eating matzah, we silence the attribute of justice and arouse the attribute of mercy.

☐ **TZIDKAS HATZADDIK:** Matzah, which is a humble food, made of only flour and water, has the power to eradicate *ta'avah* (physical desire), just as a pauper manages with little and leaves his desires unfulfilled. It also has the power to eliminate arrogance, as well as anger (which has its roots in haughtiness).

☐ **MISHKENOS HARO'IM:** Matzah has the power to sanctify all of our eating throughout the year.

[239] **HAGGADAH: THE ANSWER IS . . .**

The following two blessings are recited over matzah; the first is recited over matzah as food, and the second for the special mitzvah of eating matzah on the night of Passover. [The latter blessing is to be made with the intention that it also apply to the "sandwich" and the *Afikoman*.] The head of the household raises all the matzos on the Seder plate and recites the following blessing:

בָּרוּךְ אַתָּה יהוה אֱלֹהֵינוּ מֶלֶךְ הָעוֹלָם, הַמּוֹצִיא לֶחֶם מִן הָאָרֶץ.

The bottom matzah is put down and the following blessing is recited while the top (whole) matzah and the middle (broken) piece are still raised.

בָּרוּךְ אַתָּה יהוה אֱלֹהֵינוּ מֶלֶךְ הָעוֹלָם, אֲשֶׁר קִדְּשָׁנוּ בְּמִצְוֹתָיו, וְצִוָּנוּ עַל אֲכִילַת מַצָּה.

Each participant is required to eat an amount of matzah equal in volume to an egg. Since it is usually impossible to provide a sufficient amount of matzah from the two matzos for all members of the household, other matzos should be available at the head of the table from which to complete the required amounts. However, each participant should receive a piece from each of the top two matzos. The matzos are to be eaten while reclining on the left side and without delay; they need not be dipped in salt.

- **HAGGADAH CHODESH HAAVIV:** In the merit of the matzah that Jews eat on Pesach, they are able to survive the judgment of Rosh HaShanah. An allusion to this is found in the verse הַיּוֹם אַתֶּם יֹצְאִים בְּחֹדֶשׁ הָאָבִיב, *Today you are leaving in the month of springtime* (Exodus 13:4), which can be interpreted to mean, *This day [Rosh Hashanah], you are exonerated in judgment in the merit of [the matzah you ate in] the month of springtime.*

- **TIFERES SHLOMO:** This is the only Torah-ordained mitzvah involving eating that we are able to fulfill nowadays. Just as swallowing a pill can heal a person's body, swallowing the matzah heals a person's soul.

- **AVNEI NEZER:** Eating matzah heals a person's soul, for by eating matzah, a person becomes a new being whose life force is drawn solely from the mitzvah of matzah.

- **MESHECH CHOCHMAH:** Matzah is called *"meichla dim'heimenusa,"* food of faith. The Jews had to leave Egypt in haste, with no time to prepare food. They exhibited complete faith in following Hashem into the wilderness with no

The following two blessings are recited over matzah; the first is recited over matzah as food, and the second for the special mitzvah of eating matzah on the night of Passover. [The latter blessing is to be made with the intention that it also apply to the "sandwich" and the *Afikoman*.] The head of the household raises all the matzos on the Seder plate and recites the following blessing:

Blessed are You, HASHEM, our God, King of the universe, Who brings forth bread from the earth.

The bottom matzah is put down and the following blessing is recited while the top (whole) matzah and the middle (broken) piece are still raised.

Blessed are You, HASHEM, our God, King of the universe, Who has sanctified us with His commandments, and has commanded us concerning the eating of the matzah.

Each participant is required to eat an amount of matzah equal in volume to an egg. Since it is usually impossible to provide a sufficient amount of matzah from the two matzos for all members of the household, other matzos should be available at the head of the table from which to complete the required amounts. However, each participant should receive a piece from each of the top two matzos. The matzos are to be eaten while reclining on the left side and without delay; they need not be dipped in salt.

---

provisions other than the dough they had baked into matzah. Matzah symbolizes our belief in Hashem, and on the Seder night, it is possible to reach absolute clarity in our faith.

Q Why do we not dip the matzah in salt, as we do challah during the year?

A ☐ **MAHARAL:** Out of affection for the mitzvah, we taste the matzah alone, without adding any other flavors.

☐ **LEVUSH:** We do not dip the matzah in salt so that it will taste bland, as befits the "bread of affliction."

☐ **LEKET YOSHER:** Salt protects the Jewish people. (Just as salt is a preservative, it represents our eternal covenant with Hashem, as the verse says, 'בְּרִית מֶלַח עוֹלָם הוּא לִפְנֵי ה, *It is an eternal saltlike covenant before HASHEM* (Numbers 18:19). On the Seder night, however, we have no need for this protection, since it is a *Leil Shimurim*, a night when we are safeguarded.

[241] HAGGADAH: THE ANSWER IS . . .

מרור

The head of the household takes a half-egg volume of *maror*, dips it into *charoses*, and gives each participant a like amount.

Some recite the following before *maror*:

הִנְנִי מוּכָן וּמְזוּמָן לְקַיֵּם מִצְוַת אֲכִילַת מָרוֹר. לְשֵׁם יִחוּד קֻדְשָׁא בְּרִיךְ הוּא וּשְׁכִינְתֵּיהּ, עַל יְדֵי הַהוּא טָמִיר וְנֶעְלָם, בְּשֵׁם כָּל יִשְׂרָאֵל. וִיהִי נְעַם אֲדֹנָי אֱלֹהֵינוּ עָלֵינוּ, וּמַעֲשֵׂה יָדֵינוּ כּוֹנְנָה עָלֵינוּ, וּמַעֲשֵׂה יָדֵינוּ כּוֹנְנֵהוּ.

The following blessing is recited with the intention that it also apply to the *maror* of the "sandwich." The *maror* is eaten without reclining, and without delay.

בָּרוּךְ אַתָּה יהוה אֱלֹהֵינוּ מֶלֶךְ הָעוֹלָם, אֲשֶׁר קִדְּשָׁנוּ בְּמִצְוֹתָיו, וְצִוָּנוּ עַל אֲכִילַת מָרוֹר.

מרור / Maror

Q Why do we not recite the blessing of *borei pri ha'adamah* on the *maror*?

A
- □ **RASHBA:** It is covered by the blessing of *ha'adamah* that was already said on the *karpas*.
- □ **BA'ALEI HATOSAFOS:** Eating the *maror* is considered part of the meal (after making *hamotzi*).
- □ We do not recite a blessing because one does not derive pleasure from the *maror*, but only eats it as a commemoration of the verse וַיְמָרְרוּ אֶת חַיֵּיהֶם, *They embittered their lives* (*Exodus* 1:14). One only makes a blessing over food that provides pleasure.

Q Why do we dip the *maror* in *charoses*?

A
- □ **TALMUD** (*Pesachim* 116a): The *charoses* commemorates the mortar with which the Jews made bricks, while the *maror* symbolizes the bitterness of their slavery.
- □ **RAV YOSEF SALANT:** The Egyptians showed the Jews a pleasant demeanor, despite the fact that they intended to enslave them from the start. The *maror*, which tastes bitter, to

MAROR

The head of the household takes a half-egg volume of *maror*, dips it into *charoses*, and gives each participant a like amount.

Some recite the following before *maror*:

Behold, I am prepared and ready to fulfill the mitzvah of eating *maror*. For the sake of the unification of the Holy One, Blessed is He, and His Presence, through Him Who is hidden and inscrutable — [I pray] in the name of all Israel. May the pleasantness of the Lord, our God, be upon us, and may He establish our handiwork for us; our handiwork may He establish.

The following blessing is recited with the intention that it also apply to the maror of the "sandwich." The *maror* is eaten without reclining, and without delay.

Blessed are You, HASHEM, our God, King of the universe, Who has sanctified us with His commandments, and has commanded us concerning the eating of *maror*.

---

commemorate the bitterness of the slavery, is dipped in the sweet *charoses*, symbolizing the soft facade the Egyptians showed the Jewish people at first and which dripped with sweetness.

☐ **RAV YITZCHAK ISAAC SHER:** The Egyptians embittered the lives of our ancestors in Egypt, but the Jews did not allow

---

◈§ The Role of the *Maror*

Rav Elimelech of Lizhensk, author of *Noam Elimelech*, explains that were it not for the oppression, the Jewish nation would have assimilated. It was the slavery that made them into a people who were מְעֻנְיָן שָׁם, *distinctive there*. Thus the *maror* was an integral part of the redemption.

In the view of the Sfas Emes, the tribulations and suffering were the means through which we can see, with crystal clarity, how the Jewish people entered into a covenant with *HaKadosh Baruch Hu* and, after their redemption from Egypt, became like a new nation — just as a convert is likened to a newborn baby.

Through the slavery in Egypt, the Jewish people throughout the generations had the ability to sweeten the bitterness of all the hardships and exiles and to stand firm over the course of our difficult history. Thus the oppression was part of the redemption process.

כּוֹרֵךְ

The bottom (thus far unbroken) matzah is now taken. From it, with the addition of other matzos, each participant receives a half-egg volume of matzah with an equal-volume portion of *maror* (dipped into *charoses* which is shaken off). The following paragraph is recited and the "sandwich" is eaten while reclining.

זֵכֶר לְמִקְדָּשׁ כְּהִלֵּל. כֵּן עָשָׂה הִלֵּל בִּזְמַן שֶׁבֵּית הַמִּקְדָּשׁ הָיָה קַיָּם. הָיָה כּוֹרֵךְ (פֶּסַח) מַצָּה וּמָרוֹר וְאוֹכֵל בְּיַחַד. לְקַיֵּם מַה שֶּׁנֶּאֱמַר, עַל מַצּוֹת וּמְרֹרִים יֹאכְלֻהוּ.[1]

---

their troubles and bitterness to dominate them. Then Hashem revealed Himself to them and performed miracles that completely dissolved their bitterness. In that memory, we dip the *maror* in *charoses* to create bitterness with a "sweet" flavor.

☐ **KSAV SOFER:** We dip the *maror* in *charoses* to show the destitute that even in a time of suffering, we harbor hope of salvation and better days to come.

Q Why do we not make a blessing on the charoses?

A
☐ **KOL BO:** We do not make a blessing because the *charoses* is of secondary importance to the *maror*.

☐ **PRI CHADASH:** No blessing is said since there is no specific mitzvah to eat *charoses*.

☐ **RADVAZ:** Since they did not recite a blessing over the *charoses* in the time of the Beis HaMikdash, neither do we.

Q Why do we not ask why we eat charoses on this night in Mah Nishtanah?

A
☐ **RASHBATZ:** There is no question about *charoses* because there is nothing different about eating it. We eat the fruits from which *charoses* is made on the other nights as well.

☐ *Charoses* is a *mitzvah d'rabbanan*, and we do not remark on changes in this type of mitzvah.

KORECH

The bottom (thus far unbroken) matzah is now taken. From it, with the addition of other matzos, each participant receives a half-egg volume of matzah with an equal-volume portion of *maror* (dipped into *charoses* which is shaken off). The following paragraph is recited and the "sandwich" is eaten while reclining.

In remembrance of the Temple we do as Hillel did in Temple times: He would combine (the Passover offering,) matzah and *maror* in a sandwich and eat them together, to fulfill what is written in the Torah: They shall eat it with matzos and bitter herbs.[1]

1. *Numbers* 9:16.

כורך / Korech

Following Hillel's custom, we make a sandwich of the matzah and *maror* and eat it together. The matzah symbolizes the *yetzer hatov*; the *maror*, the *yetzer hara*. We must "sandwich" together the *yetzer hatov* and the *yetzer hara* for the purpose of serving Hashem, as the Talmud teaches regarding the words בְּכָל לְבָבְךָ, *with all of your "hearts"* (*Deuteronomy* 6:5) — *with both of your inclinations, both the good and the bad* (*Berachos* 54).

Some say that the sandwich of *maror* and matzah hints that even when a person is beset by difficulties, he should lift himself and his family to a state of joy, a state of *Shulchan Orech*.

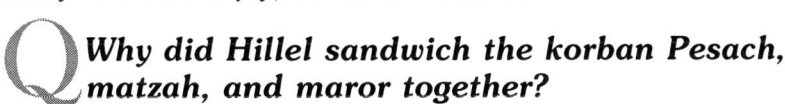

Q *Why did Hillel sandwich the korban Pesach, matzah, and maror together?*

A ☐ **KSAV SOFER:** The mitzvah of eating the *korban Pesach* is a *mitzvas asei*, a positive commandment, and one who does not fulfill it deserves *kares*, premature death and spiritual excision. Not eating matzah and *maror*, on the other hand, incurs a much lesser punishment. Hillel is teaching us to be as careful with a "light" mitzvah as with a stringent one. By sandwiching the three together, he shows that they were all equal in his eyes.

☐ **RAV MEIR LEHMANN:** Hillel was a paragon of humility and self-abnegation despite the fact that he was a leader of stature. Hillel teaches us how to sweeten the bitter in our lives, by putting the bitter together with a bit of sweetness.

[245] HAGGADAH: THE ANSWER IS . . .

שלחן עורך

The meal should be eaten in a combination of joy and solemnity, for the meal, too, is part of the Seder service. While it is desirable that *zemiros* and discussion of the laws and events of Passover be part of the meal, extraneous conversation should be avoided. It should be remembered that the *Afikoman* must be eaten while there is still some appetite for it. In fact, if one is so sated that he must literally force himself to eat it, he is not credited with the performance of the mitzvah of *Afikoman*. Therefore, it is unwise to eat more than a moderate amount during the meal.

צפון

From the *Afikoman* matzah (and from additional matzos to make up the required amount) a half-egg volume portion — according to some, a full egg's volume portion — is given to each participant. It should be eaten before midnight, while reclining, without delay, and uninterruptedly. Nothing may be eaten or drunk after the *Afikoman* (with the exception of water and the like) except for the last two Seder cups of wine.

☐ **DIVREI YOEL:** Every day Hillel said, "*Baruch Hashem!*" He would always accept whatever occurred with joy, even difficulties (*Beitzah* 16). Hillel hints at this approach with regard to the *korban Pesach*: one should accept the good and the bad with the same degree of happiness. Since the *korban Pesach* and matzah symbolize the redemption, and the *maror* represents oppression and exile, Hillel sandwiched them together and ate them in a reclining position — a posture of freedom.

When Moshe Rabbeinu came before Pharaoh at Hashem's command, Pharaoh scoffed, מִי ה' אֲשֶׁר אֶשְׁמַע בְּקֹלוֹ, *Who is Hashem, that I should heed His voice?* (*Exodus* 5:2). And he went on to torture the Jewish people in all sorts of harsh and bitter ways. And yet, when Moshe came to warn him that he would be punished for his sins, he still treated Pharaoh with respect — for he was a king — saying, וְיָרְדוּ כָל עֲבָדֶיךָ אֵלֶּה אֵלַי וְהִשְׁתַּחֲווּ לִי לֵאמֹר צֵא, *Then all these servants of yours will come down to me and bow to me, saying, "Leave!"* (*Exodus* 11:8).

Rashi says that Moshe was showing deference to the kingship, for in the end it was Pharaoh himself who came down to Moshe at night, saying, קוּמוּ צְּאוּ מִתּוֹךְ עַמִּי, *Rise up, go out from among my people* (*Exodus* 12:31) — yet Moshe did not say, "*You* will come down to me and bow to me."

[246] הגדה של פסח

SHULCHAN ORECH

The meal should be eaten in a combination of joy and solemnity, for the meal, too, is part of the Seder service. While it is desirable that *zemiros* and discussion of the laws and events of Passover be part of the meal, extraneous conversation should be avoided. It should be remembered that the *Afikoman* must be eaten while there is still some appetite for it. In fact, if one is so sated that he must literally force himself to eat it, he is not credited with the performance of the mitzvah of *Afikoman*. Therefore, it is unwise to eat more than a moderate amount during the meal.

TZAFUN

From the *Afikoman* matzah (and from additional matzos to make up the required amount) a half-egg volume portion — according to some, a full egg's volume portion — is given to each participant. It should be eaten before midnight, while reclining, without delay, and uninterruptedly. Nothing may be eaten or drunk after the *Afikoman* (with the exception of water and the like) except for the last two Seder cups of wine.

☐ Hillel saw that the *korban Pesach*, matzah, and *maror* are all connected: the bitterness of exile is part of the redemption. Therefore, he would sandwich the *korban Pesach* together with the matzah and *maror*, as these too were part of the creation of the Jewish people as a nation. All three express the spiritual formation of the Jewish nation, on their leaving slavery for freedom and independence.

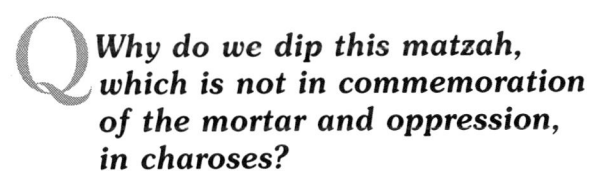

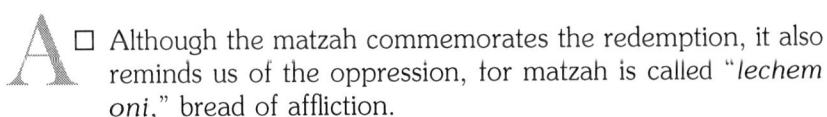

Q *Why do we dip this matzah, which is not in commemoration of the mortar and oppression, in charoses?*

A ☐ Although the matzah commemorates the redemption, it also reminds us of the oppression, for matzah is called "*lechem oni*," bread of affliction.

☐ Although the *charoses* commemorates the oppression and the mortar — the bricks that the Jews were forced to make as part of their labor for Pharaoh — it also reminds us of the redemption. The purpose of the terrible slavery and suffering was to shorten the exile and keep us from sinking into the forty-ninth level of impurity. Thus, the suffering was part of the redemption.

[247] HAGGADAH: THE ANSWER IS . . .

Some recite the following before eating the *Afikoman*:

הִנְנִי מוּכָן וּמְזוּמָן לְקַיֵּם מִצְוַת אֲכִילַת אֲפִיקוֹמָן. לְשֵׁם יִחוּד קֻדְשָׁא בְּרִיךְ הוּא וּשְׁכִינְתֵּיהּ, עַל יְדֵי הַהוּא טָמִיר וְנֶעְלָם, בְּשֵׁם כָּל יִשְׂרָאֵל. וִיהִי נֹעַם אֲדֹנָי אֱלֹהֵינוּ עָלֵינוּ, וּמַעֲשֵׂה יָדֵינוּ כּוֹנְנָה עָלֵינוּ, וּמַעֲשֵׂה יָדֵינוּ כּוֹנְנֵהוּ:

ברך

The third cup is poured and *Bircas HaMazon* (Grace After Meals) is recited. According to some customs, the Cup of Eliyahu, is poured at this point.

שִׁיר הַמַּעֲלוֹת בְּשׁוּב יהוה אֶת שִׁיבַת צִיּוֹן, הָיִינוּ כְּחֹלְמִים. אָז יִמָּלֵא שְׂחוֹק פִּינוּ, וּלְשׁוֹנֵנוּ רִנָּה; אָז יֹאמְרוּ בַגּוֹיִם: הִגְדִּיל יהוה לַעֲשׂוֹת עִם אֵלֶּה. הִגְדִּיל יהוה לַעֲשׂוֹת עִמָּנוּ, הָיִינוּ שְׂמֵחִים. שׁוּבָה יהוה אֶת שְׁבִיתֵנוּ, כַּאֲפִיקִים בַּנֶּגֶב. הַזֹּרְעִים בְּדִמְעָה, בְּרִנָּה יִקְצֹרוּ. הָלוֹךְ יֵלֵךְ וּבָכֹה נֹשֵׂא מֶשֶׁךְ הַזָּרַע; בֹּא יָבֹא בְרִנָּה, נֹשֵׂא אֲלֻמֹּתָיו.[1]

Some recite the following before *Bircas HaMazon*:

הִנְנִי מוּכָן וּמְזוּמָן לְקַיֵּם מִצְוַת עֲשֵׂה שֶׁל בִּרְכַּת הַמָּזוֹן, כַּכָּתוּב, וְאָכַלְתָּ וְשָׂבָעְתָּ, וּבֵרַכְתָּ אֶת ה' אֱלֹהֶיךָ עַל הָאָרֶץ הַטֹּבָה אֲשֶׁר נָתַן לָךְ.

If three or more males, aged thirteen or older, participated in the meal, the leader is required to formally invite the others to join him in the recitation of Grace After Meals. Following is the *"Zimun,"* or formal invitation.

The leader begins:

רַבּוֹתַי נְבָרֵךְ.

The group responds:

יְהִי שֵׁם יהוה מְבֹרָךְ מֵעַתָּה וְעַד עוֹלָם.

The leader continues:

יְהִי שֵׁם יהוה מְבֹרָךְ מֵעַתָּה וְעַד עוֹלָם.

Some recite the following before eating the *Afikoman:*

Behold, I am prepared and ready to fulfill the mitzvah of eating the *Afikoman.* For the sake of the unification of the Holy One, Blessed is He, and His Presence, through Him Who is hidden and inscrutable — [I pray] in the name of all Israel. May the pleasantness of the Lord, our God, be upon us, and may He establish our handiwork for us; our handiwork may He establish.

BARECH

The third cup is poured and *Bircas HaMazon* (Grace After Meals) is recited. According to some customs, the Cup of Eliyahu, is poured at this point.

A song of Ascents. When HASHEM brings back the exiles to Zion, we will have been like dreamers. Then our mouth will be filled with laughter, and our tongue with glad song. Then will it be said among the nations: HASHEM has done great things for them. HASHEM has done great things for us, and we rejoiced. Restore our captives, HASHEM, like streams in the dry land. Those who sow in tears shall reap in joy. Though the farmer bears the measure of seed to the field in tears, he shall come home with joy, bearing his sheaves.[1]

Some recite the following before *Bircas HaMazon:*

Behold, I am prepared and ready to fulfill the mitzvah of Grace After Meals, as it is stated: "And you shall eat and you shall be satisfied and you shall bless HASHEM, your God, for the good land that He gave you."

If three or more males, aged thirteen or older, participated in the meal, the leader is required to formally invite the others to join him in the recitation of Grace After Meals. Following is the *"Zimun,"* or formal invitation.

The leader begins:
Gentlemen, let us bless.

The group responds:
Blessed is the Name of HASHEM from this moment and forever!

The leader continues:
Blessed is the Name of HASHEM from this moment and forever!

---

1. *Psalm* 126.

[249] **HAGGADAH: THE ANSWER IS . . .**

If ten men join in the *Zimun*, אֱלֹהֵינוּ, *our God* (in parentheses), is included.

בִּרְשׁוּת מָרָנָן וְרַבָּנָן וְרַבּוֹתַי, נְבָרֵךְ [אֱלֹהֵינוּ] שֶׁאָכַלְנוּ מִשֶּׁלּוֹ.

The group responds:

בָּרוּךְ [אֱלֹהֵינוּ] שֶׁאָכַלְנוּ מִשֶּׁלּוֹ וּבְטוּבוֹ חָיִינוּ.

The leader continues:

בָּרוּךְ [אֱלֹהֵינוּ] שֶׁאָכַלְנוּ מִשֶּׁלּוֹ וּבְטוּבוֹ חָיִינוּ.

The following line is recited if ten men join in the *Zimun*.

בָּרוּךְ הוּא וּבָרוּךְ שְׁמוֹ.

בָּרוּךְ אַתָּה יהוה אֱלֹהֵינוּ מֶלֶךְ הָעוֹלָם, הַזָּן אֶת הָעוֹלָם כֻּלּוֹ, בְּטוּבוֹ, בְּחֵן בְּחֶסֶד וּבְרַחֲמִים, הוּא נֹתֵן לֶחֶם לְכָל בָּשָׂר, כִּי לְעוֹלָם חַסְדּוֹ. וּבְטוּבוֹ הַגָּדוֹל, תָּמִיד לֹא חָסַר לָנוּ, וְאַל יֶחְסַר לָנוּ מָזוֹן לְעוֹלָם וָעֶד. בַּעֲבוּר שְׁמוֹ הַגָּדוֹל, כִּי הוּא אֵל זָן וּמְפַרְנֵס לַכֹּל, וּמֵטִיב לַכֹּל, וּמֵכִין מָזוֹן לְכָל בְּרִיּוֹתָיו אֲשֶׁר בָּרָא. בָּרוּךְ אַתָּה יהוה, הַזָּן אֶת הַכֹּל.

נוֹדֶה לְּךָ יהוה אֱלֹהֵינוּ, עַל שֶׁהִנְחַלְתָּ לַאֲבוֹתֵינוּ אֶרֶץ חֶמְדָּה טוֹבָה וּרְחָבָה. וְעַל שֶׁהוֹצֵאתָנוּ יהוה אֱלֹהֵינוּ מֵאֶרֶץ מִצְרַיִם, וּפְדִיתָנוּ מִבֵּית עֲבָדִים,

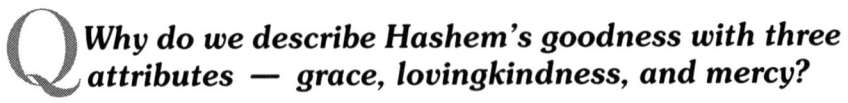

ברך / Barech

Q Why do we describe Hashem's goodness with three attributes — grace, lovingkindness, and mercy?

A ☐ **RAV ELIYAHU LOPIAN:** These three traits correspond to three types of people: *tzaddikim*, *beinonim*, and *reshaim* — the righteous, the average, and the wicked:

- חֵן, *grace* — for the righteous, who find favor in Hashem's eyes and whom He nourishes with grace.
- חֶסֶד, *lovingkindness* — for the average people, who are nourished by His power of *chesed*.

If ten men join in the Zimun, אֱלֹהֵינוּ, *our God (in parentheses), is included.*

With the permission of the distinguished people present, let us bless [our God] for we have eaten from what is His.

The group responds:
Blessed is He [our God] of Whose we have eaten and through Whose goodness we live.

The leader continues:
Blessed is He [our God] of Whose we have eaten and through Whose goodness we live.

The following line is recited if ten men join in the Zimun.
Blessed is He and Blessed is His Name.

Blessed are You, HASHEM, our God, King of the universe, Who nourishes the entire world; in His goodness, with grace, with lovingkindness, and with mercy. He gives nourishment to all flesh, for His lovingkindness is eternal. And through His great goodness, nourishment was never lacking to us, and may it never be lacking to us forever. For the sake of His Great Name, because He is God Who nourishes and sustains all, and benefits all, and He prepares food for all of His creatures which He has created. Blessed are You, HASHEM, Who nourishes all.

We thank You, HASHEM, our God, because You have given to our forefathers as a heritage a desirable, good, and spacious land; because You removed us, HASHEM, our God, from the land of Egypt and You redeemed us from the house of bondage;

- רַחֲמִים, *mercy* — for the wicked. Although they do not deserve it, Hashem nourishes the wicked with mercy.

◈§ נוֹדֶה / *We thank*

Q *Why is Eretz Yisrael not described here as a land flowing with milk and honey, as it is described in the Torah?*

[251] **HAGGADAH: THE ANSWER IS . . .**

וְעַל בְּרִיתְךָ שֶׁחָתַמְתָּ בִּבְשָׂרֵנוּ, וְעַל תּוֹרָתְךָ שֶׁלִּמַּדְתָּנוּ, וְעַל חֻקֶּיךָ שֶׁהוֹדַעְתָּנוּ, וְעַל חַיִּים חֵן וָחֶסֶד שֶׁחוֹנַנְתָּנוּ, וְעַל אֲכִילַת מָזוֹן שָׁאַתָּה זָן וּמְפַרְנֵס אוֹתָנוּ תָּמִיד, בְּכָל יוֹם וּבְכָל עֵת וּבְכָל שָׁעָה.

וְעַל הַכֹּל יהוה אֱלֹהֵינוּ, אֲנַחְנוּ מוֹדִים לָךְ וּמְבָרְכִים אוֹתָךְ, יִתְבָּרַךְ שִׁמְךָ בְּפִי כָּל חַי תָּמִיד לְעוֹלָם וָעֶד. כַּכָּתוּב, וְאָכַלְתָּ וְשָׂבָעְתָּ, וּבֵרַכְתָּ אֶת יהוה אֱלֹהֶיךָ, עַל הָאָרֶץ הַטֹּבָה אֲשֶׁר נָתַן לָךְ.¹ בָּרוּךְ אַתָּה יהוה, עַל הָאָרֶץ וְעַל הַמָּזוֹן.

רַחֵם (נָא) יהוה אֱלֹהֵינוּ עַל יִשְׂרָאֵל עַמֶּךָ, וְעַל יְרוּשָׁלַיִם עִירֶךָ, וְעַל צִיּוֹן מִשְׁכַּן כְּבוֹדֶךָ, וְעַל מַלְכוּת בֵּית דָּוִד מְשִׁיחֶךָ, וְעַל הַבַּיִת הַגָּדוֹל וְהַקָּדוֹשׁ שֶׁנִּקְרָא שִׁמְךָ עָלָיו. אֱלֹהֵינוּ אָבִינוּ, רְעֵנוּ זוּנֵנוּ פַּרְנְסֵנוּ וְכַלְכְּלֵנוּ וְהַרְוִיחֵנוּ, וְהַרְוַח לָנוּ יהוה אֱלֹהֵינוּ מְהֵרָה מִכָּל צָרוֹתֵינוּ. וְנָא אַל תַּצְרִיכֵנוּ, יהוה אֱלֹהֵינוּ, לֹא לִידֵי מַתְּנַת בָּשָׂר וָדָם, וְלֹא לִידֵי הַלְוָאָתָם, כִּי אִם לְיָדְךָ הַמְּלֵאָה הַפְּתוּחָה הַקְּדוֹשָׁה וְהָרְחָבָה, שֶׁלֹּא נֵבוֹשׁ וְלֹא נִכָּלֵם לְעוֹלָם וָעֶד.

A ☐ **AVUDRAHAM:** The words *desirable, good, and spacious* include the land on the other side of the Jordan River, while the praise *a land flowing with milk and honey* does not include that territory.

☐ **SHIRAS HAGEULAH:** The praise *good and spacious* has a spiritual connotation and indicates qualities that would endure eternally; even after the destruction of the Beis HaMikdash, the land's *kedushah* was not nullified. However, the praise *flowing with milk and honey* does not apply after the destruction.

☐ The spies used the phrase *a land flowing with milk and*

for Your covenant which You sealed in our flesh; for Your Torah that You taught us and for Your statutes that You made known to us; for life, grace, and lovingkindness which You granted us; and for the provision of food with which You nourish and sustain us constantly, in every day, in every season and in every hour.

For all, HASHEM, our God, we thank You and bless You. May Your Name be blessed continuously by the mouth of all the living, continuously for all eternity. As it is written: "And you shall eat and you shall be satisfied, and you shall bless HASHEM, your God, for the good land which He gave you."[1] Blessed are You, HASHEM, for the land and for the food.

Have mercy (we beg You) HASHEM, our God, on Your people Israel, on Your city Jerusalem, on Zion the resting place of Your Glory, on the monarchy of the house of David, Your anointed, and on the great and holy House upon which Your Name is called. Our God, our Father — tend us, nourish us, sustain us, support us, relieve us; HASHEM, our God, grant us speedy relief from all our troubles. Please, HASHEM, our God, make us not needful of the gifts of human hands nor of their loans, but only of Your Hand that is full, open, holy, and generous, that we not feel inner shame nor be humiliated for ever and ever.

---

1. *Deuteronomy* 8:10.

---

honey to denigrate Eretz Yisrael, and therefore the Haggadah avoids using it.

Q Is Eretz Yisrael truly spacious?

A ☐ **HASHIR V'HASHEVACH:** The word "spacious" indicates that Eretz Yisrael expands a person's heart. According to Chazal (*Bava Basra* 158b), Eretz Yisrael brings about an expansion of the heart to help us understand more and grow wise.

On the Sabbath add the following paragraph.

רְצֵה וְהַחֲלִיצֵנוּ יהוה אֱלֹהֵינוּ בְּמִצְוֹתֶיךָ, וּבְמִצְוַת יוֹם הַשְּׁבִיעִי הַשַּׁבָּת הַגָּדוֹל וְהַקָּדוֹשׁ הַזֶּה, כִּי יוֹם זֶה גָּדוֹל וְקָדוֹשׁ הוּא לְפָנֶיךָ, לִשְׁבָּת בּוֹ וְלָנוּחַ בּוֹ בְּאַהֲבָה כְּמִצְוַת רְצוֹנֶךָ, וּבִרְצוֹנְךָ הָנִיחַ לָנוּ יהוה אֱלֹהֵינוּ, שֶׁלֹּא תְהֵא צָרָה וְיָגוֹן וַאֲנָחָה בְּיוֹם מְנוּחָתֵנוּ, וְהַרְאֵנוּ יהוה אֱלֹהֵינוּ בְּנֶחָמַת צִיּוֹן עִירֶךָ, וּבְבִנְיַן יְרוּשָׁלַיִם עִיר קָדְשֶׁךָ, כִּי אַתָּה הוּא בַּעַל הַיְשׁוּעוֹת וּבַעַל הַנֶּחָמוֹת.

אֱלֹהֵינוּ וֵאלֹהֵי אֲבוֹתֵינוּ, יַעֲלֶה, וְיָבֹא, וְיַגִּיעַ, וְיֵרָאֶה, וְיֵרָצֶה, וְיִשָּׁמַע, וְיִפָּקֵד, וְיִזָּכֵר זִכְרוֹנֵנוּ וּפִקְדוֹנֵנוּ, וְזִכְרוֹן אֲבוֹתֵינוּ, וְזִכְרוֹן מָשִׁיחַ בֶּן דָּוִד עַבְדֶּךָ, וְזִכְרוֹן יְרוּשָׁלַיִם עִיר קָדְשֶׁךָ, וְזִכְרוֹן כָּל עַמְּךָ בֵּית יִשְׂרָאֵל לְפָנֶיךָ, לִפְלֵיטָה לְטוֹבָה לְחֵן וּלְחֶסֶד וּלְרַחֲמִים, לְחַיִּים וּלְשָׁלוֹם, בְּיוֹם חַג הַמַּצּוֹת הַזֶּה. זָכְרֵנוּ יהוה אֱלֹהֵינוּ בּוֹ לְטוֹבָה, וּפָקְדֵנוּ בוֹ לִבְרָכָה, וְהוֹשִׁיעֵנוּ בוֹ לְחַיִּים (טוֹבִים). וּבִדְבַר יְשׁוּעָה וְרַחֲמִים, חוּס וְחָנֵּנוּ וְרַחֵם עָלֵינוּ וְהוֹשִׁיעֵנוּ, כִּי אֵלֶיךָ עֵינֵינוּ, כִּי אֵל (מֶלֶךְ) חַנּוּן וְרַחוּם אָתָּה.

וּבְנֵה יְרוּשָׁלַיִם עִיר הַקֹּדֶשׁ בִּמְהֵרָה בְיָמֵינוּ. בָּרוּךְ אַתָּה יהוה, בּוֹנֵה (בְרַחֲמָיו) יְרוּשָׁלָיִם. אָמֵן.

וּבְנֵה / **Rebuild**

Q *Why is this written in the present tense? Shouldn't it either be past (Who built Jerusalem) or future (Who will rebuild Jerusalem)?*

A ☐ **RAV NAFTALI OF ROPSHITZ:** When a Jew serves Hashem, he becomes Hashem's partner in building Jerusalem. Some

>On the Sabbath add the following paragraph.
>
>May it please You to strengthen us, HASHEM, our God — through Your commandments, and through the commandment of the seventh day, this great and holy Sabbath. For this day is great and holy before You to rest on it and be content on it in love, as ordained by Your will. May it be Your will, HASHEM, our God, that there be no distress, grief, or lament on this day of our contentment. And show us, HASHEM, our God, the consolation of Zion, Your city, and the rebuilding of Jerusalem, city of Your holiness, for You are the Master of salvations and Master of consolations.

Our God and God of our fathers, may there rise, come, reach, be noted, be favored, be heard, be considered, and be remembered before You — the remembrance and consideration of ourselves; the remembrance of our fathers; the remembrance of Messiah, son of David, Your servant; the remembrance of Jerusalem, Your holy city; and the remembrance of Your entire people, the House of Israel — for deliverance, for well-being, for grace, for lovingkindness, and for mercy, for life and for peace on this day of the Festival of Matzos. Remember us on it, HASHEM, our God, for goodness; consider us on it for blessing; and help us on it for (good) life. In the matter of salvation and mercy, have pity, show grace, and be merciful upon us and help us, for our eyes are turned to You; for You are the Almighty, the gracious, and generous.

Rebuild Jerusalem, the Holy City, soon in our days. Blessed are You, HASHEM, Who rebuilds Jerusalem (in His mercy). Amen.

---

individuals lay just one brick, while others lay a whole row of them; everything is measured according to the person's service. Therefore this blessing is written in the present tense, because Hashem builds Jerusalem each and every day.

☐ **YISMACH MOSHE:** Chazal teach that there are two parallel cities of Jerusalem; the one on earth corresponds to the one

בָּרוּךְ אַתָּה יהוה אֱלֹהֵינוּ מֶלֶךְ הָעוֹלָם, הָאֵל אָבִינוּ מַלְכֵּנוּ אַדִירֵנוּ בּוֹרְאֵנוּ גּוֹאֲלֵנוּ יוֹצְרֵנוּ קְדוֹשֵׁנוּ קְדוֹשׁ יַעֲקֹב, רוֹעֵנוּ רוֹעֵה יִשְׂרָאֵל, הַמֶּלֶךְ הַטּוֹב וְהַמֵּטִיב לַכֹּל, שֶׁבְּכָל יוֹם וָיוֹם הוּא הֵטִיב, הוּא מֵטִיב, הוּא יֵיטִיב לָנוּ. הוּא גְמָלָנוּ הוּא גוֹמְלֵנוּ הוּא יִגְמְלֵנוּ לָעַד, לְחֵן וּלְחֶסֶד וּלְרַחֲמִים וּלְרֶוַח הַצָּלָה וְהַצְלָחָה, בְּרָכָה וִישׁוּעָה נֶחָמָה פַּרְנָסָה וְכַלְכָּלָה וְרַחֲמִים וְחַיִּים וְשָׁלוֹם וְכָל טוֹב, וּמִכָּל טוּב לְעוֹלָם אַל יְחַסְּרֵנוּ.

הָרַחֲמָן הוּא יִמְלֹךְ עָלֵינוּ לְעוֹלָם וָעֶד. הָרַחֲמָן הוּא יִתְבָּרַךְ בַּשָּׁמַיִם וּבָאָרֶץ. הָרַחֲמָן הוּא יִשְׁתַּבַּח לְדוֹר דּוֹרִים, וְיִתְפָּאַר בָּנוּ לָעַד וּלְנֵצַח נְצָחִים, וְיִתְהַדַּר בָּנוּ לָעַד וּלְעוֹלְמֵי עוֹלָמִים. הָרַחֲמָן הוּא יְפַרְנְסֵנוּ בְּכָבוֹד. הָרַחֲמָן הוּא יִשְׁבֹּר עֻלֵּנוּ מֵעַל צַוָּארֵנוּ, וְהוּא יוֹלִיכֵנוּ קוֹמְמִיּוּת לְאַרְצֵנוּ. הָרַחֲמָן הוּא יִשְׁלַח לָנוּ בְּרָכָה מְרֻבָּה בַּבַּיִת הַזֶּה, וְעַל שֻׁלְחָן זֶה שֶׁאָכַלְנוּ עָלָיו. הָרַחֲמָן הוּא יִשְׁלַח לָנוּ אֶת אֵלִיָּהוּ הַנָּבִיא זָכוּר לַטּוֹב, וִיבַשֶּׂר לָנוּ בְּשׂוֹרוֹת טוֹבוֹת יְשׁוּעוֹת וְנֶחָמוֹת.

The Talmud (*Berachos* 46a) gives a rather lengthy text of the blessing that a guest inserts here for the host. It is quoted with minor variations in *Shulchan Aruch* (*Orach Chaim* 201) and many authorities are at a loss to explain why the prescribed text has fallen into disuse in favor of the briefer version commonly used. The text found in *Shulchan Aruch* is:

יְהִי רָצוֹן שֶׁלֹּא יֵבוֹשׁ וְלֹא יִכָּלֵם בַּעַל הַבַּיִת הַזֶּה, לֹא בָּעוֹלָם הַזֶּה, וְלֹא בָּעוֹלָם הַבָּא, וְיַצְלִיחַ בְּכָל נְכָסָיו, וְיִהְיוּ נְכָסָיו מוּצְלָחִים וּקְרוֹבִים לָעִיר, וְאַל יִשְׁלֹט שָׂטָן בְּמַעֲשֵׂה יָדָיו, וְאַל יִזְדַּקֵּק לְפָנָיו שׁוּם דְּבַר חֵטְא וְהִרְהוּר עָוֹן, מֵעַתָּה וְעַד עוֹלָם.

---

in Heaven. *Yerushalayim shel ma'alah*, the Jerusalem of above, is presently being built by our merits: the mitzvos and

Blessed are You, HASHEM, our God, King of the universe, the Almighty, our Father, our King, our Sovereign, our Creator, our Redeemer, our Maker, our Holy One, Holy One of Yaakov, our Shepherd, the Shepherd of Israel, the good and beneficent King. For every single day He did good, does good, and will do good to us. He was bountiful with us, is bountiful with us, and will forever be bountiful with us — with grace and with lovingkindness and with mercy, with relief, salvation, success, blessing, help, consolation, sustenance, support, mercy, life, peace, and all good; and of all good things may He never deprive us.

The compassionate One! May He reign over us forever. The compassionate One! May He be blessed in heaven and on earth. The compassionate One! May He be praised throughout all generations, may He be glorified through us forever to the ultimate ends, and be honored through us to the inscrutable everlasting. The compassionate One! May He sustain us in honor. The compassionate One! May He break the yoke of oppression from our necks and guide us erect to our Land. The compassionate One! May He send us abundant blessing to this house and upon this table at which we have eaten. The compassionate One! May He send us Elijah, the Prophet — may he be remembered for good — to proclaim to us good tidings, salvations, and consolations.

> The Talmud (*Berachos* 46a) gives a rather lengthy text of the blessing that a guest inserts here for the host. It is quoted with minor variations in *Shulchan Aruch (Orach Chaim* 201) and many authorities are at a loss to explain why the prescribed text has fallen into disuse in favor of the briefer version commonly used. The text found in *Shulchan Aruch* is:
>
> May it be God's will that his host not be shamed nor humiliated in this world or in the World to Come. May he be successful in all his dealings. May his dealings be successful and conveniently close at hand. May no evil impediment reign over his handiwork, and may no semblance of sin or iniquitous thought attach itself to him from this time and forever.

הָרַחֲמָן הוּא יְבָרֵךְ

Guests recite the following.
Children at their parents' table add words in parentheses.

אֶת [אָבִי מוֹרִי] בַּעַל הַבַּיִת הַזֶּה,
וְאֶת [אִמִּי מוֹרָתִי] בַּעֲלַת הַבַּיִת הַזֶּה,

Those eating at their own table recite the following,
adding the appropriate parenthesized phrases:

אוֹתִי [וְאֶת אִשְׁתִּי / וְאֶת בַּעֲלִי. וְאֶת זַרְעִי]
וְאֶת כָּל אֲשֶׁר לִי.

All guests recite the following:

אוֹתָם וְאֶת בֵּיתָם וְאֶת זַרְעָם וְאֶת כָּל אֲשֶׁר לָהֶם.

All continue here:

אוֹתָנוּ וְאֶת כָּל אֲשֶׁר לָנוּ, כְּמוֹ שֶׁנִּתְבָּרְכוּ אֲבוֹתֵינוּ אַבְרָהָם יִצְחָק וְיַעֲקֹב בַּכֹּל מִכֹּל כֹּל, כֵּן יְבָרֵךְ אוֹתָנוּ כֻּלָּנוּ יַחַד בִּבְרָכָה שְׁלֵמָה, וְנֹאמַר, אָמֵן.

בַּמָּרוֹם יְלַמְּדוּ עֲלֵיהֶם וְעָלֵינוּ זְכוּת, שֶׁתְּהֵא לְמִשְׁמֶרֶת שָׁלוֹם. וְנִשָּׂא בְרָכָה מֵאֵת יהוה, וּצְדָקָה מֵאֱלֹהֵי יִשְׁעֵנוּ, וְנִמְצָא חֵן וְשֵׂכֶל טוֹב בְּעֵינֵי אֱלֹהִים וְאָדָם.[1]

On the Sabbath add the following sentence:

הָרַחֲמָן הוּא יַנְחִילֵנוּ יוֹם שֶׁכֻּלּוֹ שַׁבָּת וּמְנוּחָה לְחַיֵּי הָעוֹלָמִים.

The words in parentheses are added on the two Seder nights in some communities.

הָרַחֲמָן הוּא יַנְחִילֵנוּ יוֹם שֶׁכֻּלּוֹ טוֹב (יוֹם שֶׁכֻּלּוֹ אָרוּךְ, יוֹם שֶׁצַּדִּיקִים יוֹשְׁבִים וְעַטְרוֹתֵיהֶם בְּרָאשֵׁיהֶם וְנֶהֱנִים מִזִּיו הַשְּׁכִינָה, וִיהִי חֶלְקֵנוּ עִמָּהֶם).

The compassionate One! May He bless
Guests recite the following.
Children at their parents' table add words in parentheses.
(my father, my teacher) the master of this house, and (my mother, my teacher) lady of this house,
Those eating at their own table recite the following, adding the appropriate parenthesized phrases:
me (my wife/husband and family) and all that is mine,
All guests recite the following:
them, their house, their family, and all that is theirs,
All continue here:
ours and all that is ours — just as our forefathers Avraham, Yitzchak, and Yaakov were blessed in everything, from everything, with everything. So may He bless all of us together, with a perfect blessing. And let us say: Amen!

On high, may merit be pleaded upon them and upon us, for a safeguard of peace. May we receive a blessing from HASHEM and just kindness from the God of our salvation, and find favor and good understanding in the eyes of God and man.[1]

On the Sabbath add the following sentence:

The compassionate One! May He cause us to inherit the day which will be completely a Sabbath and rest day for eternal life.

The words in parentheses are added on the two Seder nights in some communities.

The compassionate One! May He cause us to inherit that day which is altogether good (that everlasting day, the day when the just will sit with crowns on their heads, enjoying the reflection of God's majesty — and may our portion be with them!).

---

1. 1. *Proverbs* 3:4

good deeds that the Jewish nation performs. Therefore, we pray for the building of Jerusalem in the present tense.

[259] **HAGGADAH: THE ANSWER IS . . .**

הָרַחֲמָן הוּא יְזַכֵּנוּ לִימוֹת הַמָּשִׁיחַ וּלְחַיֵּי הָעוֹלָם הַבָּא. מִגְדּוֹל יְשׁוּעוֹת מַלְכּוֹ וְעֹשֶׂה חֶסֶד לִמְשִׁיחוֹ לְדָוִד וּלְזַרְעוֹ עַד עוֹלָם.[1] עֹשֶׂה שָׁלוֹם בִּמְרוֹמָיו, הוּא יַעֲשֶׂה שָׁלוֹם עָלֵינוּ וְעַל כָּל יִשְׂרָאֵל. וְאִמְרוּ, אָמֵן.

יְראוּ אֶת יהוה קְדֹשָׁיו, כִּי אֵין מַחְסוֹר לִירֵאָיו. כְּפִירִים רָשׁוּ וְרָעֵבוּ, וְדֹרְשֵׁי יהוה לֹא יַחְסְרוּ כָל טוֹב. הוֹדוּ לַיהוה כִּי טוֹב, כִּי לְעוֹלָם חַסְדּוֹ.[2] פּוֹתֵחַ אֶת יָדֶךָ, וּמַשְׂבִּיעַ לְכָל חַי רָצוֹן.[3] בָּרוּךְ הַגֶּבֶר אֲשֶׁר יִבְטַח בַּיהוה, וְהָיָה יהוה מִבְטַחוֹ.[4] נַעַר הָיִיתִי גַּם זָקַנְתִּי, וְלֹא רָאִיתִי צַדִּיק נֶעֱזָב, וְזַרְעוֹ מְבַקֶּשׁ לָחֶם.[5] יהוה עֹז לְעַמּוֹ יִתֵּן, יהוה יְבָרֵךְ אֶת עַמּוֹ בַשָּׁלוֹם.[6]

Upon completion of *Bircas HaMazon* the blessing over wine is recited and the third cup is drunk while reclining on the left side. It is preferable to drink the entire cup, but at the very least, most of the cup should be drained.

יְראוּ / Fear

Q Do we not often see God-fearing people who do suffer deprivation?

A ☐ **KEDUSHAS LEVI:** It does not say that those who fear Hashem *have* no deprivation, but rather that those who fear Him *feel* no deprivation. It is a person's nature to want more than he has. If he has a hundred, he wants two. A person who truly seeks Hashem, however, is satisfied with his portion. He feels that he has enough and lacks for nothing. As Yaakov told Esav, יֶשׁ לִי כֹל, *I have everything* (Genesis 33:11).

The compassionate One! May He make us worthy of the days of Messiah and the life of the World to Come. He Who is a tower of salvations to His king and shows lovingkindness for His anointed, to David and his descendants forever.[1] He Who makes peace in His heavenly heights, may He make harmony for us and for all Israel. Say: Amen!

Fear HASHEM, His holy ones, for those who fear him feel no deprivation. Young lions may feel want and hunger, but those who seek HASHEM will not lack any good. Give thanks to God for He is good; His lovingkindness is eternal.[2] You open up Your hand and satisfy the desire of every living thing.[3] Blessed is the man who trusts in HASHEM, and HASHEM will be his trust.[4] I was a youth and also have aged, and I have not seen a righteous man forsaken, with his children begging for bread.[5] HASHEM will give might to His nation; HASHEM will bless His nation with peace.[6]

Upon completion of *Bircas HaMazon* the blessing over wine is recited and the third cup is drunk while reclining on the left side. It is preferable to drink the entire cup, but at the very least, most of the cup should be drained.

---

1. *Samuel II* 22.51. 2. *Psalms* 34:10-11. 3. Ibid. 145:16.
4. *Jeremiah* 17:7. 5. *Psalms* 37:25. 6. Ibid. 29:11.

Q *What sort of "fear" does this refer to?*

A □ **YISMACH MOSHE:** There are several levels of *yirah*, fear. The first is *yiras ha'onesh*, fear of punishment. The next is *yiras haromemus*, awe at Hashem's exaltedness. And the highest is serving Hashem out of love for Him. This service, which stems from love after one has reached the loftiest level of awe, is considered the most perfect form.

[261] **HAGGADAH: THE ANSWER IS . . .**

Some recite the following before the third cup:

הִנְנִי מוּכָן וּמְזֻמָּן לְקַיֵּם מִצְוַת כּוֹס שְׁלִישִׁי שֶׁל אַרְבַּע כּוֹסוֹת. לְשֵׁם יִחוּד קֻדְשָׁא בְּרִיךְ הוּא וּשְׁכִינְתֵּיהּ, עַל יְדֵי הַהוּא טָמִיר וְנֶעְלָם, בְּשֵׁם כָּל יִשְׂרָאֵל. וִיהִי נֹעַם אֲדֹנָי אֱלֹהֵינוּ עָלֵינוּ, וּמַעֲשֵׂה יָדֵינוּ כּוֹנְנָה עָלֵינוּ, וּמַעֲשֵׂה יָדֵינוּ כּוֹנְנֵהוּ.

בָּרוּךְ אַתָּה יהוה אֱלֹהֵינוּ מֶלֶךְ הָעוֹלָם, בּוֹרֵא פְּרִי הַגָּפֶן.

The fourth cup is poured. According to most customs, the Cup of Eliyahu is poured at this point, after which the door is opened in accordance with the verse, *"It is a guarded night."* Then the following paragraph is recited.

שְׁפֹךְ חֲמָתְךָ אֶל הַגּוֹיִם אֲשֶׁר לֹא יְדָעוּךָ וְעַל מַמְלָכוֹת אֲשֶׁר בְּשִׁמְךָ לֹא קָרָאוּ. כִּי אָכַל אֶת יַעֲקֹב וְאֶת נָוֵהוּ הֵשַׁמּוּ. שְׁפָךְ עֲלֵיהֶם זַעְמֶךָ וַחֲרוֹן אַפְּךָ יַשִּׂיגֵם. תִּרְדֹּף בְּאַף וְתַשְׁמִידֵם מִתַּחַת שְׁמֵי יהוה.

◆§ שְׁפֹךְ חֲמָתְךָ / **Pour Your wrath** §◆

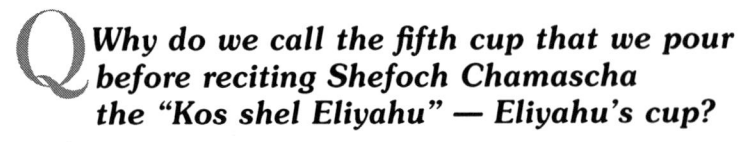

Q **Why do we call the fifth cup that we pour before reciting Shefoch Chamascha the "Kos shel Eliyahu" — Eliyahu's cup?**

A ☐ **CHOK YAAKOV:** We call it *"kos shel Eliyahu"* to hint that we believe that Hashem will redeem us speedily and will send the prophet Eliyahu to bring us word of the redemption.

☐ **VILNA GAON:** The question of whether or not it is a mitzvah to drink the fifth cup has not yet been resolved. In order to satisfy all opinions, we pour a fifth cup but do not drink it. When Eliyahu comes, he will resolve the matter for us.

☐ **RAV YERUCHAM PERLOW:** There are two prophets from the tribe of Levi — Moshe and Eliyahu — who share many similarities. By arranging the story of the Exodus (the first redemption, that of Moshe Rabbeinu) around four cups of wine, we are hinting that we will merit the final redemption — that of the prophet Eliyahu — with four cups as well.

Some recite the following before the third cup:

Behold, I am prepared and ready to fulfill the mitzvah of the third of the Four Cups. For the sake of the unification of the Holy One, Blessed is He, and His Presence, through Him Who is hidden and inscrutable — [I pray] in the name of all Israel. May the pleasantness of the Lord, our God, be upon us, and may He establish our handiwork for us; our handiwork may He establish.

Blessed are You, HASHEM, our God, King of the universe, Who creates the fruit of the vine.

The fourth cup is poured. According to most customs, the Cup of Eliyahu is poured at this point, after which the door is opened in accordance with the verse, "It is a guarded night." Then the following paragraph is recited.

Pour Your wrath upon the nations that do not recognize You and upon the kingdoms that do not invoke Your Name. For they have devoured Yaakov and destroyed His habitation. Pour Your anger upon them and let Your fiery wrath overtake them. Pursue them with wrath and annihilate them from beneath the heavens of HASHEM.

Before we fill the fourth cup in honor of the redemption by Moshe, we fill the first cup in honor of Eliyahu's redemption, to connect the two and signify that we believe and trust in the future redemption to the point where we have already filled the first cup.

☐ BIRKAS ELIYAHU: Eliyahu is present at every *bris milah* to testify to the Jewish people's loyalty to this mitzvah. An uncircumcised person is not allowed to eat from the *korban Pesach*. Thus, at the end of the Seder, Eliyahu comes to testify that everyone who participated in the Seder was circumcised and worthy of eating from the *korban Pesach*. In his honor, we pour a fifth cup.

☐ The Jewish people were redeemed because Yaakov and his children distanced themselves from the wicked Esav and because they did not change their names in Egypt. In pouring the fifth cup — the cup of the final redemption — we welcome Eliyahu, who will be sent in advance of that great day, then say *Shefoch Chamascha* in which we express our view that Esav is loathed, corrupt, and unworthy of redemption.

[263] HAGGADAH: THE ANSWER IS . . .

Q: Why do we open the door when reciting Shefoch Chamascha?

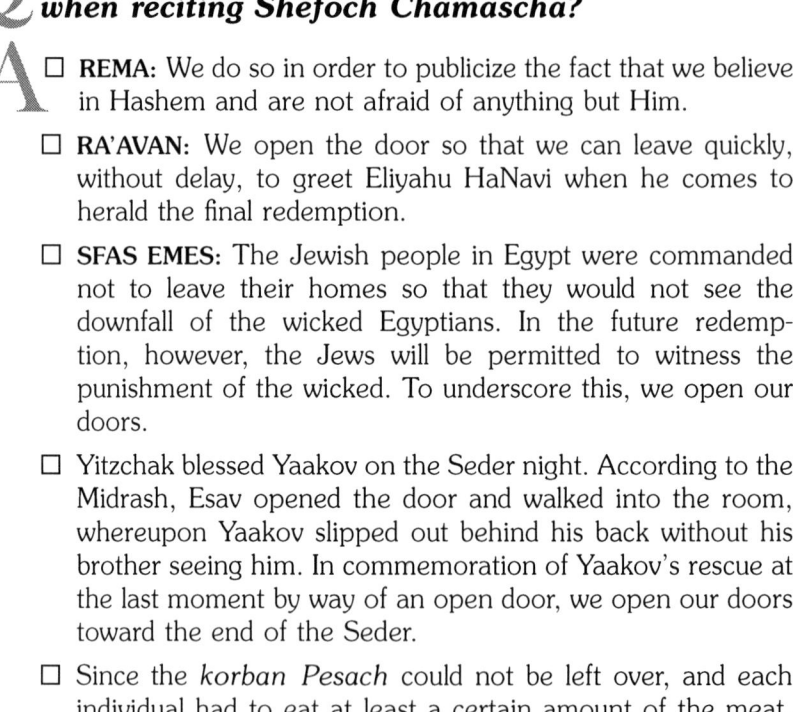

A: ☐ **REMA:** We do so in order to publicize the fact that we believe in Hashem and are not afraid of anything but Him.

☐ **RA'AVAN:** We open the door so that we can leave quickly, without delay, to greet Eliyahu HaNavi when he comes to herald the final redemption.

☐ **SFAS EMES:** The Jewish people in Egypt were commanded not to leave their homes so that they would not see the downfall of the wicked Egyptians. In the future redemption, however, the Jews will be permitted to witness the punishment of the wicked. To underscore this, we open our doors.

☐ Yitzchak blessed Yaakov on the Seder night. According to the Midrash, Esav opened the door and walked into the room, whereupon Yaakov slipped out behind his back without his brother seeing him. In commemoration of Yaakov's rescue at the last moment by way of an open door, we open our doors toward the end of the Seder.

☐ Since the *korban Pesach* could not be left over, and each individual had to eat at least a certain amount of the meat, each sacrifice was eaten only by those who had registered earlier for that specific sacrifice. This ensured that everyone received a portion and there would be no leftovers.

In many homes, the doors were locked on the Seder night to prevent strangers, who had not been designated to partake of that *korban*, from entering. After the people in the household had finished eating the *korban Pesach*, and there was no longer any fear of a stranger joining them, the door was opened. In commemoration of this custom, we too open our doors after partaking of the *Afikoman*, which we eat in memory of the *korban Pesach*.

One year at the Seder, Rav Menachem Mendel, the Rebbe of Kotzk, instructed a particular chassid to open the door.

The chassid was delighted to have been chosen for this task, and was certain that the Rebbe wanted him to see the prophet Eliyahu.

Sensing the chassid's thoughts, the Rebbe remarked, "Eliyahu does not come through the door, but rather through the mind."

Q
What is the connection between Shefoch Chamascha and the recounting of the Exodus?

A

☐ **RI BEN YAKAR:** After the sea split, the Egyptians cursed Hashem. Therefore, after mentioning the splitting of the sea in the first part of Hallel, we say, שְׁפֹךְ חֲמָתְךָ אֶל הַגּוֹיִם, *Pour Your wrath upon the nations*, to underscore the difference between ourselves and the Egyptians. We praise and extol Hashem, in contrast to the nations — led by the Egyptians — about whom it says in this passage, *They do not recognize You...and do not invoke Your Name.*

☐ **ABARBANEL:** Hashem made His might known to the whole world when He punished the Egyptians for harming the Jewish people. We ask Hashem to show the world His might once again — and to pour out His wrath on the nations that cause us to suffer.

☐ **ORCHOS CHAIM:** While there is no direct connection between *Shefoch Chamascha* and the story of the Exodus, since we fulfilled several mitzvos on this night — e.g., Kiddush, *karpas*, matzah, and *maror* — and mentioned Hashem as we did so, we add this paragraph, with an emphasis on the words אֲשֶׁר לֹא יְדָעוּךָ, *that do not recognize You*, in order to highlight the difference between ourselves and the nations of the world.

☐ **RAV AVIGDOR NEBENZAHL:** At the conclusion of the Seder, there could, Heaven forbid, be an opportunity for Satan to bring a complaint against the Jewish people for not sacrificing the *korban Pesach*. To counter this, we ask Hashem to pour out His wrath on the nations. We would like to bring the *korban Pesach* (the proof: we conducted a proper Seder), but we are prevented from doing so today by the nations that do not recognize You and who destroyed the Beis HaMikdash. Therefore, *Pour Your wrath upon the nations...*

☐ The purpose of the Seder is to glorify Hashem's Name and to praise Him for all the miracles He performed on our behalf. In *Shefoch Chamascha* we mention the suffering we have endured in order to express our gratitude to Him for having saved us.

הלל

The door is closed and the recitation of the Haggadah is continued.

לֹא לָנוּ יהוה, לֹא לָנוּ; כִּי לְשִׁמְךָ תֵּן כָּבוֹד, עַל חַסְדְּךָ עַל אֲמִתֶּךָ. לָמָּה יֹאמְרוּ הַגּוֹיִם, אַיֵּה נָא אֱלֹהֵיהֶם. וֵאלֹהֵינוּ בַשָּׁמָיִם, כֹּל אֲשֶׁר חָפֵץ עָשָׂה. עֲצַבֵּיהֶם כֶּסֶף וְזָהָב, מַעֲשֵׂה יְדֵי אָדָם. פֶּה לָהֶם וְלֹא יְדַבֵּרוּ, עֵינַיִם לָהֶם וְלֹא יִרְאוּ.

Q *Why list two reasons: that the nations do not recognize Hashem, and that they have attempted to destroy the Jewish people?*

☐ **ETZ CHAIM:** That they do not recognize You is not an explanation, but a statement: the nations should be punished despite the fact that they do not know of Hashem's existence. Their lack of knowledge does not put them into the category of ones in which circumstances absolve them of responsibility for what they have done in ignorance. The reason for this is, *For they have devoured Yaakov.* They torture and oppress the Jewish people — and take pleasure in doing so.

ᴥֻ§ הלל / Hallel

Q *Why do we recite Hallel on the Seder night?*

A ☐ **TALMUD** (*Pesachim* 95a): The recitation of Hallel was required when eating the korban Pesach. In commemoration of the Hallel that was said when the korban Pesach was eaten in the days of the Beis HaMikdash, we recite Hallel at the Seder even in the absence of a korban Pesach.

☐ We recite Hallel at the Seder as a token of our gratitude for our redemption from Egypt, which took place at night. As Chazal tell us, *When Israel was redeemed from Egypt, they were redeemed at night* (*Berachos* 9a). Therefore we say Hallel at night to thank Hashem for the redemption, which happened at night. (Even though they actually left Egypt the next day, the redemption began that night.)

הגדה של פסח [266]

HALLEL

The door is closed and the recitation of the Haggadah is continued.

Not for our sake, O Lord, not for our sake, but for Your Name's sake give glory, for the sake of Your kindness and Your truth! Why should the nations say, "Where is their God?" Our God is in the heavens; whatever He pleases, He does! Their idols are silver and gold, the handiwork of man. They have a mouth, but cannot speak; they have eyes, but cannot see;

Q Why is no blessing recited over Hallel?

A
- **MEIRI:** On the Seder night, we say Hallel as part of the mitzvah of relating the story of the Exodus. Since it is not a separate obligation on its own, it does not have its own blessing.
- **RASHBA:** The blessing of Hallel was established primarily for saying Hallel in shul.
- **TUR** (citing **MAHRITZ GEI'AS** and **AVI EZRI**): During the Seder, Hallel is interrupted by the meal.
- **MAHARAL:** The Hallel said on the Seder night is not a mitzvah; rather, it emanates from our need to thank Hashem for all the miracles He performed on our behalf. On the Seder night, after we describe Hashem's miracles and His might, we achieve a revitalized recognition of Hashem and are strengthened in our faith. When a person attains a high level of faith, Hallel emerges from his mouth naturally and does not require a command. Thus we do not say the blessing *Who has sanctified us with His commandments and has commanded us to read the Hallel.*

Q What are the differences between Hallel on the Seder night and Hallel year-round?

A
- **BA'ALEI HATOSAFOS:** Our obligation to say Hallel at the Seder stems from the miracle of the Exodus. On Yom Tov, Hallel is said as a prayer and a general expression of thanks to Hashem.

[267] HAGGADAH: THE ANSWER IS . . .

אָזְנַיִם לָהֶם וְלֹא יִשְׁמָעוּ, אַף לָהֶם וְלֹא יְרִיחוּן. יְדֵיהֶם וְלֹא יְמִישׁוּן, רַגְלֵיהֶם וְלֹא יְהַלֵּכוּ, לֹא יֶהְגּוּ בִּגְרוֹנָם. כְּמוֹהֶם יִהְיוּ עֹשֵׂיהֶם, כֹּל אֲשֶׁר בֹּטֵחַ בָּהֶם. יִשְׂרָאֵל בְּטַח בַּיהוה, עֶזְרָם וּמָגִנָּם הוּא. בֵּית אַהֲרֹן בִּטְחוּ בַיהוה, עֶזְרָם וּמָגִנָּם הוּא. יִרְאֵי יהוה בִּטְחוּ בַיהוה, עֶזְרָם וּמָגִנָּם הוּא.

☐ Seder night is the only time when Hallel is recited at night instead of by day.

All year-round, Hallel is said standing, while at the Seder we say it sitting down.

Q: Why do we recite Hallel on the Seder night while seated?

A:
☐ **SHIBBOLEI HALEKET:** Since the entire Haggadah is said while seated, we are not required to trouble ourselves to stand here.

☐ We remain seated in order not to spill the cup of wine we are holding.

☐ Hallel is said standing the rest of the year, as a testimony. On the Seder night, however, it is said as a song and not as a testimony.

Q: Why is Hallel divided into two parts, half before the meal and half after?

A:
☐ **LEVUSH:** The first half of Hallel speaks about the Exodus from Egypt, while the second half refers to the other exiles. It was therefore established that the second half be said after the meal in order to distinguish between the two redemptions.

☐ **ESHEL AVRAHAM:** In the first part of Hallel, we talk about the Exodus while the matzah and *maror* are lying in front of us — that is, before the meal. In the portion of Hallel recited after the meal, however, we do not mention the Exodus, and thus may say it even without matzah and *maror* present.

☐ The purpose of some of the changes instituted for the Seder was to prompt the children to ask questions. Saying the Hallel in two parts also prompts the children to ask.

they have ears, but cannot hear; they have a nose, but cannot smell; their hands — they cannot feel; their feet — they cannot walk; nor can they utter a sound with their throat. Those who make them should become like them, whoever trusts in them! O Israel! Trust in HASHEM; He is their help and their shield! House of Aharon! Trust in HASHEM! He is their help and their shield! You who fear HASHEM — trust in HASHEM, He is their help and their shield!

לֹא לָנוּ / Not for our sake

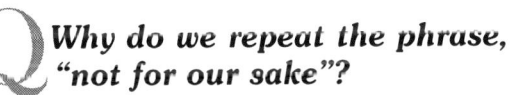

Q *Why do we repeat the phrase, "not for our sake"?*

A
- **MAHARAL:** Had it said *Not for our sake* only once, it might have been construed to mean that actually we are deserving of having Hashem do this for us, but we are asking Him to refrain. To avoid such a misunderstanding, David HaMelech repeated the words, as though to say, "We have no merit at all, so please do it for the sake of Your glorious Name!"

- **YAAVETZ:** The repetition is for emphasis — to emphasize that we are not deserving of having miracles performed for us to the same degree that our forefathers were.

- **RAV YITZCHAK ISAAC CHAVER:** The double language corresponds to the two possible times for the redemption to arrive: (1) immediately, by virtue of *din*, justice — if we repent; or (2) at the designated time, even if we do not deserve it, by virtue of Hashem's *chesed*, kindness. Corresponding to these two aspects, David said, כִּי לְשִׁמְךָ תֵּן כָּבוֹד, עַל **חַסְדְּךָ** עַל **אֲמִתֶּךָ**, *For Your Name's sake give glory, for the sake of Your* **kindness** *and Your* **truth**! — referring to Hashem's traits of *chesed* and *din*.

- **SFAS EMES:** The repetition hints that we are aware that everything comes about through Divine Providence, and we are grateful for all of it — both for the good and the bad. The first *Not for our sake* corresponds to the good, and the second to the bad.

Q Is there a distinction between "they have a mouth but cannot speak" and "nor can they utter a sound with their throat"?

A ☐ ABARBANEL: *They have a mouth but cannot speak* refers to idol worshipers, who have a mouth but do not speak properly. *Nor can they utter a sound with their throat* refers to the idols, which have no mouth with which to speak.

Q Why does David HaMelech repeat "Trust in HASHEM" three times?

A ☐ MEIRI: These three groups are divided according to the level of their *bitachon* — trust in Hashem. The first group is made up of the common folk, the second is comprised of those who study the Torah, and the third are the sages.

☐ ROKEACH: They allude to the three daily prayers — Shacharis, Minchah, and Maariv — and the three major festivals — Pesach, Shavuos, and Sukkos — which bring us merit.

☐ ABARBANEL: Each group is characterized by its level of trust in Hashem. The first is comprised of the general population of Israel. The second, *House of Aharon*, refers to those who come from the tribe of Levi. They are distinguished from the first group by virtue of their service in the Beis HaMikdash. Those in the third group — *those who fear HASHEM* — differ from the first two groups, as their inclusion is due to their piety rather than their lineage.

☐ SEFORNO: Each of the three groups lived in a different era after David's time, and he is addressing all of them:

Israel refers to those who lived in the Babylonian exile, when the Jewish nation was in need of a great salvation.

House of Aharon refers to those who lived during the second Temple period, when Kohanim were kings. They trusted in Hashem to bring about their salvation from the Medean and Greek empires.

Those who fear HASHEM refers to the future, when Hashem will again bring salvation to the Jewish people. We must believe only in Him and direct our prayers to Him.

הגדה של פסח [270]

☐ **RAV CHAIM PALAGI:** This corresponds to the three pillars on which the world rests, as listed in *Pirkei Avos: The world depends on three things — on Torah study, on the service [of God], and on kind deeds* (*Avos* 1:2):

Israel corresponds to *chesed*, lovingkindness, one of the three characteristic traits of the Jewish people, who are called "*baishanim rachmanim v'gomlei chasadim*" — bashful, merciful, and doers of good deeds.

House of Aharon corresponds to *avodah* — service.

Those who fear **HASHEM** corresponds to Torah study. Together, these three groups protect the world.

☐ **MAHARAL:** The groups differ in their level of attachment to Hashem:

Israel cleaves to Hashem like children to their father.

The second group, *House of Aharon*, clings to Hashem and serves Him out of love.

And the third — *those who fear* **HASHEM** — serves Him from *yirah*, awe.

☐ **MALBIM:** Each of these three groups has a different level of trust in Hashem. The greater the trust, the greater the help that Hashem will provide. *House of Aharon* is on a higher level than *Israel*, so the help they receive from Hashem is correspondingly greater. *Those who fear* **HASHEM** are on a higher level than the *House of Aharon*, and thus the help they will receive is even greater.

☐ **RAV SAMSON RAPHAEL HIRSCH:** The uniqueness of each of these groups lies in its mission:

Israel was collectively sent on a mission by Hashem, chosen from among the other nations.

House of Aharon was chosen from among the rest of *Klal Yisrael*, just as the Jewish people were chosen from among the nations of the world.

Those who fear **HASHEM** refers to the personal mission of every individual on the path of *yiras Hashem*. Each thanks Hashem and serves Him in his own way.

☐ **NETZIV:** The levels of each of these three groups are different, with each successive group on a higher level:

Israel believes that Hashem will not abandon them, as He promised our *Avos*.

יהוה זְכָרָנוּ יְבָרֵךְ; יְבָרֵךְ אֶת בֵּית יִשְׂרָאֵל,
יְבָרֵךְ אֶת בֵּית אַהֲרֹן. יְבָרֵךְ יִרְאֵי יהוה,
הַקְּטַנִּים עִם הַגְּדֹלִים. יֹסֵף יהוה עֲלֵיכֶם, עֲלֵיכֶם וְעַל
בְּנֵיכֶם. בְּרוּכִים אַתֶּם לַיהוה, עֹשֵׂה שָׁמַיִם וָאָרֶץ.

The **House of Aharon**, above them, draws the heavenly blessings down from on high through their service in the Beis HaMikdash.

Highest are **those who fear HASHEM**, who are attached to Hashem and trust Him constantly, and not only during the service in the Beis HaMikdash like the Kohanim.

☐ **CHAFETZ CHAIM:** The Jewish people are divided according to their spiritual levels:
Israel refers to the average Jew.
House of Aharon is the Kohanim, who teach the people Torah.
Those who fear HASHEM are those who are extremely zealous and meticulous in carrying out Hashem's will on a level higher than the Kohanim.

ה' זְכָרָנוּ / **HASHEM Who has remembered us**

Q "**HASHEM Who has remembered us will bless.**" What does the word זְכָרָנוּ, remembered, at the start of this paragraph convey?

A ☐ **RADAK:** It is related to the word "*zachar*," male, since the males go up to Yerushalayim for the Festivals, which is when we say this passage in Hallel — on Pesach, Shavuos, Sukkos.

☐ **ABARBANEL:** The word means "remember." Hashem remembered us when we were in exile in Egypt, and He still remembers and blesses us in our present exile.

☐ **YAAVETZ:** The word is from "*zachar*," male. Hashem will bless the males — ה' זְכָרָנוּ יְבָרֵךְ — and, at the same time, יְבָרֵךְ אֶת בֵּית יִשְׂרָאֵל, *He will bless the House of Israel*, the females.

☐ **NETZIV:** The word means that Hashem will remember us and — as a result of His remembering — will bless us.

[272] הגדה של פסח

Hashem Who has remembered us will bless — He will bless the House of Israel; He will bless the House of Aharon; He will bless those who fear Hashem, the small as well as the great. May Hashem add upon you, upon you and your children! You are blessed of Hashem, Maker of heaven and earth.

- □ **RAV SAMSON RAPHAEL HIRSCH:** The word is from *"zechirah,"* memory. Just as Hashem remembered us and watched over us in Egypt, so He will never abandon us in our present exile.

Q *"He will bless the House of Israel; He will bless the House of Aharon. He will bless those who fear Hashem." Why is the word בַּיִת, house, not used in conjunction with יִרְאֵי ה', those who fear Hashem?*

A
- □ **ABARBANEL:** Those who fear Hashem are a group of people whose common denominator is an inner desire to serve Hashem. It is not a matter of membership in a certain family.

- □ **VILNA GAON:** There are four groups in the Jewish nation. The first three have a "House": the Kohanim, Levi'im, and Yisraelim. The first two belong to the *House of Aharon*, while the latter belongs to the *House of Israel*. But the fourth group — *those who fear Hashem* — have no property or ancestral portion.

- □ **RAV YECHEZKEL ABRAMSKY:** The word "beis," house, is used with regard to a person whose descendants are similar to him. Thus, with regard to the Kohanim, Levi'im, and Yisraelim, the word *"beis"* is used. However, the descendants of those who fear God will not necessarily be like their ancestors. Therefore, the word *"beis"* is omitted.

Q *Why do we mention "the small" before "the great"?*

A
- □ **ABARBANEL:** David HaMelech placed the younger ones before the elders to say that the younger members should be blessed in the merit of the elders.

הַשָּׁמַיִם שָׁמַיִם לַיהוה, וְהָאָרֶץ נָתַן לִבְנֵי אָדָם. לֹא
הַמֵּתִים יְהַלְלוּ יָהּ, וְלֹא כָּל יֹרְדֵי דוּמָה. וַאֲנַחְנוּ
נְבָרֵךְ יָהּ, מֵעַתָּה וְעַד עוֹלָם; הַלְלוּיָהּ.[1]

אָהַבְתִּי כִּי יִשְׁמַע יהוה, אֶת קוֹלִי תַּחֲנוּנָי.
כִּי הִטָּה אָזְנוֹ לִי, וּבְיָמַי אֶקְרָא.
אֲפָפוּנִי חֶבְלֵי מָוֶת, וּמְצָרֵי שְׁאוֹל מְצָאוּנִי;

- ☐ **YAAVETZ:** The younger ones precede the elders to teach us the trait of humility. Even though they are younger in age, they are mentioned first.

- ☐ **NETZIV:** The elders have discovered the correct path to follow in life. The younger ones, who have not yet found their way, are in need of a blessing that they will find their way by learning from their elders.

- ☐ **MALBIM:** David HaMelech goes from smaller to greater. He begins with the younger ones, whose blessings are smaller, and continues on to the elders, whose blessings are greater and who will, in turn, influence the younger ones.

- ☐ **RAV SAMSON RAPHAEL HIRSCH:** The younger ones are placed first to emphasize the fact that they need to learn from their elders — and not, of course, the other way around.

אָהַבְתִּי / I love Him

Q *Anyone can love Hashem, for He hearkens to the person's desires. What is David HaMelech specifically telling us here about himself?*

A
- ☐ **ABARBANEL:** The nations of the world tell the Jewish people that their prayers are useless, as the prayers do not (in the nations' perception) seem to be accepted. To counter this claim, David states — even before these false claims are made — that he loves Hashem, Who hears his prayers.

- ☐ **SEFORNO:** David HaMelech loves his prayers and supplications to Hashem — even though he prays on a regular basis — because doing so banishes his sadness and anguish.

As for the heaven — the heaven is HASHEM's, but the earth He has given to mankind. Neither the dead can praise HASHEM, nor any who descend into silence; but we will bless God henceforth and forever. Halleluyah![1]

I love Him, for HASHEM hears my voice, my supplications. For He has inclined His ear to me, all my days I will call upon Him. The ropes of death encompassed me; the confines of the grave have found me;

1. *Psalm* 115.

- **MAHARAL:** Just as David loves Hashem, Who hears his supplications, so Hashem loves him and his prayers. This resembles the love of two people, in which the beloved both loves and returns love, in the same measure in which he has received it.
- **METZUDAS DAVID:** David loves Hashem because He hears his supplications.
- **YAAVETZ:** David HaMelech is saying that he loves Hashem at all times, even when troubles beset him.
- **RAV YITZCHAK ISAAC CHAVER:** David loves the fact that Hashem hears his voice even when he has not completed his prayer.
- **NETZIV:** In contrast to a king of flesh and blood, Hashem loves and desires supplication, and inclines His ear in order to hear those who ask Him for help.
- **ALTER OF KELM:** David HaMelech sees something positive in the suffering and tribulations that he has undergone (as opposed to others, who do not wish to suffer at all). After the hardships come, he prays to Hashem to rescue him. Then he praises Hashem, Who has heard his voice and heeded his supplication.
- **CHIDA:** David loves the fact that Hashem listens to his voice when he is learning Torah.

Q *One generally inclines his ear before hearing, so why is the order reversed here?*

צָרָה וְיָגוֹן אֶמְצָא. וּבְשֵׁם יהוה אֶקְרָא: אָנָּה יהוה
מַלְּטָה נַפְשִׁי. חַנּוּן יהוה וְצַדִּיק, וֵאלֹהֵינוּ מְרַחֵם.
שֹׁמֵר פְּתָאיִם יהוה, דַּלּוֹתִי וְלִי יְהוֹשִׁיעַ. שׁוּבִי
נַפְשִׁי לִמְנוּחָיְכִי, כִּי יהוה גָּמַל עָלָיְכִי. כִּי חִלַּצְתָּ
נַפְשִׁי מִמָּוֶת; אֶת עֵינִי מִן דִּמְעָה, אֶת רַגְלִי מִדֶּחִי.
אֶתְהַלֵּךְ לִפְנֵי יהוה, בְּאַרְצוֹת הַחַיִּים. הֶאֱמַנְתִּי כִּי
אֲדַבֵּר, אֲנִי עָנִיתִי מְאֹד. אֲנִי אָמַרְתִּי בְחָפְזִי, כָּל
הָאָדָם כֹּזֵב.

A ▫ **ALSHICH:** "*Shemiah*" connotes hearing from a distance, while "inclining the ear" implies listening from close by. David loves the fact that Hashem listens directly to his prayers, without the assistance of the heavenly hosts, even when He is only listening from afar. How much more so when Hashem listens to his supplications by "inclining His ear" — from up close.

▫ **RAV YITZCHAK HUTNER:** David HaMelech praises Hashem because he is privileged to be close to Him. In his case, the "inclining of the ear" is not the means but rather the purpose: drawing close to Hashem. In other words, first *HASHEM hears my voice*, and then *He inclines His ear* — then I become close to Him.

Q *Why does David call upon his soul to "return to its rest" because "HASHEM has been kind"?*

A ▫ **RADAK:** David is adjuring his soul to be at rest in times of trouble — to return to a state of *menuchah*, tranquility, after being mired in troubles (as was just said in the previous verse, *Trouble and sorrow I have found*). The end of the verse — *for HASHEM has been kind to you* — offers the reason for returning to Hashem.

▫ **MEIRI:** David is not offering an explanation, but rather instructing his soul to trust in Hashem, Who in His kindness will be its benefactor.

trouble and sorrow have I found. Then I called upon the Name of HASHEM: "Please, HASHEM, save my soul." Gracious is HASHEM and righteous, our God is merciful. The Lord protects the simple; I was brought low but He saved me. Return to your rest, my soul, for HASHEM has been kind to you. You delivered my soul from death, my eyes from tears, and my feet from stumbling. I shall walk before the Lord in the lands of the living. I kept faith although I say: "I suffer exceedingly." I said in my haste: "All mankind is deceitful."

☐ **ABARBANEL:** Just as Hashem redeemed us from Egypt, an exile in which our enemies wished to destroy us, and brought us to Eretz Yisrael, so must we trust and believe that Hashem will show us kindness and redeem us in the future.

☐ **ALSHICH:** It is not an explanation, but a proof. Just as Hashem showed David kindness in this world, his soul may rest assured that it will find peace in the next.

☐ **YAAVETZ:** David HaMelech is saying that his soul will be at rest and tranquil in both good and bad times, because Hashem is kind to him in both good times and bad.

Q In what way is all mankind deceitful?

A ☐ **RADAK:** David is expressing his faith in Hashem. Even in difficult times, when he was escaping from Shaul and it seemed that he would never attain the throne, David had faith and rejected all the criticism leveled against him. When told that he would never be king, he would reply that the speaker was "*kozeiv*," deceitful — that is, speaking falsely.

☐ **ABARBANEL:** In the course of our exile, the nations of the world have told the Jewish people that they will never be redeemed. Therefore, we answer that Hashem *will* redeem us, and that the words of the nations are false.

☐ **MAHARAL:** When Shmuel told David (as David was running to escape Shaul) that he would become the king of Israel, this prophecy appeared baseless. In response, David asked,

[277] **HAGGADAH: THE ANSWER IS . . .**

מָה אָשִׁיב לַיהוה, כָּל תַּגְמוּלוֹהִי עָלָי. כּוֹס יְשׁוּעוֹת אֶשָּׂא, וּבְשֵׁם יהוה אֶקְרָא. נְדָרַי לַיהוה אֲשַׁלֵּם, נֶגְדָה נָּא לְכָל עַמּוֹ. יָקָר בְּעֵינֵי יהוה, הַמָּוְתָה לַחֲסִידָיו. אָנָּה יהוה כִּי אֲנִי עַבְדֶּךָ; אֲנִי עַבְדְּךָ בֶּן אֲמָתֶךָ, פִּתַּחְתָּ לְמוֹסֵרָי. לְךָ אֶזְבַּח זֶבַח תּוֹדָה, וּבְשֵׁם יהוה אֶקְרָא. נְדָרַי לַיהוה אֲשַׁלֵּם, נֶגְדָה נָּא לְכָל עַמּוֹ. בְּחַצְרוֹת בֵּית יהוה, בְּתוֹכֵכִי יְרוּשָׁלָיִם; הַלְלוּיָהּ.[1]

"Is everyone deceitful?" Later, when he saw the prophecy fulfilled, David's faith in Hashem was strengthened and he expressed the thoughts found here: *I shall walk before the Lord in the lands of the living. I kept faith although I say: "I suffer exceedingly."*

☐ **MALBIM:** David spoke these words at a despairing time in his life, when his mind was not settled. He spoke hastily — as it says, *I spoke in haste* — saying that many people are deceitful. Now that he sees that there is hope, he is "retracting" what he said earlier.

☐ **RAV YECHEZKEL LEVENSTEIN:** Hashem desires that individuals toil for what they achieve. David testifies that all his achievements came about through hard work. When he believed that he accomplished something, he attributed it to prior toil — *I kept the faith, although I say...* However, when he seemed to accomplish something quickly, *in haste*, without prior toil, he treated it as if *all of man is deceitful* — and did not believe it had any substance.

מָה אָשִׁיב / *How can I repay*

Q Why do we repeat the phrase, *"I am Your servant"*?

A ☐ **ABARBANEL:** There are two types of servants: a thief who is sold into servitude, and a person who was born into servitude to a mother who is a maidservant. David is saying that his service of Hashem resembles that of this second group. He

How can I repay HASHEM for all His kindness to me? I will raise the cup of salvations and invoke the Name of HASHEM. My vows to HASHEM I will pay in the presence of His entire people. Precious in the eyes of HASHEM is the death of His devout ones. Please, HASHEM — for I am Your servant, I am Your servant, son of Your handmaid — You have released my bonds. To You I sacrifice thanksgiving offerings, and the Name of HASHEM I will invoke. My vows to HASHEM I will pay in the presence of His entire people; in the courtyards of the House of HASHEM, in your midst, O Jerusalem, Halleluyah![1]

---

1. *Psalm* 116.

---

is not like a servant that his master purchased, but rather like a son of the household, born to the service. The master of the house treats such a child like a son, since the servant was born and grew up in his house. Similarly, the Jewish people have been in exile many times, and through them all Hashem has watched over us as a father worries over his child.

☐ **ALSHICH:** In asking Hashem to grant him long life, David produces two merits: (1) *ani avdecha*, I am Your servant, and (2) *ben amasecha*, son of Your handmaid — he is a descendant of Ruth, who was called *amasecha* (*Ruth* 3:9). David asks Hashem to grant him long life as He did David's great-grandmother, Ruth.

☐ **MAHARAL:** David is expressing his attachment to Hashem. From the moment he was born, he sensed his obligation to Hashem and served Him all his life like a servant born to a maidservant — in other words, a servant from birth.

☐ **METZUDAS DAVID:** David HaMelech is expressing his gratitude for the privilege of being a servant of Hashem — and not only a servant, but also the son of a handmaid. Being the son of a handmaid taught him to be humble and submissive to Hashem from early childhood.

☐ **YAAVETZ:** There are two types of servants — the thief who is sold into servitude, and the child born to a handmaid. The difference between them is that the first kind of servant will

הַלְלוּ אֶת יהוה, כָּל גּוֹיִם; שַׁבְּחוּהוּ כָּל הָאֻמִּים.
כִּי גָבַר עָלֵינוּ חַסְדּוֹ, וֶאֱמֶת יהוה לְעוֹלָם;
הַלְלוּיָהּ.[1]

---

seize any opportunity to escape his master, while the second will not attempt to escape because he is happy. He was born into his situation and has become accustomed to it. David HaMelech is saying that he is of the second type: he is a *son of Your handmaid*. He does not try to escape because he is happy to have been born into his situation. And furthermore, he has also chosen to serve Hashem of his own free will.

☐ **MALBIM:** There are two types of servants: a servant whose master has purchased him with money, and a child born to the master's maidservant — a child born to serve. David asks Hashem to treat him as the latter kind of servant.

☐ **NETZIV:** A servant who is born to his master is more devoted than a servant purchased with money. His bond to his master is a closer one, and his work will be much more dedicated. David serves Hashem in this way, like a child born into his master's house.

◆§ הַלְלוּ / *Praise*

Q Why should the nations thank Hashem for His kindness to us?

A ☐ **RADAK:** This psalm is speaking about the future. In the days of Mashiach, everyone will realize the greatness of the Torah that was given to the world in the desert in the merit of the Jewish people. In the giving of the Torah, Hashem's providence became renowned throughout the world — and in the future, all the nations will acknowledge this.

☐ **ALSHICH:** After the Exodus from Egypt, only the Jewish people believed in Hashem. In the future redemption, however, the nations of the world will believe in Him too. They will accept His kingship and praise Him for both His kindness and His truth (as this passage goes on to say, *For His kindness to us was overwhelming, and the truth of HASHEM is eternal*).

P̲raise HASHEM, all you nations; praise Him all you peoples! For His kindness to us was overwhelming, and the truth of HASHEM is eternal, Halleluyah![1]

1. Psalm 117.

- ☐ **MAHARAL:** The nations do not thank Hashem for His kindness to *us*, but only for His kindness to *them*. From their gratitude, we are meant to learn a parallel: how much more must we be grateful to Hashem for His miracles on our behalf!
- ☐ **BINAH L'ITIM:** The nations of the world neither know nor recognize Hashem's greatness and therefore do not praise Him properly. In the future, however, after the Jews are redeemed, everyone will recognize His rule and will praise Him for it.
- ☐ **KEDUSHAS LEVI:** In the future, when the whole world acknowledges Hashem's existence, the nations will praise Him and Hashem's Name will be sanctified.
- ☐ **RAV AKIVA EIGER:** The nations extol Hashem for the mighty deeds He does in the world, because they too benefit from Hashem's kindnesses to the Jewish people.
- ☐ **BNEI YISSASCHAR:** The Jewish people are ignorant of all the plots that the nations weave against us. However, the nations themselves know what they plotted but failed to carry out because of Hashem's kindness toward the Jews, and for this they praise Hashem.
- ☐ **ALTER OF KELM:** The nations acknowledge and praise the fact that the Jewish people have mitzvos in whose merit they soar to lofty spiritual levels.
- ☐ **CHAFETZ CHAIM:** If the nations were to succeed in carrying out their evil plots, they would be severely punished — as was seen in Egypt, Rome, and other exiles. However, in the future redemption, the nations of the world will thank Hashem for His kindness to the Jewish people and for preventing them from harming the Jews, for which they would have been liable for punishment.
- ☐ **BRISKER RAV:** The nations will praise Hashem for the mighty deeds and wonders with which Hashem will redeem the Jews in the future and which the entire world will witness.

הוֹדוּ לַיהוה כִּי טוֹב, כִּי לְעוֹלָם חַסְדּוֹ.
יֹאמַר נָא יִשְׂרָאֵל, כִּי לְעוֹלָם חַסְדּוֹ.
יֹאמְרוּ נָא בֵית אַהֲרֹן, כִּי לְעוֹלָם חַסְדּוֹ.
יֹאמְרוּ נָא יִרְאֵי יהוה, כִּי לְעוֹלָם חַסְדּוֹ.

מִן הַמֵּצַר קָרָאתִי יָּהּ, עָנָנִי בַמֶּרְחָב יָהּ. יהוה לִי לֹא אִירָא, מַה יַּעֲשֶׂה לִי אָדָם. יהוה לִי בְּעֹזְרָי,

---

⊷§ הוֹדוּ לַה׳ / Give thanks to HASHEM

Q "Give thanks to HASHEM for He is good." What is implied by the words כִּי טוֹב, for He is good, which are offered as a reason for giving thanks?

A ☐ IBN EZRA: We must thank Hashem simply because He is good.

☐ ROKEACH: We are obligated to thank Hashem because He benefits and does good for the entire world.

☐ SEFORNO: We must thank Hashem for the fact that His kindness to us is steadfast and does not change.

Q What is meant by "His kindness endures forever"?

A ☐ ROKEACH: We benefit from Hashem's kindness in this world as well as in the next.

☐ ALSHICH: Hashem's kindness to the Jewish people on their leaving Egypt was revealed only temporarily. After the future redemption, however, His kindness will be revealed forever.

☐ MAHARAL: There is no limit to Hashem's kindness; it goes on forever.

☐ METZUDAS DAVID: Hashem's kindness endures forever, without pause — in contrast to the *chesed* that a human being performs, which is not constant.

☐ OTZAR HATEFILLOS: Hashem performs *chesed* for the world, not for Himself. Thus the word *l'olam*, forever, also

Give thanks to Hashem for He is good;
His kindness endures forever!
Let Israel say: His kindness endures forever!
Let the House of Aharon say:
His kindness endures forever!
Let those who fear Hashem say:
His kindness endures forever!

From the straits did I call to God; God answered me with expansiveness. Hashem is with me; I have no fear; how can man affect me? Hashem is for me

---

can be translated as "for the world": Hashem's kindness is for the world's benefit.

❏ **RAV YECHEZKEL LEVENSTEIN:** Hashem's kindness is constant and permanent. Even when He is angry at us, His love for us does not change.

◆§ מִן הַמֵּצַר / From the straits

Q Why did David HaMelech repeat the idea that his enemies surrounded him, so many times?

A ❏ **ROKEACH:** This idea appears four times in the chapter to correspond to the four directions: north, south, east, and west. David HaMelech uses two forms of the same word — סַבּוּנִי, *swarm around me*, and סְבָבוּנִי, *encompass* — to indicate the two types of warfare his enemies employed against him: (1) they sent troops of soldiers to fight him on the battlefront, and (2) they sent convoys to surround him.

❏ **ABARBANEL:** Each phrase refers to a different enemy of the Jewish people:

כָּל גּוֹיִם סְבָבוּנִי, *All the nations encompass me* was said about Sancheirev and the Assyrians, who decimated the Shomron and exiled the ten tribes. In the end, they were destroyed for doing evil to the Jewish people: בְּשֵׁם ה' כִּי אֲמִילַם, *In the Name of Hashem I cut them down!*

סַבּוּנִי גַם סְבָבוּנִי, *They encompass me; they swarm around me* was said about the Babylonian king Nevuchadnetzar, who

[283] HAGGADAH: THE ANSWER IS . . .

וַאֲנִי אֶרְאֶה בְשׂנְאָי. טוֹב לַחֲסוֹת בַּיהוה, מִבְּטֹחַ בָּאָדָם. טוֹב לַחֲסוֹת בַּיהוה, מִבְּטֹחַ בִּנְדִיבִים. כָּל גּוֹיִם סְבָבוּנִי, בְּשֵׁם יהוה כִּי אֲמִילַם. סַבּוּנִי גַם סְבָבוּנִי, בְּשֵׁם יהוה כִּי אֲמִילַם. סַבּוּנִי כִדְבֹרִים, דֹּעֲכוּ כְּאֵשׁ קוֹצִים; בְּשֵׁם יהוה כִּי אֲמִילַם.

---

came to destroy Yerushalayim several times. The Babylonians too were destroyed for their sins against the Jewish people, as David states also about them, בְּשֵׁם ה' כִּי אֲמִילַם, *In the Name of HASHEM I cut them down!*

סַבּוּנִי כִדְבֹרִים, *They swarm around me like bees* was said about Persia, Medea, and the Greeks. They too were cut down for their sins.

☐ **VILNA GAON:** סְבָבוּנִי, *they encompass me* — from afar. סַבּוּנִי, *they encompass me* — from close by. David HaMelech is saying that his enemies, who were far away, have drawn close and are surrounding him. Then, גַם סְבָבוּנִי, *they swarm around me* — other enemies have joined forces with them. Finally, סַבּוּנִי כִדְבֹרִים, *They swarm around me like bees* — they attack, trying to bring him down and kill him, much as bees surround a person.

☐ **RAV SAMSON RAPHAEL HIRSCH:** These verses describe three eras in Jewish history:

כָּל גּוֹיִם סְבָבוּנִי, *All the nations encompass me* — the era from Yehoshua until the destruction of the first Beis HaMikdash. During this period, Israel suffered from the enemies that surrounded her.

סַבּוּנִי גַם סְבָבוּנִי, *They encompass me; they swarm around me* — the era of the second Beis HaMikdash, when the nations of the world were our enemies. The nations were hostile to the Jews and deterred any attempt to be friendly to them.

סַבּוּנִי כִדְבֹרִים, *They swarm around me like bees* — this is the period of the exile. The nations hate the Jewish people, stinging them like bees that surround their victim and leave him no escape route.

☐ **BRISKER RAV:** David HaMelech is describing the nations' hatred. סַבּוּנִי גַם סְבָבוּנִי, *They encompass me; they swarm* through my helpers; therefore I can face my foes. It is better to take refuge in HASHEM than to rely on man. It is better to take refuge in HASHEM than to rely on princes. All the nations encompass me; but in the Name of HASHEM I cut them down! They encompass me; they swarm around me; but in the Name of HASHEM I cut them down! They swarm around me like bees, but they are extinguished as a fire does thorns; in the Name of HASHEM I cut them down!

---

around me — they besiege him externally as well as internally. סַבּוּנִי כִדְבֹרִים, *They swarm around me like bees* — their hatred increases and they wish to kill him, like bees swarming around their victim.

☐ **THE OZHEROVER REBBE:** David HaMelech is referring to three types of exile:

כָּל גּוֹיִם סְבָבוּנִי, *All the nations encompass me* refers to the Jewish people's exile among the nations.

סַבּוּנִי גַם סְבָבוּנִי, *They encompass me; they swarm around me* refers to the exile of *talmidei chachamim* amidst those who hate Torah.

סַבּוּנִי כִדְבֹרִים, *They swarm around me like bees* refers to the *yetzer hara*. At first it offers honey and acts as if it is concerned about us, but in truth its intent is to sting us like a bee.

☐ The nations surround us and attempt to destroy us. סַבּוּנִי, *They encompass me*, implies an attempt to destroy us physically. As though this were not enough, גַם סְבָבוּנִי, *They swarm around me* — this refers to an attempt at spiritual destruction, a war on the *neshamah*. They also wish to convert us from our faith, and try to prevent us from keeping the mitzvos through all manner of harsh decrees.

Q *Why repeat, "The right hand of HASHEM is raised triumphantly! The right hand of HASHEM does valiantly"?*

A ☐ **MAGGID OF PLOTZK:** David HaMelech is speaking about the three Holy Temples. יְמִין ה' עֹשָׂה חָיִל, *The right hand of HASHEM does valiantly*, corresponds to the first Beis

דָּחֹה דְחִיתַנִי לִנְפֹּל, וַיהוה עֲזָרָנִי. עָזִּי וְזִמְרָת יָהּ, וַיְהִי לִי לִישׁוּעָה. קוֹל רִנָּה וִישׁוּעָה בְּאָהֳלֵי צַדִּיקִים, יְמִין יהוה עֹשָׂה חָיִל. יְמִין יהוה רוֹמֵמָה, יְמִין יהוה עֹשָׂה חָיִל. לֹא אָמוּת כִּי אֶחְיֶה, וַאֲסַפֵּר מַעֲשֵׂי יָהּ. יַסֹּר יִסְּרַנִּי יָּהּ, וְלַמָּוֶת לֹא נְתָנָנִי. פִּתְחוּ לִי שַׁעֲרֵי צֶדֶק, אָבֹא בָם אוֹדֶה יָהּ. זֶה הַשַּׁעַר לַיהוה, צַדִּיקִים יָבֹאוּ בוֹ. אוֹדְךָ כִּי עֲנִיתָנִי,

---

HaMikdash, when the nations of the world did not oppress the Jewish people. יְמִין ה' רוֹמֵמָה, *The right hand of HASHEM is raised triumphantly*, corresponds to the second Beis HaMikdash. Despite the foreign powers that have oppressed our people, still *the right hand of HASHEM is raised triumphantly!* — Hashem maintains the upper hand against all those who rise up against us. The repetition of יְמִין ה' עֹשָׂה חָיִל corresponds to the building of the third Beis HaMikdash, when oppression will be banished completely.

□ **KSAV SOFER:** יְמִין ה' רוֹמֵמָה, *The right hand of HASHEM is raised triumphantly*, implies that Hashem brings about salvations that are hidden from us (they are "raised" above us so that we cannot see it). יְמִין ה' עֹשָׂה חָיִל, *The right hand of HASHEM does valiantly*, implies that Hashem brings about salvations in a natural way. The righteous always thank and praise Hashem, even if He performs miracles in a hidden way that cannot be seen.

Q Which is the gate of HASHEM?

A □ **RASHI:** It refers to the gate of the Beis HaMikdash, which belongs to Hashem.

□ **ROKEACH:** The gateway to Hashem are those shuls and study halls that are not filled with controversy and quarreling.

□ **SEFORNO:** It is the gate of Yerushalayim, through which the righteous come.

□ **RAV BARUCH OF MEZIBUZH:** Tzaddikim, in their humility, stand outside the gate and ask that it be opened so they can

You pushed me hard that I might fall, but HASHEM assisted me. My strength and song is God; He became my salvation. The sound of rejoicing and salvation is in the tents of the righteous: "The right hand of HASHEM does valiantly! The right hand of HASHEM is raised triumphantly! The right hand of HASHEM does valiantly!" I shall not die! I shall live and relate the deeds of God. God chastened me exceedingly but He did not let me die. Open for me the gates of righteousness, I will enter them and thank God. This is the gate of HASHEM; the righteous shall enter through it. I thank You for You answered me

---

come close to Hashem. David answers them, saying: *This* — humility — *is the gate of* HASHEM — the gateway to coming close to Hashem.

☐ **MALBIM:** The king had a special gate through which he entered the precincts of the Beis HaMikdash. David HaMelech is granting permission to the righteous to enter through this gate.

☐ **RAV YERUCHAM LEVOVITZ:** "The gate of Hashem" is Hashem's salvation, which the righteous are privileged to see when they find themselves in great trouble.

Q *What is David thanking Hashem for when he says* כִּי עֲנִיתָנִי*, for You answered me?*

A ☐ **SEFORNO:** David is asking Hashem to give him the privilege of thanking Him for accepting his supplications.

☐ **METZUDAS DAVID:** David HaMelech is thanking Hashem for answering his supplications and providing salvation.

☐ **CHASAM SOFER:** *Anisani*, You answered me, comes from the root word *inui*, suffering. David HaMelech is thanking Hashem even for his troubles, for he knows that salvation is near.

Q *Which is the despised stone to which David HaMelech is referring?*

[287] HAGGADAH: THE ANSWER IS . . .

אוֹדְךָ כִּי עֲנִיתָנִי, וַתְּהִי לִי לִישׁוּעָה. אוֹדְךָ כִּי עֲנִיתָנִי, וַתְּהִי לִי לִישׁוּעָה. אֶבֶן מָאֲסוּ הַבּוֹנִים, הָיְתָה לְרֹאשׁ פִּנָּה. אֶבֶן מָאֲסוּ הַבּוֹנִים, הָיְתָה לְרֹאשׁ פִּנָּה. מֵאֵת יהוה הָיְתָה זֹּאת, הִיא נִפְלָאת בְּעֵינֵינוּ. מֵאֵת יהוה הָיְתָה זֹּאת, הִיא נִפְלָאת בְּעֵינֵינוּ. זֶה הַיּוֹם עָשָׂה יהוה, נָגִילָה וְנִשְׂמְחָה בוֹ. זֶה הַיּוֹם עָשָׂה יהוה, נָגִילָה וְנִשְׂמְחָה בוֹ.

אָנָּא יהוה, הוֹשִׁיעָה נָּא.
אָנָּא יהוה, הוֹשִׁיעָה נָּא.
אָנָּא יהוה, הַצְלִיחָה נָּא.
אָנָּא יהוה, הַצְלִיחָה נָּא.

A ☐ **RADAK:** The Jewish nation, through its laws, forms the cornerstone and foundation of the world's existence, as it says, רֹעֶה אֶבֶן יִשְׂרָאֵל, *He shepherded the stone of Israel* (Genesis 49:24).

☐ **MAHARAL:** In the future, everyone will see that *the stone which the builders despised* — the persecuted Jewish nation — *has become the cornerstone* — the foundation of the world.

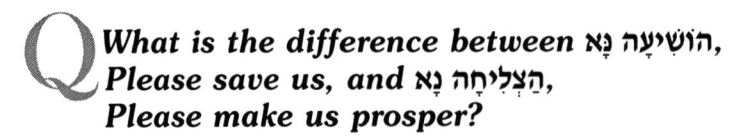

◈§ אָנָּא ה' / O HASHEM

Q *What is the difference between* הוֹשִׁיעָה נָּא, *Please save us, and* הַצְלִיחָה נָּא, *Please make us prosper?*

A ☐ **ABARBANEL:** *Please save us* refers to the redemption, which is dependent on the Jewish people's repentance. *Please make us prosper* is a request to Hashem to help us be successful in doing *teshuvah* so that we will merit our salvation.

☐ **ALSHICH:** We ask Hashem to hasten the redemption, and we do so with two requests: (1) *Please save us* — Hashem and became my salvation! I thank You for You answered me and became my salvation! The stone which the builders despised has become the cornerstone! The stone which the builders despised has become the cornerstone! This has emanated from HASHEM; it is wondrous in our eyes! This has emanated from HASHEM; it is wondrous in our eyes! This is the day HASHEM has made; we will rejoice and be glad in Him! This is the day HASHEM has made; we will rejoice and be glad in Him!

O HASHEM, please save us!
O HASHEM, please save us!
O HASHEM, please make us prosper!
O HASHEM, please make us prosper!

---

should rescue us from oppression and suffering, and (2) *Please make us prosper* — He should take us beneath His wings and shower us with His blessings.

☐ **MAGGID OF PLOTZK:** *Please save us* is a plea that we merit seeing the salvation of the Jewish nation. *Please make us prosper* is a plea that we succeed in rebuilding the Beis HaMikdash.

☐ **RAV SAMSON RAPHAEL HIRSCH:** *Please save us* expresses our desire for improvement — a personal rejuvenation. *Please make us prosper* is a blessing with no limit. David is asking Hashem for both.

A story is told of a man who came to the Chafetz Chaim to seek his blessing, as the fellow was planning to move to a different country.

The Chafetz Chaim said to him, "When we say Hallel on Sukkos, we shake the *lulav* as we say the words אָנָּא ה' הוֹשִׁיעָה נָּא, *O HASHEM, please save us!* This teaches uos that when a person finds himself in a situation where he has nothing, and all he can do is beg, 'Please save me!' he is obligated to pick himself up and go, even to wander the world.

"However, when a person is in a situation of הַצְלִיחָה נָא, *Please make us prosper!* — that is, when he already has something but wants more — then he must stay in place. He must stand in prayer in the place where he has already established himself."

---

[289] **HAGGADAH: THE ANSWER IS . . .**

בָּרוּךְ הַבָּא בְּשֵׁם יהוה, בֵּרַכְנוּכֶם מִבֵּית יהוה.
בָּרוּךְ הַבָּא בְּשֵׁם יהוה, בֵּרַכְנוּכֶם מִבֵּית
יהוה. אֵל יהוה וַיָּאֶר לָנוּ, אִסְרוּ חַג בַּעֲבֹתִים עַד
קַרְנוֹת הַמִּזְבֵּחַ. אֵל יהוה וַיָּאֶר לָנוּ, אִסְרוּ חַג
בַּעֲבֹתִים עַד קַרְנוֹת הַמִּזְבֵּחַ. אֵלִי אַתָּה וְאוֹדֶךָּ,
אֱלֹהַי אֲרוֹמְמֶךָּ. אֵלִי אַתָּה וְאוֹדֶךָּ, אֱלֹהַי אֲרוֹמְמֶךָּ.
הוֹדוּ לַיהוה כִּי טוֹב, כִּי לְעוֹלָם חַסְדּוֹ. הוֹדוּ לַיהוה
כִּי טוֹב, כִּי לְעוֹלָם חַסְדּוֹ.[1]

יְהַלְלוּךָ יהוה אֱלֹהֵינוּ כָּל מַעֲשֶׂיךָ, וַחֲסִידֶיךָ
צַדִּיקִים עוֹשֵׂי רְצוֹנֶךָ, וְכָל עַמְּךָ
בֵּית יִשְׂרָאֵל בְּרִנָּה יוֹדוּ וִיבָרְכוּ וִישַׁבְּחוּ וִיפָאֲרוּ
וִירוֹמְמוּ וְיַעֲרִיצוּ וְיַקְדִּישׁוּ וְיַמְלִיכוּ אֶת שִׁמְךָ
מַלְכֵּנוּ. כִּי לְךָ טוֹב לְהוֹדוֹת וּלְשִׁמְךָ נָאֶה לְזַמֵּר,
כִּי מֵעוֹלָם וְעַד עוֹלָם אַתָּה אֵל.

☐ **KOCHVEI OHR:** *Please save us* — in *ruchniyus*; *Please make us prosper* — in *gashmiyus*. When it comes to material things, it is possible to succeed even without a great deal of toil. In the spiritual realm, however, a person must work very hard before salvation comes.

☐ First Hashem brings salvation, which is why we begin by asking Him to save us. Afterward, we ask Hashem to let us succeed in seeing and recognizing the salvation — *Please make us prosper.*

∽§ יְהַלְלוּךָ / *They shall praise You*

Q: "The House of Israel with joy will thank, bless, praise..." There are eight terms of praise here. To what do they correspond?

A: ☐ **MICHTAV MEELIYAHU:** The eight terms of praise correspond to the order of ascension on the rungs of spirituality.

Blessed be he who comes in the Name of HASHEM; we bless you from the House of HASHEM. Blessed be he who comes in the Name of HASHEM; we bless you from the House of HASHEM. HASHEM is God and He illuminated for us; bind the festival offering with cords to the corners of the Altar. HASHEM is God and He illuminated for us; bind the festival offering with cords to the corners of the Altar. You are my God and I shall thank You; my God and I shall exalt You. You are my God, and I shall thank You; my God and I shall exalt You. Give thanks to HASHEM, for He is good; His kindness endures forever! Give thanks to HASHEM, for He is good; His kindness endures forever![1]

They shall praise You, HASHEM our God, for all Your works, along with Your pious followers, the righteous, who do Your will, and Your entire people, the House of Israel, with joy will thank, bless, praise, glorify, exalt, revere, sanctify, and coronate Your Name, our King! For to You it is fitting to give thanks, and unto Your Name it is proper to sing praises, for from eternity to eternity You are God.

---
1. Psalm 118.

נוֹדֶה, *thank* — We thank Hashem for His many kindnesses.

וִיבָרְכוּ, *bless* — "Blessing" is an expansion. We thank Hashem for the broadening of our accomplishments.

וִישַׁבְּחוּ, *praise* — We thank Him for increasing the quality of our accomplishments as well.

וִיפָאֲרוּ, *glorify* — We recognize the glory inherent in kedushah.

וִירוֹמְמוּ, *exalt* — We reach the level of yiras haromemus, awe at Hashem's greatness.

וְיַעֲרִיצוּ, *revere* — We achieve an exalted grasp and understanding.

וְיַקְדִּישׁוּ, *sanctify* — We gain a grasp and understanding that has no bounds.

[291] **HAGGADAH: THE ANSWER IS . . .**

הוֹדוּ לַיהוה כִּי טוֹב,	כִּי לְעוֹלָם חַסְדּוֹ.
הוֹדוּ לֵאלֹהֵי הָאֱלֹהִים,	כִּי לְעוֹלָם חַסְדּוֹ.
הוֹדוּ לַאֲדֹנֵי הָאֲדֹנִים,	כִּי לְעוֹלָם חַסְדּוֹ.
לְעֹשֵׂה נִפְלָאוֹת גְּדֹלוֹת לְבַדּוֹ,	כִּי לְעוֹלָם חַסְדּוֹ.
לְעֹשֵׂה הַשָּׁמַיִם בִּתְבוּנָה,	כִּי לְעוֹלָם חַסְדּוֹ.
לְרֹקַע הָאָרֶץ עַל הַמָּיִם,	כִּי לְעוֹלָם חַסְדּוֹ.
לְעֹשֵׂה אוֹרִים גְּדֹלִים,	כִּי לְעוֹלָם חַסְדּוֹ.
אֶת הַשֶּׁמֶשׁ לְמֶמְשֶׁלֶת בַּיּוֹם,	כִּי לְעוֹלָם חַסְדּוֹ.
אֶת הַיָּרֵחַ וְכוֹכָבִים לְמֶמְשְׁלוֹת בַּלָּיְלָה,	
	כִּי לְעוֹלָם חַסְדּוֹ.
לְמַכֵּה מִצְרַיִם בִּבְכוֹרֵיהֶם,	כִּי לְעוֹלָם חַסְדּוֹ.
וַיּוֹצֵא יִשְׂרָאֵל מִתּוֹכָם,	כִּי לְעוֹלָם חַסְדּוֹ.

וַיַּמְלִיכוּ, *coronate* — We attain the highest level: that of recognizing Hashem's kingship over us.

הוֹדוּ לַה׳ / Give thanks to Hashem

Q Why is this section called "Hallel HaGadol"?

A ☐ TALMUD (*Pesachim* 119a): It says in this passage, *He gives food to all living creatures.* This truly defines Hashem's greatness — that He deigns to provide sustenance to every lowly creature. Therefore this passage is called the "Great Hallel."

Q Why do we repeat כִּי לְעוֹלָם חַסְדּוֹ, *His kindness endures forever*, twenty-six times?

A ☐ TALMUD (*Pesachim* 118a): It corresponds to the twenty-six generations from Adam HaRishon to Moshe Rabbeinu, when we received the Torah.

Give thanks to HASHEM, for He is good;
　　　　　　　　　　　　　　His kindness endures forever!
Give thanks to the God of gods;
　　　　　　　　　　　　　　His kindness endures forever!
Give thanks to the Master of masters;
　　　　　　　　　　　　　　His kindness endures forever!
To Him Who alone does great wonders;
　　　　　　　　　　　　　　His kindness endures forever!
To Him Who makes the heaven with understanding;
　　　　　　　　　　　　　　His kindness endures forever!
To Him Who stretched out the earth over the waters;
　　　　　　　　　　　　　　His kindness endures forever!
To Him Who makes great luminaries;
　　　　　　　　　　　　　　His kindness endures forever!
The sun for the reign of the day;
　　　　　　　　　　　　　　His kindness endures forever!
The moon and the stars for the reign of the night;
　　　　　　　　　　　　　　His kindness endures forever!
To Him Who struck the Egyptians through
　　their firstborn;　　　His kindness endures forever!
And took Israel out from their midst;
　　　　　　　　　　　　　　His kindness endures forever!

☐ **AVUDRAHAM**: It corresponds to the Tetragrammaton, the Four-Letter Name of Hashem, whose numerical value is 26.

Q Why do we emphasize that He "alone" does great wonders?

A ☐ **RASHI**: *Wonders* refers to the creation of heaven and earth, sun and moon — all of which Hashem created when He was alone, since the angels had not yet been created.

☐ **METZUDAS DAVID**: Hashem does everything alone, not through a messenger or an angel.

☐ **MA'ASEI HASHEM**: This refers to the wonders that Hashem performs for human beings, of which they are unaware or ignorant. Hashem alone knows about them.

בְּיָד חֲזָקָה וּבִזְרוֹעַ נְטוּיָה,	כִּי לְעוֹלָם חַסְדּוֹ.
לְגֹזֵר יַם סוּף לִגְזָרִים,	כִּי לְעוֹלָם חַסְדּוֹ.
וְהֶעֱבִיר יִשְׂרָאֵל בְּתוֹכוֹ,	כִּי לְעוֹלָם חַסְדּוֹ.
וְנִעֵר פַּרְעֹה וְחֵילוֹ בְיַם סוּף,	כִּי לְעוֹלָם חַסְדּוֹ.
לְמוֹלִיךְ עַמּוֹ בַּמִּדְבָּר,	כִּי לְעוֹלָם חַסְדּוֹ.
לְמַכֵּה מְלָכִים גְּדֹלִים,	כִּי לְעוֹלָם חַסְדּוֹ.
וַיַּהֲרֹג מְלָכִים אַדִּירִים,	כִּי לְעוֹלָם חַסְדּוֹ.
לְסִיחוֹן מֶלֶךְ הָאֱמֹרִי,	כִּי לְעוֹלָם חַסְדּוֹ.
וּלְעוֹג מֶלֶךְ הַבָּשָׁן,	כִּי לְעוֹלָם חַסְדּוֹ.
וְנָתַן אַרְצָם לְנַחֲלָה,	כִּי לְעוֹלָם חַסְדּוֹ.
נַחֲלָה לְיִשְׂרָאֵל עַבְדּוֹ,	כִּי לְעוֹלָם חַסְדּוֹ.
שֶׁבְּשִׁפְלֵנוּ זָכַר לָנוּ,	כִּי לְעוֹלָם חַסְדּוֹ.
וַיִּפְרְקֵנוּ מִצָּרֵינוּ,	כִּי לְעוֹלָם חַסְדּוֹ.
נֹתֵן לֶחֶם לְכָל בָּשָׂר,	כִּי לְעוֹלָם חַסְדּוֹ.
הוֹדוּ לְאֵל הַשָּׁמָיִם,	כִּי לְעוֹלָם חַסְדּוֹ.[1]

נִשְׁמַת כָּל חַי תְּבָרֵךְ אֶת שִׁמְךָ יהוה אֱלֹהֵינוּ, וְרוּחַ כָּל בָּשָׂר תְּפָאֵר וּתְרוֹמֵם זִכְרְךָ מַלְכֵּנוּ תָּמִיד. מִן הָעוֹלָם וְעַד הָעוֹלָם אַתָּה אֵל,

---

ঔ נִשְׁמַת / The soul

Q Why the repetitive verbiage "O Rescuer and Redeemer... in every time of trouble and distress..."?

A ☐ **MALBIM:** The *tzarah*, trouble, is an external disturbance that impacts a person, like the angel that stood in a narrow space and did not allow Bilam to pass (*Numbers* 22:26). *Tzukah*,

With strong hand and outstretched arm;
>His kindness endures forever!
To Him Who divided the Sea of Reeds into parts;
>His kindness endures forever!
And caused Israel to pass through it;
>His kindness endures forever!
And threw Pharaoh and his army into the Sea of Reeds;
>His kindness endures forever!
To Him Who led His people through the Wilderness;
>His kindness endures forever!
To Him Who smote great kings;
>His kindness endures forever!
And slew mighty kings; His kindness endures forever!
Sichon, king of the Emorites;
>His kindness endures forever!
And Og, king of Bashan;
>His kindness endures forever!
And gave their land as an inheritance;
>His kindness endures forever!
An inheritance to Israel His servant;
>His kindness endures forever!
Who remembered us in our lowliness;
>His kindness endures forever!
And released us from our foes;
>His kindness endures forever!
He gives food to all living creatures;
>His kindness endures forever!
Give thanks to God of heaven;
>His kindness endures forever![1]

The soul of every living being shall bless Your Name, HASHEM our God; the spirit of all flesh shall always glorify and exalt Your remembrance, our King. From eternity to eternity You are God,

---
1. *Psalm* 136.

וּמִבַּלְעָדֶיךָ אֵין לָנוּ מֶלֶךְ גּוֹאֵל וּמוֹשִׁיעַ. פּוֹדֶה וּמַצִּיל וּמְפַרְנֵס וּמְרַחֵם, בְּכָל עֵת צָרָה וְצוּקָה, אֵין לָנוּ מֶלֶךְ אֶלָּא אָתָּה. אֱלֹהֵי הָרִאשׁוֹנִים וְהָאַחֲרוֹנִים, אֱלוֹהַּ כָּל בְּרִיּוֹת, אֲדוֹן כָּל תּוֹלָדוֹת, הַמְהֻלָּל בְּרֹב הַתִּשְׁבָּחוֹת, הַמְנַהֵג עוֹלָמוֹ בְּחֶסֶד וּבְרִיּוֹתָיו בְּרַחֲמִים. וַיהוה לֹא יָנוּם וְלֹא יִישָׁן. הַמְעוֹרֵר יְשֵׁנִים, וְהַמֵּקִיץ נִרְדָּמִים, וְהַמֵּשִׂיחַ אִלְּמִים, וְהַמַּתִּיר אֲסוּרִים, וְהַסּוֹמֵךְ נוֹפְלִים, וְהַזּוֹקֵף כְּפוּפִים. לְךָ לְבַדְּךָ אֲנַחְנוּ מוֹדִים. אִלּוּ פִינוּ מָלֵא שִׁירָה כַּיָּם, וּלְשׁוֹנֵנוּ רִנָּה כַּהֲמוֹן גַּלָּיו, וְשִׂפְתוֹתֵינוּ שֶׁבַח כְּמֶרְחֲבֵי רָקִיעַ, וְעֵינֵינוּ מְאִירוֹת כַּשֶּׁמֶשׁ וְכַיָּרֵחַ, וְיָדֵינוּ פְרוּשׂוֹת כְּנִשְׁרֵי שָׁמָיִם, וְרַגְלֵינוּ קַלּוֹת כָּאַיָּלוֹת, אֵין אֲנַחְנוּ מַסְפִּיקִים לְהוֹדוֹת לְךָ, יהוה אֱלֹהֵינוּ וֵאלֹהֵי אֲבוֹתֵינוּ, וּלְבָרֵךְ אֶת שְׁמֶךָ עַל אַחַת מֵאֶלֶף אֶלֶף אַלְפֵי אֲלָפִים וְרִבֵּי רְבָבוֹת פְּעָמִים הַטּוֹבוֹת שֶׁעָשִׂיתָ עִם אֲבוֹתֵינוּ וְעִמָּנוּ. מִמִּצְרַיִם גְּאַלְתָּנוּ יהוה אֱלֹהֵינוּ, וּמִבֵּית עֲבָדִים פְּדִיתָנוּ. בְּרָעָב זַנְתָּנוּ, וּבְשָׂבָע כִּלְכַּלְתָּנוּ, מֵחֶרֶב הִצַּלְתָּנוּ, וּמִדֶּבֶר מִלַּטְתָּנוּ, וּמֵחֳלָיִם רָעִים וְנֶאֱמָנִים דִּלִּיתָנוּ.

---

distress, is internal, a trouble that a person experiences within himself. Each of these things can exist on its own. A person may not be lacking anything, but because of an inner sadness he feels troubled. Similarly, a person may be poor or ill and yet he trusts in Hashem and remains strong of spirit. Though such a person may be beset by a *tzarah*, his inner spirit does not allow him to become downcast.

☐ **SIFSEI CHAIM:** The first, *Podeh*, Rescuer, refers to removing the negative. The second, *Matzil*, Redeemer, is the positive aspect. Before the Jewish people experienced the redemption, Hashem rescued them from Egypt. The salvation came and except for You we have no king, redeemer or helper. O Rescuer, and Redeemer, Sustainer, and Merciful One in every time of trouble and distress. We have no king but You — God of the first and of the last, God of all creatures, Master of all generations, Who is extolled through a multitude of praises, Who guides His world with kindness and His creatures with mercy. HASHEM neither slumbers nor sleeps; He rouses the sleepers and awakens the slumberers; He makes the mute speak and releases the bound; He supports the falling and raises erect the bowed down. To You alone we give thanks.

Were our mouth as full of song as the sea, and our tongue as full of jubilation as its multitude of waves, and our lips as full of praise as the breadth of the heavens, and our eyes as brilliant as the sun and the moon, and our hands as outspread in prayer as eagles of the sky and our feet as swift as deer — we still could not sufficiently thank You, HASHEM our God and God of our fathers, and bless Your Name for even one of the thousands upon thousands, and myriads upon myriads of favors, miracles, and wonders, that You performed for our ancestors and for us. You redeemed us from Egypt, HASHEM our God, and liberated us from the house of bondage. In famine You nourished us and in plenty You supported us. From the sword You saved us; from the plague You let us escape; and You spared us from severe and enduring diseases.

---

after the rescue — they left Egypt in two stages: first Hashem removed the trouble, and then He sent the salvation.

Q *Is there such a thing as a "good" disease?*

A ☐ RAV YITZCHAK BLAZER: Some illnesses are not life-threatening. While the patient suffers, he is not afraid. But there are dangerous diseases in which the fear outweighs the

עַד הֵנָּה עֲזָרוּנוּ רַחֲמֶיךָ, וְלֹא עֲזָבוּנוּ חֲסָדֶיךָ. וְאַל תִּטְּשֵׁנוּ יהוה אֱלֹהֵינוּ לָנֶצַח. עַל כֵּן אֵבָרִים שֶׁפִּלַּגְתָּ בָּנוּ, וְרוּחַ וּנְשָׁמָה שֶׁנָּפַחְתָּ בְּאַפֵּינוּ, וְלָשׁוֹן אֲשֶׁר שַׂמְתָּ בְּפִינוּ, הֵן הֵם יוֹדוּ וִיבָרְכוּ וִישַׁבְּחוּ וִיפָאֲרוּ וִירוֹמְמוּ וְיַעֲרִיצוּ וְיַקְדִּישׁוּ וְיַמְלִיכוּ אֶת שִׁמְךָ מַלְכֵּנוּ. כִּי כָל פֶּה לְךָ יוֹדֶה, וְכָל לָשׁוֹן לְךָ תִשָּׁבַע, וְכָל בֶּרֶךְ לְךָ תִכְרַע, וְכָל קוֹמָה לְפָנֶיךָ תִשְׁתַּחֲוֶה, וְכָל לְבָבוֹת יִירָאוּךָ, וְכָל קֶרֶב וּכְלָיוֹת יְזַמְּרוּ לִשְׁמֶךָ, כַּדָּבָר שֶׁכָּתוּב: כָּל עַצְמוֹתַי תֹּאמַרְנָה, יהוה מִי כָמוֹךָ, מַצִּיל עָנִי מֵחָזָק מִמֶּנּוּ, וְעָנִי וְאֶבְיוֹן מִגֹּזְלוֹ.[1] מִי יִדְמֶה לָּךְ, וּמִי יִשְׁוֶה לָּךְ, וּמִי יַעֲרָךְ לָךְ. הָאֵל הַגָּדוֹל הַגִּבּוֹר וְהַנּוֹרָא, אֵל עֶלְיוֹן, קֹנֵה שָׁמַיִם וָאָרֶץ. נְהַלֶּלְךָ וּנְשַׁבֵּחֲךָ וּנְפָאֶרְךָ וּנְבָרֵךְ אֶת שֵׁם קָדְשֶׁךָ, כָּאָמוּר: לְדָוִד, בָּרְכִי נַפְשִׁי אֶת יהוה, וְכָל קְרָבַי אֶת שֵׁם קָדְשׁוֹ.[2]

הָאֵל בְּתַעֲצֻמוֹת עֻזֶּךָ, הַגָּדוֹל בִּכְבוֹד שְׁמֶךָ, הַגִּבּוֹר לָנֶצַח וְהַנּוֹרָא בְּנוֹרְאוֹתֶיךָ. הַמֶּלֶךְ הַיּוֹשֵׁב עַל כִּסֵּא רָם וְנִשָּׂא.

שׁוֹכֵן עַד מָרוֹם וְקָדוֹשׁ שְׁמוֹ. וְכָתוּב: רַנְּנוּ צַדִּיקִים בַּיהוה לַיְשָׁרִים נָאוָה תְהִלָּה.[3] בְּפִי יְשָׁרִים תִּתְהַלָּל. וּבְדִבְרֵי צַדִּיקִים תִּתְבָּרַךְ. וּבִלְשׁוֹן חֲסִידִים תִּתְרוֹמָם. וּבְקֶרֶב קְדוֹשִׁים תִּתְקַדָּשׁ.

---

pain. This is what is meant by a "bad disease" — a disease that inspires fear and terror.

Until now Your mercy has helped us and Your kindness has not forsaken us; do not abandon us, HASHEM our God, to the ultimate end.

Therefore, the limbs which You have set within us, and the spirit and soul which You breathed into our nostrils, and the tongue which You have placed in our mouth — they shall thank and bless, praise and glorify, exalt, be devoted to, sanctify, and do homage to Your Name, our King forever. For every mouth shall offer thanks to You; every tongue shall vow allegiance to You; every knee shall bend to You; all who stand erect shall bow before You; all hearts shall fear You; and all men's innermost feelings and thoughts shall sing praises to Your Name, as it is written: "All my bones declare: 'HASHEM, who is like You?' You save the poor man from one stronger than him, the poor and needy from one who would rob him."[1] Who may be likened to You? Who is equal to You? Who can be compared to You? O great, mighty, and awesome God, supreme God, Maker of heaven and earth. We shall praise, acclaim, and glorify You and bless Your holy Name, as it is said:"A psalm of David: Bless HASHEM, O my soul, and let my whole inner being bless His holy Name!"[2]

O God, in the omnipotence of Your strength, great in the honor of Your Name, powerful forever and awesome through Your awesome deeds, O King enthroned upon a high and lofty throne!

He Who abides forever, exalted and holy is His Name. And it is written: "Rejoice in HASHEM, you righteous; for the upright, His praise is pleasant."[3] By the mouth of the upright You shall be praised; by the words of the righteous You shall be praised; by the tongue of the pious You shall be exalted; and amid the holy You shall be sanctified.

---

1. Psalms 35:10. 2. Ibid. 103:1. 3. Ibid. 33:1.

[299] **HAGGADAH: THE ANSWER IS . . .**

וּבְמַקְהֵלוֹת רִבְבוֹת עַמְּךָ בֵּית יִשְׂרָאֵל, בְּרִנָּה יִתְפָּאֵר שִׁמְךָ מַלְכֵּנוּ בְּכָל דּוֹר וָדוֹר. שֶׁכֵּן חוֹבַת כָּל הַיְצוּרִים, לְפָנֶיךָ יהוה אֱלֹהֵינוּ וֵאלֹהֵי אֲבוֹתֵינוּ, לְהוֹדוֹת לְהַלֵּל לְשַׁבֵּחַ לְפָאֵר לְרוֹמֵם לְהַדֵּר לְבָרֵךְ לְעַלֵּה וּלְקַלֵּס, עַל כָּל דִּבְרֵי שִׁירוֹת וְתִשְׁבְּחוֹת דָּוִד בֶּן יִשַׁי עַבְדְּךָ מְשִׁיחֶךָ.

יִשְׁתַּבַּח שִׁמְךָ לָעַד, מַלְכֵּנוּ, הָאֵל הַמֶּלֶךְ הַגָּדוֹל וְהַקָּדוֹשׁ, בַּשָּׁמַיִם וּבָאָרֶץ. כִּי לְךָ נָאֶה, יהוה אֱלֹהֵינוּ וֵאלֹהֵי אֲבוֹתֵינוּ, שִׁיר וּשְׁבָחָה, הַלֵּל וְזִמְרָה, עֹז וּמֶמְשָׁלָה, נֶצַח גְּדֻלָּה וּגְבוּרָה, תְּהִלָּה וְתִפְאֶרֶת, קְדֻשָּׁה וּמַלְכוּת, בְּרָכוֹת וְהוֹדָאוֹת מֵעַתָּה וְעַד עוֹלָם. בָּרוּךְ אַתָּה יהוה, אֵל מֶלֶךְ גָּדוֹל בַּתִּשְׁבָּחוֹת, אֵל הַהוֹדָאוֹת, אֲדוֹן הַנִּפְלָאוֹת, הַבּוֹחֵר בְּשִׁירֵי זִמְרָה, מֶלֶךְ אֵל חֵי הָעוֹלָמִים.

The blessing over wine is recited and the fourth cup is drunk while reclining to the left side. It is preferable that the entire cup be drunk.
Some recite the following before the fourth cup:

הִנְנִי מוּכָן וּמְזֻמָּן לְקַיֵּם מִצְוַת כּוֹס רְבִיעִי שֶׁל אַרְבַּע כּוֹסוֹת. לְשֵׁם יִחוּד קֻדְשָׁא בְּרִיךְ הוּא וּשְׁכִינְתֵּיהּ, עַל יְדֵי הַהוּא טָמִיר וְנֶעְלָם, בְּשֵׁם כָּל יִשְׂרָאֵל. וִיהִי נֹעַם אֲדֹנָי אֱלֹהֵינוּ עָלֵינוּ, וּמַעֲשֵׂה יָדֵינוּ כּוֹנְנָה עָלֵינוּ, וּמַעֲשֵׂה יָדֵינוּ כּוֹנְנֵהוּ.

בָּרוּךְ אַתָּה יהוה אֱלֹהֵינוּ מֶלֶךְ הָעוֹלָם, בּוֹרֵא פְּרִי הַגָּפֶן.

After drinking the fourth cup, the concluding blessing is recited.
On the Sabbath include the passage in parentheses.

בָּרוּךְ אַתָּה יהוה אֱלֹהֵינוּ מֶלֶךְ הָעוֹלָם, עַל הַגֶּפֶן וְעַל פְּרִי הַגֶּפֶן, וְעַל תְּנוּבַת הַשָּׂדֶה,

A nd in the assemblies of the myriads of Your people, the House of Israel, with jubilation shall Your Name, our King, be glorified in every generation. For such is the duty of all creatures — before You, HASHEM, our God, and God of our fathers, to thank, praise, laud, glorify, exalt, adore, bless, raise high, and sing praises — even beyond all expressions of the songs and praises of David the son of Jesse, Your servant, Your anointed.

M ay Your Name be praised forever, our King, the God, and King Who is great and holy in heaven and on earth; for to You, HASHEM, our God, and the God of our fathers, it is fitting to render song and praise, hallel and hymns, power and dominion, victory, greatness and might, praise and glory, holiness and sovereignty, blessings and thanksgivings from now and forever. Blessed are You, HASHEM, God, King, great in praises, God of thanksgivings, Master of wonders, Who favors songs of praise — King, God, Life of all worlds.

The blessing over wine is recited and the fourth cup is drunk while reclining to the left side. It is preferable that the entire cup be drunk.

Some recite the following before the fourth cup:

B ehold, I am prepared and ready to fulfill the mitzvah of the fourth of the Four Cups. For the sake of the unification of the Holy One, Blessed is He, and His Presence, through Him Who is hidden and inscrutable — [I pray] in the name of all Israel. May the pleasantness of the Lord, our God, be upon us, and may He establish our handiwork for us; our handiwork may He establish.

B lessed are You, HASHEM, our God, King of the universe, Who creates the fruit of the vine.

After drinking the fourth cup, the concluding blessing is recited. On the Sabbath include the passage in parentheses.

B lessed are You, HASHEM, our God, King of the universe, for the vine and the fruit of the vine, and for the produce of the field. For the

וְעַל אֶרֶץ חֶמְדָּה טוֹבָה וּרְחָבָה, שֶׁרָצִיתָ וְהִנְחַלְתָּ לַאֲבוֹתֵינוּ, לֶאֱכוֹל מִפִּרְיָהּ וְלִשְׂבּוֹעַ מִטּוּבָהּ. רַחֵם (נָא) יהוה אֱלֹהֵינוּ עַל יִשְׂרָאֵל עַמֶּךָ, וְעַל יְרוּשָׁלַיִם עִירֶךָ, וְעַל צִיּוֹן מִשְׁכַּן כְּבוֹדֶךָ, וְעַל מִזְבְּחֶךָ וְעַל הֵיכָלֶךָ. וּבְנֵה יְרוּשָׁלַיִם עִיר הַקֹּדֶשׁ בִּמְהֵרָה בְיָמֵינוּ, וְהַעֲלֵנוּ לְתוֹכָהּ, וְשַׂמְּחֵנוּ בְּבִנְיָנָהּ, וְנֹאכַל מִפִּרְיָהּ, וְנִשְׂבַּע מִטּוּבָהּ, וּנְבָרֶכְךָ עָלֶיהָ בִּקְדֻשָּׁה וּבְטָהֳרָה [וּרְצֵה וְהַחֲלִיצֵנוּ בְּיוֹם הַשַּׁבָּת הַזֶּה]. וְשַׂמְּחֵנוּ בְּיוֹם חַג הַמַּצּוֹת הַזֶּה. כִּי אַתָּה יהוה טוֹב וּמֵטִיב לַכֹּל, וְנוֹדֶה לְךָ עַל הָאָרֶץ וְעַל פְּרִי הַגָּפֶן. בָּרוּךְ אַתָּה יהוה, עַל הָאָרֶץ וְעַל פְּרִי הַגָּפֶן.

עַל הַגֶּפֶן / The after-blessing over wine

Q Why do we ask to benefit from the material goodness of the land, but do not ask for the privilege of observing the mitzvos that are connected to the land, which are seemingly paramount?

A
- ☐ **SMAG:** Indeed, for this reason there are those who omit these words.

- ☐ **BACH:** The request to eat of the fruits of Eretz Yisrael is not a material plea, but a spiritual one. As we eat, we absorb the holiness in the fruits, which emanates from the spirituality of Eretz Yisrael.

- ☐ **BRISKER RAV:** The "fruits" mentioned here are the fruits of Yerushalayim and are, indeed, related to the mitzvos of the land. This after-blessing is an abridged version of Birkas HaMazon, making these words parallel to the blessing of *Bonei Yerushalayim* (as this sentence begins, וּבְנֵה יְרוּשָׁלַיִם עִיר הַקֹּדֶשׁ, *Rebuild Jerusalem, the city of holiness*). We ask Hashem to speedily build the Beis HaMikdash, when we will ascend and eat the fruits of *ma'aser sheini* (the desirable, good, and spacious land that You were pleased to give our forefathers as a heritage, to eat of its fruit and to be satisfied with its goodness. Have mercy, we beg You, HASHEM, our God, on Israel Your people; on Jerusalem, Your city; on Zion, resting place of Your glory; Your Altar, and Your Temple. Rebuild Jerusalem the city of holiness, speedily in our days. Bring us up into it and gladden us in its rebuilding, and let us eat from its fruit and be satisfied with its goodness and bless You upon it in holiness and purity. (Favor us and strengthen us on this Sabbath day) and grant us happiness on this Festival of Matzos; for You, HASHEM, are good and do good to all, and we thank You for the land and for the fruit of the vine. Blessed are You, HASHEM, for the land and for the fruit of the vine.

---

second tithe) and *neta riva'i* (fruit produced by a tree in its fourth year after planting), which are eaten only in Yerushalayim.

Q *"Let us eat from its fruit... and bless You upon it in holiness and purity."* What is the meaning of the request to eat of the fruit of the land... in holiness and purity?

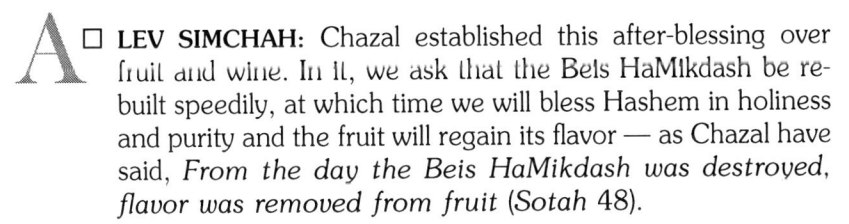

A
- ☐ **LEV SIMCHAH:** Chazal established this after-blessing over fruit and wine. In it, we ask that the Beis HaMikdash be rebuilt speedily, at which time we will bless Hashem in holiness and purity and the fruit will regain its flavor — as Chazal have said, *From the day the Beis HaMikdash was destroyed, flavor was removed from fruit* (Sotah 48).

- ☐ **SIMCHAS YAAVETZ:** The sin of Adam HaRishon brought death and impurity into the world. We are asking that this sin be rectified so that we will be able to eat in holiness and purity once again.

נרצה

חֲסַל סִדּוּר פֶּסַח כְּהִלְכָתוֹ, כְּכָל מִשְׁפָּטוֹ וְחֻקָּתוֹ. כַּאֲשֶׁר זָכִינוּ לְסַדֵּר אוֹתוֹ, כֵּן נִזְכֶּה לַעֲשׂוֹתוֹ. זָךְ שׁוֹכֵן מְעוֹנָה, קוֹמֵם קְהַל עֲדַת מִי מָנָה. בְּקָרוֹב נַהֵל נִטְעֵי כַנָּה, פְּדוּיִם לְצִיּוֹן בְּרִנָּה.

לְשָׁנָה הַבָּאָה בִּירוּשָׁלָיִם.

✢ נרצה / Nirtzah

Q *What does the word "nirtzah" mean?*

A ☐ **SHELAH:** A person who has conducted the Seder properly is *merutzeh* — pleasing — to Heaven.

☐ The *Afikoman* is eaten in commemoration of the *korban Pesach*. As with any offering, we hope that it will be *ratzui*, acceptable, as it says, וְנִרְצָה לוֹ לְכַפֵּר עָלָיו, *And it shall become acceptable for him, to atone for him* (Leviticus 1:4).

☐ There are opinions that say that *Nirtzah* is not an independent part of the Seder, but rather the second part of Hallel, in which we ask Hashem to find us pleasing to Him (*retzuyim*) and to redeem us.

Q *Why does Nirtzah come after Hallel?*

A ☐ **AVNEI NEZER:** This can be likened to a father who is angry at his son and refuses to reconciliate. The son tries in every way he can to assuage his father's anger, including showering his father with praise everywhere he goes. Eventually he learns that his praise has reconciled his father to him.

We too praise our King and never cease extolling Him until He is reconciled to us. Therefore, even after we have finished reciting Hallel, we add this section of *Nirtzah* and shower Hashem with our praises.

NIRTZAH

The Seder is now concluded in accordance with its laws, with all its ordinances and statutes. Just as we were privileged to arrange it, so may we merit to perform it. O Pure One, Who dwells on high, raise up the countless congregation, soon — guide the offshoots of Your plants, redeemed to Zion with glad song.

NEXT YEAR IN JERUSALEM

◈§ חֲסַל סִדּוּר פֶּסַח / *The Seder is now concluded*

This paragraph was written by Rav Yosef Tur-Elam, who lived in Tzefas about a thousand years ago.

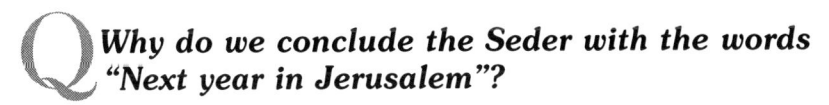

Q *Why do we conclude the Seder with the words "Next year in Jerusalem"?*

A ☐ **YISMACH MOSHE:** We say these words twice each year: at the end of Yom Kippur and at the conclusion of the Seder. The common denominator between the two is that some say that the redemption will take place in the month of Nissan and some, in the month of Tishrei. They are both accurate: the redemption of the Jewish people will take place in Nissan, while the rest of the world will be redeemed in Tishrei. It is at these times that we say, *Next year in Jerusalem*, in anticipation and longing for the redemption. On Seder night, we ask that next year we find ourselves in Yerushalayim, and that our redemption will bring in its wake the redemption of Tishrei for the entire world.

☐ **DIVREI YOEL:** The *Yerushalmi* (*Rosh Hashanah* 1:1) states that at first the Jewish people began counting the years and months from their Exodus from Egypt. Later, they dated things from important events, such as the building of the Beis HaMikdash. We pray that Mashiach will come soon, and the Jewish people will begin a brand-new count — from the final redemption.

On the first night recite the following.
On the second night continue on page 308.

וּבְכֵן וַיְהִי בַּחֲצִי הַלַּיְלָה.

אָז רוֹב נִסִּים הִפְלֵאתָ בַּלַּיְלָה,
בְּרֹאשׁ אַשְׁמוֹרֶת זֶה הַלַּיְלָה,
גֵּר צֶדֶק נִצַּחְתּוֹ כְּנֶחֱלַק לוֹ לַיְלָה,
וַיְהִי בַּחֲצִי הַלַּיְלָה.

דַּנְתָּ מֶלֶךְ גְּרָר בַּחֲלוֹם הַלַּיְלָה,
הִפְחַדְתָּ אֲרַמִּי בְּאֶמֶשׁ לַיְלָה,
וַיָּשַׂר יִשְׂרָאֵל לְמַלְאָךְ וַיּוּכַל לוֹ לַיְלָה,
וַיְהִי בַּחֲצִי הַלַּיְלָה.

זֶרַע בְּכוֹרֵי פַתְרוֹס מָחַצְתָּ בַּחֲצִי הַלַּיְלָה,
חֵילָם לֹא מָצְאוּ בְּקוּמָם בַּלַּיְלָה,
טִיסַת נְגִיד חֲרֹשֶׁת סִלִּיתָ בְּכוֹכְבֵי לַיְלָה,
וַיְהִי בַּחֲצִי הַלַּיְלָה.

יָעַץ מְחָרֵף לְנוֹפֵף אִוּוּי הוֹבַשְׁתָּ פְגָרָיו בַּלַּיְלָה,
כָּרַע בֵּל וּמַצָּבוֹ בְּאִישׁוֹן לַיְלָה,
לְאִישׁ חֲמוּדוֹת נִגְלָה רָז חֲזוֹת לַיְלָה,
וַיְהִי בַּחֲצִי הַלַּיְלָה.

מִשְׁתַּכֵּר בִּכְלֵי קֹדֶשׁ נֶהֱרַג בּוֹ בַּלַּיְלָה,
נוֹשַׁע מִבּוֹר אֲרָיוֹת פּוֹתֵר בִּעֲתוּתֵי לַיְלָה,
שִׂנְאָה נָטַר אֲגָגִי וְכָתַב סְפָרִים בַּלַּיְלָה,
וַיְהִי בַּחֲצִי הַלַּיְלָה.

☐ These words are said twice a year, at the end of Yom Kippur and at the conclusion of the Seder. These are the two happiest times of the year. On the Seder night we celebrate our Exodus from the oppression of Egypt, and at the conclusion

On the first night recite the following.
On the second night continue on page 308.

It came to pass at midnight.

You have, of old, performed many wonders
    by night.
At the head of the watches of   this night.
To the righteous convert (Avraham)
    You gave triumph by dividing for him   the night.
        It came to pass at midnight.
You judged the king of Gerar (Avimelech),
    in a dream   by night.
You frightened the Aramean (Lavan),
    in the dark   of night.
Israel (Yaakov) fought with an angel
    and overcame him   by night.
        It came to pass at midnight.
Egypt's firstborn You crushed at   midnight.
Their host they found not upon arising at   night.
The army of the prince of Charoshes (Sisera)
    You swept away with stars of   the night.
        It came to pass at midnight.
The blasphemer (Sancheriv) planned to raise
    his hand against Jerusalem —
    but You withered his corpses   by night.
Bel was overturned with its pedestal,
    in the darkness   of night.
To the man of Your delights (Daniel)
    was revealed the mystery of the visions   of night.
        It came to pass at midnight.
He (Belshazzar) who caroused from the holy vessels
    was killed that very   night.
From the lions' den was rescued he (Daniel)
    who interpreted the "terrors" of   the night.
The Agagite (Haman) nursed hatred
    and wrote decrees   at night.
        It came to pass at midnight.

לַיְלָה,	עוֹרַרְתָּ נִצְחֲךָ עָלָיו בְּנֶדֶד שְׁנַת	
מִלַּיְלָה,	פּוּרָה תִדְרוֹךְ לְשׁוֹמֵר מַה	
לַיְלָה,	צָרַח כַּשּׁוֹמֵר וְשָׂח אָתָא בְקֶר וְגַם	
	וַיְהִי בַּחֲצִי הַלָּיְלָה.	
לַיְלָה,	קָרֵב יוֹם אֲשֶׁר הוּא לֹא יוֹם וְלֹא	
הַלַּיְלָה,	רָם הוֹדַע כִּי לְךָ הַיּוֹם אַף לְךָ	
הַלַּיְלָה,	שׁוֹמְרִים הַפְקֵד לְעִירְךָ כָּל הַיּוֹם וְכָל	
לַיְלָה,	תָּאִיר כְּאוֹר יוֹם חֶשְׁכַּת	
	וַיְהִי בַּחֲצִי הַלָּיְלָה.	

On the second night recite the following.
On the first night continue on page 312.

וּבְכֵן וַאֲמַרְתֶּם זֶבַח פֶּסַח:

בַּפֶּסַח.	אֹמֶץ גְּבוּרוֹתֶיךָ הִפְלֵאתָ	
פֶּסַח.	בְּרֹאשׁ כָּל מוֹעֲדוֹת נִשֵּׂאתָ	
פֶּסַח.	גִּלִּיתָ לְאֶזְרָחִי חֲצוֹת לֵיל	
	וַאֲמַרְתֶּם זֶבַח פֶּסַח.	
בַּפֶּסַח.	דְּלָתָיו דָּפַקְתָּ כְּחֹם הַיּוֹם	
בַּפֶּסַח.	הִסְעִיד נוֹצְצִים עֻגוֹת מַצּוֹת	
פֶּסַח.	וְאֶל הַבָּקָר רָץ זֵכֶר לְשׁוֹר עֵרֶךְ	
	וַאֲמַרְתֶּם זֶבַח פֶּסַח.	
בַּפֶּסַח.	זוֹעֲמוּ סְדוֹמִים וְלֹהֲטוּ בָּאֵשׁ	
פֶּסַח.	חֻלַּץ לוֹט מֵהֶם וּמַצּוֹת אָפָה בְּקֵץ	

---

of Yom Kippur we rejoice over our purification from our sins. On both of these occasions we yearn for the service in the Beis HaMikdash again. This year, sadly, we have not yet merited that. It is our hope that, with Hashem's help, we will merit it next year.

You began Your triumph over him
   when You disturbed (Ahasuerus') sleep   at night.
Trample the winepress to help those who ask the
   watchman, "What of the   long night?"
He will shout, like a watchman, and say:
   "Morning shall come   after night."
      It came to pass at midnight.

Hasten the day (of Messiah),
that is neither day   nor night.
Most High — make known that Yours
are day   and night.
Appoint guards for Your city,
all the day and all   the night.
Brighten like the light of day the darkness of night.
      It came to pass at midnight.

<small>On the second night recite the following.
On the first night continue on page 312.</small>

And you shall say: This is the feast of Pesach.

Y ou displayed wondrously Your mighty powers
                                      on Pesach.
Above all festivals You elevated   Pesach.
To the Oriental (Avraham) You revealed
   the future midnight   of Pesach.
   And you shall say: This is the feast of Pesach.

At his door You knocked in the heat of the day
                                      on Pesach;
He satiated the angels with matzah-cakes on Pesach.
And he ran to the herd —
   symbolic of the sacrificial feast   of Pesach.
   And you shall say: This is the feast of Pesach.

The Sodomites provoked (God)
   and were devoured by fire   on Pesach;
Lot was withdrawn from them —
   he had baked matzos at the time   of Pesach.

[309] **HAGGADAH: THE ANSWER IS . . .**

טאטֵאתָ אַדְמַת מוֹף וְנוֹף בְּעָבְרְךָ	בַּפֶּסַח.
וַאֲמַרְתֶּם זֶבַח פֶּסַח.	
יָהּ רֹאשׁ כָּל אוֹן מָחַצְתָּ בְּלֵיל שִׁמּוּר	פֶּסַח.
כַּבִּיר עַל בֵּן בְּכוֹר פָּסַחְתָּ בְּדַם	פֶּסַח.
לְבִלְתִּי תֵּת מַשְׁחִית לָבֹא בִּפְתָחַי	בַּפֶּסַח.
וַאֲמַרְתֶּם זֶבַח פֶּסַח.	
מְסֻגֶּרֶת סֻגְּרָה בְּעִתּוֹתֵי	פֶּסַח.
נִשְׁמְדָה מִדְיָן בִּצְלִיל שְׂעוֹרֵי עֹמֶר	פֶּסַח.
שֹׂרְפוּ מִשְׁמַנֵּי פּוּל וְלוּד בִּיקַד יְקוֹד	פֶּסַח.
וַאֲמַרְתֶּם זֶבַח פֶּסַח.	
עוֹד הַיּוֹם בְּנֹב לַעֲמוֹד עַד גָּעָה עוֹנַת	פֶּסַח.
פַּס יָד כָּתְבָה לְקַעֲקֵעַ צוּל	בַּפֶּסַח.
צָפֹה הַצָּפִית עָרוֹךְ הַשֻּׁלְחָן	בַּפֶּסַח.
וַאֲמַרְתֶּם זֶבַח פֶּסַח.	
קָהָל כִּנְּסָה הֲדַסָּה צוֹם לְשַׁלֵּשׁ	בַּפֶּסַח.
רֹאשׁ מִבֵּית רָשָׁע מָחַצְתָּ בְּעֵץ חֲמִשִּׁים	בַּפֶּסַח.
שְׁתֵּי אֵלֶּה רֶגַע תָּבִיא לְעוּצִית	בַּפֶּסַח.
תָּעֹז יָדְךָ וְתָרוּם יְמִינְךָ כְּלֵיל הִתְקַדֶּשׁ חַג פֶּסַח.	
וַאֲמַרְתֶּם זֶבַח פֶּסַח.	

☐ These words are said twice a year — at the end of Yom Kippur, and at the end of the Seder. This teaches us that going up to Yerushalayim is for every Jew, whether he comes there in the wake of hardship and suffering in exile (like the suffering of Yom Kippur) or in the aftermath of redemption and its attendant joy (i.e., Seder night).

You swept clean the soil of Mof and Nof (in Egypt)
    when You passed through	on Pesach.
    And you shall say: This is the feast of Pesach.

God, You crushed every firstborn of On (in Egypt)
    on the watchful night	of Pesach.
But Master — Your own firstborn,
    You skipped by merit of the blood	of Pesach,
Not to allow the Destroyer to enter my doors
        on Pesach.
    And you shall say: This is the feast	of Pesach.

The beleaguered (Yericho) was besieged	on Pesach.
Midyan was destroyed with a barley cake,
    from the Omer	of Pesach.
The mighty nobles of Pul and Lud (Ashur) were
    consumed in a great conflagration	on Pesach.
    And you shall say: This is the feast of Pesach.
He (Sancheiriv) would have stood that day at Nov,
    but for the advent	of Pesach.
A hand inscribed the destruction of Zul (Bavel)
        on Pesach.
As the watch was set, and the royal table decked
        on Pesach.
    And you shall say: This is the feast of Pesach.

Hadassah (Esther) gathered a congregation
    for a three-day fast	on Pesach.
You caused the head of the evil clan (Haman)
    to be hanged on a fifty-cubit gallows	on Pesach.
Doubly, will You bring in an instant
    upon Utzis (Edom)	on Pesach.
Let Your hand be strong, and Your right arm exalted,
    as on that night when You hallowed the festival
        of Pesach.
    And you shall say: This is the feast of Pesach.

On both nights continue here:

כִּי לוֹ נָאֶה, כִּי לוֹ יָאֶה:

אַדִּיר בִּמְלוּכָה, בָּחוּר כַּהֲלָכָה, גְּדוּדָיו יֹאמְרוּ לוֹ, לְךָ וּלְךָ, לְךָ כִּי לְךָ, לְךָ אַף לְךָ, לְךָ יהוה הַמַּמְלָכָה, כִּי לוֹ נָאֶה, כִּי לוֹ יָאֶה.

דָּגוּל בִּמְלוּכָה, הָדוּר כַּהֲלָכָה, וָתִיקָיו יֹאמְרוּ לוֹ, לְךָ וּלְךָ, לְךָ כִּי לְךָ, לְךָ אַף לְךָ, לְךָ יהוה הַמַּמְלָכָה, כִּי לוֹ נָאֶה, כִּי לוֹ יָאֶה.

זַכַּאי בִּמְלוּכָה, חָסִין כַּהֲלָכָה, טַפְסְרָיו יֹאמְרוּ לוֹ, לְךָ וּלְךָ, לְךָ כִּי לְךָ, לְךָ אַף לְךָ, לְךָ יהוה הַמַּמְלָכָה, כִּי לוֹ נָאֶה, כִּי לוֹ יָאֶה.

יָחִיד בִּמְלוּכָה, כַּבִּיר כַּהֲלָכָה, לִמּוּדָיו יֹאמְרוּ לוֹ, לְךָ וּלְךָ, לְךָ כִּי לְךָ, לְךָ אַף לְךָ, לְךָ יהוה הַמַּמְלָכָה, כִּי לוֹ נָאֶה, כִּי לוֹ יָאֶה.

מוֹשֵׁל בִּמְלוּכָה, נוֹרָא כַּהֲלָכָה, סְבִיבָיו יֹאמְרוּ לוֹ, לְךָ וּלְךָ, לְךָ כִּי לְךָ, לְךָ אַף לְךָ, לְךָ יהוה הַמַּמְלָכָה, כִּי לוֹ נָאֶה, כִּי לוֹ יָאֶה.

עָנָיו בִּמְלוּכָה, פּוֹדֶה כַּהֲלָכָה, צַדִּיקָיו יֹאמְרוּ לוֹ, לְךָ וּלְךָ, לְךָ כִּי לְךָ, לְךָ אַף לְךָ, לְךָ יהוה הַמַּמְלָכָה, כִּי לוֹ נָאֶה, כִּי לוֹ יָאֶה.

קָדוֹשׁ בִּמְלוּכָה, רַחוּם כַּהֲלָכָה, שִׁנְאַנָּיו יֹאמְרוּ

כִּי לוֹ נָאֶה / **To Him praise is due**

Q Hashem is described here as הָדוּר, which signifies something venerable, and also as בָּחוּר, which signifies youth. Is this not a contradiction?

A □ **MA'ASEH NISSIM:** HaKadosh Baruch Hu appears in various forms, according to what is appropriate for that particular event. At the splitting of the sea, for example, Hashem

On both nights continue here:
To Him praise is due!
To Him praise is fitting!

Mighty in majesty, perfectly distinguished, His companies of angels say to Him: Yours and only Yours; Yours, yes Yours; Yours, surely Yours; Yours, HASHEM, is the sovereignty. To Him praise is due! To Him praise is fitting!

Supreme in kingship, perfectly glorious, His faithful say to Him: Yours and only Yours; Yours, yes Yours; Yours, surely Yours; Yours, HASHEM, is the sovereignty. To Him praise is due! To Him praise is fitting!

Pure in kingship, perfectly mighty, His angels say to Him: Yours and only Yours; Yours, yes Yours; Yours, surely Yours; Yours, HASHEM, is the sovereignty. To Him praise is due! To Him praise is fitting!

Alone in kingship, perfectly omnipotent, His scholars say to Him: Yours and only Yours; Yours, yes Yours; Yours, surely Yours; Yours, HASHEM, is the sovereignty. To Him praise is due! To Him praise is fitting!

Commanding in kingship, perfectly wondrous, His surrounding (angels) say to Him: Yours and only Yours; Yours, yes Yours; Yours, surely Yours; Yours, HASHEM, is the sovereignty. To Him praise is due! To Him praise is fitting!

Gentle in kingship, perfectly the Redeemer, His righteous say to Him: Yours and only Yours; Yours, yes Yours; Yours, surely Yours; Yours, HASHEM, is the sovereignty. To Him praise is due! To Him praise is fitting!

Holy in kingship, perfectly merciful, His troops of angels say to Him: Yours and only Yours; Yours, yes

---

appeared as a young warrior, because there was a need to show His might and alter the laws of nature. At Mount Sinai, when He gave the Torah, however, Hashem appeared as a sage accompanied by the heavenly host.

לוֹ, לְךָ וּלְךָ, לְךָ כִּי לְךָ, לְךָ אַף לְךָ, לְךָ יהוה הַמַּמְלָכָה, כִּי לוֹ נָאֶה, כִּי לוֹ יָאֶה.

תַּקִּיף בִּמְלוּכָה, תּוֹמֵךְ כַּהֲלָכָה, תְּמִימָיו יֹאמְרוּ לוֹ, לְךָ וּלְךָ, לְךָ כִּי לְךָ, לְךָ אַף לְךָ, לְךָ יהוה הַמַּמְלָכָה, כִּי לוֹ נָאֶה, כִּי לוֹ יָאֶה.

אַדִּיר הוּא יִבְנֶה בֵיתוֹ בְּקָרוֹב, בִּמְהֵרָה, בִּמְהֵרָה, בְּיָמֵינוּ בְּקָרוֹב. אֵל בְּנֵה, אֵל בְּנֵה, בְּנֵה בֵיתְךָ בְּקָרוֹב.

בָּחוּר הוּא. גָּדוֹל הוּא. דָּגוּל הוּא. יִבְנֶה בֵיתוֹ בְּקָרוֹב, בִּמְהֵרָה, בִּמְהֵרָה, בְּיָמֵינוּ בְּקָרוֹב. אֵל בְּנֵה, אֵל בְּנֵה, בְּנֵה בֵיתְךָ בְּקָרוֹב.

הָדוּר הוּא. וָתִיק הוּא. זַכַּאי הוּא. חָסִיד הוּא. יִבְנֶה בֵיתוֹ בְּקָרוֹב, בִּמְהֵרָה, בִּמְהֵרָה, בְּיָמֵינוּ בְּקָרוֹב. אֵל בְּנֵה, אֵל בְּנֵה, בְּנֵה בֵיתְךָ בְּקָרוֹב.

טָהוֹר הוּא. יָחִיד הוּא. כַּבִּיר הוּא. לָמוּד הוּא. מֶלֶךְ הוּא. נוֹרָא הוּא. סַגִּיב הוּא. עִזּוּז הוּא. פּוֹדֶה הוּא. צַדִּיק הוּא. יִבְנֶה בֵיתוֹ בְּקָרוֹב, בִּמְהֵרָה, בִּמְהֵרָה, בְּיָמֵינוּ בְּקָרוֹב. אֵל בְּנֵה, אֵל בְּנֵה, בְּנֵה בֵיתְךָ בְּקָרוֹב.

קָדוֹשׁ הוּא. רַחוּם הוּא. שַׁדַּי הוּא. תַּקִּיף הוּא. יִבְנֶה בֵיתוֹ בְּקָרוֹב, בִּמְהֵרָה, בִּמְהֵרָה, בְּיָמֵינוּ בְּקָרוֹב. אֵל בְּנֵה, אֵל בְּנֵה, בְּנֵה בֵיתְךָ בְּקָרוֹב.

אֶחָד מִי יוֹדֵעַ? אֶחָד אֲנִי יוֹדֵעַ. אֶחָד אֱלֹהֵינוּ שֶׁבַּשָּׁמַיִם וּבָאָרֶץ.

Yours; Yours, surely Yours; Yours, HASHEM, is the sovereignty. To Him praise is due! To Him praise is fitting.

Almighty in kingship, perfectly sustaining, His perfect ones say to Him: Yours and only Yours; Yours, yes Yours; Yours, surely Yours; Yours, HASHEM, is the sovereignty. To Him praise is due! To Him praise is fitting!

He is most mighty. May He soon rebuild His House, speedily, yes speedily, in our days, soon. God, rebuild, God, rebuild, rebuild Your House soon!

He is distinguished, He is great, He is exalted. May He soon rebuild His House, speedily, yes speedily, in our days, soon. God, rebuild, God, rebuild, rebuild Your House soon!

He is all glorious, He is faithful, He is faultless, He is righteous. May He soon rebuild His House, speedily, yes speedily, in our days, soon. God, rebuild, God, rebuild, rebuild Your House soon!

He is pure, He is unique, He is powerful, He is all-wise, He is King, He is awesome, He is sublime, He is all-powerful, He is the Redeemer, He is the all-righteous. May He soon rebuild His House, speedily, yes speedily, in our days, soon. God, rebuild, God, rebuild, rebuild Your House soon!

He is holy, He is compassionate, He is Almighty, He is omnipotent. May He soon rebuild His House, speedily, yes speedily, in our days, soon. God, rebuild, God, rebuild, rebuild Your House soon!

Who knows one? I know one: One is our God, in heaven and on earth.

אֶחָד מִי יוֹדֵעַ / *Who knows one?*

This poem, in question-and-answer form, details thirteen reasons that Hashem took us out of Egypt. Thirteen is also alluded to in the word *echad*, which begins this poem: the numerical value of *echad*,

שְׁנַיִם מִי יוֹדֵעַ? שְׁנַיִם אֲנִי יוֹדֵעַ. שְׁנֵי לֻחוֹת הַבְּרִית, אֶחָד אֱלֹהֵינוּ שֶׁבַּשָּׁמַיִם וּבָאָרֶץ.
שְׁלשָׁה מִי יוֹדֵעַ? שְׁלשָׁה אֲנִי יוֹדֵעַ. שְׁלשָׁה אָבוֹת, שְׁנֵי לֻחוֹת הַבְּרִית, אֶחָד אֱלֹהֵינוּ שֶׁבַּשָּׁמַיִם וּבָאָרֶץ.

---

one, which describes Hashem, is 13. In this poem we emphasize that Hashem is one from beginning to end.

Q Why do we say this passage on the Seder night?

A ☐ **MIDRASH:** The Jewish people worshiped foreign gods in Egypt, and the angels asked Hashem why He had decided to rescue the Jews, who appeared no different than the Egyptians. This song enumerates the reasons that the nation deserved to be redeemed: first, because of their faith in the unity of our God; second, because they would receive the Tablets of the Covenant; third, in the merit of the Patriarchs, and so on.

☐ **RAV YISSACHAR DOV OF BELZ:** This can be compared to a wealthy man who takes care not to reveal the extent of his property to the public eye. But after imbibing a great deal of wine, he begins listing his considerable possessions. The Jewish people are the same way: after they have consumed four cups of wine at the Seder, they begin revealing their treasures in public: one is our God, two are the Tablets of the Covenant, three are the Patriarchs, and so on.

☐ **MA'ASEH NISSIM:** The song is a list of thirteen good qualities that distinguish us from the other nations:

Our God — Who chose the Jewish people to spread His Name in the world.

The Tablets of the Covenant — He gave the Torah to us, and not to the other nations.

The Three Patriarchs — He gave the Torah only to the Jewish people, who came from the three *Avos* (and not to the rest of their offspring, from whom the other nations are

Who knows two? I know two: two are the Tablets of the Covenant; One is our God, in heaven and on earth.

Who knows three? I know three: three are the Patriarchs; two are the Tablets of the Covenant; One is our God, in heaven and on earth.

---

descended)...

The Four Matriarchs — ...and the four *Imahos*.

The Five Books of the Torah — the Written Torah was given only to the Jewish people.

The Six Orders of the Mishnah — the Oral Torah was given only to the Jewish people.

The seven days of the week — Shabbos was given only to the Jewish people, as a symbol of the covenant that Hashem made with us.

Eight days of circumcision — this is another symbol of the covenant between Hashem and the Jewish people.

Nine months of pregnancy — the Jewish lineage.

The Ten Commandments — were given only to the Jewish people.

Eleven stars — the conduct of Heaven is guided by our actions; therefore, only we can truly influence the cosmos.

The twelve tribes — the Jewish nation was built and composed of the twelve tribes.

The thirteen attributes — this refers to Hashem's attributes of mercy that He shows toward the Jewish people alone, and not toward the other nations.

☐ This song discusses the reasons for the plagues in Egypt and explains why each one came:

Two — Pharaoh was struck by two (Moshe and Aharon) so that the Jewish people could leave Egypt and receive two Tablets.

Three — the Jewish people were redeemed through three (דָּם וָאֵשׁ וְתִימְרוֹת עָשָׁן, *Blood, fire, and columns of smoke*) in the merit of the three Patriarchs.

Four — the plagues came through four powers (fire, wind, water, and earth) in the merit of the four Matriarchs.

אַרְבַּע מִי יוֹדֵעַ? אַרְבַּע אֲנִי יוֹדֵעַ. אַרְבַּע אִמָּהוֹת, שְׁלֹשָׁה אָבוֹת, שְׁנֵי לֻחוֹת הַבְּרִית, אֶחָד אֱלֹהֵינוּ שֶׁבַּשָּׁמַיִם וּבָאָרֶץ.
חֲמִשָּׁה מִי יוֹדֵעַ? חֲמִשָּׁה אֲנִי יוֹדֵעַ. חֲמִשָּׁה חֻמְשֵׁי תוֹרָה, אַרְבַּע אִמָּהוֹת, שְׁלֹשָׁה אָבוֹת, שְׁנֵי לֻחוֹת הַבְּרִית, אֶחָד אֱלֹהֵינוּ שֶׁבַּשָּׁמַיִם וּבָאָרֶץ.

Five — the Torah was given with five sounds, and the Egyptians were struck down in the merit of the five Books of the Torah — that is, so that the Jewish people would receive the Torah in the desert.

Six — the plagues in Egypt came from six directions (north, south, east, west, above, and below) so that the Jews would receive the Torah and the six Orders of the Mishnah.

Seven — each plague lasted seven days, corresponding to the seven days of the week in which the Jewish people toiled.

Eight — according to the Midrash, after Yosef died the Jews wanted to stop circumcising themselves (which is done on the eighth day after a boy's birth), so as to appear more like the Egyptians. This was one of the factors that led to their oppression, which in turn led to the ten plagues.

Nine — of the Ten Plagues, only one was inflicted directly by Hashem. The other nine were inflicted through the agency of Moshe and Aharon, mortal men, who are usually born at the end of nine months. This recalls the Jewish babies who were hurled into the Nile when born after nine months.

Ten — the Egyptians were struck with Ten Plagues so that they would send the Jews out and the Jewish people would be able to receive the Ten Commandments in the desert.

Eleven — Pharaoh himself was inflicted with eleven plagues: ten in Egypt and an additional one at the sea, corresponding to the eleven stars (i.e., tribes) who were oppressed in Egypt (the tribe of Levi was not enslaved).

Twelve — Hashem split the sea in two, enabling the twelve tribes to pass between them.

☐ Saying this poem reminds us that even in exile we can rejoice as we recall the Exodus from Egypt. In the merit of the

Who knows four? I know four: four are the Matriarchs; three are the Patriarchs; two are the Tablets of the Covenant; One is our God, in heaven and on earth.

Who knows five? I know five: five are the Books of the Torah; four are the Matriarchs; three are the Patriarchs; two are the Tablets of the Covenant; One is our God, in heaven and on earth.

Exodus, we were privileged to have One God, two Tablets, the five Books of the Torah, and so on.

☐ The Jewish people were redeemed from Egypt in the merit of their faith in Hashem — their belief that *echad Elokeinu, One is our God* — and in the merit of the Tablets of the Covenant, the three Patriarchs, the four Matriarchs, and so on. This song was established to strengthen our faith, so that in the merit of all of these things we too will be speedily redeemed from our exile.

☐ The author of this song collected statements by Chazal about the Jews' merits that led to their being redeemed from Egypt. These merits were arranged in a question-and-answer format: **Who knows one** praiseworthy thing in whose merit we were redeemed? *One is our God, in heaven and on earth.* **Who knows of a second merit?** *The Tablets of the Covenant.* Moshe Rabbeinu asked Hashem, "In what merit will the Jews depart from Egypt?" Hashem answered, בְּהוֹצִיאֲךָ אֶת הָעָם מִמִּצְרַיִם תַּעַבְדוּן אֶת הָאֱלֹהִים עַל הָהָר הַזֶּה, *When you take the people out of Egypt, you will serve God on this mountain* (Exodus 3:12). The Jewish people received the Luchos on Mount Sinai and were redeemed in that merit.
Who knows of a third merit? *The three Patriarchs,* as it says, וַיִּזְכֹּר אֱלֹהִים אֶת בְּרִיתוֹ אֶת אַבְרָהָם אֶת יִצְחָק וְאֶת יַעֲקֹב, *And God remembered His covenant with Avraham, with Yitzchak, and with Yaakov* (Exodus 2:24). The Jews were redeemed from Egypt in their merit.
Who knows of a fourth merit? The merit of *our four holy Matriarchs.*
Who knows of a fifth merit? In the merit of accepting the Torah (*the five Books of the Torah*), the Jews were redeemed from Egypt.

שִׁשָּׁה מִי יוֹדֵעַ? שִׁשָּׁה אֲנִי יוֹדֵעַ. שִׁשָּׁה סִדְרֵי מִשְׁנָה, חֲמִשָּׁה חֻמְשֵׁי תוֹרָה, אַרְבַּע אִמָּהוֹת, שְׁלֹשָׁה אָבוֹת, שְׁנֵי לֻחוֹת הַבְּרִית, אֶחָד אֱלֹהֵינוּ שֶׁבַּשָּׁמַיִם וּבָאָרֶץ.

שִׁבְעָה מִי יוֹדֵעַ? שִׁבְעָה אֲנִי יוֹדֵעַ. שִׁבְעָה יְמֵי שַׁבַּתָּא, שִׁשָּׁה סִדְרֵי מִשְׁנָה, חֲמִשָּׁה חֻמְשֵׁי תוֹרָה, אַרְבַּע אִמָּהוֹת, שְׁלֹשָׁה אָבוֹת, שְׁנֵי לֻחוֹת הַבְּרִית, אֶחָד אֱלֹהֵינוּ שֶׁבַּשָּׁמַיִם וּבָאָרֶץ.

שְׁמוֹנָה מִי יוֹדֵעַ? שְׁמוֹנָה אֲנִי יוֹדֵעַ. שְׁמוֹנָה יְמֵי מִילָה, שִׁבְעָה יְמֵי שַׁבַּתָּא, שִׁשָּׁה סִדְרֵי מִשְׁנָה, חֲמִשָּׁה חֻמְשֵׁי תוֹרָה, אַרְבַּע אִמָּהוֹת, שְׁלֹשָׁה אָבוֹת, שְׁנֵי לֻחוֹת הַבְּרִית, אֶחָד אֱלֹהֵינוּ שֶׁבַּשָּׁמַיִם וּבָאָרֶץ.

Who knows of a sixth merit? *The six Orders of the Mishnah.* As it says in *Gittin* (60), Hashem made a covenant with the Jewish nation only on the basis of the oral teachings — that is, the six Orders of the Mishnah.

Who knows of a seventh merit? Our forefathers were redeemed in the merit of Shabbos, which we observe on *the seventh day of the week*.

Who knows of an eighth merit? *The eight days of circumcision.* The Jewish people, devoid of mitzvos, had no merit with which to be redeemed. Then Hashem gave them two mitzvos, one of which was *bris milah*.

Who knows of a ninth merit? *The nine months of pregnancy.* The Jews continued the chain of the generations despite the difficulties and were not deterred even when Pharaoh decreed, כָּל הַבֵּן הַיִּלּוֹד הַיְאֹרָה תַּשְׁלִיכֻהוּ, *Every son that will be born — into the river shall you throw him!* (Exodus 1:22). In this merit, they were redeemed.

Who knows of a tenth merit? The Jewish people were redeemed in the merit of *the Ten Commandments* they received on Mount Sinai.

Who knows six? I know six: six are the Orders of the Mishnah; five are the Books of the Torah; four are the Matriarchs; three are the Patriarchs; two are the Tablets of the Covenant; One is our God, in heaven and on earth.

Who knows seven? I know seven: seven are the days of the week; six are the Orders of the Mishnah; five are the Books of the Torah; four are the Matriarchs; three are the Patriarchs; two are the Tablets of the Covenant; One is our God, in heaven and on earth.

Who knows eight? I know eight: eight are the days of circumcision; seven are the days of the week; six are the Orders of the Mishnah; five are the Books of the Torah; four are the Matriarchs; three are the Patriarchs; two are the Tablets of the Covenant; One is our God, in heaven and on earth.

Who knows of an eleventh merit? These are *the eleven stars* — corresponding to the eleven tribes — in Yosef's dream. These tribes did not change their names, and in that merit they were redeemed.

Who knows of a twelfth merit? *The twelve tribes.* The Jewish people safeguarded themselves against immorality, maintaining the purity of their families, and did not assimilate with the Egyptians.

Who knows of a thirteenth merit? These are *the thirteen attributes of God.* After listing all the merits that led to the Jews' exodus from Egypt, the author concludes his song with the merit that will redeem the nation in the future: the merit of Hashem's thirteen *middos.*

Q **Why does it say** שְׁמוֹנָה יְמֵי מִילָה**, Eight are the days of circumcision, when the mitzvah of bris milah is only on the eighth day and not on all eight?**

A ☐ The Jewish parents in Egypt demonstrated their devotion to this mitzvah all eight days, as they risked their lives to safeguard their baby before the *bris milah.*

[321] **HAGGADAH: THE ANSWER IS . . .**

תִּשְׁעָה מִי יוֹדֵעַ? תִּשְׁעָה אֲנִי יוֹדֵעַ. תִּשְׁעָה יַרְחֵי לֵדָה, שְׁמוֹנָה יְמֵי מִילָה, שִׁבְעָה יְמֵי שַׁבַּתָּא, שִׁשָּׁה סִדְרֵי מִשְׁנָה, חֲמִשָּׁה חֻמְשֵׁי תוֹרָה, אַרְבַּע אִמָּהוֹת, שְׁלֹשָׁה אָבוֹת, שְׁנֵי לֻחוֹת הַבְּרִית, אֶחָד אֱלֹהֵינוּ שֶׁבַּשָּׁמַיִם וּבָאָרֶץ.

עֲשָׂרָה מִי יוֹדֵעַ? עֲשָׂרָה אֲנִי יוֹדֵעַ. עֲשָׂרָה דִבְּרַיָּא, תִּשְׁעָה יַרְחֵי לֵדָה, שְׁמוֹנָה יְמֵי מִילָה, שִׁבְעָה יְמֵי שַׁבַּתָּא, שִׁשָּׁה סִדְרֵי מִשְׁנָה, חֲמִשָּׁה חֻמְשֵׁי תוֹרָה, אַרְבַּע אִמָּהוֹת, שְׁלֹשָׁה אָבוֹת, שְׁנֵי לֻחוֹת הַבְּרִית, אֶחָד אֱלֹהֵינוּ שֶׁבַּשָּׁמַיִם וּבָאָרֶץ.

אַחַד עָשָׂר מִי יוֹדֵעַ? אַחַד עָשָׂר אֲנִי יוֹדֵעַ. אַחַד עָשָׂר כּוֹכְבַיָּא, עֲשָׂרָה דִבְּרַיָּא, תִּשְׁעָה יַרְחֵי לֵדָה, שְׁמוֹנָה יְמֵי מִילָה, שִׁבְעָה יְמֵי שַׁבַּתָּא, שִׁשָּׁה סִדְרֵי מִשְׁנָה, חֲמִשָּׁה חֻמְשֵׁי תוֹרָה, אַרְבַּע אִמָּהוֹת, שְׁלֹשָׁה אָבוֹת, שְׁנֵי לֻחוֹת הַבְּרִית, אֶחָד אֱלֹהֵינוּ שֶׁבַּשָּׁמַיִם וּבָאָרֶץ.

Q "Nine are the months of pregnancy." The first eight stanzas list the Jews' advantages over the other nations. The "nine months of pregnancy," however, applies equally to all people. In that case, why is it mentioned here?

A ☐ The Jewish midwives told Pharaoh that the purpose of Jewish marriage is to establish righteous generations for the future. In this respect, Jewish women were different from Egyptian women, whose only goal was to fulfill their desires. Regarding the Jewish women, it is written, כִּי חָיוֹת הֵנָּה, *For they are experts* (Exodus 1:19). The word *chayos* comes from the root word *chai*, living. The words of the verse imply that they *lived* for future generations, for the children. The verse goes on to say, בְּטֶרֶם תָּבוֹא אֲלֵהֶן הַמְיַלֶּדֶת וְיָלָדוּ, *Before the midwife comes to them, they have given*

Who knows nine? I know nine: nine are the months of pregnancy; eight are the days of circumcision; seven are the days of the week; six are the Orders of the Mishnah; five are the Books of the Torah; four are the Matriarchs; three are the Patriarchs; two are the Tablets of the Covenant; One is our God, in heaven and on earth.

Who knows ten? I know ten: ten are the Ten Commandments; nine are the months of pregnancy; eight are the days of circumcision; seven are the days of the week; six are the Orders of the Mishnah; five are the Books of the Torah; four are the Matriarchs; three are the Patriarchs; two are the Tablets of the Covenant; One is our God, in heaven and on earth.

Who knows eleven? I know eleven: eleven are the stars (in Yosef's dream); ten are the Ten Commandments; nine are the months of pregnancy; eight are the days of circumcision; seven are the days of the week; six are the Orders of the Mishnah; five are the Books of the Torah; four are the Matriarchs; three are the Patriarchs; two are the Tablets of the Covenant; One is our God, in heaven and on earth.

---

birth: even while the mother was pregnant, it was as though the child was already born.

Therefore, the author of this poem uses the words *yarchei leidah* — literally, the months of childbirth — and not *yarchei ibbur*, the months of pregnancy. The Jewish nation differs from the nations of the world during the nine months of pregnancy, which for them are the months of childbirth. Already during the pregnancy, the child is a living person to them, a new generation born.

☐ Despite the hardships of life in Egypt, the Jewish wives encouraged their husbands and happily embraced the pain of pregnancy and childbirth. In their merit, our forefathers were redeemed from Egypt. On this night we highlight the outstanding dedication of these women — as opposed to the women of other nations who, had they been asked to withstand similar stresses, would have been incapable of doing so.

שְׁנֵים עָשָׂר מִי יוֹדֵעַ? שְׁנֵים עָשָׂר אֲנִי יוֹדֵעַ. שְׁנֵים עָשָׂר שִׁבְטַיָּא, אַחַד עָשָׂר כּוֹכְבַיָּא, עֲשָׂרָה דִבְּרַיָּא, תִּשְׁעָה יַרְחֵי לֵדָה, שְׁמוֹנָה יְמֵי מִילָה, שִׁבְעָה יְמֵי שַׁבַּתָּא, שִׁשָּׁה סִדְרֵי מִשְׁנָה, חֲמִשָּׁה חֻמְשֵׁי תוֹרָה, אַרְבַּע אִמָּהוֹת, שְׁלֹשָׁה אָבוֹת, שְׁנֵי לֻחוֹת הַבְּרִית, אֶחָד אֱלֹהֵינוּ שֶׁבַּשָּׁמַיִם וּבָאָרֶץ.

שְׁלֹשָׁה עָשָׂר מִי יוֹדֵעַ? שְׁלֹשָׁה עָשָׂר אֲנִי יוֹדֵעַ. שְׁלֹשָׁה עָשָׂר מִדַּיָּא, שְׁנֵים עָשָׂר שִׁבְטַיָּא, אַחַד עָשָׂר כּוֹכְבַיָּא, עֲשָׂרָה דִבְּרַיָּא, תִּשְׁעָה יַרְחֵי לֵדָה, שְׁמוֹנָה יְמֵי מִילָה, שִׁבְעָה יְמֵי שַׁבַּתָּא, שִׁשָּׁה סִדְרֵי מִשְׁנָה, חֲמִשָּׁה חֻמְשֵׁי תוֹרָה, אַרְבַּע אִמָּהוֹת, שְׁלֹשָׁה אָבוֹת, שְׁנֵי לֻחוֹת הַבְּרִית, אֶחָד אֱלֹהֵינוּ שֶׁבַּשָּׁמַיִם וּבָאָרֶץ.

חַד גַּדְיָא. חַד גַּדְיָא, דְּזַבִּין אַבָּא בִּתְרֵי זוּזֵי, חַד גַּדְיָא חַד גַּדְיָא.

וְאָתָא **שׁוּנְרָא** וְאָכְלָה לְגַדְיָא, דְּזַבִּין אַבָּא בִּתְרֵי זוּזֵי, חַד גַּדְיָא חַד גַּדְיָא.

₪§ חַד גַּדְיָא / *A kid*

Q *Why do we say this song on the Seder night?*

A ☐ **VILNA GAON:** This poem highlights several events in Jewish history, beginning with Yitzchak and ending with Mashiach:

A kid, a kid refers to the two kids that Yaakov brought to Yitzchak on the night of Pesach, and which later became a mitzvah for all generations: one kid for the *korban Pesach* and the other for the *korban chagigah*. Through them, Yaakov Avinu merited Yitzchak's blessings and Esav's firstborn status, and he passed both on to Yosef.

Who knows twelve? I know twelve: twelve are the tribes; eleven are the stars (in Yosef's dream); ten are the Ten Commandments; nine are the months of pregnancy; eight are the days of circumcision; seven are the days of the week; six are the Orders of the Mishnah; five are the Books of the Torah; four are the Matriarchs; three are the Patriarchs; two are the Tablets of the Covenant; One is our God, in heaven and on earth.

Who knows thirteen? I know thirteen: thirteen are the attributes of God; twelve are the tribes; eleven are the stars (in Yosef's dream); ten are the Ten Commandments; nine are the months of pregnancy; eight are the days of circumcision; seven are the days of the week; six are the Orders of the Mishnah; five are the Books of the Torah; four are the Matriarchs; three are the Patriarchs; two are the Tablets of the Covenant; One is our God, in heaven and on earth.

A **kid, a kid,** that father bought for two zuzim, a kid, a kid.

A **cat** then came and devoured the kid that father bought for two zuzim, a kid, a kid.

The cat is a symbol of envy, referring to the envy of Yosef's brothers, who sold him to Egypt in order to nullify the blessings and the firstborn status he had received.

The dog is Pharaoh, king of Egypt, whom Chazal referred to by this epithet and who oppressed the Jewish tribes; this would serve to rectify the sin of the brothers' envy of Yosef.

The stick is Moshe's staff, with which the miracles and wonders in Egypt were performed. Moshe gave it to Yehoshua, and it was passed down through the generations to David HaMelech. This stick was used to perform miracles and wonders on behalf of the Jewish people until the destruction of the first Beis HaMikdash, which was destroyed for the sin of idol worship. As a result, the power of the stick was taken away.

The fire: The Beis HaMikdash was destroyed through the fire of the *yetzer hara*, which arose through the sin of idol worship.

וְאָתָא **כַלְבָּא** וְנָשַׁךְ לְשׁוּנְרָא, דְּאָכְלָה לְגַדְיָא, דְּזַבִּין אַבָּא בִּתְרֵי זוּזֵי, חַד גַּדְיָא חַד גַּדְיָא.

וְאָתָא **חוּטְרָא** וְהִכָּה לְכַלְבָּא, דְּנָשַׁךְ לְשׁוּנְרָא, דְּאָכְלָה לְגַדְיָא, דְּזַבִּין אַבָּא בִּתְרֵי זוּזֵי, חַד גַּדְיָא חַד גַּדְיָא.

וְאָתָא **נוּרָא** וְשָׂרַף לְחוּטְרָא, דְּהִכָּה לְכַלְבָּא, דְּנָשַׁךְ לְשׁוּנְרָא, דְּאָכְלָה לְגַדְיָא, דְּזַבִּין אַבָּא בִּתְרֵי זוּזֵי, חַד גַּדְיָא חַד גַּדְיָא.

The water refers to the Torah. The Men of the Great Assembly nullified the inclination for idol worship.

The ox is the kingdom of Edom, which is compared to an ox, and which has grievously persecuted the Jews with evil decrees in an attempt to part them from Torah and mitzvos.

The shochet (slaughterer) is Mashiach ben Yosef, who would fight Edom.

The Angel of Death will kill Mashiach ben Yosef.

And then **HaKadosh Baruch Hu** will come and save us with an eternal salvation, may it be speedily and in our day!

☐ **MA'ASEH NISSIM:** This song describes the trials and tribulations of the Jewish people and concludes with the redemption that comes from Hashem:

A kid — the Beis HaMikdash is like the kid, purchased with two *zuzim*. David HaMelech collected two gold coins from each tribe when he purchased the site of the Beis HaMikdash.

The cat is Nevuchadnetzar, who destroyed the Beis HaMikdash. The Aramaic word for cat is *shunra*, which in Hebrew can be rendered as *sonei ra*, an evil enemy.

The dog is Koresh, who nursed from a dog.

The stick is Greece.

The fire refers to the Chashmonaim. They were Kohanim, who are compared to fire.

The water is Edom, from the verse... מִקֹּלוֹת מַיִם רַבִּים, *More than the roars of many waters...* (Psalms 93:4). The Midrash teaches us that this refers to Edom, whose voice reaches from one end of the world to the other.

הגדה של פסח [326]

A dog then came and bit the cat, that devoured the kid that father bought for two zuzim, a kid, a kid.

A stick then came and beat the dog, that bit the cat, that devoured the kid that father bought for two zuzim, a kid, a kid.

A fire then came and burnt the stick, that beat the dog, that bit the cat, that devoured the kid that father bought for two zuzim, a kid, a kid.

The ox is Yishmael.
The shochet is Mashiach ben Yosef.
The Angel of Death kills Mashiach ben Yosef.
HaKadosh Baruch Hu will redeem us in the future.

☐ KLAUSENBERGER REBBE: This song teaches us that, despite all the suffering — the cat, the dog, the stick, etc. — one God-fearing Jew remains: the *shochet* who is scrupulous about the mitzvos. The Angel of Death comes and kills him: the Jewish people are left, seemingly, with no hope. This situation leads us to conclude that we have no one to depend on and we must have faith that Hashem will slaughter the Angel of Death, hasten our salvation, and redeem us speedily!

☐ The Seder night is a festival of faith, when we relate the miracles that Hashem has performed for us. We believe that there is judgment and that there is a Judge Who dispenses reward and punishment. Just as Pharaoh oppressed the Jews and was punished for it, so too, in every time of trouble, Hashem repays and punishes those who flout His will. We can find examples in this song. Everyone receives his just deserts: the cat is punished for devouring the kid, and so on down the line — because Hashem is the Judge and He executes true and righteous justice.

☐ This song is a dialogue that took place in Egypt between a Jew and an Egyptian. The Egyptians saw the Jews preparing the kids in order to offer the *korban Pesach* and were enraged, for the Egyptians worshiped sheep. The Jew retorted mockingly, "Is your god a cheap kid that your father bought for two *zuzim*? Even a cat is stronger than that!"

וְאָתָא **מַיָּא** וְכָבָה לְנוּרָא, דְּשָׂרַף לְחוּטְרָא, דְּהִכָּה לְכַלְבָּא, דְּנָשַׁךְ לְשׁוּנְרָא, דְּאָכְלָה לְגַדְיָא, דְּזַבִּין אַבָּא בִּתְרֵי זוּזֵי, חַד גַּדְיָא חַד גַּדְיָא.

וְאָתָא **תוֹרָא** וְשָׁתָה לְמַיָּא, דְּכָבָה לְנוּרָא, דְּשָׂרַף לְחוּטְרָא, דְּהִכָּה לְכַלְבָּא, דְּנָשַׁךְ לְשׁוּנְרָא, דְּאָכְלָה לְגַדְיָא, דְּזַבִּין אַבָּא בִּתְרֵי זוּזֵי, חַד גַּדְיָא חַד גַּדְיָא.

The Egyptian began to wonder if it would be better to worship the cat instead. The Jew continued, "And a dog is stronger than a cat" — whereupon the Egyptian pondered the advisability of worshiping the dog.

And so the dialogue continued, until the Jew explained to the Egyptian that HaKadosh Baruch Hu is the one true God Whom all must serve.

☐ This poem describes our history, from our slavery in Egypt until our sojourn in the desert:

A kid — this represents the Jewish people, whom Hashem (the father in the poem) acquired.

The cat — the Egyptians sought out the Jews in their hiding places, like an animal on the scent of its prey.

The dog — Pharaoh killed even his own people (the "cat," above) with his decree: כָּל הַבֵּן הַיִּלּוֹד הַיְאֹרָה תַּשְׁלִיכֻהוּ, *Every son that will be born — into the river shall you throw him!* (*Exodus* 1:22). This decree included Egyptian babies.

The stick — the staff that Moshe used to initiate the plagues on Pharaoh.

The fire that burned the stick — these are the necromancers, who (in their view) nullified Moshe's words and burned the staff.

The water that put out the fire — this refers to the splitting of the sea, when the Egyptians drowned. Since that time, magic has had no power over us as a nation.

The ox that drank the water — the sin of the golden calf (the "ox") removed the purity that the Jewish people had achieved at the sea.

The shochet that slaughtered the ox — Moshe Rabbeinu

[328] הגדה של פסח

Water then came and quenched the fire, that burnt the stick, that beat the dog, that bit the cat, that devoured the kid that father bought for two zuzim, a kid, a kid.

An ox then came and drank the water, that quenched the fire, that burnt the stick, that beat the dog, that bit the cat, that devoured the kid that father bought for two zuzim, a kid, a kid.

---

stood at the camp gates and called, מִי לַה' אֵלָי, *Whoever is for HASHEM, join me!* (*Exodus* 32:26). The tribe of Levi answered the call and killed those who had worshiped the golden calf.

The Angel of Death — this is the Satan, who stirred up strife with Korach's conflict and nullified the Jews' merit.

And slaughtered the shochet — Hashem will slaughter the Angel of Death: He will abolish the evil inclination.

☐ There is a similar explanation that says that this poem describes events that took place in Jewish history, but this approach includes a variety of historical eras. The purpose of the poem is to strengthen the faith of the Jewish people (the kid) in Hashem (the shepherd who purchased it), Who watches over and rescues Israel from all its troubles. The poem enumerates the dangers that stalk the kid: the troubles that have beset the Jewish people:

A kid is a term for the nation of Israel, which is like a young lamb purchased by the Shepherd: Hashem.

The cat symbolizes the enemies who attack us. At first they behave in a friendly manner, but this quickly changes drastically. The cat's manner changes and becomes that of a dog.

The dog refers to the gentiles who, up to a point, had behaved in a warm and friendly way to us, but who turned into enemies and attacked the Jewish people, like a dog that appears mild and friendly, but suddenly loses its calm and leaps upon a person to bite him.

The stick symbolizes the blows the Jews have suffered.

The fire refers to the Jews' tribulations during the Middle Ages. These are the bonfires of the Inquisition, when it demanded that the Jews renounce their faith. But the Jews sacrificed their lives instead and leaped into the flames.

וְאָתָא הַשּׁוֹחֵט וְשָׁחַט לְתוֹרָא, דְּשָׁתָא לְמַיָּא, דְּכָבָה לְנוּרָא, דְּשָׂרַף לְחוּטְרָא, דְּהִכָּה לְכַלְבָּא, דְּנָשַׁךְ לְשׁוּנְרָא, דְּאָכְלָה לְגַדְיָא, דְּזַבִּין אַבָּא בִּתְרֵי זוּזֵי, חַד גַּדְיָא חַד גַּדְיָא.

וְאָתָא מַלְאַךְ הַמָּוֶת וְשָׁחַט לְשׁוֹחֵט, דְּשָׁחַט לְתוֹרָא, דְּשָׁתָה לְמַיָּא, דְּכָבָה לְנוּרָא, דְּשָׂרַף לְחוּטְרָא, דְּהִכָּה לְכַלְבָּא, דְּנָשַׁךְ לְשׁוּנְרָא, דְּאָכְלָה לְגַדְיָא, דְּזַבִּין אַבָּא בִּתְרֵי זוּזֵי, חַד גַּדְיָא חַד גַּדְיָא.

וְאָתָא הַקָּדוֹשׁ בָּרוּךְ הוּא וְשָׁחַט לְמַלְאַךְ הַמָּוֶת, דְּשָׁחַט לְשׁוֹחֵט, דְּשָׁחַט לְתוֹרָא, דְּשָׁתָה לְמַיָּא, דְּכָבָה לְנוּרָא, דְּשָׂרַף לְחוּטְרָא, דְּהִכָּה לְכַלְבָּא, דְּנָשַׁךְ לְשׁוּנְרָא, דְּאָכְלָה לְגַדְיָא, דְּזַבִּין אַבָּא בִּתְרֵי זוּזֵי, חַד גַּדְיָא חַד גַּדְיָא.

Although the Haggadah formally ends at this point, one should continue to occupy himself with the story of the Exodus, and the laws of Passover, until sleep overtakes him.

The water is what our enemies used to baptize those Jews who did not withstand the test and chose to convert.

The ox represents the enemies who have attacked us like an ox. And yet, despite everything, Hashem has redeemed and saved us. The blows we have absorbed through our history demonstrate that we can never rely on our own strength, but can only have faith and trust in HaKadosh Baruch Hu.

☐ This poem is recited at the end of the Seder on Pesach, the festival of faith. It shows how far we are from understanding Hashem's ways and how little we know of His providence.

The story seems paradoxical. The cat is wicked, as it devoured an innocent kid. The dog, which punishes the wicked cat, is righteous. The stick, which beats the righteous dog, is wicked, and so the fire that burns the stick is righteous. The water, which puts out the fire, is then wicked, while the ox is righteous, the *shochet* is wicked, and the Angel of Death is righteous. According to this, why is the Angel of Death

A slaughterer then came and slaughtered the ox, that drank the water, that quenched the fire, that burnt the stick, that beat the dog, that bit the cat, that devoured the kid that father bought for two zuzim, a kid, a kid.

The angel of death then came and killed the slaughterer, who slaughtered the ox, that drank the water, that quenched the fire, that burnt the stick, that beat the dog, that bit the cat, that devoured the kid that father bought for two zuzim, a kid, a kid.

The Holy One, Blessed is He, then came and slew the angel of death, who killed the slaughterer, who slaughtered the ox, that drank the water, that quenched the fire, that burnt the stick, that beat the dog, that bit the cat, that devoured the kid that father bought for two zuzim, a kid, a kid.

Although the Haggadah formally ends at this point, one should continue to occupy himself with the story of the Exodus, and the laws of Passover, until sleep overtakes him.

---

slaughtered? After all, it seems to have conducted itself in righteousness!

We can learn a lesson from this story. First, we do not understand Hashem's providence or the way He chooses to conduct this world. Second, a person may not appoint himself "Hashem's policeman" and the dispenser of justice in the world — especially if his intention is to hurt others. A person should not be a "*tzaddik*" while "slaughtering" others along the way.

☐ At the conclusion of the Haggadah, after relating the events of the Exodus from Egypt, this poem hints at all the ways that our forefathers tested Hashem. Out of respect for the Jewish people, these things are mentioned in a veiled manner:

A kid — a small, oppressed nation, "purchased" with two *zuzim* — Egypt's gold and silver.

The cat symbolizes the ten trials with which the Jews tested Hashem in the desert. It was the *eirev rav*, the mixed multitude that left Egypt along with the Jews, who were responsible for this (for their nature was like that of a cat, which pursues and pounces).

The dog is Pharaoh, who was like a pursuing dog after the *eirev rav* returned to him and slandered the Jews.

The stick — Hashem told Moshe to lift his staff in the direction of the sea. The stick beat the dog (the Egyptians) and caused them to drown.

The fire — the Mishnah in *Avos* lists the ten trials in the desert, including that of Kivros HaTa'avah, where a group of Jews complained that they wanted meat. The fire refers to the flame of their desires.

The water — this refers to Mei Merivah, where the Jewish people quarreled with Moshe and complained about water.

The ox — this is the golden calf, which drank the "water"; that is, the sin of the golden calf nullified the Torah, which is compared to water, and caused the *luchos* to be shattered.

The shochet is Moshe Rabbeinu, who brought the tribe of Levi into the camp and destroyed the golden calf, while the Levites killed those who had worshiped the idol.

The Angel of Death is the Satan, who was with the *eirev rav*.

HaKadosh Baruch Hu — in the future, Hashem will slaughter the evil inclination in front of the righteous.

There was a man in the city of Slonim who constantly quarreled with his fellow townsfolk. The rav of the city, Rav Yehoshua Eizel Charif, asked him, "Why are you so eager for conflict?"

"Heaven forbid!" the man said. "I mean it only for the sake of Heaven — to keep the public from sinning!"

Rav Eizel smiled. "If you look at the poem *Chad Gadya*, you will see that there is a definite order to the way these things occur:

"The kid is innocent of all wrongdoing, so the cat is guilty of devouring it. The dog is innocent, for he is fighting for justice, but the stick is guilty of beating the dog — and so on.

"According to this, it turns out that the Angel of Death is guiltless, because he simply repaid the *shochet* for slaughtering the ox. In that case, why did Hashem fault him?

"Rather, we tell it: You Angel of Death, stop seeking justice and leave people alone!"

הגדה של פסח

Q *What do the kid and the two zuzim represent?*

A
- ☐ **CHIDA:** The two *zuzim* represent the *luchos*. Just as a groom gives his bride a ring under the *chuppah* when he takes her as his wife, so Hashem "acquired" the Jewish people with the giving of the *luchos*.
- ☐ **MIGDAL EDER:** The kid is the Jewish people. The father is HaKadosh Baruch Hu. The two *zuzim* are the half-shekel (one shekel is equivalent to four *zuzim*) that was given as an atonement for the sin of the golden calf. Through the half-shekel that the Jews donated in the desert, the Mishkan was built as a home for Hashem's Shechinah.
- ☐ **BIRKAS HASHIR:** The kid is Yosef. The brothers slaughtered the kid and dipped Yosef's coat in its blood after they sold him, in order to convince Yaakov that Yosef had been killed by a wild animal. The rest of the song describes other events that took place in our long exile, beginning with the selling of Yosef (the kid) and ending when Hashem will slaughter the Satan (i.e., the Angel of Death).

When controversy broke out in Frankfurt over the conduct of Rav Nosson Adler, the Chasam Sofer's rebbi, he went away to a place where he would not be recognized.

But he could not escape the controversy and he overheard people talking about him. Rav Nosson Adler said in response, "In the song of *Chad Gadya*, the cat that ate the kid did something wrong. Therefore, the dog that bit the cat was justified, the stick that hit the dog was wrong, the fire was correct in burning it, and the water should not have put out the fire. The ox was correct in punishing the water by drinking it; the *shochet* should not have slaughtered the ox, and the Angel of Death was justified in killing the *shochet*.

"Why then did *HaKadosh Baruch Hu* slaughter the Angel of Death? "We can agree that the cat was wrong in eating the kid, and there is good reason to be angry with it and punish it. But if there is a quarrel between a man and his cat, why should the dog interfere in a fight that is not his own? He is guiltier than anyone — so the stick was correct in beating him, the fire was wrong to burn it, and so on. Thus, we find in the end that *HaKadosh Baruch Hu* was correct in slaughtering the Angel of Death."

שיר השירים / Song of Songs

Many have the custom to recite *Shir HaShirim* following the Seder.

פרק א

א שִׁיר הַשִּׁירִים אֲשֶׁר לִשְׁלֹמֹה: ב יִשָּׁקֵנִי מִנְּשִׁיקוֹת פִּיהוּ כִּי־טוֹבִים דֹּדֶיךָ מִיָּיִן: ג לְרֵיחַ שְׁמָנֶיךָ טוֹבִים שֶׁמֶן תּוּרַק שְׁמֶךָ עַל־כֵּן עֲלָמוֹת אֲהֵבוּךָ: ד מָשְׁכֵנִי אַחֲרֶיךָ נָּרוּצָה הֱבִיאַנִי הַמֶּלֶךְ חֲדָרָיו נָגִילָה וְנִשְׂמְחָה בָּךְ נַזְכִּירָה דֹדֶיךָ מִיַּיִן מֵישָׁרִים אֲהֵבוּךָ: ה שְׁחוֹרָה אֲנִי וְנָאוָה בְּנוֹת יְרוּשָׁלָםִ כְּאָהֳלֵי קֵדָר כִּירִיעוֹת שְׁלֹמֹה: ו אַל־תִּרְאוּנִי שֶׁאֲנִי שְׁחַרְחֹרֶת שֶׁשְּׁזָפַתְנִי הַשָּׁמֶשׁ בְּנֵי אִמִּי נִחֲרוּ־בִי שָׂמֻנִי נֹטֵרָה אֶת־הַכְּרָמִים כַּרְמִי שֶׁלִּי לֹא נָטָרְתִּי: ז הַגִּידָה לִּי שֶׁאָהֲבָה נַפְשִׁי אֵיכָה תִרְעֶה אֵיכָה תַּרְבִּיץ בַּצָּהֳרָיִם שַׁלָּמָה אֶהְיֶה כְּעֹטְיָה עַל עֶדְרֵי חֲבֵרֶיךָ: ח אִם־לֹא תֵדְעִי לָךְ הַיָּפָה בַּנָּשִׁים צְאִי־לָךְ בְּעִקְבֵי הַצֹּאן וּרְעִי אֶת־גְּדִיֹּתַיִךְ עַל מִשְׁכְּנוֹת הָרֹעִים: ט לְסֻסָתִי בְּרִכְבֵי פַרְעֹה דִּמִּיתִיךְ רַעְיָתִי: י נָאווּ לְחָיַיִךְ בַּתֹּרִים צַוָּארֵךְ בַּחֲרוּזִים: יא תּוֹרֵי זָהָב נַעֲשֶׂה־לָּךְ עִם נְקֻדּוֹת הַכָּסֶף: יב עַד־שֶׁהַמֶּלֶךְ בִּמְסִבּוֹ נִרְדִּי נָתַן רֵיחוֹ: יג צְרוֹר הַמֹּר | דּוֹדִי לִי בֵּין שָׁדַי יָלִין: יד אֶשְׁכֹּל הַכֹּפֶר דּוֹדִי לִי בְּכַרְמֵי עֵין גֶּדִי: טו הִנָּךְ יָפָה רַעְיָתִי הִנָּךְ יָפָה עֵינַיִךְ יוֹנִים: טז הִנְּךָ יָפֶה דוֹדִי אַף נָעִים אַף־עַרְשֵׂנוּ רַעֲנָנָה: יז קֹרוֹת בָּתֵּינוּ אֲרָזִים רַהִיטֵנוּ בְּרוֹתִים:

Q *Why must we not drink after the four cups of wine have been consumed?*

A ☐ **TUR:** After the Seder, one should involve himself with learning the laws of Pesach. If he drinks wine, he is liable to fall asleep.

☐ **VILNA GAON:** We do not drink after the four cups so that it will not appear as if we are adding on to the prescribed four cups.

☐ **DARKEI MOSHE:** We do not drink anything else so that the taste of the matzah will linger in our mouth.

פרק ב

א אֲנִי חֲבַצֶּלֶת הַשָּׁרוֹן שׁוֹשַׁנַּת הָעֲמָקִים: ב כְּשׁוֹשַׁנָּה בֵּין הַחוֹחִים כֵּן רַעְיָתִי בֵּין הַבָּנוֹת: ג כְּתַפּוּחַ בַּעֲצֵי הַיַּעַר כֵּן דּוֹדִי בֵּין הַבָּנִים בְּצִלּוֹ חִמַּדְתִּי וְיָשַׁבְתִּי וּפִרְיוֹ מָתוֹק לְחִכִּי: ד הֱבִיאַנִי אֶל־בֵּית הַיָּיִן וְדִגְלוֹ עָלַי אַהֲבָה: ה סַמְּכוּנִי בָּאֲשִׁישׁוֹת רַפְּדוּנִי בַּתַּפּוּחִים כִּי־חוֹלַת אַהֲבָה אָנִי: ו שְׂמֹאלוֹ תַּחַת לְרֹאשִׁי וִימִינוֹ תְּחַבְּקֵנִי: ז הִשְׁבַּעְתִּי אֶתְכֶם בְּנוֹת יְרוּשָׁלַםִ בִּצְבָאוֹת אוֹ בְּאַיְלוֹת הַשָּׂדֶה אִם־תָּעִירוּ וְאִם־תְּעוֹרְרוּ אֶת־הָאַהֲבָה עַד שֶׁתֶּחְפָּץ: ח קוֹל דּוֹדִי הִנֵּה־זֶה בָּא מְדַלֵּג עַל־הֶהָרִים מְקַפֵּץ עַל־הַגְּבָעוֹת: ט דּוֹמֶה דוֹדִי לִצְבִי אוֹ לְעֹפֶר הָאַיָּלִים הִנֵּה־זֶה עוֹמֵד אַחַר כָּתְלֵנוּ מַשְׁגִּיחַ מִן־הַחֲלֹּנוֹת מֵצִיץ מִן־הַחֲרַכִּים: י עָנָה דוֹדִי וְאָמַר לִי קוּמִי לָךְ רַעְיָתִי יָפָתִי וּלְכִי־לָךְ: יא כִּי־הִנֵּה הַסְּתָו עָבָר הַגֶּשֶׁם חָלַף הָלַךְ לוֹ: יב הַנִּצָּנִים נִרְאוּ בָאָרֶץ עֵת הַזָּמִיר הִגִּיעַ וְקוֹל הַתּוֹר נִשְׁמַע בְּאַרְצֵנוּ: יג הַתְּאֵנָה חָנְטָה פַגֶּיהָ וְהַגְּפָנִים סְמָדַר נָתְנוּ רֵיחַ קוּמִי לָךְ רַעְיָתִי יָפָתִי וּלְכִי־לָךְ: יד יוֹנָתִי בְּחַגְוֵי הַסֶּלַע בְּסֵתֶר הַמַּדְרֵגָה הַרְאִינִי אֶת־מַרְאַיִךְ הַשְׁמִיעִנִי אֶת־קוֹלֵךְ כִּי־קוֹלֵךְ עָרֵב וּמַרְאֵיךְ נָאוֶה: טו אֶחֱזוּ־לָנוּ שֻׁעָלִים שֻׁעָלִים קְטַנִּים מְחַבְּלִים כְּרָמִים וּכְרָמֵינוּ סְמָדַר: טז דּוֹדִי לִי וַאֲנִי לוֹ הָרֹעֶה בַּשּׁוֹשַׁנִּים: יז עַד שֶׁיָּפוּחַ

Q: *Why is it a custom to recite Shir HaShirim after the Seder?*

A:
- **REMA**: The Exodus is hinted at in *Shir HaShirim*, in the verse לְסֻסָתִי בְּרִכְבֵי פַרְעֹה דִּמִּיתִיךְ רַעְיָתִי, *With My mighty steeds who battled Pharaoh's riders, I revealed that you are My beloved* (Song of Songs 1:9).

- **ALEI SHUR**: *Shir HaShirim* is a love song between the Jewish people and Hashem. On the Seder night, as we contemplate Hashem's miracles and relate the story of the Exodus from Egypt, we show our love for Hashem and read *Shir HaShirim*.

[335] **HAGGADAH: THE ANSWER IS . . .**

הַיּוֹם וְנָסוּ הַצְּלָלִים סֹב דְּמֵה־לְךָ דוֹדִי לִצְבִי אוֹ לְעֹפֶר הָאַיָּלִים עַל־הָרֵי בָתֶר:

פרק ג

א עַל־מִשְׁכָּבִי בַּלֵּילוֹת בִּקַּשְׁתִּי אֵת שֶׁאָהֲבָה נַפְשִׁי בִּקַּשְׁתִּיו וְלֹא מְצָאתִיו: ב אָקוּמָה נָּא וַאֲסוֹבְבָה בָעִיר בַּשְּׁוָקִים וּבָרְחֹבוֹת אֲבַקְשָׁה אֵת שֶׁאָהֲבָה נַפְשִׁי בִּקַּשְׁתִּיו וְלֹא מְצָאתִיו: ג מְצָאוּנִי הַשֹּׁמְרִים הַסֹּבְבִים בָּעִיר אֵת שֶׁאָהֲבָה נַפְשִׁי רְאִיתֶם: ד כִּמְעַט שֶׁעָבַרְתִּי מֵהֶם עַד שֶׁמָּצָאתִי אֵת שֶׁאָהֲבָה נַפְשִׁי אֲחַזְתִּיו וְלֹא אַרְפֶּנּוּ עַד־שֶׁהֲבֵיאתִיו אֶל־בֵּית אִמִּי וְאֶל־חֶדֶר הוֹרָתִי: ה הִשְׁבַּעְתִּי אֶתְכֶם בְּנוֹת יְרוּשָׁלַ͏ִם בִּצְבָאוֹת אוֹ בְּאַיְלוֹת הַשָּׂדֶה אִם־תָּעִירוּ | וְאִם־תְּעוֹרְרוּ אֶת־הָאַהֲבָה עַד שֶׁתֶּחְפָּץ: ו מִי זֹאת עֹלָה מִן־הַמִּדְבָּר כְּתִימְרוֹת עָשָׁן מְקֻטֶּרֶת מֹר וּלְבוֹנָה מִכֹּל אַבְקַת רוֹכֵל: ז הִנֵּה מִטָּתוֹ שֶׁלִּשְׁלֹמֹה שִׁשִּׁים גִּבֹּרִים סָבִיב לָהּ מִגִּבֹּרֵי יִשְׂרָאֵל: ח כֻּלָּם אֲחֻזֵי חֶרֶב מְלֻמְּדֵי מִלְחָמָה אִישׁ חַרְבּוֹ עַל־יְרֵכוֹ מִפַּחַד בַּלֵּילוֹת: ט אַפִּרְיוֹן עָשָׂה לוֹ הַמֶּלֶךְ שְׁלֹמֹה מֵעֲצֵי הַלְּבָנוֹן: י עַמּוּדָיו עָשָׂה כֶסֶף רְפִידָתוֹ זָהָב מֶרְכָּבוֹ אַרְגָּמָן תּוֹכוֹ רָצוּף אַהֲבָה מִבְּנוֹת יְרוּשָׁלָ͏ִם: יא צְאֶינָה וּרְאֶינָה בְּנוֹת צִיּוֹן בַּמֶּלֶךְ שְׁלֹמֹה בָּעֲטָרָה שֶׁעִטְּרָה־לּוֹ אִמּוֹ בְּיוֹם חֲתֻנָּתוֹ וּבְיוֹם שִׂמְחַת לִבּוֹ:

פרק ד

א הִנָּךְ יָפָה רַעְיָתִי הִנָּךְ יָפָה עֵינַיִךְ יוֹנִים מִבַּעַד לְצַמָּתֵךְ שַׂעְרֵךְ כְּעֵדֶר הָעִזִּים שֶׁגָּלְשׁוּ מֵהַר גִּלְעָד: ב שִׁנַּיִךְ כְּעֵדֶר הַקְּצוּבוֹת שֶׁעָלוּ מִן־הָרַחְצָה שֶׁכֻּלָּם מַתְאִימוֹת וְשַׁכֻּלָה אֵין בָּהֶם: ג כְּחוּט הַשָּׁנִי שִׂפְתוֹתַיִךְ וּמִדְבָּרֵךְ נָאוֶה כְּפֶלַח הָרִמּוֹן רַקָּתֵךְ מִבַּעַד לְצַמָּתֵךְ: ד כְּמִגְדַּל דָּוִיד צַוָּארֵךְ בָּנוּי לְתַלְפִּיּוֹת אֶלֶף הַמָּגֵן תָּלוּי עָלָיו כֹּל שִׁלְטֵי הַגִּבֹּרִים: ה שְׁנֵי שָׁדַיִךְ כִּשְׁנֵי עֳפָרִים תְּאוֹמֵי צְבִיָּה הָרוֹעִים בַּשּׁוֹשַׁנִּים: ו עַד שֶׁיָּפוּחַ הַיּוֹם וְנָסוּ הַצְּלָלִים אֵלֶךְ לִי אֶל־הַר הַמּוֹר וְאֶל־גִּבְעַת הַלְּבוֹנָה: ז כֻּלָּךְ יָפָה רַעְיָתִי וּמוּם אֵין בָּךְ: ח אִתִּי

הגדה של פסח [336]

מִלְּבָנוֹן כַּלָּה אִתִּי מִלְּבָנוֹן תָּבוֹאִי תָּשׁוּרִי | מֵרֹאשׁ אֲמָנָה מֵרֹאשׁ שְׂנִיר וְחֶרְמוֹן מִמְּעֹנוֹת אֲרָיוֹת מֵהַרְרֵי נְמֵרִים: י לִבַּבְתִּנִי אֲחֹתִי כַלָּה לִבַּבְתִּינִי בְּאַחַת מֵעֵינַיִךְ בְּאַחַד עֲנָק מִצַּוְּרֹנָיִךְ: יא מַה־יָּפוּ דֹדַיִךְ אֲחֹתִי כַלָּה מַה־טֹּבוּ דֹדַיִךְ מִיַּיִן וְרֵיחַ שְׁמָנַיִךְ מִכָּל־בְּשָׂמִים: יא נֹפֶת תִּטֹּפְנָה שִׂפְתוֹתַיִךְ כַּלָּה דְּבַשׁ וְחָלָב תַּחַת לְשׁוֹנֵךְ וְרֵיחַ שַׂלְמֹתַיִךְ כְּרֵיחַ לְבָנוֹן: יב גַּן | נָעוּל אֲחֹתִי כַלָּה גַּל | נָעוּל מַעְיָן חָתוּם: יג שְׁלָחַיִךְ פַּרְדֵּס רִמּוֹנִים עִם פְּרִי מְגָדִים כְּפָרִים עִם־נְרָדִים: יד נֵרְדְּ | וְכַרְכֹּם קָנֶה וְקִנָּמוֹן עִם כָּל־עֲצֵי לְבוֹנָה מֹר וַאֲהָלוֹת עִם כָּל־רָאשֵׁי בְשָׂמִים: טו מַעְיַן גַּנִּים בְּאֵר מַיִם חַיִּים וְנֹזְלִים מִן־לְבָנוֹן: טז עוּרִי צָפוֹן וּבוֹאִי תֵימָן הָפִיחִי גַנִּי יִזְּלוּ בְשָׂמָיו יָבֹא דוֹדִי לְגַנּוֹ וְיֹאכַל פְּרִי מְגָדָיו:

פרק ה

א בָּאתִי לְגַנִּי אֲחֹתִי כַלָּה אָרִיתִי מוֹרִי עִם־בְּשָׂמִי אָכַלְתִּי יַעְרִי עִם־דִּבְשִׁי שָׁתִיתִי יֵינִי עִם־חֲלָבִי אִכְלוּ רֵעִים שְׁתוּ וְשִׁכְרוּ דּוֹדִים: ב אֲנִי יְשֵׁנָה וְלִבִּי עֵר קוֹל | דּוֹדִי דוֹפֵק פִּתְחִי־לִי אֲחֹתִי רַעְיָתִי יוֹנָתִי תַמָּתִי שֶׁרֹּאשִׁי נִמְלָא־טָל קְוֻצּוֹתַי רְסִיסֵי לָיְלָה: ג פָּשַׁטְתִּי אֶת־כֻּתָּנְתִּי אֵיכָכָה אֶלְבָּשֶׁנָּה רָחַצְתִּי אֶת־רַגְלַי אֵיכָכָה אֲטַנְּפֵם: ד דּוֹדִי שָׁלַח יָדוֹ מִן־הַחֹר וּמֵעַי הָמוּ עָלָיו: ה קַמְתִּי אֲנִי לִפְתֹּחַ לְדוֹדִי וְיָדַי נָטְפוּ־מוֹר וְאֶצְבְּעֹתַי מוֹר עֹבֵר עַל כַּפּוֹת הַמַּנְעוּל: ו פָּתַחְתִּי אֲנִי לְדוֹדִי וְדוֹדִי חָמַק עָבָר נַפְשִׁי יָצְאָה בְדַבְּרוֹ בִּקַּשְׁתִּיהוּ וְלֹא מְצָאתִיהוּ קְרָאתִיו וְלֹא עָנָנִי: ז מְצָאֻנִי הַשֹּׁמְרִים הַסֹּבְבִים בָּעִיר הִכּוּנִי פְצָעוּנִי נָשְׂאוּ אֶת־רְדִידִי מֵעָלַי שֹׁמְרֵי הַחֹמוֹת: ח הִשְׁבַּעְתִּי אֶתְכֶם בְּנוֹת יְרוּשָׁלִָם אִם־תִּמְצְאוּ אֶת־דּוֹדִי מַה־תַּגִּידוּ לוֹ שֶׁחוֹלַת אַהֲבָה אָנִי: ט מַה־דּוֹדֵךְ מִדּוֹד הַיָּפָה בַּנָּשִׁים מַה־דּוֹדֵךְ מִדּוֹד שֶׁכָּכָה הִשְׁבַּעְתָּנוּ: י דּוֹדִי צַח וְאָדוֹם דָּגוּל מֵרְבָבָה: יא רֹאשׁוֹ כֶּתֶם פָּז קְוֻצּוֹתָיו תַּלְתַּלִּים שְׁחֹרוֹת כָּעוֹרֵב: יב עֵינָיו כְּיוֹנִים עַל־אֲפִיקֵי מָיִם רֹחֲצוֹת בֶּחָלָב יֹשְׁבוֹת עַל־מִלֵּאת: יג לְחָיָו כַּעֲרוּגַת הַבֹּשֶׂם מִגְדְּלוֹת

[337] **HAGGADAH: THE ANSWER IS . . .**

מְרֻקָּחִים שִׂפְתוֹתָיו שׁוֹשַׁנִּים נֹטְפוֹת מוֹר עֹבֵר: יד יָדָיו גְּלִילֵי זָהָב מְמֻלָּאִים בַּתַּרְשִׁישׁ מֵעָיו עֶשֶׁת שֵׁן מְעֻלֶּפֶת סַפִּירִים: טו שׁוֹקָיו עַמּוּדֵי שֵׁשׁ מְיֻסָּדִים עַל־אַדְנֵי־פָז מַרְאֵהוּ כַּלְּבָנוֹן בָּחוּר כָּאֲרָזִים: טז חִכּוֹ מַמְתַקִּים וְכֻלּוֹ מַחֲמַדִּים זֶה דוֹדִי וְזֶה רֵעִי בְּנוֹת יְרוּשָׁלָם:

פרק ו

א אָנָה הָלַךְ דּוֹדֵךְ הַיָּפָה בַּנָּשִׁים אָנָה פָּנָה דוֹדֵךְ וּנְבַקְשֶׁנּוּ עִמָּךְ: ב דּוֹדִי יָרַד לְגַנּוֹ לַעֲרֻגוֹת הַבֹּשֶׂם לִרְעוֹת בַּגַּנִּים וְלִלְקֹט שׁוֹשַׁנִּים: ג אֲנִי לְדוֹדִי וְדוֹדִי לִי הָרֹעֶה בַּשּׁוֹשַׁנִּים: ד יָפָה אַתְּ רַעְיָתִי כְּתִרְצָה נָאוָה כִּירוּשָׁלָם אֲיֻמָּה כַּנִּדְגָּלוֹת: ה הָסֵבִּי עֵינַיִךְ מִנֶּגְדִּי שֶׁהֵם הִרְהִיבֻנִי שַׂעְרֵךְ כְּעֵדֶר הָעִזִּים שֶׁגָּלְשׁוּ מִן־הַגִּלְעָד: ו שִׁנַּיִךְ כְּעֵדֶר הָרְחֵלִים שֶׁעָלוּ מִן־הָרַחְצָה שֶׁכֻּלָּם מַתְאִימוֹת וְשַׁכֻּלָה אֵין בָּהֶם: ז כְּפֶלַח הָרִמּוֹן רַקָּתֵךְ מִבַּעַד לְצַמָּתֵךְ: ח שִׁשִּׁים הֵמָּה מְלָכוֹת וּשְׁמֹנִים פִּילַגְשִׁים וַעֲלָמוֹת אֵין מִסְפָּר: ט אַחַת הִיא יוֹנָתִי תַמָּתִי אַחַת הִיא לְאִמָּהּ בָּרָה הִיא לְיוֹלַדְתָּהּ רָאוּהָ בָנוֹת וַיְאַשְּׁרוּהָ מְלָכוֹת וּפִילַגְשִׁים וַיְהַלְלוּהָ: י מִי־זֹאת הַנִּשְׁקָפָה כְּמוֹ־שָׁחַר יָפָה כַלְּבָנָה בָּרָה כַּחַמָּה אֲיֻמָּה כַּנִּדְגָּלוֹת: יא אֶל־גִּנַּת אֱגוֹז יָרַדְתִּי לִרְאוֹת בְּאִבֵּי הַנָּחַל לִרְאוֹת הֲפָרְחָה הַגֶּפֶן הֵנֵצוּ הָרִמֹּנִים: יב לֹא יָדַעְתִּי נַפְשִׁי שָׂמַתְנִי מַרְכְּבוֹת עַמִּי נָדִיב:

פרק ז

א שׁוּבִי שׁוּבִי הַשּׁוּלַמִּית שׁוּבִי שׁוּבִי וְנֶחֱזֶה־בָּךְ מַה־תֶּחֱזוּ בַּשּׁוּלַמִּית כִּמְחֹלַת הַמַּחֲנָיִם: ב מַה־יָּפוּ פְעָמַיִךְ בַּנְּעָלִים בַּת־נָדִיב חַמּוּקֵי יְרֵכַיִךְ כְּמוֹ חֲלָאִים מַעֲשֵׂה יְדֵי אָמָּן: ג שָׁרְרֵךְ אַגַּן הַסַּהַר אַל־יֶחְסַר הַמָּזֶג בִּטְנֵךְ עֲרֵמַת חִטִּים סוּגָה בַּשּׁוֹשַׁנִּים: ד שְׁנֵי שָׁדַיִךְ כִּשְׁנֵי עֳפָרִים תָּאֳמֵי צְבִיָּה: ה צַוָּארֵךְ כְּמִגְדַּל הַשֵּׁן עֵינַיִךְ בְּרֵכוֹת בְּחֶשְׁבּוֹן עַל־שַׁעַר בַּת־רַבִּים אַפֵּךְ כְּמִגְדַּל הַלְּבָנוֹן צוֹפֶה פְּנֵי דַמָּשֶׂק: ו רֹאשֵׁךְ עָלַיִךְ כַּכַּרְמֶל וְדַלַּת רֹאשֵׁךְ כָּאַרְגָּמָן מֶלֶךְ אָסוּר בָּרְהָטִים:

הגדה של פסח [338]

ז מַה־יָּפִית וּמַה־נָּעַמְתְּ אַהֲבָה בַּתַּעֲנוּגִים: ח זֹאת קוֹמָתֵךְ דָּמְתָה לְתָמָר וְשָׁדַיִךְ לְאַשְׁכֹּלוֹת: ט אָמַרְתִּי אֶעֱלֶה בְתָמָר אֹחֲזָה בְּסַנְסִנָּיו וְיִהְיוּ־נָא שָׁדַיִךְ כְּאֶשְׁכְּלוֹת הַגֶּפֶן וְרֵיחַ אַפֵּךְ כַּתַּפּוּחִים: י וְחִכֵּךְ כְּיֵין הַטּוֹב הוֹלֵךְ לְדוֹדִי לְמֵישָׁרִים דּוֹבֵב שִׂפְתֵי יְשֵׁנִים: יא אֲנִי לְדוֹדִי וְעָלַי תְּשׁוּקָתוֹ: יב לְכָה דוֹדִי נֵצֵא הַשָּׂדֶה נָלִינָה בַּכְּפָרִים: יג נַשְׁכִּימָה לַכְּרָמִים נִרְאֶה אִם־פָּרְחָה הַגֶּפֶן פִּתַּח הַסְּמָדַר הֵנֵצוּ הָרִמּוֹנִים שָׁם אֶתֵּן אֶת־דֹּדַי לָךְ: יד הַדּוּדָאִים נָתְנוּ־רֵיחַ וְעַל־פְּתָחֵינוּ כָּל־מְגָדִים חֲדָשִׁים גַּם־יְשָׁנִים דּוֹדִי צָפַנְתִּי לָךְ:

פרק ח

א מִי יִתֶּנְךָ כְּאָח לִי יוֹנֵק שְׁדֵי אִמִּי אֶמְצָאֲךָ בַחוּץ אֶשָּׁקְךָ גַּם לֹא־יָבֻזוּ לִי: ב אֶנְהָגְךָ אֲבִיאֲךָ אֶל־בֵּית אִמִּי תְּלַמְּדֵנִי אַשְׁקְךָ מִיַּיִן הָרֶקַח מֵעֲסִיס רִמֹּנִי: ג שְׂמֹאלוֹ תַּחַת רֹאשִׁי וִימִינוֹ תְּחַבְּקֵנִי: ד הִשְׁבַּעְתִּי אֶתְכֶם בְּנוֹת יְרוּשָׁלָיִם מַה־תָּעִירוּ | וּמַה־תְּעֹרְרוּ אֶת־הָאַהֲבָה עַד שֶׁתֶּחְפָּץ: ה מִי זֹאת עֹלָה מִן־הַמִּדְבָּר מִתְרַפֶּקֶת עַל־דּוֹדָהּ תַּחַת הַתַּפּוּחַ עוֹרַרְתִּיךָ שָׁמָּה חִבְּלַתְךָ אִמֶּךָ שָׁמָּה חִבְּלָה יְלָדַתְךָ: ו שִׂימֵנִי כַחוֹתָם עַל־לִבֶּךָ כַּחוֹתָם עַל־זְרוֹעֶךָ כִּי־עַזָּה כַמָּוֶת אַהֲבָה קָשָׁה כִשְׁאוֹל קִנְאָה רְשָׁפֶיהָ רִשְׁפֵּי אֵשׁ שַׁלְהֶבֶתְיָה: ז מַיִם רַבִּים לֹא יוּכְלוּ לְכַבּוֹת אֶת־הָאַהֲבָה וּנְהָרוֹת לֹא יִשְׁטְפוּהָ אִם־יִתֵּן אִישׁ אֶת־כָּל־הוֹן בֵּיתוֹ בָּאַהֲבָה בּוֹז יָבוּזוּ לוֹ: ח אָחוֹת לָנוּ קְטַנָּה וְשָׁדַיִם אֵין לָהּ מַה־נַּעֲשֶׂה לַאֲחֹתֵנוּ בַּיּוֹם שֶׁיְּדֻבַּר־בָּהּ: ט אִם־חוֹמָה הִיא נִבְנֶה עָלֶיהָ טִירַת כָּסֶף וְאִם־דֶּלֶת הִיא נָצוּר עָלֶיהָ לוּחַ אָרֶז: י אֲנִי חוֹמָה וְשָׁדַי כַּמִּגְדָּלוֹת אָז הָיִיתִי בְעֵינָיו כְּמוֹצְאֵת שָׁלוֹם: יא כֶּרֶם הָיָה לִשְׁלֹמֹה בְּבַעַל הָמוֹן נָתַן אֶת־הַכֶּרֶם לַנֹּטְרִים אִישׁ יָבִא בְּפִרְיוֹ אֶלֶף כָּסֶף: יב כַּרְמִי שֶׁלִּי לְפָנָי הָאֶלֶף לְךָ שְׁלֹמֹה וּמָאתַיִם לְנֹטְרִים אֶת־פִּרְיוֹ: יג הַיּוֹשֶׁבֶת בַּגַּנִּים חֲבֵרִים מַקְשִׁיבִים לְקוֹלֵךְ הַשְׁמִיעִנִי: יד בְּרַח | דּוֹדִי וּדְמֵה־לְךָ לִצְבִי אוֹ לְעֹפֶר הָאַיָּלִים עַל הָרֵי בְשָׂמִים:

[339] **HAGGADAH: THE ANSWER IS . . .**

Selected Bibliography

Abarbanel
A commentary on *Tanach* written by Rav Yitzchak Abarbanel. He lived first in Portugal and then in Italy and produced a Haggadah called *Zevach Pesach*. He passed away in the year 1508 (5668).

Acharis L'Shalom
A Haggadah written by Rav Yitzchak Eliyahu Landau in Vilna in the year 1871 (5631).

Akeidas Yitzchak
A commentary by Rav Yitzchak Arama, who served as rav and *rosh yeshivah* in Zamora, in northern Spain. He passed away in the year 1494 (5254).

Alei Shur
A classic *mussar* work by Rav Shlomo Wolbe, who was born in Berlin and moved to Eretz Yisrael in 1946 (5706), where he became *mashgiach* of Yeshivas Be'er Yaakov and later Lakewood Yeshivah. He passed away in 2005 (5765).

Alshich
A commentary on the Torah by Rav Moshe ben Chaim Alshich. The Alshich lived in Tzefas and received *semichah* from Rav Yosef Karo. He passed away in the year 1593 (5353).

Alter of Kelm
Rav Simcha Zissel Ziv Broide of Kelm was one of the leaders of the *mussar* movement and a foremost disciple of Rav Yisrael Salanter. He passed away in 1898 (5658).

Alter of Novardok
Rav Yosef Yozel Horowitz served as *mashgiach* in the Slabodka yeshivah before he founded the Novardok yeshivah in 1896 (5656). He passed away in 1919 (5689).

Alter of Slabodka
Rav Nosson Tzvi Finkel founded Yeshivas Knesses Yisrael in Slabodka before moving the yeshivah to Chevron in Eretz Yisrael. He passed away in 1927 (5687).

Anaf Yosef
A homiletic commentary on Midrash Rabbah by Rav Henoch Zundel ben Rav Yosef, a Russian Torah scholar and Talmudist. He passed away in Bialystok, Poland, in 1867 (5627).

Arizal
An acronym for Rav Yitzchak Luria, the famed kabbalist from Tzefas. The Ari was born in Jerusalem and orphaned as a child. He became a student of the Radvaz in Egypt. After the death of the Ramak, the Ari became leader of the kabbalists in Tzefas. His foremost student was Rav Chaim Vital. The Ari passed away in 1572 (5332).

Aruch HaShulchan
A halachic work by Rav Yechiel Michel HaLevi Epstein. He served as *av beis din* in Novardok and was the father of the Torah Temimah and a brother-in-law of the Netziv. He passed away in 1908 (5668).

Avnei Nezer
Written by the Sochatchover Rebbe, Rav Avraham Bornstein, who was known by the name of his work, *Avnei Nezer*. He was a student of the Gerrer Rebbe, the Chiddushei HaRim. He served as the Rebbe of Sochatchov until he passed away in 1910 (5670).

Avudraham
Rav David Avudraham lived in the era of the *Rishonim*. In the year 1340 (5100) he wrote the *Avudraham*, a

compilation of the *tefillos* along with their commentaries and laws.

Ba'al HaTurim
A commentary on the Torah by Rav Yaakov ben Asher, son of the Rosh. He also authored *Arba'ah Turim*, or "*Tur,*" a halachic commentary on the *Shulchan Aruch*. He lived in Toledano and passed away in 1343 (5103).

Baal Shem Tov
Rav Yisrael Baal Shem Tov was the founder of the Chassidus movement. He lived in Mezibuzh, in the Ukraine. He passed away in the year 1760 (5520).

Ba'alei HaTosafos
Medieval commentaries on the Talmud, also known as "*Tosafos.*"

Bach
An abbreviation of the halachic work *Bayis Chadash*, by Rav Yoel Sirkis, *rav* of Belz, Brest-Litovsk, and Cracow. *Bayis Chadash* is a commentary on *Arba'ah Turim* by Rav Yaakov ben Ashur. Rav Sirkis passed away in 1640 (5400).

Bartenura
A foremost commentary on the Mishnah by Rav Ovadiah of Bartenura. Born in Italy in 1445 (5205), he moved to Eretz Yisrael at the age of thirty-five. He passed away in 1516 (5276).

Baruch She'amar
A commentary on the Haggadah by Rav Baruch HaLevi Epstein, one of the great Torah scholars of Pinsk and the son of Rav Yechiel Michel Epstein, the *av beis din* of Novardok and author of *Aruch HaShulchan*. He also wrote *Torah Temimah*, a commentary on the Torah. He was killed in the Holocaust in 1942 (5702).

B'Chipazon Pesach
A commentary on the Haggadah by Rav Avraham Sid. He passed away in 1871 (5631).

Be'er Mayim
A commentary on the Haggadah based on that of the Baal Shem Tov, written by Rav Yosef Meir Shapiro, the Maggid of Zlazitch, a disciple of the Maggid of Mezritch. The Haggadah was printed in Mezibuzh in 1817 (5577).

Be'er Shmuel
By Rav Shmuel Rosenberg, *rosh yeshivah* of Unsdorf and a student of the Ksav Sofer. He passed away in 1919 (5679).

Beis HaLevi
Rav Yosef Dov HaLevi Soloveitchik became *rosh yeshivah* of Yeshivas Volozhin in the year 1852 (5612). He also served as rav of Slutzk and head of the Brisker community. He passed away in 1892 (5652).

Belzer Rebbe
Rav Yissachar Dov Rokeach was the third Belzer Rebbe, the son of Rav Yehoshua. At the start of World War I, when the city of Belz became a battlefield, he moved to Hungary and lived for a time in the city of Munkacz. He passed away in 1926 (5687).

Ben Ish Chai
Rav Yosef Chaim of Baghdad was the student of Rav Abdallah Somech. He served as rabbi for the community of Baghdad for many years and passed away in the year 1909 (5669).

Binah L'Itim
Written by Rav Azaryah Pigo, a great Italian Torah scholar at the start of the seventeenth century. He passed away in 1647 (5407).

Birkas HaShir
A commentary on the Haggadah by Rav Aryeh Leib Tzintz. A foremost rabbinical figure in Poland in the nineteenth century, he served primarily in Warsaw. He passed away in 1853 (5593).

Bnei Yissaschar
Written by Rav Tzvi Elimelech of Dinov. He served as rav of several *kehillos* in Galicia and was a student

[342] הגדה של פסח

of both the Chozeh of Lublin and the Maggid of Koznitz. He passed away in 1841 (5601).

Brisker Rav
Rav Yitzchak Zev Soloveitchik was the grandson of the Beis HaLevi. In 1941 (5701) he moved to Eretz Yisrael, where he founded the great yeshivah of Brisk. He passed away in 1959 (5719).

Chafetz Chaim
Rav Yisrael Meir HaKohen Kagan of Radin was known by the name of his well-known *sefer*, *Chafetz Chaim*. He wrote an important halachic work entitled *Mishnah Berurah* and founded a great yeshivah in Radin. He passed away in 1933 (5693).

Chanukas HaTorah
A commentary on the Torah by Rav Yehoshua Heshel, a great rav in Poland in the seventeenth century. After his father's death, he was appointed chief rabbi of Lublin. He passed away in 1663 (5423).

Chasam Sofer
Rav Moshe Sofer became the rav of Pressburg in 1803 (5563); he was the son-in-law of Rav Akiva Eiger. He wrote responsa and original insights on the Talmud, and is known by his main work, *Chasam Sofer*. He passed away in 1839 (5599).

Chayei Adam
A halachic work on *Orach Chaim* authored by Rav Avraham Danzig, a student of the Noda BiYehudah. Besides *Chayei Adam*, he authored many halachic works, including *Chachmas Adam* and *Toldos Adam*. He passed away in 1821 (5581).

Chemdas Shlomo
Authored by Rav Shlomo Lifshitz, who served as the chief rabbi of Warsaw. He passed away in the year 1839 (5599).

Chida
Rav Chaim Yosef David Azulai was one of the great Sephardic Torah scholars and a student of the Ohr HaChaim. Among other works, he authored the *Simchas HaRegel* Haggadah. He passed away in Italy in 1906 (5666), and in 1960 (5720) his bones were brought to Eretz Yisrael.

Chiddushei HaRim
Written by Rav Yitzchak Meir Alter, a student of the Peshischer Rebbe, Rav Mendel of Kotzk. He is considered the first Rebbe of the Ger chassidic dynasty. He wrote original insights on the *Shulchan Aruch* and passed away in the year 1866 (5626).

Chok Yaakov
A commentary on the laws of Pesach in *Orach Chaim* by Rav Yaakov Reischer, an Austrian rav and *posek*. He passed away in 1733 (5493).

Chok Yosef
A halachic work on the laws of Pesach by Rav Yosef of Breslau. It was printed in Amsterdam in 1730 (5490).

Chomas HaDas V'Ha'emunah
Written by Rav Shlomo HaLevi Halperin.

Chozeh of Lublin
Rav Yaakov Yitzchak Horowitz was a student of the Maggid of Mezritch and a descendant of the Shelah HaKadosh. Near the end of his life, he served as rav of Lublin. He passed away in 1815 (5575).

Chukas HaPesach
A commentary on the Haggadah by Rav Yaakov Emden (the Yaavetz) in Vienna. Rav Yaakov Emden was the son of the Chacham Tzvi and an eminent Torah scholar in Germany. He is most well known for his commentary on the *siddur*. He passed away in 1776 (5536).

Da'as Zekeinim
A commentary on the Torah written by a group of Ashkenazic and French sages in the twelfth and thirteenth centuries, most of them students of Rashi.

Darkei Moshe
A commentary on the *Tur* by Rav Moshe Isserlis, a foremost *posek* in Europe also known as the Rema. He is most well known for his commentary on the *Shulchan Aruch* entitled *HaMapah*. He lived in Cracow and passed away in 1572 (5332).

Divrei Chaim
Authored by Rav Chaim Halberstam, the Rebbe of Sanz. He was the first of the chassidic rebbes of Poland, and he served as Rebbe for about fifty years before he passed away in the year 1876 (5636).

Divrei Shaul
A commentary on the Haggadah by Rav Yosef Shaul HaLevi Nathanson, rav of Lvov. He also authored *Divrei Shaul* on the Torah and *Aggadah* and *Shoel U'Meishiv*, a book of halachic responsa. He passed away in 1875 (5635).

Divrei Yoel
Written by the Satmar Rebbe, Rav Yoel Teitelbaum. He became the Satmar Rebbe in the year 1935 (5695) and passed away in 1979 (5739).

Dover Shalom
Written by Rav Shalom Rokeach, also known as the Sar Shalom, who founded the Belzer chassidic dynasty and was a student of the Chozeh of Lublin. He passed away in 1855 (5615).

Dubno Maggid
Rav Yaakov Kranz was a great *darshan* (preacher) who became famous for his many parables. Author of the commentaries *Ohel Yaakov* and *Kol Yaakov*, he passed away in 1804 (5564).

Eshel Avraham
A commentary on *Orach Chaim* by Rav Avraham Dovid Wahrman, the rav of Buczacz. He passed away in 1840 (5600).

Eshel B'Ramah
A commentary on the Haggadah written by Rav Avraham Lichtenstein in Bulgaria in 1935 (5695).

Etz Chaim
A fundamental work of Kabbalah written by Rav Chaim Vital, a great kabbalist in Tzefas and a foremost disciple of the Arizal. He passed away in Damascus in 1620 (5380) and was buried there.

Ga'al Yisrael Haggadah
A commentary on the Haggadah by Rav Yisrael Zev HaLevi Horowitz, an *av beis din* and *rosh yeshivah* in Ujhely, Hungary. He was a student of the Chasam Sofer. He moved to Eretz Yisrael at the end of his life and passed away in 1860 (5620).

Hafla'ah
Written by Rav Pinchas HaLevi Horowitz, a student of the Maggid of Mezritch and rav of Frankfurt. He passed away in 1805 (5565).

Haggadah Chodesh HaAviv
Written by Rav Asher Anshel Katz, a rav in Hungary, who was killed during the Holocaust in 1944 (5704).

Haggadah Sheleimah
A Haggadah with commentary written by Rav Menachem Mendel Kasher. Rav Kasher was born in Warsaw and moved to Israel in 1924 (5684). He wrote the encyclopedic work on the Torah *Torah Sheleimah*. He passed away in 1983 (5743).

HaShir V'Hashevach
A commentary on the Haggadah by Rav Zalman Sorotzkin, who served as rav of Lutzk as well as the head of the Moetzes Gedolei HaTorah. He passed away in 1966 (5726).

Ibn Ezra
A commentary on *Tanach* by Rav Avraham Ibn Ezra. He lived in Spain and was married to the daughter of Rav Yehudah HaLevi. He passed away in the year 1167 (4927).

Imrei Emes
Written by Rav Avraham Mordechai Alter, the son and successor of the Sfas Emes in the Gerrer chassidic

הגדה של פסח [344]

dynasty. He moved to Eretz Yisrael in the year 1940 (5700) and passed away in 1948 (5708).

Iyun Tefillah
Authored by Rav Yaakov Tzvi Mecklenburg, the rav of Konigsburg. He is also famous for his commentary on the Torah, *HaKsav V'Hakabbalah*. He passed away in 1865 (5625).

Kedushas Levi
A commentary on the Torah and the festivals by Rav Levi Yitzchak of Berditchev, a student of the Maggid of Mezritch. A staunch advocate of seeing the good in all Jews, he earned the title "Defender of Israel." He passed away in 1810 (5570).

Klausenberger Rebbe
Rav Yekusiel Yehudah Halberstam, grandson of Rav Chaim of Sanz. He rebuilt the Sanz chassidic dynasty after the Holocaust. Among his many philanthropic projects, he founded Mifal HaShas to encourage Jewish men and boys worldwide to study Talmud and *Shulchan Aruch*. He passed away in 1994 (5754).

Kli Chemdah
A commentary on *Nach* written by Rav Shmuel Laniado, a sixteenth-century Syrian Torah scholar and a descendant of Jews who were exiled from Spain. He studied under the author of the *Shulchan Aruch*, Rav Yosef Karo. *Kli Chemdah* was printed in Venice in 1595 (1355).

Kli Yakar
A commentary on the Torah by Rav Shlomo Efraim of Luntschitz, who served as a rav and *rosh yeshivah* in Prague. He passed away in 1619 (5379).

Kochvei Ohr
Written by Rav Yitzchak Blazer, also known as Rav Itzele Peterburger. He was a student of the leader of the *mussar* movement, Rav Yisrael Salanter, and was responsible for publishing Rav Yisrael's letters in the form of *Ohr Yisrael*. In 1861 (5621) he became chief rabbi of Petersburg and later joined the Alter of Slabodka in leading the Slabodka yeshivah. He passed away in 1907 (5667).

Kol Bo
A *sefer* of customs and laws. There are those who attribute this work to Rabbeinu Peretz, while others attribute it to the Rivash. It was first printed in Naples, Italy, in the year 1490 (5250), and again in Constantinople (Istanbul) in 1519 (5279).

Ksav Sofer
Rav Avraham Shmuel Binyamin Sofer, son of the Chasam Sofer, served as *av beis din* and *rosh yeshivah* in Pressburg after his father's passing. He passed away in 1871 (5631).

Leket Yosher
Written by Rav Yisrael Isserlin (the Mahari), who served as *rav* in the city of Marburg and later in Neustadt, near Vienna. He passed away in 1460 (5220).

Lev Simchah
Written by Rav Simcha Bunim Alter, the fifth Gerrer Rebbe and the son of the Imrei Emes. He passed away in 1992 (5752).

Levush
A work of halachah whose full title is *Levush Malchus* by Rav Mordechai Yaffe, a student of the Rema. He was a *rosh yeshivah* in Prague and later became chief rabbi of Posen. He passed away in 1612 (5372).

Ma'aseh Nissim
A commentary on the Haggadah by Rav Yaakov Loberbaum, author of *Nesivos HaMishpat* and a great-grandson of the Chacham Tzvi. In 1809 (5569) he became rav of Lissa. He passed away in 1832 (5592).

Ma'asei Hashem
A commentary on the Torah and the Pesach Haggadah by Rav Eliezer

[345] HAGGADAH: THE ANSWER IS . . .

Ashkenazi, a sixteenth-century Torah scholar and physician. He served as a rav in Egypt and later in Posen. He passed away in 1585 (5346).

Machzor Vitri
A halachic volume and prayer machzor attributed to Rabbeinu Simcha ben Rav Shmuel from the city of Vitri, who was a student of Rashi. It is considered a primary source in tefillah literature. Machzor Vitri was completed in 1208 (4968) and published in 1893 (5653).

Maggid of Plotzk
Rav Pinchas bar Yehudah was a disciple of the Vilna Gaon and authored the Maggid Tzedek siddur. He passed away in 1823 (5583).

Maharal
Rav Yehudah Loew, son of Rav Betzalel Loew, wrote a commentary on the Torah known as Gur Aryeh, as well as many writings on both the revealed and hidden aspects of the Torah. He also wrote a commentary on the Haggadah, Divrei Negidim. He passed away in 1609 (5369).

Maharil
Rav Yaakov ben Moshe Moelin was the spiritual leader of Ashkenazic Jews in his day. He wrote Minhagei HaMaharil and other commentaries and rulings. He passed away in 1427 (5187).

Maharsha
Rav Shmuel Eliezer HaLevi Eidlish wrote a commentary on Shas known as Chiddushei Halachos V'Aggados. He passed away in 1632 (5392).

Maharsham
Rav Shalom Mordechai HaKohen Schwadron lived in Galicia, where he served as rav of Berezhan and founded a yeshivah. In his youth, he was a chassid of Rav Shalom Rokeach, the Belzer Rebbe, and of Rav Meir of Premishlan. He passed away in 1911 (5671).

Malbim
Rav Meir Leibush ben Yechiel Michel served as rav in Posna and later in Bucharest, Romania. He authored a commentary on Tanach. He passed away in 1880 (5640).

Marbeh Lesaper
A commentary on the Haggadah by Rav Yedidya Weil, son of the author of Korban Nesanel and a student of Rav Yonasan Eibeshitz.

Mechilta
A halachic Midrash on sefer Shemos, from Parashas Bo to Parashas Vayakhel.

Meiri
Rav Menachem ben Shlomo Meiri was a major commentator on the Talmud. He lived in Catalonia (part of France today) and was especially famous for his work Beis HaBechirah. He passed away in the year 1315 (5075).

Meshech Chochmah
A commentary on the Torah by Rav Meir Simcha HaKohen of Dvinsk, who was known by the name of that work. He also wrote Ohr Same'ach on the Rambam and served as av beis din in Dvinsk. He passed away in 1926 (5686).

Metzudas David
A commentary on Nach written at the end of the seventeenth century by Rav Dovid Altschuler and his son Rav Yechiel, who lived in Prague and Galicia. Rav Dovid passed away in 1753 (5513).

Michtav MeEliyahu
A work of mussar and Jewish thought by Rav Eliyahu Dessler. Rav Dessler was the great-grandson of Rav Yisrael Salanter and was a rosh kollel in Gateshead. In 1950 (5710) he moved to Eretz Yisrael, where he served as mashgiach in Ponevezh Yeshivah. He passed away in 1954 (5714).

Midrash HaGadol
A compilation of midrashim from the fourteenth century.

הגדה של פסח [346]

Midrash Shocher Tov
A compilation of midrashim also known as *Midrash Tehillim*.

Midrash Yelamdeinu
A compilation of midrashim from the ninth century also known as *Midrash Tanchuma Yelamdeinu*.

Migdal Eder
A commentary on the Haggadah by Rav Yisrael Dovid Miller published in Vilna in 1912 (5672).

Minchas Asher
A commentary on the Haggadah written by Rav Asher Weiss. It includes explanations, halachic rulings, halachic responsa, and learned selections on the laws of Pesach. Rav Weiss is the *rosh yeshivah* of Chug Chasam Sofer in Bnei Brak and head of a *kollel* which trains men for *semichah* in the Sorotzkin section of Jerusalem. He also serves as the rav of Chassidei Tchechnov in Ramot, Jerusalem.

Minchas Yitzchak
Works of halachic responsa and commentary on the Torah authored by Rav Yitzchak Yaakov Weiss, rav of the Eidah HaChareidis. He passed away in 1989 (5749).

Mishnah Berurah
A halachic work by Rav Yisrael Meir HaKohen Kagan of Radin (see Chafetz Chaim).

Mizrachi
A commentary on the Torah by Rav Eliyahu Mizrachi, also known by the abbreviation of his name, Re'em. He was the rabbinical leader of Turkey and served as *rosh yeshivah* in Kushta, the capital. He passed away in 1526 (5286).

Nesivos Shalom
Written by the Slonimer Rebbe, Rav Shalom Berzovsky. He moved to Eretz Yisrael in 1935 (5695), where he contributed much to the rehabilitation of Slonimer Chassidus after its decimation in the Holocaust. He became the Slonimer Rebbe following his father-in-law's death in 1981 (5741) and passed away in the year 2000 (5760).

Netziv
Rav Naftali Tzvi Yehudah Berlin served as *rosh yeshivah* of Volozhin Yeshivah from the year 1853 (5613) until it closed its doors about forty years later. He wrote the *Ha'amek Davar* commentary on the Torah, as well as the *Imrei Shefer* Haggadah. He passed away in 1893 (5653).

Noam Elimelech
Written by Rav Elimelech of Lizhensk, a disciple of the Maggid of Mezritch. He worked tirelessly to disseminate Chassidus in Poland. He passed away in 1786 (5546).

Noda BiYehudah
A work of responsa by Rav Yechezkel Segal Landau. He served as *rav* and *av beis din* in Prague. Rav Avraham ben Yechiel Danzig, author of *Chayei Adam*, was among his disciples. He passed away in 1793 (5553).

Ohr HaChaim
A commentary on the Torah by Rav Chaim ben Attar, a kabbalist and halachic *posek*. In the year 1741 (5501), he moved to Eretz Yisrael, where he established Yeshivah Ohr HaChaim. He passed away two years later.

Ohr HaChamah
A commentary on the Haggadah written by Rav Zundel Kroizer, a contemporary sage living in Jerusalem.

Ohr Yahel
A collection of talks delivered by Rav Yehudah Leib Chasman, who served as the *mashgiach* of Chevron Yeshivah. He passed away in 1935 (5695).

Orchos Chaim
Written by Rav Aharon HaKohen of Lunel, a French Torah scholar who was one of the Chachmei Provence (Sages of Provence) during the times

of the *Tosafos*. He passed away in 1330 (5090).

Otzar HaTefillos
An annotated *siddur* with the commentary of Rav Aryeh Leib Gordon, a nineteenth-century *dikduk* master. The *siddur* was printed in Vilna in 1911 (5671).

Ozherover Rebbe
Rav Moshe Yechiel HaLevi Epstein authored *Eish Das* and *Be'er Moshe*. He served as the secretary of Agudath Israel and passed away in the year 1971 (5731).

Oznayim LaTorah
A commentary on the Torah by Rav Zalman Sorotzkin (see *HaShir V'Hashevach*).

Peirush Kadmon
A commentary of unknown origin, apparently written about eight hundred years ago.

Pele Yo'etz
A work of *mussar* built on chapters arranged alphabetically, written by Rav Eliezer Yitzchak Papo, who served as chief rabbi in Silistria, Bulgaria, until his death in 1824 (5584).

Pesikta D'Rav Kahana
A collection of midrashim from around the sixth to the seventh centuries.

Pidyon Shevuyim
Authored by Rav Yochanan Kirschenbaum.

Pirkei D'Rabbi Eliezer
Fifty-four chapters of midrashim, attributed primarily to the *Tanna* Rabbi Eliezer ben Horkanos.

Pri Chadash
A commentary on *Yoreh De'ah* by Rav Chizkiyahu da Silva, a seventeenth-century Italian Torah scholar. He also wrote *Mayim Chaim*. He passed away in 1698 (5458).

Pri Chaim
A work of homiletics, written by Rav Chaim Knoller of Premishlan in 1884 (5644). He passed away at the end of World War I, in 1918 (5678).

Pri Megadim
A commentary and explanation on the *Orach Chaim* and *Yoreh De'ah* sections of the *Shulchan Aruch* by Rav Yosef Teumim, one of the foremost commentators on the *Shulchan Aruch*. He passed away in the year 1792 (5552).

Ra'avan
Rav Eliezer ben Nosson of Magentza (Mainz) was one of the first of the *Tosafos*. He compiled a *siddur* with his own commentary and was a student of the Riva. He passed away in 1170 (4930).

Rabbeinu Bachya
A student of the Rashba, a Torah commentator, and a Spanish kabbalist. He wrote a commentary on the Torah using the four methods known as *Pardes* (*peshat, derash, remez, sod*). He is also the author of *Kad HaKemach*. He passed away in the year 1340 (5100).

Radak
An abbreviation of Rav David Kimchi, who is most known for his commentary on *Nach*. He also wrote *Sefer HaShorashim*, a dictionary of *lashon hakodesh*. He passed away in 1235 (4995).

Radvaz
An abbreviation of Rav David ibn Zimra, a foremost Torah scholar in Spain in the sixteenth century and author of *Shitah Mekubetzes*. He passed away in 1573 (5333).

Rambam
Rav Moshe ben Maimon, one of the greatest halachic authorities of all time. His magnum opus was *Yad HaChazakah* (also known as *Mishneh Torah*), encompassing every area of halachic ruling. He also authored, among other works, *Moreh Nevuchim* and *Sefer HaMitzvos*.

הגדה של פסח [348]

The text of the Haggadah he wrote resembles that of Rav Amram Gaon. He passed away in 1204 (4964).

Ramban
R' Moshe ben Nachman, one of the foremost Torah scholars in the Middle Ages. In the year 1267 (5027) he moved to Jerusalem. He wrote a commentary on the Torah and another on *Shas*. He passed away in 1270 (5030).

Ran
An abbreviation of Rabbeinu Nissim, a medieval Talmudist and *posek*. The Rivash was among his disciples. He passed away in 1376 (5136).

Rashba
Rav Shlomo ben Aderes, a student of the Ramban and of Rabbeinu Yonah and a teacher of Rabbeinu Bachya. He wrote halachic responsa and a commentary on the Talmud. He passed away in 1310 (5070).

Rashbam
Rav Shmuel ben Meir was a grandson of Rashi and one of the *Ba'alei HaTosafos*. He wrote a commentary on the Torah and on several tractates of *Shas*. He passed away in 1158 (4918).

Rashbatz
Rav Shimon ben Rav Tzemach Doron, a major fifteenth-century *posek* and physician. He passed away in 1444 (5204).

Rashi
Rav Shlomo Yitzchaki, the great commentator of Torah and Talmud. He lived at the beginning of the period of the *Rishonim*. He passed away in 1105 (4866).

Rav Yechezkel Abramsky
Author of *Chazon Yechezkel*, he served as rav of Slutzk and London. He later moved to Eretz Yisrael, where he served as the *rosh yeshivah* of Slabodka. He passed away in 1976 (5736).

Rav Avraham Adler
Rav Adler served as the rav of the Beis Yaakov neighborhood in Jerusalem.

Rav Shlomo Alkabetz
A foremost kabbalist in Tzefas who wrote the liturgical poem *Lechah Dodi*. The majority of his work and contribution is in the area of hidden wisdom. He passed away in the year 1584 (5344).

Rav Shlomo Zalman Auerbach
A well-known *posek* who wrote numerous halachic rulings. He authored *Minchas Shlomo* and served as *rosh yeshivah* of Kol Torah in Jerusalem for many years. He passed away in 1994 (5755).

Rav Aharon Bakst
A student of the Alter of Kelm, he served as rav in Shavel, Lithuania, and wrote *Lev Aharon*. He passed away in 1941 (5701).

Rav Reuven Bengis
He served as *av beis din* of the Eidah HaChareidis in Jerusalem and authored *Palgos Reuven*. He passed away in 1953 (5713).

Rav Chaim Berlin
The son of the Netziv of Volozhin, he served as rav of Moscow and then as *rosh yeshivah* of the Volozhiner Yeshivah. After the yeshivah closed its doors, he moved to Eretz Yisrael. He passed away in 1912 (5672).

Rav Yitzchak Blazer
Also known as Rav Itzele Peterburger (see *Kochvei Ohr*).

Rav Shlomo Brevda
He was one of the most well-known *maggidei shiur* of the twenty-first century. He authored numerous *sefarim*, among them a commentary on the Haggadah entitled *Leil Shimurim*. He passed away in 2012 (5773).

Rav Yitzchak Isaac Chaver
A student of the Vilna Gaon, Rav Chaver served as *av beis din* in Soblek and later in Tiktin. Among

[349] HAGGADAH: THE ANSWER IS . . .

his works are *Yad Chazakah* and *Yad Ramah*. He passed away in 1853 (5613).

Rav Yehoshua Leib Diskin
The *av beis din* of Brisk, he authored responsa under the title *Maharil Diskin*. He moved to Eretz Yisrael in 1877 (5637) and passed away in Jerusalem in 1898 (5658).

Rav Yonasan Eibeshitz
A great leader in the eighteenth century born in Cracow. He studied the hidden Torah and wrote many commentaries, including *Ya'aros Devash*. He passed away in 1764 (5524).

Rav Akiva Eiger
Served as *av beis din* in Posna from 1814 (5574) until the end of his life. He was also the father-in-law of the Chasam Sofer, and he wrote editorial comments on *Shas* and the *Shulchan Aruch*. He passed away in 1837 (5597).

Rav Moshe Feinstein
Rosh yeshivah of Mesivtha Tifereth Jerusalem and the author of works of halachic responsa entitled *Igros Moshe* as well as *Dorash Moshe* on the Torah. The acknowledged Torah leader of the generation and its leading halachic decisor, he passed away in 1986 (5746).

Rav Tzvi Pesach Frank
Born in Kovno in 1873 (5633), he moved to Eretz Yisrael when he was twenty years old, in 1893 (5653). He wrote *Har Tzvi*, a work of halachic responsa, and served as rav of Jerusalem from the year 1936 (5696). He passed away in 1961 (5721).

Rav Hai Gaon
He was the son of Rav Sherira Gaon and became his father's successor as head of the yeshivah at Pumbedisa in 998 (4758). He passed away in 1038 (4798).

Rav Sherira Gaon
He lived in the tenth century and was head of the yeshivah at Pumbedisa. His father, Rav Chanina, and his grandfather, Rav Yehudah, were also *geonim* at Pumbedisa. He passed away in 1006 (4766).

Rav Mordechai Gifter
Rosh yeshivah of Telz in Cleveland and a leader of the Moetzes Gedolei HaTorah. He passed away in 2001 (5761).

Rav Avraham Grodzinsky
A student of the Alter of Slabodka, Rav Nosson Tzvi Finkel, he served as *mashgiach* in Slabodka Yeshivah. He passed away in 1944 (5704).

Rav Reuven Grozovsky
The son-in-law of Rav Baruch Ber Leibowitz, he served as *rosh yeshivah* of Kamenitz Yeshivah and later of Beis Medrash Elyon in the United States. He passed away in 1958 (5718).

Rav Aryeh Leib Gurwicz
Rosh yeshivah of Gateshead. He passed away in 1983 (5743).

Rav Samson Raphael Hirsch
He was the leader of German Orthodoxy in the nineteenth century and served as rav of Oldenburg and later in Frankfurt-am-Main. He passed away in 1888 (5648).

Rav Yitzchak Hutner
Rosh yeshivah of Yeshivas Gur Aryeh (also known as Yeshivas Rabbi Chaim Berlin) and author of *Pachad Yitzchak*. He passed away in 1981 (5741).

Rav Avraham Joffen
Rosh yeshivah of Novardok for about half a century. In 1964 (5724) he moved to Eretz Yisrael, where he passed away in 1970 (5730).

Rav Yosef Shlomo Kahaneman
Also known as the Ponevezher Rav, he founded Ponevezh Yeshivah in Bnei Brak in the summer of 1940 (5700), after the original yeshivah was destroyed in the Holocaust. He passed away in 1969 (5729).

הגדה של פסח [350]

Rav Aharon of Karlin
Rav Aharon ben Rav Asher founded the Karliner chassidic dynasty. He was a disciple of the Maggid of Mezritch. He passed away in 1772 (5532).

Rav Reuven Katz
Author of *Degel Reuven*, a work of halachic responsa. He served as *rosh yeshivah* of the Lomza yeshivah and as chief rabbi of Petach Tikva. He passed away in 1964 (5724).

Rav Uri Kellerman
One of the *roshei yeshivah* of Yeshivas Knesses Chizkiyahu at Kfar Chassidim and the author of *Ohr LaYesharim*. He passed away in 1993 (5753).

Rav Shlomo Kluger
He served as rav in various communities in Poland and as a *dayan* in Galicia for most of his life. He passed away in 1869 (5629).

Rav Yosef Kornitzer
A descendant of the Chasam Sofer, he wrote a work of responsa entitled *Rabbeinu Yosef Nechemiah* and served as a rav in Cracow. He passed away in 1933 (5693).

Rav Aharon Kotler
Rosh yeshivah of Yeshivas Eitz Chaim in Kletzk. Later he founded Beth Medrash Govoha in Lakewood and helped replant the Torah world in the U.S. He passed away in 1962 (5723).

Rav Menachem Mendel of Kotzk
A student of the Chozeh of Lublin and of Rav Simcha Bunim of Peshischa, he served as the Kotzker Rebbe from the age of forty. He passed away in 1859 (5619).

Rav Meir (Marcus) Lehmann
He served as a rav in Germany and studied in Rav Azriel Hildesheimer's Rabbinical Theological Seminary in Halberstadt. He was a prolific writer whose literary works helped influence generations of adults and youth.

Rav Yechezkel Levenstein
Mashgiach of the Mirrer Yeshivah in Poland. In 1941 (5701) he moved the Mirrer Yeshivah to Shanghai, China. In 1954 (5714) he became *mashgiach* of Ponevezh Yeshivah in Israel. He passed away in 1974 (5734).

Rav Yerucham Levovitz
A foremost *mussar* scholar who served as *mashgiach* of the Mirrer Yeshivah. He was known for his work *Da'as Chachmah U'Mussar*. He passed away in 1936 (5696).

Rav Eliyahu Lopian
A *mashgiach* in Yeshivas Knesses Chizkiyahu at Kfar Chassidim, he is known for his *sefer Lev Eliyahu*, a work of *mussar* presenting a collection of his talks. He passed away in 1970 (5730).

Rav Reuven Margalios
A prolific writer whose memory and bibliographic knowledge was legendary, he is mainly known for his *Margalios Hayam* on tractate *Sanhedrin* and *Nitzotzei Zohar* — extensive notes on the *Zohar*. He founded and maintained the Rambam Library. He passed away in 1971 (5731).

Rav Baruch of Mezibuzh
A grandson of the Baal Shem Tov and a disciple of the Maggid of Mezritch and Rav Pinchas of Koritz. He became Rebbe in Mezibuzh around 1782 (5542). He passed away in 1811 (5572).

Rav Avigdor Nebenzahl
Rav Nebenzahl was born in 1935 (5695). He is the chief rabbi of Jerusalem's Old City.

Rav Chaim Palagi
He served as *av beis din* and chief rabbi in Izmir, Turkey. He authored eighty *sefarim*, the most well known of which is *Kaf HaChaim*. He passed away in 1868 (5628).

Rav Yerucham Perlow
He was a disciple of Rav Yehoshua Leib Diskin and the Netziv, and eventually Rav Chaim Soloveitchik. He

never held a rabbinic post, preferring to focus on his Torah studies. Toward the end of his life he moved to Eretz Yisrael and passed away in 1934 (5694).

Rav Naftali of Ropshitz
Author of *Zera Kodesh* and a student of the Noam Elimelech and the Maggid of Mezritch. He passed away in 1827 (5587).

Rav Yisrael of Ruzhin
Rav Yisrael Friedman of Ruzhin was a great-grandson of the Maggid of Mezritch and founder of the Sadigora chassidic dynasty in Vienna. He passed away in 1850 (5610).

Rav Yosef Salant
A great twentieth-century *maggid* from Jerusalem who authored *Be'er Yosef*. He passed away in 1981 (5741).

Rav Yisrael Salanter
The founder of the *mussar* movement, he wrote a work of *mussar* entitled *Ohr Yisrael*. He passed away in 1883 (5643).

Rav Yechezkel Sarna
A student of the Alter of Kelm, he was the author of the *Dalyos Yechezkel* and *rosh yeshivah* of Chevron (Knesses Yisrael) for about half a century. He passed away in 1969 (5729).

Rav Yitzchak Isaac Sher
The son-in-law of the Alter of Slabodka, he studied in the Volozhin and Slabodka yeshivahs and became *rosh yeshivah* of Slabodka. He passed away in 1952 (5712).

Rav Yosef Shimanowitz
A student of the Chasam Sofer. He passed away in 1927 (5687).

Rav Chaim Shmulevitz
For more than forty years, he was *rosh yeshivah* of the Mirrer Yeshivah in Poland, Shanghai, and Jerusalem. He passed away in 1979 (5739).

Rav Yosef of Slutzk
Rav Yosef Peimer was a student of the Vilna Gaon and of Rav Chaim Volozhiner. He passed away in 1864 (5724).

Rav Chaim Sofer
A student of the Chasam Sofer (no relation) and later of Rav Yehudah Assad. He served as rav in Munkacz and wrote *Machaneh Chaim* and *Peles Chaim*. He passed away in 1886 (5646).

Rav Chaim Soloveitchik
Rav Soloveitchik served as *av beis din* in Brisk after the death of his father, the Beis HaLevi. He was a foremost *gadol* in nineteenth-century Europe and passed away in 1918 (5678).

Rav Zalman Sorotzkin
Rav of Lutzk (see *HaShir V'Hashevach*).

Rav Moshe Sternbuch
He is the *av beis din* of the Eidah HaChareidis in Jerusalem, and he also served as a rav in Johannesburg. He wrote *Mo'adim U'Zemanim* on the festivals and the *Ta'am VaDa'as* commentary on the Torah.

Rav Ezra Traub
Author of *Sefer Ezra* and a Torah scholar first in Damascus and later in Jerusalem.

Rav Betzalel HaKohen of Vilna
He was appointed rav of Vilna at the age of twenty-three. The Chafetz Chaim was among his disciples. He passed away in 1878 (5638).

Rav Itzele of Volozhin
Rav Yitzchak of Volozhin, also known as "Rav Itzele," was the son of Rav Chaim Volozhiner and one of the *roshei yeshivah* of the Volozhin yeshivah. He was also the son-in-law of the Netziv. He passed away in 1855 (5615).

Rav Chaim Volozhiner
A student of the Sha'agas Aryeh and the Vilna Gaon, he founded Volozhin Yeshivah. He passed away in 1821 (5581).

Rav Shmuel HaLevi Wosner
Rav Wosner is a prominent *posek* and the author of *Shevet HaLevi*, a

work of halachic responsa. He is also the rav of the Zichron Meir neighborhood and *rosh yeshivah* of Chachmei Lublin in Bnei Brak.

Rav Shlomo Zalman Zelaznik
The author of the *Zera Yaakov* and *rosh yeshivah* of Eitz Chaim. He passed away in 1975 (5735).

Rav Menachem Ziemba
Author of *Zera Avraham* and a prominent rav in Europe in the generation before the Holocaust. He was one of the last leaders killed in the Warsaw ghetto, in 1943 (5703).

Rav Betzalel Zolty
In 1956 (5716), he was appointed a *dayan* on the Supreme Beis Din of Israel, after serving on the rabbinical courts of Tel Aviv and Jerusalem. He became chief rabbi of Jerusalem in 1978 (5738) and passed away in 1982 (5743).

Re'ach Duda'im
A commentary on the Haggadah, written in 1902 (5662) by Rav Duvid Dov Meizlish, who served as *av beis din* of Lask.

Rebbe of Minsk
Rav Yerucham Yehudah Perlman was born in the city of Brisk and was the rav of Minsk. He became known as the "Gadol of Minsk." He passed away in 1896 (5656).

Rema
Rav Moshe Isserlis, a foremost *posek* in Europe, most well known for his commentary on the *Shulchan Aruch*. He also wrote a commentary on the *Tur* entitled *Darkei Moshe*. He lived in Cracow and passed away in 1572 (5332).

Ri ben Yakar
Rav Yaakov ben Yakar is most famously known as one of Rashi's teachers. He passed away in 1064 (4824).

Rid
Rav Yeshayah ben di Trani, a *Rishon* who lived in Italy. He commented on the Torah, Mishnah, and Talmud and was also a *posek*. He passed away in 1240 (5000).

Ritva
Rav Yom Tov ben Rav Avraham Ishbili, a foremost Torah scholar in Spain and a student of the Re'eh and the Rashba. He wrote original insights on *Shas*. He passed away in 1330 (5090).

Rokeach
A halachic guide to ethics and Jewish law written by Rav Elazar ben Yehudah of Worms, a leading Talmudist and kabbalist. He passed away in 1238 (4998).

Sdei Chemed
An eighteen-volume work, which serves as a Talmudic encyclopedia and giant treasury of halachic responsa, authored by Rav Chaim Chizkiyahu Medini. He served as rav of Kushta, Turkey, and later as the rav of Chevron in Eretz Yisrael. He passed away in 1905 (5665).

Seforno
A commentary on the Torah by Rav Ovadiah Seforno, one of the great Torah scholars of Italy at the start of the sixteenth century. He passed away in 1550 (5310).

Sfas Emes
Written by Rav Yehudah Aryeh Leib Alter, a grandson of the Chiddushei HaRim and the second Gerrer Rebbe. He wrote a commentary on the Torah and *Shas*. He passed away in the year 1905 (5665).

Sfas HaYam
A commentary on the Haggadah by Rav Zev Wolf Altschuler written in 1812 (5572). He was also the *av beis din* in Lutzin.

Sha'ar Bas Rabbim
A commentary on the Torah and the five *megillos* written by Rav Chaim Aryeh Leib Fenster. It was published in Warsaw in 1902 (5662).

[353] **HAGGADAH: THE ANSWER IS . . .**

Sha'ar HaTziyun
A reference section to the Mishnah Berurah by Rav Yisrael Meir HaKohen Kagan of Radin (see Chafetz Chaim).

Shelah
Rav Yeshayah HaLevi Horowitz was chief rabbi of Prague before he moved to Eretz Yisrael in 1621 (5381). He lived first in Jerusalem and then in Tzefas. He authored *Shnei Luchos HaBris* and is known by the abbreviation of the title, *Shelah*. He passed away in 1630 (5390).

Shem MiShmuel
A commentary on the Torah and the Festivals written by the second Sochatchover Rebbe, Rav Shmuel Bornstein, the son of Rav Avraham, founder of the chassidic dynasty. He passed away in 1926 (5686).

Shibbolei HaLeket
A commentary by Rav Tzidkiyah ben Avraham HaRofei, who lived about seven hundred years ago. He passed away in 1280 (5040).

Shoel U'Meishiv
Halachic responsa by Rav Yosef Shaul Nathanson, rav of Lvov. He also authored *Divrei Shaul*, commentaries on the Torah, *Aggadah*, and the Haggadah. He passed away in 1875 (5635).

Shulchan Aruch HaRav
A halachic work by Rav Shneur Zalman of Liadi, founder of Chabad Chassidus and a disciple of the Maggid of Mezritch. He passed away in 1812 (5571).

Sifsei Chachamim
A commentary on Rashi on the Torah by Rav Shabsai Bass, who also owned a printing press so that he could print *sefarim*. He passed away in 1718 (5478).

Sifsei Chaim
A work on Jewish thought and *mussar* written by Rav Chaim Friedlander, who served as *mashgiach* of the Ponevezh. A student of Rav Eliyahu Dessler, he was one of the editors of *Michtav MeEliyahu*. He passed away in 1985 (5745).

Simchas Yaavetz
A commentary on the Haggadah by Rav Dovid Kohn.

Smag
An abbreviation of *Sefer Mitzvos HaGadol*, a halachic work by Rav Moshe ben Yaakov, one of the Ba'alei HaTosafos who lived in the first half of the thirteenth century. He was a disciple of Rav Yehudah HeChassid.

Steipler Gaon
Rav Yisrael Yaakov Kanievsky wrote *Kehillas Yaakov*, a commentary on *Shas*, as well as a commentary on the Torah entitled *Birkas Peretz*. He passed away in 1985 (5745).

Targum Yonasan ben Uziel
An Aramaic translation of *Nevi'im* by Rabbi Yonasan ben Uziel, one of the disciples of Hillel HaZaken.

Taz
An abbreviation of *Turei Zahav*, a commentary on the *Shulchan Aruch*, by Rav Dovid HaLevi Segal, son-in-law of the Bach. He passed away in 1667 (5427).

Tiferes Shlomo
Rav Shlomo Rabinowitz of Radomsk, a student of Rav Meir Apter. In the year 1834 (5594) he was appointed rav of Radomsk. He passed away in 1866 (5626).

Toldos Adam
Written by Rav Avraham Danzig, a student of the Noda BiYehudah. Besides *Toldos Adam*, he authored many halachic works, including *Chayei Adam* and *Chachmas Adam*. He passed away in 1821 (5581).

Tur
See *Ba'al HaTurim*.

Tzidkas HaTzaddik
Short thoughts on various topics in *avodas Hashem* written by Rav

הגדה של פסח [354]

Tzadok HaKohen of Lublin, a foremost chassidic leader. He passed away in the year 1900 (5660).

Tzitz Eliezer
A series of twenty-two volumes of halachic responsa by Rav Eliezer Yehudah Waldenberg. He served as an *av beis din* of the Supreme Rabbinical Court in Jerusalem. He passed away in 2006 (5767).

Tzuf Amarim
A commentary on the Haggadah written by Rav Moshe Chaim Kleinman of Brisk in the year 1924 (5684).

Vayaged L'Avraham
A commentary by Rav Avraham ben Rav Binyamin Chalimi in the year 1862 (5622) in Livorno.

Vilna Gaon
Rav Eliyahu of Vilna was the *gadol hador* in the eighteenth century. He encouraged his students to move to Eretz Yisrael and authored commentaries on the Torah and halachah. He passed away in 1797 (5557).

Yaavetz
Rav Yaakov Emden; see *Chukas HaPesach*.

Yalkut Reuveni
An anthology on the Torah, edited by Rav Avraham Reuven HaKohen Sofer. Most of the material comes from kabbalistic works, such as the writings of the Ramak, the Arizal, and Rema.

Yalkut Shimoni
A collection of midrashim on *Tanach*, including teachings from the Talmud, *Sifra*, *Sifri*, *Mechilta*, and *Midrash Rabbah*. According to the Chida, they were compiled by Rav Shimon Ashkenazi, a fourteenth-century scholar from Frankfurt.

Yesod V'Shoresh HaAvodah
By Rav Alexander Ziskind on *tefillah* and the festivals. He was a kabbalist and student of Rav Aryeh Leib Epstein of Konigsberg. He passed away in 1793 (5553).

Yismach Moshe
Written by Rav Moshe Teitelbaum, a student of the Chozeh of Lublin and rav of Premishlan and later Ujhely. He also wrote *Heishiv Moshe* and *Tefillah L'Moshe*. He passed away in 1841 (5601).

Yismach Yisrael
Written by the Alexander Rebbe Rav Yerachmiel Yisrael Yitzchak Danziger. He passed away in 1910 (5670).

Yitav Panim
A work on the Shabbos and festivals by Rav Yekusiel Yehudah Teitelbaum, the grandson of the Yismach Moshe and the Rebbe of Sighet in Hungary. He also founded a yeshivah. He is known by the title of his work, *Yitav Lev*, a commentary on the Torah. He passed away in 1883 (5643).

This volume is part of
THE ARTSCROLL SERIES®
an ongoing project of
translations, commentaries and expositions on
Scripture, Mishnah, Talmud, Midrash, Halachah,
liturgy, history, the classic Rabbinic writings,
biographies and thought.

For a brochure of current publications
visit your local Hebrew bookseller
or contact the publisher:

Mesorah Publications, ltd
4401 Second Avenue
Brooklyn, New York 11232
(718) 921-9000
www.artscroll.com